PEARSON CUSTOM BUSINESS RESOURCES

Compiled by

Microeconomics
Cabrillo College

Pearson Custom Publishing

New York   Boston   San Francisco
London   Toronto   Sydney   Tokyo   Singapore   Madrid
Mexico City   Munich   Paris   Cape Town   Hong Kong   Montreal

Senior Vice President, Editorial and Marketing: Patrick F. Boles
Senior Sponsoring Editor: Robin J. Lazrus
Development Editor: Abbey Lee Briggs
Marketing Manager: Jack Cooney
Associate Editor: Ana Díaz-Caneja
Operations Manager: Eric M. Kenney
Database Product Manager: Jennifer Berry
Art Director: Renée Sartell
Cover Designer: Renée Sartell

Cover Art: Courtesy of EyeWire/Getty Images and PhotoDisc/Getty Images. Photodisc, "Globe surrounded by business people on computer monitors," courtesy of Photodisc/Getty Images. Dave Cutler (Artist), "Man Dropping Coins Into Glass Jar," courtesy of David Cutler/Images.com. Dave Cutler (Artist), "Three Coins in Glass Jar," courtesy of David Cutler/Images.com.

This special edition published in cooperation with Pearson Custom Publishing.

Printed in the United States of America.

Please visit our web site at *www.pearsoncustom.com.*

Attention bookstores: For permission to return any unsold stock, contact us at *pe-uscustomreturns@pearson.com.*

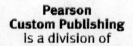
Pearson Custom Publishing is a division of

www.pearsonhighered.com

ISBN 10: 0-558-14447-0
ISBN 13: 978-0-558-14447-0

Contents

Where Prices Come From: The Interaction of Demand and Supply

From Chapter 3 of *Microeconomics*, 2/e. R. Glenn Hubbard. Anthony Patrick O'Brien. Copyright © 2008 by Pearson Prentice Hall. All rights reserved.

Where Prices Come From: The Interaction of Demand and Supply

Apple and the Demand for iPods

During the last three months of 2006, Apple sold $3.43 billion worth of iPods. iPods seemed to be everywhere, but during 2007 it became clear that the market for digital music players was becoming much more competitive.

Steve Jobs and Steve Wozniak started Apple in 1976. Working out of Jobs's parents' garage, the two friends created the Apple I computer. By 1980, although Jobs was still only in his mid-twenties, Apple had become the first firm in history to join the Fortune 500 list of largest U.S. firms in less than five years. Apple's success in the computer business has been up and down, but when the company introduced the iPod digital music player in 2001, it had a runaway success on its hands. The most obvious reasons for the iPod's success are its ease of use and sleek design. But also important has been iTunes, Apple's online music store. Apple decided to offer individual songs, as well as whole albums, for download at a price of just $0.99 per song. After paying a royalty to the record company, Apple makes very little profit from the songs it sells on iTunes. Apple was willing to accept a small profit on the sale of each song to make the purchase of the iPod more attractive to consumers.

At a price of several hundred dollars, the iPod might be relatively expensive, but purchasing the music is very inexpensive. In addition, the songs on iTunes are playable only on iPods, and iPods can only play songs downloaded from iTunes (although with enough technical skill, it's possible to get around both restrictions). So, owners of other digital music players do not have easy access to iTunes, and iPod owners have little incentive to download music from other online sites. In addition, because Apple makes the iPod and owns iTunes, the two systems work smoothly together, which is not the case for many of Apple's competitors. Microsoft's Vice President Bryan Lee says, "That's something that Apple has played up very well. One brand, one device, one service."

By early 2007, more than 100 million iPods had been sold and more than 2 billion songs had been downloaded from iTunes. Clearly, the strategy of selling an expensive digital music player and selling the music cheaply has been very successful for Apple. But how long will the iPod's dominance last? By 2007, competitors were flooding into the market. New digital music players, such as Microsoft's Zune, Toshiba's Gigabeat, and iRiver's H10, among many others, were rapidly gaining customers. In addition, firms were introducing new "music phones" that combined the features of a cell phone with the features of a digital music player. Although this wave of competition might be bad news for Apple, it could be good news for consumers by increasing the choices available and lowering prices. **AN INSIDE LOOK** discusses how Apple responded to competition by teaming with AT&T to create its own music phone, the iPhone.

Sources: Nick Wingfield and Robert Guth, "iPod, TheyPod: Rivals Imitate Apple's Success," *Wall Street Journal*, September 18, 2006, p. B1; and Nick Wingfield, "iPod Demand Lifts Apple's Results," *Wall Street Journal*, January 18, 2007, p. A2.

LEARNING Objectives

After studying this chapter, you should be able to:

1   Discuss the variables that influence **demand**

2   Discuss the variables that influence **supply**

3   Use a graph to illustrate **market equilibrium**

4   Use **demand and supply graphs** to predict changes in prices and quantities.

Economics in YOUR Life!

Will you buy an iPod or a Zune?

Suppose you are about to buy a new digital music player and that you are choosing between Apple's iPod and Microsoft's Zune. As the industry leader, the iPod has many advantages over a new entrant like Zune. One strategy Microsoft can use to overcome those advantages is to compete based on price. Would you choose a Zune if it had a lower price than a comparable iPod? Would you choose a Zune if the songs sold on Zune Marketplace were cheaper than the songs sold on iTunes? As you read the chapter, see if you can answer these questions. You can check your answers against those we provide at the end of the chapter.

3

I n this chapter, we explore the model of demand and supply, which is the most powerful tool in economics, and use it to explain how prices are determined.

Economic models rely on assumptions and that these assumptions are simplifications of reality. In some cases, the assumptions of the model may not seem to describe exactly the economic situation being analyzed. For example, the model of demand and supply assumes that we are analyzing a *perfectly competitive market*. In a **perfectly competitive market**, there are many buyers and sellers, all the products sold are identical, and there are no barriers to new firms entering the market. These assumptions are very restrictive and apply exactly to only a few markets, such as the markets for wheat and other agricultural products. Experience has shown, however, that the model of demand and supply can be very useful in analyzing markets where competition among sellers is intense, even if there are relatively few sellers and the products being sold are not identical. In fact, in recent studies the model of demand and supply has been successful in analyzing markets with as few as four buyers and four sellers. In the end, the usefulness of a model depends on how well it can predict outcomes in a market. As we will see in this chapter, the model of demand and supply is often very useful in predicting changes in quantities and prices in many markets.

We begin considering the model of demand and supply by discussing consumers and the demand side of the market, then we turn to firms and the supply side. As you will see, we will apply this model throughout this book to understand business, the economy, and economic policy.

Perfectly competitive market
A market that meets the conditions of (1) many buyers and sellers, (2) all firms selling identical products, and (3) no barriers to new firms entering the market.

---

1 LEARNING OBJECTIVE

1 | Discuss the variables that influence demand.

The Demand Side of the Market

In a market system, consumers ultimately determine which goods and services will be produced. The most successful businesses are the ones that respond best to consumer demand. But what determines consumer demand for a product? Certainly, many factors influence the willingness of consumers to buy a particular product. For example, consumers who are considering buying a digital music player, such as Apple's iPod or Microsoft's Zune, will make their decisions based on, among other factors, the income they have available to spend and the effectiveness of the advertising campaigns of the companies that sell digital music players. The main factor in consumer decisions, though, will be the price of the digital music player. So, it makes sense to begin with price when analyzing the decisions of consumers to buy a product. It is important to note that when we discuss demand, we are considering not what a consumer *wants* to buy but what the consumer is both willing and *able* to buy.

Demand Schedules and Demand Curves

Tables that show the relationship between the price of a product and the quantity of the product demanded are called **demand schedules**. The table in Figure 1 shows the number of players consumers would be willing to buy over the course of a month at five different prices. The amount of a good or a service that a consumer is willing and able to purchase at a given price is referred to as the **quantity demanded**. The graph in Figure 1 plots the numbers from the table as a **demand curve**, a curve that shows the relationship between the price of a product and the quantity of the product demanded. (Note that for convenience, we made the demand curve in Figure 1 a straight line, or linear. There is no reason that all demand curves need to be straight lines.) The demand curve in Figure 1 shows the **market demand**, or the demand by all the consumers of a

Demand schedule A table showing the relationship between the price of a product and the quantity of the product demanded.

Quantity demanded The amount of a good or service that a consumer is willing and able to purchase at a given price.

Demand curve A curve that shows the relationship between the price of a product and the quantity of the product demanded.

Market demand The demand by all the consumers of a given good or service.

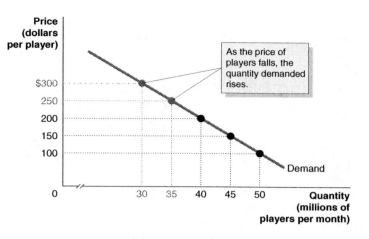

Demand Schedule	
Price (dollars per player)	Quantity (millions of players per month)
$300	30
250	35
200	40
150	45
100	50

As the price of players falls, the quantity demanded rises.

Figure 1

A Demand Schedule and Demand Curve

As the price changes, consumers change the quantity of digital music players they are willing to buy. We can show this as a *demand schedule* in a table or as a *demand curve* on a graph. The table and graph both show that as the price of players falls, the quantity demanded rises. When the price of a player is $300, consumers buy 30 million. When the price drops to $250, consumers buy 35 million. Therefore, the demand curve for digital music players is downward sloping.

given good or service. The market for a product, such as restaurant meals, that is purchased locally would include all the consumers in a city or a relatively small area. The market for a product that is sold internationally, such as digital music players, would include all the consumers in the world.

The demand curve in Figure 1 slopes downward because consumers will buy more players as the price falls. When the price of players is $300, consumers buy 30 million players per month. If the price of players falls to $250, consumers buy 35 million players. Buyers demand a larger quantity of a product as the price falls because the product becomes less expensive relative to other products and because they can afford to buy more at a lower price.

The Law of Demand

The inverse relationship between the price of a product and the quantity of the product demanded is known as the **law of demand**: Holding everything else constant, when the price of a product falls, the quantity demanded of the product will increase, and when the price of a product rises, the quantity demanded of the product will decrease. The law of demand holds for any market demand curve. Economists have never found an exception to it. In fact, Nobel Prize–winning economist George Stigler once remarked that the surest way for an economist to become famous would be to discover a market demand curve that sloped upward rather than downward.

Law of demand The rule that, holding everything else constant, when the price of a product falls, the quantity demanded of the product will increase, and when the price of a product rises, the quantity demanded of the product will decrease.

What Explains the Law of Demand?

It makes sense that consumers will buy more of a good when the price falls and less of a good when the price rises, but let's look more closely at why this is true. When the price of digital music players falls, consumers buy a larger quantity because of the *substitution effect* and the *income effect*.

Substitution Effect The **substitution effect** refers to the change in the quantity demanded of a good that results from a change in price, making the good more or less expensive *relative* to other goods that are *substitutes*. When the price of digital music players falls, consumers will substitute buying music players for buying other goods, such as radios or compact stereos.

Substitution effect The change in the quantity demanded of a good that results from a change in price, making the good more or less expensive relative to other goods that are substitutes.

The Income Effect The **income effect** of a price change refers to the change in the quantity demanded of a good that results from the effect of a change in the good's price on consumers' purchasing power. Purchasing power is the quantity of goods a consumer can buy with a fixed amount of income. When the price of a good falls, the increased purchasing power of consumers' incomes will usually lead them to purchase a larger quantity of the good. When the price of a good rises, the decreased purchasing power of consumers' incomes will usually lead them to purchase a smaller quantity of the good.

Income effect The change in the quantity demanded of a good that results from the effect of a change in the good's price on consumers' purchasing power.

Note that although we can analyze them separately, the substitution effect and the income effect happen simultaneously whenever a price changes. Thus, a fall in the price of digital music players leads consumers to buy more players, both because the players are now cheaper relative to substitute products and because the purchasing power of the consumers' incomes has increased.

Holding Everything Else Constant: The *Ceteris Paribus* Condition

Notice that the definition of the law of demand contains the phrase *holding everything else constant*. In constructing the market demand curve for digital music players, we focused only on the effect that changes in the price of players would have on the quantity of players consumers would be willing and able to buy. We were holding constant other variables that might affect the willingness of consumers to buy players. Economists refer to the necessity of holding all variables other than price constant in constructing a demand curve as the **ceteris paribus** condition; *ceteris paribus* is Latin for "all else equal."

What would happen if we allowed a change in a variable—other than price—that might affect the willingness of consumers to buy music players? Consumers would then change the quantity they demand at each price. We can illustrate this effect by shifting the market demand curve. A shift of a demand curve is *an increase or a decrease in demand*. A movement along a demand curve is *an increase or a decrease in the quantity demanded*. As Figure 2 shows, we shift the demand curve to the right if consumers decide to buy more of the good at each price, and we shift the demand curve to the left if consumers decide to buy less at each price.

Variables That Shift Market Demand

Many variables other than price can influence market demand. These five are the most important:

- Income
- Prices of related goods
- Tastes
- Population and demographics
- Expected future prices

We next discuss how changes in each of these variables affect the market demand curve for digital music players.

Ceteris paribus ("all else equal")
The requirement that when analyzing the relationship between two variables—such as price and quantity demanded—other variables must be held constant.

Figure 2

Shifting the Demand Curve

When consumers increase the quantity of a product they wish to buy at a given price, the market demand curve shifts to the right, from D_1 to D_2. When consumers decrease the quantity of a product they wish to buy at any given price, the demand curve shifts to the left, from D_1 to D_3.

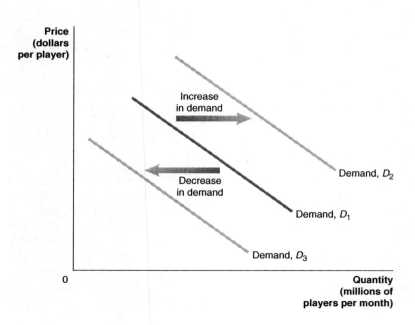

6

Income The income that consumers have available to spend affects their willingness and ability to buy a good. Suppose that the market demand curve in Figure 1 represents the willingness of consumers to buy digital music players when average household income is $43,000. If household income rises to $45,000, the demand for players will increase, which we show by shifting the demand curve to the right. A good is a **normal good** when demand increases following a rise in income and decreases following a fall in income. Most goods are normal goods, but the demand for some goods falls when income rises and rises when income falls. For instance, as your income rises, you might buy less canned tuna fish or fewer hot dogs and buy more shrimp or prime rib. A good is an **inferior good** when demand decreases following a rise in income and increases following a fall in income. So, for you hot dogs and tuna fish would be examples of inferior goods—not because they are of low quality but because you buy less of them as your income increases.

Normal good A good for which the demand increases as income rises and decreases as income falls.

Inferior good A good for which the demand increases as income falls and decreases as income rises.

Prices of Related Goods The prices of other goods can also affect consumers' demand for a product. Suppose that the market demand curve in Figure 1 represents the willingness and ability of consumers to buy digital music players during a year when the average price of compact stereos, such as the Bose Wave music system, is $500. If the average price of these stereo systems falls to $400, how will the market demand for digital music players change? Fewer players will be demanded at every price. We show this by shifting the demand curve for players to the left.

Goods and services that can be used for the same purpose—such as digital music players and compact stereos—are **substitutes**. When two goods are substitutes, the more you buy of one, the less you will buy of the other. A decrease in the price of a substitute causes the demand curve for a good to shift to the left. An increase in the price of a substitute causes the demand curve for a good to shift to the right.

Substitutes Goods and services that can be used for the same purpose.

Many consumers play songs downloaded from a Web site, such as iTunes or Zune Marketplace, on their digital music players. Suppose the market demand curve in Figure 1 represents the willingness of consumers to buy players at a time when the average price to download a song is $0.99. If the price to download a song falls to $0.49, consumers will buy more song downloads *and* more digital music players: The demand curve for music players will shift to the right.

Products that are used together—such as digital music players and song downloads—are **complements**. When two goods are complements, the more consumers buy of one, the more they will buy of the other. A decrease in the price of a complement causes the demand curve for a good to shift to the right. An increase in the price of a complement causes the demand curve for a good to shift to the left.

Complements Goods and services that are used together.

Making *the* Connection | Why Supermarkets Need to Understand Substitutes and Complements

Supermarkets sell what sometimes seems like a bewildering variety of goods. The first row of the following table shows the varieties of eight products stocked by five Chicago supermarkets.

	COFFEE	FROZEN PIZZA	HOT DOGS	ICE CREAM	POTATO CHIPS	REGULAR CEREAL	SPAGHETTI SAUCE	YOGURT
Varieties in five Chicago supermarkets	391	337	128	421	285	242	194	288
Varieties introduced in a 2-year period	113	109	47	129	93	114	70	107
Varieties removed in a 2-year period	135	86	32	118	77	75	36	51

Source: Juin-Kuan Chong, Teck-Hua Ho, and Christopher S. Tang, "A Modeling Framework for Category Assortment Planning," *Manufacturing & Service Operations Management*, 2001, Vol. 3, No. 3, pp. 191–210.

Supermarkets are also constantly adding new varieties of goods to their shelves and removing old varieties. The second row of the table shows that these five Chicago supermarkets added 113 new varieties of coffee over a two-year period, while the third row shows that they eliminated 135 existing varieties. How do supermarkets decide which varieties to add and which to remove?

Christopher Tang is a professor at the Anderson Graduate School of Management at the University of California, Los Angeles (UCLA). In an interview with the *Baltimore Sun*, Tang argues that supermarkets should not necessarily remove the slowest-selling goods from their shelves but should consider the relationships among the goods. In particular, they should consider whether the goods being removed are substitutes or complements with the remaining goods. A lobster bisque soup, for example, could be a relatively slow seller but might be a complement to other soups because it can be used with them to make a sauce. In that case, removing the lobster bisque would hurt sales of some of the remaining soups. Tang suggests the supermarket would be better off removing a slow-selling soup that is a substitute for another soup. For example, the supermarket might want to remove one of two brands of cream of chicken soup.

Source: Lobster bisque example from Lorraine Mirabella, "Shelf Science in Supermarkets," *Baltimore Sun*, March 17, 2002, p. 16.

YOUR TURN: For more practice, do problem 1.5 at the end of this chapter.

Tastes Consumers can be influenced by an advertising campaign for a product. If Apple, Microsoft, Toshiba, and other makers of digital music players begin to heavily advertise on television and online, consumers are more likely to buy players at every price, and the demand curve will shift to the right. An economist would say that the advertising campaign has affected consumers' *taste* for digital music players. Taste is a catchall category that refers to the many subjective elements that can enter into a consumer's decision to buy a product. A consumer's taste for a product can change for many reasons. Sometimes trends play a substantial role. For example, the popularity of low-carbohydrate diets caused a decline in demand for some goods, such as bread and donuts, and an increase in demand for beef. In general, when consumers' taste for a product increases, the demand curve will shift to the right, and when consumers' taste for a product decreases, the demand curve for the product will shift to the left.

Population and Demographics Population and demographic factors can affect the demand for a product. As the population of the United States increases, so will the number of consumers, and the demand for most products will increase. The **demographics** of a population refers to its characteristics, with respect to age, race, and gender. As the demographics of a country or region change, the demand for particular goods will increase or decrease because different categories of people tend to have different preferences for those goods. For instance, in 2006, a record 17 percent of the U.S. population was 60 years of age or older increasing the demand for health care and other products heavily used by older people.

Demographics The characteristics of a population with respect to age, race, and gender.

Getty Images, Inc.

Blockbuster responds to a growing Hispanic population by featuring DVDs dubbed in Spanish.

Making the Connection | Companies Respond to a Growing Hispanic Population

The spending power of Hispanic Americans is rapidly increasing. So, it is no surprise that firms have begun to respond: When Apple announced in early 2007 that it would sell a 90-minute video of highlights of the 2007 Super Bowl on its iTunes store, the download was made available in Spanish as well as in English. In late 2006, "Coffee Break Spanish," a weekly Spanish language podcast, was one of the most frequently downloaded podcasts on iTunes. Today, more than one third of all DVDs are sold to consumers whose first language is Spanish, and Blockbuster has responded by increasing its offerings of Spanish-language films. Kmart sells a clothing line named after Thalia, a Mexican singer. The Ford Motor Company hired Mexican actress Salma Hayek to appear in commercials. A used car dealer in Pennsylvania displayed a sign stating "Salga Manejando Hoy Mismo" (or "Drive Out Today" in English).

The increase in spending by Hispanic households was due partly to increased population growth and partly to rising incomes. By 2020, the Hispanic share of the U.S. consumer market is expected to grow to more than 13 percent—almost twice what it was in 2000. The Selig Center for Economic Growth at the University of Georgia has forecast that spending by Hispanic households will increase about 70 percent more between 2006 and 2011 than spending by non-Hispanic households.

As the demand for goods purchased by Hispanic households increases, a larger quantity can be sold at every price. Firms have responded by devoting more resources to serving this demographic group.

Sources: "Apple Completes Pass for Super Bowl Highlights," *St. Petersburg* (Florida) *Times*, February 1, 2007; Catherine E. Shoichet and John Martin, "Downloading," *Houston Chronicle*, January 7, 2007; Jeffrey M. Humphreys, "The Multicultural Economy 2006," *Georgia Business and Economic Conditions*, Third Quarter 2006, Vol. 66, No. 3; and Eduardo Porter, "Buying Power of Hispanics Is Set to Soar," *Wall Street Journal*, April 18, 2003, p. B1.

YOUR TURN: For more practice, do problem 1.8 at the end of this chapter.

Expected Future Prices Consumers choose not only which products to buy but also when to buy them. If enough consumers become convinced that digital music players will be selling for lower prices three months from now, the demand for players will decrease now, as some consumers postpone their purchases to wait for the expected price decrease. Alternatively, if enough consumers become convinced that the price of players will be higher three months from now, the demand for players will increase now, as some consumers try to beat the expected price increase.

Table 1 summarizes the most important variables that cause market demand curves to shift. You should note that the table shows the shift in the demand curve that results from an *increase* in each of the variables. A *decrease* in these variables would cause the demand curve to shift in the opposite direction.

A Change in Demand versus a Change in Quantity Demanded

It is important to understand the difference between a *change in demand* and a *change in quantity demanded*. A change in demand refers to a shift of the demand curve. A shift occurs if there is a change in one of the variables, *other than the price of the product*, that affects the willingness of consumers to buy the product. A change in quantity demanded refers to a movement along the demand curve as a result of a change in the product's price. Figure 3 illustrates this important distinction. If the price of digital music players falls from $300 to $250, the result will be a movement along the demand curve from

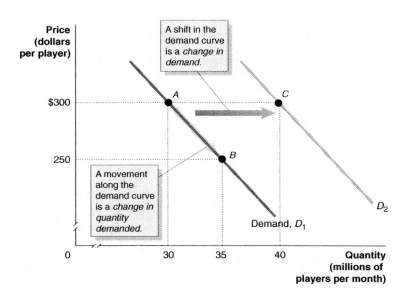

Figure 3

A Change in Demand versus a Change in the Quantity Demanded

If the price of digital music players falls from $300 to $250, the result will be a movement along the demand curve from point *A* to point *B*—an increase in quantity demanded from 30 million to 35 million. If consumers' income increases, or if another factor changes that makes consumers want more of the product at every price, the demand curve will shift to the right—an increase in demand. In this case, the increase in demand from D_1 to D_2 causes the quantity of players demanded at a price of $300 to increase from 30 million at point *A* to 40 million at point *C*.

TABLE 1

**Variables That Shift Market
Demand Curves**

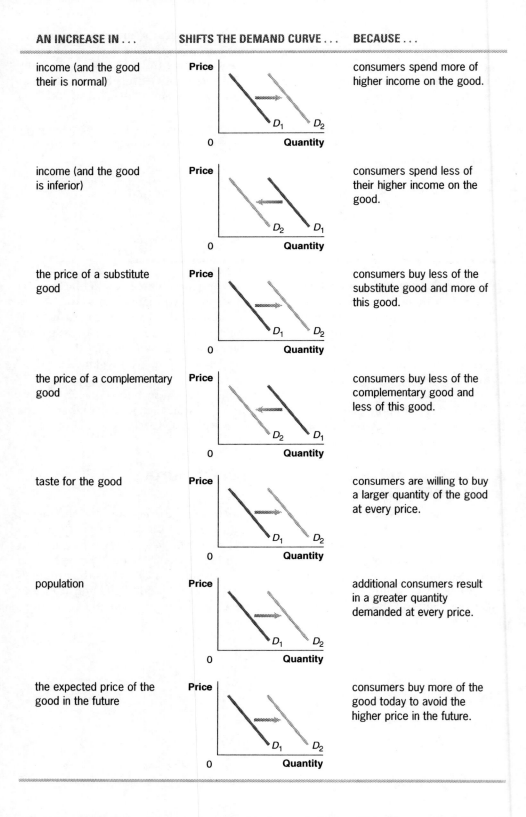

AN INCREASE IN ...	SHIFTS THE DEMAND CURVE ...	BECAUSE ...
income (and the good their is normal)		consumers spend more of higher income on the good.
income (and the good is inferior)		consumers spend less of their higher income on the good.
the price of a substitute good		consumers buy less of the substitute good and more of this good.
the price of a complementary good		consumers buy less of the complementary good and less of this good.
taste for the good		consumers are willing to buy a larger quantity of the good at every price.
population		additional consumers result in a greater quantity demanded at every price.
the expected price of the good in the future		consumers buy more of the good today to avoid the higher price in the future.

point A to point B—an increase in quantity demanded from 30 million to 35 million. If consumers' incomes increase, or if another factor changes that makes consumers want more of the product at every price, the demand curve will shift to the right—an increase in demand. In this case, the increase in demand from D_1 to D_2 causes the quantity of digital music players demanded at a price of $300 to increase from 30 million at point A to 40 million at point C.

Making the Connection

Apple Forecasts the Demand for iPhones and other Consumer Electronics

Will Apple's iPhone match the success of its iPod?

One of the most important decisions that the managers of any large firm have to make is which new products to develop. A firm must devote people, time, and money to designing the product, negotiating with suppliers, formulating a marketing campaign, and many other tasks. But any firm has only limited resources and so faces a trade-off: Resources used to develop one product will not be available to develop another product. Ultimately, the products a firm chooses to develop will be those which it believes will be the most profitable. So, to decide which products to develop, firms need to forecast the demand for those products.

David Sobotta, who worked at Apple for 20 years, eventually becoming its national sales manager, has described the strategy Apple has used to decide which consumer electronics products will have the greatest demand. Sobotta describes discussions at Apple during 2002 about whether to develop a tablet personal computer. A tablet PC is a laptop with a special screen that allows the computer to be controlled with a stylus or pen and that has the capability of converting handwritten input into text. The previous year, Bill Gates, chairman of Microsoft, had predicted that "within five years . . . [tablet PCs] will be the most popular form of PC sold in America." Representatives of the federal government's National Institutes of Health also urged Apple to develop a tablet PC, arguing that it would be particularly useful to doctors, nurses, and hospitals. Apple's managers decided not to develop a tablet PC, however, because they believed the technology was too complex for the average computer user and did not believe that the demand from doctors and nurses would be very large. This forecast turned out to be correct. Despite Bill Gates's prediction, in 2006, tablets made up only 1 percent of the computer market, and they were forecast to increase to only 5 percent by 2009.

According to Sobotta, "Apple executives had a theory that the route to success will not be through selling thousands of relatively expensive things, but millions of very inexpensive things like iPods." In fact, although many business analysts were skeptical that the iPod would succeed, demand grew faster than even Apple's most optimistic forecasts. By the beginning of 2007, 100 million iPods had been sold. So, it was not very surprising when in early 2007, Apple Chief Executive Officer Steve Jobs announced that the company would be combining the iPod with a cell phone to create the iPhone. With more than 900 million cell phones sold each year, Apple expects the demand for the iPhone to be very large. As Sobotta noted, "And there's an 'Apple gap': mobile phone users often find their interfaces confusing. . . . Apple's unique ability to simplify while innovating looks like a good fit there."

Apple forecast that it would sell 10 million iPhones during the product's first year on the market, with much larger sales expected in future years. Time will tell whether Apple's forecast of a large demand for the iPhone will turn out to be correct.

Source: David Sobotta, "Technology: What Jobs Told Me on the iPhone," *The Guardian* (London), January 4, 2007, p. 1; and Connie Guglielmo, "Apple First-Quarter Profit Rises on IPod, Mac Sales," Bloomberg.com, January 17, 2007.

YOUR TURN: For more practice, do problem 1.10 at the end of this chapter.

---

2 LEARNING OBJECTIVE

The Supply Side of the Market

Just as many variables influence the willingness and ability of consumers to buy a particular good or service, many variables also influence the willingness and ability of firms to sell a good or service. The most important of these variables is price. The amount of a good or service that a firm is willing and able to supply at a given price is the **quantity supplied**. Holding other variables constant, when the price of a good rises, producing

Quantity supplied The amount of a good or service that a firm is willing and able to supply at a given price.

the good is more profitable, and the quantity supplied will increase. When the price of a good falls, the good is less profitable, and the quantity supplied will decrease. In addition, devoting more and more resources to the production of a good results in increasing marginal costs. So, if, for example, Apple, Microsoft, and Toshiba increase production of digital music players during a given time period, they are likely to find that the cost of producing the additional players increases as they run existing factories for longer hours and pay higher prices for components and higher wages for workers. With higher marginal costs, firms will supply a larger quantity only if the price is higher.

Supply Schedules and Supply Curves

Supply schedule A table that shows the relationship between the price of a product and the quantity of the product supplied.

Supply curve A curve that shows the relationship between the price of a product and the quantity of the product supplied.

A **supply schedule** is a table that shows the relationship between the price of a product and the quantity of the product supplied. The table in Figure 4 is a supply schedule showing the quantity of digital music players that firms would be willing to supply per month at different prices. The graph in Figure 4 plots the numbers from the supply schedule as a *supply curve*. A **supply curve** shows the relationship between the price of a product and the quantity of the product supplied. The supply schedule and supply curve both show that as the price of players rises, firms will increase the quantity they supply. At a price of $250 per player, firms will supply 45 million players per year. At the higher price of $300, they will supply 50 million. (Once again, we are assuming for convenience that the supply curve is a straight line, even though not all supply curves are actually straight lines.)

The Law of Supply

Law of supply The rule that, holding everything else constant, increases in price cause increases in the quantity supplied, and decreases in price cause decreases in the quantity supplied.

The *market supply curve* in Figure 4 is upward sloping. We expect most supply curves to be upward sloping according to the **law of supply**, which states that, holding everything else constant, increases in price cause increases in the quantity supplied, and decreases in price cause decreases in the quantity supplied. Notice that the definition of the law of supply—like the definition of the law of demand—contains the phrase *holding everything else constant*. If only the price of the product changes, there is a movement along the supply curve, which is *an increase or a decrease in the quantity supplied*. As Figure 5 shows, if any other variable that affects the willingness of firms to supply a good changes, the supply curve will shift, which is *an increase or decrease in supply*. When firms increase the quantity of a product they wish to sell at a given price, the supply curve shifts to the right. The shift from S_1 to S_3 represents *an increase in supply*. When firms decrease the quantity of a product they wish to sell at a given price, the supply curve shifts to the left. The shift from S_1 to S_2 represents *a decrease in supply*.

Figure 4

Supply Schedule and Supply Curve

As the price changes, Apple, Microsoft, Toshiba, and the other firms producing digital music players change the quantity they are willing to supply. We can show this as a *supply schedule* in a table or as a *supply curve* on a graph. The supply schedule and supply curve both show that as the price of players rises, firms will increase the quantity they supply. At a price of $250, firms will supply 45 million players. At a price of $300 per player, firms will supply 50 million players.

Supply Schedule	
Price (dollars per player)	Quantity (millions of players per month)
$300	50
250	45
200	40
150	35
100	30

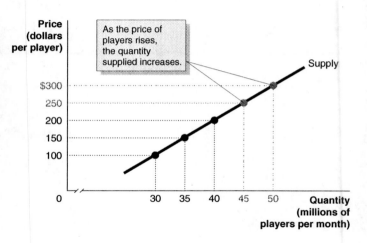

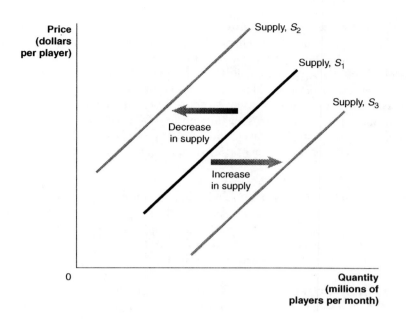

Figure 5

Shifting the Supply Curve

When firms increase the quantity of a product they wish to sell at a given price, the supply curve shifts to the right. The shift from S_1 to S_3 represents an *increase in supply*. When firms decrease the quantity of a product they wish to sell at a given price, the supply curve shifts to the left. The shift from S_1 to S_2 represents a *decrease in supply*.

Variables That Shift Supply

The following are the most important variables that shift supply:

- Prices of inputs
- Technological change
- Prices of substitutes in production
- Number of firms in the market
- Expected future prices

We next discuss how each of these variables affects the supply of digital music players.

Prices of Inputs The factor most likely to cause the supply curve for a product to shift is a change in the price of an *input*. An input is anything used in the production of a good or service. For instance, if the price of a component of digital music players, such as the microprocessor, rises, the cost of producing music players will increase, and players will be less profitable at every price. The supply of players will decline, and the market supply curve for players will shift to the left. Similarly, if the price of an input declines, the supply of players will increase, and the supply curve will shift to the right.

Technological Change A second factor that causes a change in supply is *technological change*. **Technological change** is a positive or negative change in the ability of a firm to produce a given level of output with a given quantity of inputs. Positive technological change occurs whenever a firm is able to produce more output using the same amount of inputs. This shift will happen when the *productivity* of workers or machines increases. If a firm can produce more output with the same amount of inputs, its costs will be lower, and the good will be more profitable to produce at any given price. As a result, when positive technological change occurs, the firm will increase the quantity supplied at every price, and its supply curve will shift to the right. Normally, we expect technological change to have a positive impact on a firm's willingness to supply a product. Negative technological change is relatively rare, although it could result from a natural disaster or a war that reduces the ability of a firm to supply as much output with a given amount of inputs. Negative technological change will raise a firm's costs, and the good will be less profitable to produce. Therefore, negative technological change causes a firm's supply curve to shift to the left.

Technological change A positive or negative change in the ability of a firm to produce a given level of output with a given quantity of inputs.

Prices of Substitutes in Production Firms often choose which good or service they will produce. Alternative products that a firm could produce are called *substitutes in production*. To this point, we have considered the market for all types of digital music players. But suppose we now consider separate markets for music players with screens capable of showing videos and for smaller players, without screens, that play only music. If the price of video music players increases, video music players will become more profitable, and Apple, Microsoft, and the other companies making music players will shift some of their productive capacity away from smaller players and toward video players. The companies will offer fewer smaller players for sale at every price, so the supply curve for smaller players will shift to the left.

Number of Firms in the Market A change in the number of firms in the market will change supply. When new firms *enter* a market, the supply curve shifts to the right, and when existing firms leave, or *exit*, a market, the supply curve for digital music players shifts to the left. For instance, when Microsoft introduced the Zune, the market supply curve for digital music players shifted to the right.

Expected Future Prices If a firm expects that the price of its product will be higher in the future than it is today, it has an incentive to decrease supply now and increase it in the future. For instance, if Apple believes that prices for digital music players are temporarily

TABLE 2

Variables That Shift Market Supply Curves

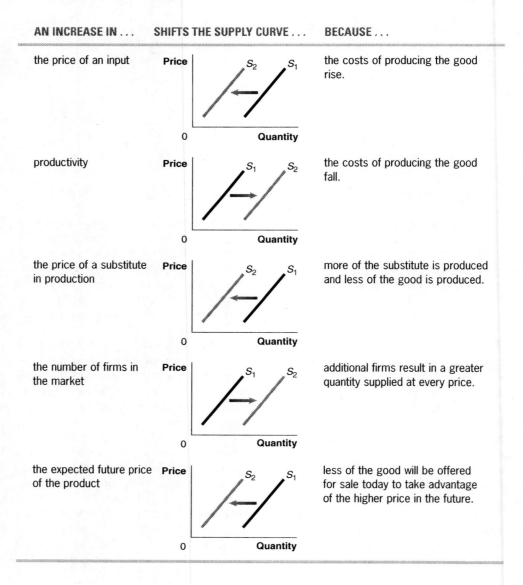

AN INCREASE IN ...	SHIFTS THE SUPPLY CURVE ...	BECAUSE ...
the price of an input		the costs of producing the good rise.
productivity		the costs of producing the good fall.
the price of a substitute in production		more of the substitute is produced and less of the good is produced.
the number of firms in the market		additional firms result in a greater quantity supplied at every price.
the expected future price of the product		less of the good will be offered for sale today to take advantage of the higher price in the future.

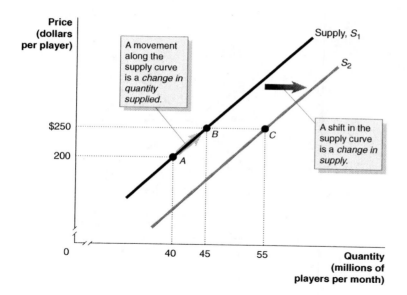

Figure 6

A Change in Supply versus a Change in the Quantity Supplied

If the price of digital music players rises from $200 to $250, the result will be a movement up the supply curve from point A to point B—an increase in quantity supplied by Apple, Microsoft, and Toshiba and the other firms from 40 million to 45 million. If the price of an input decreases or another factor changes that makes sellers supply more of the product at every price, the supply curve will shift to the right—an increase in supply. In this case, the increase in supply from S_1 to S_2 causes the quantity of digital music players supplied at a price of $250 to increase from 45 million at point B to 55 million at point C.

low—perhaps because of a price war among firms making players—it may store some of its production today to sell tomorrow, when it expects prices will be higher.

Table 2 summarizes the most important variables that cause market supply curves to shift. You should note that the table shows the shift in the supply curve that results from an *increase* in each of the variables. A *decrease* in these variables would cause the supply curve to shift in the opposite direction.

A Change in Supply versus a Change in Quantity Supplied

We noted earlier the important difference between a change in demand and a change in quantity demanded. There is a similar difference between a *change in supply* and a *change in quantity supplied*. A change in supply refers to a shift of the supply curve. The supply curve will shift when there is a change in one of the variables, *other than the price of the product*, that affects the willingness of suppliers to sell the product. A change in quantity supplied refers to a movement along the supply curve as a result of a change in the product's price. Figure 6 illustrates this important distinction. If the price of music players rises from $200 to $250, the result will be a movement up the supply curve from point A to point B—an increase in quantity supplied from 40 million to 45 million. If the price of an input decreases or another factor makes sellers supply more of the product at every price change, the supply curve will shift to the right—an increase in supply. In this case, the increase in supply from S_1 to S_2 causes the quantity of digital music players supplied at a price of $250 to increase from 45 million at point B to 55 million at point C.

3 | Use a graph to illustrate market equilibrium.

3 LEARNING OBJECTIVE

Market Equilibrium: Putting Demand and Supply Together

The purpose of markets is to bring buyers and sellers together. Instead of being chaotic and disorderly, the interaction of buyers and sellers in markets ultimately results in firms being led to produce those goods and services consumers desire most. To understand how this process happens, we first need to see how markets work to reconcile the plans of buyers and sellers.

In Figure 7, we bring together the market demand curve for digital music players and the market supply curve. Notice that the demand curve crosses the supply curve at

Figure 7

Market Equilibrium

Where the demand curve crosses the supply curve determines market equilibrium. In this case, the demand curve for digital music players crosses the supply curve at a price of $200 and a quantity of 40 million. Only at this point is the quantity of players consumers are willing to buy equal to the quantity of players Apple, Microsoft, Toshiba, and the other firms are willing to sell: The quantity demanded is equal to the quantity supplied.

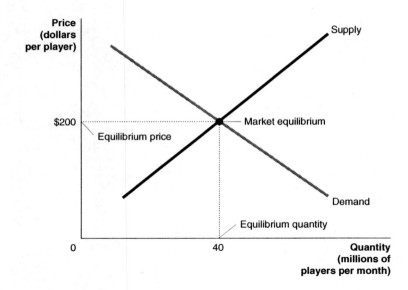

Market equilibrium A situation in which quantity demanded equals quantity supplied.

Competitive market equilibrium A market equilibrium with many buyers and many sellers.

Surplus A situation in which the quantity supplied is greater than the quantity demanded.

Shortage A situation in which the quantity demanded is greater than the quantity supplied.

only one point. This point represents a price of $200 and a quantity of 40 million players. Only at this point is the quantity of players consumers are willing to buy equal to the quantity of players firms are willing to sell. This is the point of **market equilibrium**. Only at market equilibrium will the quantity demanded equal the quantity supplied. In this case, the *equilibrium price* is $200, and the *equilibrium quantity* is 40 million. As we noted at the beginning of the chapter, markets that have many buyers and many sellers are competitive markets, and equilibrium in these markets is a **competitive market equilibrium**. In the market for digital music players, there are many buyers but fewer than 20 firms. Whether 20 firms is enough for our model of demand and supply to apply to this market is a matter of judgment. In this chapter, we are assuming that the market for digital music players has enough sellers to be competitive.

How Markets Eliminate Surpluses and Shortages

A market that is not in equilibrium moves toward equilibrium. Once a market is in equilibrium, it remains in equilibrium. To see why, consider what happens if a market is not in equilibrium. For instance, suppose that the price in the market for digital music players was $250, rather than the equilibrium price of $200. As Figure 8 shows, at a price of $250, the quantity of players supplied would be 45 million, and the quantity of players demanded would be 35 million. When the quantity supplied is greater than the quantity demanded, there is a **surplus** in the market. In this case, the surplus is equal to 10 million players (45 million − 35 million = 10 million). When there is a surplus, firms have unsold goods piling up, which gives them an incentive to increase their sales by cutting the price. Cutting the price will simultaneously increase the quantity demanded and decrease the quantity supplied. This adjustment will reduce the surplus, but as long as the price is above $200, there will be a surplus, and downward pressure on the price will continue. Only when the price has fallen to $200 will the market be in equilibrium.

If, however, the price were $100, the quantity supplied would be 30 million, and the quantity demanded would be 50 million, as shown in Figure 8. When the quantity demanded is greater than the quantity supplied, there is a **shortage** in the market. In this case, the shortage is equal to 20 million digital music players (50 million − 30 million = 20 million). When a shortage occurs, some consumers will be unable to buy a digital music player at the current price. In this situation, firms will realize that they can raise the price without losing sales. A higher price will simultaneously increase the quantity supplied and decrease the quantity demanded. This adjustment will reduce the shortage, but as long as the price is below $200, there will be a shortage, and upward pressure on the price will continue. Only when the price has risen to $200 will the market be in equilibrium.

16

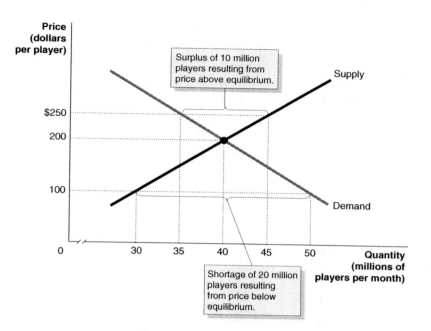

Figure 8

The Effect of Surpluses and Shortages on the Market Price

When the market price is above equilibrium, there will be a *surplus*. In the figure, a price of $250 for digital music players results in 45 million being supplied but only 35 million being demanded, or a surplus of 10 million. As Apple, Microsoft, Toshiba, and the other firms cut the price to dispose of the surplus, the price will fall to the equilibrium of $200. When the market price is below equilibrium, there will be a *shortage*. A price of $100 results in 50 million players being demanded but only 30 million being supplied, or a shortage of 20 million. As consumers who are unable to buy a player offer to pay higher prices, the price will rise to the equilibrium of $200.

At a competitive market equilibrium, all consumers willing to pay the market price will be able to buy as much of the product as they want, and all firms willing to accept the market price will be able to sell as much of the product as they want. As a result, there will be no reason for the price to change unless either the demand curve or the supply curve shifts.

Demand and Supply Both Count

Always keep in mind that it is the interaction of demand and supply that determines the equilibrium price. Neither consumers nor firms can dictate what the equilibrium price will be. No firm can sell anything at any price unless it can find a willing buyer, and no consumer can buy anything at any price without finding a willing seller.

Solved Problem | **3**

Demand and Supply Both Count:
A Tale of Two Letters

Which letter is likely to be worth more: one written by Abraham Lincoln or one written by his assassin, John Wilkes Booth? Lincoln is one of the greatest presidents, and many people collect anything written by him. The demand for letters written by Lincoln surely would seem to be much greater than the demand for letters written by Booth. Yet when R. M. Smythe and Co. auctioned off on the same day a letter written by Lincoln and a letter written by Booth, the Booth letter sold for $31,050, and the Lincoln letter sold for only $21,850. Use a demand and supply graph to explain how the Booth letter has a higher market price than the Lincoln letter, even though the demand for letters written by Lincoln is greater than the demand for letters written by Booth.

SOLVING THE PROBLEM:

Step 1: **Review the chapter material.** This problem is about prices being determined at market equilibrium, so you may want to review the section "Market Equilibrium: Putting Demand and Supply Together."

Step 2: **Draw demand curves that illustrate the greater demand for Lincoln's letters.** Begin by drawing two demand curves. Label one "Demand for Lincoln's letters" and the other "Demand for Booth's letters." Make sure that the Lincoln demand curve is much farther to the right than the Booth demand curve.

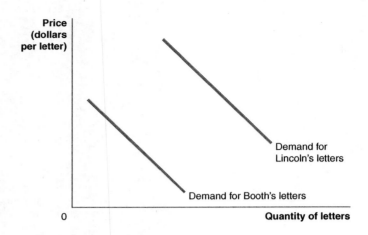

Step 3: **Draw supply curves that illustrate the equilibrium price of Booth's letters being higher than the equilibrium price of Lincoln's letters.** Based on the demand curves you have just drawn, think about how it might be possible for the market price of Lincoln's letters to be lower than the market price of Booth's letters. The only way this can be true is if the supply of Lincoln's letters is much greater than the supply of Booth's letters. Draw on your graph a supply curve for Lincoln's letters and a supply curve for Booth's letters that will result in an equilibrium price of Booth's letters of $31,050 and an equilibrium price of Lincoln's letters of $21,850. You have now solved the problem.

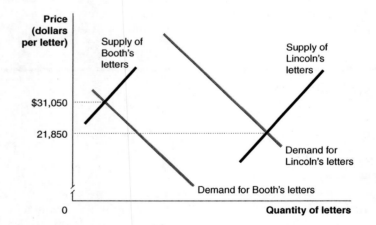

EXTRA CREDIT: The explanation for this puzzle is that both demand and supply count when determining market price. The demand for Lincoln's letters is much greater than the demand for Booth's letters, but the supply of Booth's letters is very small. Historians believe that only eight letters written by Booth exist today. (Note that the supply curves for letters written by Booth and by Lincoln slope up even though only a fixed number of each of these types of letters is available and, obviously, no more can be produced. The upward slope of the supply curves occurs because the higher the price, the larger the quantity of letters that will be offered for sale by people who currently own them.)

▶▶ End Solved Problem 3

YOUR TURN: For more practice, do related problem 3.4 at the end of this chapter.

18

The Effect of Demand and Supply Shifts on Equilibrium

We have seen that the interaction of demand and supply in markets determines the quantity of a good that is produced and the price at which it sells. We have also seen that several variables cause demand curves to shift, and other variables cause supply curves to shift. As a result, demand and supply curves in most markets are constantly shifting, and the prices and quantities that represent equilibrium are constantly changing. In this section, we see how shifts in demand and supply curves affect equilibrium price and quantity.

The Effect of Shifts in Supply on Equilibrium

When Microsoft decided to start selling the Zune music player, the market supply curve for music players shifted to the right. Figure 9 shows the supply curve shifting from S_1 to S_2. When the supply curve shifts to the right, there will be a surplus at the original equilibrium price, P_1. The surplus is eliminated as the equilibrium price falls to P_2, and the equilibrium quantity rises from Q_1 to Q_2. If existing firms exit the market, the supply curve will shift to the left, causing the equilibrium price to rise and the equilibrium quantity to fall.

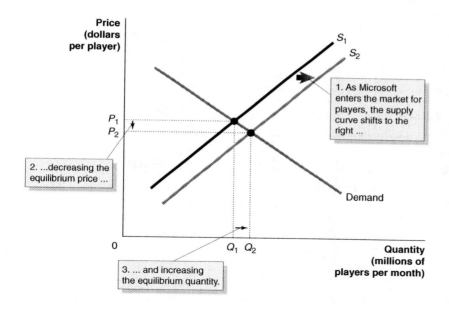

Figure 9

The Effect of an Increase in Supply on Equilibrium

If a firm enters a market, as Microsoft entered the market for digital music players when it launched the Zune, the equilibrium price will fall, and the equilibrium quantity will rise.

1. As Microsoft enters the market for digital music players, a larger quantity of players will be supplied at every price, so the market supply curve shifts to the right, from S_1 to S_2, which causes a surplus of players at the original price, P_1.
2. The equilibrium price falls from P_1 to P_2.
3. The equilibrium quantity rises from Q_1 to Q_2.

In-figure labels:
1. As Microsoft enters the market for players, the supply curve shifts to the right ...
2. ...decreasing the equilibrium price ...
3. ... and increasing the equilibrium quantity.

Making the Connection | The Falling Price of LCD Televisions

Research on flat-screen televisions using liquid crystal displays (LCDs) began in the 1960s. However, it was surprisingly difficult to use this research to produce a television priced low enough for many consumers to purchase. One researcher noted, "In the 1960s, we used to say 'In ten years, we're going to have the TV on the wall.' We said the same thing in the seventies and then in the eighties." A key technical problem in manufacturing LCD televisions was making glass sheets large enough, thin enough, and clean enough to be used as LCD screens. Finally, in 1999, Corning, Inc., developed a process to manufacture glass that was less than 1 millimeter thick and very clean because it was produced without being touched by machinery.

Corning's breakthrough led to what the *Wall Street Journal* described as a "race to build new, better factories." The firms producing the flat screens are all located in Taiwan, South Korea, and Japan. The leading firms are Korea's Samsung Electronics and LG Phillips LCD, Taiwan's AU Optronics, and Japan's Sharp Corporation. In 2004, AU Optronics opened a new factory with 2.4 million square feet of clean room in which the LCD screens are manufactured. This factory is nearly five times as large as the largest factory in which Intel makes computer chips. In all, 10 new factories manufacturing LCD screens came into operation between late 2004 and late 2005. The figure shows that this increase in supply drove the price of a typical large LCD television from $4,000 in the fall of 2004 to $1,600 at the end of 2006, increasing the quantity demanded worldwide from 8 million to 46 million.

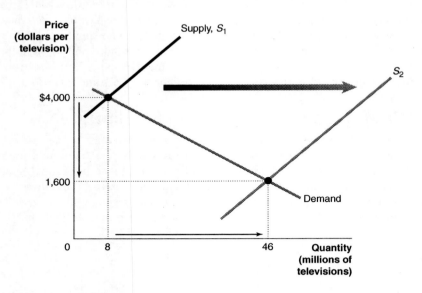

Sources: David Richards, "Sony and Panasonic Flat Screen Kings," Smarthouse.com, February 13, 2007; Evan Ramstad, "Big Display: Once a Footnote, Flat Screens Grow into Huge Industry," *Wall Street Journal*, August 30, 2004, p. A1; and Michael Schuman, "Flat Chance: Prices on Cool TVs Are Dropping as New Factories Come on Line," *Time*, October 18, 2004, pp. 64–66.

YOUR TURN: For more practice, do problem 4.7 at the end of this chapter.

The Effect of Shifts in Demand on Equilibrium

When population growth and income growth occur, the market demand for music players shifts to the right. Figure 10 shows the effect of a demand curve shifting to the right, from D_1 to D_2. This shift causes a shortage at the original equilibrium price, P_1. To eliminate the shortage, the equilibrium price rises to P_2, and the equilibrium quantity

Figure 10

The Effect of an Increase in Demand on Equilibrium

Increases in income and population will cause the equilibrium price and quantity to rise:
1. As population and income grow, the quantity demanded increases at every price, and the market demand curve shifts to the right, from D_1 to D_2, which causes a shortage of digital music players at the original price, P_1.
2. The equilibrium price rises from P_1 to P_2.
3. The equilibrium quantity rises from Q_1 to Q_2.

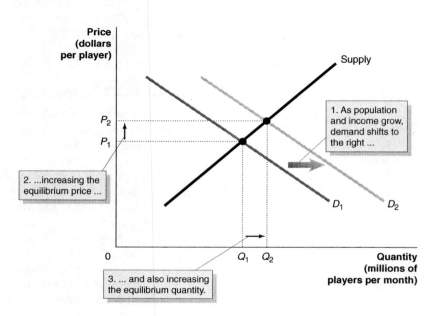

rises from Q_1 to Q_2. By contrast, if the price of a complementary good, such as downloads from music Web sites, were to rise, the demand for music players would decrease. This change would cause the demand curve for players to shift to the left, and the equilibrium price and quantity would both decrease.

The Effect of Shifts in Demand and Supply over Time

Whenever only demand or only supply shifts, we can easily predict the effect on equilibrium price and quantity. But what happens if *both* curves shift? For instance, in many markets, the demand curve shifts to the right over time, as population and income grow. The supply curve also often shifts to the right as new firms enter the market and positive technological change occurs. Whether the equilibrium price in a market rises or falls over time depends on whether demand shifts to the right more than does supply. Panel (a) of Figure 11 shows that when demand shifts to the right more than supply, the equilibrium price rises. But, as panel (b) shows, when supply shifts to the right more than demand, the equilibrium price falls.

Table 3 summarizes all possible combinations of shifts in demand and supply over time and the effects of the shifts on equilibrium price (P) and quantity (Q). For example, the entry in red in the table shows that if the demand curve shifts to the right and the supply curve also shifts to the right, then the equilibrium quantity will increase, while the equilibrium price may increase, decrease, or remain unchanged. To make sure you understand each entry in the table, draw demand and supply graphs to check whether you can reproduce the predicted changes in equilibrium price and quantity. If the entry in the table says the predicted change in equilibrium price or quantity can be either an increase or a decrease, draw two graphs similar to panels (a) and (b) of Figure 11, one showing the equilibrium price or quantity increasing and the other showing it decreasing. Note also that in the ambiguous cases where either price or quantity might increase or decrease, it is also possible that price or quantity might remain unchanged. Be sure you understand why this is true.

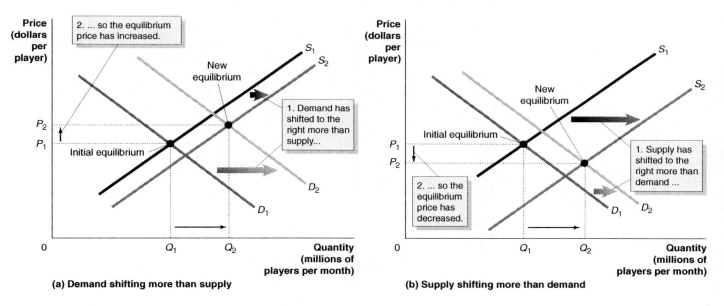

(a) Demand shifting more than supply

(b) Supply shifting more than demand

Figure 11 | Shifts in Demand and Supply over Time

Whether the price of a product rises or falls over time depends on whether demand shifts to the right more than supply.

In panel (a), demand shifts to the right more than supply, and the equilibrium price rises.
1. Demand shifts to the right more than supply.
2. Equilibrium price rises from P_1 to P_2.

In panel (b), supply shifts to the right more than demand, and the equilibrium price falls.
1. Supply shifts to the right more than demand.
2. Equilibrium price falls from P_1 to P_2.

TABLE 3

How Shifts in Demand and Supply Affect Equilibrium Price (P) and Quantity (Q)

	SUPPLY CURVE UNCHANGED	SUPPLY CURVE SHIFTS TO THE RIGHT	SUPPLY CURVE SHIFTS TO THE LEFT
DEMAND CURVE UNCHANGED	Q unchanged P unchanged	Q increases P decreases	Q decreases P increases
DEMAND CURVE SHIFTS TO THE RIGHT	Q increases P increases	Q increases P increases or decreases	Q increases or decreases P increases
DEMAND CURVE SHIFTS TO THE LEFT	Q decreases P decreases	Q increases or decreases P decreases	Q decreases P decreases or decreases

Solved Problem | 4

High Demand and Low Prices in the Lobster Market?

During the spring, when demand for lobster is relatively low, Maine lobstermen are able to sell their lobster catches for about $4.50 per pound. During the summer, when demand for lobster is much higher, Maine lobstermen are able to sell their lobster catches for only about $3.00 per pound. It may seem strange that the market price is higher when demand is low than when demand is high. Can you resolve this paradox with the help of a demand and supply graph?

SOLVING THE PROBLEM:

Step 1: **Review the chapter material.** This problem is about how shifts in demand and supply curves affect the equilibrium price, so you may want to review the section "The Effect of Shifts in Demand and Supply over Time."

Step 2: **Draw the demand and supply graph.** Draw a demand and supply graph, showing the market equilibrium in the spring. Label the equilibrium price $4.50. Label both the demand and supply curves "spring."

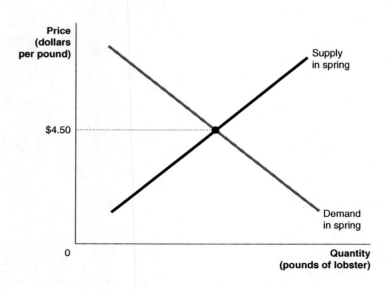

22

Step 3: **Add to your graph a demand curve for summer.**

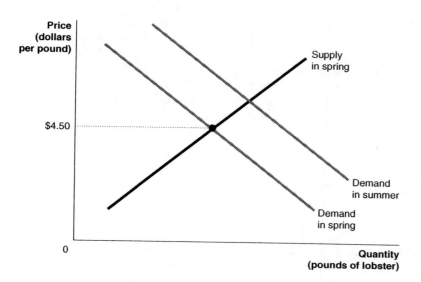

Step 4: **Explain the graph.** After studying the graph, it is possible to see how the equilibrium price can fall from $4.50 to $3.00, despite the increase in demand: The supply curve must have shifted to the right by enough to cause the equilibrium price to fall to $3.00. Draw the new supply curve, label it "summer," and label the new equilibrium price $3.00. The demand for lobster does increase in summer compared with the spring. But the increase in the supply of lobster between spring and summer is even greater. So, the equilibrium price falls.

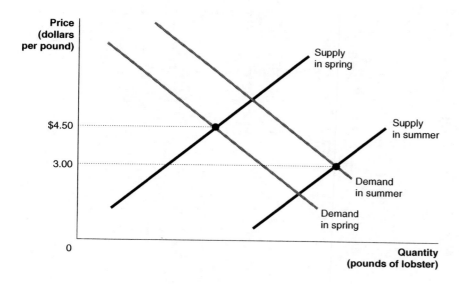

Source: Carey Goldberg, "Down East, the Lobster Hauls Are Up Big," *New York Times*, May 31, 2001.

YOUR TURN: For more practice, do related problem 4.5 at the end of this chapter.

>> **End Solved Problem 4**

Shifts in a Curve versus Movements along a Curve

When analyzing markets using demand and supply curves, it is important to remember that *when a shift in a demand or supply curve causes a change in equilibrium price, the change in price does not cause a further shift in demand or supply*. For instance, suppose an increase in supply causes the price of a good to fall, while everything else that affects the willingness of consumers to buy the good is constant. The result will be an increase in the quantity demanded but not an increase in demand. For demand to increase, the whole curve must shift. The point is the same for supply: If the price of the good falls but everything else that affects the willingness of sellers to supply the good is constant, the quantity supplied decreases, but the supply does not. For supply to decrease, the whole curve must shift.

Don't Let This Happen to **YOU!**

Remember: A Change in a Good's Price Does *Not* Cause the Demand or Supply Curve to Shift

Suppose a student is asked to draw a demand and supply graph to illustrate how an increase in the price of oranges would affect the market for apples, other variables being constant. He draws the graph on the left below and explains it as follows: "Because apples and oranges are substitutes, an increase in the price of oranges will cause an initial shift to the right in the demand curve for apples, from D_1 to D_2. However, because this initial shift in the demand curve for apples results in a higher price for apples, P_2, consumers will find apples less desirable, and the demand curve will shift to the left, from D_2 to D_3, resulting in a final equilibrium price of P_3." Do you agree or disagree with the student's analysis?

You should disagree. The student has correctly understood that an increase in the price of oranges will cause the demand curve for apples to shift to the right. But the sec-

ond demand curve shift the student describes, from D_2 to D_3, will not take place. Changes in the price of a product do not result in shifts in the product's demand curve. Changes in the price of a product result only in movements along a demand curve.

The graph on the right below shows the correct analysis. The increase in the price of oranges causes the demand curve for apples to increase from D_1 to D_2. At the original price, P_1, the increase in demand initially results in a shortage of apples equal to $Q_3 - Q_1$. But, as we have seen, a shortage causes the price to increase until the shortage is eliminated. In this case, the price will rise to P_2, where the quantity demanded and the quantity supplied are both equal to Q_2. Notice that the increase in price causes a decrease in the *quantity demanded* from Q_3 to Q_2, but does *not* cause a decrease in demand.

YOUR TURN: Test your understanding by doing related problems 4.13 and 4.14 at the end of this chapter.

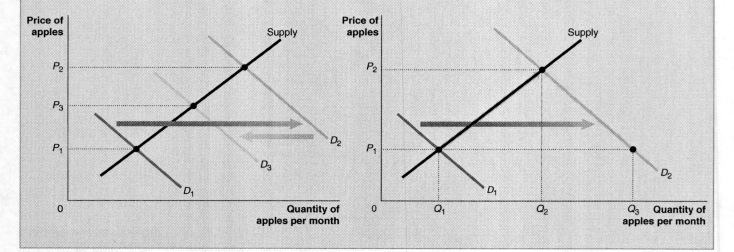

Economics in YOUR Life!

At the beginning of the chapter, we asked you to consider two questions: Would you choose to buy a Zune if it had a lower price than a comparable iPod? and Would you choose a Zune if the songs sold on Zune Marketplace were cheaper than the songs sold on iTunes? To determine the answers, you have to recognize that iPods and Zunes are substitutes, while Zunes and songs sold on Zune Marketplace are complements. If a Zune had a lower price than an iPod, this would cause consumers to purchase the Zune rather than the iPod, provided that the two players have the same features. If consumers believe that the Zune and the iPod are very close substitutes, a fall in the price of Zunes would cause the demand for iPods to decline, as the quantity of Zunes demanded increased. If Microsoft reduced the price of a song sold on Zune Marketplace so that it was lower than the price of the same song on iTunes, even if iPods and Zunes had the same price, the demand for Zunes would increase, and the demand for iPods would decrease.

Conclusion

The interaction of demand and supply determines market equilibrium. The model of demand and supply provides us with a powerful tool for predicting how changes in the actions of consumers and firms will cause changes in equilibrium prices and quantities. As we have seen in this chapter, the model can often be used to analyze markets that do not meet all the requirements for being perfectly competitive. As long as there is intense competition among sellers, the model of demand and supply can often successfully predict changes in prices and quantities. We will use the model in the next chapter to analyze economic efficiency and the results of government-imposed price floors and price ceilings. Before moving on, read *An Inside Look* on the next page to learn how Apple and AT&T benefit from collaborating on the iPhone.

WALL STREET JOURNAL, FEBRUARY 17, 2007

Apple Coup: How Steve Jobs Played Hardball in iPhone Birth

During a visit to Las Vegas last December for a rodeo event, Cingular Wireless chief executive Stan Sigman received a welcome guest: Steve Jobs. The Apple Inc. chief stopped by Mr. Sigman's Four Seasons hotel suite to show off the iPhone, a sleek cellphone designed to surf the Web and double as an iPod music player.

The phone had been in development by Apple and Cingular [now AT&T] for two years and was weeks away from being revealed to the world. And yet this was the first time Mr. Sigman got to see it. For three hours, Mr. Jobs played with the device, with its touch-screen that allows users to view contacts, dial numbers and flip through photos with the swipe of a finger. Mr. Sigman looked on in awe, according to a person familiar with the meeting . . .

Mr. Jobs is famous for making a splash with new products that upend industry models. Several years ago, he personally lobbied music industry executives and obtained licenses for songs that gave Apple the flexibility to build its successful iTunes store.

Apple eyed the cellphone market as both an opportunity to expand its iPod business and, if ignored, a potential threat to the company, people familiar with its strategy say. Cellphones are gradually offering more sophisticated capabilities and features, including increased storage capacity and entertainment functions. That stands to make them more competitive with iPods over time. Already, music phones like Samsung Electronics Co.'s BlackJack, Sony Ericsson's Walkman models and LG Electronic Inc.'s Chocolate are edging onto Apple's turf . . .

In early 2005, Mr. Jobs called Mr. Sigman to pitch the initial concept of the iPhone. The two executives later met in New York, and agreed to pursue the idea. Mr. Sigman is a Texan who wears cowboy boots and business suits, while Mr. Jobs is a former hippie who sports black turtlenecks and jeans. Despite their vastly different styles, the two executives found common ground. Over the next year and a half, the two sides negotiated to reach an agreement that would make sense for both of them . . .

While Mr. Jobs considered Cingular a logical choice as a partner to carry the device—its GSM technology is the prevailing standard in much of the world—Apple continued to shop its ideas to other carriers. Mr. Jobs reached out to Verizon Wireless chief executive Denny Strigl in the middle of 2005 and proposed a partnership with the carrier, a joint venture of Verizon Communications Inc. and Vodafone Group PLC. The companies held a few discussions over the next year, but the talks eventually soured.

There were a few sticking points. Verizon balked at the notion of cutting out its big retail partners, like Circuit City, who would not be allowed to sell the phone. And the company's chief marketing officer, John Stratton, was firm that Verizon wouldn't give up its ability to sell content like music and videos through its proprietary V Cast service, people familiar with the discussions say. . . .

In January, Mr. Jobs finally unveiled the phone at Macworld, the conference he has used to launch such key products as the iPod Mini. Since then, the two companies have continued to test the iPhone at an undisclosed facility, a person familiar with the matter said. The handful of Cingular people who have access to the sample phones at the company's headquarters were required to sign confidentiality agreements, a person familiar with the matter says. Meanwhile, competitors already are responding. Samsung and LG both have announced phones in recent weeks with designs that look similar to the iPhone. Apple has said it intends to sell 10 million of the devices by 2008, with price tags for two different versions set steeply at $499 and $599.

Cingular, which has more than 60 million customers, hopes the iPhone will give it a lift when it hits stores in June, at a time when attracting new subscribers is getting more difficult for all operators.

Source: "Apple Coup: How Steve Jobs Played Hardball in iPhone Birth" by Armol Sharma, Nick Wingfield, and Li Yuan from *Wall Street Journal*, February 17, 2007, p. A1. Copyright © 2007 Dow Jones. Reprinted by permission of Dow Jones via Copyright Clearance Center.

© Glow Images/Alamy

Key Points in the Article

The article discusses Apple's new iPhone, which combines features of the iPod and a cell phone. Apple has teamed up with Cingular, now AT&T, to provide cell phone service for the iPhone. The phone will also function as an iPod that plays music in Apple's proprietary format. The iPhone helps both companies. Apple gains because it now has a digital music player that doubles as a cell phone and competes with the other music phones on the market. AT&T gains a potentially large customer base for its cell phone services.

Analyzing the News

Ⓐ Apple has viewed the evolution of the cell phone as a threat to the iPod because over time, cell phone manufacturers have added features that are similar to those of the iPod. For example, manu-facturers have increased the storage capacity of cell phones so that people can store their music, pictures, and videos. Cell phones can also function as cameras and video recorders. These cell phones are a threat to the iPod because they are sub-stitute goods that offer many of the same features.

If people are forced to choose just one product, then they might choose a cell phone that can play music over an iPod that cannot function as a phone. The figure shows the result. The demand curve for iPods shifts to the left, which reduces the price and quantity sold of iPods. Because the iPod is a critical product for Apple, this would significantly harm the entire com-pany. Introducing the iPhone is a strategy to protect a very lucrative market for Apple.

Ⓑ Apple could have worked with a num-ber of different cell phone service providers. Ultimately, Apple chose to part-ner with Cingular for a couple of reasons. First, Cingular uses technology that is the industry standard. Second, Cingular was willing to make concessions that other cell phone service providers were not willing to make. The chapter opener pointed out that one of the key factors in the iPod's success was that Apple both made the iPod and sold music through iTunes. This means that the two products were developed by the same company and worked seamlessly together. One reason that Apple did not end up partnering with Verizon is that Verizon insisted on the right to continue to sell downloads of music and videos. This raised the possibility of compatibility problems with downloads available through iTunes.

Ⓒ AT&T also benefits from the introduc-tion of the iPhone. The iPhone will work only with AT&T's cellular phone ser-vice, so if you want to purchase an iPhone, you have to purchase AT&T's service. That means the iPhone and AT&T's services are complementary goods—and as sales of iPhones increase, the demand for AT&T's services should also increase.

Thinking Critically

1. What effect will the introduction of the iPhone have on sales of the iPod? Are there any reasons why someone might want to own both an iPhone and an iPod? Would it be better to think of the iPhone and the iPod as substitutes or complements? Briefly explain.

2. Apple plans to sell two versions of the iPhone: one for $499 and one for $599, which are significantly higher than the price of the most expensive iPod and much higher than the prices of cell phones. Are most customers likely to see the iPhone as a closer substi-tute for other cell phones or for other digital music players? Is the high price of the iPhone relevant to your answer? Briefly explain.

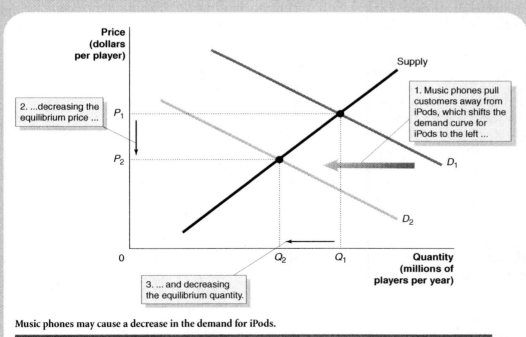
Music phones may cause a decrease in the demand for iPods.

Key Terms

Ceteris paribus ("all else equal")

Competitive market equilibrium

Complements

Demand curve

Demand schedule

Demographics

Income effect

Inferior good

Law of demand

Law of supply

Market demand

Market equilibrium

Normal good

Perfectly competitive market

Quantity demanded

Quantity supplied

Shortage

Substitutes

Substitution effect

Supply curve

Supply schedule

Surplus

Technological change

1 LEARNING OBJECTIVE | 1 | Discuss the variables that influence demand

The Demand Side of the Market

Summary

The model of demand and supply is the most powerful in economics. The model applies exactly only to **perfectly competitive markets**, where there are many buyers and sellers, all the products sold are identical, and there are no barriers to new sellers entering the market. But the model can also be useful in analyzing markets that don't meet all of these requirements. The **quantity demanded** is the amount of a good or service that a consumer is willing and able to purchase at a given price. A **demand schedule** is a table that shows the relationship between the price of a product and the quantity of the product demanded. A **demand curve** is a graph that shows the relationship between the price of a good and the quantity of the good consumers are willing and able to buy over a period of time. **Market demand** is the demand by all consumers of a given good or service. The **law of demand** states that *ceteris paribus*—holding everything else constant—the quantity of a product demanded increases when the price falls and decreases when the price rises. Demand curves slope downward because of the **substitution effect**, which is the change in quantity demanded that results from a price change making one good more or less expensive relative to another good, and the **income effect**, which is the change in quantity demanded of a good that results from the effect of a change in the good's price on consumer purchasing power. Changes in income, the prices of related goods, tastes, population and demographics, and expected future prices all cause the demand curve to shift. **Substitutes** are goods that can be used for the same purpose. **Complements** are goods that are used together. A **normal good** is a good for which demand increases as income increases. An **inferior good** is a good for which demand decreases as income increases. **Demographics** are the characteristics of a population with respect to age, race, and gender. A change in demand refers to a shift of the demand curve. A change in quantity demanded refers to a movement along the demand curve as a result of a change in the product's price.

 Visit www.myeconlab.com to complete these exercises online and get instant feedback.

Review Questions

1.1 What is a demand schedule? What is a demand curve?

1.2 What do economists mean when they use the Latin expression *ceteris paribus*?

1.3 What is the difference between a change in demand and a change in quantity demanded?

1.4 What is the law of demand? What are the main variables that will cause the demand curve to shift? Give an example of each.

Problems and Applications

1.5 (Related to the *Making the Connection*) For each of the following pairs of products, state which are complements, which are substitutes, and which are unrelated.
   a. Pepsi and Coke
   b. Oscar Mayer hot dogs and Wonder hot dog buns
   c. Jif peanut butter and Smucker's strawberry jam
   d. iPods and Texas Instruments financial calculators

1.6 (Related to the *Chapter Opener*) Suppose Apple discovers that it is selling relatively few downloads of television programs on iTunes. Are downloads of television programs substitutes or complements for downloads of music? For downloads of movies? How might the answers to these questions affect Apple's decision about whether to continue offering downloads of television programs on iTunes?

1.7 State whether each of the following events will result in a movement along the demand curve for McDonald's Big Mac hamburgers or whether it will cause the curve to shift. If the demand curve shifts, indicate whether it will shift to the left or to the right and draw a graph to illustrate the shift.
   a. The price of Burger King's Whopper hamburger declines.

b. McDonald's distributes coupons for $1.00 off on a purchase of a Big Mac.

c. Because of a shortage of potatoes, the price of French fries increases.

d. Kentucky Fried Chicken raises the price of a bucket of fried chicken.

1.8 (Related to the *Making the Connection*) Name three products whose demand is likely to increase rapidly if the following demographic groups increase at a faster rate than the population as a whole:

a. Teenagers

b. Children under five

c. People over age 65

1.9 Suppose the data in the following table present the price of a base model Ford Explorer sport-utility vehicle (SUV) and the quantity of Explorers sold. Do

these data indicate that the demand curve for Explorers is upward sloping? Explain.

YEAR	PRICE	QUANTITY
2006	$27,865	325,265
2007	28,325	330,648
2008	28,765	352,666

1.10 (Related to the *Making the Connection*) In early 2007, Apple forecast that it would sell 10 million iPhones during the product's first year on the market. What factors could affect the accuracy of this forecast? Is the forecast likely to be more or less accurate than Apple's forecast of how many iPods they would sell during the same time period? Briefly explain.

>> **End Learning Objective 1**

2 LEARNING OBJECTIVE | 2 | Discuss the variables that influence supply

The Supply Side of the Market

Summary

The **quantity supplied** is the amount of a good that a firm is willing and able to supply at a given price. A **supply schedule** is a table that shows the relationship between the price of a product and the quantity of the product supplied. A **supply curve** shows on a graph the relationship between the price of a product and the quantity of the product supplied. When the price of a product rises, producing the product is more profitable, and a greater amount will be supplied. The **law of supply** states that, holding everything else constant, the quantity of a product supplied increases when the price rises and decreases when the price falls. Changes in the prices of inputs, technology, the prices of substitutes in production, expected future prices, and the number of firms in a market all cause the supply curve to shift. **Technological change** is a positive or negative change in the ability of a firm to produce a given level of output with a given quantity of inputs. A change in supply refers to a shift of the supply curve. A change in quantity supplied refers to a movement along the supply curve as a result of a change in the product's price.

myeconlab Visit www.myeconlab.com to complete these exercises online and get instant feedback.

Review Questions

2.1 What is a supply schedule? What is a supply curve?

2.2 What is the law of supply? What are the main variables that will cause a supply curve to shift? Give an example of each.

Problems and Applications

2.3 Briefly explain whether each of the following statements describes a change in supply or a change in the quantity supplied.

a. To take advantage of high prices for snow shovels during a very snowy winter, Alexander Shovels, Inc., decides to increase output.

b. The success of Apple's iPod leads more firms to begin producing digital music players.

c. In the six months following Hurricane Katrina, production of oil in the Gulf of Mexico declined by 25 percent.

2.4 Will each firm in a given industry always supply the same quantity as every other firm at each price? What factors might cause the quantity of digital music players supplied by each firm at each price to be different?

2.5 If the price of a good increases, is the increase in the quantity of the good supplied likely to be smaller or larger, the longer the time period being considered? Briefly explain.

>> **End Learning Objective 2**

3 LEARNING OBJECTIVE   3 | Use a graph to illustrate market equilibrium

Market Equilibrium: Putting Demand and Supply Together

Summary

Market equilibrium occurs where the demand curve intersects the supply curve. A **competitive market equilibrium** has a market equilibrium with many buyers and many sellers. Only at this point is the quantity demanded equal to the quantity supplied. Prices above equilibrium result in **surpluses**, with the quantity supplied being greater than the quantity demanded. Surpluses cause the market price to fall. Prices below equilibrium result in **shortages**, with the quantity demanded being greater than the quantity supplied. Shortages cause the market price to rise.

 Visit www.myeconlab.com to complete these exercises online and get instant feedback.

Review Questions

3.1 What do economists mean by market equilibrium?

3.2 What happens in a market if the current price is above the equilibrium price? What happens if the current price is below the equilibrium price?

Problems and Applications

3.3 Briefly explain whether you agree with the following statement: "When there is a shortage of a good, con-

sumers eventually give up trying to buy it, so the demand for the good declines, and the price falls until the market is finally in equilibrium."

3.4 **(Related to *Solved Problem 3*)** In *The Wealth of Nations*, Adam Smith discussed what has come to be known as the "diamond and water paradox":

> Nothing is more useful than water: but it will purchase scarce anything; scarce anything can be had in exchange for it. A diamond, on the contrary, has scarce any value in use; but a very great quantity of other goods may frequently be had in exchange for it.

Graph the market for diamonds and the market for water. Show how it is possible for the price of water to be much lower than the price of diamonds, even though the demand for water is much greater than the demand for diamonds.

3.5 Briefly explain under what conditions zero would be the equilibrium quantity.

3.6 If a market is in equilibrium, is it necessarily true that all buyers and all sellers are satisfied with the market price? Briefly explain.

>> End Learning Objective 3

4 LEARNING OBJECTIVE   4 | Use demand and supply graphs to predict changes in prices and quantities

The Effect of Demand and Supply Shifts on Equilibrium

Summary

In most markets, demand and supply curves shift frequently, causing changes in equilibrium prices and quantities. Over time, if demand increases more than supply, equilibrium price will rise. If supply increases more than demand, equilibrium price will fall.

 Visit www.myeconlab.com to complete these exercises online and get instant feedback.

Review Questions

4.1 Draw a demand and supply curve to show the effect on the equilibrium price in a market in the following two situations:
  a. The demand curve shifts to the right.
  b. The supply curve shifts to the left.

4.2 If, over time, the demand curve for a product shifts to the right more than the supply curve does, what will happen to the equilibrium price? What will happen to the equilibrium price if the supply curve shifts to the right more than the demand curve? For each case, draw a demand and supply graph to illustrate your answer.

Problems and Applications

4.3 As oil prices rose during 2006, the demand for alternative fuels increased. Ethanol, one alternative fuel, is made from corn. According to an article in the *Wall Street Journal*, the price of tortillas, which are made from corn, also rose during 2006: "The price spike [in tortillas] is part of a ripple effect from the ethanol boom."

a. Draw a demand and supply graph for the corn market and use it to show the effect on this market of an increase in the demand for ethanol. Be sure to indicate the equilibrium price and quantity before and after the increase in the demand for ethanol.

b. Draw a demand and supply graph for the tortilla market and use it to show the effect on this market of an increase in the price of corn. Once again, be sure to indicate the equilibrium price and quantity before and after the increase in the demand for ethanol.

Source: Mark Gongloff, "Tortilla Soup," *Wall Street Journal*, January 25, 2007.

4.4 A recent study indicated that "stricter college alcohol policies, such as raising the price of alcohol, or banning alcohol on campus, decrease the number of students who use marijuana."

a. On the basis of this information, are alcohol and marijuana substitutes or complements?

b. Suppose that campus authorities reduce the supply of alcohol on campus. Use demand and supply graphs to illustrate the impact on the campus alcohol and marijuana markets.

Source: Jenny Williams, Rosalie Pacula, Frank Chaloupka, and Henry Wechsler, "Alcohol and Marijuana Use Among College Students: Economic Complements or Substitutes?" *Health Economics*, Volume 13, Issue 9, September 2005, pp. 825–843.

4.5 **(Related to *Solved Problem 4*)** The demand for watermelons is highest during summer and lowest during winter. Yet watermelon prices are normally lower in summer than in winter. Use a demand and supply graph to demonstrate how this is possible. Be sure to carefully label the curves in your graph and to clearly indicate the equilibrium summer price and the equilibrium winter price.

4.6 According to an article in the *Wall Street Journal*:

As occupancy rates at luxury hotels have grown 13% over the last five years, prices have risen by 19%, according to Smith Travel Research. (That comes despite an 18.5% increase in the number of rooms over the same period.)

Use a demand and supply graph to explain how these three things could be true: an increase in the equilibrium quantity of hotel rooms occupied, an increase in the equilibrium price of hotel rooms, and an increase in the number of hotel rooms available.

Source: Nancy Keates, "Cracking Down on Chair Hogs," *Wall Street Journal*, February 23, 2007, p. W1.

4.7 **(Related to the *Making the Connection*)** The average price of a high-definition plasma or LCD television fell between 2001 and 2006, from more than $8,000 to about $1,500. During that period, Sharp, Matsushita Electric Industrial, and Samsung all began producing plasma or LCD televisions. Use a demand and supply graph to explain what happened to the quantity of plasma and LCD televisions sold during this period.

4.8 According to an article in the *Wall Street Journal*, during 2006, the demand for full-size pickup trucks declined as a result of rising gas prices and a decline in housing construction (construction firms are an important part of the market for full-size pickup trucks). At the same time, Toyota began production of trucks at a new truck factory in Texas.

a. Draw a demand and supply graph illustrating these developments in the market for full-size pickup trucks. Be sure to indicate changes in the equilibrium price and equilibrium quantity.

b. Briefly discuss whether this problem provides enough information to determine whether the equilibrium quantity of trucks increased or decreased.

Source: Neal E. Boudette and Jeffrey C. McCracken, "Detroit's Cash Cow Stumbles," *Wall Street Journal*, August 1, 2006, p. B1.

4.9 Beginning in the late 1990s, many consumers were having their vision problems corrected with laser surgery. An article in the *Wall Street Journal* noted two developments in the market for laser eye surgery. The first involved increasing concerns related to side effects from the surgery, including blurred vision and, occasionally, blindness. The second development was that the companies renting eye-surgery machinery to doctors had reduced their charges. One large company had cut its charge from $250 per patient to $100. Use a demand and supply graph to illustrate the effects of these two developments on the market for laser eye surgery.

Source: Laura Johannes and James Bandler, "Slowing Economy, Safety Concerns Zap Growth in Laser Eye Surgery," *Wall Street Journal*, January 8, 2001, p. B1.

4.10 The market for autographs, including letters or other documents signed by famous people, is subject to frequent large price changes, as are markets for most collectibles. The following table is adapted from one that originally appeared in an article in the *Wall Street Journal*. It gives the 1997 price for an autograph, the 2001 price, and a brief comment by the *Wall Street Journal* reporter. Use the information contained in the Comment column of the table to draw a demand and supply graph for each of the three autographs listed that can account for the change in its market price from 1997 to 2001.

AUTOGRAPH	1997 PRICE	2001 PRICE	COMMENT
The Beatles	$2,500	$7,475	"As boomers get rich, so do prices for pieces . . . signed by the Fab Four."
Princess Diana	14,000	2,000	"Demand rose after her death in 1997, but now the market's full of items like her signed Christmas cards."
Robert E. Lee	200,000	100,000	"The Civil War's out."

Source: Brooks Barnes, "Signature Market: Hard to Read," *Wall Street Journal*, July 13, 2001.

4.11 Historically, the production of many perishable foods, such as dairy products, was highly seasonal. Thus, as the supply of those products fluctuated, prices tended to fluctuate tremendously—typically by 25 to 50 percent or more—over the course of the year. One impact of mechanical refrigeration, which was commercialized on a large scale in the last decade of the nineteenth century, was that suppliers could store perishables from one season to the next. Economists have estimated that as a result of refrigerated storage, wholesale prices rose by roughly 10 percent during peak supply periods, while they fell by almost the same amount during the off season. Use a demand and supply graph for each season to illustrate how refrigeration affected the market for perishable food.

Source: Lee A. Craig, Barry Goodwin, and Thomas Grennes, "The Effect of Mechanical Refrigeration on Nutrition in the U.S.," *Social Science History*, Vol. 28, No. 2 (Summer 2004), pp. 327–328.

4.12 Briefly explain whether each of the following statements is true or false.

a. If the demand and supply for a product both increase, the equilibrium quantity of the product must also increase.

b. If the demand and supply for a product both increase, the equilibrium price of the product must also increase.

c. If the demand for a product decreases and the supply of the product increases, the equilibrium price of the product may increase or decrease, depending on whether supply or demand has shifted more.

4.13 (Related to the *Don't Let This Happen to You!*) A student writes the following: "Increased production leads to a lower price, which in turn increases demand." Do you agree with his reasoning? Briefly explain.

4.14 (Related to the *Don't Let This Happen To You!*) A student was asked to draw a demand and supply graph to illustrate the effect on the laptop computer market of a fall in the price of computer hard drives, *ceteris paribus*. She drew the graph at the top of the next column and explained it as follows:

Hard drives are an input to laptop computers, so a fall in the price of hard drives will cause the supply curve for personal computers to shift to the right (from S_1 to S_2). Because this shift in the supply curve results in a lower price (P_2), consumers will want to buy more laptops, and the demand curve will shift to the right (from D_1 to D_2). We know that more laptops will be sold, but we can't be sure whether the price of laptops will rise or fall. That depends on whether the supply curve or the demand curve has shifted farther to the right. I assume that the effect on supply is greater than the effect on demand, so

I show the final equilibrium price (P_3) as being lower than the initial equilibrium price (P_1).

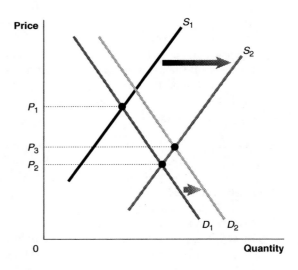

Explain whether you agree or disagree with the student's analysis. Be careful to explain exactly what—if anything—you find wrong with her analysis.

4.15 Following are four graphs and four market scenarios, each of which would cause either a movement along the supply curve for Pepsi or a shift of the supply curve. Match each scenario with the appropriate graph.

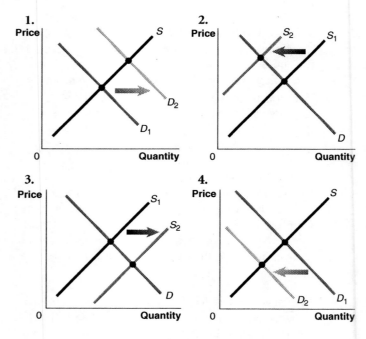

a. A decrease in the supply of Coke
b. A drop in the average household income in the United States from $42,000 to $41,000
c. An improvement in soft-drink bottling technology
d. An increase in the price of sugar

4.16 David Surdam, an economist at Loyola University of Chicago, makes the following observation of the world cotton market at the beginning of the Civil War:

> As the supply of American-grown raw cotton decreased and the price of raw cotton increased, there would be a *movement along* the supply curve of non-American raw cotton suppliers, and the quantity supplied by these producers would increase.

Illustrate this observation with one demand and supply graph for the market for American-grown cotton and another demand and supply graph for the market for non-American cotton. Make sure your graphs clearly show (1) the initial equilibrium before the decrease in the supply of American-grown cotton and (2) the final equilibrium. Also clearly show any shifts in the demand and supply curves for each market.

Source: David G. Surdam, "King Cotton: Monarch or Pretender? The State of the Market for Raw Cotton on the Eve of the American Civil War," *The Economic History Review,* Vol. 51, No. 1 (February 1998), p. 116.

4.17 Proposals have been made to increase government regulation of firms providing childcare services by, for instance, setting education requirements for childcare workers. Suppose that these regulations increase the quality of childcare and cause the demand for childcare services to increase. At the same time, assume that complying with the new government regulations increases the costs of firms providing childcare services. Draw a demand and supply graph to illustrate the effects of these changes in the market for childcare services. Briefly explain whether the total quantity of childcare services purchased will increase or decrease as a result of regulation.

4.18 Below are the supply and demand functions for two markets. One of the markets is for BMW automobiles, and the other is for a cancer-fighting drug, without which lung cancer patients will die. Briefly explain which diagram most likely represents which market.

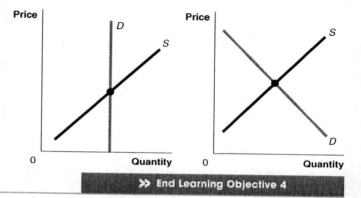

>> End Learning Objective 4

33

Economic Efficiency, Government Price Setting, and Taxes

From Chapter 4 of *Microeconomics*, 2/e. R. Glenn Hubbard. Anthony Patrick O'Brien. Copyright © 2008 by Pearson Prentice Hall.

Economic Efficiency, Government Price Setting, and Taxes

Should the Government Control Apartment Rents?

Robert F. Moss owns an apartment building in New York City. Unlike most other business owners, he is not free to charge the prices he would like for the service he offers. In New York, San Francisco, Los Angeles, and nearly 200 smaller cities, apartments are subject to rent control by the local government. Rent control puts a legal limit on the rent that landlords can charge for an apartment.

New York City has two million apartments, about one million of which are subject to rent control. The other one million apartments have their rents determined in the market by the demand and supply for apartments. Mr. Moss's building includes apartments that are rent controlled and apartments that are not. The market-determined rents are usually far above the controlled rents. The government regulations that determine what Mr. Moss can charge for a rent-controlled apartment are very complex. The following is Mr. Moss's description:

When [an apartment] is vacated, state rent laws entitle landlords to raise rents in three primary ways: a vacancy increase of 20 percent for a new tenant's two-year lease (a bit less for a one-year lease); one-fortieth per month of the cost of any improvements, and a "longevity bonus" for longtime residents (calculated at six-tenths of 1 percent times the tenant's last legal rent multiplied by the number of years of residency beyond eight). . . . Apartments renting for $2,000 a month are automatically deregulated if they are vacant. Occupied apartments whose rent reaches that figure can be deregulated if the income of the tenants has been $175,000 or more for two years.

As this description shows, someone earning a living by renting out apartments in New York City has to deal with much more complex government regulation of prices than someone who owns, for instance, a McDonald's restaurant.

Larger companies also struggle with the complexity of rent-control regulations. This was the case for several companies that built multiple apartment buildings in New York during the 1970s. In exchange for renting apartments to moderate- and low-income tenants at controlled rents, the companies were allowed to charge market rents after 20 years. Unfortunately for the companies, when the 20 years were over, attempts to start charging market rents were often met with lawsuits from unhappy tenants. New York Mayor Michael Bloomberg proposed that the law be changed to keep many of these apartment buildings under rent control.

Tenants in rent-controlled apartments in New York are very reluctant to see rent control end because rents for rent-controlled apartments are much lower than rents for apartments that aren't rent controlled. As we will see in this chapter, however rent control can also cause significant problems for renters. **AN INSIDE LOOK AT POLICY** explores the debate over rent control laws in Los Angeles.

Source: Robert F. Moss, "A Landlord's Lot is Sometimes Not an Easy One," *New York Times*, August 3, 2003, Section 11, p. 1.

LEARNING Objectives

After studying this chapter, you should be able to:

1   Distinguish between the concepts of **consumer surplus** and **producer surplus**

2   Understand the concept of **economic efficiency**

3   Explain the economic effect of government-imposed **price ceilings** and **price floors**

4   Analyze the economic impact of **taxes**

APPENDIX Use **quantitative** demand and supply **analysis**

Economics in YOUR Life!

Does Rent Control Make It Easier to Find an Affordable Apartment?

Suppose you have job offers in two cities. One factor in deciding which job to accept is whether you can find an affordable apartment. If one city has rent control, are you more likely to find an affordable apartment in that city, or would you be better off looking for an apartment in a city without rent control? As you read the chapter, see if you can answer this question. You can check your answer against the one we provide at the end of the chapter.

I n a competitive market, the price adjusts to ensure that the quantity demanded equals the quantity supplied. Stated another way, in equilibrium, every consumer willing to pay the market price is able to buy as much of the product as the consumer wants, and every firm willing to accept the market price can sell as much as it wants. Even so, consumers would naturally prefer to pay a lower price, and sellers would prefer to receive a higher price. Normally, consumers and firms have no choice but to accept the equilibrium price if they wish to participate in the market. Occasionally, however, consumers succeed in having the government impose a **price ceiling**, which is a legally determined maximum price that sellers may charge. Rent control is an example of a price ceiling. Firms also sometimes succeed in having the government impose a **price floor**, which is a legally determined minimum price that sellers may receive. In markets for farm products such as milk, the government has been setting price floors that are above the equilibrium market price since the 1930s.

Another way in which the government intervenes in markets is by imposing taxes. The government relies on the revenue raised from taxes to finance its operations. As we will see, though, imposing taxes alters the equilibrium in a market.

Unfortunately, whenever the government imposes a price ceiling, a price floor, or a tax, there are predictable negative economic consequences. It is important for government policymakers and voters to understand these negative consequences when evaluating the effects of these policies. Economists have developed the concepts of *consumer surplus, producer surplus*, and *economic surplus*, which we discuss in the next section. In the sections that follow, we use these concepts to analyze the economic effects of price ceilings, price floors, and taxes. (As we will see in later chapters, these concepts are also useful in many other contexts.)

Price ceiling A legally determined maximum price that sellers may charge.

Price floor A legally determined minimum price that sellers may receive.

---

1 LEARNING OBJECTIVE

1 | Distinguish between the concepts of consumer surplus and producer surplus.

Consumer Surplus and Producer Surplus

Consumer surplus measures the dollar benefit consumers receive from buying goods or services in a particular market. Producer surplus measures the dollar benefit firms receive from selling goods or services in a particular market. Economic surplus in a market is the sum of consumer surplus plus producer surplus. As we will see, *when the government imposes a price ceiling or a price floor, the amount of economic surplus in a market is reduced*—in other words, price ceilings and price floors reduce the total benefit to consumers and firms from buying and selling in a market. To understand why this is true, we need to understand how consumer surplus and producer surplus are determined.

Consumer Surplus

Consumer surplus measures the difference between the highest price a consumer is willing to pay and the price the consumer actually pays. For example, suppose you are in Wal-Mart and you see a DVD of *Spider-Man 3* on the rack. No price is indicated on the package, so you bring it over to the register to check the price. As you walk to the register, you think to yourself that $20 is the highest price you would be willing to pay. At the register, you find out that the price is actually $12, so you buy the DVD. Your consumer surplus in this example is $8: the difference between the $20 you were willing to pay and the $8 you actually paid.

We can use the demand curve to measure the total consumer surplus in a market. Demand curves show the willingness of consumers to purchase a product at different prices. Consumers are willing to purchase a product up to the point where the marginal benefit of consuming a product is equal to its price. The **marginal benefit** is the additional

Consumer surplus The difference between the highest price a consumer is willing to pay and the price the consumer actually pays.

Marginal benefit The additional benefit to a consumer from consuming one more unit of a good or service.

38

Consumer	Highest Price Willing to Pay
Theresa	$6
Tom	5
Terri	4
Tim	3

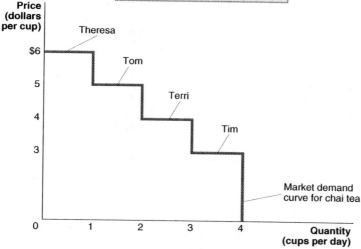

Figure 1

Deriving the Demand Curve for Chai Tea

With four consumers in the market for chai tea, the demand curve is determined by the highest price each consumer is willing to pay. For prices above $6, no tea is sold because $6 is the highest price any consumer is willing to pay. For prices of $3 and below, all four consumers are willing to buy a cup of tea.

benefit to a consumer from consuming one more unit of a good or service. As a simple example, suppose there are only four consumers in the market for chai tea: Theresa, Tom, Terri, and Tim. Because these four consumers have different tastes for tea and different incomes, the marginal benefit each of them receives from consuming a cup of tea will be different. Therefore, the highest price each is willing to pay for a cup of tea is also different. In Figure 1, the information from the table is used to construct a demand curve for chai tea. For prices above $6 per cup, no tea is sold because $6 is the highest price any of the consumers is willing to pay. At a price of $5, both Theresa and Tom are willing to buy, so two cups are sold. At prices of $3 and below, all four consumers are willing to buy, and four cups are sold.

Suppose the market price of tea is $3.50 per cup. As Figure 2 shows, the demand curve allows us to calculate the total consumer surplus in this market. In panel (a), we can see that the highest price Theresa is willing to pay is $6, but because she pays only $3.50, her consumer surplus is $2.50 (shown by the area of rectangle A). Similarly, Tom's consumer surplus is $1.50 (rectangle B), and Terri's consumer surplus is $0.50 (rectangle C). Tim is unwilling to buy a cup of tea at a price of $3.50, so he doesn't participate in this market and receives no consumer surplus. In this simple example, the total consumer surplus is equal to $2.50 + $1.50 + $0.50 = $4.50 (or the sum of the areas of rectangles A, B, and C). Panel (b) shows that a lower price will increase consumer surplus. If the price of tea drops from $3.50 per cup to $3.00, Theresa, Tom, and Terri each receive $0.50 more in consumer surplus (shown by the shaded areas), so total consumer surplus in the market rises to $6.00. Tim now buys a cup of tea but doesn't receive any consumer surplus because the price is equal to the highest price he is willing to pay. In fact, Tim is indifferent between buying the cup or not—his well-being is the same either way.

The market demand curves shown in Figures 1 and 2 do not look like smooth curves. This is because this example uses a small number of consumers, each consuming a single cup of tea. With many consumers, the market demand curve for chai tea will have the normal smooth shape shown in Figure 3. In this figure, the quantity demanded at a price of $2.00 is 15,000 cups per day. We can calculate total consumer surplus in Figure 3 the same way we did in Figures 1 and

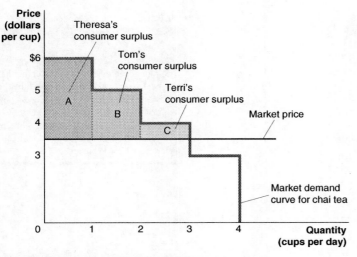

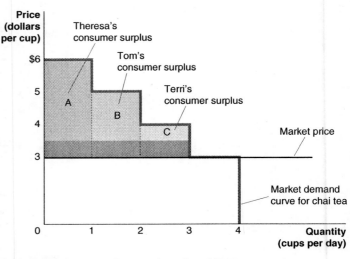

(a) Consumer surplus with a market price of $3.50

(b) Consumer surplus with a market price of $3.00

Figure 2 | Measuring Consumer Surplus

Panel (a) shows the consumer surplus for Theresa, Tom, and Terri when the price of tea is $3.50 per cup. Theresa's consumer surplus is equal to the area of rectangle *A* and is the difference between the highest price she would pay—$6—and the market price of $3.50. Tom's consumer surplus is equal to the area of rectangle *B*, and Terri's con-

sumer surplus is equal to the area of rectangle *C*. Total consumer surplus in this market is equal to the sum of the areas of rectangles *A*, *B*, and *C*, or the total area below the demand curve and above the market price. In panel (b), consumer surplus increases by the shaded area as the market price declines from $3.50 to $3.00.

2: by adding up the consumer surplus received on each unit purchased. Once again, we can draw an important conclusion: *The total amount of consumer surplus in a market is equal to the area below the demand curve and above the market price.* Consumer surplus is shown as the blue area in Figure 3 and represents the benefit to consumers in excess of the price they paid to purchase the product—in this case, chai tea.

Figure 3

Total Consumer Surplus in the Market for Chai Tea

The demand curve tells us that most buyers of chai tea would have been willing to pay more than the market price of $2.00. For each buyer, consumer surplus is equal to the difference between the highest price he or she is willing to pay and the market price actually paid. Therefore, the total amount of consumer surplus in the market for chai tea is equal to the area below the demand curve and above the market price. Consumer surplus represents the benefit to consumers in excess of the price they paid to purchase the product.

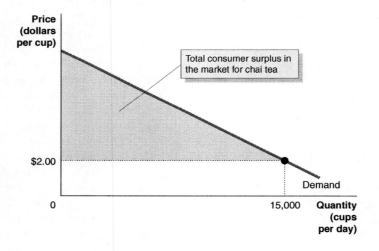

Making the Connection | The Consumer Surplus from Satellite Television

Consumer surplus allows us to measure the benefit consumers receive in excess of the price they paid to purchase a product. Recently, Austan Goolsbee and Amil Petrin, economists at the Graduate

School of Business at the University of Chicago, estimated the consumer surplus that households receive from subscribing to satellite television. To do this, they estimated the demand curve for satellite television and then computed the shaded area shown in the graph.

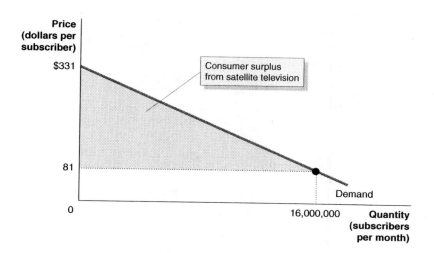

In 2001, the year for which the study was conducted, 16 million consumers paid an average price of $81 per month to subscribe to DIRECTV or DISH Network, the two main providers of satellite television. The demand curve shows that many consumers would have been willing to pay more than $81 rather than do without satellite television. Goolsbee and Petrin calculated that the consumer surplus for households subscribing to satellite television averaged $127 per month, which is the difference between the price they would have paid and the $81 they did pay. The shaded area on the graph represents the total consumer surplus in the market for satellite television. Goolsbee and Petrin estimate that the value of this area is $2 billion. This is one year's benefit to the consumers who subscribe to satellite television.

Source: Austan Goolsbee and Amil Petrin, "The Consumer Gains from Direct Broadcast Satellites and the Competition with Cable TV," *Econometrica*, Vol. 72, No. 2, March 2004, pp. 351–381.

YOUR TURN: Test your understanding by doing related problem 1.8 at the end of this chapter.

Producer Surplus

Just as demand curves show the willingness of consumers to buy a product at different prices, supply curves show the willingness of firms to supply a product at different prices. The willingness to supply a product depends on the cost of producing it. Firms will supply an additional unit of a product only if they receive a price equal to the additional cost of producing that unit. **Marginal cost** is the additional cost to a firm of producing one more unit of a good or service. Consider the marginal cost to the firm Heavenly Tea of producing one more cup: In this case, the marginal cost includes the ingredients to make the tea and the wages paid to the worker preparing the tea. Often, the marginal cost of producing a good increases as more of the good is produced during a given period of time. This is the key reason that supply curves are upward sloping.

Panel (a) of Figure 4 shows Heavenly Tea's producer surplus. For simplicity, we show Heavenly producing only a small quantity of tea. The figure shows that Heavenly's marginal cost of producing the first cup of tea is $1.00. Its marginal cost of producing

Marginal cost The additional cost to a firm of producing one more unit of a good or service.

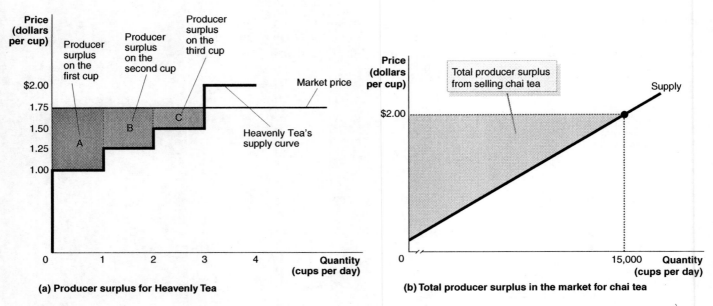

(a) Producer surplus for Heavenly Tea

(b) Total producer surplus in the market for chai tea

Figure 4 | Calculating Producer Surplus

Panel (a) shows Heavenly Tea's producer surplus. Producer surplus is the difference between the lowest price a firm would be willing to accept and the price it actually receives. The lowest price Heavenly Tea is willing to accept to supply a cup of tea is equal to its marginal cost of producing that cup. When the market price of tea is $1.75, Heavenly receives producer surplus of $0.75 on the first cup (the area of rectan-

gle *A*), $0.50 on the second cup (rectangle *B*), and $0.25 on the third cup (rectangle *C*). In panel (b), the total amount of producer surplus tea sellers receive from selling chai tea can be calculated by adding up for the entire market the producer surplus received on each cup sold. In the figure, total producer surplus is equal to the area above the supply curve and below the market price, shown in red.

Producer surplus The difference between the lowest price a firm would be willing to accept and the price it actually receives.

the second cup is $1.25, and so on. The marginal cost of each cup of tea is the lowest price Heavenly is willing to accept to supply that cup. The supply curve, then, is also a marginal cost curve. Suppose the market price of tea is $1.75 per cup. On the first cup of tea, the price is $0.75 higher than the lowest price Heavenly is willing to accept. **Producer surplus** is the difference between the lowest price a firm would be willing to accept and the price it actually receives. Therefore, Heavenly's producer surplus on the first cup is $0.75 (shown by the area of rectangle *A*). Its producer surplus on the second cup is $0.50 (rectangle *B*). Its producer surplus on the third cup is $0.25 (rectangle *C*). Heavenly will not be willing to supply the fourth cup because the marginal cost of producing it is less than the market price. Heavenly Tea's total producer surplus is equal to $0.75 + $0.50 + $0.25 = $1.50 (or the sum of rectangles *A*, *B*, and *C*). A higher price will increase producer surplus. For example, if the market price of chai tea rises from $1.75 to $2.00, Heavenly Tea's producer surplus will increase from $1.50 to $2.25. (Make sure you understand how the new level of producer surplus was calculated.)

The supply curve shown in panel (a) of Figure 4 does not look like the smooth curves we saw because this example uses a single firm producing only a small quantity of tea. With many firms, the market supply curve for chai tea will have the normal smooth shape shown in panel (b) of Figure 4. In panel (b), the quantity supplied at a price of $2.00 is 15,000 cups per day. We can calculate total producer surplus in panel (b) the same way we did in panel (a): by adding up the producer surplus received on each cup sold. Therefore, *the total amount of producer surplus in a market is equal to the area above the market supply curve and below the market price*. The total producer surplus tea sellers receive from selling chai tea is shown as the red area in panel (b) of Figure 4.

What Consumer Surplus and Producer Surplus Measure

We have seen that consumer surplus measures the benefit to consumers from participating in a market, and producer surplus measures the benefit to producers from participating in a market. It is important, however, to be clear what we mean by this. In a sense, consumer surplus measures the *net* benefit to consumers from participating in a market rather than the *total* benefit. That is, if the price of a product were zero, the consumer surplus in a market would be all of the area under the demand curve. When the price is not zero, consumer surplus is the area below the demand curve and above the market price. So, consumer surplus in a market is equal to the total benefit received by consumers minus the total amount they must pay to buy the good.

Similarly, producer surplus measures the *net* benefit received by producers from participating in a market. If producers could supply a good at zero cost, the producer surplus in a market would be all of the area below the market price. When cost is not zero, producer surplus is the area below the market price and above the supply curve. So, producer surplus in a market is equal to the total amount firms receive from consumers minus the cost of producing the good.

---

2 | Understand the concept of economic efficiency.

2 LEARNING OBJECTIVE

The Efficiency of Competitive Markets

A *competitive market* is a market with many buyers and many sellers. An important advantage of the market system is that it results in efficient economic outcomes. But what do we mean by *economic efficiency*? The concepts we have developed so far in this chapter give us two ways to think about the economic efficiency of competitive markets. We can think in terms of marginal benefit and marginal cost. We can also think in terms of consumer surplus and producer surplus. As we will see, these two approaches lead to the same outcome, but using both can increase our understanding of economic efficiency.

Marginal Benefit Equals Marginal Cost in Competitive Equilibrium

Figure 5 again shows the market for chai tea. Recall from our discussion that the demand curve shows the marginal benefit received by consumers, and the supply curve shows the marginal cost of production. To achieve economic efficiency in this market, the marginal

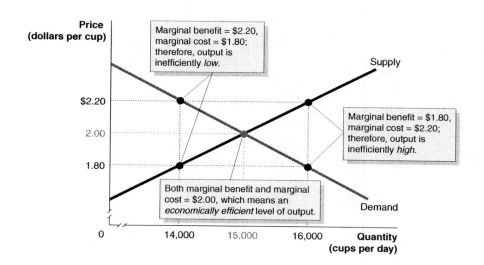

Figure 5

Marginal Benefit Equals Marginal Cost Only at Competitive Equilibrium

In a competitive market, equilibrium occurs at a quantity of 15,000 cups and price of $2.00 per cup, where marginal benefit equals marginal cost. This is the economically efficient level of output because every cup has been produced where the marginal benefit to buyers is greater than or equal to the marginal cost to producers.

benefit from the last unit sold should equal the marginal cost of production. The figure shows that this equality occurs at competitive equilibrium where 15,000 cups per day are produced, and marginal benefit and marginal cost are both equal to $2.00. Why is this outcome economically efficient? Because every cup of chai tea has been produced where the marginal benefit to buyers is greater than or equal to the marginal cost to producers.

Another way to see why the level of output at competitive equilibrium is efficient is to consider what would be true if output were at a different level. For instance, suppose that output of chai tea were 14,000 cups per day. Figure 5 shows that at this level of output, the marginal benefit from the last cup sold is $2.20, whereas the marginal cost is only $1.80. This level of output is not efficient because 1,000 more cups could be produced for which the additional benefit to consumers would be greater than the additional cost of production. Consumers would willingly purchase those cups, and tea sellers would willingly supply them, making both consumers and sellers better off. Similarly, if the output of chai tea were 16,000 cups per day, the marginal cost of the 16,000th cup is $2.20, whereas the marginal benefit is only $1.80. Tea sellers would only be willing to supply this cup at a price of $2.20, which is $0.40 higher than consumers would be willing to pay. In fact, consumers would not be willing to pay the price tea sellers would need to receive for any cup beyond the 15,000th.

To summarize, we can say this: *Equilibrium in a competitive market results in the economically efficient level of output, where marginal benefit equals marginal cost.*

Economic Surplus

Economic surplus The sum of consumer surplus and producer surplus.

Economic surplus in a market is the sum of consumer surplus and producer surplus. In a competitive market, with many buyers and sellers and no government restrictions, economic surplus is at a maximum when the market is in equilibrium. To see this, let's look one more time at the market for chai tea shown in Figure 6. The consumer surplus in this market is the blue area below the demand curve and above the line indicating the equilibrium price of $2.00. The producer surplus is the red area above the supply curve and below the price line.

Deadweight Loss

To show that economic surplus is maximized at equilibrium, consider the situation in which the price of chai tea is *above* the equilibrium price, as shown in Figure 7. At a price of $2.20 per cup, the number of cups consumers are willing to buy per day drops from 15,000 to 14,000. At competitive equilibrium, consumer surplus is equal to the sum of areas A, B, and C. At a price of $2.20, fewer cups are sold at a higher price, so consumer surplus declines to just the area of A. At competitive equilibrium, producer surplus is equal to the sum of areas D and E. At the higher price of $2.20, producer surplus changes to be equal to the sum of areas B and D. The sum of consumer and producer surplus—economic surplus—has been reduced to the sum of areas A, B, and D. Notice that this is less than the original economic surplus by an amount equal to areas C and E.

Figure 6

Economic Surplus Equals the Sum of Consumer Surplus and Producer Surplus

The economic surplus in a market is the sum of the blue area representing consumer surplus and the red area representing producer surplus.

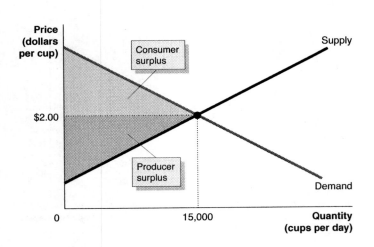

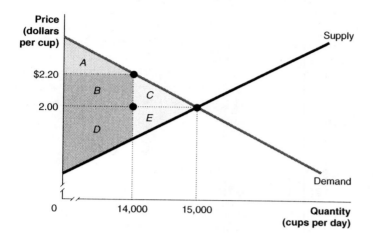

	At Competitive Equilibrium	At a Price of $2.20
Consumer Surplus	A + B + C	A
Producer Surplus	D + E	B + D
Deadweight Loss	None	C + E

Figure 7

When a Market Is Not in Equilibrium, There Is a Deadweight Loss

Economic surplus is maximized when a market is in competitive equilibrium. When a market is not in equilibrium, there is a deadweight loss. When the price of chai tea is $2.20, instead of $2.00, consumer surplus declines from an amount equal to the sum of areas A, B, and C to just area A. Producer surplus increases from the sum of areas D and E to the sum of areas B and D. At competitive equilibrium, there is no deadweight loss. At a price of $2.20, there is a deadweight loss equal to the sum of areas C and E.

Economic surplus has declined because at a price of $2.20, all the cups between the 14,000th and the 15,000th, which would have been produced in competitive equilibrium, are not being produced. These "missing" cups are not providing any consumer or producer surplus, so economic surplus has declined. The reduction in economic surplus resulting from a market not being in competitive equilibrium is called the **deadweight loss**. In the figure, it is equal to the sum of areas C and E.

Deadweight loss The reduction in economic surplus resulting from a market not being in competitive equilibrium.

Economic Surplus and Economic Efficiency

Consumer surplus measures the benefit to consumers from buying a particular product, such as chai tea. Producer surplus measures the benefit to firms from selling a particular product. Therefore, economic surplus—which is the sum of the benefit to firms plus the benefit to consumers—is the best measure we have of the benefit to society from the production of a particular good or service. This gives us a second way of characterizing the economic efficiency of a competitive market: *Equilibrium in a competitive market results in the greatest amount of economic surplus, or total net benefit to society, from the production of a good or service.* Anything that causes the market for a good or service not to be in competitive equilibrium reduces the total benefit to society from the production of that good or service.

Now we can give a more general definition of *economic efficiency* in terms of our two approaches: **Economic efficiency** is a market outcome in which the marginal benefit to consumers of the last unit produced is equal to its marginal cost of production and in which the sum of consumer surplus and producer surplus is at a maximum.

Economic efficiency A market outcome in which the marginal benefit to consumers of the last unit produced is equal to its marginal cost of production and in which the sum of consumer surplus and producer surplus is at a maximum.

3 | Explain the economic effect of government-imposed price ceilings and price floors.

3 LEARNING OBJECTIVE

Government Intervention in the Market: Price Floors and Price Ceilings

Notice that we have *not* concluded that every *individual* is better off if a market is at competitive equilibrium. We have only concluded that economic surplus, or the *total* net benefit to society, is greatest at competitive equilibrium. Any individual producer would rather charge a higher price, and any individual consumer would rather pay a lower price, but usually producers can sell and consumers can buy only at the competitive equilibrium price.

Producers or consumers who are dissatisfied with the competitive equilibrium price can lobby the government to legally require that a different price be charged. The U.S. government only occasionally overrides the market outcome by setting prices. When the government does intervene, it can either attempt to aid sellers by requiring that a price be above equilibrium—a price floor—or aid buyers by requiring that a price be below equilibrium—a price ceiling. To affect the market outcome, a price floor must be set above the equilibrium price and a price ceiling must be set below the equilibrium price. Otherwise, the price ceiling or price floor will not be *binding* on buyers and sellers. The preceding section demonstrates that moving away from competitive equilibrium will reduce economic efficiency. We can use the concepts of consumer surplus, producer surplus, and deadweight loss to see more clearly the economic inefficiency of binding price floors and price ceilings.

Price Floors: Government Policy in Agricultural Markets

The Great Depression of the 1930s was the greatest economic disaster in U.S. history, affecting every sector of the U.S. economy. Many farmers were unable to sell their products or could sell them only at very low prices. Farmers were able to convince the federal government to intervene to raise prices by setting price floors for many agricultural products. Government intervention in agriculture—often referred to as the "farm program"—has continued ever since. To see how a price floor in an agricultural market works, suppose that the equilibrium price in the wheat market is $3.00 per bushel but the government decides to set a price floor of $3.50 per bushel. As Figure 8 shows, the price of wheat rises from $3.00 to $3.50, and the quantity of wheat sold falls from 2.0 billion bushels per year to 1.8 billion. Initially, suppose that production of wheat also falls to 1.8 billion bushels.

Just as we saw in the earlier example of the market for chai tea (refer to Figure 7), the producer surplus received by wheat farmers increases by an amount equal to the area of the red rectangle A and falls by an amount equal to the area of the yellow triangle C. The area of the red rectangle A represents a transfer from consumer surplus to producer surplus. The total fall in consumer surplus is equal to the area of the red rectangle A plus the area of the yellow triangle B. Wheat farmers benefit from this program, but consumers lose. There is also a deadweight loss equal to the areas of the yellow triangles B and C, which represents the decline in economic efficiency due to the price floor. There

Figure 8

The Economic Effect of a Price Floor in the Wheat Market

If wheat farmers convince the government to impose a price floor of $3.50 per bushel, the amount of wheat sold will fall from 2.0 billion bushels per year to 1.8 billion. If we assume that farmers produce 1.8 billion bushels, producer surplus then increases by the red rectangle A—which is transferred from consumer surplus—and falls by the yellow triangle C. Consumer surplus declines by the red rectangle A plus the yellow triangle B. There is a deadweight loss equal to the yellow triangles B and C, representing the decline in economic efficiency due to the price floor. In reality, a price floor of $3.50 per bushel will cause farmers to expand their production from 2.0 billion to 2.2 billion bushels, resulting in a surplus of wheat.

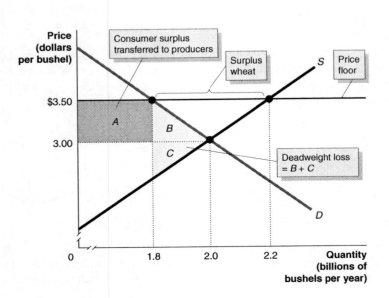

is a deadweight loss because the price floor has reduced the amount of economic surplus in the market for wheat. Or, looked at another way, the price floor has caused the marginal benefit of the last bushel of wheat to be greater than the marginal cost of producing it. We can conclude that a price floor reduces economic efficiency.

The actual federal government farm programs have been more complicated than just legally requiring farmers not to sell their output below a minimum price. We assumed initially that farmers reduce their production of wheat to the amount consumers are willing to buy. In fact, as Figure 8 shows, a price floor will cause the quantity of wheat that farmers want to supply to increase from 2.0 billion to 2.2 billion bushels. Because the higher price also reduces the amount of wheat consumers wish to buy, the result is a surplus of 0.4 billion bushels of wheat (the 2.2 billion bushels supplied minus the 1.8 billion demanded).

The federal government's farm programs have often resulted in large surpluses of wheat and other agricultural products. The government has usually either bought the surplus food or paid farmers to restrict supply by taking some land out of cultivation. Because both of these options are expensive, Congress passed the Freedom to Farm Act of 1996. The intent of the act was to phase out price floors and government purchases of surpluses and return to a free market in agriculture. To allow farmers time to adjust, the federal government began paying farmers *subsidies*, or cash payments based on the number of acres planted. Although the subsidies were originally scheduled to be phased out, Congress has continued to pay them.

Making the Connection | Price Floors in Labor Markets: The Debate over Minimum Wage Policy

The minimum wage may be the most controversial "price floor." Supporters see the minimum wage as a way of raising the incomes of low-skilled workers. Opponents argue that it results in fewer jobs and imposes large costs on small businesses.

In summer 2008, the national minimum wage as set by Congress is $6.55 per hour for most occupations. (The minimum wage is scheduled to increase to $7.25 per hour in 2009.) It is illegal for an employer to pay less than this wage in those occupations. For most workers, the minimum wage is irrelevant because it is well below the wage employers are voluntarily willing to pay them. But for low-skilled workers—such as workers in fast-food restaurants—the minimum wage is above the wage they would otherwise receive. The following figure shows the effect of the minimum wage on employment in the market for low-skilled labor.

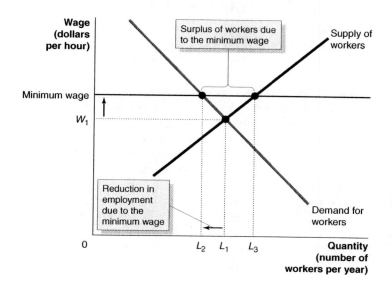

Without a minimum wage, the equilibrium wage would be W_1, and the number of workers hired would be L_1. With a minimum wage set above the equilibrium wage, the quantity of workers demanded by employers declines from L_1 to L_2, and the quantity of labor supplied increases to L_3, leading to a surplus of workers unable to find jobs equal to $L_3 - L_2$. The quantity of labor supplied increases because the higher wage attracts more people to work. For instance, some teenagers may decide that working after school is worthwhile at the minimum wage of $6.55 per hour but would not be worthwhile at a lower wage.

This analysis is very similar to our analysis of the wheat market in Figure 8. Just as a price floor in the wheat market leads to less wheat consumed, a price floor in the labor market should lead to fewer workers hired. Views differ sharply among economists, however, concerning how large a reduction in employment the minimum wage causes. For instance, David Card of the University of California, Berkeley, and Alan Krueger of Princeton University conducted a study of fast-food restaurants in New Jersey and Pennsylvania that indicates that the effect of minimum wage increases on employment is very small. Card and Krueger's study has been very controversial, however. Other economists have examined similar data and have come to the different conclusion that the minimum wage leads to a significant decrease in employment.

Whatever the extent of employment losses from the minimum wage, because it is a price floor, it will cause a deadweight loss, just as a price floor in the wheat market does. Therefore, many economists favor alternative policies for attaining the goal of raising the incomes of low-skilled workers. One policy many economists support is the *earned income tax credit*. The earned income tax credit reduces the amount of tax that low-income wage earners would otherwise pay to the federal government. Workers with very low incomes who do not owe any tax receive a payment from the government. Compared with the minimum wage, the earned income tax credit can increase the incomes of low-skilled workers without reducing employment. The earned income tax credit also places a lesser burden on the small businesses that employ many low-skilled workers, and it might cause a smaller loss of economic efficiency.

Sources: David Card and Alan B. Krueger, *Myth and Measurement: The New Economics of the Minimum Wage*, Princeton, NJ: Princeton University Press, 1995; David Neumark and William Wascher, "Minimum Wages and Employment: A Case Study of the Fast-Food Industry in New Jersey and Pennsylvania: Comment," *American Economic Review*, Vol. 90, No. 5, December 2000, pp. 1362–1396; and David Card and Alan B. Krueger, "Minimum Wages and Employment: A Case Study of the Fast-Food Industry in New Jersey and Pennsylvania: Reply," *American Economic Review*, Vol. 90, No. 5, December 2000, pp. 1397–1420.

YOUR TURN: Test your understanding by doing related problem 3.12 at the end of this chapter.

Price Ceilings: Government Rent Control Policy in Housing Markets

Support for governments setting price floors typically comes from sellers, and support for governments setting price ceilings typically comes from consumers. For example, when there is a sharp increase in gasoline prices, there are often proposals for the government to impose a price ceiling on the market for gasoline. As we saw in the opener to this chapter, New York is one of the cities that imposes rent controls, which put a ceiling on the maximum rent that landlords can charge for an apartment. Figure 9 shows the market for apartments in a city that has rent controls.

Without rent control, the equilibrium rent would be $1,500 per month, and 2,000,000 apartments would be rented. With a maximum legal rent of $1,000 per month, landlords reduce the quantity of apartments supplied to 1,900,000. The fall in the quantity of apartments supplied is the result of some apartments being converted to offices or sold off as condominiums, some small apartment buildings being converted to single-family homes, and, over time, some apartment buildings being abandoned. In New York City, rent control has resulted in whole city blocks being abandoned by landlords

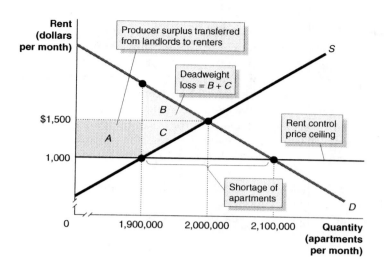

Figure 9

The Economic Effect of a Rent Ceiling

Without rent control, the equilibrium rent is $1,500 per month. At that price, 2,000,000 apartments would be rented. If the government imposes a rent ceiling of $1,000, the quantity of apartments supplied falls to 1,900,000, and the quantity of apartments demanded increases to 2,100,000, resulting in a shortage of 200,000 apartments. Producer surplus equal to the area of the blue rectangle *A* is transferred from landlords to renters, and there is a deadweight loss equal to the areas of yellow triangles *B* and *C*.

who were unable to cover their costs with the rents they were allowed to charge. In London, when rent controls were applied to rooms and apartments located in a landlord's own home, the quantity of these apartments supplied dropped by 75 percent.

In Figure 9, with the rent ceiling of $1,000, the quantity of apartments demanded rises to 2,100,000. There is a shortage of 200,000 apartments. Consumer surplus increases by rectangle *A* and falls by triangle *B*. Rectangle *A* would have been part of producer surplus if rent control were not in place. With rent control, it is part of consumer surplus. Rent control causes the producer surplus received by landlords to fall by rectangle *A* plus triangle *C*. Triangles *B* and *C* represent the deadweight loss. There is a deadweight loss because rent control has reduced the amount of economic surplus in the market for apartments. Rent control has caused the marginal benefit of the last apartment rented to be greater than the marginal cost of supplying it. We can conclude that a price ceiling, such as rent control, reduces economic efficiency. The appendix to this chapter shows how we can make quantitative estimates of the deadweight loss, and it shows the changes in consumer surplus and producer surplus that result from rent control.

Renters as a group benefit from rent controls—total consumer surplus is larger—but landlords lose. Because of the deadweight loss, the total loss to landlords is greater than the gain to renters. Notice also that although renters as a group benefit, the number of renters is reduced, so some renters are made worse off by rent controls because they are unable to find an apartment at the legal rent.

Don't Let This Happen to **YOU!**

Don't Confuse "Scarcity" with a "Shortage"

At first glance, the following statement seems correct: "There is a shortage of every good that is scarce." In everyday conversation, we describe a good as "scarce" if we have trouble finding it. For instance, if you are looking for a present for a child, you might call the latest hot toy "scarce" if you are willing to buy it at its listed price but can't find it online or in any store. But recall that economists have a broad definition of *scarce*. In the economic sense, almost everything—except undesirable things like garbage—is scarce. A shortage of a good occurs only if the quantity demanded is greater than the quantity supplied at the current price. Therefore, the preceding statement—"There is a shortage of every good that is scarce"—is incorrect. In fact, there is no shortage of most scarce goods.

YOUR TURN: Test your understanding by doing related problem 3.16 at the end of this chapter.

Black Markets

To this point, our analysis of rent controls is incomplete. In practice, renters may be worse off and landlords may be better off than Figure 9 makes it seem. We have assumed that renters and landlords actually abide by the price ceiling, but sometimes they don't. Because rent control leads to a shortage of apartments, renters who would otherwise not be able to find apartments have an incentive to offer landlords rents above the legal maximum. When governments try to control prices by setting price ceilings or price floors, buyers and sellers often find a way around the controls. The result is a **black market** where buying and selling take place at prices that violate government price regulations.

In a housing market with rent controls, the total amount of consumer surplus received by renters may be reduced and the total amount of producer surplus received by landlords may be increased if apartments are being rented at prices above the legal price ceiling.

Black market A market in which buying and selling take place at prices that violate government price regulations.

Solved Problem | 3

What's the Economic Effect of a "Black Market" for Apartments?

In many cities with rent controls, the actual rents paid can be much higher than the legal maximum. Because rent controls cause a shortage of apartments, desperate tenants are often willing to pay landlords rents that are higher than the law allows, perhaps by writing a check for the legally allowed rent and paying an additional amount in cash. Look again at Figure 9.

Suppose that competition among tenants results in the black market rent rising to $2,000 per month. At this rent, tenants demand 1,900,000 apartments. Use a graph showing the market for apartments to compare this situation with the one shown in Figure 9. Be sure to note any differences in consumer surplus, producer surplus, and deadweight loss.

SOLVING THE PROBLEM:

Step 1: **Review the chapter material.** This problem is about price controls in the market for apartments, so you may want to review the section "Price Ceilings: Government Rent Control Policy in Housing Markets."

Step 2: **Draw a graph similar to Figure 9, with the addition of the black market price.**

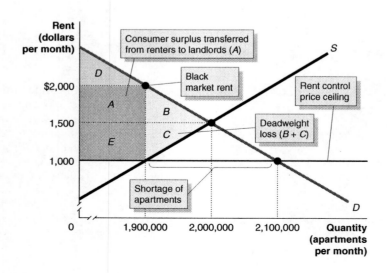

Step 3: **Analyze the changes from Figure 9.** Because the black market rent is now $2,000—even higher than the original competitive equilibrium rent of $1,500—compared with Figure 9, consumer surplus declines by an amount equal to the red rectangle *A* plus the red rectangle *E*. The remaining consumer surplus is the blue triangle *D*. Note that the rectangle *A*, which would have been part of consumer surplus without rent control, represents a transfer from renters to landlords. Compared with the situation shown in Figure 9, producer surplus has increased by an amount equal to rectangles *A* and *E*, and consumer surplus has declined by the same amount. Deadweight loss is equal to triangles *B* and *C*, the same as in Figure 9.

EXTRA CREDIT: This analysis leads to a surprising result: With an active black market in apartments, rent control may leave renters as a group worse off—with less consumer surplus—than if there were no rent control. There is one more possibility to consider, however. If enough landlords become convinced that they can get away with charging rents above the legal ceiling, the quantity of apartments supplied will increase. Eventually, the market could even end up at the competitive equilibrium, with an equilibrium rent of $1,500 and equilibrium quantity of 2,000,000 apartments. In that case the rent control price ceiling becomes nonbinding, not because it was set below the equilibrium price but because it was not legally enforced.

YOUR TURN: For more practice, do related problems 3.14 and 3.23 at the end of this chapter.

>> **End Solved Problem 3**

Rent controls can also lead to an increase in racial and other types of discrimination. With rent controls, more renters are looking for apartments than there are apartments to rent. Landlords can afford to indulge their prejudices by refusing to rent to people they don't like. In cities without rent controls, landlords face more competition, which makes it more difficult to turn down tenants on the basis of irrelevant characteristics, such as race.

Making the Connection

Does Holiday Gift Giving Have a Deadweight Loss?

The deadweight loss that results from rent control occurs, in part, because consumers rent fewer apartments than they would in a competitive equilibrium. Their choices are *constrained* by government. When you receive a gift, you are also constrained because the person who gave the gift has already chosen the product. In many cases, you would have chosen a different gift for yourself. Economist Joel Waldfogel of the University of Pennsylvania points out that gift giving results in a deadweight loss. The amount of the deadweight loss is equal to the difference between the gift's price and the dollar value the recipient places on the gift. Waldfogel surveyed his students, asking them to list every gift they had received for Christmas, to estimate the retail price of each gift, and to state how much they would have been willing to

pay for each gift. Waldfogel's students estimated that their families and friends had paid $438 on average for the students' gifts. The students themselves, however, would have been willing to pay only $313 to buy the presents. If the deadweight losses experienced by Waldfogel's students were extrapolated to the whole population, the deadweight loss of Christmas gift giving could be as much as $13 billion.

Neil Guegan, Corbis Zefa Collection

Gift giving may lead to deadweight loss.

If the gifts had been cash, the people receiving the gifts would not have been constrained by the gift givers' choices, and there would have been no deadweight loss. If your sister had given you cash instead of that sweater you didn't like, you could have bought whatever you wanted. Why then do people continue giving presents rather than cash? One answer is that most people receive more satisfaction from giving or receiving a present than from giving or receiving cash. If we take this satisfaction into account, the deadweight loss from gift giving will be lower than in Waldfogel's calculations. In fact, a later study by economists John List of the University of Maryland and Jason Shogren of the University of Wyoming showed that as much as half the value of a gift to a recipient was its sentimental value. As Professor Shogren concluded, "People get a whole heck of a lot of value out of doing something for others and other people doing something for them. Aunt Helga gave you that ugly scarf, but hey, it's Aunt Helga."

Sources: Mark Whitehouse, "How Christmas Brings Out the Grinch in Economists," *Wall Street Journal*, December 23, 2006, p. A1; Joel Waldfogel, "The Deadweight Loss of Christmas," *American Economic Review*, Vol. 83, No. 4, December 1993, pp. 328–336; and John A. List and Jason F. Shogren, "The Deadweight Loss of Christmas: Comment," *American Economic Review*, Vol. 88, No, 5, 1998, pp. 1350–1355.

YOUR TURN: Test your understanding by doing related problem 3.15 at the end of this chapter.

The Results of Government Price Controls: Winners, Losers, and Inefficiency

When the government imposes price floors or price ceilings, three important results occur:

* Some people win.

* Some people lose.

* There is a loss of economic efficiency.

The winners with rent control are the people who are paying less for rent because they live in rent-controlled apartments. Landlords may also gain if they break the law by charging rents above the legal maximum for their rent-controlled apartments, provided that those illegal rents are higher than the competitive equilibrium rents would be. The losers from rent control are the landlords of rent-controlled apartments who abide by the law and renters who are unable to find apartments to rent at the controlled price. Rent control reduces economic efficiency because fewer apartments are rented than would be rented in a competitive market (refer again to Figure 9). The resulting deadweight loss measures the decrease in economic efficiency.

Positive and Normative Analysis of Price Ceilings and Price Floors

Are rent controls, government farm programs, and other price ceilings and price floors bad? Questions of this type have no right or wrong answers. Economists are generally skeptical of government attempts to interfere with competitive market equilibrium. Economists know the role competitive markets have played in raising the average person's standard of living. They also know that too much government intervention has the potential to reduce the ability of the market system to produce similar increases in living standards in the future.

But recall the difference between positive and normative analysis. Positive analysis is concerned with *what is*, and normative analysis is concerned with *what should be*. Our analysis of rent control and of the federal farm programs in this chapter is positive analysis. We discussed the economic results of these programs. Whether these programs are desirable or undesirable is a normative question. Whether the gains to the winners more than make up for the losses to the losers and for the decline in economic efficiency is a matter of judgment and not strictly an economic question. Price ceilings and price floors continue to exist partly because people who understand their downside still believe they are good policies and therefore support them. The policies also persist because many people who support them do not understand the economic analysis in this chapter and so do not understand the drawbacks to these policies.

4 | Analyze the economic impact of taxes.

4 LEARNING OBJECTIVE

The Economic Impact of Taxes

Supreme Court Justice Oliver Wendell Holmes once remarked, "Taxes are what we pay for a civilized society." When the government taxes a good, however, it affects the market equilibrium for that good. Just as with a price ceiling or price floor, one result of a tax is a decline in economic efficiency. Analyzing taxes is an important part of the field of economics known as *public finance*. In this section, we will use the model of demand and supply and the concepts of consumer surplus, producer surplus, and deadweight loss to analyze the economic impact of taxes.

The Effect of Taxes on Economic Efficiency

Whenever a government taxes a good or service, less of that good or service will be produced and consumed. For example, a tax on cigarettes will raise the cost of smoking and reduce the amount of smoking that takes place. We can use a demand and supply graph to illustrate this point. Figure 10 shows the market for cigarettes.

Without the tax, the equilibrium price of cigarettes would be $4.00 per pack, and 4 billion packs of cigarettes would be sold per year (point *A*). If the federal government requires sellers of cigarettes to pay a $1.00-per-pack tax, then their cost of selling cigarettes will increase by $1.00 per pack. This causes the supply curve for cigarettes to

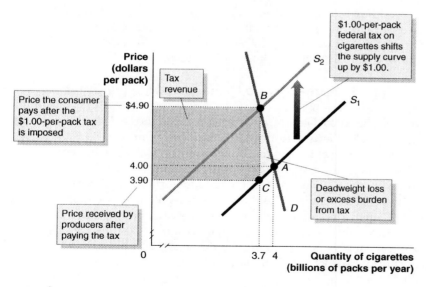

Figure 10 | The Effect of a Tax on the Market for Cigarettes

Without the tax, market equilibrium occurs at point *A*. The equilibrium price of cigarettes is $4.00 per pack, and 4 billion packs of cigarettes are sold per year. A $1.00-per-pack tax on cigarettes will cause the supply curve for cigarettes to shift up by $1.00, from S_1 to S_2. The new equilibrium occurs at point *B*. The price of cigarettes will increase by $0.90, to $4.90 per pack, and the quantity sold will fall to 3.7 billion packs. The tax on cigarettes has increased the price paid by consumers from $4.00 to $4.90 per pack. Producers receive a price of $4.90 per pack (point *B*), but after paying the $1.00 tax, they are left with $3.90 (point *C*). The government will receive tax revenue equal to the green shaded box. Some consumer surplus and some producer surplus will become tax revenue for the government and some will become deadweight loss, shown by the yellow-shaded area.

shift up by $1.00 because sellers will now require a price that is $1.00 greater to supply the same quantity of cigarettes. In Figure 10, for example, without the tax, sellers would be willing to supply a quantity of 3.7 billion packs of cigarettes at a price of $3.90 per pack (point C). With the tax, they will supply only 3.7 billion packs of cigarettes if the price is $4.90 per pack (point B). The shift in the supply curve will result in a new equilibrium price of $4.90 and a new equilibrium quantity of 3.7 billion packs (point B).

The federal government will collect tax revenue equal to the tax per pack multiplied by the number of packs sold, or $3.7 billion. The area shaded in green in Figure 10 represents the government's tax revenue. Consumers will pay a higher price of $4.90 per pack. Although sellers appear to be receiving a higher price per pack, after they have paid the tax, the price they receive falls from $4.00 per pack to $3.90 per pack. There is a loss of consumer surplus because consumers are paying a higher price. The price producers receive falls, so there is also a loss of producer surplus. Therefore, the tax on cigarettes has reduced *both* consumer surplus and producer surplus. Some of the reduction in consumer and producer surplus becomes tax revenue for the government. The rest of the reduction in consumer and producer surplus is equal to the deadweight loss from the tax, shown by the yellow-shaded triangle in the figure.

We can conclude that the true burden of a tax is not just the amount paid to government by consumers and producers but also includes the deadweight loss. The deadweight loss from a tax is referred to as the *excess burden* of the tax. *A tax is efficient if it imposes a small excess burden relative to the tax revenue it raises.* One contribution economists make to government tax policy is to provide advice to policymakers on which taxes are most efficient.

Tax Incidence: Who Actually Pays a Tax?

The answer to the question "Who pays a tax?" seems obvious: Whoever is legally required to send a tax payment to the government pays the tax. But there can be an important difference between who is legally required to pay the tax and who actually *bears the burden* of the tax. The actual division of the burden of a tax is referred to as **tax incidence**. The federal government currently levies an excise tax of 18.4 cents per gallon of gasoline sold. Gas station owners collect this tax and forward it to the federal government, but who actually bears the burden of the tax?

Tax incidence The actual division of the burden of a tax between buyers and sellers in a market.

Determining Tax Incidence on a Demand and Supply Graph Suppose that the retail price of gasoline—including the federal excise tax—is $3.08 per gallon, 140 billion gallons of gasoline are sold in the United States per year, and the federal excise tax is 10 cents per gallon. Figure 11 allows us to analyze the incidence of the tax.

Consider the market for gasoline if there were no federal excise tax on gasoline. This equilibrium occurs at the intersection of the demand curve and supply curve, S_1. The equilibrium price is $3.00 per gallon, and the equilibrium quantity is 144 billion gallons. If the federal government imposes a 10-cents-per-gallon tax, the supply curve for gasoline will shift up by 10 cents per gallon. At the new equilibrium, where the demand curve intersects the supply curve, S_2, the price has risen by 8 cents per gallon, from $3.00 to $3.08. Notice that only in the extremely unlikely case that demand is a vertical line will the market price rise by the full amount of the tax. Consumers are paying 8 cents more per gallon. Sellers of gasoline receive a new higher price of $3.08 per gallon, but after paying the 10-cents-per-gallon tax, they are left with $2.98 per gallon, or 2 cents less than they had been receiving in the old equilibrium.

Although the sellers of gasoline are responsible for collecting the tax and sending the tax receipts to the government, they do not bear most of the burden of the tax. In this case, consumers pay 8 cents of the tax because the market price has risen by 8 cents, and sellers pay 2 cents of the tax because after sending the tax to the government, they are receiving 2 cents less per gallon of gasoline sold. Expressed in percentage terms, consumers pay 80 percent of the tax, and sellers pay 20 percent of the tax.

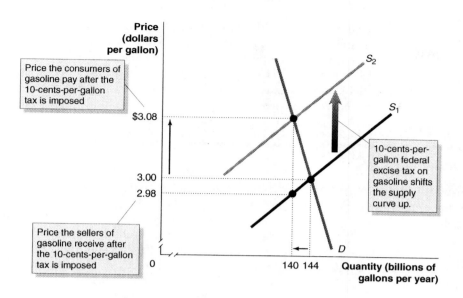

Figure 11

The Incidence of a Tax on Gasoline

With no tax on gasoline, the price would be $3.00 per gallon, and 144 billion gallons of gasoline would be sold each year. A 10-cents-per-gallon excise tax shifts up the supply curve from S_1 to S_2, raises the price consumers pay from $3.00 to $3.08, and lowers the price producers receive from $3.00 to $2.98. Therefore, consumers pay 8 cents of the 10-cents-per-gallon tax on gasoline, and producers pay 2 cents.

Labels in figure:
- Price the consumers of gasoline pay after the 10-cents-per-gallon tax is imposed
- Price the sellers of gasoline receive after the 10-cents-per-gallon tax is imposed
- 10-cents-per-gallon federal excise tax on gasoline shifts the supply curve up.

Solved Problem | 4

When Do Consumers Pay All of a Sales Tax Increase?

Briefly explain whether you agree with the following statement: "If the federal government raises the sales tax on gasoline by $0.25, then the price of gasoline will rise by $0.25. Consumers can't get by without gasoline, so they have to pay the whole amount of any increase in the sales tax." Illustrate your answer with a graph.

SOLVING THE PROBLEM:

Step 1: **Review the chapter material.** This problem is about tax incidence, so you may want to review the section "Tax Incidence: Who Actually Pays a Tax?"

Step 2: **Draw a graph like Figure 11 to illustrate the circumstances when consumers will pay all of an increase in a sales tax.**

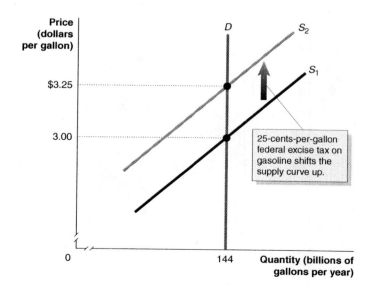

Labels in figure:
- 25-cents-per-gallon federal excise tax on gasoline shifts the supply curve up.

Step 3: **Use the graph to evaluate the statement.** The graph shows that consumers will pay all of an increase in a sales tax only if the demand curve is a vertical line. It is very unlikely that the demand for gasoline looks like this because we expect that for every good, an increase in price will cause a decrease in the quantity demanded. Because the demand curve for gasoline is not a vertical line, the statement is incorrect.

>> **End Solved Problem 4**

YOUR TURN: For more practice, do related problem 4.5 at the end of the chapter.

Does It Matter Whether the Tax Is on Buyers or Sellers? We have already seen the important distinction between the true burden of a tax and whether buyers or sellers are legally required to pay a tax. We can reinforce this point by noting explicitly that the incidence of a tax does *not* depend on whether a tax is collected from the buyers of a good or from the sellers. Figure 12 illustrates this point by showing the effect on equilibrium in the market for gasoline if a 10-cents-per-gallon tax is imposed on buyers rather than on sellers. That is, we are now assuming that instead of sellers having to collect the 10-cents-per-gallon tax at the pump, buyers are responsible for keeping track of how many gallons of gasoline they purchase and sending the tax to the government. (Of course, it would be very difficult for buyers to keep track of their purchases or for the government to check whether they were paying all of the tax they owed. That is why the government collects the tax on gasoline from sellers.)

Figure 12 is similar to Figure 11 except that it shows the gasoline tax being imposed on buyers rather than sellers. In Figure 12, the supply curve does not shift because nothing has happened to change the willingness of sellers to change the quantity of gasoline they supply. The demand curve has shifted, however, because consumers now have to pay a 10-cent tax on every gallon of gasoline they buy. Therefore, at every quantity, they are willing to pay a price 10 cents less than they would have without the tax. We indicate this in the figure by shifting the demand curve down by 10 cents, from D_1 to D_2. Once the tax has been imposed and the demand curve has shifted down, the new equilibrium quantity of gasoline is 140 billion gallons, which is exactly the same as in Figure 11.

The new equilibrium price after the tax is imposed appears to be different in Figure 12 than in Figure 11, but if we include the tax, buyers will pay and sellers will receive the same price in both figures. To see this, notice that in Figure 11, buyers paid sellers a price of $3.08 per gallon. In Figure 12, they pay sellers only $2.98, but they must also pay the government a tax of 10 cents per gallon. So, the total price buyers pay remains $3.08 per gallon.

Figure 12

The Incidence of a Tax on Gasoline Paid by Buyers

With no tax on gasoline, the demand curve is D_1. If a 10-cents-per-gallon tax is imposed that consumers are responsible for paying, the demand curve shifts down by the amount of the tax, from D_1 to D_2. In the new equilibrium, consumers pay a price of $3.08 per gallon, including the tax. Producers receive $2.98 per gallon. This is the same result we saw when producers were responsible for paying the tax.

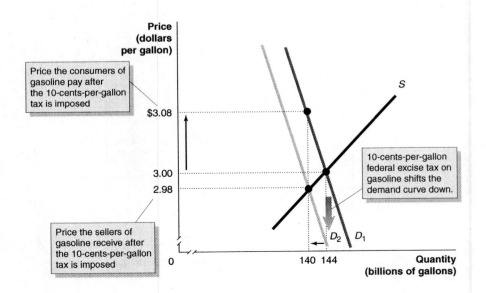

In Figure 11, sellers receive $3.08 per gallon from buyers, but after they pay the tax of 10 cents per gallon, they are left with $2.98, which is the same amount they receive in Figure 12.

Making the Connection | Is the Burden of the Social Security Tax Really Shared Equally between Workers and Firms?

Everyone who receives a paycheck has several different taxes withheld from it by their employers, who forward these taxes directly to the government. In fact, many people are shocked after getting their first job, when they discover the gap between their gross pay and their net pay after taxes have been deducted. The largest tax many people of low or moderate income pay is the FICA, which stands for the Federal Insurance Contributions Act. The FICA funds the Social Security and Medicare programs, which provide income and health care to the elderly and disabled. The FICA is sometimes referred to as the *payroll tax*. When Congress passed the FICA, it wanted employers and workers to equally share the burden of the tax. Currently, the FICA is 15.3 percent of wages, with 7.65 percent paid by workers by being withheld from their paychecks and the other 7.65 percent paid by employers.

How much FICA do you think this employee pays?

Bill Aron, PhotoEdit, Inc.

But does requiring workers and employers to each pay half the tax mean that the burden of the tax is also shared equally? Our discussion in this chapter shows us that the answer is no. In the labor market, employers are buyers, and workers are sellers. As we saw in the example of federal taxes on gasoline, whether the tax is collected from buyers or from sellers does not affect the incidence of the tax. Most economists believe, in fact, that the burden of the FICA falls almost entirely on workers. The following figure, which shows the market for labor, illustrates why.

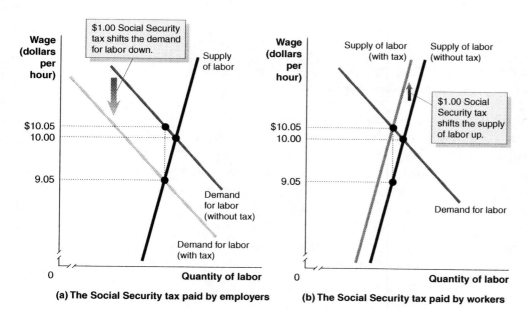

(a) The Social Security tax paid by employers

(b) The Social Security tax paid by workers

In the market for labor, the demand curve reflects the quantity of labor demanded by employers at various wages, and the supply curve reflects the quantity of labor supplied by workers at various wages. The intersection of the demand curve and the supply curve determines the equilibrium wage. In both panels, the equilibrium wage without a Social Security payroll tax is $10 per hour. For simplicity, let's assume that the payroll tax equals $1 per hour of work. In panel (a), we assume that employers must pay the tax. The tax causes the demand for labor curve to shift down by $1 at every quantity of labor because firms now must pay a $1 tax for every hour of labor they hire. We have drawn the supply curve for labor as being very steep because most economists believe the quantity of labor supplied by workers does not change much as the wage rate changes. Workers pay $0.95 of the tax because their wages fall from $10 before the tax to $9.05 after the tax. Firms pay only $0.05 of the tax because the amount they pay for an hour of labor increases from $10 before the tax to $10.05 after the tax. In panel (a), after the tax is imposed, the equilibrium wage declines from $10 per hour to $9.05 per hour. Firms are now paying a total of $10.05 for every hour of work they hire: $9.05 in wages to workers and $1 in tax to the government. In other words, workers have paid $0.95 of the $1 tax, and firms have paid only $0.05.

Panel (b) shows that this result is exactly the same if the tax is imposed on workers rather than on firms. In this case, the tax causes the supply curve for labor to shift up by $1 at every quantity of labor because workers must now pay a tax of $1 for every hour they work. After the tax is imposed, the equilibrium wage increases to $10.05 per hour. But workers receive only $9.05 after they have paid the $1.00 tax. Once again, workers have paid $0.95 of the $1 tax, and firms have paid only $0.05.

Although the figure presents a simplified analysis, it reflects the conclusion of most economists who have studied the incidence of the FICA: Even though Congress requires half the tax to be paid by employers and the other half to be paid by workers, in fact, the burden of the tax falls almost entirely on workers. This conclusion would not be changed even if Congress revised the law to require either employers or workers to pay all of the tax. The forces of demand and supply working in the labor market, and not Congress, determine the incidence of the tax.

YOUR TURN: Test your understanding by doing related problem 4.6 at the end of this chapter.

Economics in YOUR Life!

At the beginning of the chapter, we posed the following question: If you have two job offers in different cities, one with rent control and one without, will you be more likely to find an affordable apartment in the city with rent control? In answering the question, this chapter has shown that although rent control can keep rents lower than they might otherwise be, it can also lead to a permanent shortage of apartments. You may have to search for a long time to find a suitable apartment, and landlords may even ask you to give them payments "under the table," which would make your actual rent higher than the controlled rent. Finding an apartment in a city without rent control should be much easier, although the rent may be higher.

Conclusion

The model of demand and supply showed that markets free from government intervention eliminate surpluses and shortages and do a good job of responding to the wants of consumers. We have seen in this chapter that both consumers and firms sometimes try to use the government to change market outcomes in their favor. The concepts of consumer and producer surplus and deadweight loss allow us to measure the benefits consumers and producers receive from competitive market equilibrium. They also allow us to measure the effects of government price floors and price ceilings and the economic impact of taxes.

Read *An Inside Look at Policy* for a discussion of the debate over rent control in Los Angeles.

Is Rent Control a Lifeline or Stranglehold?

LOS ANGELES TIMES, JANUARY 14, 2007

The Landlords: Two Sides of a Coin

With apologies to David Letterman, the Top Five reasons why landlords hate rent control are:

No. 1. As private citizens, they believe they shouldn't be forced to do the government's job of providing low-cost housing.

No. 2. In few sectors of private enterprise does a city tell a business how much it may charge.

No. 3. Rent-control buildings sell for less, even in high-rolling realty days.

No. 4. Capping what they may collect in rents translates to capping what they can spend on maintenance and repair—and then they get dinged for lousy upkeep.

No. 5: It's virtually impossible to evict undesirable tenants from a rent-controlled building; owners of buildings not under rent control can boot them out for nearly any reason. . . .

Some Westside owners [in Los Angeles], in particular, complain that longtime renters get a lifetime break, even when they easily can afford market rates. Rent-control laws do not require financial-means testing, so professionals, for example, could still be living in rent-controlled units they secured when they were struggling students. Also, some renters secretly sublet their cheap units for market rate, flouting the terms of their contracts, landlords say. . . .

In an identical unit in the building, a recent tenant was paying about $900 a month while charging $1,000 for one of the bedrooms she rented out on the side, Lambert [a Santa Monica landlord of a rent-controlled building] said.

Selling rent-controlled buildings is no cakewalk, either, said Bruce Bernard, who has bought and sold scores of such buildings in Los Angeles. He recently got his asking price of $6.5 million for a 42-unit building in Hollywood that was not under rent control. One mile away, he also recently sold a 20-unit rent-controlled building with similar amenities for $2.3 million, which was $1.1 million less than his listing price.

More dramatically, Lambert got zero offers on his 15-unit rent-controlled building listed for $890,000 just before the 1994 Northridge earthquake. The temblor shoved the building off the foundation, resulting in all of the tenants vacating the red-tagged structure. Despite $500,000 in needed repairs and not a penny of rent coming in, Lambert quickly sold the building after it was legally rent decontrolled—for $950,000. "It was worth more with all that damage and no rent control than the day before the quake, when it had paying tenants. What does that tell you?"

Hard as it is to sell rent-controlled units for a market-rate profit, owners of those buildings face more urgent daily concerns: covering rising insurance, taxes, upkeep, water, plumbing, landscaping and other costs with 3% or 4% annual rent increases. The result often is that repairs are not made in a timely fashion. . . .

The Rent Stabilization Ordinance allows owners to "pass through" half of the costs of capital improvements to tenants. For example, when an owner replaces a roof for $20,000, he or she may divide half of that cost by the number of units in the building and charge the tenants of each unit up to $55 per month—spread out over multiple years—to cover the cost of the repair.

Even so, Stephens [a landlord near the Hollywood Bowl] said, "sometimes you get killed" economically. Landlords complain that some renters, hip to the strict Rent Escrow Account Program—which allows them to pay the city up to 50% of their rent and landlords nothing while units with health or safety violations are being brought up to code—deliberately ruin buildings to avoid paying full rent.

Attorney Harold Greenberg, who owns buildings and represents landlords, recalled a tenant who took a sledgehammer to the walls of his apartment, then reported the damage to the city, getting a rent discount while repairs were underway.

Bennett said he fixed a broken pole in the parking lot of one of his buildings and tenants subsequently rammed their cars into it five more times. Bennett finally closed the lot.

"We pay for repairs and pay for the inspections," said Jim Clarke, manager of government relations for the Apartment Assn. of Greater Los Angeles. "We've become the housing department's cash cow." . . .

© Ambient Images Inc./Alamy

Key Points in the Article

The article discusses the effects of rent-control laws in the Los Angeles market. Los Angeles, like New York City, which we discussed in the chapter opener, places limits on the rents that landlords can charge some tenants. The purpose of rent-control laws is to ensure that low-income people can find affordable housing. As the article and the chapter explain, rent controls impose substantial costs on landlords, which, in turn, may also harm renters.

Analyzing the News

a The law in Los Angeles does not require that tenants in rent-controlled apartments prove they have low incomes, so some rent-controlled apartments are rented to people with high incomes. In other words, there is nothing in the law to guarantee that rent-controlled apartments go to the intended beneficiaries of the law. A rent-control law may actually increase the rent some tenants pay. The figure in Solved Problem 3 shows that the rent-control laws create a shortage of apartments and that the resulting black market rent is often higher than the rent without rent-control laws. That is why the Santa Monica tenant in the article was able to charge $1,000 to rent a single room of her rent-controlled apartment when she paid just $900 to rent the entire apartment.

b Not surprisingly, rent-control laws reduce the price for which a landlord can sell a rent-controlled apartment complex. Clearly, this hurts the landlord, but it can also harm renters. The lower selling price for rent-controlled apartment complexes makes building those complexes less profitable. If developers can't make a profit building rent-controlled apartment complexes, then they won't build them. Over time, the number of rent-controlled complexes should decrease as old complexes become run down and developers lack the incentive to build new ones. The supply of rent-controlled apartments should decrease, making the apartment shortage worse. The figure below shows the effect of the decrease in rent-controlled apartment complexes as a shift of the supply curve to the left, from S_1 to S_2. This shift causes the shortage of apartments to increase from $(Q_1 - Q_2)$ to $(Q_1 - Q_3)$. In addition, the black market rent also increases from Black Market$_1$ to Black Market$_2$.

c Rent-control laws also limit the ability of landlords to raise rents to pay for repairs. Indeed, as the article indicates, some of the laws are written in a way that actually gives tenants an incentive to purposely damage the apartment complex. Both the limit on recovering repair costs and the incentives for tenants to damage the property increase the costs of running rent-controlled apartment complexes. These costs can cause the supply curve in this market to shift even further to the left and make the effects we described in part b even larger.

Thinking Critically About Policy

1. The article describes the significant costs associated with rent-control laws. Despite these costs, rent-control laws are very popular with tenants and local politicians. Why would some tenants support rent-control laws? Do all tenants in the market gain from rent-control laws?

2. Economists are critical of rent-control laws for several reasons. One reason is that the laws create a deadweight loss. The magnitude of this deadweight loss depends on the slopes of the demand and supply curves. Look at the figure for Solved Problem 3. The deadweight loss equals $B + C$, which is the yellow area. What causes the deadweight loss? What would the supply curve have to look like for the deadweight loss to equal zero?

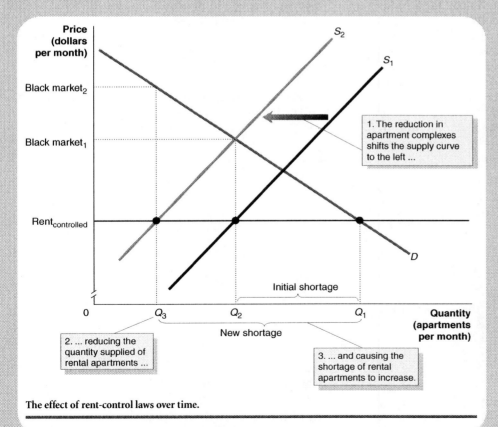

The effect of rent-control laws over time.

Key Terms

Black market	Economic efficiency	Marginal cost	Producer surplus
Consumer surplus	Economic surplus	Price ceiling	Tax incidence
Deadweight loss	Marginal benefit	Price floor	

1 LEARNING OBJECTIVE 1 | Distinguish between the concepts of consumer surplus and producer surplus

Consumer Surplus and Producer Surplus

Summary

Although most prices are determined by demand and supply in markets, the government sometimes imposes *price ceilings* and *price floors*. A **price ceiling** is a legally determined maximum price that sellers may charge. A **price floor** is a legally determined minimum price that sellers may receive. Economists analyze the effects of price ceilings and price floors using *consumer surplus* and *producer surplus*. **Marginal benefit** is the additional benefit to a consumer from consuming one more unit of a good or service. The demand curve is also a marginal benefit curve. **Consumer surplus** is the difference between the highest price a consumer is willing to pay for a product and the price the consumer actually pays. The total amount of consumer surplus in a market is equal to the area below the demand curve and above the market price. **Marginal cost** is the additional cost to a firm of producing one more unit of a good or service. The supply curve is also a marginal cost curve. **Producer surplus** is the difference between the lowest price a firm is willing to accept and the price it actually receives. The total amount of producer surplus in a market is equal to the area above the supply curve and below the market price.

myeconlab Visit www.myeconlab.com to complete these exercises online and get instant feedback.

Review Questions

1.1 What is marginal benefit? Why is the demand curve referred to as a marginal benefit curve?

1.2 What is marginal cost? Why is the supply curve referred to as a marginal cost curve?

1.3 What is consumer surplus? How does consumer surplus change as the equilibrium price of a good rises or falls?

1.4 What is producer surplus? How does producer surplus change as the equilibrium price of a good rises or falls?

Problems and Applications

1.5 Suppose that a frost in Florida reduces the size of the orange crop, which causes the supply curve for oranges to shift to the left. Briefly explain whether each of the following will increase or decrease. Use demand and supply to illustrate your answers.
   a. Consumer surplus
   b. Producer surplus

1.6 A student makes the following argument: "When a market is in equilibrium, there is no consumer surplus. We know this because in equilibrium, the market price is equal to the price consumers are willing to pay for the good." Briefly explain whether you agree with the student's argument.

1.7 The following graph illustrates the market for a breast cancer–fighting drug, without which breast cancer patients cannot survive. What is the consumer surplus in this market? How does it differ from the consumer surplus in the markets you have studied up to this point?

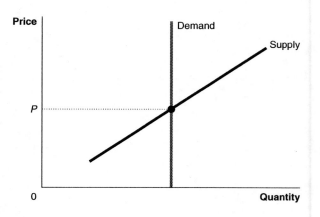

1.8 **(Related to the *Making the Connection*)** The *Making the Connection* states that the value of the area representing consumer surplus from satellite television is $2 billion. Use the information from the graph in the *Making the Connection* to show how this value was calculated.

1.9 The graph in the next column shows the market for tickets to a concert that will be held in a local arena that seats 15,000 people. What is the producer surplus in this market? How does it differ from the producer surplus in the markets you have studied up to this point?

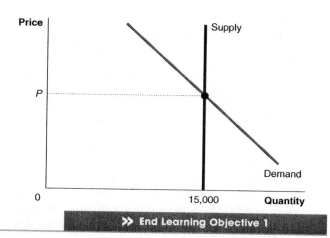

>> End Learning Objective 1

2 LEARNING OBJECTIVE   2 | Understand the concept of economic efficiency

The Efficiency of Competitive Markets

Summary

Equilibrium in a competitive market is **economically efficient**. **Economic surplus** is the sum of consumer surplus and producer surplus. Economic efficiency is a market outcome in which the marginal benefit to consumers from the last unit produced is equal to the marginal cost of production and where the sum of consumer surplus and producer surplus is at a maximum. When the market price is above or below the equilibrium price, there is a reduction in economic surplus. The reduction in economic surplus resulting from a market not being in competitive equilibrium is called the **deadweight loss**.

Review Questions

2.1 Define economic surplus and deadweight loss?

2.2 What is economic efficiency? Why do economists define efficiency in this way?

Problems and Applications

2.3 Suppose you were assigned the task of coming up with a single number that would allow someone to compare the economic activity in one country to that in another country. How might such a number be related to economic efficiency and consumer and producer surplus?

2.4 Briefly explain whether you agree with the following statement: "If at the current quantity marginal benefit is greater than marginal cost, there will be a deadweight loss in the market. However, there is no deadweight loss when marginal cost is greater than marginal benefit."

2.5 Briefly explain whether you agree with the following statement: "If consumer surplus in a market increases, producer surplus must decrease."

2.6 Does an increase in economic surplus in a market always mean that economic efficiency in the market has increased? Briefly explain.

2.7 Using the graph below, explain why economic surplus would be smaller if Q_1 or Q_3 were the quantity produced than if Q_2 is the quantity produced.

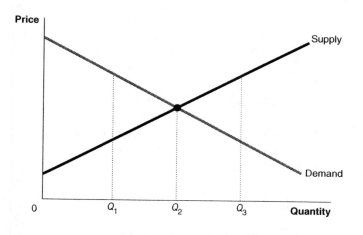

>> End Learning Objective 2

Government Intervention in the Market: Price Floors and Price Ceilings

Summary

Producers or consumers who are dissatisfied with the market outcome can attempt to convince the government to impose price floors or price ceilings. Price floors usually increase producer surplus, decrease consumer surplus, and cause a deadweight loss. Price ceilings usually increase consumer surplus, reduce producer surplus, and cause a deadweight loss. The results of the government imposing price ceilings and price floors are that some people win, some people lose, and a loss of economic efficiency occurs. Price ceilings and price floors can lead to a **black market**, where buying and selling takes place at prices that violate government price regulations. Positive analysis is concerned with what is, and normative analysis is concerned with what should be. Positive analysis shows that price ceilings and price floors cause deadweight losses. Whether these policies are desirable or undesirable, though, is a normative question.

myeconlab Visit www.myeconlab.com to complete these exercises
Get Ahead of the Curve online and get instant feedback.

Review Questions

3.1 Why do some consumers tend to favor price controls while others tend to oppose them?

3.2 Do producers tend to favor price floors or price ceilings? Why?

3.3 What is a black market? Under what circumstances do black markets arise?

3.4 Can economic analysis provide a final answer to the question of whether the government should intervene in markets by imposing price ceilings and price floors? Why or why not?

Problems and Applications

3.5 The graph in the next column shows the market for apples. Assume the government has imposed a price floor of $10 per crate.
  a. How many crates of apples will be sold after the price floor has been imposed?
  b. Will there be a shortage or a surplus? If there is a shortage or a surplus, how large will it be?
  c. Will apple producers benefit from the price floor? If so, explain how they will benefit.

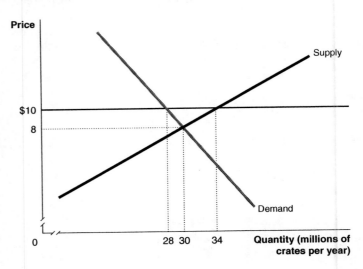

3.6 Use the information on the kumquat market in the table to answer the following questions.

PRICE (PER CRATE)	QUANTITY DEMANDED (MILLIONS OF CRATES PER YEAR)	QUANTITY SUPPLIED (MILLIONS OF CRATES PER YEAR)
$10	120	20
15	110	60
20	100	100
25	90	140
30	80	180
35	70	220

  a. What are the equilibrium price and quantity? How much revenue do kumquat producers receive when the market is in equilibrium? Draw a graph showing the market equilibrium and the area representing the revenue received by kumquat producers.
  b. Suppose the federal government decides to impose a price floor of $30 per crate. Now how many crates of kumquats will consumers purchase? How much revenue will kumquat producers receive? Assume that the government does not purchase any surplus kumquats. On your graph from question (a), show the price floor, the change in the quantity of kumquats purchased, and the revenue received by kumquat producers after the price floor is imposed.
  c. Suppose the government imposes a price floor of $30 per crate and purchases any surplus kumquats from producers. Now how much revenue will kumquat producers receive? How much will the

government spend purchasing surplus kumquats? On your graph from question (a), show the area representing the amount the government spends to purchase the surplus kumquats.

3.7 Suppose that the government sets a price floor for milk that is above the competitive equilibrium price.
   a. Draw a graph showing this situation. Be sure your graph shows the competitive equilibrium price, the price floor, the quantity that would be sold in competitive equilibrium, and the quantity that is sold with the price floor.
   b. Compare the economic surplus in this market when there is a price floor and when there is no price floor.

3.8 During 2007, the Venezuelan government allowed consumers to buy only a limited quantity of sugar. The government also imposed a ceiling on the price of sugar. As a result, both the quantity of sugar consumed and the market price of sugar were below the competitive equilibrium price and quantity. Draw a graph to illustrate this situation. On your graph, be sure to indicate the areas representing consumer surplus, producer surplus, and deadweight loss.

3.9 Refer again to question 3.8. An article in the *New York Times* contained the following (Hugo Chávez is the president of Venezuela):

> José Vielma Mora, the chief of Seniat, the government's tax agency, oversaw a raid this month on a warehouse here where officials seized about 165 tons of sugar. Mr. Vielma said the raid exposed hoarding by vendors who were unwilling to sell the sugar at official prices. He and other officials in Mr. Chávez's government have repeatedly blamed the shortages on producers, intermediaries and grocers.

Do you agree that the shortages in the Venezuelan sugar market are the fault of "producers, intermediaries and grocers"? Briefly explain.

Source: Simon Romero, "Chavez Threatens to Jail Price Control Violators," *New York Times*, February 17, 2007.

3.10 To drive a taxi legally in New York City, you must have a medallion issued by the city government. City officials have issued only 12,187 medallions. Let's assume this puts an absolute limit on the number of taxi rides that can be supplied in New York City on any day because no one breaks the law by driving a taxi without a medallion. Let's also assume that each taxi can provide 6 trips per day. In that case, the supply of taxi rides is fixed at 73,122 (or 6 rides per taxi × 12,187 taxis). We show this in the following graph, with a vertical line at this quantity. *Assume that there are no government controls on the prices that drivers can charge for rides.* Use the graph to answer the following questions.

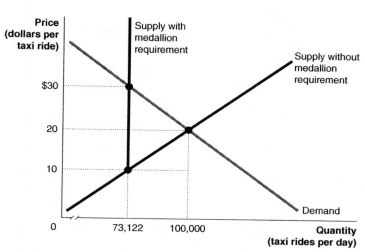

a. What would the equilibrium price and quantity be in this market if there were no medallion requirement?
b. What are the price and quantity with the medallion requirement?
c. Indicate on the graph the areas representing consumer surplus and producer surplus if there were no medallion requirement.
d. Indicate on the graph the areas representing consumer surplus, producer surplus, and deadweight loss with the medallion requirement.

3.11 If the goal of the federal government's farm program is to raise the incomes of poor family farmers, is the current system of price floors and subsidy payments based on the number of acres farmed a good way to reach the goal? Briefly explain. What other ways might the federal government attempt to reach its goals?

3.12 (Related to the *Making the Connection*) Some economists studying the effects of the minimum wage law have found that it tends to reduce the employment of black teenagers relative to white teenagers. Does the graph in the *Making the Connection* help you understand why black teenagers may have been disproportionately affected by the minimum wage? Briefly explain.

3.13 (Related to the *Chapter Opener*) Suppose the competitive equilibrium rent for a standard two-bedroom apartment in Lawrence is $600. Now suppose the city council passes a rent-control law imposing a price ceiling of $500. Use a demand and supply graph to illustrate the impact of the rent-control law. Suppose that shortly after the law is passed, a large employer in the area announces that it will close a plant in Lawrence and lay off 5,000 workers. Show on your graph how this will affect the market for rental property in Lawrence.

3.14 (Related to *Solved Problem 3*) Use the information on the market for apartments in Bay City in the table on the next page to answer the following questions.

RENT	QUANTITY DEMANDED	QUANTITY SUPPLIED
$500	375,000	225,000
600	350,000	250,000
700	325,000	275,000
800	300,000	300,000
900	275,000	325,000
1,000	250,000	350,000

a. In the absence of rent control, what is the equilibrium rent and what is the equilibrium quantity of apartments rented? Draw a demand and supply graph of the market for apartments to illustrate your answer. In equilibrium, will there be any renters who are unable to find an apartment to rent or any landlords who are unable to find a renter for an apartment?

b. Suppose the government sets a ceiling on rents of $600 per month. What is the quantity of apartments demanded, and what is the quantity of apartments supplied?

c. Assume that all landlords abide by the law. Use a demand and supply graph to illustrate the impact of this price ceiling on the market for apartments. Be sure to indicate on your graph each of the following: (i) the area representing consumer surplus after the price ceiling has been imposed, (ii) the area representing producer surplus after the price ceiling has been imposed, and (iii) the area representing the deadweight loss after the ceiling has been imposed.

d. Assume that the quantity of apartments supplied is the same as you determined in (b). But now assume that landlords ignore the law and rent this quantity of apartments for the highest rent they can get. Briefly explain what this rent will be.

3.15 (Related to the *Making the Connection*) Joel Waldfogel argues that there may be a deadweight loss to holiday gift giving. An article in the *Wall Street Journal* suggests that retail stores might be better off if the tradition of holiday gift giving ended: "In theory, smoother sales throughout the year would be better for retailers, enabling them to avoid the extra costs of planning and stocking up for the holidays." Owners of many stores disagree, however. The owner of a store in New York City was quoted in the article as arguing: "Christmas is the lifeblood of the retail business. It's a time of year when people don't have a choice. They *have* to spend." Do you believe the efficiency of the economy would be improved if the tradition of holiday gift giving ended? Briefly explain your reasoning.

Source: Mark Whitehouse, "How Christmas Brings Out the Grinch in Economists," *Wall Street Journal*, December 23, 2006, p. A1.

3.16 (Related to the *Don't Let This Happen to You!*) Briefly explain whether you agree or disagree with the following statement: "If there is a shortage of a good, it must be scarce, but there is not a shortage of every scarce good."

3.17 A student makes the following argument:

A price floor reduces the amount of a product that consumers buy because it keeps the price above the competitive market equilibrium. A price ceiling, on the other hand, increases the amount of a product that consumers buy because it keeps the price below the competitive market equilibrium.

Do you agree with the student's reasoning? Use a demand and supply graph to illustrate your answer.

3.18 An advocate of medical care system reform makes the following argument:

The 15,000 kidneys that are transplanted in the United States each year are received free from organ donors. Despite this, because of hospital and doctor's fees, the average price of a kidney transplant is $250,000. As a result, only rich people or people with very good health insurance can afford these transplants. The government should put a ceiling of $100,000 on the price of kidney transplants. That way, middle-income people will be able to afford them, the demand for kidney transplants will increase, and more kidney transplants will take place.

Do you agree with the advocate's reasoning? Use a demand and supply graph to illustrate your answer.

3.19 (Related to the *Chapter Opener*) The cities of Peabody and Woburn are five miles apart. Woburn enacts a rent-control law that puts a ceiling on rents well below their competitive market value. Predict the impact of this law on the competitive equilibrium rent in Peabody, which does not have a rent-control law. Illustrate your answer with a demand and supply graph.

3.20 (Related to the *Chapter Opener*) Rent controls were first imposed in New York City in the early 1940s, during a housing shortage brought on by World War II. Why do you think that, once established, rent controls continued in New York City for many decades?

3.21 (Related to the *Chapter Opener*) The competitive equilibrium rent in the city of Lowell is currently $1,000 per month. The government decides to enact rent control and to establish a price ceiling for apartments of $750 per month. Briefly explain whether rent control is likely to make each of the following people better or worse off.

a. Someone currently renting an apartment in Lowell

b. Someone who will be moving to Lowell next year and who intends to rent an apartment

c. A landlord who intends to abide by the rent-control law

d. A landlord who intends to ignore the law and illegally charge the highest rent possible for his apartments

3.22 **(Related to the *Chapter Opener*)** The following is from an article in the *New York Times*:

> Imagine finding the perfect apartment, only to learn that the landlord is denying you the place because you are on a blacklist of supposedly high-risk renters. Nothing is wrong with your credit rating, but your name showed up on the list because a private screening service found it in housing court records about a dispute you had with a previous landlord—a dispute that was resolved in your favor.

Is it more likely that a "blacklist" of "high-risk" tenants will exist in a city with rent control or one without rent control? Briefly explain.

Source: Motoko Rich, "A Blacklist of Renters," *New York Times*, April 8, 2004.

3.23 **(Related to *Solved Problem 3*)** Suppose that initially the gasoline market is in equilibrium, at a price of $3.00 per gallon and a quantity of 45 million gallons per month. Then a war in the Middle East disrupts imports of oil into the United States, shifting the supply curve for gasoline from S_1 to S_2. The price of gasoline begins to rise, and consumers protest. The federal government responds by setting a price ceiling of $3.00 per gallon. Use the graph to answer the following questions.

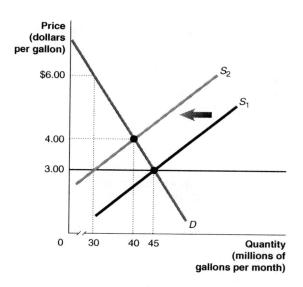

a. If there were no price ceiling, what would be the equilibrium price of gasoline, the quantity of

gasoline demanded, and the quantity of gasoline supplied? Now assume that the price ceiling is imposed and that there is no black market in gasoline. What are the price of gasoline, the quantity of gasoline demanded, and the quantity of gasoline supplied? How large is the shortage of gasoline?

b. Assume that the price ceiling is imposed and there is no black market in gasoline. Show on the graph the areas representing consumer surplus, producer surplus, and deadweight loss.

c. Now assume that there is a black market and the price of gasoline rises to the maximum that consumers are willing to pay for the amount supplied by producers at $3.00 per gallon. Show on the graph the areas representing producer surplus, consumer surplus, and deadweight loss.

d. Are consumers made better off with the price ceiling than without it? Briefly explain.

3.24 In the United States, Amazon.com, BarnesandNoble.com, and many other retailers sell books, DVDs, and music CDs for less than the price marked on the package. In Japan, retailers are not allowed to discount prices in this way. Who benefits and who loses from this Japanese law?

3.25 An editorial in *Economist* discusses the fact that in most countries—including the United States—it is illegal for individuals to buy or sell body parts, such as kidneys.

a. Draw a demand and supply graph for the market for kidneys. Show on your graph the legal maximum price of zero and indicate the quantity of kidneys supplied at this price. (Hint: Because we know that some kidneys are donated, the quantity supplied will not be zero.)

b. The editorial argues that buying and selling kidneys should be legalized:

> With proper regulation, a kidney market would be a big improvement over the current sorry state of affairs. Sellers could be checked for disease and drug use, and cared for after operations. . . . Buyers would get better kidneys, faster. Both sellers and buyers would do better than in the illegal market, where much of the money goes to middlemen.

Do you agree with this argument? Should the government treat kidneys like other goods and allow the market to determine the price?

Source: "Psst, Wanna Buy a Kidney?" *Economist*, November 18, 2006, p. 15.

>> **End Learning Objective 3**

67

4 LEARNING OBJECTIVE   4 | Analyze the economic impact of taxes

The Economic Impact of Taxes

Summary

Most taxes result in a loss of consumer surplus, a loss of producer surplus, and a deadweight loss. The true burden of a tax is not just the amount paid to government by consumers and producers but also includes the deadweight loss. The deadweight loss from a tax is the excess burden of the tax. **Tax incidence** is the actual division of the burden of a tax. In most cases, consumers and firms share the burden of a tax levied on a good or service.

myeconlab Visit www.myeconlab.com to complete these exercises
Get Ahead of the Curve online and get instant feedback.

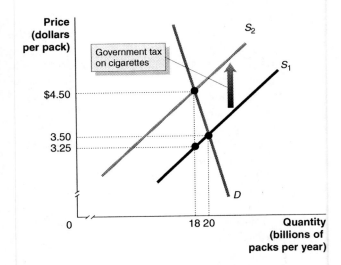

Review Questions

4.1 What is meant by tax incidence?

4.2 Does it matter whether buyers or sellers are legally responsible for paying a tax? Briefly explain.

Problems and Applications

4.3 Suppose the current equilibrium price of cheese pizzas is $10, and 10 million pizzas are sold per month. After the federal government imposes a $0.50 per pizza tax, the equilibrium price of pizzas rises to $10.40, and the equilibrium quantity falls to 9 million. Illustrate this situation with a demand and supply graph. Be sure your graph shows the equilibrium price before and after the tax, the equilibrium quantity before and after the tax, and the areas representing consumer surplus after the tax, producer surplus after the tax, tax revenue collected by the government, and deadweight loss.

4.4 Use the graph of the market for cigarettes in the next column to answer the following questions.
  a. According to the graph, how much is the government tax on cigarettes?
  b. What price do producers receive after paying the tax?
  c. How much tax revenue does the government collect?

4.5 **(Related to Solved Problem 4)** Suppose the federal government decides to levy a sales tax on pizza of $1.00 per pie. Briefly explain whether you agree with the following statement by a representative of the pizza industry:

> The pizza industry is very competitive. As a result, pizza sellers will have to pay the whole tax because they are unable to pass any of it on to consumers in the form of higher prices. Therefore, a sales tax of $1.00 per pie will result in pizza sellers receiving $1.00 less on each pie sold, after paying the tax.

Illustrate your answer with a graph.

4.6 **(Related to the Making the Connection)** If the price consumers pay and the price sellers receive are not affected by whether consumers or sellers collect a tax on a good or service, why does the government usually require sellers and not consumers to collect a tax?

>> End Learning Objective 4

Appendix

Quantitative Demand and Supply Analysis

Graphs help us understand economic change *qualitatively*. For instance, a demand and supply graph can tell us that if household incomes rise, the demand curve for a normal good will shift to the right, and its price will rise. Often, though, economists, business managers, and policymakers want to know more than the qualitative direction of change; they want a *quantitative estimate* of the size of the change.

In this chapter, we carried out a qualitative analysis of rent controls. We saw that imposing rent controls involves a trade-off: Renters as a group gain, but landlords lose, and the market for apartments becomes less efficient, as shown by the deadweight loss. To better evaluate rent controls, we need to know more than just that these gains and losses exist; we need to know how large they are. A quantitative analysis of rent controls will tell us how large the gains and losses are.

Use **quantitative** demand and supply **analysis**.

Demand and Supply Equations

The first step in a quantitative analysis is to supplement our use of demand and supply curves with demand and supply *equations*. Economists often statistically estimate equations for demand curves. Supply curves can also be statistically estimated. For example, suppose that economists have estimated that the demand for apartments in New York City is:

$$Q^D = 3{,}000{,}000 - 1{,}000P,$$

and the supply of apartments is:

$$Q^S = -450{,}000 + 1{,}300P.$$

We have used Q^D for the quantity of apartments demanded per month, Q^S for the quantity of apartments supplied per month, and P for the apartment rent in dollars per month. In reality, both the quantity of apartments demanded and the quantity of apartments supplied will depend on more than just the rental price of apartments in New York City. For instance, the demand for apartments in New York City will also depend on the average incomes of families in the New York area and on the rents of apartments in surrounding cities. For simplicity, we will ignore these other factors.

With no government intervention, we know that at competitive market equilibrium, the quantity demanded must equal the quantity supplied, or:

$$Q^D = Q^S.$$

We can use this equation, which is called an *equilibrium condition*, to solve for the equilibrium monthly apartment rent by setting the demand equation equal to the supply equation:

$$3{,}000{,}000 - 1{,}000P = -450{,}000 + 1{,}300P$$

$$3{,}450{,}000 = 2{,}300P$$

$$P = \frac{3{,}450{,}000}{2{,}300} = \$1{,}500.$$

69

Figure A-1

Graphing Supply and Demand
Equations

After statistically estimating supply and demand equations, we can use the equations to draw supply and demand curves. In this case, the equilibrium rent for apartments is $1,500 per month, and the equilibrium quantity of apartments rented is 1,500,000. The supply equation tells us that at a rent of $346, the quantity of apartments supplied will be zero. The demand equation tells us that at a rent of $3,000, the quantity of apartments demanded will be zero. The areas representing consumer surplus and producer surplus are also indicated on the graph.

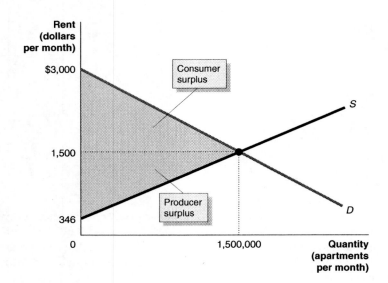

We can then substitute this price back into either the supply equation or the demand equation to find the equilibrium quantity of apartments rented:

$$Q^D = 3,000,000 - 1,000P = 3,000,000 - 1,000(1,500) = 1,500,000$$

$$Q^S = -450,000 + 1,300P = -450,000 + 1,300(1,500) = 1,500,000.$$

Figure A-1 illustrates the information from these equations in a graph. The figure shows the values for rent when the quantity supplied is zero and when the quantity demanded is zero. These values can be calculated from the demand equation and the supply equation by setting Q^D and Q^S equal to zero and solving for price:

$$Q^D = 0 = 3,000,000 - 1,000P$$

$$P = \frac{3,000,000}{1,000} = \$3,000$$

and:

$$Q^S = 0 = -450,000 + 1,300P$$

$$P = \frac{-450,000}{-1,300} = \$346.15.$$

Calculating Consumer Surplus and Producer Surplus

Figure A-1 shows consumer surplus and producer surplus in this market. Recall that the sum of consumer surplus and producer surplus equals the net benefit that renters and landlords receive from participating in the market for apartments. We can use the values from the demand and supply equations to calculate the value of consumer surplus and producer surplus. Remember that consumer surplus is the area below the demand curve and above the line representing market price. Notice that this area forms a right triangle because the demand curve is a straight line—it is *linear*. The area of a triangle is equal to ½ multiplied by the base of the triangle multiplied by the height of the triangle. In this case, the area is:

$$\tfrac{1}{2} \times (1,500,000) \times (3,000 - 1,500) = \$1,125,000,000.$$

70

So, this calculation tells us that the consumer surplus in the market for rental apartments in New York City would be about $1.125 billion.

We can calculate producer surplus in a similar way. Remember that producer surplus is the area above the supply curve and below the line representing market price. Because our supply curve is also a straight line, producer surplus on the figure is equal to the area of the right triangle:

$$\tfrac{1}{2} \times 1,500,000 \times (1,500 - 346) = \$865,500,000.$$

This calculation tells us that the producer surplus in the market for rental apartments in New York City is about $865 million.

We can use this same type of analysis to measure the impact of rent control on consumer surplus, producer surplus, and economic efficiency. For instance, suppose the city imposes a rent ceiling of $1,000 per month. Figure A-2 can help guide us as we measure the impact.

First, we can calculate the quantity of apartments that will actually be rented by substituting the rent ceiling of $1,000 into the supply equation:

$$Q^S = -450,000 + (1,300 \times 1,000) = 850,000.$$

We also need to know the price on the demand curve when the quantity of apartments is 850,000. We can do this by substituting 850,000 for quantity in the demand equation and solving for price:

$$850,000 = 3,000,000 - 1,000P$$

$$P = \frac{-2,150,000}{-1,000} = \$2,150.$$

Compared with its value in competitive equilibrium, consumer surplus has been reduced by a value equal to the area of the yellow triangle B but increased by a value equal to the area of the blue rectangle A. The area of the yellow triangle B is:

$$\tfrac{1}{2} \times (1,500,000 - 850,000) \times (2,150 - 1,500) = \$211,250,000,$$

and the area of the blue rectangle A is base multiplied by height, or:

$$(\$1,500 - \$1,000) \times (850,000) = \$425,000,000.$$

The value of consumer surplus in competitive equilibrium was $1,125,000,000. As a result of the rent ceiling, it will be increased to:

$$(\$1,125,000,000 + \$425,000,000) - \$211,250,000 = \$1,338,750,000.$$

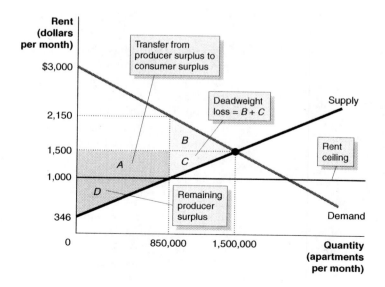

Figure A-2

Once we have estimated equations for the demand and supply of rental housing, a diagram can guide our numeric estimates of the economic effects of rent control. Consumer surplus falls by an amount equal to the area of the yellow triangle B and increases by an amount equal to the area of the blue rectangle A. The difference between the values of these two areas is $213,750,000. Producer surplus falls by an amount equal to the area of the blue rectangle A plus the area of the yellow triangle C. The value of these two areas is $587,500,000. The remaining producer surplus is equal to the area of triangle D, or $278,000,000. Deadweight loss is equal to the area of triangle B plus the area of triangle C, or $373,750,000.

Compared with its value in competitive equilibrium, producer surplus has been reduced by a value equal to the area of the yellow triangle C plus a value equal to the area of the blue rectangle. The area of the yellow triangle C is:

$$\tfrac{1}{2} \times 1,500,000 - 850,000) \times (1,500 - 1,000) = \$162,500,000.$$

We have already calculated the area of the blue rectangle A as \$425,000,000. The value of producer surplus in competitive equilibrium was \$865,500,000. As a result of the rent ceiling, it will be reduced to:

$$\$865,500,000 - \$162,500,000 - \$425,000,000 = \$278,000,000.$$

The loss of economic efficiency, as measured by the deadweight loss, is equal to the value represented by the areas of the yellow triangles B and C, or:

$$\$211,250,000 + \$162,500,000 = \$373,750,000.$$

The following table summarizes the results of the analysis (the values are in millions of dollars).

CONSUMER SURPLUS		PRODUCER SURPLUS		DEADWEIGHT LOSS	
COMPETITIVE EQUILIBRIUM	RENT CONTROL	COMPETITIVE EQUILIBRIUM	RENT CONTROL	COMPETITIVE EQUILIBRIUM	RENT CONTROL
\$1,125	\$1,338.75	\$865.50	\$278	\$0	\$373.75

Qualitatively, we know that imposing rent controls will make consumers better off, make landlords worse off, and decrease economic efficiency. The advantage of the analysis we have just gone through is that it puts dollar values on the qualitative results. We can now see how much consumers have gained, how much landlords have lost, and how great the decline in economic efficiency has been. Sometimes the quantitative results can be surprising. Notice, for instance, that after the imposition of rent control, the deadweight loss is actually greater than the remaining producer surplus.

Economists often study issues where the qualitative results of actions are apparent, even to non-economists. You don't have to be an economist to understand who wins and loses from rent control or that if a company cuts the price of its product, its sales will increase. Business managers, policymakers, and the general public do, however, need economists to measure quantitatively the effects of different actions—including policies such as rent control—so that they can better assess the results of these actions.

 Visit www.myeconlab.com to complete these exercises online and get instant feedback.

Review Questions

A.1 In a linear demand equation, what economic information is conveyed by the intercept on the price axis?

A.2 Suppose you were assigned the task of choosing a price that maximized economic surplus in a market. What price would you choose? Why?

A.3 Consumer surplus is used as a measure of a consumer's net benefit from purchasing a good or service. Explain why consumer surplus is a measure of net benefit.

A.4 Why would economists use the term *deadweight loss* to describe the impact on consumer and producer surplus from a price control?

Problems and Applications

A.5 Suppose that you have been hired to analyze the impact on employment from the imposition of a minimum wage in the labor market. Further suppose that you estimate the supply and demand functions for labor, where L stands for the quantity of labor (measured in thousands of workers) and W stands for the wage rate (measured in dollars per hour):

Demand: $L^D = 100 - 4W$
Supply: $L^S = 6W$

First, calculate the free-market equilibrium wage and quantity of labor. Now suppose the proposed minimum wage is \$12. How large will the surplus of labor in this market be?

A.6 The following graphs illustrate the markets for two different types of labor. Suppose an identical minimum wage is imposed in both markets. In which market will the minimum wage have the largest impact on employment? Why?

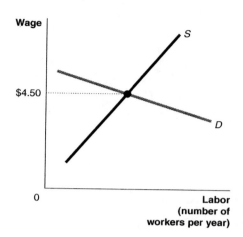

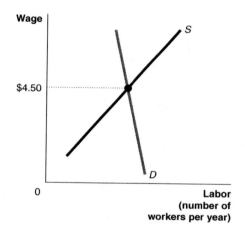

A.7 Suppose that you are the vice president of operations of a manufacturing firm that sells an industrial lubricant in a competitive market. Further suppose that your economist gives you the following supply and demand functions:

Demand: $Q^D = 45 - 2P$
Supply: $Q^S = -15 + P$

What is the consumer surplus in this market? What is the producer surplus?

A.8 The following graph shows a market in which a price floor of $3.00 per unit has been imposed. Calculate the values of each of the following.
  a. The deadweight loss
  b. The transfer of producer surplus to consumers or the transfer of consumer surplus to producers
  c. Producer surplus after the price floor is imposed
  d. Consumer surplus after the price floor is imposed

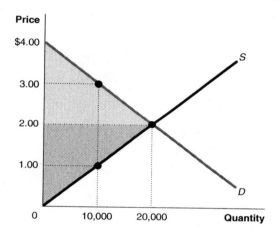

A.9 Construct a table like the one in this appendix, but assume that the rent ceiling is $1,200 rather than $1,000.

>> End Appendix Learning Objective

Externalities, Environmental Policy, and **Public Goods**

From Chapter 5 of *Microeconomics*, 2/e. R. Glenn Hubbard. Anthony Patrick O'Brien. Copyright © 2008 by Pearson Prentice Hall. All rights reserved.

Externalities, Environmental Policy, and Public Goods

Economic Policy and the Environment

Pollution is a part of economic life. Consumers create air pollution by burning gasoline to power their cars and natural gas to heat their homes. Firms create air pollution when they produce electricity, pesticides, or plastics, among other products. Utilities produce sulfur dioxide when they burn coal to generate electricity. Sulfur dioxide contributes to acid rain, which can damage trees, crops, and buildings. The burning of fossil fuels generates carbon dioxide and other greenhouse gases that can increase global warming.

How should government policy deal with the problem of pollution? Can economic analysis help in formulating more efficient pollution policies? In the past, Congress frequently employed policies that ordered firms to use particular methods to reduce pollution. But many economists are critical of this approach—known as *command and control*—because some companies are able to reduce their emissions much more inexpensively if they are allowed to choose the method. To deal with reducing sulfur dioxide emissions in the most efficient way, economists recommended, and Congress adopted, a *market-based approach* called *tradable emissions allowances*.

Under this system, which went into operation in 1995, the federal government gives utility companies allowances to produce a target amount of sulfur dioxide emissions. Utilities are free to buy and sell allowances, although they must end up with allowances equal to the amount of sulfur dioxide they wish to emit: one allowance for every ton of sulfur dioxide emitted. Utilities that initially lack sufficient allowances either must reduce the amount of sulfur dioxide they emit or buy allowances from other utilities that are polluting less.

For example, Duke Energy generates electricity using coal-burning plants, which emit sulfur dioxide. Because Duke Energy already burns low-sulfur coal, reducing emissions of sulfur dioxide even further would be expensive. Many electric utilities in the Midwest, however, burn high-sulfur coal, and their emissions can be reduced greatly by installing anti-pollution devices known as "scrubbers." As a result, these utilities can drastically reduce their emissions and still have allowances left that they can sell to utilities like Duke Energy. According to the manager in charge of environmental compliance at the company, reducing emissions of sulfur dioxide would cost Duke Energy about $300 per ton. A Midwestern utility could reduce emissions for only about $100 per ton. These utilities were willing to sell allowances to Duke Energy for $200 each. As the manager put it, "They would make $100, and Duke would save $100." Not only would the utilities gain, but sulfur dioxide emissions would be reduced at a lower total cost to the economy.

Some economists have advocated a similar program of tradable permits to reduce emissions of carbon dioxide from burning fossil fuels. Other economists have endorsed a carbon tax, which is a tax on energy sources that emit carbon dioxide. With a government carbon tax, the generation of power by burning gasoline, natural gas, coal, or other carbon-based fuels would be taxed. As we will see in this chapter, economic analysis can play a significant role in shaping environmental policies.

AN INSIDE LOOK AT POLICY discusses how tradable emissions permits are also being used to reduce emissions of carbon dioxide, one of the gases suspected of contributing to global warming.

Sources: Jeffrey Bail, "New Consensus In Climate Controversy, Industry Cedes Ground," *Wall Street Journal*, January 23, 2007, p. A1; and Daniel Altman, "Just How Far Can Trading of Emissions Be Extended?" *New York Times*, May 31, 2002.

Mariusz Szachowski, Shutterstock

LEARNING Objectives

After studying this chapter, you should be able to:

1   Identify examples of positive and negative **externalities** and use graphs to show how externalities affect **economic efficiency**

2   Discuss the **Coase theorem** and explain how private bargaining can lead to economic efficiency in a market with an externality.

3   Analyze **government policies** to achieve economic efficiency in a market with an externality.

4   Explain how goods can be categorized on the basis of whether they are **rival or excludable**, and use graphs to illustrate the efficient quantities of **public goods** and **common resources**.

Economics in YOUR Life!

What's the "Best" Level of Pollution?

Carbon taxes and carbon trading are alternative approaches for achieving the goal of reducing carbon dioxide emissions. But how do we know the "best" level of carbon emissions? If carbon dioxide emissions hurt the environment, should the government take action to eliminate them completely? As you read the chapter, see if you can answer these questions. You can check your answers against those we provide at the end of the chapter.

Externality A benefit or cost that affects someone who is not directly involved in the production or consumption of a good or service.

Pollution is just one example of an *externality*. An **externality** is a benefit or cost that affects someone who is not directly involved in the production or consumption of a good or service. In the case of air pollution, there is a *negative externality* because, for example, people with asthma may bear a cost even though they were not involved in the buying or selling of the electricity that caused the pollution. *Positive externalities* are also possible. For instance, medical research can provide a positive externality because people who are not directly involved in producing it or paying for it can benefit. A competitive market usually does a good job of producing the economically efficient amount of a good or service. This may not be true, though, if there is an externality in the market. When there is a negative externality, the market may produce a quantity of the good that is greater than the efficient amount. When there is a positive externality, the market may produce a quantity that is less than the efficient amount. Government interventions in the economy—such as price floors on agricultural products or price ceilings on rents—can reduce economic efficiency. But when there are externalities, government intervention may actually increase economic efficiency and enhance the well-being of society. The way in which government intervenes is important, however. As the example of the program to reduce acid rain by reducing sulfur dioxide emissions shows, economists can help policy-makers ensure that government programs are as efficient as possible.

In this chapter, we explore how best to deal with the problem of pollution and other externalities. We also look at *public goods*, which are goods that may not be produced at all unless the government produces them.

1 | Identify examples of positive and negative externalities and use graphs to show how externalities affect economic efficiency.

Externalities and Economic Efficiency

When you consume a Big Mac, only you benefit, but when you consume a college education, other people also benefit. College-educated people are less likely to commit crimes and, by being better-informed voters, more likely to contribute to better government policies. So, although you capture most of the benefits of your college education, you do not capture all of them.

When you buy a Big Mac, the price you pay covers all McDonald's costs of producing the Big Mac. When you buy electricity from a utility that burns coal and generates acid rain, the price you pay for the electricity does not cover the cost of the damage caused by the acid rain.

So, there is a *positive externality* in the production of college educations because people who do not pay for college educations will nonetheless benefit from them. There is a *negative externality* in the generation of electricity because, for example, people with homes on a lake from which fish and wildlife have disappeared because of acid rain have incurred a cost, even though they might not have bought their electricity from the polluting utility.

The Effect of Externalities

Externalities interfere with the *economic efficiency* of a market equilibrium. A competitive market achieves economic efficiency by maximizing the sum of consumer surplus and producer surplus. *But that result holds only if there are no externalities in production or consumption.* An externality causes a difference between the *private cost* of production and the *social cost*, or the *private benefit* from consumption and the *social benefit*. The **private cost** is the cost borne by the producer of a good or service. The **social cost** is the private cost plus any external cost resulting from production, such as the cost of pollution. Unless

Private cost The cost borne by the producer of a good or service.

Social cost The total cost of producing a good or service, including both the private cost and any external cost.

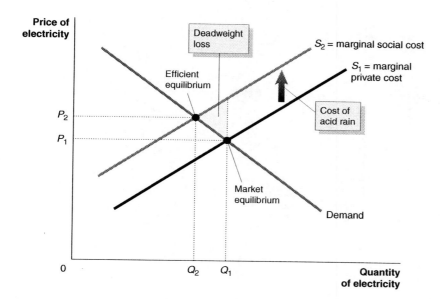

Price of electricity

Deadweight loss

S_2 = marginal social cost

S_1 = marginal private cost

Efficient equilibrium

Cost of acid rain

P_2

P_1

Market equilibrium

Demand

0   Q_2 Q_1

Quantity of electricity

Figure 1

The Effect of Pollution on Economic Efficiency

Because utilities do not bear the cost of acid rain, they produce electricity beyond the economically efficient level. Supply curve S_1 represents just the marginal private cost that the utility has to pay. Supply curve S_2 represents the marginal social cost, which includes the costs to those affected by acid rain. The figure shows that if the supply curve were S_2, rather than S_1, market equilibrium would occur at a price of P_2 and a quantity of Q_2, the economically efficient level of output. But when the supply curve is S_1, the market equilibrium occurs at a price of P_1 and a quantity of Q_1 where there is a deadweight loss equal to the area of the yellow triangle. Because of the deadweight loss, this equilibrium is not efficient.

there is an externality, the private cost and the social cost are equal. The **private benefit** is the benefit received by the consumer of a good or service. The **social benefit** is the private benefit plus any external benefit, such as the benefit to others resulting from your college education. Unless there is an externality, the private benefit and the social benefit are equal.

How a Negative Externality in Production Reduces Economic Efficiency

Consider first how a negative externality in production affects economic efficiency. We often assume that the producer of a good or service must bear all the costs of production. We now know that this observation is not always true. In producing electricity, some private costs are borne by the utility, but some external costs of acid rain are borne by farmers, fishermen, and the general public. The social cost of producing electricity is the sum of the private cost plus the external cost. Figure 1 shows the effect on the market for electricity of a negative externality in production.

S_1 is the market supply curve and represents only the private costs that utilities have to bear in generating electricity. Firms will supply an additional unit of a good or service only if they receive a price equal to the additional cost of producing that unit, so a supply curve represents the *marginal cost* of producing a good or service. If utilities also had to bear the cost of acid rain, the supply curve would be S_2, which represents the true marginal social cost of generating electricity. The equilibrium with a price P_2 and quantity Q_2 is efficient. The equilibrium with a price P_1 and quantity Q_1 is not efficient. To see why, remember that an equilibrium is economically efficient if economic surplus—which is the sum of consumer surplus plus producer surplus—is at a maximum. When economic surplus is at a maximum, the net benefit to society from the production of the good or service is at a maximum. With an equilibrium quantity of Q_2, economic surplus is at a maximum, so this equilibrium is efficient. But with an equilibrium quantity of Q_1, economic surplus is reduced by the deadweight loss, shown in Figure 1 by the yellow triangle, and the equilibrium is not efficient. The deadweight loss occurs because the supply curve is above the demand curve for the production of the units of electricity between Q_2 and Q_1. That is, the additional cost—including the external cost—of producing these units is greater than the marginal benefit to consumers, as represented by the demand curve. In other words, because of the cost of the acid rain, economic efficiency would be improved if less electricity were produced.

We can conclude the following: *When there is a negative externality in producing a good or service, too much of the good or service will be produced at market equilibrium.*

Private benefit The benefit received by the consumer of a good or service.

Social benefit The total benefit from consuming a good or service, including both the private benefit and any external benefit.

Figure 2

The Effect of a Positive Externality on Efficiency

People who do not consume college educations can still benefit from them. As a result, the marginal social benefit from a college education is greater than the marginal private benefit seen by college students. Because only the marginal private benefit is represented in the market demand curve D_1, the quantity of college educations produced, Q_1, is too low. If the market demand curve were D_2 instead of D_1, the level of college educations produced would be Q_2, which is the efficient level. At the market equilibrium of Q_1, there is a deadweight loss equal to the area of the yellow triangle.

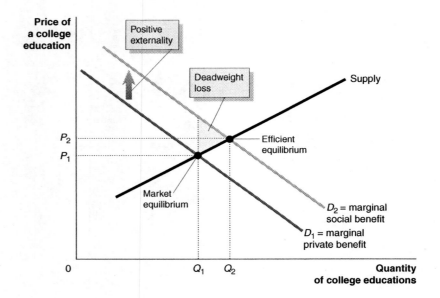

How a Positive Externality in Consumption Reduces Economic Efficiency

We have seen that a negative externality interferes with achieving economic efficiency. The same holds true for a positive externality. We often assume that the demand curve represents all the benefits that come from consuming a good. But we have seen that a college education generates benefits that are not captured by the student receiving the education and so is not represented in the market demand curve for college education. Figure 2 shows the effect of a positive externality in consumption on the market for a college education.

If students receiving a college education could capture all its benefits, the demand curve would be D_2, which represents the marginal social benefits. The actual demand curve is D_1, however, which represents only the marginal private benefits received by students. The efficient equilibrium would come at price P_2 and quantity Q_2. At this equilibrium, economic surplus is maximized. The market equilibrium, at price P_1 and quantity Q_1, will not be efficient because the demand curve is above the supply curve for production of the units between Q_1 and Q_2. That is, the marginal benefit—including the external benefit—for producing these units is greater than the marginal cost. As a result, there is a deadweight loss equal to the area of the yellow triangle. Because of the positive externality, economic efficiency would be improved if more college educations were produced. We can conclude the following: *When there is a positive externality in consuming a good or service, too little of the good or service will be produced at market equilibrium.*

Externalities May Result in Market Failure

We have seen that because of externalities, the efficient level of output may not occur in either the market for electricity or the market for college educations. These are examples of **market failure**: situations in which the market fails to produce the efficient level of output. Later, we will discuss possible solutions to problems of externalities. But first we need to consider why externalities occur.

Market failure A situation in which the market fails to produce the efficient level of output.

What Causes Externalities?

Governments need to guarantee *property rights* for a market system to function well. **Property rights** refers to the rights individuals or businesses have to the exclusive use of their property, including the right to buy or sell it.

Property rights The rights individuals or businesses have to the exclusive use of their property, including the right to buy or sell it.

Property can be tangible, physical property, such as a store or factory. Property can also be intangible, such as the right to an idea. Most of the time, the U.S. government and the governments of other high-income countries do a good job of enforcing property rights, but in certain situations, property rights do not exist or cannot be legally enforced.

Consider the following situation: Lee owns land that includes a lake. A paper company wants to lease some of Lee's land to build a pulp and paper mill. The paper mill will discharge pollutants into Lee's lake. Because Lee owns the lake, he can charge the paper company the cost of cleaning up the pollutants. The result is that the cost of the pollution is a private cost to the paper company and is included in the price of the paper it sells. There is no externality, the efficient level of paper is produced, and there is no market failure.

Now suppose that the paper company builds its paper mill on privately owned land on the banks of a lake that is owned by the state. In the absence of any government regulations, the company will be free to discharge pollutants into the lake. The cost of the pollution will be external to the company because it doesn't have to pay the cost of cleaning it up. More than the economically efficient level of paper will be produced, and a market failure will occur. Or, suppose that Lee owns the lake, but the pollution is caused by acid rain generated by an electric utility hundreds of miles away. The law does not allow Lee to charge the utility for the damage caused by the acid rain. Even though someone is damaging Lee's property, the law does not allow him to enforce his property rights in this situation. Once again, there is an externality, and the market failure will result in too much electricity being produced.

Similarly, if you buy a house, the government will protect your right to exclusive use of that house. No one else can use the house without your permission. Because of your property rights in the house, your private benefit from the house and the social benefit are the same. When you buy a college education, however, other people are, in effect, able to benefit from your college education. You have no property right that will enable you to prevent them from benefiting or to charge them for the benefits they receive. As a result, there is a positive externality, and the market failure will result in too few college educations being supplied.

We can conclude the following: *Externalities and market failures result from incomplete property rights or from the difficulty of enforcing property rights in certain situations.*

---

2 | Discuss the Coase theorem and explain how private bargaining can lead to economic efficiency in a market with an externality.

Private Solutions to Externalities: The Coase Theorem

As noted at the beginning of this chapter, government intervention may actually increase economic efficiency and enhance the well-being of society when externalities are present. It is also possible, however, for people to find private solutions to the problem of externalities.

Can the market cure market failure? In an important article written in 1960, Ronald Coase of the University of Chicago, winner of the 1991 Nobel Prize in Economics, argued that under some circumstances, private solutions to the problem of externalities will occur. To understand Coase's argument, it is important to recognize that completely eliminating an externality usually is not economically efficient. Consider pollution, for example. There is, in fact, an *economically efficient level of pollution reduction*. At first, this seems paradoxical. Pollution is bad, and you might think the efficient amount of a bad thing is zero. But it isn't zero.

The Economically Efficient Level of Pollution Reduction

The optimal decision is to continue any activity up to the point where the marginal benefit equals the marginal cost. This applies to reducing pollution just as much as to other activities. As sulfur dioxide emissions—or any other type of pollution—decline, society benefits: Fewer trees die, fewer buildings are damaged, and fewer people suffer breathing problems. But a key point is that the additional benefit—that is, the *marginal benefit*—received from eliminating another ton of sulfur dioxide declines as sulfur dioxide emissions are reduced. To see why this is true, consider what happens with no reduction in sulfur dioxide emissions. In this situation, many smoggy days will occur in the cities of the Midwest and Northeast. Even healthy people may experience breathing problems. As sulfur dioxide emissions are reduced, the number of smoggy days will fall, and healthy people will no longer experience breathing problems. Eventually, if emissions of sulfur dioxide fall to low levels, even people with asthma will no longer be affected. Further reductions in sulfur dioxide will have little additional benefit. The same will be true of the other benefits from reducing sulfur dioxide emissions: As the reductions increase, the additional benefits from fewer buildings and trees being damaged and lakes polluted will decline.

<table>
<tr><td>Making
the
Connection</td><td>

The Clean Air Act: How a Government Policy Reduced Infant Mortality

The following bar graphs show that tremendous progress has been made in the United States in reducing air pollution since
</td></tr>
</table>

Congress passed the Clean Air Act in 1970: Total emissions of the six main air pollutants have fallen by more than half. Over the same period, real U.S. gross domestic product—which measures the value, corrected for inflation, of all the final goods and services produced in the country—almost doubled, energy consumption increased by half, and the number of miles traveled by all vehicles almost doubled.

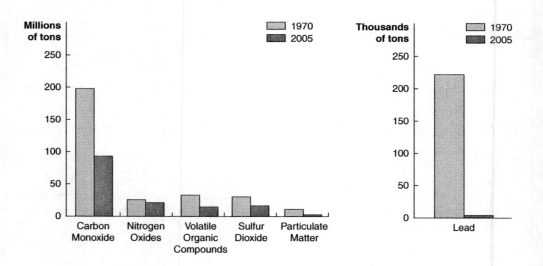

As we have seen, when levels of pollution are high, the marginal benefit of reducing pollution also is high. We would expect, then, that the benefit of reducing air pollution in 1970 was much higher than the benefit from a proportional reduction in air pollution would be today, when the level of pollution is much lower. Kenneth Y. Chay of the University of California, Berkeley, and Michael Greenstone of MIT have shown that the benefits from the air pollution reductions that occurred in the period immediately after passage of the Clean Air Act were indeed high. Chay and Greenstone argue that the exposure of pregnant women to high levels of air pollution can be damaging to their unborn fetuses, possibly by retarding lung functioning. This damage would increase the chance that the infant would die in the first weeks after being born. In the two years following passage of the Clean Air Act, there was a sharp reduction in air pollution and also a reduction in infant mortality. The decline in infant mortality was mainly due to a reduction in deaths within one month of birth. Of course, other factors also may have been responsible for the decline in infant mortality, but Chay and Greenstone use statistical analysis to isolate the effect of the decline in air pollution. They conclude that "1,300 fewer infants died in 1972 than would have in the absence of the Clean Air Act."

Source: Kenneth Y. Chay and Michael Greenstone, "Air Quality, Infant Mortality, and the Clean Air Act of 1970," National Bureau of Economic Research working paper 10053, October 2003.

YOUR TURN: Test your understanding by doing related problem 2.8 at the end of this chapter.

What about the marginal cost to electric utilities of reducing pollution? To reduce sulfur dioxide emissions, utilities have to switch from burning high-sulfur coal to burning more costly fuel, or they have to install pollution control devices, such as scrubbers. As the level of pollution falls, further reductions become increasingly costly. Reducing emissions or other types of pollution to very low levels can require complex and expensive new technologies. For example, Arthur Fraas of the federal Office of Management and Budget and Vincent Munley of Lehigh University have shown that the marginal cost of removing 97 percent of pollutants from municipal wastewater is more than twice as high as the marginal cost of removing 95 percent.

The *net benefit* to society from reducing pollution is equal to the difference between the benefit of reducing pollution and the cost. To maximize the net benefit to society, sulfur dioxide emissions—or any other type of pollution—should be reduced up to the point where the marginal benefit from another ton of reduction is equal to the marginal cost. Figure 3 illustrates this point.

In Figure 3, we measure *reductions* in sulfur dioxide emissions on the horizontal axis. We measure the marginal benefit and marginal cost in dollars from eliminating another ton of sulfur dioxide emissions on the vertical axis. As reductions in pollution increase, the marginal benefit declines and the marginal cost increases. The economically efficient amount of pollution reduction occurs where the marginal benefit equals the marginal cost. The figure shows that in this case, the economically efficient reduction of sulfur dioxide emissions is 8.5 million tons per year, which is the amount of reduction Congress decided should occur by 2010. At that level of emission reduction, the marginal benefit and the marginal cost of the last ton of sulfur dioxide emissions eliminated are both $200 per ton. Suppose instead that the emissions target were only 7.0 million tons. The figure shows that, at that level of reduction, the last ton of reduction has added $250 to the benefits received by society, but it has added only $175 to the costs of utilities. There has been a net benefit to society from this ton of pollution reduction of $75. In fact, the figure shows a net benefit to society from pollution reduction for every ton from 7.0 million to 8.5 million. Only when sulfur dioxide emissions are reduced by 8.5 million tons per year will marginal benefit fall enough and marginal cost rise enough that the two are equal.

Now suppose Congress had set the target for sulfur dioxide emissions reduction at 10 million tons per year. The figure shows that the marginal benefit at that level of reduction has fallen to only $150 per ton and the marginal cost has risen to $225 per ton. The last ton of reduction has actually *reduced* the net benefit to society by $75 per ton. In fact, every ton of reduction beyond 8.5 million reduces the net benefit to society.

To summarize: If the marginal benefit of reducing sulfur dioxide emissions is greater than the marginal cost, further reductions will make society better off. But if the

83

Figure 3

The Marginal Benefit from Pollution Reduction Should Equal the Marginal Cost

If the reduction of sulfur dioxide emissions is at 7.0 million tons per year, the marginal benefit of $250 per ton is greater than the marginal cost of $175 per ton. Further reductions in emissions will increase the net benefit to society. If the reduction of sulfur dioxide emissions is at 10.0 million tons, the marginal cost of $225 per ton is greater than the marginal benefit of $150 per ton. An increase in sulfur dioxide emissions will increase the net benefit to society. Only when the reduction is at 8.5 million tons is the marginal benefit equal to the marginal cost. This level is the economically efficient level of pollution reduction.

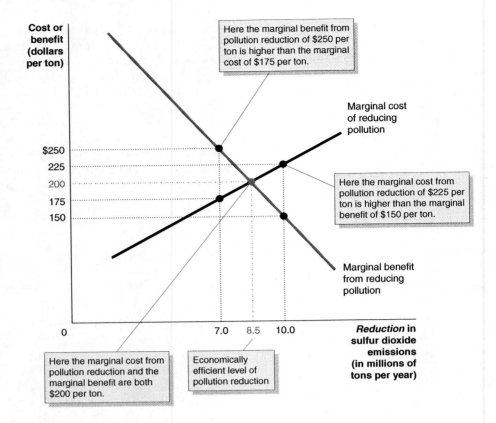

marginal cost of reducing sulfur dioxide emissions is greater than the marginal benefit, reducing sulfur dioxide emissions will actually make society worse off.

The Basis for Private Solutions to Externalities

In arguing that private solutions to the problem of externalities were possible, Ronald Coase emphasized that when more than the optimal level of pollution is occurring, the benefits from reducing the pollution to the optimal level are greater than the costs. Figure 4 illustrates this point.

Don't Let This Happen to **YOU!**

Remember That It's the *Net* Benefit That Counts

Why would we not want to *completely* eliminate anything unpleasant? As long as any person suffers any unpleasant consequences from air pollution, the marginal benefit of reducing air pollution will be positive. So, removing every particle of air pollution results in the largest *total* benefit to society. But removing every particle of air pollution is not optimal for the same reason that it is not optimal to remove every particle of dirt or dust from a room when cleaning it. The cost of cleaning your room is not just the price of the cleaning products but also the opportunity cost of your time. The more time you devote to cleaning your room, the less time you have available for other activities. As you devote more and more additional hours to cleaning your room, the alternative activities you have to give up are likely to increase in value, raising the opportunity cost of cleaning: Cleaning instead of watching TV may not be too costly, but cleaning instead of eating any meals or getting any sleep is very costly. Optimally, you should eliminate dirt in your room up to the point where the marginal benefit of the last dirt removed equals the marginal cost of removing it. Society should take the same approach to air pollution. The result is the largest *net* benefit to society.

YOUR TURN: Test your understanding by doing related problem 2.6 at the end of this chapter.

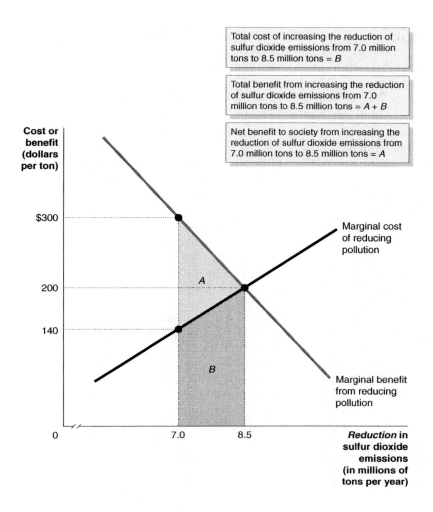

Total cost of increasing the reduction of sulfur dioxide emissions from 7.0 million tons to 8.5 million tons = *B*

Total benefit from increasing the reduction of sulfur dioxide emissions from 7.0 million tons to 8.5 million tons = *A* + *B*

Net benefit to society from increasing the reduction of sulfur dioxide emissions from 7.0 million tons to 8.5 million tons = *A*

Figure 4

The Benefits of Reducing Pollution to the Optimal Level Are Greater Than the Costs

Increasing the reduction in sulfur dioxide emissions from 7.0 million tons to 8.5 million tons results in total benefits equal to the sum of the areas *A* and *B* under the marginal benefits curve. The total cost of this decrease in pollution is equal to the area *B* under the marginal cost curve. The total benefits are greater than the total costs by an amount equal to the area of triangle *A*. Because the total benefits from reducing pollution are greater than the total costs, it's possible for those receiving the benefits to arrive at a private agreement with polluters to pay them to reduce pollution.

The marginal benefit curve shows the additional benefit from each reduction in a ton of sulfur dioxide emissions. The area under the marginal benefit curve between the two emission levels is the *total* benefit received from reducing emissions from one level to another. For instance, in Figure 4, the total benefit from increasing the reduction in sulfur dioxide emissions from 7.0 million tons to 8.5 million tons is the sum of the areas of *A* and *B*. The marginal cost curve shows the additional cost from each reduction in a ton of emissions. The *total* cost of reducing emissions from one level to another is the area under the marginal cost curve between the two emissions levels. The total cost from increasing the reduction in emissions from 7.0 million tons to 8.5 million tons is the area *B*. The net benefit from reducing emissions is the difference between the total cost and the total benefit, which is equal to the area of triangle *A*.

In Figure 4, the benefits from further reductions in sulfur dioxide emissions are much greater than the costs. The formula for calculating the area of a triangle is ½ × base × height, and the formula for the area of a rectangle is base × height. Using these formulas, we can calculate the value of the total benefits from the reduction in emissions and the value of the total costs. The value of the benefits (*A* + *B*) is $375 million. The value of the costs (*B*) is $255 million. If the people who would benefit from a reduction in pollution could get together, they could offer to pay the electric utilities $255 million to reduce the pollution to the optimal level. After making the payment, they would still be left with a net benefit of $120 million. In other words, a private agreement to reduce pollution to the optimal level is possible, without any need for government intervention.

Making the Connection

The Fable of the Bees

Apple trees must be pollinated by bees to bear fruit. Bees need the nectar from apple trees (or other plants) to produce honey.

In a famous article published in the early 1950s, the British economist James Meade, winner of the 1977 Nobel Prize in Economics, argued that there were positive externalities in both apple growing and beekeeping. The more apple trees growers planted, the more honey would be produced in the hives of local beekeepers. And the more hives beekeepers kept, the larger the apple crops in neighboring apple orchards. Meade assumed that beekeepers were not being compensated by apple growers for the pollination services they were providing to apple growers and that apple growers were not being compensated by beekeepers for the use of their nectar in honey making. Therefore, he concluded that unless the government intervened, the market would not supply enough apple trees and beehives.

Steven Cheung of the University of Washington showed, however, that government intervention was not necessary because beekeepers and apple growers had long since arrived at private agreements. In fact, in Washington State, farmers with fruit orchards had been renting beehives to pollinate their trees since at least World War I. According to Cheung, "Pollination contracts usually include stipulations regarding the number and strength of the [bee] colonies, the rental fee per hive, the time of delivery and removal of hives, the protection of bees from pesticide sprays, and the strategic placing of hives."

Today, honeybees pollinate more than $14 billion worth of crops annually. Many beekeepers travel from state to state, renting out their bees to farmers. Increasing demand for almonds has expanded the crop in California until it now stretches for 300 miles across 580,000 acres. Currently, more than one million beehives are required to pollinate the California almond crop. Beehives are shipped into the state in February and March to pollinate the almond trees, and then they are shipped to Oregon and Washington to pollinate the cherry, pear, and apple orchards in those states during April and May.

AP Wide World Photos

Some apple growers and beekeepers make private arrangements to arrive at an economically efficient outcome.

Sources: J. E. Meade, "External Economies and Diseconomies in a Competitive Situation," *Economic Journal*, Vol. 62, March 1952, pp. 54–67; Steven N. S. Cheung, "The Fable of the Bees: An Economic Investigation," *Journal of Law and Economics*, Vol. 16, 1973, pp. 11–33; and Alexei Barrionuevo, "Honey Bees Vanish, Leaving Keepers in Peril," *New York Times*, February 27, 2007.

YOUR TURN: Test your understanding by doing related problem 2.9 at the end of this chapter.

Do Property Rights Matter?

In discussing the bargaining between the electric utilities and the people suffering the effects of the utlities' pollution, we assumed that the electric utilities were not legally liable for the damage they were causing. In other words, the victims of pollution could not legally enforce the right of their property not to be damaged, so they would have to pay the utilities to reduce the pollution. But would it make any difference if the utilities were legally liable for the damages? Surprisingly, as Coase was the first to point out, it does not matter for the amount of pollution reduction. The only difference would be that now the electric utilities would have to pay the victims of pollution for the right to pollute rather than the victims having to pay the utilities. Because the marginal benefits and marginal costs of pollution reduction would not change, the bargaining would still result in the efficient level of pollution reduction—in this case, 8.5 million tons.

In the absence of the utilities being legally liable, the victims of pollution have an incentive to pay the utilities to reduce pollution up to the point where the marginal benefit of the last ton of reduction is equal to the marginal cost. If the utilities are legally liable, they have an incentive to pay the victims of pollution to allow them to pollute up to the same point.

The Problem of Transactions Costs

Unfortunately, there are frequently practical difficulties in the way of a private solution to the problem of externalities. In cases of pollution, for example, there are often both many polluters and many people suffering from the negative effects of pollution. Bringing together all those suffering from pollution with all those causing the pollution and negotiating an agreement often fails due to *transactions costs*. **Transactions costs** are the costs in time and other resources that parties incur in the process of agreeing to and carrying out an exchange of goods or services. In this case, the transactions costs would include the time and other costs of negotiating an agreement, drawing up a binding contract, purchasing insurance, and monitoring the agreement. Unfortunately, when many people are involved, the transactions costs are often higher than the net benefits from reducing the externality. Thus, the cost of transacting ends up exceeding the gain from the transaction. In such cases, a private solution to an externality problem is not feasible.

Transactions costs The costs in time and other resources that parties incur in the process of agreeing to and carrying out an exchange of goods or services.

The Coase Theorem

Coase's argument that private solutions to the problem of externalities are possible is summed up in the **Coase theorem**: If transactions costs are low, private bargaining will result in an efficient solution to the problem of externalities. We have seen the basis for the Coase theorem in the preceding example of pollution by electric utilities: Because the benefits from reducing an externality are often greater than the costs, private bargaining can arrive at an efficient outcome. But we have also seen that this outcome will occur only if transactions costs are low, and in the case of pollution, they usually are not. In general, private bargaining is most likely to reach an efficient outcome if the number of parties bargaining is small.

Coase theorem The argument of economist Ronald Coase that if transactions costs are low, private bargaining will result in an efficient solution to the problem of externalities.

In practice, we must add a couple of other qualifications to the Coase theorem. In addition to low transactions costs, private solutions to the problem of externalities will occur only if all parties to the agreement have full information about the costs and benefits associated with the externality, and all parties must be willing to accept a reasonable agreement. For example, if those suffering from the effects of pollution do not have information on the costs of reducing pollution, it is unlikely that the parties can reach an agreement. Unreasonable demands can also hinder an agreement. For instance, in the example of pollution by electric utilities, we saw that the total benefit of reducing sulfur dioxide emissions was $375 million. Even if transactions costs are very low, if the utilities insist on being paid more than $375 million to reduce emissions, no agreement will be reached because the amount paid exceeds the value of the reduction to those suffering from the emissions.

3 | Analyze government policies to achieve economic efficiency in a market with an externality.

Government Policies to Deal with Externalities

When private solutions to externalities are not feasible, how should the government intervene? The first economist to analyze market failure systematically was A. C. Pigou, a British economist at Cambridge University. Pigou argued that to deal with a negative externality in production, the government should impose a tax equal to the cost of the externality. The effect of such a tax is shown in Figure 5, which reproduces the negative externality from acid rain shown in Figure 1.

By imposing a tax equal to the cost of acid rain on the production of electricity, the government will cause electric utilities to *internalize* the externality. As a consequence, the cost of the acid rain will become a private cost borne by the utilities, and

Figure 5

When There Is a Negative Externality, a Tax Can Bring about the Efficient Level of Output

Because utilities do not bear the cost of acid rain, they produce electricity beyond the economically efficient level. If the government imposes a tax equal to the cost of acid rain, the utilities will internalize the externality. As a consequence, the supply curve will shift up from S_1 to S_2. The market equilibrium quantity changes from Q_1, where an inefficiently high level of electricity is produced, to Q_2, the economically efficient equilibrium quantity. The price of electricity will rise from P_1— which does not include the cost of acid rain— to P_2—which does include the cost.

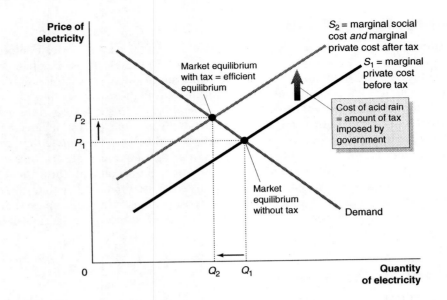

the supply curve for electricity will shift from S_1 to S_2. The result will be a decrease in the equilibrium output of electricity from Q_1 to the efficient level, Q_2. The price of electricity will rise from P_1—which does not include the cost of acid rain—to P_2— which does include the cost.

Solved Problem | 3

Using a Tax to Deal with a Negative Externality

Companies that produce toilet paper bleach the paper to make it white. Some paper plants discharge the bleach into rivers and lakes, causing substantial environmental damage. Suppose the following graph illustrates the situation in the toilet paper market.

Explain how the federal government can use a tax on toilet paper to bring about the efficient level of production. What should the value of the tax be?

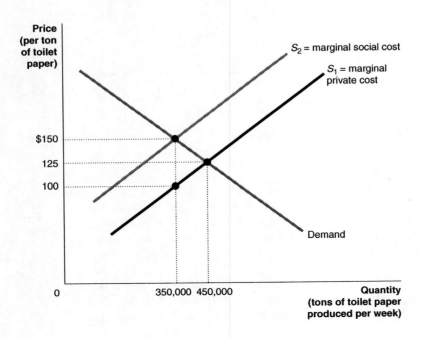

SOLVING THE PROBLEM:

Step 1: **Review the chapter material.** This problem is about the government using a tax to deal with a negative externality in production, so you may want to review the section "Government Policies to Deal with Externalities."

Step 2: **Use the information from the graph to determine the necessary tax.** The efficient level of toilet paper production will occur where the marginal social benefit from consuming toilet paper, as represented by the demand curve, is equal to the marginal social cost of production. The graph shows that this will occur at a price of $150 per ton and production of 350,000 tons. In the absence of government intervention, the price will be $125 per ton, and production will be 450,000 tons. It is tempting—but incorrect!—to think that the government could bring about the efficient level of production by imposing a per-ton tax equal to the difference between the price when production is at its optimal level and the current market price. But this would be a tax of only $25. The graph shows that at the optimal level of production, the difference between the marginal private cost and the marginal social cost is $50. Therefore, a tax of $50 per ton is required to shift the supply curve up from S_1 to S_2.

YOUR TURN: For more practice, do related problem 3.8 at the end of this chapter.

>> End Solved Problem 3

Pigou also argued that the government can deal with a positive externality in consumption by giving consumers a subsidy, or payment, equal to the value of the externality. The effect of the subsidy is shown in Figure 6, which reproduces the positive externality from college education shown in Figure 2.

By paying college students a subsidy equal to the external benefit from a college education, the government will cause students to *internalize* the externality. That is, the external benefit from a college education will become a private benefit received by college students, and the demand curve for college educations will shift from D_1 to D_2. The equilibrium number of college educations supplied will increase from Q_1 to the efficient level, Q_2. In fact, the government does heavily subsidize college educations. All states have government-operated universities that charge tuitions well below the cost of providing the education. The state and federal governments also provide students with grants and low-interest loans that subsidize college educations. The economic justification for these programs is that college educations provide an external benefit to society.

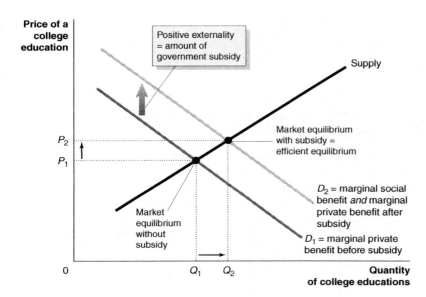

Figure 6

When There Is a Positive Externality, a Subsidy Can Bring about the Efficient Level of Output

People who do not consume college educations can benefit from them. As a result, the social benefit from a college education is greater than the private benefit seen by college students. If the government pays a subsidy equal to the external benefit, students will internalize the externality. The subsidy will cause the demand curve to shift up, from D_1 to D_2. The result will be that market equilibrium quantity shifts from Q_1, where an inefficiently low level of college educations is supplied, to Q_2, the economically efficient equilibrium quantity.

Pigovian taxes and subsidies
Government taxes and subsidies intended to bring about an efficient level of output in the presence of externalities.

Because A. C. Pigou was the first economist to propose using government taxes and subsidies to deal with externalities, they are sometimes referred to as **Pigovian taxes and subsidies**. Note that a Pigovian tax eliminates deadweight loss and improves economic efficiency. Most taxes reduce consumer surplus and producer surplus and create a deadweight loss. In fact, one reason that economists support Pigovian taxes as a way to deal with negative externalities is that the government can use the revenues raised by Pigovian taxes to lower other taxes that reduce economic efficiency.

Command and Control versus Tradable Emissions Allowances

Command and control approach An approach that involves the government imposing quantitative limits on the amount of pollution firms are allowed to emit or requiring firms to install specific pollution control devices.

Although the federal government has sometimes used taxes and subsidies to deal with externalities, in dealing with pollution, it has traditionally used a *command and control approach* with firms that pollute. A **command and control approach** to reducing pollution involves the government imposing quantitative limits on the amount of pollution firms are allowed to generate or requiring firms to install specific pollution control devices. For example, in 1983, the federal government required auto manufacturers such as Ford and General Motors to install catalytic converters to reduce auto emissions on all new automobiles.

Congress could have used direct pollution controls to deal with the problem of acid rain. To achieve its objective of a reduction of 8.5 million tons per year in sulfur dioxide emissions by 2010, it could have required every utility to reduce sulfur dioxide emissions by the same specified amount. However, this approach would not have been an economically efficient solution to the problem. As we saw at the beginning of this chapter, utilities can have very different costs of reducing sulfur dioxide emissions. Some utilities, like Duke Energy, that already use low-sulfur coal can reduce emissions further only at a high cost. Other utilities, particularly those in the Midwest, are able to reduce emissions at a lower cost.

Congress decided to use a market-based approach to reducing sulfur dioxide emissions by setting up a system of tradable emissions allowances. The federal government gave utilities allowances equal to the total amount of allowable sulfur dioxide emissions. The utilities were then free to buy and sell the allowances. An active market where the allowances can be bought and sold is conducted on the Chicago Mercantile Exchange. Utilities that could reduce emissions at low cost did so and sold their allowances. Utilities that could only reduce emissions at high cost bought allowances. Using tradable emissions allowances to reduce acid rain has been a great success and has made it possible for utilities to meet Congress's emissions goal at a much lower cost than expected. As Figure 7 shows, just before Congress enacted the allowances program in 1990, the Edison Electrical Institute estimated that the cost to utilities of complying with the program would be $7.4 billion by 2010. By 1994, the federal government's General Accounting Office estimated that the cost would be less than $2 billion. In practice, the cost appears likely to be almost 90 percent less than the initial estimate, or only about $870 *million*.

Are Tradable Emissions Allowances Licenses to Pollute?

Some environmentalists have criticized tradable emissions allowances, labeling them "licenses to pollute." They argue that just as the government does not issue licenses to rob banks or to drive drunk, it should not issue licenses to pollute. But this criticism ignores one of the central lessons of economics: Resources are scarce, and trade-offs exist. Resources that are spent reducing one type of pollution are not available to reduce other types of pollution or for any other use. Because reducing acid rain using tradable emissions allowances cost utilities $870 million, rather than $7.4 billion, as originally estimated, society saved more than $6.5 billion.

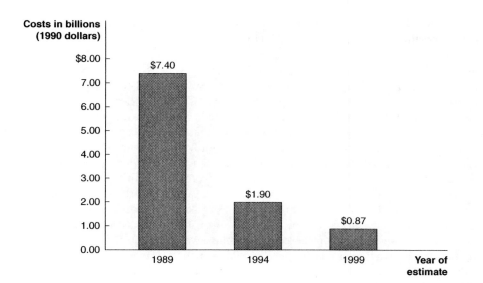

Figure 7

Estimated Cost of the Acid Rain Program in 2010

The Edison Electric Institute estimated in 1989 that the program to reduce acid rain pollution would cost utilities a total of $7.4 billion by 2010. The system of tradable emissions allowances used in the program resulted in the bulk of the reduction in pollution being carried out by the utilities that could do it at the lowest cost. As a result, the program is likely to cost $870 million, which is almost 90 percent less than the original estimate. (*Note:* To correct for the effect of inflation, the costs are measured in dollars of 1990 purchasing power.)

Source: Environmental Protection Agency, *Progress Report on the EPA Acid Rain Program,* November 1999, Figure 2.

Making the Connection

Can Tradable Permits Reduce Global Warming?

In the past 25 years, the global surface temperature has increased about three-quarters of 1 degree Fahrenheit (or four-tenths of 1 degree Centigrade) compared with the average for the previous 30 years. The following graph shows changes in temperature over the years since 1880.

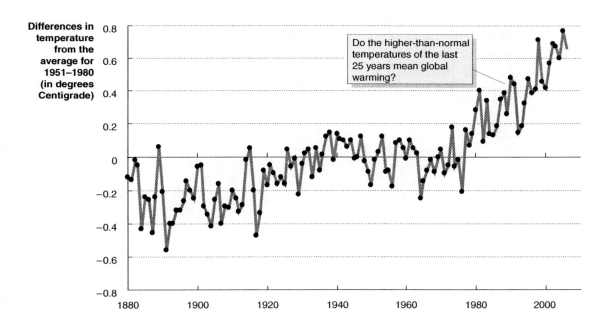

Global temperatures have gone through many periods of warming and cooling. In fact, the below-normal temperatures that prevailed before 1970 led some scientists to predict the eventual arrival of a new ice age. Nevertheless, many scientists are convinced that the recent warming is not part of the natural fluctuations in temperature but is instead due to the burning of fossil fuels, such as coal, natural gas, and petroleum. Burning these fuels releases CO_2 (carbon dioxide), which accumulates in the atmosphere as a "greenhouse gas." Greenhouse gases cause some of the heat released from the earth to be reflected back, increasing temperatures.

91

If greenhouse gases continue to accumulate in the atmosphere, according to some estimates, global temperatures could increase by 3 degrees Fahrenheit or more during the next 100 years. Such increases in temperature could lead to significant changes in climate, which might result in more storms and flooding as well as other problems. By 1995, a number of nations had concluded that the threat of global warming was significant enough to take steps toward reducing emissions of CO_2 and other greenhouse gases. The result was the 1997 Kyoto Treaty, which, if accepted, would have required the high-income countries to reduce their CO_2 emissions by more than 5 percent compared with their 1990 levels. However, President George W. Bush was not willing to commit the United States to the treaty. He argued that the costs to the United States of complying with the treaty were too high, particularly because some scientists were still skeptical that CO_2 emissions actually were causing the increase in temperature. Even scientists who believed that CO_2 emissions contribute to rising temperatures were skeptical that the Kyoto Treaty would have much effect on global warming. President Bush also argued that developing countries should be included in any agreement. Some developing countries, such as China and India, are experiencing rapid economic growth, which in turn has led to rapid increases in CO_2 emissions. European countries that ratified the Kyoto Treaty have had difficulty fulfilling their commitments to reduce CO_2 emissions to the levels indicated by the treaty. Of the larger European countries, only Great Britain, where emissions have declined by more than 15 percent since 1990, seems likely to succeed in fulfilling its commitments by 2012.

The mechanism by which reductions in CO_2 emissions would occur has also been in dispute. The United States has favored a global system of tradable emission permits for CO_2 that would be similar to the system for sulfur dioxide discussed earlier in this chapter. As we have seen, this type of system has the potential to reduce CO_2 emissions at a lower cost. Most European countries, however, have been reluctant to fully accept such a system, preferring instead to require that each country reduce emissions by a specified amount. In recent years, though, support has grown in Europe for using tradable allowances, and an active market in these allowances has developed under the European Union Greenhouse Gas Emission Trading Scheme, which began operation in 2005. It seems unlikely that the debate over the costs and benefits of reducing CO_2 emissions will be resolved any time soon.

Sources: Juliet Eilperin and Steven Mufson, "Tax on Carbon Emissions Gains Support," *Washington Post*, April 1, 2007, p. A05; United Nations Framework Convention on Climate Change, *National Greenhouse Gas Inventory Data for the Period 1990–2004*, October 19, 2006; and (for data in the graph) NASA, Goddard Institute for Space Studies, http://data.giss.nasa.gov/gistemp/graphs/.

YOUR TURN: Test your understanding by doing related problem 3.11 at the end of this chapter.

---

4 LEARNING OBJECTIVE

4 | Explain how goods can be categorized on the basis of whether they are rival or excludable, and use graphs to illustrate the efficient quantities of public goods and common resources.

Four Categories of Goods

Rivalry The situation that occurs when one person's consuming a unit of a good means no one else can consume it.

Excludability The situation in which anyone who does not pay for a good cannot consume it.

We can explore further the question of when the market is likely to succeed in supplying the efficient quantity of a good by noting that goods differ on the basis of whether their consumption is *rival* and *excludable*. **Rivalry** occurs when one person's consuming a unit of a good means no one else can consume it. If you consume a Big Mac, for example, no one else can consume it. **Excludability** means that anyone who does not pay for a good cannot consume it. If you don't pay for a Big Mac, for example, MacDonald's can exclude you from consuming it. The consumption of a Big Mac is rival and excludable. The consumption of some goods, however, can be either *nonrival or nonexcludable*. Nonrival means that one person's consumption does not interfere with another person's consumption. Nonexcludable means that it is impossible to exclude

	Excludable	Nonexcludable
Rival	**Private Goods** *Examples:* *Big Macs* *Running shoes*	**Common Resources** *Examples:* *Tuna in the ocean* *Public pasture land*
Nonrival	**Quasi-Public Goods** *Examples:* *Cable TV* *Toll road*	**Public Goods** *Examples:* *National defense* *Court system*

Figure 8

Four Categories of Goods

Goods and services can be divided into four categories on the basis of whether people can be excluded from consuming them and whether they are rival in consumption. A good or service is rival in consumption if it can be consumed by only one person at the same time.

others from consuming the good, whether they have paid for it or not. Figure 8 shows four possible categories into which goods can fall.

We next consider each of the four categories:

1. *Private goods.* A good that is both rival and excludable is a **private good**. Food, clothing, haircuts, and many other goods and services fall into this category. One person's consuming a unit of these goods precludes other people from consuming that unit, and anyone who does not buy these goods can't consume them. Although we didn't state it explicitly, when we analyzed the demand and supply for goods and services, we assumed that the goods and services were all private goods.

   Private good A good that is both rival and excludable.

2. *Public goods.* A **public good** is both nonrivalrous and nonexcludable. Public goods are often, although not always, supplied by a government rather than by private firms. The classic example of a public good is national defense. Your consuming national defense does not interfere with your neighbor's consuming it, so consumption is nonrivalrous. You also cannot be excluded from consuming it, whether you pay for it or not. No private firm would be willing to supply national defense because everyone can consume national defense without paying for it. The behavior of consumers in this situation is referred to as *free riding*. **Free riding** involves individuals benefiting from a good—in this case, the provision of national defense—without paying for it.

   Public good A good that is both nonrivalrous and nonexcludable.

   Free riding Benefiting from a good without paying for it.

3. *Quasi-public goods.* Some goods are excludable but not rival. An example is cable television. People who do not pay for cable television do not receive it, but one person's watching it doesn't affect other people's watching it. The same is true of a toll road. Anyone who doesn't pay the toll doesn't get on the road, but one person using the road doesn't interfere with someone else using the road (unless so many people are using the road that it becomes congested). Goods that fall into this category are called *quasi-public goods.*

4. *Common resources.* If a good is rival but not excludable, it is a **common resource**. Forest land in many poor countries is a common resource. If one person cuts down a tree, no one else can use the tree. But if no one has a property right to the forest, no one can be excluded from using it. As we will discuss in more detail later, people often overuse common resources.

   Common resource A good that is rival but not excludable.

Making the Connection | Should the Government Run the Health Care System?

In many countries, such as Canada, Japan, the United Kingdom, and France, the government either supplies health care directly by operating hospitals and employing doctors and nurses, or pays for most health care expenses even if hospitals are not government owned and doctors are not government employees. In the United States, the federal government supplies health care to veterans of the armed forces through the Veterans Administration (VA) system and pays for the health care of people over age 65 under the Medicare program. The federal government also contributes to the Medicaid program under which state governments pay for health care for some poor people. Most medium and large-size firms provide health insurance as a fringe benefit to their employees. About 88 percent of individuals who have private health insurance receive it as part of a benefits package from their employers. Those individuals not covered by health insurance plans and not eligible for government aid must pay for their own health care bills out of pocket, just as they pay their other bills, or receive charity care. The chart shows that in 2006, government spending on Medicare, Medicaid, and other government health care programs was about 47 percent of total health care spending.

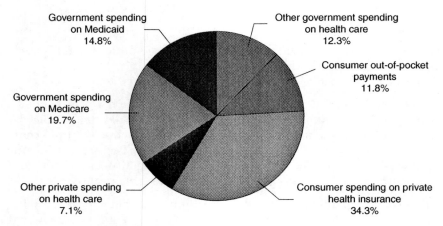

Source: John A. Poisal, et al., *Health Spending Projections through 2016*, Washington, DC: National Health Statistics Group, Centers for Medicare & Medicaid Services, U.S. Department of Health and Human Services.

What should be the government's role in health care? Is health care a public good that government should supply—or, at least, pay for? Is it a private good, like food, clothing, or television sets, that private firms should supply and consumers should pay for without government aid? Should private firms supply most health care, subject to some government regulation? Economists differ in their answers to these questions because the delivery of health care involves a number of complex issues. But we can consider briefly some of the most important points. We have seen that a public good is both nonrivalrous and nonexcludable. In this sense, health care does not qualify as a public good. More than one person cannot simultaneously consume the same surgical operation, for example. And someone who will not pay for an operation can be excluded from consuming it. (Most states require hospitals to treat patients who are too poor to pay for treatment, and many doctors will treat poor people at a reduced price. But because there is nothing in the nature of health care that keeps people who do not pay for it from being excluded from consuming it, health care does not fit the definition of a public good.)

There are aspects of the delivery of health care that have convinced some economists that government intervention is justified, however. For example, consuming certain types of health care generates positive externalities. In particular, being vaccinated against a communicable disease, such as influenza or chicken pox, not only reduces the chance that the person vaccinated will catch the disease but also reduces the probability that an epidemic of the disease will occur. Therefore, the market may supply an inefficiently small quantity of vaccinations unless vaccinations receive a government subsidy. Information problems can also be important in the market for private health insurance. Consumers as buyers of health insurance often know much more about the state of their health than do the companies selling health insurance. This information problem may raise costs to insurance companies when the pool of people being insured is small, making insurance companies less willing to offer health insurance to consumers the companies suspect may file too many claims. Economists debate how important information problems are in health care markets and whether government intervention is required to reduce them.

94

Many economists believe that market-based solutions are the best approach to improving the health care system. Currently, the U.S. health care system is a world leader in innovation in medical technology and prescription drugs. The market-oriented approach to reforming health care starts with the goal of preserving incentives for U.S. firms to continue with innovations in medical screening equipment, surgical procedures, and prescription drugs. Presently, markets are delivering inaccurate signals to consumers because when buying health care, unlike when buying most other goods and services, consumers pay a price well *below* the true cost of providing the service. Consumers usually pay less than the true cost of medical treatment because a third party—typically, an insurance company—often pays most of the bill. For example, consumers who have health insurance provided by their employers usually pay only a small amount—perhaps $20—for a visit to a doctor's office, when the true cost of the visit might be $80 or $90. The result is that consumers demand a larger quantity of health care services than they would if they paid a price that better represented the cost of providing the services. Doctors and other health care providers also have a reduced incentive to control costs because they know that an insurance company will pick up most of the bill.

Under current tax laws, individuals do not pay taxes on health insurance benefits they receive from their employers, and this encourages them to want very generous coverage that reduces incentives to control costs. But individuals get no tax break for buying insurance on their own or for out-of-pocket medical spending. Some economists have proposed making the tax treatment of health insurance and health spending more uniform, a change that could, potentially, significantly reduce spending on health care without reducing the effectiveness of the health care received. Such tax law changes would make it more likely that company-provided health insurance would focus on large medical bills—such as those resulting from hospitalizations—while consumers would pay prices closer to the costs of providing routine medical care.

Because health care is so important to consumers and because health care spending looms so large in the U.S. economy, the role of the government in the health care system is likely to be the subject of intense debate for some time to come.

Source: To read more on the role of the government in the market for health care, see Sherman Folland, Allen C. Goodman, and Miron Stano, *The Economics of Health and Health Care*, 5th ed., Upper Saddle River, NJ: Prentice Hall, 2007, Chapter 19; and John F. Coogan, R. Glenn Hubbard, and Daniel P. Kessler, *Healthy, Wealthy, and Wise: Five Steps to a Better Health Care System*, Washington, DC: The AEI Press, 2005.

YOUR TURN: Test your understanding by doing related problem 4.9 at the end of this chapter.

For the remainder of this chapter, we focus on the categories of public goods and common resources. To determine the optimal quantity of a public good, we have to modify demand and supply analysis to take into account that a public good is both nonrivalrous and nonexcludable.

The Demand for a Public Good

We can determine the market demand curve for a good or service by adding up the quantity of the good demanded by each consumer at each price. To keep things simple, let's take the case of a market with only two consumers. Figure 9 shows that the market demand curve for hamburgers depends on the individual demand curves of Jill and Joe.

At a price of $4.00, Jill demands 2 hamburgers per week and Joe demands 4. Adding horizontally, the combination of a price of $4.00 per hamburger and a quantity demanded of 6 hamburgers will be a point on the market demand curve for hamburgers. Similarly, adding horizontally at a price of $1.50, we have a price of $1.50 and a quantity demanded of 11 as another point on the market demand curve. A consumer's demand curve for a good represents the marginal benefit the consumer receives from the good, so when we add together the consumers' demand curves, we not only have the

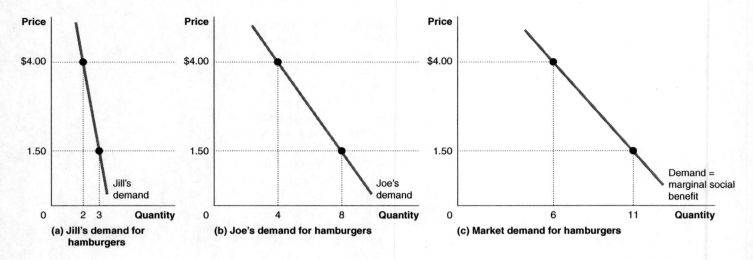

Figure 9 | Constructing the Market Demand Curve for a Private Good

The market demand curve for private goods is determined by adding horizontally the quantity of the good demanded at each price by each consumer. For instance, in panel (a), Jill demands 2 hamburgers when the price is $4.00, and in panel (b), Joe demands 4 hamburgers when the price is $4.00. So, a quantity of 6 hamburgers and a price of $4.00 is a point on the market demand curve in panel (c).

market demand curve but also the marginal social benefit curve for this good, assuming that there is no externality in consumption.

How can we find the demand curve or marginal social benefit curve for a public good? Once again, for simplicity, assume that Jill and Joe are the only consumers. Unlike with a private good, where Jill and Joe can end up consuming different quantities, with a public good, they will consume *the same quantity*. Suppose that Jill owns a service station on an isolated rural road, and Joe owns a car dealership next door. These are the only two businesses around for miles. Both Jill and Joe are afraid that unless they hire a security guard at night, their businesses may be burgled. Like national defense, the services of a security guard are in this case a public good: Once hired, the guard will be able to protect both businesses, so the good is nonrival. It also will not be possible to exclude either business from being protected, so the good is nonexcludable.

To arrive at a demand curve for a public good, we don't add quantities at each price, as with a private good. Instead, we add the price each consumer is willing to pay for each quantity of the public good. This value represents the total dollar amount consumers as a group would be willing to pay for that quantity of the public good. Put another way, to find the demand curve, or marginal social benefit curve, for a private good, we add the demand curves of individual consumers horizontally, while for public goods, we add individual demand curves vertically. Figure 10 shows how the marginal social benefit curve for security guard services depends on the individual demand curves of Jill and Joe.

The figure shows that Jill is willing to pay $8 per hour for the guard to provide 10 hours of protection per night. Joe would suffer a greater loss from a burglary, so he is willing to pay $10 per hour for the same amount of protection. Adding the dollar amount that each is willing to pay gives us a price of $18 per hour and a quantity of 10 hours as a point on the marginal social benefit curve for security guard services. Because Jill is willing to spend $4 per hour for 15 hours of guard services and Joe is willing to pay $5, a price of $9 per hour and a quantity of 15 hours is also a point on the marginal social benefit curve for security guard services.

The Optimal Quantity of a Public Good

We know that to achieve economic efficiency, a good or service should be produced up to the point where the sum of consumer surplus and producer surplus is maximized, or, alternatively, where the marginal social cost equals the marginal social benefit. Therefore,

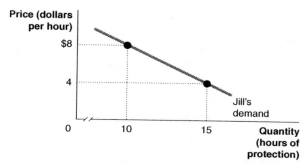

(a) Jill's demand for security guard services

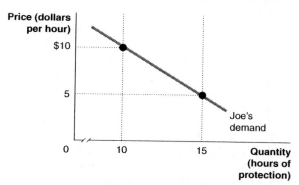

(b) Joe's demand for security guard services

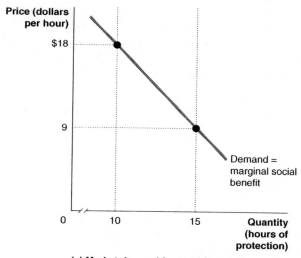

(c) Market demand for security guard services

Figure 10

To find the demand curve for a public good, we add up the price at which each consumer is willing to purchase each quantity of the good. In panel (a), Jill is willing to pay $8 per hour for a security guard to provide 10 hours of protection. In panel (b), Joe is willing to pay $10 for that level of protection. Therefore, in panel (c), the price of $18 per hour and the quantity of 10 hours will be a point on the market demand curve for security guard services.

the optimal quantity of security guard services—or any other public good—will occur where the marginal social benefit curve intersects the supply curve. As with private goods, in the absence of an externality in production, the supply curve represents the marginal social cost of supplying the good. Figure 11 shows that the optimal quantity of security guard services supplied is 15 hours, at a price of $9 per hour.

Will the market provide the economically efficient quantity of security guard services? One difficulty is that the individual preferences of consumers, as shown by their demand curves, are not revealed in this market. This difficulty does not arise with private goods because consumers must reveal their preferences in order to purchase private goods. If the market price of Big Macs is $4.00, Joe either reveals he is willing to pay that much by buying it, or he does without it. In our example, neither Jill nor Joe can be excluded from consuming the services provided by a security guard once either hires one, and, therefore, neither has an incentive to reveal her or his preferences. In this case, though, with only two consumers, it is likely that private

Figure 11

The Optimal Quantity of a Public Good

The optimal quantity of a public good is produced where the sum of consumer surplus and producer surplus is maximized, which occurs where the demand curve intersects the supply curve. In this case, the optimal quantity of security guard services is 15 hours at a price of $9 per hour.

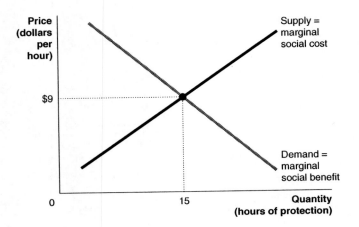

bargaining will result in an efficient quantity of the public good. This outcome is not likely for a public good—such as national defense—that is supplied by the government to millions of consumers.

Governments sometimes use *cost–benefit analysis* to determine what quantity of a public good should be supplied. For example, before building a dam on a river, the federal government will attempt to weigh the costs against the benefits. The costs include the opportunity cost of other projects the government cannot carry out if it builds the dam. The benefits include improved flood control or new recreational opportunities on the lake formed by the dam. However, for many public goods, including national defense, the government does not use a formal cost–benefit analysis. Instead, the quantity of national defense supplied is determined by a political process involving Congress and the president. Even here, of course, Congress and the president realize that trade-offs are involved: The more resources used for national defense, the fewer resources available for other public goods or for private goods.

Solved Problem | **5**

Determining the Optimal Level of Public Goods

Suppose, once again, that Jill and Joe run isolated businesses that are next door to each other and in need of the services of a security guard. Their demand schedules for security guard services are as follows:

JOE	
PRICE (DOLLARS PER HOUR)	QUANTITY (HOURS OF PROTECTION)
$20	0
18	1
16	2
14	3
12	4
10	5
8	6
6	7
4	8
2	9

JILL	
PRICE (DOLLARS PER HOUR)	QUANTITY (HOURS OF PROTECTION)
$20	1
18	2
16	3
14	4
12	5
10	6
8	7
6	8
4	9
2	10

The supply schedule for security guard services is as follows:

PRICE (DOLLARS PER HOUR)	QUANTITY (HOURS OF PROTECTION)
$8	1
10	2
12	3
14	4
16	5
18	6
20	7
22	8
24	9

a. Draw a graph that shows the optimal level of security guard services. Be sure to label the curves on the graph.

b. Briefly explain why 8 hours of security guard protection is not an optimal quantity.

SOLVING THE PROBLEM:

Step 1: **Review the chapter material.** This problem is about the determination of the optimal level of public goods, so you may want to review the section "The Optimal Quantity of a Public Good."

Step 2: **Begin by deriving the demand curve or marginal social benefit curve for security guard services.** To calculate the marginal social benefit of guard services, we need to add the prices that Jill and Joe are willing to pay at each quantity:

DEMAND OR MARGINAL SOCIAL BENEFIT	
PRICE (DOLLARS PER HOUR)	QUANTITY (HOURS OF PROTECTION)
$38	1
34	2
30	3
26	4
22	5
18	6
14	7
10	8
6	9

Step 3: **Answer question (a) by plotting the demand (marginal social benefit) and supply (marginal social cost) curves.** The graph shows that the optimal level of security guard services is 6 hours.

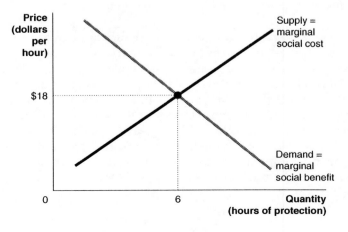

99

Step 4: **Answer question (b) by explaining why 8 hours of security guard protection is not an optimal quantity.** For each hour beyond 6, the supply curve is above the demand curve. Therefore, the marginal social benefit received will be less than the marginal social cost of supplying these hours. This results in a deadweight loss and a reduction in economic surplus.

YOUR TURN: For more practice, do related problem 4.4 at the end of this chapter.

>> End Solved Problem 5

Common Resources

In England during the Middle Ages, each village had an area of pasture, known as a *commons*, on which any family in the village was allowed to graze its cows or sheep without charge. Of course, the grass one family's cow ate was not available for another family's cow, so consumption was rival. But every family in the village had the right to use the commons, so it was nonexcludable. Without some type of restraint on usage, the commons would end up overgrazed. To see why, consider the economic incentives facing a family that was thinking of buying another cow and grazing it on the commons. The family would gain the benefits from increased milk production, but adding another cow to the commons would create a negative externality by reducing the amount of grass available for the cows of other families. Because this family—and the other families in the village—did not take this negative externality into account when deciding whether to add another cow to the commons, too many cows would be added. The grass on the commons would eventually be depleted, and no family's cow would get enough to eat.

Tragedy of the commons The tendency for a common resource to be overused.

The Tragedy of the Commons The tendency for a common resource to be overused is called the **tragedy of the commons**. A modern example is the forests in many poor countries. When a family chops down a tree in a public forest, it takes into account the benefits of gaining firewood or wood for building, but it does not take into account the costs of deforestation. Haiti, for example, was once heavily forested. Today, 80 percent of the country's forests have been cut down, primarily to be burned to create charcoal, which is used for heating and cooking. Because the mountains no longer have tree roots to hold the soil, heavy rains lead to devastating floods. The following is from a newspaper account of tree cutting in Haiti:

> "No Tree Cutting" signs hang over the park entrance, but without money and manpower, there is no way to enforce that. Loggers make nightly journeys, hacking away at trees until they fall. The next day, they're on a truck out. Days later, they've been chopped up, burned and packaged in white bags offered for sale by soot-covered women. "This is the only way I can feed my four kids," said Vena Verone, one of the vendors. "I've heard about the floods and deforestation that caused them, but there's nothing I can do about that."

Figure 12 shows that with a common resource such as wood from a forest, the efficient level of use, Q_2, is determined by the intersection of the demand curve—which represents the marginal social benefit received by consumers—and S_2, which represents the marginal social cost of cutting the wood. As in our discussion of negative externalities, the social cost is equal to the private cost of cutting the wood plus the external cost. In this case, the external cost represents the fact that the more wood each person cuts, the less wood there is available for others, and the greater the deforestation, which increases the chances of floods. Because each individual tree cutter ignores the external cost, the equilibrium quantity of wood cut is Q_1, which is greater than the efficient quantity. At the equilibrium level of output, there is a deadweight loss, as shown in Figure 12 by the yellow triangle.

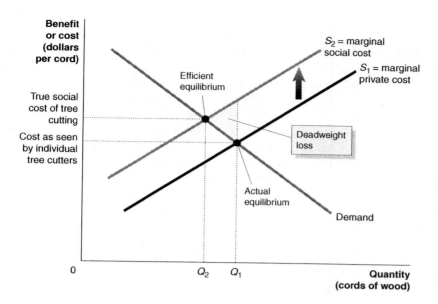

Figure 12

Overuse of a Common Resource

For a common resource such as wood from a forest, the efficient level of use, Q_2, is determined by the intersection of the demand curve—which represents the marginal benefit received by consumers—and S_2, which represents the marginal social cost of cutting the wood. Because each individual tree cutter ignores the external cost, the equilibrium quantity of wood cut is Q_1, which is greater than the efficient quantity. At the equilibrium level of output, there is a deadweight loss, as shown by the yellow triangle.

Is There a Way Out of the Tragedy of the Commons? Notice that our discussion of the tragedy of the commons is very similar to our earlier discussion of negative externalities. The source of the tragedy of the commons is the same as the source of negative externalities: lack of clearly defined and enforced property rights. For instance, suppose that instead of being held as a collective resource, a piece of pastureland is owned by one person. That person will take into account the effect of adding another cow on the food available to cows already using the pasture. As a result, the optimal number of cows will be placed on the pasture. Over the years, most of the commons lands in England were converted to private property. Most of the forest land in Haiti and other developing countries is actually the property of the government. The failure of the government to protect the forests against trespassers or convert them to private property is the key to their overuse.

Should these fishermen have unlimited access to the ocean?

Paul A. Souders, Corbis/Bettmann

In some situations, though, enforcing property rights is not feasible. An example is the oceans. Because no country owns the oceans beyond its own coastal waters, the fish and other resources of the ocean will remain a common resource. In situations in which enforcing property rights is not feasible, two types of solutions to the tragedy of the commons are possible. If the geographic area involved is limited and the number of people involved is small, access to the commons can be restricted through community norms and laws. If the geographic area or the number of people involved is large, legal restrictions on access to the commons are required. As an example of the first type of solution, the tragedy of the commons was avoided in the Middle Ages by traditional limits on the number of animals each family was allowed to put on the common pasture. Although these traditions were not formal laws, they were usually enforced adequately by social pressure.

With the second type of solution, the government imposes restrictions on access to the common resources. These restrictions can take several different forms, of which taxes, quotas, and tradable permits are the most common. By setting a tax equal to the external cost, governments can ensure that the efficient quantity of a resource is used. Quotas, or legal limits, on the quantity of the resource that can be taken during a given time period have been used in the United States to limit access to pools of oil when the pool is beneath property owned by many different persons. The governments of Canada, New Zealand, and Iceland have used a system of tradable permits to restrict access to ocean fisheries. Under this system, a total allowable catch (TAC) limits the number of fish that fishermen can catch during a season. The fishmen are then assigned permits called Individual Transferable Quotas (ITQs) that are equal to the total allowable catch. This system operates like the tradable emissions allowances described earlier in this chapter. The fishermen are free to use the ITQs or to sell them, which ensures that the fishermen with the lowest costs use the ITQs. The use of ITQs has sometimes proven controversial, which has limited their use in managing fisheries along the coastal United States. Critics argue that allowing trading of ITQs can result in their concentration in the hands of a relatively few large commercial fishing firms. Such a concentration may, though, be economically efficient if these firms have lower costs than smaller, family-based firms.

Economics in YOUR Life!

At the beginning of the chapter, we asked you to think about what the "best" level of carbon emissions is. Conceptually, this is a straightforward question to answer: The correct level of carbon emissions is the level for which the marginal benefit of reducing carbon emissions exactly equals the marginal cost of reducing carbon emissions. In practice, however, this is a very difficult question to answer. Scientists disagree about how much carbon emissions are contributing to the damage from climate change. In addition, the cost of reducing carbon emissions depends on the method of reduction used. As a result, neither the marginal cost curve nor the marginal benefit curve for reducing carbon emissions is known with certainty. This uncertainty makes it difficult for policymakers to determine the correct level of carbon emissions and is the source of much of the current debate. In any case, economists agree that the total cost of *completely* eliminating carbon emissions are much greater than the total benefits.

Conclusion

Government intervention in the economy can reduce economic efficiency. In this chapter, however, we have seen that the government has an indispensable role to play in the economy when the absence of well-defined and enforceable property rights keeps the market from operating efficiently. Because no one has a property right for clean air, in the absence of government intervention, firms will produce too great a quantity of products that generate air pollution. We have also seen that public goods are nonrivalrous and nonexcludable and are, therefore, often supplied directly by the government.

Read *An Inside Look at Policy*, which begins on the following page, to learn about problems with carbon trading.

FINANCIAL TIMES, FEBRUARY 7, 2007

Next Carbon Trading Phase Promises to Clean Up Anomalies

When the European Union launched its scheme to trade carbon emission rights to combat climate change, it probably did not envisage that it might eventually provide an incentive to pollute.

But that is exactly what has happened. Just over two years into a scheme that was launched in 2005 as the first of its kind in the world, the price for a permit to emit one tonne of carbon dioxide has plummeted to a record low of just €1.50 ($1.94) a tonne—a fraction of the peak €30 level hit last April.

Chris Rogers, utility analyst at JPMorgan, says that at current prices it is far cheaper for utilities to burn coal—and buy the emissions permits that allow them to pollute—than it is for them to buy cleaner fuels such as natural gas. He estimates that a utility can buy coal that is €10 per megawatt hour cheaper than gas. "There is no economic incentive for users to import less coal than they did last year," he says.

But the scheme was set up to encourage utilities and large industrial consumers of energy to switch from heavy polluting energies such as coal to cleaner fuels such as gas.

Companies were given a set level of permits. If they wanted or needed to pollute more, they had to buy more on the market. If a company was cleaner than envisaged, it could sell excess permits. However, too many emission permits were issued and the low prices have defeated the scheme's original purpose. As a result, coal imports into Europe have been rising, with the UK last year importing record volumes of coal. . . .

The incentive to pollute in the EU, however, changes next year [in 2008] when phase two of the emissions trading scheme starts. In the second phase, the EU will issue fewer permits. Phase one permits cannot be carried over to phase two. As a result, carbon prices for phase two are a lot higher. The December 2008 carbon price is €15 a tonne.

Traders still fear there could be downward pressure on 2008 carbon prices as the second phase allows permits earned from clean energy projects in the developing world—officially called certified emission reductions—to be exchanged for the EU permits.

Louis Redshaw, head of environmental markets at Barclays Capital, said there would be a limit to the amount of CERs that can be converted into EU permits, which varies between each EU member. Mr Redshaw said that by 2009 there would be more carbon schemes, including schemes in Japan and Canada, where CERs could be exchanged. "When we start getting into 2009, 2010, the EU scheme will not be the only one around and therefore CERs will go to the market that offers the best price. So we may not see so many come into the EU," he said. He said the diminishing potential dilution effect of CERs was reflected in the pricing of phase two, where prices for 2009 trade at a premium to 2008.

The December 2009 carbon price is quoted at €15.50, 2010 at €16.00, 2011 at €16.50 and 2012 at €17.

There is a premium for prices for 2011 and onwards because of the inclusion of the aviation sector in four years' time. In spite of the performance of EU emissions prices in phase one, investors and analysts are confident there will be a phase three of the scheme.

"Neither the Kyoto agenda nor the EU scheme will disappear at the end of 2012 . . . enough people are now involved that there is sure to be a further market of some kind," said Paul Newman, managing director of Icap Energy. "In any case, discontinuing the market in five years' time would be like turning off the ventilator just as the patient is starting to get better."

Source: Kevin Morrison, "Next Carbon Trading Phase Promises to Clean Up Anomalies," *Financial Times*, Feb. 7, 2007, p. 38. Reprinted by permission.

Mariusz Szachowski, Shutterstock

Key Points in the Article

Carbon trading is a relatively straightforward idea. The government determines how much carbon dioxide utilities and firms can emit and issues a corresponding quantity of permits. The government then forces firms to pay for the right to emit carbon dioxide, which gives firms an incentive to reduce carbon emissions. European governments hoped that carbon trading would lead firms to switch from energy sources with high carbon content, like coal, to energy sources with low carbon content, like natural gas. Some practical problems with setting up a carbon trading scheme have resulted in the system not working the way European governments had expected.

Analyzing the News

ⓐ The goal of the carbon trading program was to raise the price of energy sources such as coal that emit more carbon dioxide than energy sources such as natural gas. If the price of coal goes up and the prices of permits to emit carbon dioxide are high, then utilities and firms will switch from coal to natural gas. As a result, carbon dioxide emissions will decline. Unfortunately, the European Union issued so many carbon permits that it was cheaper for firms to buy permits and continue to burn coal than to switch to natural gas.

ⓑ The European Union issued the carbon permits in phases. The problems with the program all deal with the first-phase carbon permits. To rectify the problems, the European Union has issued fewer carbon permits for phase two of the program. This reduction in the supply of permits has caused the price to rise from €1.50 a ton for phase one permits to €15 a ton for phase two permits. Figure 1 shows that this is exactly what economic theory predicts. The reduction in the number of permits available causes the supply curve to shift to the left. At the old price of €1.50, there would be a shortage equal to $(Q_1 - Q_2)$, which leads firms to bid up the price of carbon emission permits. The higher price provides an economic incentive for utilities and other firms to reduce the amount of carbon dioxide they emit.

ⓒ The carbon trading program in Europe does not cover all industries. Airlines were initially exempted from having to purchase permits, but that is going to change in 2011. As a result, the current price of carbon permits for the years 2011 and 2012 is higher than the permits for 2008. Figure 2 shows that this is exactly what an economist would expect. As more firms compete for the fixed supply of carbon permits, the price of those carbon permits rises. To avoid paying for the higher-priced permits, some utilities and firms will reduce the amount of carbon dioxide they emit.

Thinking Critically About Policy

1. The article points out some of the difficulties with carbon trading programs. Due to these difficulties, the initial phase of the carbon trading program in Europe did not provide a strong incentive to switch from coal to natural gas. As a result, it is likely that firms used too much coal. Would a carbon tax result in similar difficulties?

2. The government raises no revenue from tradable permits, because it gives the permits to firms at no charge. Because tradable permits raise no government revenue—which might be used to reduce other taxes that result in deadweight losses—some economists and policymakers favor carbon taxes over carbon trading. What is an alternative means of allocating the initial carbon permits that would raise revenue for the government?

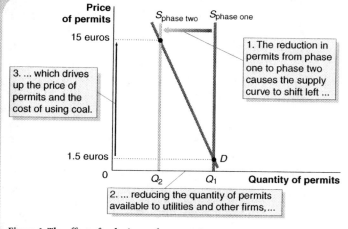

Figure 1. The effect of reducing carbon permits.

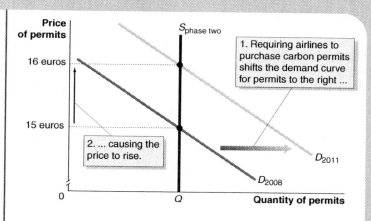

Figure 2. The effect of requiring more firms to purchase permits.

Key Terms

Coase theorem

Command and control approach

Common resource

Excludability

Externality

Free riding

Market failure

Pigovian taxes and subsidies

Private benefit

Private cost

Private good

Property rights

Public good

Rivalry

Social benefit

Social cost

Tragedy of the commons

Transactions costs

1 LEARNING OBJECTIVE 1 | Identify examples of positive and negative externalities and use graphs to show how externalities affect economic efficiency

Externalities and Economic Efficiency

Summary

An **externality** is a benefit or cost to parties who are not involved in a transaction. Pollution and other externalities in production cause a difference between the **private cost** borne by the producer of a good or services and the **social cost**, which includes any external cost, such as the cost of pollution. An externality in consumption causes a difference between the **private benefit** received by the consumer and the **social benefit**, which includes any external benefit. If externalities exist in production or consumption, the market will not produce the optimal level of a good or service. This outcome is referred to as **market failure**. Externalities arise when property rights do not exist or cannot be legally enforced. **Property rights** are the rights individuals or businesses have to the exclusive use of their property, including the right to buy or sell it.

myeconlab Visit www.myeconlab.com to complete these exercises *Get Ahead of the Curve* online and get instant feedback.

Review Questions

1.1 What is an externality? Give an example of a positive externality and give an example of a negative externality.

1.2 When will the private cost of producing a good differ from the social cost? Give an example. When will the private benefit from consuming a good differ from the social benefit? Give an example.

1.3 What is economic efficiency? How do externalities affect the economic efficiency of a market equilibrium?

1.4 What is market failure? When is market failure likely to arise?

1.5 Briefly discuss the relationship between property rights and the existence of externalities.

Problems and Applications

1.6 The chapter states that your consuming a Big Mac does not create an externality. But suppose you arrive at your favorite McDonald's at lunchtime and get in a long line to be served. By the time you reach the counter, there are 10 people in line behind you. Because you decided to have a Big Mac for lunch—instead of, say, a pizza—each of those 10 people must wait in line an additional 2 minutes. Or suppose that after a lifetime of consuming Big Macs, you develop heart disease. Because you are now over age 65, the government must pay most of your medical bills through the Medicare system. Is it still correct to say that your consuming a Big Mac created no externalities? Might there be a justification here for the government to intervene in the market for Big Macs? Explain.

1.7 The chapter discusses the cases of consumption generating a positive externality and production generating a negative externality. Is it possible for consumption to generate a negative externality? If so, give an example. Is it possible for production to generate a positive externality? If so, give an example.

1.8 In a recent study at a large state university, students were randomly assigned roommates. Researchers found that, on average, males assigned to roommates who reported drinking alcohol in the year before entering college had GPAs one-quarter point lower than those assigned to non-drinking roommates. For males who drank frequently before college, being assigned to a roommate who also drank frequently before college reduced their GPAs by two-thirds of a point. Draw a graph showing the price of alcohol and the quantity of alcohol consumption on college campuses. Include in the graph the private and social cost of drinking. Label any deadweight loss that arises in this market.

Source: Michael Kremer and Dan M. Levy, "Peer Effects and Alcohol Use Among College Students," National Bureau of Economic Research working paper 9876, July 2003.

1.9 Tom and Jacob are college students. Each of them will probably get married later and have two or three children. Each knows that if he studies more in college, he'll get a better job and earn more than if he doesn't study. Earning more means the ability to spend more on their future families—things like orthodontia, nice clothes, admission to an expensive college, and travel. Tom thinks about the potential benefits to his potential children when he decides how much studying to do. Jacob doesn't.

    a. What type of externality arises from studying?

    b. Draw a graph showing this externality, contrasting the responses of Tom and Jacob. Who studies more? Who acts more efficiently? Why?

1.10 For several years, *The Sopranos* television series was available only on the HBO cable network. The series was a hit and attracted more viewers than many programs available on the broadcast networks NBC, CBS, ABC, and Fox. But Chris Albrecht, the chair of HBO, found that he was unable to use the popularity of *The Sopranos* to increase the number of subscribers to HBO. To receive HBO, cable viewers usually had to pay for a "premium package" that included not just HBO but other services, like Showtime, that were owned by other companies. As Albrecht put it, "That means we're just part of everything else. First the consumer is asked to pay $60 for the basic cable service and then it's another $40 for the platinum package, and they're selling Showtime and Starz in with us." Is there an externality involved here? If so, is it an externality in production or consumption, and is it positive or negative? If there is an externality, discuss possible solutions.

Source: Excerpt from Bill Carter, "Cable Conquered, What's Next for 'The Sopranos'?" *New York Times*, October 7, 2002. Copyright © 2002 by The New York Times Co. Reprinted with permission.

1.11 A columnist for the *Wall Street Journal* observes: "No one collects money from those who benefit from the flood control a wetland provides, or the nutrient recycling a forest does. . . . In a nutshell, market failures help drive habitat loss." What does the columnist mean by *market failures*? What does she mean by *habitat loss*? Explain why she believes one is causing the other. Illustrate your argument with a graph showing the market for land to be used for development.

Source: Sharon Begley, "Furry Math? Market Has Failed to Capture True Value of Nature," *Wall Street Journal*, August 9, 2002, p. B1.

>> **End Learning Objective 1**

2 LEARNING OBJECTIVE   2 | Discuss the Coase theorem and explain how private bargaining can lead to economic efficiency in a market with an externality

Private Solutions to Externalities: The Coase Theorem

Summary

Externalities and market failures result from incomplete property rights or from the difficulty of enforcing property rights in certain situations. When an externality exists, and the efficient quantity of a good is not being produced, the total cost of reducing the externality is usually less than the total benefit. According to the **Coase theorem**, if **transactions costs** are low, private bargaining will result in an efficient solution to the problem of externalities.

X myeconlab   Visit www.myeconlab.com to complete these exercises
Get Ahead of the Curve online and get instant feedback.

Review Questions

2.1 What do economists mean by "an economically efficient level of pollution"?

2.2 What is the Coase theorem? What are transactions costs? When are we likely to see private solutions to the problem of externalities?

Problems and Applications

2.3 Is it ever possible for an *increase* in pollution to make society better off? Briefly explain using a graph like Figure 3.

2.4 If the marginal cost of reducing a certain type of pollution is zero, should all of that pollution be eliminated? Briefly explain.

2.5 Discuss the factors that determine the marginal cost of reducing crime. Discuss the factors that determine the marginal benefit of reducing crime. Would it be economically efficient to reduce the amount of crime to zero? Briefly explain.

2.6 **(Related to the** *Don't Let This Happen to You!***)** Briefly explain whether you agree or disagree with the following statement: "Sulfur dioxide emissions cause acid rain and breathing difficulties for people with respiratory problems. The total benefit to society is greatest if we completely eliminate sulfur dioxide emissions. Therefore, the economically efficient level of emissions is zero."

2.7 In discussing cleaning up oil spills, Gary Shigenka of the National Oceanographic and Atmospheric Agency observed, "The first 90% of any cleanup comes easy. But the tradeoffs for the remaining bits are brutal." He estimates that the last 1 percent of oil removed can cost seven times as much as the first 99 percent. Why should it be any more costly to clean up the last 1 percent of an oil spill than to clean up the first 1 percent? What trade-offs do you think Shigenka was referring to?

Source: Keith Johnson and Gautam Naik, "For Spain, Exxon Valdez Offers Some Surprising Lessons," *Wall Street Journal*, November 22, 2002.

2.8 **(Related to the *Making the Connection*)** In the first years following the passage of the Clean Air Act in 1970, air pollution declined sharply and there were important health benefits, including a decline in infant mortality. Should the government take action to reduce air pollution further? How should government go about deciding this question?

2.9 **(Related to the *Making the Connection*)** We know that owners of apple orchards and owners of beehives are able to negotiate private agreements. Is it likely that as a result of these private agreements the market supplies the efficient quantities of apple trees and beehives? Are there any real-world difficulties that might stand in the way of achieving this efficient outcome?

>> **End Learning Objective 2**

---

3 LEARNING OBJECTIVE 3 | Analyze government policies to achieve economic efficiency in a market with an externality

Government Policies to Deal with Externalities

Summary

When private solutions to externalities are unworkable, the government sometimes intervenes. One way to deal with a negative externality in production is to impose a tax equal to the cost of the externality. The tax causes the producer of the good to internalize the externality. The government can deal with a positive externality in consumption by giving consumers a subsidy, or payment, equal to the value of the externality. Government taxes and subsidies intended to bring about an efficient level of output in the presence of externalities are called **Pigovian taxes and subsidies**. Although the federal government has sometimes used subsidies and taxes to deal with externalities, in dealing with pollution, it has more often used a command and control approach. A **command and control approach** involves the government imposing quantitative limits on the amount of pollution allowed or requiring firms to install specific pollution control devices. Direct pollution controls of this type are not economically efficient, however. As a result, Congress decided to use a system of tradable emissions allowances to reduce sulfur dioxide emissions.

myeconlab Visit www.myeconlab.com to complete these exercises online and get instant feedback.

Review Questions

3.1 What is a Pigovian tax? At what level must a Pigovian tax be set to achieve efficiency?

3.2 Why do most economists prefer tradable emissions allowances rather than the command and control approach to pollution?

Problems and Applications

3.3 Why does the government subsidize the purchase of college educations but not the purchase of hamburgers?

3.4 Writing in the *New York Times*, Michael Lewis argues: "Good new technologies are a bit like good new roads: Their social benefits far exceed what any one person or company can get paid for creating them." Does this observation justify the government subsidizing the production of new technologies? If so, how might the government do this?

Source: Michael Lewis, "In Defense of the Boom," *New York Times*, October 27, 2002.

3.5 In 2007, Governor Deval Patrick of Massachusetts proposed that criminals would have to pay a "safety fee" to the government. The size of the fee would be based on the seriousness of the crime (that is, the fee would be larger for more serious crimes).
  a. Is there an economically efficient amount of crime? Briefly explain.
  b. Briefly explain whether the "safety fee" is a Pigovian tax of the type discussed in this chapter.

Source: Michael Levenson, "Patrick Proposes New Fee on Criminals," *Boston Globe*, January 14, 2007.

3.6 We saw in this chapter that market failure occurs when firms ignore the costs generated by pollution in deciding how much to produce. Government intervention is usually necessary to bring about a more efficient level of production. Before 1989, the Communist governments of Eastern Europe directly controlled the production of most goods and were free to choose how much of each good would be produced and what production process would be used. When these Communist governments collapsed, it was revealed that the countries of Eastern Europe suffered from very high levels of pollution, much higher than had existed in the United States and other high-income countries even before there was government anti-pollution legislation. Discuss reasons why the nonmarket Communist system generated more pollution than market economies.

3.7 Bjorn Lomborg, director of the Environmental Assessment Institute in Denmark, argued in a column in the *New York Times*: "Traditionally, the developed nations of the West have shown a greater concern for environmental sustainability, while the third world countries have a stronger desire for economic development." Is environmental protection a normal good? If so, is there any connection between this fact and Lomborg's observation? Briefly explain. How do the marginal cost and marginal benefit of environmental protection change with economic development?

Source: Bjorn Lomborg, "The Environmentalists Are Wrong," *New York Times*, August 26, 2002.

3.8 **(Related to *Solved Problem 3*)** The fumes from dry cleaners can contribute to air pollution. Suppose the following graph illustrates the situation in the dry cleaning market.

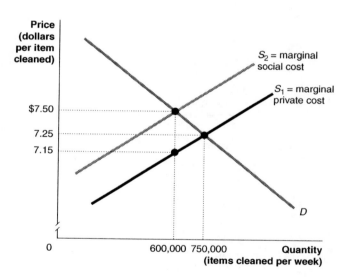

a. Explain how a government can use a tax on dry cleaning to bring about the efficient level of production. What should the value of the tax be?

b. How large is the deadweight loss (in dollars) from excessive dry cleaning, according to the figure?

3.9 The graph in the next column illustrates the situation in the dry cleaning market. In contrast to problem 3.8, the marginal social cost of the pollution rises as the quantity of items cleaned per week increases. In addi-

tion, there are two demand curves, one for a smaller city, D_S, the other for a larger city, D_L.

a. Explain why the marginal social cost curve has a different slope than the marginal private cost curve.

b. What tax per item cleaned will achieve economic efficiency in the smaller city? In the larger city? Explain why the efficient tax is different in the two cities.

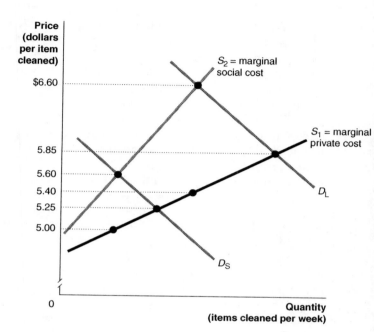

3.10 **(Related to the *Chapter Opener*)** Anyone can purchase sulfur dioxide emissions allowances on the Chicago Mercantile Exchange. Several environmental groups have raised money to buy allowances. As part of their fundraising, these groups have urged contributors to buy the allowances as gifts. As one newspaper story put it, "For the environmentalist in your life, here's a gift that is sold by the ton, fits in an envelope and will last forever." What would be the impact of environmental groups buying emission allowances on the total amount of sulfur dioxide pollution in the United States? What would be the impact on the price of the emission allowances?

Source: Randall Edwards, "Dear Santa: Please Bring Me Sulfur Dioxide for Christmas," *Columbus (Ohio) Dispatch*, December 19, 1999.

3.11 **(Related to the *Making the Connection*)** As discussed in the chapter, a system of tradable permits was very successful in efficiently reducing emissions of sulfur dioxide in the United States. Why have some economists proposed a similar system of tradable permits to reduce carbon dioxide emissions? Briefly discuss similarities and differences between the problem of reducing sulfur dioxide emissions and the problem of reducing carbon dioxide emissions.

>> **End Learning Objective 3**

4 LEARNING OBJECTIVE 4 | Explain how goods can be categorized on the basis of whether they are rival or excludable and use graphs to illustrate the efficient quantities of public goods and common resources

Four Categories of Goods

Summary

There are four categories of goods: private goods, public goods, quasi-public goods, and common resources. **Private goods** are both rival and excludable. **Rivalry** means that when one person consumes a unit of a good, no one else can consume that unit. **Excludability** means that anyone who does not pay for a good cannot consume it. **Public goods** are both nonrivalrous and nonexcludable. Private firms are usually not willing to supply public goods because of free riding. **Free riding** involves benefiting from a good without paying for it. **Quasi-public goods** are excludable but not rival. **Common resources** are rival but not excludable. The **tragedy of the commons** refers to the tendency for a common resource to be overused. The tragedy of the commons results from a lack of clearly defined and enforced property rights. We find the market demand curve for a private good by adding the quantity of the good demanded by each consumer at each price. We find the demand curve for a public good by adding vertically the price each consumer would be willing to pay for each quantity of the good. The optimal quantity of a public good occurs where the demand curve intersects the curve representing the marginal cost of supplying the good.

 Visit www.myeconlab.com to complete these exercises online and get instant feedback.

Review Questions

4.1 Define rivalry and excludability and use these terms to discuss the four categories of goods.

4.2 What is a public good? What is free riding? How is free riding related to the tendency of a public good to create market failure?

4.3 What is the tragedy of the commons? How can it be avoided?

Problems and Applications

4.4 **(Related to *Solved Problem 5*)** Suppose that Jill and Joe are the only two people in the small town of Andover. Andover has land available to build a park of no more than 9 acres. Jill and Joe's demand schedules for the park are as follows:

JOE	
PRICE PER ACRE	NUMBER OF ACRES
$10	0
9	1
8	2
7	3
6	4
5	5
4	6
3	7
2	8
1	9

JILL	
PRICE PER ACRE	NUMBER OF ACRES
$15	0
14	1
13	2
12	3
11	4
10	5
9	6
8	7
7	8
6	9

The supply curve is as follows:

PRICE	NUMBER OF ACRES
$11	1
13	2
15	3
17	4
19	5
21	6
23	7
25	8
27	9

a. Draw a graph showing the optimal size of the park. Be sure to label the curves on the graph.

b. Briefly explain why a park of 2 acres is not optimal.

4.5 Commercial whaling has been described as a modern example of the tragedy of the commons. Briefly explain whether you agree or disagree.

4.6 According to an article in the *Wall Street Journal*, economist Paul Romer of Stanford University has argued: "The market mechanism and property rights are excellent at conserving scarce resources and putting them to the most profitable use. . . . They aren't so good at encouraging the production and distribution of new ideas, which are critical to progress." What characteristics of the production and distribution of new ideas might make it difficult for the market to produce the optimal amount?

Source: David Wessel, "Precepts from Professor Summers," *Wall Street Journal*, October 17, 2002.

4.7 The more frequently bacteria are exposed to antibiotics, the more quickly the bacteria will develop resistance to the antibiotics. A columnist for the *Wall Street Journal* observes:

> Each parent will press a pediatrician for a drug if there's any chance it will cure a child. Yet if every parent and pediatrician does the same, they will speed the evolution of drug-resistant microbes. And what drug company will enlist its marketers to prod doctors to prescribe its antibiotics less?

Briefly discuss in what sense antibiotics can be considered a common resource.

Source: David Wessel, "Losing the Race with Bugs: Bacteria Beats New Drugs," *Wall Street Journal*, April 25, 2002.

4.8 Put each of these goods or services into one of the boxes in Figure 8. That is, categorize them as private goods, public goods, quasi-public goods, or common resources.
a. A television broadcast of the World Series
b. Home mail delivery
c. Education in a public school
d. Education in a private school
e. Hiking in a park surrounded by a fence
f. Hiking in a park not surrounded by a fence
g. An apple

4.9 (Related to the *Making the Connection*) Explain whether you agree or disagree with the following statement: "Providing health care is obviously a public good. If one person becomes ill and doesn't receive treatment, that person may infect many other people. If many people become ill, then the output of the economy will be negatively affected. Therefore, providing health care is a public good that should be supplied by the government."

>> End Learning Objective 4

Elasticity: The Responsiveness of Demand and Supply

From Chapter 6 of *Microeconomics*, 2/e. R. Glenn Hubbard. Anthony Patrick O'Brien. Copyright © 2008 by Pearson Prentice Hall. All rights reserved.

Elasticity: The Responsiveness of Demand and Supply

Do People Care about the Prices of Books?

Some observers have been predicting for years that the printed book will be replaced with the electronic book. The printed book is still holding its own, however. In 2006, U.S. consumers spent almost $54 billion to buy 3.2 billion copies of new printed books. By contrast, although thousands of books were available in electronic format, total sales amounted to only a few million dollars.

While the printed book lives on, book publishers face a problem unique to the industry: Unlike most retailers, bookstores have the right to return unsold books. For example, when a local supermarket orders shampoo, apple juice, or dog food, it knows that if it has overestimated consumer demand, it will be stuck with the unsold items. By contrast, to give bookstores an incentive to order more books, publishers have given the stores the right to return unsold copies. On average, bookstores return 35 percent of books to publishers.

The high return rate of books means that publishers have to be very careful when deciding how many copies of a book to print and ship to bookstores. In 2007, Scholastic, the largest publisher of children's books in the world, published the final installment of the hugely popular Harry Potter series. Barnes & Noble bookstores have a special membership program that gives customers a 20 percent discount on most hardcover books. But on *Harry Potter and the Deathly Hallows*, Barnes & Noble offered a 40 percent discount. The company was willing to accept a small profit on each book in hopes of selling a very large quantity. Scholastic could not simply print all the books ordered by bookstores like Barnes & Noble because it feared that the bookstores might overestimate the quantity of books actually demanded by consumers. Executives at Scholastic knew that the number of copies of the book demanded by consumers would depend in part on the price of the book. But how responsive are consumers to changes in book prices? Will a lower price significantly increase sales? Publishers debate this point.

For example, Stephen Rubin, president and publisher of Doubleday, has made the following argument about book prices: "I am just convinced that there is no difference between $22 and $23. Let's face it. If you want a book in translation from a Czech writer, you are going to buy the book—price is not a factor if it is a book that you really want." On the other hand, Barnes & Noble's program of discounting books for members will be effective only if consumers are sufficiently responsive to lower prices for books. As Bill Armstrong, an industry analyst, put it: "[Barnes & Noble's discount program] will only be a success if these lower prices produce greater unit volume enough to offset the lower price per book." **AN INSIDE LOOK** discusses the effectiveness of Borders bookstores' Borders Rewards program.

Sources: Henry Sanderson, "Barnes & Noble Disappoints Investors with Outlook," *Wall Street Journal*, March 5, 2007; and data on book sales from U.S. Census Bureau, *The 2007 Statistical Abstract*.

Getty Images, Inc.

Economics in YOUR Life!

How Much Do Book Prices Matter to You?

We have just seen that there is a debate in the publishing industry about how responsive consumers are to changes in book prices. Barnes & Noble was willing to reduce the price of *Harry Potter and the Deathly Hallows* because it believed doing so would significantly increase sales. Some book executives, like Stephen Rubin of Doubleday, seem to think that prices do not matter. What factors would make you more or less sensitive to price when purchasing a book? Is Barnes & Noble's strategy likely to succeed? As you read the chapter, see if can answer these questions. You can check your answers against those we provide at the end of the chapter.

Elasticity A measure of how much one economic variable responds to changes in another economic variable.

Whether you are managing a publishing company, bookstore, or coffee shop, you need to know how an increase or decrease in the price of your products will affect the quantity consumers are willing to buy. Cutting the price of a good increases the quantity demanded and that raising the price reduces the quantity demanded. But the critical question is this: *How much* will the quantity demanded change as a result of a price increase or decrease? Economists use the concept of **elasticity** to measure how one economic variable—such as the quantity demanded—responds to changes in another economic variable—such as the price. For example, the responsiveness of the quantity demanded of a good to changes in its price is called the *price elasticity of demand*. Knowing the price elasticity of demand allows you to compute the effect of a price change on the quantity demanded.

The quantity of a good that consumers demand depends not just on the price of the good but also on consumer income and on the prices of related goods. As a manager, you would also be interested in measuring the responsiveness of demand to these other factors. As we will see, we can use the concept of elasticity here as well. We also are interested in the responsiveness of the quantity supplied of a good to changes in its price, which is called the *price elasticity of supply*.

Elasticity is an important concept not just for business managers but for policymakers as well. If the government wants to discourage teenage smoking, it can raise the price of cigarettes by increasing the tax on them. If we know the price elasticity of demand for cigarettes, we can calculate how many fewer cigarettes will be demanded at a higher price. In this chapter, we will also see how policymakers use the concept of elasticity.

---

1 LEARNING OBJECTIVE

1 | Define the price elasticity of demand and understand how to measure it.

The Price Elasticity of Demand and Its Measurement

We know from the law of demand that when the price of a product falls, the quantity demanded of the product increases. But the law of demand tells firms only that the demand curves for their products slope downward. More useful is a measure of the responsiveness of the quantity demanded to a change in price. This measure is called the **price elasticity of demand**.

Measuring the Price Elasticity of Demand

Price elasticity of demand The responsiveness of the quantity demanded to a change in price, measured by dividing the percentage change in the quantity demanded of a product by the percentage change in the product's price.

We might measure the price elasticity of demand by using the slope of the demand curve because the slope of the demand curve tells us how much quantity changes as price changes. Using the slope of the demand curve to measure price elasticity has a drawback, however: The measurement of slope is sensitive to the units chosen for quantity and price. For example, suppose a $1 decrease in the price of *Harry Potter and the Deathly Hallows* leads to an increase in the quantity demanded from 10.1 million books to 10.2 million books. The change in quantity is 0.1 million books, and the change in price is −$1, so the slope is 0.1/−1 = −0.1. But if we measure price in cents, rather than dollars, the slope is 0.1/−100 = −0.001. If we measure price in dollars and books in thousands, instead of millions, the slope is 100/−1 = −100. Clearly, the value we compute for the slope can change dramatically, depending on the units we use for quantity and price.

To avoid this confusion over units, economists use *percentage changes* when measuring the price elasticity of demand. Percentage changes are not dependent on units. No matter what units we use to measure the quantity of wheat, 10 percent more wheat is 10 percent more wheat. Therefore, the price elasticity of demand is measured by dividing the percentage change in the quantity demanded by the percentage change in the price. Or:

$$\text{Price elasticity of demand} = \frac{\text{Percentage change in quantity demanded}}{\text{Percentage change in price}}.$$

It's important to remember that *the price elasticity of demand is not the same as the slope of the demand curve.*

If we calculate the price elasticity of demand for a price cut, the percentage change in price will be negative, and the percentage change in quantity demanded will be positive. Similarly, if we calculate the price elasticity of demand for a price increase, the percentage change in price will be positive, and the percentage change in quantity will be negative. Therefore, the price elasticity of demand is always negative. In comparing elasticities, though, we are usually interested in their relative size. So, we often drop the minus sign and compare their *absolute values*. In other words, although −3 is actually a smaller number than −2, a price elasticity of −3 is larger than a price elasticity of −2.

Elastic Demand and Inelastic Demand

If the quantity demanded is responsive to changes in price, the percentage change in quantity demanded will be *greater* than the percentage change in price, and the price elasticity of demand will be greater than 1 in absolute value. In this case, demand is **elastic**. For example, if a 10 percent fall in the price of bagels results in a 20 percent increase in the quantity of bagels demanded, then:

$$\text{Price elasticity of demand} = \frac{20\%}{-10\%} = -2,$$

and we can conclude that the price of bagels is **elastic**.

When the quantity demanded is not very responsive to price, however, the percentage change in quantity demanded will be *less* than the percentage change in price, and the price elasticity of demand will be less than 1 in absolute value. In this case, demand is **inelastic**. For example, if a 10 percent fall in the price of wheat results in a 5 percent increase in the quantity of wheat demanded, then:

$$\text{Price elasticity of demand} = \frac{5\%}{-10\%} = -0.5,$$

and we can conclude that the demand for wheat is **inelastic**.

In the special case in which the percentage change in the quantity demanded is equal to the percentage change in price, the price elasticity of demand equals −1 (or 1 in absolute value). In this case, demand is **unit-elastic**.

An Example of Computing Price Elasticities

Suppose you own a small bookstore and you are trying to decide whether to cut the price you are charging for a new John Grisham mystery novel. You are currently at point *A* in Figure 1: selling 16 copies of the novel per day at a price of $30 per copy. How many more copies you will sell by cutting the price to $20 depends on the price elasticity of demand for this novel. Let's consider two possibilities: If D_1 is the demand curve for this novel in your store, your sales will increase to 28 copies per day, point *B*. But if D_2 is your demand curve, your sales will increase only to 20 copies per day, point *C*. We might expect—correctly, as we will see—that between these points, demand curve D_1 is *elastic*, and demand curve D_2 is *inelastic*.

To confirm that D_1 is elastic between these points and that D_2 is inelastic, we need to calculate the price elasticity of demand for each curve. In calculating price elasticity between two points on a demand curve, though, we run into a problem because we get

Elastic demand Demand is elastic when the percentage change in quantity demanded is *greater* than the percentage change in price, so the price elasticity is *greater* than 1 in absolute value.

Inelastic demand Demand is inelastic when the percentage change in quantity demanded is *less* than the percentage change in price, so the price elasticity is *less* than 1 in absolute value.

Unit-elastic demand Demand is unit-elastic when the percentage change in quantity demanded is *equal to* the percentage change in price, so the price elasticity is equal to 1 in absolute value.

Figure 1

Along D_1, cutting the price from $30 to $20 increases the number of copies sold from 16 per day to 28 per day, so demand is elastic between point A and point B. Along D_2, cutting the price from $30 to $20 increases the number of copies sold from 16 per day to only 20 per day, so demand is inelastic between point A and point C.

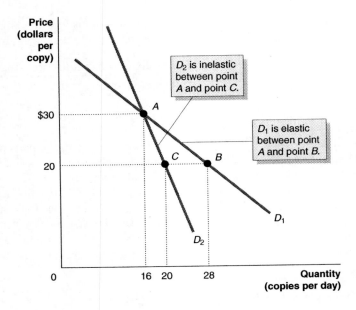

a different value for price increases than for price decreases. For example, suppose we calculate the price elasticity for D_2 as the price is cut from $30 to $20. This reduction is a 33 percent price cut that increases the quantity demanded from 16 books to 20 books, or by 25 percent. Therefore, the price elasticity of demand between points A and C is $25/-33 = -0.8$. Now let's calculate the price elasticity for D_2 as the price is *increased* from $20 to $30. This is a 50 percent price increase that decreases the quantity demanded from 20 books to 16 books, or by 20 percent. So, now our measure of the price elasticity of demand between points A and C is $-20/50 = -0.4$. It can be confusing to have different values for the price elasticity of demand between the same two points on the same demand curve.

The Midpoint Formula

We can use the *midpoint formula* to ensure that we have only one value of the price elasticity of demand between the same two points on a demand curve. The midpoint formula uses the *average* of the initial and final quantities and the initial and final prices. If Q_1 and P_1 are the initial quantity and price and Q_2 and P_2 are the final quantity and price, the midpoint formula is:

$$\text{Price elasticity of demand} = \frac{(Q_2 - Q_1)}{\left(\frac{Q_1 + Q_2}{2}\right)} \div \frac{(P_2 - P_1)}{\left(\frac{P_1 + P_2}{2}\right)}.$$

The midpoint formula may seem challenging at first, but the numerator is just the change in quantity divided by the average of the initial and final quantities, and the denominator is just the change in price divided by the average of the initial and final prices.

Let's apply the formula to calculating the price elasticity of D_2 in Figure 1. Between point A and point C on D_2, the change in quantity is 4, and the average of the two quantities is 18. Therefore, there is a 22.2 percent change in quantity. The change in price is $-$10, and the average of the two prices is $25. Therefore, there is a -40 percent change in price. So, the price elasticity of demand is $22.2/-40.0 = -0.6$. Notice these three results from calculating the price elasticity of demand using the midpoint formula: First, as we suspected from examining Figure 1, demand curve D_2 is inelastic between points A and C. Second, our value for the price elasticity calculated using the midpoint formula is between the two values we calculated earlier. Third, the midpoint formula will give us the same value whether we are moving from the higher price to the lower price or from the lower price to the higher price.

118

We can also use the midpoint formula to calculate the elasticity of demand between point A and point B on D_1. In this case, there is a 54.5 percent change in quantity and a −40 percent change in price. So, the elasticity of demand is 54.5/−40.0 = −1.4. Once again, as we suspected, demand curve D_1 is price elastic between points A and B.

Solved Problem | **1**

Calculating the Price Elasticity of Demand

Scholastic Corporation's suggested retail price for *Harry Potter and the Deathly Hallows* is $35. Suppose you own a small bookstore, and you believe that if you keep the price of the book at $35, you will be able to sell 40 copies per day. You are considering cutting the price to $25. The graph below shows two possible increases in the quantity sold as a result of your price cut. Use the information in the graph to calculate the price elasticity between these two prices on each of the demand curves. Use the midpoint formula in your calculations. State whether each demand curve is elastic or inelastic between these two prices.

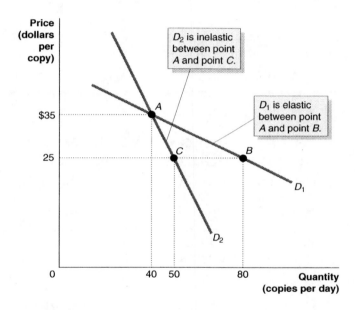

SOLVING THE PROBLEM:

Step 1: **Review the chapter material.** This problem requires calculating the price elasticity of demand, so you may want to review the material in the section "The Midpoint Formula."

Step 2: **As the first step in using the midpoint formula, calculate the average quantity and the average price for demand curve D_1.**

$$\text{Average quantity} = \frac{40 + 80}{2} = 60$$

$$\text{Average price} = \frac{\$35 + \$25}{2} = \$30$$

Step 3: **Now calculate the percentage change in the quantity demanded and the percentage change in price for demand curve D_1.**

$$\text{Percentage change in quantity demanded} = \frac{80 - 40}{60} \times 100 = 66.7\%$$

$$\text{Percentage change in price} = \frac{\$25 - \$35}{\$30} \times 100 = -33.3\%$$

119

Step 4: **Divide the percentage change in the quantity demanded by the percentage change in price to arrive at the price elasticity for demand curve D_1.**

$$\text{Price elasticity of demand} = \frac{66.7\%}{-33.3\%} = -2$$

Because the elasticity is greater than 1 in absolute value, D_1 is price *elastic* between these two prices.

Step 5: **Calculate the price elasticity of demand curve D_2 between these two prices.**

$$\text{Percentage change in quantity demanded} = \frac{50 - 40}{45} \times 100 = 22.2\%$$

$$\text{Percentage change in price} = \frac{\$25 - \$35}{\$30} \times 100 = -33.3\%$$

$$\text{Price elasticity of demand} = \frac{22.2\%}{-33.3\%} = -0.7$$

Because the elasticity is less than 1 in absolute value, D_2 is price *inelastic* between these two prices.

>> End Solved Problem 1

YOUR TURN: For more practice, do related problem 1.6 at the end of this chapter.

When Demand Curves Intersect, the Flatter Curve Is More Elastic

Remember that elasticity is not the same thing as slope. While slope is calculated using changes in quantity and price, elasticity is calculated using percentage changes. But it *is* true that if two demand curves intersect, the one with the smaller slope (in absolute value)—the flatter demand curve—is more elastic, and the one with the larger slope (in absolute value)—the steeper demand curve—is less elastic. In Figure 1, demand curve D_1 is more elastic than demand curve D_2.

Polar Cases of Perfectly Elastic and Perfectly Inelastic Demand

Perfectly inelastic demand The case where the quantity demanded is completely unresponsive to price, and the price elasticity of demand equals zero.

Although they do not occur frequently, you should be aware of the extreme, or polar, cases of price elasticity. If a demand curve is a vertical line, it is **perfectly inelastic** . In this case, the quantity demanded is completely unresponsive to price, and the price elasticity of demand equals zero. However much price may increase or decrease, the quantity remains the same. For only a very few products will the quantity demanded be completely unresponsive to the price, making the demand curve a vertical line. The drug insulin is an example. Diabetics must take a certain amount of insulin each day. If the price of insulin declines, it will not affect the required dose and thus will not increase the quantity demanded. Similarly, a price increase will not affect the required dose or decrease the quantity demanded. (Of course, some diabetics will not be able to afford insulin at a higher price. If so, even in this case, the demand curve may not be completely vertical and, therefore, not perfectly inelastic.)

Perfectly elastic demand The case where the quantity demanded is infinitely responsive to price, and the price elasticity of demand equals infinity.

If a demand curve is a horizontal line, it is **perfectly elastic**. In this case, the quantity demanded would be infinitely responsive to price, and the price elasticity of demand equals infinity. If a demand curve is perfectly elastic, an increase in price causes the quantity demanded to fall to zero. Once again, perfectly elastic demand curves are rare, and it is important not to confuse *elastic* with *perfectly elastic*. Table 1 summarizes the different price elasticities of demand.

120

IF DEMAND IS...	THEN THE ABSOLUTE VALUE OF PRICE ELASTICITY IS
elastic	greater than 1
inelastic	less than 1
unit-elastic	equal to 1
perfectly elastic	equal to infinity
perfectly inelastic	equal to 0

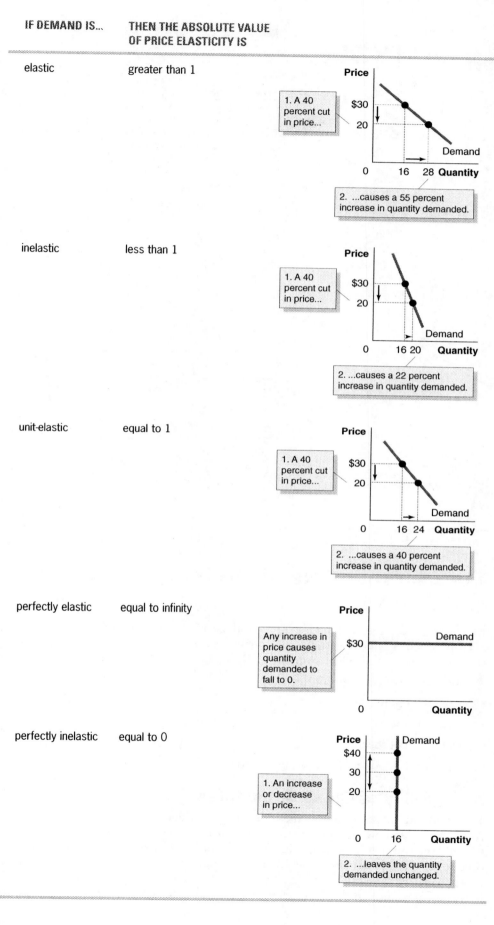

1. A 40 percent cut in price...

$30
20

Demand

0   16   28   Quantity

2. ...causes a 55 percent increase in quantity demanded.

1. A 40 percent cut in price...

$30
20

Demand

0   16 20   Quantity

2. ...causes a 22 percent increase in quantity demanded.

1. A 40 percent cut in price...

$30
20

Demand

0   16 24   Quantity

2. ...causes a 40 percent increase in quantity demanded.

Any increase in price causes quantity demanded to fall to 0.

$30   Demand

0   Quantity

1. An increase or decrease in price...

$40
30
20

Demand

0   16   Quantity

2. ...leaves the quantity demanded unchanged.

TABLE 1

Summary of the Price Elasticities of Demand

(Note that the percentage increases shown in the boxes in the graphs were calculated using the midpoint formula.)

Don't Let This Happen to **YOU!**

Don't Confuse Inelastic with *Perfectly* Inelastic

You may be tempted to simplify the concept of elasticity by assuming that any demand curve described as being inelastic is *perfectly* inelastic. You should never assume this because perfectly inelastic demand curves are rare. For example, consider the following problem: "Use a demand and supply graph to show how a decrease in supply affects the equilibrium quantity of gasoline. Assume that the demand for gasoline is inelastic." The following graph would be an *incorrect* answer to this problem.

The demand for gasoline is inelastic, but it is not *perfectly* inelastic. When the price of gasoline rises, the quantity demanded falls. So, the graph that would be the correct answer to this problem would show a normal downward-sloping demand curve rather than a vertical demand curve.

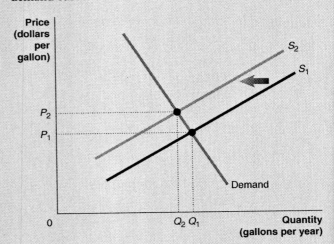

YOUR TURN: Test your understanding by doing related problem 1.11 at the end of this chapter.

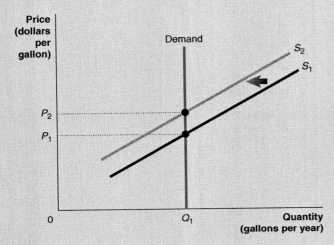

---

2 | Understand the determinants of the price elasticity of demand.

The Determinants of the Price Elasticity of Demand

We have seen that the demand for some products may be elastic, while the demand for other products may be inelastic. In this section, we examine why price elasticities differ among products. The key determinants of the price elasticity of demand are as follows:

- Availability of close substitutes

- Passage of time

- Necessities versus luxuries

- Definition of the market

- Share of the good in the consumer's budget

Availability of Close Substitutes

The availability of substitutes is the most important determinant of price elasticity of demand because how consumers react to a change in the price of a product depends on what alternatives they have. When the price of gasoline rises, consumers have few alternatives, so the quantity demanded falls only a little. But if Domino's raises the price of pizza, consumers have many alternatives, so the quantity demanded is likely to fall quite a lot. In fact, a key constraint on a firm's pricing policies is how many close substitutes exist for its product. In general, *if a product has more substitutes available, it will have more elastic demand. If a product has fewer substitutes available, it will have less elastic demand.*

Passage of Time

It usually takes consumers some time to adjust their buying habits when prices change. If the price of chicken falls, for example, it takes a while before consumers decide to change from eating chicken for dinner once per week to eating it twice per week. If the price of gasoline increases, it also takes a while for consumers to decide to shift toward buying more fuel-efficient cars to reduce the quantity of gasoline they buy. *The more time that passes, the more elastic the demand for a product becomes.*

Luxuries versus Necessities

Goods that are luxuries usually have more elastic demand curves than goods that are necessities. For example, the demand for milk is inelastic because milk is a necessity, and the quantity that people buy is not very dependent on its price. Tickets to a concert are a luxury, so the demand for concert tickets is much more elastic than the demand for milk. *The demand curve for a luxury is more elastic than the demand curve for a necessity.*

Definition of the Market

In a narrowly defined market, consumers have more substitutes available. If the price of Kellogg's Raisin Bran rises, many consumers will start buying another brand of raisin bran. If the prices of all brands of raisin bran rise, the responsiveness of consumers will be lower. If the prices of all breakfast cereals rise, the responsiveness of consumers will be even lower. *The more narrowly we define a market, the more elastic demand will be.*

What happens when the price of raisin bran increases?

Making the Connection | The Price Elasticity of Demand for Breakfast Cereal

MIT economist Jerry Hausman has estimated the price elasticity of demand for breakfast cereal. He divided breakfast cereals into three categories: children's cereals, such as Trix and Froot Loops; adult cereals, such as Special K and Grape-Nuts; and family cereals, such as Corn Flakes and Raisin Bran. Some of the results of his estimates are given in the following table.

CEREAL	PRICE ELASTICITY OF DEMAND
Post Raisin Bran	−2.5
All family breakfast cereals	−1.8
All types of breakfast cereals	−0.9

Source: Jerry A. Hausman, "The Price Elasticity of Demand for Breakfast Cereal," in *The Economics of New Goods*, TF Bresnahan & RJ Gordon, eds. Used with permission of The University of Chicago Press.

Just as we would expect, the price elasticity for a particular brand of raisin bran was larger in absolute value than the elasticity for all family cereals, and the elasticity for all family cereals was larger than the elasticity for all types of breakfast cereals. If Post increases the price of its Raisin Bran by 10 percent, sales will decline by 25 percent, as many consumers switch to another brand of raisin bran. If the prices of all family breakfast cereals rise by 10 percent, sales will decline by 18 percent, as consumers switch to child or adult cereals. In both of these cases, demand is elastic. But if the prices of all types of breakfast cereals rise by 10 percent, sales will decline by only 9 percent. Demand for all breakfast cereals is inelastic.

Source: Jerry A. Hausman, "Valuation of New Goods under Perfect and Imperfect Competition," in Timothy F. Bresnahan and Robert J. Gordon, eds., *The Economics of New Goods*, Chicago: University of Chicago Press, 1997.

YOUR TURN: Test your understanding by doing related problem 2.4 at the end of this chapter.

Share of a Good in a Consumer's Budget

Goods that take only a small fraction of a consumer's budget tend to have less elastic demand than goods that take a large fraction. For example, most people buy salt infrequently and in relatively small quantities. The share of the average consumer's budget that is spent on salt is very low. As a result, even a doubling of the price of salt is likely to result in only a small decline in the quantity of salt demanded. "Big-ticket items," such as houses, cars, and furniture, take up a larger share in the average consumer's budget. Increases in the prices of these goods are likely to result in significant declines in quantity demanded. In general, *the demand for a good will be more elastic the larger the share of the good in the average consumer's budget.*

Is the Demand for Books Perfectly Inelastic?

At the beginning of the chapter we quoted Stephen Rubin, publisher of Doubleday, as saying, "I am just convinced that there is no difference between $22 and $23. . . . Price is not a factor if it is a book that you really want." Taken literally, Rubin seems to be arguing that the demand for books is perfectly inelastic because only when demand is perfectly inelastic is price "not a factor." It's unlikely that this is what he means because if demand were really perfectly inelastic, he could charge $200 or $2,000 instead of charging $23 and still sell the same number of books. It is more likely he is arguing that demand is inelastic, so that even though he will sell fewer books at a price of $23 than at a price of $22, the decline in sales will be small.

Notice also that the book he mentions is a "translation from a Czech writer." Specialized books of this type will have relatively few substitutes (although a consumer can buy a used copy or borrow a copy from the library). A cut in price is unlikely to attract many new customers, and an increase in price is unlikely to cause many existing customers to not buy. This lack of substitutes is the main factor that makes demand inelastic. The situation may be different for light fiction written by popular novelists, like John Grisham, Stephen King, or Dean Koontz. Many consumers see books written by these authors as close substitutes. Someone looking for a "good read" on an airplane trip or at the beach may switch from Stephen King to Dean Koontz if the price of the Stephen King book is significantly higher.

---

3 LEARNING OBJECTIVE

3 | Understand the relationship between the price elasticity of demand and total revenue.

The Relationship between Price Elasticity of Demand and Total Revenue

Total revenue The total amount of funds received by a seller of a good or service, calculated by multiplying price per unit by the number of units sold.

A firm is interested in price elasticity because it allows the firm to calculate how changes in price will affect its **total revenue**, which is the total amount of funds it receives from selling a good or service. Total revenue is calculated by multiplying price per unit by the number of units sold. When demand is inelastic, price and total revenue move in the same direction: An increase in price raises total revenue, and a decrease in price reduces total revenue. When demand is elastic, price and total revenue move inversely: An increase in price reduces total revenue, and a decrease in price raises total revenue.

To understand the relationship between price elasticity and total revenue, consider Figure 2. Panel (a) shows a demand curve for a John Grisham novel (as in Figure 1). This demand curve is inelastic between point *A* and point *B*. The total revenue received by a bookseller at point *A* equals the price of $30 multiplied by the 16 copies sold, or $480. This amount equals the areas of the rectangles *C* and *D* in the figure because together the rectangles have a height of $30 and a base of 16 copies. Because this demand curve is inelastic between point *A* and point *B* (it was demand curve D_2 in Figure 1), cutting the price to $20 (point *B*) reduces total revenue. The new total revenue is shown by the areas of rectangles *D* and *E*, and it is equal to $20 multiplied by 20 copies, or $400. Total revenue falls because the increase in the quantity demanded is not large enough to make up for the decrease in price.

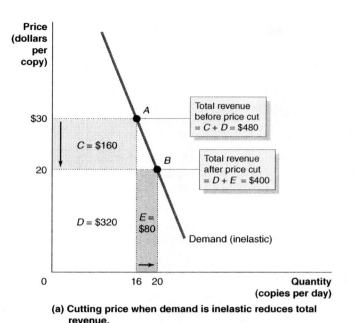

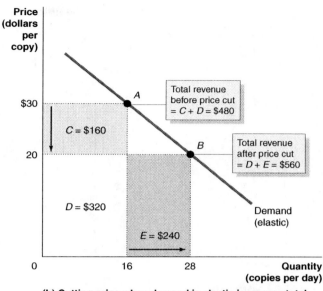

(a) Cutting price when demand is inelastic reduces total revenue.

(b) Cutting price when demand is elastic increases total revenue.

Figure 2 | The Relationship between Price Elasticity and Total Revenue

When demand is inelastic, a cut in price will decrease total revenue. In panel (a), at point A, the price is $30, 16 copies are sold, and total revenue received by the bookseller equals $30 × 16 copies, or $480. At point B, cutting price to $20 increases the quantity demanded to 20 copies, but the fall in price more than offsets the increase in quantity. As a result, revenue falls to $20 × 20 copies, or $400. When demand is elastic,

a cut in price will increase total revenue. In panel (b), at point A, the area of rectangles C and D is still equal to $480. But at point B, the area of rectangles D and E is equal to $20 × 28 copies, or $560. In this case, the increase in the quantity demanded is large enough to offset the fall in price, so total revenue increases.

As a result, the $80 increase in revenue gained as a result of the price cut—dark-green rectangle E—is less than the $160 in revenue lost—light-green rectangle C.

Panel (b) of Figure 2 shows a demand curve that is elastic between point A and point B (it was demand curve D_1 in Figure 1). In this case, cutting the price increases total revenue. At point A, the areas of rectangles C and D are still equal to $480, but at point B, the areas of rectangles D and E are equal to $20 multiplied by 28 copies, or $560. Here, total revenue rises because the increase in the quantity demanded is large enough to offset the lower price. As a result, the $240 increase in revenue gained as a result of the price cut—dark-green rectangle E—is greater than the $160 in revenue lost—light-green rectangle C.

The third, less common, possibility is that demand is unit elastic. In that case, a change in price is exactly offset by a proportional change in quantity demanded, leaving revenue unaffected. Therefore, when demand is unit elastic, neither a decrease in price nor an increase in price affects revenue. Table 2 summarizes the relationship between price elasticity and revenue.

Elasticity and Revenue with a Linear Demand Curve

Along most demand curves, elasticity is not constant at every point. For example, a straight-line, or linear, demand curve for DVDs is shown in panel (a) of Figure 3. The numbers from the table are plotted in the graphs. The demand curve shows that when the price falls by $1, consumers always respond by buying 2 more DVDs per month. When the price is high and the quantity demanded is low, demand is elastic. This is true because a $1 fall in price is a smaller percentage change when the price is high, and an increase of 2 DVDs is a larger percentage change when the quantity of DVDs is small. By similar reasoning, we can see why demand is inelastic when the price is low and the quantity demanded is high. Panel (a) in Figure 3 shows that when price is between $8 and $4 and quantity is between 0 and 6, demand is elastic. Panel (b) shows that over this same range, total revenue will increase as price falls. For example, in panel (a), as price falls from $7 to $6,

TABLE 2

The Relationship between Price Elasticity and Revenue

IF DEMAND IS ...	THEN ...	BECAUSE ...
elastic	an increase in price reduces revenue	the decrease in quantity demanded is proportionally *greater* than the increase in price.
elastic	a decrease in price increases revenue	the increase in quantity demanded is proportionally *greater* than the decrease in price.
inelastic	an increase in price increases revenue	the decrease in quantity demanded is proportionally *smaller* than the increase in price.
inelastic	a decrease in price reduces revenue	the increase in quantity demanded is proportionally *smaller* than the decrease in price.
unit elastic	an increase in price does not affect revenue	the decrease in quantity demanded is proportionally *the same as* the increase in price.
unit elastic	a decrease in price does not affect revenue	the increase in quantity demanded is proportionally *the same as* the decrease in price.

quantity demand increases from 2 to 4, and in panel (b), total revenue increases from $14 to $24. Similarly, when price is between $4 and zero and quantity is between 8 and 16, demand is inelastic. Over this same range, total revenue will decrease as price falls. For example, as price falls from $3 to $2 and quantity increases from 10 to 12, total revenue decreases from $30 to $24.

Solved Problem | 3

Price and Revenue Don't Always Move in the Same Direction

Briefly explain whether you agree or disagree with the following statement: "The only way to increase the revenue from selling a product is to increase the product's price."

SOLVING THE PROBLEM:

Step 1: **Review the chapter material.** This problem deals with the effect of a price change on a firm's revenue, so you may want to review the section "The Relationship between Price Elasticity and Total Revenue."

Step 2: **Analyze the statement.** We have seen that a price increase will increase revenue only if demand is inelastic. In Figure 3, for example, increasing the rental price of DVDs from $1 to $2 *increases* revenue from $14 to $24 because demand is inelastic along this portion of the demand curve. But increasing the price from $5 to $6 *decreases* revenue from $30 to $24 because demand is elastic along this portion of the demand curve. If the price is currently $5, increasing revenue would require a price *cut*, not a price increase. As this example shows, the statement is incorrect and you should disagree with it.

>> End Solved Problem 3

YOUR TURN: For more practice, do related problem 3.6 at the end of this chapter.

Price	Quantity Demanded	Total Revenue
$8	0	$0
7	2	14
6	4	24
5	6	30
4	8	32
3	10	30
2	12	24
1	14	14
0	16	0

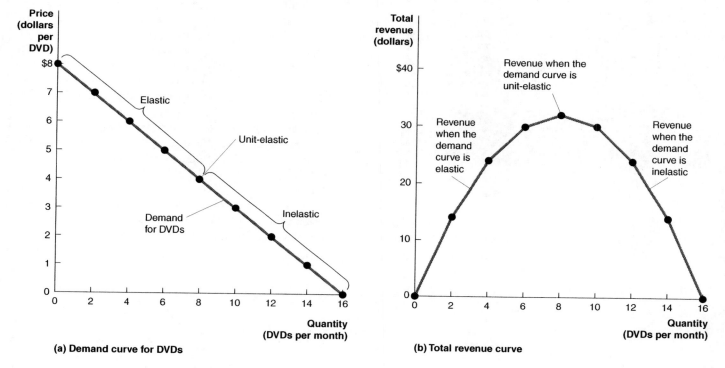

(a) Demand curve for DVDs

(b) Total revenue curve

Figure 3 | Elasticity Is Not Constant Along a Linear Demand Curve

The data from the table are plotted in the graphs. Panel (a) shows that as we move down the demand curve for DVDs, the price elasticity of demand declines. In other words, at higher prices, demand is elastic, and at lower prices, demand is inelastic. Panel (b) shows that as the quantity of DVDs sold increases from zero, revenue will increase until it reaches a maximum of $32 when 8 DVDs are sold. As sales increase beyond 8 DVDs, revenue falls because demand is inelastic on this portion of the demand curve.

Estimating Price Elasticity of Demand

To estimate the price elasticity of demand, economists need to know the demand curve for a product. To calculate the price elasticity of demand for new products, firms often rely on market experiments. With market experiments, firms try different prices and observe the change in quantity demanded that results.

Making *the* Connection | Determining the Price Elasticity of Demand for DVDs by Market Experiment

DVDs were a relatively new product in 2001. The movie studios producing them were unsure of the price elasticity of the demand curves they were facing, so they experimented with different prices to help determine the price elasticity.

127

Following are four films and the prices for DVDs and VHS tapes that the studios suggested stores such as Blockbuster Video charge for them:

FILM	DVD PRICE	VHS PRICE
Rugrats in Paris	$22.46	$22.99
The Mummy Returns	26.98	22.98
Miss Congeniality	16.69	22.98
The Perfect Storm	24.98	22.99

Getty Images, Inc.

When DVDs were first introduced, the movie studios were uncertain about their price elasticity of demand.

VHS tapes had been on the market for many years, and the studios had determined their pricing strategies, given their estimates of the price elasticity of demand. As a result, the prices of VHS tapes were usually very similar; for these four films, the prices were almost identical. The prices of DVDs were much less standardized because the studios were unsure of their price elasticities. Tom Adams, the head of Adams Market Research, a company that does research on the home video market, summed up the situation: "The studios have different views of the market, so they are setting different suggested retail prices, and the stores are discounting those prices to different degrees."

After several years of market experiments, the movie studios had more accurate estimates of the price elasticity of DVDs, and the prices of most DVDs became similar. For instance, in 2007, nearly all newly released DVDs had a list price of about $29, which was often discounted to about $17 when they were sold online or in discount department stores, such as Wal-Mart. When HD-DVDs were introduced, the studios apparently felt confident that they understood their price elasticity, because in 2007 most had list prices of $39.95, discounted to $27.95 in many online stores.

Sources: Geraldine Fabrikant, "Sale of DVDs Are Challenging Movie Rental Business," *New York Times*, April 16, 2001; prices from Amazon.com.

YOUR TURN: Test your understanding by doing related problem 3.12 at the end of this chapter.

4 LEARNING OBJECTIVE

4 | Define the cross-price elasticity of demand and the income elasticity of demand, and understand their determinants and how they are measured.

Other Demand Elasticities

Elasticity is an important concept in economics because it allows us to quantify the responsiveness of one economic variable to changes in another economic variable. In addition to price elasticity, two other demand elasticities are important: *cross-price elasticity of demand* and *income elasticity of demand*.

Cross-Price Elasticity of Demand

Cross-price elasticity of demand
The percentage change in quantity demanded of one good divided by the percentage change in the price of another good.

Suppose you work at Apple and you need to predict the effect of an increase in the price of Microsoft's Zune on the quantity of iPods demanded, holding other factors constant. You can do this by calculating the **cross-price elasticity of demand**, which is the percentage change in the quantity of iPods demanded divided by the percentage change in the price of Zunes—or, in general:

$$\text{Cross-price elasticity of demand} = \frac{\text{Percentage change in quantity demanded of one good}}{\text{Percentage change in price of another good}}.$$

IF THE PRODUCTS ARE . . .	THEN THE CROSS-PRICE ELASTICITY OF DEMAND WILL BE . . .	EXAMPLE
substitutes	positive	Two brands of digital music players
complements	negative	Digital music players and song downloads from online music stores
unrelated	zero	Digital music players and peanut butter

TABLE 3

Summary of Cross-Price Elasticity of Demand

The cross-price elasticity of demand is positive or negative, depending on whether the two products are substitutes or complements. Recall that substitutes are products that can be used for the same purpose, such as two brands of digital music players. Complements are products that are used together, such as digital music players and song downloads from online music sites. An increase in the price of a substitute will lead to an increase in quantity demanded, so the cross-price elasticity of demand will be positive. An increase in the price of a complement will lead to a decrease in the quantity demanded, so the cross-price elasticity of demand will be negative. Of course, if the two products are unrelated—such as digital music players and peanut butter—the cross-price elasticity of demand will be zero. Table 3 summarizes the key points concerning the cross-price elasticity of demand.

Cross-price elasticity of demand is important to firm managers because it allows them to measure whether products sold by other firms are close substitutes for their products. For example, Amazon.com and Barnesandnoble.com are the leading online booksellers. We might predict that if Amazon raises the price of a new John Grisham novel, many consumers will buy it from Barnesandnoble.com instead. But Jeff Bezos, Amazon's chief executive officer, has argued that because of Amazon's reputation for good customer service and because more customers are familiar with the site, ordering a book from Barnesandnoble.com is not a good substitute for ordering a book from Amazon. In effect, Bezos is arguing that the cross-price elasticity between Amazon's books and Barnesandnoble.com's books is low. Economists Judith Chevalier of Yale University and Austan Goolsbee of the University of Chicago used data on prices and quantities of books sold on these Web sites to estimate the cross-price elasticity. They found that the cross-price elasticity of demand between books at Amazon and books at Barnesandnoble.com was 3.5. This estimate means that if Amazon raises its prices by 10 percent, the quantity of books demanded on Barnesandnoble.com will increase by 35 percent. This result indicates that, contrary to Jeff Bezos's argument, consumers do consider books sold on the two Web sites to be close substitutes.

Income Elasticity of Demand

The **income elasticity of demand** measures the responsiveness of quantity demanded to changes in income. It is calculated as follows:

$$\text{Income elasticity of demand} = \frac{\text{Percentage change in quantity demanded}}{\text{Percentage change in income}}.$$

Income elasticity of demand
A measure of the responsiveness of quantity demanded to changes in income, measured by the percentage change in quantity demanded divided by the percentage change in income.

If the quantity demanded of a good increases as income increases, then the good is a *normal good*. Normal goods are often further subdivided into *luxury goods* and *necessity goods*. A good is a luxury if the quantity demanded is very responsive to changes in income, so that a 10 percent increase in income results in more than a 10 percent increase in quantity demanded. Expensive jewelry and vacation homes are examples of luxuries. A good is a necessity if the quantity demanded is not very responsive to changes in income, so that a 10 percent increase in income results in less than a 10 percent increase in quantity demanded. Food and clothing are examples of necessities.

TABLE 4

Summary of Income Elasticity of Demand

IF THE INCOME ELASTICITY OF DEMAND IS . . .	THEN THE GOOD IS . . .	EXAMPLE
positive but less than 1	normal and a necessity	Milk
positive and greater than 1	normal and a luxury	Caviar
negative	inferior	High-fat meat

A good is *inferior* if the quantity demanded falls when income increases. Ground beef with a high fat content is an example of an inferior good. We should note that normal goods, inferior goods, necessities, and luxuries are just labels economists use for goods with different income elasticities; they are not intended to be value judgments about the worth of these goods.

Because most goods are normal goods, during periods of economic expansion, when consumer income is rising, most firms can expect—holding other factors constant—that the quantity demanded of their products will increase. Sellers of luxuries can expect particularly large increases. During the late 1990s, rapid increases in income resulted in large increases in demand for luxuries, such as meals in expensive restaurants, luxury apartments, and high-performance automobiles. During recessions, falling consumer income can cause firms to experience increases in demand for inferior goods. For example, the demand for bus trips increases as consumers cut back on air travel, and supermarkets find the demand for hamburger increases relative to the demand for steak. Table 4 summarizes the key points about the income elasticity of demand.

Making the Connection | Price Elasticity, Cross-Price Elasticity, and Income Elasticity in the Market for Alcoholic Beverages

Many public policy issues are related to the consumption of alcoholic beverages. These issues include underage drinking, drunk driving, and the possible beneficial effects of red wine in lowering the risk of heart disease. X. M. Gao, an economist who works at American Express, and two colleagues have estimated statistically the following elasticities. (*Spirits* refers to all beverages that contain alcohol, other than beer and wine.)

Price elasticity of demand for beer	−0.23
Cross-price elasticity of demand between beer and wine	0.31
Cross-price elasticity of demand between beer and spirits	0.15
Income elasticity of demand for beer	−0.09
Income elasticity of demand for wine	5.03
Income elasticity of demand for spirits	1.21

The demand for beer is inelastic. A 10 percent increase in the price of beer will result in a 2.3 percent decline in the quantity of beer demanded. Not surprisingly, both wine and spirits are substitutes for beer. A 10 percent increase in the price of wine will result in a 3.1 percent *increase* in the quantity of beer demanded. A 10 percent increase in income will result in a little less than a 1 percent *decline* in the quantity of beer demanded. So, beer is an inferior good. Both wine and spirits are categorized as luxuries because their income elasticities are greater than 1.

Source: X. M. Gao, Eric J. Wailes, and Gail L. Cramer, "A Microeconometric Model Analysis of U.S. Consumer Demand for Alcoholic Beverages," *Applied Economics*, January 1995.

YOUR TURN: Test your understanding by doing related problem 4.8 at the end of this chapter.

5 LEARNING OBJECTIVE

Using Elasticity to Analyze the Disappearing Family Farm

The concepts of price elasticity and income elasticity can help us understand many economic issues. For example, some people are concerned that the family farm is becoming an endangered species in the United States. Although food production continues to grow rapidly, the number of farms and the number of farmers continue to dwindle. In 1950, the United States was home to more than 5 million farms, and more than 23 million people lived on farms. By 2006, fewer than 2 million farms remained, and fewer than 3 million people lived on them. Several federal government programs exist that are designed to slow the movement of people out of farming. Many of these programs have been aimed at helping small, family-operated farms, but rapid growth in farm production, combined with low price and income elasticities for most food products, has made family farming difficult in the United States.

Productivity measures the ability of firms to produce goods and services with a given amount of economic inputs, such as workers, machines, and land. Productivity has grown very rapidly in U.S. agriculture. In 1950, the average U.S. wheat farmer harvested about 17 bushels from each acre of wheat planted. By 2006, because of the development of superior strains of wheat and improvements in farming techniques, the average American wheat farmer harvested 42 bushels per acre. So, even though the total number of acres devoted to growing wheat declined from about 62 million to about 50 million, total wheat production rose from about 1.0 billion bushels to about 2.1 billion.

Unfortunately for U.S. farmers, this increase in wheat production resulted in a substantial decline in wheat prices. Two key factors explain this decline in wheat prices: (1) The demand for wheat is inelastic and (2) the income elasticity of demand for wheat is low. Even though the U.S. population has increased greatly since 1950 and the income of the average American is much higher than it was in 1950, the demand for wheat has increased only moderately. For all of the additional wheat to be sold, the price has had to decline. Because the demand for wheat is inelastic, the price decline has been substantial. Figure 4 illustrates these points.

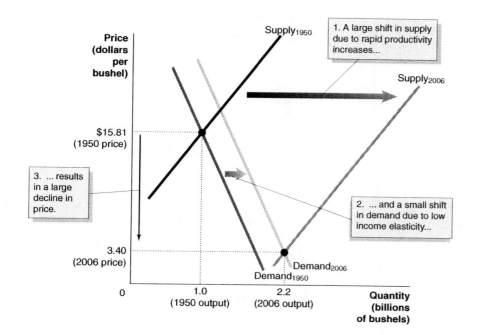

Figure 4

Elasticity and the Disappearing Farm

In 1950, U.S. farmers produced 1.0 billion bushels of wheat at a price of $15.81 per bushel. Over the next 50 years, rapid increases in farm productivity caused a large shift to the right in the supply curve for wheat. The income elasticity of demand for wheat is low, so the demand for wheat increased relatively little over this period. Because the demand for wheat is also inelastic, the large shift in the supply curve and the small shift in the demand curve resulted in a sharp decline in the price of wheat, from $15.81 per bushel in 1950 to $3.40 per bushel in 2006.

A large shift in supply, a small shift in demand, and an inelastic demand curve combined to drive down the price of wheat from $15.81 per bushel in 1950 to $3.40 per bushel in 2006. (The 1950 price is measured in terms of prices in 2006, to adjust for the general increase in prices since 1950.) With low prices, only the most efficiently run farms have been able to remain profitable. Smaller, family-run farms have found it difficult to survive, and many of these farms have disappeared. The markets for most food products are similar to the market for wheat. They are characterized by rapid output growth and low income and price elasticities. The result is the paradox of American farming: ever more abundant and cheaper food, supplied by fewer and fewer farms. American consumers have benefited, but most family farmers have not.

Solved Problem | 5

Using Price Elasticity to Analyze Policy toward Illegal Drugs

An ongoing policy debate concerns whether to legalize the use of drugs such as marijuana and cocaine. Some researchers estimate that legalizing cocaine would cause its price to fall by as much as 95 percent. Proponents of legalization argue that legalizing drug use would lower crime rates by eliminating the main reason for the murderous gang wars that plague many big cities and by reducing the incentive for drug addicts to commit robberies and burglaries. Opponents of legalization argue that lower drug prices would lead more people to use drugs.

a. Suppose the price elasticity of demand for cocaine is −2. If legalization causes the price of cocaine to fall by 95 percent, what will be the percentage increase in the quantity of cocaine demanded?

b. If the price elasticity is −0.02, what will be the percentage increase in the quantity demanded?

c. Discuss how the size of the price elasticity of demand for cocaine is relevant to the debate over its legalization.

SOLVING THE PROBLEM:

Step 1: **Review the chapter material.** This problem deals with applications of the price elasticity of demand formula, so you may want to review the section "Measuring the Price Elasticity of Demand."

Step 2: **Answer question (a) using the formula for the price elasticity of demand.**

$$\text{Price elasticity of demand} = \frac{\text{Percentage change in quantity demanded}}{\text{Percentage change in price}}.$$

We can plug into this formula the values we are given for the price elasticity and the percentage change in price:

$$-2 = \frac{\text{Percentage change in quantity demanded}}{-95\%}.$$

Or, rearranging:

$$\text{Percentage change in quantity demanded} = -2 \times -95\% = 190\%$$

Step 3: **Use the same method to answer question (b).** We only need to substitute −0.02 for −2 as the price elasticity of demand:

$$\text{Percentage change in quantity demanded} = -0.02 \times -95\% = 1.9\%$$

Step 4: **Answer question (c) by discussing how the size of the price elasticity of demand for cocaine helps us to understand the effects of legalization.** Clearly, the higher the absolute value of the price elasticity of demand for cocaine, the greater the increase in cocaine use that would result from legalization. If the price elasticity is as high as in question (a), legalization will lead to a large increase in use. If, however, the price elasticity is as low as in question (b), legalization will lead to only a small increase in use.

EXTRA CREDIT: One estimate puts the price elasticity at −0.28, which suggests that even a large fall in the price of cocaine might lead to only a moderate increase in cocaine use. However, even a moderate increase in cocaine use would have costs. Some studies have shown that cocaine users are more likely to commit crimes, to abuse their children, to have higher medical expenses, and to be less productive workers. Moreover, many people object to the use of cocaine and other narcotics on moral grounds and would oppose legalization even if it led to no increase in use. Ultimately, whether the use of cocaine and other drugs should be legalized is a normative issue. Economics can contribute to the discussion but cannot decide the issue.

Source for estimate of price elasticity of cocaine: Henry Saffer and Frank Chaloupka, "The Demand for Illicit Drugs," *Economic Inquiry*, Vol. 37, No. 3, July 1999, pp. 401–411.

YOUR TURN: For more practice, do related problems 5.2 and 5.3 at the end of this chapter.

>> End Solved Problem 5

6 LEARNING OBJECTIVE

6 | Define the price elasticity of supply and understand its main determinants and how it is measured.

The Price Elasticity of Supply and Its Measurement

We can use the concept of elasticity to measure the responsiveness of firms to a change in price just as we used it to measure the responsiveness of consumers. We know from the law of supply that when the price of a product increases, the quantity supplied increases. To measure how much quantity supplied increases when price increases, we use the *price elasticity of supply*.

Measuring the Price Elasticity of Supply

Just as with the price elasticity of demand, we calculate the **price elasticity of supply** using percentage changes:

$$\text{Price elasticity of supply} = \frac{\text{Percentage change in quantity supplied}}{\text{Percentage change in price}}.$$

Price elasticity of supply
The responsiveness of the quantity supplied to a change in price, measured by dividing the percentage change in the quantity supplied of a product by the percentage change in the product's price.

Notice that because supply curves are upward sloping, the price elasticity of supply will be a positive number. We categorize the price elasticity of supply the same way we categorized the price elasticity of demand: If the price elasticity of supply is less than 1, then supply is *inelastic*. For example, the price elasticity of supply of gasoline from U.S. oil refineries is about 0.20, and so it is inelastic. A 10 percent increase in the price of gasoline will result in only a 2 percent increase in the quantity supplied. If the price elasticity of supply is greater than 1, then supply is *elastic*. If the price elasticity of supply is equal to 1, then supply is *unit elastic*. As with other elasticity calculations, when we calculate the price elasticity of supply, we hold the values of other factors constant.

Determinants of the Price Elasticity of Supply

Whether supply is elastic or inelastic depends on the ability and willingness of firms to alter the quantity they produce as price increases. Often, firms have difficulty increasing the quantity of the product they supply during any short period of time. For example, a pizza parlor cannot produce more pizzas on any one night than is possible using the ingredients on hand. Within a day or two it can buy more ingredients, and within a few months it can hire more cooks and install additional ovens. As a result, the supply curve for pizza and most other products will be inelastic if we measure it over a short period of time, but increasingly elastic the longer the period of time over which we measure it. Products that require resources that are themselves in fixed supply are an exception to this rule. For example, a French winery may rely on a particular variety of grape. If all the land on which that grape can be grown is already planted in vineyards, then the supply of that wine will be inelastic even over a long period.

Making the Connection | Why Are Oil Prices So Unstable?

Bringing oil to market is a long process. Oil companies hire geologists to locate fields for exploratory oil well drilling. If an exploratory well indicates that significant amounts of oil are present, the company begins full-scale development of the field. The process from exploration to pumping significant amounts of oil can take years. Because it takes so long to bring additional quantities of oil to market, the price elasticity of supply for oil is very low. Substitutes are limited for oil-based products—such as gasoline—so the price elasticity of demand for oil is also low.

As the following graph shows, the combination of inelastic supply and inelastic demand results in shifts in supply causing large changes in price. In the graph, a reduction in supply that shifts the market supply curve from S_1 to S_2 causes the equilibrium quantity of oil to fall only by 5 percent, from 80 million barrels per day to 76 million, but the equilibrium price rises by 22 percent, from $40 per barrel to $50 per barrel.

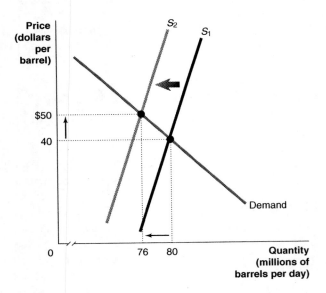

The world oil market is heavily influenced by the Organization of Petroleum Exporting Countries (OPEC). OPEC has 11 members, including Saudi Arabia, Kuwait, and other Arab countries, as well as Iran, Venezuela, Nigeria, and Indonesia. Together

134

these countries own 75 percent of the world's proven oil reserves. Periodically, OPEC has attempted to force up the price of oil by reducing the quantity of oil its members supply. Since the 1970s, the attempts by OPEC to reduce the quantity of oil on world markets have been successful only sporadically: Periods during which OPEC members cooperate and reduce supply alternate with periods in which the members fail to cooperate and supply increases. As a result, the supply curve for oil shifts fairly frequently. Combined with the low price elasticities of oil supply and demand, these shifts in supply have caused the price of oil to fluctuate significantly over the past 30 years, from as low as $11 per barrel to more than $75 per barrel.

Over longer periods of time, higher oil prices also lead to greater increases in the quantity supplied; in other words, the price elasticity of supply for oil increases. This increase happens because higher prices increase the economic incentive to explore for oil and to recover oil from more costly sources, such as under the oceans, in the Arctic, or at greater depths in the earth. When supply is more elastic, a given shift in supply results in a smaller increase in price. This effect is illustrated in the following graph. Compared with the preceding graph, the same decrease in supply increases the equilibrium price to $45 per barrel rather than $50 per barrel (and also causes a smaller decrease in the equilibrium quantity).

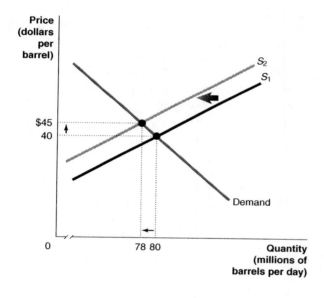

YOUR TURN: Test your understanding by doing related problem 6.3 at the end of this chapter.

Polar Cases of Perfectly Elastic and Perfectly Inelastic Supply

Although it occurs infrequently, it is possible for supply to fall into one of the polar cases of price elasticity. If a supply curve is a vertical line, it is *perfectly inelastic*. In this case, the quantity supplied is completely unresponsive to price, and the price elasticity of supply equals zero. However much price may increase or decrease, the quantity remains the same. Over a brief period of time, the supply of some goods and services may be perfectly inelastic. For example, a parking lot may have only a fixed number of parking spaces. If demand increases, the price to park in the lot may rise, but no more spaces will become available. Of course, if demand increases permanently, over a longer period of time, the owner of the lot may buy more land to add additional spaces.

If a supply curve is a horizontal line, it is *perfectly elastic*. In this case, the quantity supplied is infinitely responsive to price, and the price elasticity of supply equals infinity. If a supply curve is perfectly elastic, a very small increase in price causes a very large increase in quantity supplied. Just as with demand curves, it is important not to confuse a supply curve being elastic with its being perfectly elastic and not to confuse a supply curve being inelastic with its being perfectly inelastic. Table 5 summarizes the different price elasticities of supply.

Using Price Elasticity of Supply to Predict Changes in Price

Figure 5 illustrates the important point that, when demand increases, the amount that price increases depends on the price elasticity of supply. The figure shows the demand and supply for parking spaces at a beach resort. In panel (a), on a typical summer weekend, equilibrium occurs at point A, where Demand (typical) intersects a supply curve that is inelastic. The increase in demand for parking spaces on the Fourth of July shifts the demand curve to the right, moving the equilibrium to point B. Because the supply curve is inelastic, the increase in demand results in a large increase in price—from $2.00 per hour to $4.00—but only a small increase in the quantity of spaces supplied—from 1,200 to 1,400.

In panel (b), supply is elastic, perhaps because the resort has vacant land that can be used for parking during periods of high demand. As a result, the shift in equilibrium from point A to point B results in a smaller increase in price and a larger increase in the quantity supplied. An increase in price from $2.00 per hour to $2.50 is sufficient to increase the quantity of parking supplied from 1,200 to 2,100. Knowing the price elasticity of supply makes it possible to predict more accurately how much price will change following an increase or a decrease in demand.

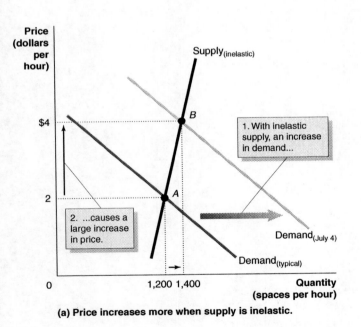

(a) Price increases more when supply is inelastic.

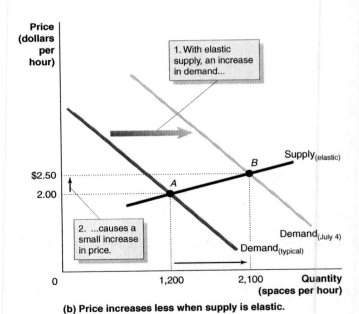

(b) Price increases less when supply is elastic.

Figure 5 | Changes in Price Depend on the Price Elasticity of Supply

In panel (a), Demand (typical) represents the typical demand for parking spaces on a summer weekend at a beach resort. Demand (July 4) represents demand on the Fourth of July. Because supply is inelastic, the shift in equilibrium from point A to point B results in a large increase in price—from $2.00 per hour to $4.00—but only a small increase in the quantity of spaces supplied—from 1,200 to 1,400. In panel (b), supply is elastic. As a result, the shift in equilibrium from point A to point B results in a smaller increase in price and a larger increase in the quantity supplied. An increase in price from $2.00 per hour to $2.50 is sufficient to increase the quantity of parking supplied from 1,200 to 2,100.

IF SUPPLY IS . . .	THEN THE VALUE OF PRICE ELASTICITY IS
elastic	greater than 1
inelastic	less than 1
unit-elastic	equal to 1
perfectly elastic	equal to infinity
perfectly inelastic	equal to 0

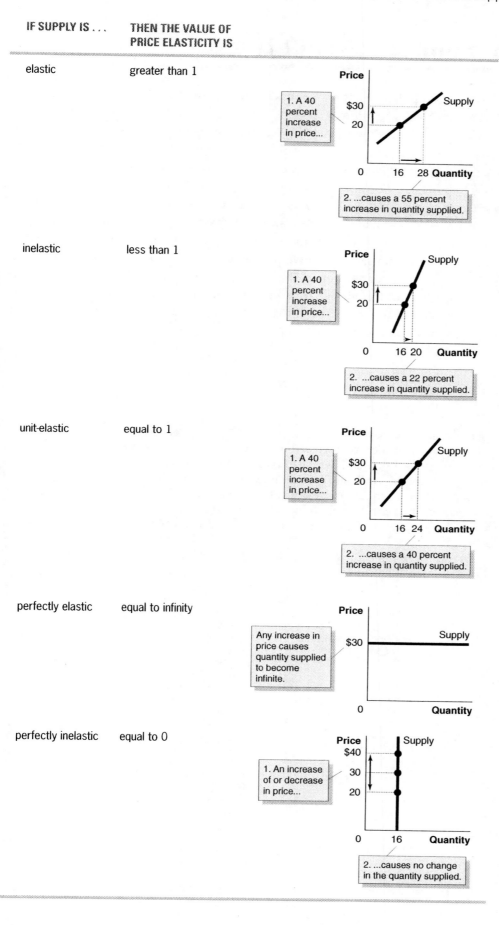

TABLE 5

Summary of the Price Elasticities of Supply

(Note that the percentage increases shown in the boxes in the graphs were calculated using the midpoint formula.)

Economics in YOUR Life!

At the beginning of the chapter, we asked you to think about two questions: What factors would make you more or less sensitive to price when purchasing a book? and Is Barnes & Noble's strategy of heavily discounting copies of *Harry Potter and the Deathly Hallows* in hopes of selling a very large quantity likely to succeed? If you have never read any Harry Potter books, you are probably not a fan of the series and are unlikely to purchase the book at any price. If you read all the earlier books in the series as soon as they came out, you are very likely to consider purchasing the book even at a high price. However, if you usually wait to purchase inexpensive paperback editions of books you like to read, you are more likely to purchase the hardcover book when Barnes & Noble discounts it. The answer to the second question depends on the prevalence of this last type of consumer. The more price-conscious consumers there are in the market, the more responsive to price the quantity demanded for the hardcover version will be, and the more likely it is for Barnes & Noble's revenue to increase in response to the drop in price.

Conclusion

In this chapter, we have explored the important concept of elasticity. Table 6 summarizes the various elasticities we discussed in this chapter. Computing elasticities is important in economics because it allows us to measure how one variable changes in response to changes in another variable. For example, by calculating the price elasticity of demand for its product, a firm can make a quantitative estimate of the effect of a price change on the revenue it receives. Similarly, by calculating the price elasticity of demand for cigarettes, the government can better estimate the effect of an increase in cigarette taxes on smoking.

Read *An Inside Look* to use the concept of elasticity to analyze the Borders bookstores' Borders Rewards program.

PRICE ELASTICITY OF DEMAND

TABLE 6

Summary of Elasticities

Formula: $\dfrac{\text{Percentage change in quantity demanded}}{\text{Percentage change in price}}$

Midpoint Formula: $\dfrac{(Q_2 - Q_1)}{\left(\dfrac{Q_1 + Q_2}{2}\right)} \div \dfrac{(P_2 - P_1)}{\left(\dfrac{P_1 + P_2}{2}\right)}$

	ABSOLUTE VALUE OF PRICE ELASTICITY	EFFECT ON TOTAL REVENUE OF AN INCREASE IN PRICE
Elastic	Greater than 1	Total revenue falls
Inelastic	Less than 1	Total revenue rises
Unit elastic	Equal to 1	Total revenue unchanged

CROSS-PRICE ELASTICITY OF DEMAND

Formula: $\dfrac{\text{Percentage change in quantity demanded of one good}}{\text{Percentage change in price of another good}}$

TYPES OF PRODUCTS	VALUE OF CROSS-PRICE ELASTICITY
Substitutes	Positive
Complements	Negative
Unrelated	Zero

INCOME ELASTICITY OF DEMAND

Formula: $\dfrac{\text{Percentage change in quantity demanded}}{\text{Percentage change in income}}$

TYPES OF PRODUCTS	VALUE OF INCOME ELASTICITY
Normal and a necessity	Positive but less than 1
Normal and a luxury	Positive and greater than 1
Inferior	Negative

PRICE ELASTICITY OF SUPPLY

Formula: $\dfrac{\text{Percentage change in quantity supplied}}{\text{Percentage change in price}}$

	VALUE OF PRICE ELASTICITY
Elastic	Greater than 1
Inelastic	Less than 1
Unit elastic	Equal to 1

WALL STREET JOURNAL, MARCH 28, 2007

Borders Slashes Buyer Rewards, Cuts Discounts

The nation's second-largest book retailer, Borders Group Inc., has decided there can be too much of a good thing when it comes to its free membership-rewards program.

Less than a week after it reported disappointing fourth-quarter and annual results, Borders said that it is phasing out its popular Holiday Savings Rewards and Personal Shopping Days benefits and replacing them with a simpler, less-generous promotion called Borders Bucks.

The move will dramatically alter a program that has been a tremendous hit with consumers. Since the launch of the Borders Rewards membership club in February 2006, nearly 17 million people have signed up, and Borders continues to add an estimated 150,000 new customers each week. Borders' announcement comes at a time when many reward programs—including those from credit-card companies and airlines' frequent-flier plans—are tightening eligibility rules or becoming stingier with benefits.

Under the new Borders plan, each time customers reach $150 in purchases at Borders superstores or Waldenbooks stores, they will receive $5 in Borders Bucks at the beginning of the following month. They can then use that $5 until the end of that month, at which point the offer expires. Users will be contacted by e-mail and urged to print out a $5 coupon, although those who forget will be able to use their $5 credit by presenting their Borders Rewards card in stores. Customers will be able to earn Borders Bucks online after Borders opens its own Web site next year. . . .

But, under the old plan, discounts could be much deeper. Members were given Personal Shopping Days, which enabled those who had spent $50 in a month to apply a 10% discount on all purchases made on a specific day in the following month. Gift cards were the exception. Customers also received a credit equal to 5% of their store purchases made through Nov. 14 in a special Holiday Savings account. That credit could then be used on purchases made from Nov. 15 through Jan. 31. The only caveat was that customers had to have at least $10 in their account—which meant they had to have spent a minimum of $200 to qualify.

A big downside for Borders was that the company had to absorb all of the Holiday Savings account spending during its fourth quarter, a period when shoppers would have been in the stores anyway buying gifts. Under the new program, the impact on the company will be more regulated by enabling customers to claim their Borders Bucks year-round.

George Jones, the retailer's CEO, foreshadowed the changes to the program in January when he told investors that he intended to "make modifications in the program going forward." Earlier this month, Borders cited the "customer redemption of Borders Rewards benefits" as one of the reasons that gross margins as a percentage of sales decreased 3% in the fourth quarter.

In addition, Mr. Tam [Borders' chief marketing officer] said that Borders will now add special savings promotions to make up for the difference between the old and new programs. Although he declined to be specific, he said the retailer will be launching what it calls Bonus Rewards Events for all members. This could include days when discounts can be applied to all purchases, something previously available only to customers who had spent $50 in the prior month. Borders will also continue to send out weekly coupons via its e-mail newsletter.

Some customers weren't impressed. "Why bother?" asked Ron Goodenow, a market research consultant and writer in Northborough, Mass. "I find that on a lot of things that I'm interested in like music and DVDs that their prices are higher than the competition." The five dollars, he says, won't mean anything to him. "It's gratuitous considering how much they've hyped the program."

A spokeswoman for Borders said she believes that based on the retailer's market research, most customers will be happy with the changes.

Getty Images, Inc.

Key Points in the Article

Many retailers have programs that provide repeat buyers with price discounts. From a firm's point of view, whether a discount program is a good idea depends on how customers respond—that is, it depends on the price elasticity of demand. The Borders Rewards program reduces the price of books, but if the lower prices cause enough additional books to be sold, then total revenue will rise. This is why firms offer discount programs: They believe the programs raise total profits. However, not all discount programs increase total profits, and Borders recently changed its discount program for this reason.

Analyzing the News

(a) The Borders Rewards program is immensely popular, as indicated by the 17 million customers who signed up for the program during 2006. Will the Borders Rewards program increase the firm's revenue? Figure 1 shows the effect of a decrease in price on the quantity of books sold, and Figure 2 shows the effect on total revenue. A decrease in price will increase total revenue only if the firm is operating on the elastic region of the demand curve. Even if the firm starts off on the elastic region, it could cut prices so much that total revenue declines. That is exactly what Figure 2 shows.

(b) The old Borders Rewards program had several features designed to ensure that customers bought enough items to make the program profitable. First, customers who spent $50 in a month would receive a 10 percent discount on a specific day the following month. Second, those who spent at least $200 before November 14 received a special credit good for purchases at Borders through the holiday season. By imposing minimum purchase requirements on customers before they could qualify for discounts, Borders hoped that the Rewards program would increase sales enough to make the program profitable. Unfortunately, most of the credits were good during the holiday season, when customers were in the stores anyway, already purchasing books. The Rewards program gave customers discounts on books that they would probaby have bought anyway and did not lead customers to purchase many additional books.

In other words, the price discounts applied when the demand for books was relatively inelastic.

(c) In response to these problems, Borders has substantially changed its discount program. Customers will no longer receive the large holiday discounts. This means that the bulk of the discounts will no longer occur when the demand is relatively inelastic. However, this is no guarantee of success because the discounts offered in the new program may be too small, and too few customers may purchase the discounted books.

Thinking Critically

1. The purpose of discount programs is to increase sales and profits. However, a firm's competitors often have discount programs as well. Suppose Borders and Barnes & Noble both institute discount programs at the same time. Will revenue at Borders necessarily increase, even if Borders is currently on the elastic region of the demand curve?

2. The Internet has made it easy for consumers to buy books online. As a result, many traditional booksellers like Barnes & Noble and Borders (starting in 2008), along with Amazon, sell books on their Web sites. What effect has the Internet had on the demand curve for the books Borders sells in its (non-Internet) stores?

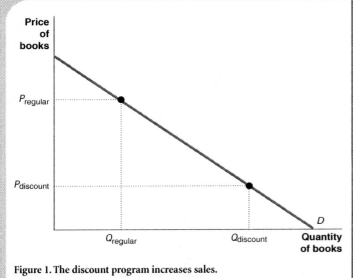

Figure 1. The discount program increases sales.

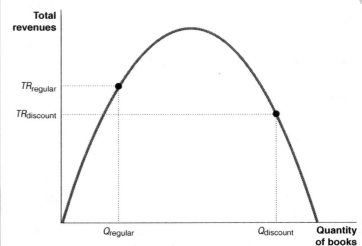

Figure 2. The discount program may not increase total revenues.

Key Terms

Cross-price elasticity of demand	Income elasticity of demand	Perfectly inelastic demand	Total revenue
Elastic demand	Inelastic demand	Price elasticity of demand	Unit-elastic demand
Elasticity	Perfectly elastic demand	Price elasticity of supply	

1 LEARNING OBJECTIVE 1 | Define the price elasticity of demand and understand how to measure it

The Price Elasticity of Demand and Its Measurement

Summary

Elasticity measures how much one economic variable responds to changes in another economic variable. The **price elasticity of demand** measures how responsive quantity demanded is to changes in price. The price elasticity of demand is equal to the percentage change in quantity demanded divided by the percentage change in price. If the quantity demanded changes more than proportionally when price changes, the price elasticity of demand is greater than 1 in absolute value, and demand is **elastic**. If the quantity demanded changes less than proportionally when price changes, the price elasticity of demand is less than 1 in absolute value, and demand is **inelastic**. If the quantity demanded changes proportionally when price changes, the price elasticity of demand is equal to 1 in absolute value, and demand is **unit elastic**. **Perfectly inelastic demand curves** are vertical lines, and **perfectly elastic** demand curves are horizontal lines. Relatively few products have perfectly elastic or perfectly inelastic demand curves.

myeconlab Visit www.myeconlab.com to complete these exercises
Get Ahead of the Curve online and get instant feedback.

Review Questions

1.1 Write the formula for the price elasticity of demand. Why isn't elasticity just measured by the slope of the demand curve?

1.2 If a 10 percent increase in the price of Cap'n Crunch cereal causes a 25 percent reduction in the number of boxes of cereal demanded, what is the price elasticity of demand for Cap'n Crunch cereal? Is demand for Cap'n Crunch elastic or inelastic?

1.3 What is the midpoint method for calculating price elasticity of demand? How else can you calculate the price elasticity of demand? What is the advantage of the midpoint method?

1.4 Draw a graph of a perfectly inelastic demand curve. Think of a product that would have a perfectly inelastic demand curve. Explain why demand for this product would be perfectly inelastic.

Problems and Applications

1.5 Suppose the following table gives data on the price of rye and the number of bushels of rye sold in 2008 and 2009.

YEAR	PRICE (DOLLARS PER BUSHEL)	QUANTITY (BUSHELS)
2008	$3.00	8 million
2009	2.00	12 million

a. Calculate the change in the quantity of rye demanded divided by the change in the price of rye. Measure the quantity of rye in bushels.

b. Calculate the change in the quantity of rye demanded divided by the change in the price of rye, but this time measure the quantity of rye in millions of bushels. Compare your answer to the one you computed in a.

c. Finally, assuming that the demand curve for rye did not shift between 2008 and 2009, use the information in the table to calculate the price elasticity of demand for rye. Use the midpoint formula in your calculation. Compare the value for the price elasticity of demand to the values you calculated in a and b.

1.6 **(Related to *Solved Problem 1*)** You own a hot dog stand that you set up outside the student union every day at lunch time. Currently, you are selling hot dogs for a price of $3, and you sell 30 hot dogs a day. You are considering cutting the price to $2. The following graph shows two possible increases in the quantity sold as a result of your price cut. Use the information in the graph to calculate the price elasticity between these two prices on each of the demand curves. Use the midpoint formula to calculate the price elasticities.

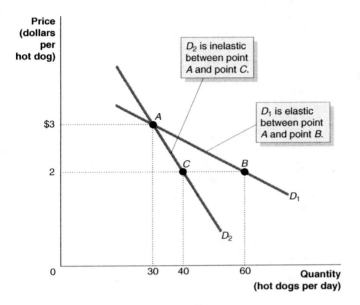

D₂ is inelastic between point A and point C.

D₁ is elastic between point A and point B.

1.7 In fall 2006, Pace University in New York raised its annual tuition from $24,751 to $29,454. Freshman enrollment declined from 1,469 in fall 2005 to 1,131 in fall 2006. Assuming that the demand curve for places in the freshmen class at Pace did not shift between 2005 and 2006, use this information to calculate the price elasticity of demand. Use the midpoint formula in your calculation. Is the demand for places in Pace's freshmen class elastic or inelastic? Did the total amount of tuition Pace received from its freshman class rise or fall in 2006 compared with 2005?

Source: Karen W. Arenson, "At Universities, Plum Post at Top Is Now Shaky," *New York Times*, January 9, 2007.

1.8 Consider the following excerpt from a newspaper story on increases in college tuition:

Facing stiff competition, Hendrix College, a small liberal arts institution in Conway, Ark., decided two years ago to bolster its academic offerings, promising students at least three hands-on experiences out-

side the classroom, including research, internships and service projects. It also raised tuition and fees 29 percent, to $21,636. . . . As a result, 409 students enrolled in the freshman class this year, a 37 percent increase. "What worked was the buzz," said J. Timothy Cloyd, the Hendrix president. "Students saw that they were going to get an experience that had value, and the price positioning conveyed to them the value of the experience."

Does this excerpt provide enough information to calculate the price elasticity of demand for places in Hendrix College's freshman class? Briefly explain.

Source: Jonathan D. Glater and Alan Finder, "In New Twist on Tuition Game, Popularity Rises with the Price," *New York Times*, December 12, 2006.

1.9 In summer 2007, Sony decided to cut the price of its PlayStation 3 video game console from $600 to $500. One industry analyst forecast that the price cut would increase sales from 80,000 units per month to 120,000 units per month. Assuming the analyst's forecast is correct, use the midpoint formula to calculate the price elasticity of demand for PlayStation 3.

Source: "Sony Cuts Price on PlayStation 3 by $100," *New York Times*, July 9, 2007.

1.10 In 1916, the Ford Motor Company sold 500,000 Model T Fords at a price of $440 each. Henry Ford believed that he could increase sales of the Model T by 1,000 cars for every dollar he cut the price. Use this information to calculate the price elasticity of demand for Model T Fords. Use the midpoint formula in your calculation.

1.11 **(Related to the *Don't Let This Happen to You!*)** The publisher of a magazine gives his staff the following information:

Current price	$2.00 per issue
Current sales	150,000 copies per month
Current total costs	$450,000 per month

He tells the staff, "Our costs are currently $150,000 more than our revenues each month. I propose to eliminate this problem by raising the price of the magazine to $3.00 per issue. This will result in our revenue being exactly equal to our cost." Do you agree with the publisher's analysis? Explain. (*Hint:* Remember that a firm's revenue is equal to the price of the product multiplied by the quantity sold.)

>> End Learning Objective 1

143

The Determinants of the Price Elasticity of Demand

Summary

The main determinants of the price elasticity of demand for a product are the availability of close substitutes, the passage of time, whether the good is a necessity or a luxury, how narrowly the market for the good is defined, and the share of the good in the consumer's budget.

 Visit www.myeconlab.com to complete these exercises *Get Ahead of the Curve* online and get instant feedback.

Review Questions

2.1 Is the demand for most agricultural products elastic or inelastic? Why?

2.2 What are the key determinants of the price elasticity of demand for a product? Which determinant is the most important?

Problems and Applications

2.3 Briefly explain whether the demand for each of the following products is likely to be elastic or inelastic.

a. Milk
b. Frozen cheese pizza
c. Cola
d. Prescription medicine

2.4 **(Related to the *Making the Connection*)** A study of the price elasticities of products sold in supermarkets contained the following data:

PRODUCT	PRICE ELASTICITY OF DEMAND
Soft drinks	−3.18
Canned soup	−1.62
Cheese	−0.72
Toothpaste	−0.45

a. For which products is the demand inelastic? Discuss reasons why the demand for each product is either elastic or inelastic.
b. Use the information in the table to predict the change in the quantity demanded for each product following a 10 percent price increase.

Source: Stephen J. Hoch, Byung-do Kim, Alan L. Montgomery, and Peter E. Rossi, "Determinants of Store-Level Price Elasticity," *Journal of Marketing Research*, Vol. 32, February 1995, pp. 17–29.

>> End Learning Objective 2

The Relationship between Price Elasticity of Demand and Total Revenue

Summary

Total revenue is the total amount of funds received by a seller of a good or service. When demand is inelastic, a decrease in price reduces total revenue, and an increase in price increases total revenue. When demand is elastic, a decrease in price increases total revenue, and an increase in price decreases total revenue. When demand is unit elastic, an increase or a decrease in price leaves total revenue unchanged.

 Visit www.myeconlab.com to complete these exercises *Get Ahead of the Curve* online and get instant feedback.

Review Questions

3.1 If the demand for orange juice is inelastic, will an increase in the price of orange juice increase or decrease the revenue received by orange juice sellers?

3.2 The price of organic apples falls and apple growers find that their revenue increases. Is the demand for organic apples elastic or inelastic?

Problems and Applications

3.3 A newspaper story on the effect of higher milk prices on the market for ice cream contained the following: "As a result [of the increase in milk prices], retail prices for ice cream are up 4 percent from last year. . . . And ice cream consumption is down 3 percent." Given this information, compute the price elasticity of demand for ice cream. Will the revenue received by ice cream suppliers have increased or decreased following the price increase? Briefly explain.

Source: John Curran, "Ice Cream, They Scream: Milk Fat Costs Drive Up Ice Cream Prices," Associated Press, July 23, 2001.

3.4 Use the following graph for Yolanda's Frozen Yogurt Stand to answer the questions that follow.

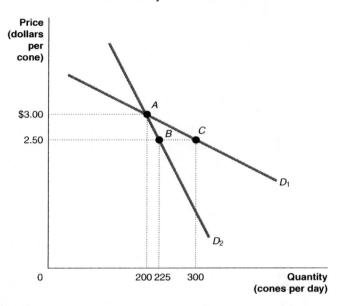

a. Use the midpoint formula to calculate the price elasticity of demand for D_1 between point A and point C and the price elasticity of demand for D_2 between point A and point B. Which demand curve is more elastic, D_1 or D_2? Briefly explain.

b. Suppose Yolanda is initially selling 200 cones per day at a price of $3.00 per cone. If she cuts her price to $2.50 per cone and her demand curve is D_1, what will be the change in her revenue? What will be the change in her revenue if her demand curve is D_2?

3.5 An article in the *Wall Street Journal* noted the following:

> Instead of relying on a full-coach, round-trip unrestricted fare of about $2,000 between Cleveland and Los Angeles . . . Continental [Airlines] since June has offered a $716 unrestricted fare in that market. . . . Through October, the test resulted in about the same revenue that Continental thinks it would have collected with its higher fare.

What is the value of the price elasticity of demand on this airline route? Is Continental likely to be better off charging the low fare or the high fare? Briefly explain.

Source: Scott McCartney, "Airlines Try Cutting Business Fares, Find They Don't Lose Revenue," *Wall Street Journal*, November 22, 2002.

3.6 (Related to *Solved Problem 3*) Briefly explain whether you agree or disagree with Manager 2's reasoning:

> **Manager 1:** "The only way we can increase the revenue we receive from selling our frozen pizzas is by cutting the price."

> **Manager 2:** "Cutting the price of a product never increases the amount of revenue you receive. If we want to increase revenue, we have to increase price."

3.7 (Related to the *Chapter Opener*) Consider the following description of a pricing decision by academic book publishers:

> A publisher may have issued a monograph several years ago, when both costs and book prices were lower, and priced it at $14.95. The book is still selling reasonably well and would continue to do so at $19.95. Why not, then, raise the price? The only danger is miscalculation: By raising the price you may reduce sales to the point where you make less money overall, even while making more per copy.

Assume that the situation described in the last sentence happens. What does this tell us about the price elasticity of demand for that book? Briefly explain.

Source: Beth Luey, *Handbook for Academic Authors*, 4th ed., Cambridge, UK: Cambridge University Press, 2002, p. 250.

3.8 Each summer, the city of Bethlehem, Pennsylvania, holds Musikfest, an outdoor music festival. The city had been charging $7 per day to park in city parking lots. One year it raised the fee to $10 per day. According to an article in a local newspaper, "Fewer parkers used city lots, but this year's parking rate increase [from $7 to $10] gave the [parking] authority record [parking] lot revenues for the annual festival." Use the information in the following table to calculate the price elasticity of demand for parking spaces in Bethlehem city parking lots during Musikfest; use the midpoint price elasticity of demand formula. Assume that nothing happened to shift the demand curve for parking places. Be sure to state whether demand is elastic or inelastic.

MUSIKFEST PARKING RATE REVENUE		
YEAR	RATE	REVENUE
1999	$10	$83,760
1998	7	77,791

Source: Matt Assad, "Grinch Alive and Well in Bethlehem Parking Authority," (*Allentown, Pennsylvania*) *Morning Call*, September 29, 1999, page B4.

3.9 An article about the newspaper industry that appeared in the *Wall Street Journal* noted the following: "Declining circulation hasn't stopped Knight Ridder papers from raising subscription prices. Such increases, while boosting revenue per copy, almost always trigger a readership decline."

a. What is a newspaper's "circulation"?

b. To what is "revenue per copy" equal?

c. Why would a newspaper's management increase its subscription price if the result was a decline in the quantity of newspapers sold?

Source: Patricia Callahan and Kevin Helliker, "Subscriptions Fall, but Knight Ridder Lifts Advertising Rates," *Wall Street Journal*, June 18, 2001.

3.10 (Related to the *Chapter Opener*) Look again at the quote from Stephen Rubin of Doubleday at the beginning of this chapter. Doubleday is selling John Grisham's book *The Innocent Man* at a price of $28.95.

a. Assume that the demand for this book is perfectly inelastic. Draw a demand curve showing the effect on the quantity demanded of raising the price from $28.95 to $39.95. Assume that sales are 500,000 at a price of $28.95. What is the change in revenue as a result of the price change?

b. Now assume that the price elasticity of demand is −2. Draw another demand curve showing the effect of raising the price from $28.95 to $39.95. Be sure to show the quantity demanded at each price. Now what is the change in revenue as a result of the price change?

3.11 The Delaware River Joint Toll Bridge Commission increased the toll on the bridges on Route 22 and Interstate 78 from New Jersey to Pennsylvania from $0.50 to $1.00. Use the information in the table to answer the questions. (Assume that nothing other than the toll change occurred during the months that would affect consumer demand.)

NUMBER OF VEHICLES CROSSING THE BRIDGE			
MONTH	**TOLL**	**ROUTE 22 BRIDGE**	**INTERSTATE 78 BRIDGE**
November	$0.50	519,337	728,022
December	1.00	433,691	656,257

a. Calculate the price elasticity of demand for each bridge, using the midpoint formula.

b. How much total revenue did the commission collect from these bridges in November? How much did it collect in December? Relate your answer to your answer in part a.

Source: Garrett Therolf, "Frugal Drivers Flood Free Bridge," (*Allentown, Pennsylvania*) *Morning Call*, January 20, 2003.

3.12 (Related to the *Making the connection*) Suppose you check out the prices of two products on Amazon.com: Conventional DVD players and HD (or Blu-Ray) DVD players. For which type of players would you expect manufacturers to be offering similar players at about the same prices and for which type of players would you expect prices to be more spread out? Briefly explain.

>> End Learning Objective 3

---

4 LEARNING OBJECTIVE   4 | Define the cross-price elasticity of demand and the income elasticity of demand, and understand their determinants and how they are measured

Other Demand Elasticities

Summary

Other important demand elasticities are the **cross-price elasticity of demand**, which is equal to the percentage change in quantity demanded of one good divided by the percentage change in the price of another good, and the **income elasticity of demand**, which is equal to the percentage change in the quantity demanded divided by the percentage change in income.

myeconlab Visit www.myeconlab.com to complete these exercises
Get Ahead of the Curve online and get instant feedback.

Review Questions

4.1 Define the cross-price elasticity of demand. What does it mean if the cross-price elasticity of demand is negative? What does it mean if the cross-price elasticity of demand is positive?

4.2 Define the income elasticity of demand. Use income elasticity to distinguish a normal good from an inferior good. Is it possible to tell from the income elasticity of demand whether a product is a luxury good or a necessity good?

Problems and Applications

4.3 In spring 2002, lettuce prices doubled, from about $1.50 per head to about $3.00. The reaction of one consumer was quoted in a newspaper article: "I will not buy [lettuce] when it's $3 a head," she said, adding that other green vegetables can fill in for lettuce. "If bread were $5 a loaf we'd still have to buy it. But lettuce is not that important in our family."

a. For this consumer's household, which product has the higher price elasticity of demand: bread or lettuce? Briefly explain.

b. Is the cross-price elasticity of demand between lettuce and other green vegetables positive or negative for this consumer? Briefly explain.

Source: Justin Bachman, "Sorry, Romaine Only," Associated Press, March 29, 2002.

4.4 In the following graph, the demand for hot dog buns has shifted outward because the price of hot dogs has fallen from $2.20 to $1.80 per package. Calculate the cross-price elasticity of demand between hot dogs and hot dog buns.

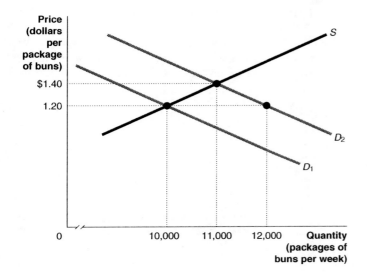

4.5 Are the cross-price elasticities of demand between the following pairs of products likely to be positive or negative? Briefly explain.

a. Pepsi and Coca-Cola

b. French fries and ketchup

c. Steak and chicken

d. HD-DVD players and HD-DVDs

4.6 After World War II, the Japanese government intervened in the economy to provide aid to certain industries that it believed would be most important in the recovery from war. One of the requirements for receiving government aid was that an industry had to be producing a good with a high income elasticity of demand. Why do you think the Japanese government made this a requirement?

4.7 Rank the following four goods from lowest income elasticity of demand to highest income elasticity of demand. Briefly explain your ranking.

a. Bread

b. Pepsi

c. Mercedes-Benz automobiles

d. Personal computers

4.8 (Related to the *Making the Connection*) Is the cross-price elasticity of demand between wine and spirits likely to be positive or negative? Can you think of reasons why the income elasticity of demand for wine is so much higher than the income elasticity of demand for spirits?

>> End Learning Objective 4

---

5 LEARNING OBJECTIVE   5 | Use price elasticity and income elasticity to analyze economic issues

Using Elasticity to Analyze the Disappearing Family Farm

Summary

Price elasticity and income elasticity can be used to analyze many economic issues. One example is the disappearance of the family farm in the United States. Because the income elasticity of demand for food is low, the demand for food has not increased proportionally as incomes in the United States have grown. As farmers have become more productive, they have increased the supply of most foods. Because the price elasticity of demand for food is

low, increasing supply has resulted in continually falling food prices.

myeconlab   Visit www.myeconlab.com to complete these exercises
Get Ahead of the Curve online and get instant feedback.

Review Question

5.1 The demand for agricultural products is inelastic, and the income elasticity of demand for agricultural products is low. How do these facts help explain the disappearing family farm?

Problems and Applications

5.2 **(Related to *Solved Problem 6-5*)** According to a study by the U.S. Centers for Disease Control and Prevention, the price elasticity of demand for cigarettes is −0.25. Americans purchase about 480 billion cigarettes each year.

   a. If the federal tax on cigarettes were increased enough to raise the price of cigarettes by 50 percent, what would be the effect on the quantity of cigarettes demanded?

   b. Is raising the tax on cigarettes a more effective way to reduce smoking if the demand for cigarettes is elastic or if it is inelastic? Briefly explain.

Source: "Response to Increases in Cigarette Prices by Race/Ethnicity, Income, and Age Groups—United States, 1976–1993," *Morbidity and Mortality Weekly Report*, July 31, 1998.

5.3 **(Related to *Solved Problem 6-5*)** The price elasticity of demand for cocaine has been estimated at −0.28. Suppose that a successful war on illegal drugs reduces the supply of cocaine in the United States enough to result in a 20 percent increase in its price. What will be the percentage reduction in the quantity of cocaine demanded?

Source: Henry Saffer and Frank Chaloupka, "The Demand for Illicit Drugs," *Economic Inquiry*, Vol. 37, No. 3, July 1999, pp. 401–411.

5.4 The price elasticity of demand for most agricultural products is quite low. What effect is this likely to have on how much the prices of these products change from year to year? Illustrate your answer with a demand and supply graph.

5.5 The head of the United Kumquat Growers Association makes the following statement:

> The federal government is considering implementing a price floor in the market for kumquats. The government will not be able to buy any surplus kumquats produced at the price floor or to pay us any other subsidy. Because the demand for kumquats is elastic, I believe this program will make us worse off, and I say we should oppose it.

Explain whether you agree or disagree with this reasoning.

5.6 Will there be a greater loss of economic efficiency from a price ceiling when demand is elastic or inelastic? Illustrate your answer with a demand and supply graph.

>> **End Learning Objective 5**

6 LEARNING OBJECTIVE 6 | Define the price elasticity of supply and understand its main determinants and how it is measured

The Price Elasticity of Supply and Its Measurement

Summary

The **price elasticity of supply** is equal to the percentage change in quantity supplied divided by the percentage change in price. The supply curves for most goods are inelastic over a short period of time, but they become increasingly elastic over longer periods of time. Perfectly inelastic demand curves are vertical lines, and perfectly elastic supply curves are horizontal lines. Relatively few products have perfectly elastic or perfectly inelastic supply curves.

myeconlab Visit www.myeconlab.com to complete these exercises online and get instant feedback.

Review Questions

6.1 Write the formula for the price elasticity of supply. If an increase of 10 percent in the price of frozen pizzas results in a 9 percent increase in the quantity of frozen pizzas supplied, what is the price elasticity of supply for frozen pizzas? Is the supply of pizzas elastic or inelastic?

6.2 What is the main determinant of the price elasticity of supply?

Problems and Applications

6.3 **(Related to the *Making the Connection*)** Suppose the demand for oil declines. Will the equilibrium price of oil decline more if the supply of oil is elastic or if it is inelastic? Illustrate your answer with a demand and supply graph.

6.4 Use the midpoint formula for calculating elasticity to calculate the price elasticity of supply between point *A* and point *B* for each panel of Figure 5.

6.5 Briefly explain whether you agree with the following statement: "The longer the period of time following an increase in the demand for apples, the greater the increase in the equilibrium quantity of apples and the smaller the increase in the equilibrium price."

6.6 On most days, the price of a rose is $1, and 8,000 roses are purchased. On Valentine's Day, the price of a rose jumps to $2, and 30,000 roses are purchased.

    a. Draw a demand and supply diagram that shows why the price jumps.

b. Based on this information, what do we know about the price elasticity of demand for roses? What do we know about the price elasticity of supply for roses? Calculate values for the price elasticity of demand and the price elasticity of supply or explain why you can't calculate these values.

>> **End Learning Objective 6**

Firms, the Stock Market, and Corporate Governance

From Chapter 7 of *Microeconomics*, 2/e. R. Glenn Hubbard. Anthony Patrick O'Brien. Copyright © 2008 by Pearson Prentice Hall.

Firms, the **Stock Market**, and **Corporate Governance**

Google: From Dorm Room to Wall Street

There could be no question that Google was cool. The world's most widely used Internet search engine, Google had become the essence of cool as a way to research information stored on Web sites. Founded in 1998 by Larry Page and Sergey Brin, Google grew quickly. By 2006, Google employed 10,000 people and earned $10.6 billion in revenue. Google's founders had transformed the Internet search engine and brought value to users through a combination of intellect, technology, and the talents of many employees. Google's key advantage over competitors such as A9 and Ask Jeeves was its search algorithms that allowed users to easily find the Web sites most relevant to a subject. Google had other advantages as well, such as its automatic foreign-language translation. Google had become so dominant that other major Web sites, such as AOL and Yahoo, were using it as their search engine. Google has also succeeded in expand-

ing into foreign markets. In China, Google has been successful even though it remains in a struggle for market share with the local Chinese firm Baidu.com.

And Google was hot. In 2004, Google sold part of the firm to outside investors by offering stock—and partial ownership—to the public. This stock offering vaulted Larry Page and Sergey Brin to the ranks of the super-rich. Google's stock offering also gained significant press attention, as the firm bypassed conventional financial practice and used an automated online auction to help set the share price and determine who should receive stock. The offering's size grabbed attention, too: It was the most anticipated stock sale since the 1995 launch of Netscape, a deal that sparked the late-1990s Internet gold rush on Wall Street.

As Google grew larger, it was less the informal organization put together by the founders and more a complex organization with greater need for management and funds to grow. Indeed, Google's offering of stock to outside investors provided the firm

with a major inflow of funds for growth.

Once a firm grows very large, its owners often do not continue to manage it. Large corporations are owned by millions of individual investors who have purchased the firms' stock. With ownership so dispersed, the top managers who actually run a firm have the opportunity to make decisions that are in the managers' best interests but that may not be in the best interests of the stockholders who own the firm.

Against this backdrop, Google faced significant costs associated with selling stock to the public. High-profile corporate accounting scandals in 2001 and 2002 at major U.S. firms, such as Enron, WorldCom, and Tyco, led to the passage of stronger—and more costly—securities regulation under the Sarbanes-Oxley Act, enacted by Congress in 2002. Google's growth prospects and the health of the financial system were intertwined. **AN INSIDE LOOK** discusses the compensation Google pays its top executives.

AP Wide World Photos

LEARNING Objectives

After studying this chapter, you should be able to:

1   Categorize the major **types of firms** in the United States.

2   Describe the typical **management structure** of corporations and understand the concepts of **separation of ownership from control** and the **principal-agent problem**.

3   Explain how firms obtain the **funds** they need to **operate** and **expand**.

4   Understand the information provided in corporations' **financial statements**.

5   Understand the role of government in **corporate governance**.

APPENDIX Understand the concept of **present value** and the information contained on a firm's **income statement** and **balance sheet**.

Economics in YOUR Life!

Is It Risky to Own Stock?

Although stockholders legally own corporations, managers often have a great deal of freedom in deciding how corporations are run. As a result, managers can make decisions, such as spending money on large corporate headquarters or decorating their offices with expensive paintings, that are in their interests but not in the interests of the shareholders. If managers make decisions that waste money and lower the profits of a firm, the price of the firm's stock will fall, which hurts the investors who own the stock. Suppose you own stock in a corporation, such as Google. Why is it difficult to get the managers to act in your interest rather than in their own? Given this problem, should you ever take on the risk of buying stock? As you read the chapter, see if you can answer these questions. You can check your answers against those we provide at the end of the chapter.

I n this chapter, we look at the firm: how it is organized, how it raises funds, and the information it provides to investors. As we have already discussed, firms in a market system are responsible for organizing the factors of production to produce goods and services. Firms are the vehicles entrepreneurs use to earn profits. To succeed, entrepreneurs must meet consumer wants by producing new or better goods and services or by finding ways of producing existing goods and services at a lower cost so they can be sold at a lower price. Entrepreneurs also need access to sufficient funds, and they must be able to efficiently organize production. As the typical firm in many industries has become larger during the past 100 years, the task of efficiently organizing production has become more difficult. Toward the end of this chapter, we look at why a series of corporate scandals occurred beginning in 2002 and at the steps firms and the government have taken to avoid similar problems in the future.

1 | Categorize the major types of firms in the United States.

Types of Firms

In studying a market economy, it is important to understand the basics of how firms operate. In the United States, there are three legal categories of firms: *sole proprietorships, partnerships,* and *corporations.* A **sole proprietorship** is a firm owned by a single individual. Although most sole proprietorships are small, some are quite large in terms of sales, number of persons employed, and profits earned. **Partnerships** are firms owned jointly by two or more—sometimes many—persons. Most law and accounting firms are partnerships. The famous Lloyd's of London insurance company is a partnership. Although some partnerships, such as Lloyd's, can be quite large, most large firms are organized as *corporations.* A **corporation** is a legal form of business that provides the owners with limited liability.

Who Is Liable? Limited and Unlimited Liability

A key distinction among the three types of firms is that the owners of sole proprietorships and partnerships have unlimited liability. Unlimited liability means there is no legal distinction between the personal assets of the owners of the firm and the assets of the firm. An **asset** is anything of value owned by a person or a firm. If a sole proprietorship or a partnership owes a lot of money to the firm's suppliers or employees, the suppliers and employees have a legal right to sue the firm for payment, even if this requires the firm's owners to sell some of their personal assets, such as stocks or bonds. In other words, with sole proprietorships and partnerships, the owners are not legally distinct from the firms they own.

It may seem only fair that the owners of a firm be responsible for a firm's debts. But early in the nineteenth century, it became clear to many state legislatures in the United States that unlimited liability was a significant problem for any firm that was attempting to raise funds from large numbers of investors. An investor might be interested in making a relatively small investment in a firm but be unwilling to become a partner in the firm for fear of placing at risk all of his or her personal assets if the firm were to fail. To get around this problem, state legislatures began to pass *general incorporation laws,* which allowed firms to be organized as corporations. Under the corporate form of business, the owners of a firm have **limited liability**, which means that if the firm fails, the owners can never lose more than the amount they had invested in the firm. The personal assets of the owners of the firm are not affected by the failure of the firm. In fact, in the eyes of the law, a corporation is a legal "person" separate from its owners. Limited

Sole proprietorship A firm owned by a single individual and not organized as a corporation.

Partnership A firm owned jointly by two or more persons and not organized as a corporation.

Corporation A legal form of business that provides the owners with limited liability.

Asset Anything of value owned by a person or a firm.

Limited liability The legal provision that shields owners of a corporation from losing more than they have invested in the firm.

	SOLE PROPRIETORSHIP	PARTNERSHIP	CORPORATION
ADVANTAGES	• Control by owner • No layers of management	• Ability to share work • Ability to share risks	• Limited personal liability • Greater ability to raise funds
DISADVANTAGES	• Unlimited personal liability • Limited ability to raise funds	• Unlimited personal liability • Limited ability to raise funds	• Costly to organize • Possible double taxation of income

TABLE 1

Differences among Business Organizations

liability has made it possible for corporations to raise funds by issuing shares of stock to large numbers of investors. For example, if you buy a share of Google stock, you are a part owner of the firm, but even if Google were to go bankrupt, you would not be personally responsible for any of Google's debts. Therefore, you could not lose more than the amount you paid for the stock.

Corporate organizations also have some disadvantages. In the United States, corporate profits are taxed twice—once at the corporate level and again when investors receive a share of corporate profits. Corporations generally are larger than sole proprietorships and partnerships and therefore more difficult to organize and run. Table 1 reviews the advantages and disadvantages of different forms of business organization.

Making the Connection | What's in a "Name"? Lloyd's of London Learns about Unlimited Liability the Hard Way

The world-famous insurance company Lloyd's of London got its start in Edward Lloyd's coffeehouse in London in the late 1600s. Ship owners would come to the coffeehouse looking for someone to insure (or "underwrite") their ships and cargos in exchange for a flat fee (or "premium"). The customers of the coffeehouse, themselves merchants or ship owners, who agreed to insure ships or cargos would have to make payment from their personal funds if an insured ship was lost at sea. By the late 1700s, the system had become more formal: Each underwriter would recruit investors, known as "Names," and use the funds raised to back insurance policies sold to a wide variety of clients. In the twentieth century, Lloyd's became famous for some of its unusual insurance policies. It issued a policy insuring the legs of Betty Grable, a 1940s movie star. One man bought an insurance policy against seeing a ghost.

By the late 1980s, 34,000 persons around the world had invested in Lloyd's as Names. A series of disasters in the late 1980s and early 1990s—including the *Exxon Valdez* oil spill in Alaska, Hurricane Hugo in South Carolina, and an earthquake in San Francisco—resulted in huge payments on insurance policies written by Lloyd's. In 1989, Lloyd's lost $3.85 billion. In 1990, it lost an additional $4.4 billion. It then became clear to many of the Names that Lloyd's was not a corporation and that the Names did not have the limited liability enjoyed by corporate shareholders. On the contrary, the Names were personally responsible for paying the losses on the insurance policies. Many Names lost far more than they had invested. Some investors, such as Charles Schwab, the discount stockbroker, were wealthy enough to sustain their losses, but others were less fortunate. One California investor ended up living in poverty after having to sell his $1 million house to pay his share of the losses. Another Name, Sir Richard Fitch, a British admiral, committed suicide after most of his wealth was wiped out. As many as 30 Names may have committed suicide as a result of their losses.

By 2007, only 1,100 Names—undoubtedly sadder but wiser—remained as investors in Lloyd's. New rules have allowed insurance companies to underwrite

Investors in Lloyd's of London lost billions of dollars during the 1980s and 1990s.

Ed Pritchard, Getty Images Inc.–Stone Allstock

Lloyd's policies for the first time. Today, Names provide only about 20 percent of Lloyd's funds.

Sources: "The Rip van Winkle of Risk," *Economist*, January 4, 2007; Charles Fleming, "The Master of Disaster Is Trying to Avoid One," *Wall Street Journal*, November 17, 2003; and "Lloyd's of London: Insuring for the Future," *Economist*, September 16, 2004.

YOUR TURN: Test your understanding by doing related problem 1.4 and 1.5 at the end of this chapter.

Corporations Earn the Majority of Revenue and Profits

Figure 1 gives basic statistics on the three types of business organizations. Panel (a) shows that almost three-quarters of all firms are sole proprietorships. Panels (b) and (c) show that although only 20 percent of all firms are corporations, corporations account for the majority of revenue and profits earned by all firms. *Profit* is the difference between revenue and the total cost to a firm of producing the goods and services it offers for sale.

There are more than 5 million corporations in the United States, but only 26,000 have annual revenues of more than $50 million. We can think of these 26,000 firms—including Microsoft, General Electric, and Google—as representing "big business." These large firms earn almost 85 percent of the total profits of all corporations in the United States.

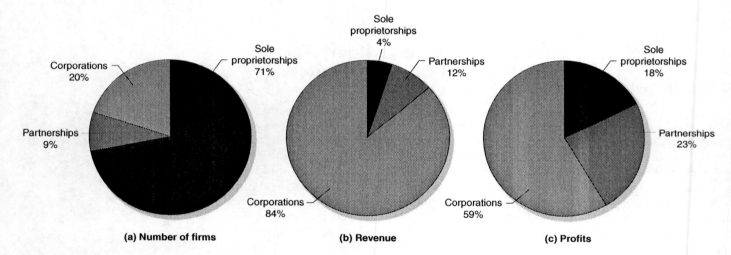

(a) Number of firms   **(b) Revenue**   **(c) Profits**

Figure 1 | Business Organizations: Sole Proprietorships, Partnerships, and Corporations

The three types of firms in the United States are sole proprietorships, partnerships, and corporations. Panel (a) shows that only 20 percent of all firms are corporations.

Yet, as panels (b) and (c) show, corporations account for a majority of the total revenue and profits earned by all firms.
Source: U.S. Census Bureau, *The 2007 Statistical Abstract of the United States.*

---

2 LEARNING OBJECTIVE

2 | Describe the typical management structure of corporations and understand the concepts of separation of ownership from control and the principal-agent problem.

The Structure of Corporations and the Principal-Agent Problem

Corporate governance The way in which a corporation is structured and the effect a corporation's structure has on the firm's behavior.

Because large corporations account for most sales and profits in the economy, it is important to know how they are managed. Most large corporations have a similar management structure. The way in which a corporation is structured and the effect a corporation's structure has on the firm's behavior is referred to as **corporate governance**.

Corporate Structure and Corporate Governance

Corporations are legally owned by their *shareholders*, the owners of the corporation's stock. Unlike family businesses, a corporation's shareholders, although they are the firm's owners, do not manage the firm directly. Instead, they elect a *board of directors* to represent their interests. The board of directors appoints a *chief executive officer* (CEO) to run the day-to-day operations of the corporation. Sometimes the board of directors also appoints other members of *top management*, such as the *chief financial officer* (CFO). At other times, the CEO appoints other members of top management. Members of top management, including the CEO and CFO, often serve on the board of directors. Members of management serving on the board of directors are referred to as *inside directors*. Members of the board of directors who do not have a direct management role in the firm are referred to as *outside directors*. The outside directors are intended to act as checks on the decisions of top managers, but the distinction between an outside director and an inside director is not always clear. For example, the CEO of a firm that sells a good or service to a large corporation may sit on the board of directors of that corporation. Although an outside director, this person may be reluctant to displease the top managers because the top managers have the power to stop purchasing from his firm. In some instances, top managers have effectively controlled their firms' boards of directors.

Unlike founder-dominated businesses, the top management of large corporations does not generally own a large share of the firm's stock, so large corporations have a **separation of ownership from control**. Although the shareholders actually own the firm, top management controls the day-to-day operations of the firm. Because top managers do not own the entire firm, they may have an incentive to decrease the firm's profits by spending money to purchase private jets or schedule management meetings at luxurious resorts. Economists refer to the conflict between the interests of shareholders and the interests of top management as a **principal–agent problem**. This problem occurs when agents—in this case, a firm's top management—pursue their own interests rather than the interests of the principal who hired them—in this case, the shareholders of the corporation. To reduce the impact of the principal–agent problem, many boards of directors in the 1990s began to tie the salaries of top managers to the profits of the firm or to the price of the firm's stock. They hoped this would give top managers an incentive to make the firm as profitable as possible, thereby benefiting its shareholders.

Separation of ownership from control A situation in a corporation in which the top management, rather than the shareholders, control day-to-day operations.

Principal–agent problem A problem caused by an agent pursuing his own interests rather than the interests of the principal who hired him.

Solved Problem | 2

Does the Principal–Agent Problem Apply to the Relationship between Managers and Workers?

Briefly explain whether you agree or disagree with the following argument:

> The principal–agent problem applies not just to the relationship between shareholders and top managers. It also applies to the relationship between managers and workers. Just as shareholders have trouble monitoring whether top managers are earning as much profit as possible, managers have trouble monitoring whether workers are working as hard as possible.

SOLVING THE PROBLEM:

Step 1: **Review the chapter material.** This problem concerns the principal–agent problem, so you may want to review the section "Corporate Structure and Corporate Governance," which is on this page.

Step 2: **Evaluate the argument.** You should agree with the argument. A corporation's shareholders have difficulty monitoring the activities of top managers. In practice, they attempt to do so indirectly through the corporation's board of directors. But the firm's top managers may influence—or even control—the firm's board of directors. Even if top managers do not control a board of directors, it may be difficult for the board to know whether actions managers take—say, opening a branch office in Paris—will increase the profitability of the firm or just increase the enjoyment of the top managers.

To answer the problem, we must extend this analysis to the relationship between managers and workers: Managers would like workers to work as hard as possible. Workers would often rather not work hard, particularly if they do not see a direct financial reward for doing so. Managers can have trouble monitoring whether workers are working hard or goofing off. Is that worker in his cubicle diligently staring at a computer screen because he is hard at work on a report or because he is surfing the Web for sports scores or writing a long e-mail to his girlfriend? So, the principal–agent problem does apply to the relationship between managers and workers.

EXTRA CREDIT: Boards of directors try to reduce the principal–agent problem by designing compensation policies for top managers that give them financial incentives to increase profits. Similarly, managers try to reduce the principal–agent problem by designing compensation policies that give workers an incentive to work harder. For example, some manufacturers pay factory workers on the basis of how much they produce rather than on the basis of how many hours they work.

YOUR TURN: For more practice, do related problems 2.4 and 2.5 at the end of this chapter.

>> **End Solved Problem 2**

---

3 | Explain how firms obtain the funds they need to operate and expand.

How Firms Raise Funds

Owners and managers of firms try to earn a profit. To earn a profit, a firm must raise funds to pay for its operations, including paying its employees and buying machines. Indeed, a central challenge for anyone running a firm, whether that person is a sole proprietor or a top manager of a large corporation, is raising the funds needed to operate and expand the business. Suppose you decide to open an online trading service using $100,000 you have saved in a bank. You use the $100,000 to rent a building for your firm, to buy computers, and to pay other start-up expenses. Your firm is a great success, and you decide to expand by moving to a larger building and buying more computers. As the owner of a small business, you can obtain the funds for this expansion in three ways:

1 If you are making a profit, you could reinvest the profits back into your firm. Profits that are reinvested in a firm rather than taken out of a firm and paid to the firm's owners are *retained earnings*.

2 You could obtain funds by taking on one or more partners who invest in the firm. This arrangement would increase the firm's *financial capital*.

3 Finally, you could borrow the funds from relatives, friends, or a bank.

The managers of a large firm have some additional ways to raise funds, as we will see in the next section.

Sources of External Funds

Unless firms rely on retained earnings, they have to obtain the *external funds* they need from others who have funds available to invest. It is the role of an economy's *financial system* to transfer funds from savers to borrowers—directly through financial markets or indirectly through financial intermediaries such as banks.

Firms can raise external funds in two ways. The first relies on financial intermediaries such as banks and is called **indirect finance**. If you put $1,000 in a checking account or a savings account, or if you buy a $1,000 certificate of deposit (CD), the bank will loan most of those funds to borrowers. The bank will combine your funds with those of other depositors and, for example, make a $100,000 loan to a local business. Small businesses rely heavily on bank loans as their primary source of external funds.

The second way for firms to acquire external funds is through *financial markets*. Raising funds in these markets, such as the New York Stock Exchange on Wall Street in New York, is called **direct finance**. Direct finance usually takes the form of the borrower selling the lender a *financial security*. A financial security is a document—sometimes in electronic form—that states the terms under which the funds have passed from the buyer of the security—who is lending funds—to the borrower. *Bonds* and *stocks* are the two main types of financial securities. Typically, only large corporations are able to sell bonds and stocks on financial markets. Investors are generally unwilling to buy securities issued by small and medium-sized firms because the investors lack sufficient information on the financial health of smaller firms.

Bonds **Bonds** are financial securities that represent promises to repay a fixed amount of funds. When General Electric (GE) sells a bond to raise funds, it promises to pay the purchaser of the bond an interest payment each year for the term of the bond, as well as a final payment of the amount of the loan, or the *principal*, at the end of the term. GE may need to raise many millions of dollars to build a factory, but each individual bond has a principal, or *face value*, of $1,000, which is the amount each bond purchaser is lending GE. So, GE must sell many bonds to raise all the funds it needs. Suppose GE promises it will pay interest of $60 per year to anyone who will buy one of its bonds. The interest payments on a bond are referred to as **coupon payments**. The **interest rate** is the cost of borrowing funds, usually expressed as a percentage of the amount borrowed. If we express the coupon as a percentage of the face value of the bond, we find the interest rate on the bond, called the *coupon rate*. In this case, the interest rate is:

$$\frac{\$60}{\$1,000} = 0.06, \text{ or } 6\%.$$

Many bonds that corporations issue have terms, or *maturities*, of 30 years. For example, if you bought a bond from GE, GE would pay you $60 per year for 30 years, and at the end of the thirtieth year, GE would pay you back the $1,000 principal.

Stocks When you buy a newly issued bond from a firm, you are lending funds to that firm. When you buy **stock** issued by a firm, you are actually buying part ownership of the firm. When a corporation sells stock, it is doing the same thing the owner of a small business does when she takes on a partner: The firm is increasing its financial capital by bringing additional owners into the firm. Any individual shareholder usually owns only a small fraction of the total shares of stock issued by a corporation.

A shareholder is entitled to a share of the corporation's profits, if there are any. Corporations generally keep some of their profits—known as retained earnings—to finance future expansion. The remaining profits are paid to shareholders as **dividends**. If investors expect the firm to earn economic profits on its retained earnings, the firm's share price will rise, providing a *capital gain* for investors. If a corporation is unable to

Indirect finance A flow of funds from savers to borrowers through financial intermediaries such as banks. Intermediaries raise funds from savers to lend to firms (and other borrowers).

Direct finance A flow of funds from savers to firms through financial markets, such as the New York Stock Exchange.

Bond A financial security that represents a promise to repay a fixed amount of funds.

Coupon payment An interest payment on a bond.

Interest rate The cost of borrowing funds, usually expressed as a percentage of the amount borrowed.

Stock A financial security that represents partial ownership of a firm.

Dividends Payments by a corporation to its shareholders.

make a profit, it usually does not pay a dividend. Under the law, corporations must make payments on any debt they have before making payments to their owners. That is, a corporation must make promised payments to bondholders before it may make any dividend payments to shareholders. In addition, when firms sell stock, they acquire from investors an open-ended commitment of funds to the firm. Therefore, unlike bonds, stocks do not have a maturity date, so the firm is not obliged to return the investor's funds at any particular date.

Stock and Bond Markets Provide Capital— and Information

The original purchasers of stocks and bonds may resell them to other investors. In fact, most of the buying and selling of stocks and bonds that takes place each day is investors reselling existing stocks and bonds to each other rather than corporations selling new stocks and bonds to investors. The buyers and sellers of stocks and bonds together make up the *stock and bond markets*. There is no single place where stocks and bonds are bought and sold. Some trading of stocks and bonds takes place in buildings known as *exchanges*, such as the New York Stock Exchange or Tokyo Stock Exchange. In the United States, the stocks and bonds of the largest corporations are traded on the New York Stock Exchange. The development of computer technology has spread the trading of stocks and bonds outside exchanges to *securities dealers* linked by computers. These dealers comprise the *over-the-counter market*. The stocks of many computer and other high-technology firms—including Apple, Google, and Microsoft—are traded in the most important of the over-the-counter markets, the *National Association of Securities Dealers Automated Quotation* system, which is referred to by its acronym, Nasdaq.

Don't Let This Happen to **YOU!**

When Google Shares Change Hands, Google Doesn't Get the Money

Google is a popular investment, with investors buying and selling shares often as their views about the firm's valuation shift. That's great for Google, right? Think of all that money flowing into Google's coffers as shares change hands and the stock price goes up. *Wrong.* Google raises funds in a primary market, but shares change hands in a secondary market. Those trades don't put money into Google's hands, but they do give important information to the firm's managers. Let's see why.

Primary markets are those in which newly issued claims are sold to initial buyers by the issuer. Businesses can raise funds in a primary financial market in two ways—by borrowing (selling bonds) or by selling shares of stock—which result in different types of claims on the borrowing firm's future income. Although you hear about the stock market fluctuations each night on the evening news, bonds actually account for more of the funds raised by borrowers. In mid-2007, the value of bonds in the United States was about $27 trillion compared to $15 trillion for stocks, or equities.

In *secondary markets*, stocks and bonds that have already been issued are sold by one investor to another. If Google sells shares to the public, it is turning to a primary market for new funds. Once Google shares are issued, investors trade the shares in the secondary market. The founders of Google do not receive any new funds when Google shares are traded on secondary markets. The initial seller of a stock or bond raises funds from a lender only in the primary market. Secondary markets convey information to firms' managers and to investors by determining the price of financial instruments. For example, a major increase in Google's stock price conveys the market's good feelings about the firm, and the firm may decide to raise funds to expand. Hence, secondary markets are valuable sources of information for corporations that are considering raising funds.

Primary and secondary markets are both important, but they play different roles. As an investor, you principally trade stocks and bonds in a secondary market. As a corporate manager, you may help decide how to raise new funds to expand the firm where you work.

YOUR TURN: Test your understanding by doing related problem 3.10 at the end of this chapter.

Shares of stock represent claims on the profits of the firms that issue them. Therefore, as the fortunes of the firms change and they earn more or less profit, the prices of the stock the firms have issued should also change. Similarly, bonds represent claims to receive coupon payments and one final payment of principal. Therefore, a particular bond that was issued in the past may have its price go up or down, depending on whether the coupon payments being offered on newly issued bonds are higher or lower than on existing bonds. If you hold a bond with a coupon of $80 per year, and newly issued bonds have coupons of $100 per year, the price of your bond will fall because it is less attractive to investors. The price of a bond will be affected by changes in investors' perceptions of the issuing firm's ability to make the coupon payments. For example, if investors begin to believe that a firm may soon go out of business and stop making coupon payments to its bondholders, the price of the firm's bonds will fall to very low levels.

Changes in the value of a firm's stocks and bonds offer important information for a firm's managers, as well as for investors. An increase in the stock price means that investors are more optimistic about the firm's profit prospects, and the firm's managers may wish to expand the firm's operations as a result. By contrast, a decrease in the firm's stock price indicates that investors are less optimistic about the firms' profit prospects, so management may want to shrink the firm's operations. Likewise, changes in the value of the firm's bonds imply changes in the cost of external funds to finance the firm's investment in research and development or in new factories. A higher bond price indicates a lower cost of new external funds, while a lower bond price indicates a higher cost of new external funds.

Making the Connection

Following Abercrombie & Fitch's Stock Price in the Financial Pages

If you read the stock listings in your local paper or the *Wall Street Journal*, you will notice that newspapers manage to pack into a small space a lot of information about what happened to stocks during the previous day's trading. The figure on the next page reproduces a small portion of the listings from the *Wall Street Journal* from March 6, 2007, for stocks listed on the New York Stock Exchange. The listings provide information on the buying and selling of the stock of five firms during the previous day. Let's focus on the highlighted listing for Abercrombie & Fitch, the clothing store, and examine the information in each column:

- The first column gives the name of the company.

- The second column gives the firm's "ticker" symbol (ANF), which you may have seen scrolling along the bottom of the screen on cable financial news channels.

- The third column (Open) gives the price (in dollars) of the stock at the time that trading began, which is 9:30 A.M. on the New York Stock Exchange. Abercrombie & Fitch had opened for trading the previous day at a price of $74.54.

- The fourth column (High) and the fifth column (Low) give the highest price and the lowest price the stock sold for during the previous day.

- The sixth column (Close) gives the price the stock sold for the last time it was traded before the close of trading on the previous day (4:30 P.M.), which in this case was $73.42.

- The seventh column (Net Chg) gives the amount by which the closing price changed from the closing price the day before. In this case, the price of Abercrombie

& Fitch's stock had fallen by $1.52 per share from its closing price the day before. Changes in Abercrombie & Fitch's stock price give the firm's managers a signal that they may want to expand or contract the firm's operations.

- The eighth column (% Chg) gives the change in the price in percentage terms rather than in dollar terms.

- The ninth column (Vol) gives the number of shares of stock traded on the previous day.

- The tenth column (52 Week High) and the eleventh column (52 Week Low) give the highest price the stock has sold for and the lowest price the stock has sold for during the previous year. These numbers tell how *volatile* the stock price is—that is, how much it fluctuates over the course of the year.

- The twelfth column (Div) gives the dividend expressed in dollars. In this case, .70 means that Abercrombie paid a dividend of $0.70 per share.

- The thirteenth column (Yield) gives the *dividend yield*, which is calculated by dividing the dividend by the *closing price* of the stock—that is, the price at which Abercrombie's stock last sold before the close of trading on the previous day.

- The fourteenth column (PE) gives the *P-E ratio* (or *price-earnings ratio*), which is calculated by dividing the price of the firm's stock by its earnings per share. (Remember that because firms retain some earnings, earnings per share is not necessarily the same as dividends per share.) Abercrombie's P-E ratio was 16, meaning that its price per share was 16 times its earnings per share. You would have to pay $16 to buy $1 of Abercrombie & Fitch's earnings.

- The final column (Year-To-Date % Chg) gives the percentage change in the price of the stock from the beginning of the year to the previous day. In this case, the price of Abercrombie's stock had increased by 5.4 percent since the beginning of 2007.

	Symbol	Open	High	Low	Close	Net Chg	%Chg	Vol	52 Week High	52 Week Low	Div	Yield	PE	Year-To-Date %Chg
ABB LTD ADS	ABB	15.95	16.21	15.94	15.96	-0.56	-3.39	4,478,028	19.3	10.1	0.1	0.6	25	-11.2
ABBOTT LABORATORIES	ABT	52.80	53.59	52.72	52.75	-0.26	-0.49	6,910,610	55.1	40.6	1.30	2.5	48	8.3
ABERCROMBIE & FITCH CO.	ANF	74.54	75.07	73.37	73.42	-1.52	-2.03	1,580,908	83.8	50	0.7	1.0	16	5.4
ABITIBI-CONSOLIDATED INC.	ABY	2.72	2.74	2.70	2.70	-0.03	-1.1	965,400	4.53	2.23	...	...	...	5.5
ACADIA REALTY TRUST SBI	AKR	26.65	26.77	26.30	26.36	-0.49	-1.82	429,604	28.1	19.5	.80	3.0	22	5.4

Source: "Stock Prices from Abercrombie and Fitch" from *The Wall Street Journal*, March 6, 2007. Copyright © 2007 Dow Jones. Reprinted by permission of Dow Jones via Copyright Clearance Center

YOUR TURN: Test your understanding by doing related problem 3.11 at the end of this chapter.

Using Financial Statements to Evaluate a Corporation

To raise funds, a firm's managers must persuade financial intermediaries or buyers of its bonds or stock that it will be profitable. Before a firm can sell new issues of stock or bonds, it must first provide investors and financial regulators with information about its finances. To borrow from a bank or another financial intermediary, the firm must disclose financial information to the lender as well.

In most high-income countries, government agencies require firms that want to sell securities in financial markets to disclose specific financial information to the public. In the United States, the Securities and Exchange Commission requires publicly owned firms to report their performance in financial statements prepared using standard accounting methods, often referred to as *generally accepted accounting principles*. Such disclosure reduces information costs, but it doesn't eliminate them—for two reasons. First, some firms may be too young to have much information for potential investors to evaluate. Second, managers may try to present the required information in the best possible light so that investors will overvalue their securities.

Private firms also collect information on business borrowers and sell the information to lenders and investors. As long as the information-gathering firm does a good job, lenders and investors purchasing the information will be better able to judge the quality of borrowing firms. Firms specializing in information—including Moody's Investors Service, Standard & Poor's Corporation, Value Line, and Dun & Bradstreet—collect information from businesses and sell it to subscribers. Buyers include individual investors, libraries, and financial intermediaries. You can find some of these publications in your college library or through online information services.

Making the Connection

A Bull in China's Financial Shop

Prospects for Sichuan Changhong Electric Co., manufacturer of plasma televisions and liquid crystal displays, looked excellent in 2007, with rapidly growing output, employment, and profits earned from trade in the world economy. And Changhong was not alone. In the 2000s, the Chinese economy was sizzling. China's output grew by 10.7 percent during 2006, dominated by an astonishing 24 percent growth in investment in plant and equipment. The Chinese economic juggernaut caught the attention of the global business community—and charged onto the U.S. political stage, as China's growth fueled concerns about job losses in the United States.

Yet at the same time, many economists and financial commentators worried that the Chinese expansion—which was fueling rising living standards in a rapidly developing economy with 1.3 billion people—would come to an end. Indeed, the debate seemed to be over whether China's boom would have a "soft landing" (with gradually declining growth) or a "hard landing" (possibly leading to an economic financial crisis).

Why the debate? Although China's saving rate was estimated to be a very high 40 percent of gross domestic product (GDP)—double or triple the rate in most other countries—the financial system was doing a poor job of allocating capital. Excessive expansion in office construction and factories was fueled less by careful

David McIntyre, Black Star

Will China's weak financial system derail economic growth?

financial analysis than by the directions of national and local government officials trying to encourage growth. With nonperforming loans—where the borrower cannot make promised payments to lenders—at unheard-of levels, China's banks were in financial trouble. Worse still, they continued to lend to weak, politically connected borrowers.

China's prospects for long-term economic growth depend importantly on a better-developed financial system to generate information for borrowers and lenders. Many economists have urged Chinese officials to improve accounting transparency and information disclosure so that stock and bond markets can flourish. In the absence of well-functioning financial markets, banks are crucial allocators of capital. There, too, information disclosure and less government direction of lending will help oil the Chinese growth machine in the long run.

Chinese firms, like Changhong, may well play a major role on the world's economic stage. But China's creaky financial system needs repair if Chinese firms are to grow rapidly enough to raise the standard of living for Chinese workers over the long run.

YOUR TURN: Test your understanding by doing related problem 4.7 at the end of this chapter.

What kind of information do investors and firm managers need? A firm must answer three basic questions: What to produce? How to produce it? and What price to charge? To answer these questions, a firm's managers need two pieces of information: The first is the firm's revenues and costs, and the second is the value of the property and other assets the firm owns and the firm's debts, or other **liabilities**, that it owes to other persons and firms. Potential investors in the firm also need this information to decide whether to buy the firm's stocks or bonds. Managers and investors find this information in the firm's *financial statements*, principally its income statement and balance sheet, which we discuss next.

The Income Statement

A firm's **income statement** sums up its revenues, costs, and profit over a period of time. Corporations issue annual income statements, although the 12-month *fiscal year* covered may be different from the calendar year to represent the seasonal pattern of the business better. We explore income statements in greater detail in the appendix to this chapter.

Getting to Accounting Profit An income statement shows a firm's revenue, costs, and profit for the firm's fiscal year. To determine profitability, the income statement starts with the firm's revenue and subtracts its operating expenses and taxes paid. The remainder, *net income*, is the **accounting profit** of the firm.

. . . And Economic Profit Accounting profit provides information on a firm's current net income measured according to accepted accounting standards. Accounting profit is not, however, the ideal measure of a firm's profits because it neglects some of the firm's costs. By taking into account all costs, *economic profit* provides a better indication than accounting profit of how successful a firm is. Firms making an economic profit will remain in business and may even expand. Firms making an *economic loss* are unlikely to remain in business in the long run. To understand how economic profit is calculated, remember that economists always measure cost as *opportunity cost*. The **opportunity cost** of any activity is the highest-valued alternative that must be given up to engage in that activity. Costs are either *explicit* or *implicit*. When a firm spends money, an **explicit cost** results. If a firm incurs an opportunity cost but does not spend money, an **implicit cost** results. For example, firms incur an explicit

Liability Anything owed by a person or a firm.

Income statement A financial statement that sums up a firm's revenues, costs, and profit over a period of time.

Accounting profit A firm's net income measured by revenue minus operating expenses and taxes paid.

Opportunity cost The highest-valued alternative that must be given up to engage in an activity.

Explicit cost A cost that involves spending money.

Implicit cost A nonmonetary opportunity cost.

labor cost when they pay wages to employees. Firms have many other explicit costs as well, such as the cost of the electricity used to light their buildings or the costs of advertising or insurance.

Some costs are implicit, however. The most important of these is the opportunity cost to investors of the funds they have invested in the firm. Economists refer to the minimum amount that investors must earn on the funds they invest in a firm, expressed as a percentage of the amount invested, as a *normal rate of return*. If a firm fails to provide investors with at least a normal rate of return, it will not be able to remain in business over the long run because investors will not continue to invest their funds in the firm. For example, Bethlehem Steel was once the second-leading producer of steel in the United States and a very profitable firm with stock that sold for more than $50 per share. By 2002, investors became convinced that the firm's uncompetitive labor costs in world markets meant that the firm would never be able to provide investors with a normal rate of return. Many investors expected that the firm would eventually have to declare bankruptcy, and as a result, the price of Bethlehem Steel's stock plummeted to $1 per share. Shortly thereafter, the firm declared bankruptcy, and its remaining assets were sold off to a competing steel firm. The return (in dollars) that investors require to continue investing in a firm is a true cost to the firm and should be subtracted from the firm's revenues to calculate its profits.

The necessary rate of return that investors must receive to continue investing in a firm varies from firm to firm. If the investment is risky—as would be the case with a biotechnology start-up—investors may require a high rate of return to compensate them for the risk. Investors in firms in more established industries, such as electric utilities, may require lower rates of return. The exact rate of return investors require to invest in any particular firm is difficult to calculate, which also makes it difficult for an accountant to include the return as a cost on an income statement. Firms have other implicit costs besides the return investors require that can also be difficult to calculate. As a result, the rules of accounting generally require that accounts include only explicit costs in the firm's financial records. *Economic costs* include both explicit costs *and* implicit costs. **Economic profit** is equal to a firm's revenues minus all of its costs, implicit and explicit. Because accounting profit excludes some implicit costs, it is larger than economic profit.

Economic profit A firm's revenues minus all of its implicit and explicit costs.

The Balance Sheet

A firm's **balance sheet** sums up its financial position on a particular day, usually the end of a quarter or year. Recall that an asset is anything of value that a firm owns, and a liability is a debt or obligation owed by a firm. Subtracting the value of a firm's liabilities from the value of its assets leaves its *net worth*. We can think of the net worth as what the firm's owners would be left with if the firm were closed, its assets were sold, and its liabilities were paid off. Investors can determine a firm's net worth by inspecting its balance sheet. We analyze a balance sheet in detail in the appendix to this chapter.

Balance sheet A financial statement that sums up a firm's financial position on a particular day, usually the end of a quarter or year.

5 | Understand the role of government in corporate governance

5 LEARNING OBJECTIVE

Corporate Governance Policy

A firm's financial statements provide important information on the firm's ability to add value for investors and the economy. Accurate and easy-to-understand financial statements are inputs for decisions by the firm's managers and investors. Indeed, the information in accounting statements helps guide resource allocation in the economy.

Firms disclose financial statements in periodic filings to the federal government and in *annual reports* to shareholders. An investor is more likely to buy a firm's stock if the firm's income statement shows a large after-tax profit and if its balance sheet shows a large net worth. The top management of a firm has at least two reasons to attract investors and keep the firm's stock price high. First, a higher stock price increases the funds the firm can raise when it sells a given amount of stock. Second, to reduce the principal–agent problem, boards of directors often tie the salaries of top managers to the firm's stock price or to the profitability of the firm.

Top managers clearly have an incentive to maximize the profits reported on the income statement and the net worth reported on the balance sheet. If top managers make good decisions, the firm's profits will be high, and the firm's assets will be large relative to its liabilities. The business scandals that came to light in 2002 revealed, however, that some top managers have inflated profits and hidden liabilities that should have been listed on their balance sheets.

At Enron, an energy trading firm, CFO Andrew Fastow was accused of creating partnerships that were supposedly independent of Enron but in fact were owned by the firm. He was accused of transferring large amounts of Enron's debts to these partnerships, which reduced the liabilities on Enron's balance sheet, thereby increasing the firm's net worth. Fastow's deception made Enron more attractive to investors, increasing its stock price—and Fastow's compensation. In 2001, however, Enron was forced into bankruptcy. The firm's shareholders lost billions of dollars, and many employees lost their jobs. In 2004, Fastow pleaded guilty to conspiracy and was sentenced to 10 years in federal prison. Enron's CEO, Kenneth Lay, was found guilty of securities fraud in 2006 but died prior to being sentenced.

At WorldCom, a telecommunications firm, David Myers, the firm's controller, pleaded guilty to falsifying "WorldCom's books, to reduce WorldCom's reported actual costs and therefore increase WorldCom's reported earnings." Myers's actions caused WorldCom's income statement to overstate the firm's profits by more than $10 billion. WorldCom CEO Bernard Ebbers is serving a 25-year prison sentence for fraud. The scandals at Enron and WorldCom were the largest cases of corporate fraud in U.S. history.

How was it possible for corporations such as Enron and WorldCom to falsify their financial statements? The federal government regulates how financial statements are prepared, but this regulation cannot by itself guarantee the accuracy of the statements. All firms that issue stock to the public have certified public accountants *audit* their financial statements. The accountants are employees of accounting firms, *not* of the firms being audited. The audits are intended to provide investors with an independent opinion as to whether a firm's financial statements fairly represent the true financial condition of the firm. Unfortunately, as the Enron and WorldCom scandals revealed, top managers who are determined to deceive investors about the true financial condition of their firms can also deceive outside auditors.

The private sector's response to the corporate scandals was almost immediate. In addition to the reexamination of corporate governance practices at many corporations, the New York Stock Exchange and the Nasdaq put forth initiatives to ensure the accuracy and accessibility of information.

To guard against future scandals, new federal legislation was enacted in 2002. The landmark *Sarbanes-Oxley Act of 2002* requires that corporate directors have a certain level of expertise with financial information and mandates that CEOs personally certify the accuracy of financial statements. The Sarbanes-Oxley Act also requires that financial analysts and auditors disclose whether any conflicts of interest might exist that would limit their independence in evaluating a firm's financial condition. The purpose of this provision is to ensure that analysts and auditors are acting in the best interests of shareholders. The act promotes management accountability by specifying the responsibilities of corporate officers and by increasing penalties, including long jail sentences, for managers who do not meet their responsibilities.

Perhaps the most noticeable corporate governance reform under the Sarbanes-Oxley Act is the creation of the Public Company Accounting Oversight Board, a national board that oversees the auditing of public companies' financial reports. The board's mission is to promote the independence of auditors to ensure that they disclose accurate information. On balance, most observers acknowledge that the Sarbanes-Oxley Act brought back confidence in the U.S. corporate governance system, though questions remain for the future about whether the act may chill legitimate business risk-taking by diverting management attention from the core business toward regulatory compliance. And the high accounting costs of implementing Sarbanes-Oxley are borne by all shareholders.

By 2007, it had become clear that Sarbanes-Oxley had raised the costs to firms of issuing stocks and bonds in the United States. Section 404 of Sarbanes-Oxley is intended to reassure investors that accounting "errors"—whether from fraud, mistakes, or omissions—will be minimized by requiring firms to maintain effective controls over financial reporting. Many economists believe, though, that the rules for implementing Section 404 set forth by the Securities and Exchange Commission and the Public Company Accounting Oversight Board have turned out to be much more costly to firms than anticipated and that these costs may exceed the benefits of the regulations. As a result, the share of new issues of stocks and bonds being listed on the New York Stock Exchange or Nasdaq has declined relative to listings on foreign stock markets, such as the London Stock Exchange. Some economists, though, are skeptical that the decline in the share of new listings on the New York Stock Exchange and Nasdaq is due to the effects of Sarbanes-Oxley. These economists argue that as other global exchanges become more mature, they are naturally able to attract new listings from local firms. Therefore, in this view, the declining fraction of foreign firms willing to list new issues on the New York Stock Exchange or Nasdaq is not an indication that the burden of U.S. regulations is too heavy.

Outside the United States, the European Commission and Japan have also tightened corporate governance rules. The challenge of ensuring the accurate reporting of firms' economic profits without excessively raising firms' costs is a global one.

Solved Problem | 5

What Makes a Good Board of Directors?

Western Digital Corporation makes computer hard drives. *BusinessWeek* magazine published the following analysis by Standard & Poor's Equity Research Services of Western Digital's corporate governance:

> Overall, we view Western Digital's corporate-governance policies favorably and believe the company compares well in this regard relative to peers. We see the following factors as positives: the board is controlled by a supermajority (greater than 67%) of independent outsiders; the nominating and compensation committees are comprised solely of independent outside directors; all directors with more than one year of service own stock. . . .

a. What is an "independent outsider" on a board of directors?

b. Why is it good for a firm to have a large majority of independent outsiders on the board of directors?

c. Why would it be good for a firm to have the auditing and compensation committees composed of outsiders?

d. Why would it be good for a firm if its directors own the firm's stock?

Source: Jawahar Hingorani, "Western Digital: A Drive Buy." *BusinessWeek*, January 9, 2007.

SOLVING THE PROBLEM:

Step 1: **Review the chapter material.** The context of this problem is the business scandals of 2002 and the underlying principal–agent problem that arises because of the separation of ownership from control in large corporations, so you may want to review the section "Corporate Governance Policy."

Step 2: **Answer question (a) by defining "independent outsiders."** *Insiders* are members of top management who also serve on the board of directors. *Outsiders* are members of the board of directors who are not otherwise employed by the firm. *Independent outsiders* are outsiders who have no business connections with the firm.

Step 3: **Answer question (b) by explaining why it is good for a firm to have a large majority of independent outsiders on the board of directors.** Having members of top management on the board of directors provides the board with information about the firm that only top managers possess. Having too many insiders on a board, however, means that top managers may end up controlling the board rather than the other way around. A corporation's board of directors is supposed to provide the monitoring and control of top managers that shareholders cannot provide directly. This is most likely to happen when a larger majority of the board of directors consists of independent outsiders.

Step 4: **Answer question (c) by explaining why it may be good for a firm to have the auditing and compensation committees composed of outsiders.** The auditing committee is responsible for ensuring that the firm's financial statements are accurate, and the compensation committee is responsible for setting the pay of top management. It is of vital importance to a firm that these activities be carried out in an honest and impartial way. Having these two important committees composed exclusively of independent outside members increases the chances that the committees will act in the best interests of the shareholders rather than in the best interests of top management.

Step 5: **Answer question (d) by explaining why it may be good for a firm to have directors owning the firm's stock.** When directors own the firm's stock, they will then share with other stockholders the desire to see the firm maximize profits. The directors will be more likely to insist that top managers take actions to increase profits rather than to pursue other objectives that may be in the interests of the managers but not the stockholders. Of course, when directors own the firm's stock the directors may be tempted not to object if top managers take steps to improperly inflate the firm's profits, as happened during the business scandals of 2002. On balance, though, most economists believe that it improves corporate governance when a firm's directors own the firm's stock.

YOUR TURN: For more practice, do related problems 5.3 and 5.4 at the end of this chapter.

>> End Solved Problem 5

Economics in YOUR Life!

At the beginning of the chapter, we asked you to consider two questions: Why is it difficult to get the managers of a firm to act in your interest rather than in their own? and Given this problem, should you ever take on the risk of buying stock? The reason managers may not act in shareholders' interest is that in large corporations, there is separation of ownership from control: The shareholders own the firm, but the top managers actually control it. This results in the principal–agent problem discussed in the chapter. The principal–agent problem clearly adds to the risk you would face by buying stock rather than doing something safe with your money, such as putting it in the bank. But the rewards to owning stock can also be substantial, potentially earning you far more over the long run than a bank account will. Buying the stock of well-known firms, such as Google, that are closely followed by Wall Street investment analysts helps to reduce the principal–agent problem. It is less likely that the managers of these firms will take actions that are clearly not in the best interests of shareholders because the managers' actions are difficult to conceal. Buying the stock of large, well-known firms certainly does not completely eliminate the risk from principal–agent problems, however. Enron, WorldCom, and some of the other firms that were involved in the scandals discussed in this chapter were all well known and closely followed by Wall Street analysts, but the misbehavior of their managers went undetected, at least for a while.

Conclusion

In a market system, firms make independent decisions about which goods and services to produce, how to produce them, and what prices to charge. In modern high-income countries, such as the United States, large corporations account for a majority of the sales and profits earned by firms. Generally, the managers of these corporations do a good job of representing the interests of stockholders, while providing the goods and services demanded by consumers. As the business scandals of 2002 showed, however, some top managers enriched themselves at the expense of stockholders and consumers by manipulating financial statements. Passage of the Sarbanes-Oxley Act of 2002 and other new government regulations have helped restore investor and management confidence in firms' financial statements. However, economists debate whether the benefits from these regulations are greater than their costs.

An Inside Look on the next page discusses the compensation Google pays its top executives.

ASSOCIATED PRESS, APRIL 4, 2007

Google CEO, Co-Founders Get $1 Salary

The trio of billionaires who run Google Inc. collected less than $600,000 in combined compensation last year while they raked in big jackpots by selling some of their holdings in the online search leader.

The total amount that Google paid its chief executive, Eric Schmidt, and co-founders Larry Page and Sergey Brin during 2006 would have been less than $5,200 if not for personal security and transportation costs, according to documents filed Wednesday with the Securities and Exchange Commission.

Schmidt's package totaled $557,466, including $532,755 for personal security. Page's pay totaled $38,519, with most of the money covering personal transportation, logistics and security. Brin's 2006 pay consisted solely of a $1 salary and $1,723 bonus. Google paid the same salary and holiday bonus to Schmidt and Page.

The Associated Press bases its executive pay totals on salary, bonus, incentives, perks, above-market returns on deferred compensation and the estimated value of stock options and awards granted during the year.

Schmidt, Page and Brin have refused to take anything more than a token paycheck for the past three years to promote the egalitarian spirit championed by the Mountain View-based company.

It's a sacrifice that the three executives can afford to make because Google's high-flying stock has elevated them into the ranks of the world's richest people. Meanwhile, hundreds of Google's early employees have become millionaires.

As of March 1, Page, 34, owned 29.2 million Google shares currently worth $13.8 billion while Brin, 33, held 28.6 million shares worth about $13.5 billion. Schmidt, 51, owns 10.7 million shares currently worth $5 billion. The three men have been converting some of their holdings into cash by regularly selling some of their stockholdings since the company went public in August 2004.

Last year, Brin, Page and Schmidt made more than $2 billion combined from their Google stock sales, according to data compiled from SEC filings by Thomson Financial. Brin sold 1.99 million shares for a total windfall of $788 million last year while Page pocketed $666 million by selling 1.72 million shares. Schmidt cashed out 1.39 million shares during 2006 for a total $580 million.

Google's stock price rose by 11 percent last year, a gain that lagged the Standard & Poor's 500 index—a blue-chip bellwether that the company joined during 2006. The S&P 500 rose by 13.6 percent last year.

Since its IPO, Google shares have surged to a more than fivefold increase, a meteoric performance that has created more than $120 billion in shareholder wealth. Google shares fell $1.58 Wednesday to close at $471.02 the Nasdaq Stock Market.

The rapid run-up in Google's stock has been driven by its search engine, which has become synonymous with looking things up on the Internet. The search engine also propels a lucrative online advertising network that enabled Google to turn a 2006 profit of $3.1 billion, more than doubling its earnings from the previous year. The robust growth has enabled Google to add more than 8,000 workers during the past three years. At the end of 2006, Google had 10,674 employees—all of whom were eligible for the same holiday bonus paid to Schmidt, Page and Brin.

Google's brain trust has already agreed to settle for a $1 salary again this year, rejecting an opportunity for a raise, according to the SEC filing.

Key Points in the Article

The article discusses how Google CEO Eric Schmidt and the firm's co-founders Sergey Brin and Larry Page are compensated. Google is different from most large corporations in that most of the compensation for the CEO comes in the form of stock. The figure tracks the performance of Google's stock. Prior to August 2004, when Google had its initial public offering (IPO), Eric Schmidt and the co-founders agreed to cut their salaries to $1 a year plus some fringe benefits and stock in the company. Essentially, they bet that the price of the stock would rise. This turned out to be a good bet. Google's IPO was in August 2004. The price opened at $100 per share and closed at $104.06 that day. Google's stock has performed very well since the initial offering, and on April 4, 2007 (the date of the article) the price closed at $471.02 per share. As a result, the CEO and co-founders of Google have become billionaires.

The chapter discusses the principal–agent problem facing modern corporations. In large corporations, the executives of a firm are not usually the owners of the firm. In this situation, executives (especially the CEO) can take actions that are in their own interests rather than the interests of the shareholders. For example, the executives could use their influence to obtain large base salaries that are not sensitive to the firm's stock price. This reduces the executives' incentive to perform well. After all, the executives have large salaries, regardless of whether the firm does well.

Analyzing the News

(a) At Google, the CEO actually has a low base salary. Eric Schmidt earns a salary of $1 per year. He receives other compensation in the form of bonuses and compensation for security. Schmidt's combined compensation package was only $557,466, which is much less than those of most executives at similar firms.

(b) Instead of having a large base salary, most of Eric Schmidt's income comes from the sale of Google stock that he owned at the time Google went public or has received since then. He owns 10.7 million shares of Google stocks, making him a major shareholder in the firm. For each $1 increase in the stock price, Schmidt's wealth increases by $10.7 million. This is a strong incentive for him to take actions that will increase the stock price. This is good news to other Google shareholders, because Schmidt's income is tied to increases in the value of Google's stock. It seems Google has significantly reduced the principal–agent problem.

Thinking Critically

1. Compensating executives with stock, or equity, is a way to solve the principal–agent problem, but the practice is not without flaws. Critics of equity compensation point out that it can create incentives for executives to take actions not in the best interests of other shareholders and may have contributed to the corporate scandals discussed in the chapter. How could equity compensation contribute to these scandals?

2. An executive at Google who knew that Google was about to announce a larger than expected profit could have earned a bundle quickly by buying Google stock at $470 per share and then selling it at a higher price a day or so later. Such insider trading is illegal, however. Do you think that insider trading should be illegal? Are there benefits to other investors or to the economy as a whole associated with such trading? Are there problems associated with such trading?

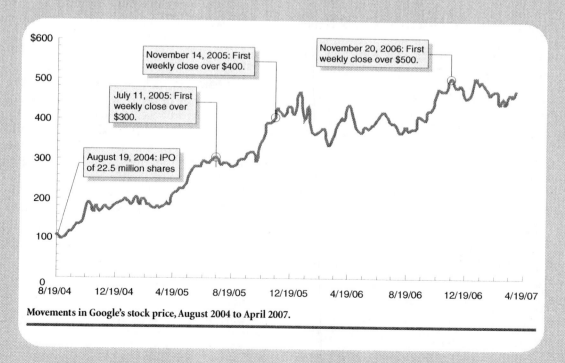

Movements in Google's stock price, August 2004 to April 2007.

Key Terms

Accounting profit	Coupon payment	Income statement	Partnership
Asset	Direct finance	Indirect finance	Principal–agent problem
Balance sheet	Dividends	Interest rate	Separation of ownership from control
Bond	Economic profit	Liability	Sole proprietorship
Corporate governance	Explicit cost	Limited liability	Stock
Corporation	Implicit cost	Opportunity cost	

---

1 LEARNING OBJECTIVE 1 | Categorize the major types of firms in the United States

Types of Firms

Summary

There are three types of firms: A **sole proprietorship** is a firm owned by a single individual and not organized as a corporation. A **partnership** is a firm owned jointly by two or more persons and not organized as a corporation. A **Corporation** is a legal form of business that provides the owners with limited liability. An **asset** is anything of value owned by a person or a firm. The owners of sole proprietorships and partners have unlimited liability, which means there is no legal distinction between the personal assets of the owners of the business and the assets of the business. The owners of corporations have **limited liability**, which means they can never lose more than their investment in the firm. Although only 20 percent of firms are corporations, they account for the majority of revenue and profit earned by all firms.

 Visit www.myeconlab.com to complete these exercises online and get instant feedback.

Review Questions

1.1 What are the three major types of firms in the United States? Briefly discuss the most important characteristics of each type.

1.2 What is limited liability? Why does the government grant limited liability to the owners of corporations?

Problems and Applications

1.3 Suppose that shortly after graduating from college, you decide to start your own business. Will you be likely to organize the business as a sole proprietorship, a partnership, or a corporation? Explain your reasoning.

1.4 **(Related to the *Making the Connection*)** Evaluate the following argument:

> I would like to invest in the stock market, but I think that buying shares of stock in a corporation is too risky. Suppose I buy $10,000 of General Motors stock, and the company ends up going bankrupt. Because as a stockholder, I'm part owner of the company, I might be responsible for paying hundreds of thousands of dollars of the company's debts.

1.5 **(Related to the *Making the Connection*)** In an article in the *New York Times*, sociologist Dalton Conley proposed the *elimination* of limited liability for corporate shareholders. Do you think that corporations should be granted limited liability? What are the benefits of limited liability? What is its downside? Would you be more willing to buy bonds from a corporation with limited liability? Would you be more willing to buy the stock of a corporation with limited liability?

Source: Dalton Conley, "Reward but No Risk," *New York Times*, May 10, 2003.

>> End Learning Objective 1

The Structure of Corporations and the Principal-Agent Problem

Summary

Corporate governance refers to the way in which a corporation is structured and the impact a corporation's structure has on the firm's behavior. Most corporations have a similar management structure: The shareholders elect a board of directors that appoints the corporation's top managers, such as the chief executive officer (CEO). Because the top management often does not own a large fraction of the stock in the corporation, large corporations have a **separation of ownership from control**. Because top managers have less incentive to increase the corporation's profits than to increase their own salaries and their own enjoyment, corporations can suffer from a **principal-agent problem**. A principal-agent problem exists when the principals—in this case, the shareholders of the corporation—have difficulty in getting the agent—the corporation's top management—to carry out their wishes.

 Visit www.myeconlab.com to complete these exercises online and get instant feedback.

Review Questions

2.1 What do we mean by the separation of ownership from control in large corporations?

2.2 How is the separation of ownership from control related to the principal-agent problem?

Problems and Applications

2.3 The principal-agent problem arises almost everywhere in the business world—but it also crops up even closer to home. Discuss the principal-agent problem that exists in the college classroom. Who is the principal? Who is the agent? What is the problem between this principal and this agent?

2.4 (Related to *Solved Problem 2*) Briefly explain whether you agree or disagree with the following argument: "The separation of ownership from control in large corporations and the principal-agent problem means that top managers can work short days, take long vacations, and otherwise slack off."

2.5 (Related to *Solved Problem 2*) An economic consultant gives the board of directors of a firm the following advice:

> You can increase the profitability of the firm if you change your method of compensating top management. Instead of paying your top management a straight salary, you should pay them a salary plus give them the right to buy the firm's stock in the future at a price above the stock's current market price.

Explain the consultant's reasoning. To what difficulties might this compensation scheme lead?

2.6 The following is from an article in the *New York Times*: "In theory, boards [of directors] design pay packages to attract and inspire good chief executives and to align their interests with those of shareholders. . . . But what kind of pay packages are appropriate at companies still run by the founding family?" The article quotes one expert as arguing: "There is little or no justification for treating an owner-manager in exactly the same way as a standard CEO." What does the article mean by saying that pay packages should "align [chief executives'] interests with those of shareholders"? What kind of pay packages would achieve this objective? Do you agree that an "owner-manager" should have a pay package different from that of a CEO who is not a member of the family that started the firm? Briefly explain.

Source: Diana B. Henriques, "What's Fair Pay for Running the Family Store?" *New York Times*, January 12, 2003.

>> End Learning Objective 2

How Firms Raise Funds

Summary

Firms rely on retained earnings—which are profits retained by the firm and not paid out to the firm's owners—or on using the savings of households for the funds they need to operate and expand. With **direct finance**, the savings of households flow directly to businesses when investors buy **stocks** and **bonds** in financial markets. With **indirect finance**, savings flow indirectly to businesses when households deposit money in saving and checking accounts in banks and the banks lend these funds to businesses. Federal, state, and local governments also sell bonds in financial markets and households also borrow funds from banks. When a firm sells a bond, it is borrowing money from the buyer of the bond. The firm makes a **coupon payment** to the buyer of the bond. The **interest rate** is the cost of borrowing funds, usually expressed as a percentage of the amount borrowed. When a firm sells stock, it is selling part ownership of the firm to the buyer of the stock. **Dividends** are payments by a corporation to its shareholders. The original purchasers of stocks and bonds may resell them in stock and bond markets, such as the New York Stock Exchange.

myeconlab Visit www.myeconlab.com to complete these exercises online and get instant feedback.

Review Questions

3.1 What is the difference between direct finance and indirect finance? If you borrow money from a bank to buy a new car, are you using direct finance or indirect finance?

3.2 Why is a bond considered to be a loan but a share of stock is not? Why do corporations issue both bonds and shares of stock?

3.3 How do the stock and bond markets provide information to businesses? Why do stock and bond prices change over time?

Problems and Applications

3.4 Suppose that a firm in which you have invested is losing money. Would you rather own the firm's stock or the firm's bonds? Explain.

3.5 Suppose you originally invested in a firm when it was small and unprofitable. Now the firm has grown considerably and is large and profitable. Would you be better off if you had bought the firm's stock or the firm's bonds? Explain.

3.6 If you deposit $20,000 in a savings account at a bank, you might earn 3 percent interest per year. Someone who borrows $20,000 from a bank to buy a new car might have to pay an interest rate of 8 percent per year on the loan. Knowing this, why don't you just lend your money directly to the car buyer, cutting out the bank?

3.7 (Related to the *Chapter Opener*) When Google's owners wanted to raise funds for expansion in 2004, they decided to sell stock in their company rather than borrow the money. Why do some companies fund their expansion by borrowing, while others fund expansion by issuing new stock?

3.8 (Related to the *Chapter Opener*) What impact would the following events be likely to have on the price of Google's stock?

a. A competitor launches a search engine that's just as good as Google's.

b. The corporate income tax is abolished.

c. Google's board of directors becomes dominated by close friends and relatives of its top management.

d. The price of wireless Internet connections unexpectedly drops, so more and more people use the Internet.

e. Google announces a huge profit of $1 billion, but everybody anticipated that Google would earn a huge profit of $1 billion.

3.9 In 2005, the French government began issuing bonds with 50-year maturities. Would this bond be purchased only by very young investors who expect to still be alive when the bond matures? Briefly explain.

3.10 (Related to the *Don't Let This Happen to You!*) Briefly explain whether you agree or disagree with the following statement: "The total value of the shares of Microsoft stock traded on the Nasdaq last week was $250 million, so the firm actually received more revenue from stock sales than from selling software."

3.11 (Related to the *Making the Connection*) Loans from banks are the most important external source of funds to businesses because most businesses are too small to borrow in financial markets by issuing stocks or bonds. Most investors are reluctant to buy the stocks or bonds of small businesses because of the difficulty of gathering accurate information on the financial strength and profitability of the businesses. Nevertheless, news about the stock market is included in nearly every network news program and is often the lead story in the business section of most newspapers. Is there a contradiction here? Why is the average viewer of TV news or the average reader of a newspaper interested in the fluctuations in prices in the stock market?

>> End Learning Objective 3

Using Financial Statements to Evaluate a Corporation

Summary

A firm's **income statement** sums up its revenues, costs, and profit over a period of time. A firm's **balance sheet** sums up its financial position on a particular day, usually the end of a quarter or year. A balance sheet records a firms assets and liabilities. A **liability** is anything owed by a person or a firm. Firms report their **accounting profit** on their income statements. Accounting profit does not always include all of a firm's **opportunity cost**. **Explicit cost** is a cost that involves spending money. **Implicit cost** is a nonmonetary opportunity cost. Because accounting profit excludes some implicit costs, it is larger than **economic profit**.

myeconlab Visit www.myeconlab.com to complete these exercises
Get Ahead of the Curve online and get instant feedback.

Review Questions

4.1 What is the difference between a firm's assets and its liabilities? Give an example of an asset and an example of a liability.

4.2 What is the difference between a firm's balance sheet and a firm's income statement?

Problems and Applications

4.3 Paolo currently has $100,000 invested in bonds that earn him 10 percent interest per year. He wants to open a pizza restaurant and is considering either selling the bonds and using the $100,000 to start his restaurant or borrowing the $100,000 from a bank, which would charge him an annual interest rate of 7 percent. He finally decides to sell the bonds and not take out the bank loan. He reasons, "Because I already have the $100,000 invested in the bonds, I don't have

to pay anything to use the money. If I take out the bank loan, I have to pay interest, so my costs of producing pizza will be higher if I take out the loan than if I sell the bonds." What do you think of Paolo's reasoning?

4.4 Paolo and Alfredo are twins who both want to open pizza restaurants. Because their parents always liked Alfredo best, they buy two pizza ovens and give both to him. Unfortunately, Paolo must buy his own pizza ovens. Does Alfredo have lower cost of producing pizza than Paolo does because Alfredo received his pizza ovens as a gift while Paolo had to pay for his? Briefly explain.

4.5 Dane decides to give up a job earning $100,000 per year as a corporate lawyer and converts the duplex that he owns into a UFO museum. (He had been renting out the duplex for $20,000 a year.) His direct expenses include $50,000 per year paid to his assistants and $10,000 per year for utilities. Fans flock to the museum to see his collection of extraterrestrial paraphernalia, which he could easily sell on eBay for $1,000,000. Over the course of the year, the museum brings in revenues of $100,000.
   a. How much is Dane's accounting profit for the year?
   b. Is Dane earning an economic profit? Explain.

4.6 The Securities and Exchange Commission requires that every firm that wishes to issue stock and bonds to the public make available its balance sheet and income statement. Briefly explain how information useful to investors can be found in these financial statements.

4.7 (Related to the *Making the Connection*) The Making the Connection on China argues that "In the absence of well-functioning financial markets, banks are crucial allocators of capital." What is the difference between a financial market and a bank? What is an "allocator of capital"? How do banks allocate capital?

>> **End Learning Objective 4**

Corporate Governance Policy

Summary

Because their compensation often rises with the profitability of the corporation, top managers have an incentive to overstate the profits reported on their firm's income statements. During 2002, it became clear that the

top managers of several large corporations had done this, even though intentionally falsifying financial statements is illegal. The *Sarbanes-Oxley Act* of 2002 and greater scrutiny of financial statements have helped to restore investor and management confidence in firms' financial statements.

Review Questions

5.1 What is the Sarbanes-Oxley Act? Why was it passed?

5.2 Why are some policymakers and business owners concerned about the Sarbanes-Oxley Act?

Problems and Applications

5.3 (Related to *Solved Problem 5*) When Buford Yates, director of accounting at WorldCom, pleaded guilty to fraud, he stated in federal court that top managers at WorldCom ordered him to make certain adjustments to the firm's financial statements:

> I came to believe that the adjustments I was being directed to make in World-Com's financial statements had no justification and contravened generally accepted accounting principles. I concluded that the purpose of these adjustments was to incorrectly inflate World-Com's reported earnings.

What are "generally accepted accounting principles"? How would the "adjustments" Yates was ordered to make benefit top managers at WorldCom? Would these adjustments also benefit WorldCom's stockholders? Briefly explain.

Source: Devlin Barrett, "Ex-WorldCom Exec Pleads Guilty," Associated Press, October 8, 2002.

5.4 (Related to *Solved Problem 5*) In 2002, *BusinessWeek* listed Apple Computer as having one of the worst boards of directors:

> Founder Steve Jobs owns just two shares in the company. . . . The CEO of Micro Warehouse, which accounted for nearly 2.9% of Apple's net sales in 2001, sits on the compensation committee. . . . There is an interlocking directorship—with Gap CEO Mickey Drexler and Jobs sitting on each other's boards.

Why might investors be concerned that a top manager like Steve Jobs owns only two shares in the firm? Why might investors be concerned if a member of the board of directors also has a business relationship with the firm? What is an "interlocking directorship"? Why is it a bad thing?

Source: "The Best Boards and the Worst Boards," *BusinessWeek*, October 7, 2002, p. 107.

5.5 The following is from a *BusinessWeek* editorial:

> Welcome to the revolution. After years of paying lip service to reform, Enron Corp. and the ensuing wave of business scandal has finally produced a dramatic change in corporate governance. . . . Investors are rewarding companies with good governance and punishing those without it.

How are investors able to reward or punish firms? What impact will these rewards and punishments have on boards of directors and top managers?

Source: "Boardrooms Are Starting to Wake Up," *BusinessWeek*, October 7, 2002, p. 107.

5.6 An article in *BusinessWeek* stated that the Allstate Corporation, a large insurance company, would now require a simple majority vote, rather than a two-thirds majority vote, to elect members to its board of directors and to remove directors in between annual meetings when elections are held. The article also stated that the price of Allstate's stock rose following the announcement. Briefly discuss whether there may have been a possible connection between these changes in Allstate's corporate governance and the increase in the firm's stock price.

Source: "Allstate Announces Changes to Governance," *BusinessWeek*, February 20, 2007.

5.7 According to a survey in 2007, 78 percent of corporate executives responding believed that the costs of complying with the Sarbanes-Oxley Act outweighed the benefits. The total costs of compliance were about $2.92 million dollars per company. Is it possible to put a dollar value on the benefits to complying with Sarbanes-Oxley? Which groups are likely to receive the most benefits from Sarbanes-Oxley: investors, corporations, or some other group?

Source: Kara Scannell, "Costs to Comply with Sarbanes-Oxley Decline Again," *Wall Street Journal*, May 16, 2007, p. C7.

>> **End Learning Objective 5**

Appendix

Tools to Analyze Firms' Financial Information

As we saw in the chapter, modern business organizations are not just "black boxes" transforming inputs into output. Most business revenues and profits are earned by large corporations. Unlike founder-dominated firms, the typical large corporation is run by managers who generally do not own a controlling interest in the firm. Large firms raise funds from outside investors, and outside investors seek information on firms and the assurance that the managers of firms will act in the interests of the investors.

This chapter showed how corporations raise funds by issuing stocks and bonds. This appendix provides more detail to support that discussion. We begin by analyzing *present value* as a key concept in determining the prices of financial securities. We then provide greater information on *financial statements* issued by corporations, using Google as an example.

Using Present Value to Make Investment Decisions

Firms raise funds by selling equity (stock) and debt (bonds and loans) to investors and lenders. If you own shares of stock or a bond, you will receive payments in the form of dividends or coupons over a number of years. Most people value funds they already have more highly than funds they will not receive until some time in the future. For example, you would probably not trade $1,000 you already have for $1,000 you will not receive for one year. The longer you have to wait to receive a payment, the less value it will have for you. One thousand dollars you will not receive for two years is worth less to you than $1,000 you will receive after one year. The value you give today to money you will receive in the future is called the future payment's **present value**. The present value of $1,000 you will receive in one year will be less than $1,000.

Why is this true? Why is the $1,000 you will not receive for one year less valuable to you than the $1,000 you already have? The most important reason is that if you have $1,000 today, you can use that $1,000 today. You can buy goods and services with the money and receive enjoyment from them. The $1,000 you receive in one year does not have direct use to you now.

Also, prices will likely rise during the year you are waiting to receive your $1,000. So, when you finally do receive the $1,000 in one year, you will not be able to buy as much with it as you could with $1,000 today. Finally, there is some risk that you will not receive the $1,000 in one year. The risk may be very great if an unreliable friend borrows $1,000 from you and vaguely promises to pay you back in one year. The risk may be very small if you lend money to the federal government by buying a United States Treasury bond. In either case, though, there is at least some risk that you will not receive the funds promised.

When someone lends money, the lender expects to be paid back both the amount of the loan and some additional interest. Say that you decide that you are willing to lend your $1,000 today if you are paid back $1,100 one year from now. In this case, you are charging $100/$1,000 = 0.10, or 10 percent interest on the funds you have loaned. Economists would say that you value $1,000 today as equivalent to the $1,100 to be received one year in the future.

Present value The value in today's dollars of funds to be paid or received in the future.

Notice that $1,100 can be written as $1,000 (1 + 0.10). That is, the value of money received in the future is equal to the value of money in the present multiplied by 1 plus the interest rate, with the interest rate expressed as a decimal. Or:

$$\$1,100 = 1,000\,(1 + 0.10).$$

Notice, also, that if we divide both sides by (1 + 0.10), we can rewrite this formula as:

$$\$1,000 = \frac{\$1,100}{(1 + 0.10)}.$$

The rewritten formula states that the present value is equal to the future value to be received in one year divided by one plus the interest rate. This formula is important because you can use it to convert any amount to be received in one year into its present value. Writing the formula generally, we have:

$$\text{Present Value} = \frac{\text{Future Value}_1}{(1 + i)}.$$

The present value of funds to be received in one year—Future Value$_1$—can be calculated by dividing the amount of those funds to be received by 1 plus the interest rate. With an interest rate of 10 percent, the present value of $1,000,000 to be received one year from now is:

$$\frac{\$1,000,000}{(1 + 0.10)} = \$909,090.91.$$

This method is a very useful way of calculating the value today of funds that won't be received for one year. But financial securities such as stocks and bonds involve promises to pay funds over many years. Therefore, it would be even more useful if we could expand this formula to calculate the present value of funds to be received more than one year in the future.

This expansion is easy to do. Go back to the original example where we assumed you were willing to loan out your $1,000 for one year, provided that you received 10 percent interest. Suppose you are asked to lend the funds for two years and that you are promised 10 percent interest per year for each year of the loan. That is, you are lending $1,000, which at 10 percent interest will grow to $1,100 after one year, and you are agreeing to loan that $1,100 out for a second year at 10 percent interest. So, after two years, you will be paid back $1,100 (1 + 0.10), or $1,210. Or:

$$\$1,210 = \$1,000\,(1 + 0.10)(1 + 0.10),$$

or:

$$\$1,210 = \$1,000\,(1 + 0.10)^2.$$

This formula can also be rewritten as:

$$\$1,000 = \frac{\$1,210}{(1 + 0.10)^2}.$$

To put this formula in words, the $1,210 you receive two years from now has a present value equal to $1,210 divided by the quantity 1 plus the interest rate squared. If you were to agree to lend out your $1,000 for three years at 10 percent interest, you would receive:

$$\$1,331 = \$1,000\,(1 + 0.10)^3.$$

Notice, again, that:

$$\$1,000 = \frac{\$1,331}{(1 + 0.10)^3}.$$

You can probably see a pattern here. We can generalize the concept to say that the present value of funds to be received n years in the future—whether n is 1, 20, or 85 does not matter—equals the amount of the funds to be received divided by the quantity 1 plus the interest rate raised to the nth power. For instance, with an interest rate of 10 percent, the value of $1,000,000 to be received 25 years in the future is:

$$\text{Present Value} = \frac{\$1,000,000}{(1+0.10)^{25}} = \$92,296.$$

Or, more generally:

$$\text{Present Value} = \frac{\text{Future Value}_n}{(1+i)^n},$$

where Future Value$_n$ represents funds that will be received in n years.

Solved Problem | A-1

How to Receive Your Contest Winnings

Suppose you win a contest and are given the choice of the following prizes:

Prize 1: $50,000 to be received right away, with four additional payments of $50,000 to be received each year for the next four years

Prize 2: $175,000 to be received right away

Explain which prize you would choose and the basis for your decision.

SOLVING THE PROBLEM:

Step 1: **Review the material.** This problem involves applying the concept of present value, so you may want to review the section "Using Present Value to Make Investment Decisions."

Step 2: **Explain the basis for choosing the prize.** Unless you need immediate cash, you should choose the prize with the highest present value.

Step 3: **Calculate the present value of each prize.** Prize 2 consists of one payment of $175,000 received right away, so its present value is $175,000. Prize 1 consists of five payments spread out over time. To find the present value of the prize, we must find the present value of each of these payments and add them together. To calculate present value, we must use an interest rate. Let's assume an interest rate of 10 percent. In that case, the present value of Prize 1 is:

$$\$50,000 + \frac{\$50,000}{(1+0.10)} + \frac{\$50,000}{(1+0.10)^2} + \frac{\$50,000}{(1+0.10)^3} + \frac{\$50,000}{(1+0.10)^4} =$$

$$\$50,000 + \$45,454.55 + \$41,322.31 + \$37,565.74 + \$34,150.67 = \$208,493.$$

Step 4: **State your conclusion.** Prize 1 has the greater present value, so you should choose it rather than Prize 2.

YOUR TURN: For more practice, do related problems A.6, A.8, A.9, and A.10 at the end of this appendix.

>> End Solved Problem A-1

Using Present Value to Calculate Bond Prices

Anyone who buys a financial asset, such as shares of stock or a bond, is really buying a promise to receive certain payments—dividends in the case of shares of stock or coupons in the case of a bond. The price investors are willing to pay for a financial asset should be equal to the value of the payments they will receive as a result of owning the asset. Because most of the coupon or dividend payments will be received in the future, it is their present value that matters. Put another way, we have the following important idea: *The price of a financial asset should be equal to the present value of the payments to be received from owning that asset.*

Let's consider an example. Suppose that in 1980, General Electric issued a bond with an $80 coupon that will mature in 2010. It is now 2008, and that bond has been bought and sold by investors many times. You are considering buying it. If you buy the bond, you will receive two years of coupon payments plus a final payment of the bond's principal or face value of $1,000. Suppose, once again, that you need an interest rate of 10 percent to invest your funds. If the bond has a coupon of $80, the present value of the payments you receive from owning the bond—and, therefore, the present value of the bond—will be:

$$\text{Present Value} = \frac{\$80}{(1+0.10)} + \frac{\$80}{(1+0.10)^2} + \frac{\$1,000}{(1+0.10)^2} = \$965.29.$$

That is, the present value of the bond will equal the present value of the three payments you will receive during the two years you own the bond. You should, therefore, be willing to pay $965.29 to own this bond and have the right to receive these payments from GE. This process of calculating present values of future payments is used to determine bond prices, with one qualification. The relevant interest rate used by investors in the bond market to calculate the present value and, therefore, the price of an existing bond is usually the coupon rate on comparable newly issued bonds. Therefore, the general formula for the price of a bond is:

$$\text{Bond Price} = \frac{\text{Coupon}_1}{(1+i)} + \frac{\text{Coupon}_2}{(1+i)^2} + \cdots + \frac{\text{Coupon}_n}{(1+i)^n} + \frac{\text{Face Value}}{(1+i)^n},$$

where Coupon_1 is the coupon payment to be received after one year, Coupon_2 is the coupon payment to be received after two years, up to Coupon_n, which is the coupon payment received in the year the bond matures. The ellipsis takes the place of the coupon payments—if any—received between the second year and the year the bond matures. Face Value is the face value of the bond, to be received when the bond matures. The interest rate on comparable newly issued bonds is i.

Using Present Value to Calculate Stock Prices

When you own a firm's stock, you are legally entitled to your share of the firm's profits. Remember that the profits a firm pays out to its shareholders are referred to as dividends. The price of a share of stock should be equal to the present value of the dividends investors expect to receive as a result of owning that stock. Therefore, the general formula for the price of a stock is:

$$\text{Stock Price} = \frac{\text{Dividend}_1}{(1+i)} + \frac{\text{Dividend}_2}{(1+i)^2} + \cdots$$

Notice that this formula looks very similar to the one we used to calculate the price of a bond, with a couple of important differences. First, unlike a bond, stock has no maturity date, so we have to calculate the present value of an infinite number of dividend payments. At first, it may seem that the stock's price must be infinite as well, but remember that dollars you don't receive for many years are worth very little today. For instance, a dividend payment of $10 that will be received 40 years in the future is worth only a little more than $0.20 today at a 10 percent interest rate. The second difference between the stock price formula and the bond price formula is that whereas the coupon payments you receive from owning the bond are known with certainty—they are written on the bond and cannot be changed—you don't know for sure what the dividend payments from owning a stock will be. How large a dividend payment you will receive depends on how profitable the company will be in the future.

Although it is possible to forecast the future profitability of a company, this cannot be done with perfect accuracy. To emphasize this point, some economists rewrite the basic stock price formula by adding a superscript e to each Dividend term to emphasize that these are *expected* dividend payments. Because the future profitability of companies is often very difficult to forecast, it is not surprising that differences of opinion exist over what the price of a particular stock should be. Some investors will be very optimistic about the future profitability of a company and will, therefore, believe that the company's stock should have a high price. Other investors might be very pessimistic and believe that the company's stock should have a low price.

A Simple Formula for Calculating Stock Prices

It is possible to simplify the formula for determining the price of a stock, if we assume that dividends will grow at a constant rate:

$$\text{Stock Price} = \frac{\text{Dividend}}{(i - \text{Growth Rate})}.$$

In this equation, Dividend is the dividend expected to be received one year from now, and Growth Rate is the rate at which those dividends are expected to grow. If a company pays a dividend of $1 per share to be received one year from now and Growth Rate is 10 percent, the company is expected to pay a dividend of $1.10 the following year, $1.21 the year after that, and so on.

Now suppose that IBM pays a dividend of $5 per share, the consensus of investors is that these dividends will increase at a rate of 5 percent per year for the indefinite future, and the interest rate is 10 percent. Then the price of IBM's stock should be:

$$\text{Stock Price} = \frac{\$5.00}{(0.10 - 0.05)} = \$100.00.$$

Particularly during the years 1999 and 2000, there was much discussion of whether the high prices of many Internet stocks—such as the stock of Amazon.com—were justified, given that many of these companies had not made any profit yet and so had not paid any dividends. Is there any way that a rational investor would pay a high price for the stock of a company currently not earning profits? The formula for determining stock prices shows that it is possible, provided that the investor's assumptions are optimistic enough! For example, during 1999, one stock analyst predicted that Amazon.com would soon be earning $10 per share of stock. That is, Amazon.com's total earnings divided by the number of shares of its stock outstanding would be $10. Suppose Amazon.com pays out that $10 in dividends and that the $10 will grow rapidly over the years, by, say, 7 percent per year. Then our formula indicates that the price of Amazon.com stock should be:

$$\text{Stock Price} = \frac{\$10.00}{(\$0.10 - 0.07)} = \$333.33.$$

If you are sufficiently optimistic about the future prospects of a company, a high stock price can be justified even if the company is not currently earning a profit. But investors in growth stocks must be careful. Suppose investors believe that growth prospects for Amazon are only 4 percent per year instead of 7 percent because the firm turns out not to be as profitable as initially believed. Then our formula indicates that the price of Amazon.com stock should be:

$$\text{Stock Price} = \frac{\$10.00}{(\$0.10 - 0.04)} = \$166.67,$$

This price is only half the price assuming a more optimistic growth rate. Hence investors use information about a firm's profitability and growth prospects to determine what the firm is worth.

181

Going Deeper into Financial Statements

Corporations disclose substantial information about their business operations and financial position to actual and potential investors. Some of this information meets the demands of participants in financial markets and of information-collection agencies, such as Moody's Investors Service, which develops credit ratings that help investors judge how risky corporate bonds are. Other information meets the requirements of the U.S. Securities and Exchange Commission.

Key sources of information about a corporation's profitability and financial position are its principal financial statements—the *income statement* and the *balance sheet*. These important information sources were first introduced in the chapter. Here we go into more detail, using recent data for Google as an example.

Analyzing Income Statements

As discussed in the chapter, a firm's income statement summarizes its revenues, costs, and profit over a period of time. Figure A-1 shows Google's income statement for 2006.

Google's income statement presents the results of the company's operations during the year. Listed first are the revenues it earned, largely from selling advertising on its Web site, from January 1, 2006, to December 31, 2006: $10,605 million. Listed next are Google's operating expenses, the most important of which is its *cost of revenue*—which is commonly known as *cost of sales* or *cost of goods sold*: $4,225 million. Cost of revenue is the direct cost of producing the products sold, including in this case the salaries of the computer programmers Google hires to write the software for its Web site. Google also has substantial costs for researching and developing its products ($1,229 million) and for advertising and marketing them ($850 million). General and administrative expenses ($850 million) include costs such as the salaries of top managers.

The difference between a firm's revenue and its costs is its profit. "Profit" shows up in several forms on an income statement. A firm's *operating income* is the difference between its revenue and its operating expenses. Most corporations, including Google, also have investments, such as government and corporate bonds, that normally generate some income for them. In this case, Google earned $461 million on its investments, which increased its *income before taxes* to $4,011 million. The federal government taxes the profits of corporations. During 2006, Google paid $934 million—or about 23 percent

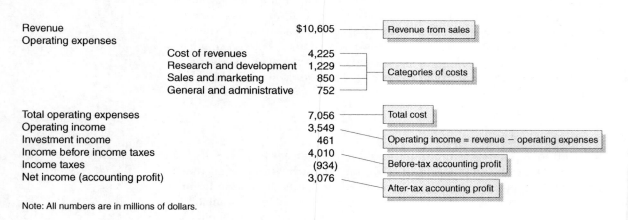

Revenue	$10,605	Revenue from sales
Operating expenses		
Cost of revenues	4,225	
Research and development	1,229	
Sales and marketing	850	Categories of costs
General and administrative	752	
Total operating expenses	7,056	Total cost
Operating income	3,549	
Investment income	461	Operating income = revenue − operating expenses
Income before income taxes	4,010	Before-tax accounting profit
Income taxes	(934)	
Net income (accounting profit)	3,076	After-tax accounting profit

Note: All numbers are in millions of dollars.

Figure A-1 | Google's Income Statement for 2006

Google's income statement shows the company's revenue, costs, and profit for 2006. The difference between its revenue ($10,605 million) and its operating expenses ($7,055 million) is its operating income ($3,550 million). Most corporations also have investments, such as government or corporate bonds, that generate some income for them. In this case, Google earned $461 million, giving the firm an income before taxes

of $4,011 million. After paying taxes of $934 million, Google was left with a net income, or accounting profit, of $3,076 million for the year.

Source: Google's Income Statement for 2006. Google Inc., "Consolidated Statements of Income," February 1, 2007 Used with permission of Google, Inc.

of its profits—in taxes. *Net income* after taxes was $3,077 million. The net income that firms report on their income statements is referred to as their after-tax *accounting profit*.

Analyzing Balance Sheets

As discussed in the chapter, whereas a firm's income statement reports a firm's activities for a period of time, a firm's balance sheet summarizes its financial position on a particular day, usually the end of a quarter or year. To understand how a balance sheet is organized, first recall that an asset is anything of value that the firm owns, and a liability is a debt or an obligation that the firm owes. Subtracting the value of a firm's liabilities from the value of its assets leaves its *net worth*. Because a corporation's stockholders are its owners, net worth is often listed as **stockholders' equity** on a balance sheet. Using these definitions, we can state the balance sheet equation (also called the basic accounting equation) as follows:

$$\text{Assets} - \text{Liabilities} = \text{Stockholders' Equity},$$

or:

$$\text{Assets} = \text{Liabilities} + \text{Stockholders' Equity}.$$

Stockholders' equity The difference between the value of a corporation's assets and the value of its liabilities; also known as net worth.

This formula tells us that the value of a firm's assets must equal the value of its liabilities plus the value of stockholders' equity. An important accounting rule dating back to the beginning of modern bookkeeping in fifteenth-century Italy holds that balance sheets should list assets on the left side and liabilities and net worth, or stockholders' equity, on the right side. Notice that this means that *the value of the left side of the balance sheet must always equal the value of the right side.* Figure A-2 shows Google's balance sheet as of December 31, 2006.

A couple of the entries on the asset side of the balance sheet may be unfamiliar: *Current assets* are assets that the firm could convert into cash quickly, such as the balance in its checking account or its accounts receivable, which is money currently owed to the firm for products that have been delivered but not yet paid for. *Goodwill* represents the difference between the purchase price of a company and the market value of its assets. It represents the ability of a business to earn an economic profit from its assets. For example, if you buy a restaurant that is located on a busy intersection and you employ a chef with a reputation for preparing delicious food, you may pay more than the market value of the tables, chairs, ovens, and other assets. This additional amount you pay will be entered on the asset side of your balance sheet as goodwill.

Current liabilities are short-term debts such as accounts payable, which is money owed to suppliers for goods received but not yet paid for, or bank loans that will be paid back in less than one year. Long-term bank loans and the value of outstanding corporate bonds are *long-term liabilities*.

ASSETS		LIABILITIES AND STOCKHOLDERS' EQUITY	
Current Assets	$13,040	Current Liabilities	$1,305
Property and Equipment	2,395	Long-term liabilities	129
Investments	1,032	Total Liabilities	1,434
Goodwill	1,545	Stockholders' Equity	17,040
Other long-term assets	461		
Total Assets	18,473	Total liabilites and stockholders' equity	18,473

Figure A-2 | Google's Balance Sheet as of December 31, 2006

Corporations list their assets on the left of their balance sheets and their liabilities on the right. The difference between the value of the firm's assets and the value of its liabilities equals the net worth of the firm, or stockholders' equity. Stockholders' equity is listed on the right side of the balance sheet. Therefore, the value of the left side of the balance sheet must always equal the value of the right side.

Note: All numbers are in millions of dollars.

Source: Google's Balance Sheet as of December 31, 2006, Google, Inc., "Consolidated Balance Sheets," February 1, 2007. Used with permission of Google, Inc.

Key Terms

Present value   Stockholders' equity

myeconlab   Visit www.myeconlab.com to complete these exercises
Get Ahead of the Curve   online and get instant feedback.

Review Questions

A.1 Why is money you receive at some future date worth less than money you receive today? If the interest rate rises, what effect does this have on the present value of payments you receive in the future?

A.2 Give the formula for calculating the present value of a bond that will pay a coupon of $100 per year for 10 years and that has a face value of $1,000.

A.3 Compare the formula for calculating the present value of the payments you will receive from owning a bond to the formula for calculating the present value of the payments you will receive from owning a stock. What are the key similarities? What are the key differences?

A.4 How is operating income calculated? How does operating income differ from net income? How does net income differ from accounting profit?

A.5 What's the key difference between a firm's income statement and its balance sheet? What is listed on the left side of a balance sheet? What is listed on the right side?

Problems and Applications

A.6 (Related to *Solved Problem A-1*) If the interest rate is 10 percent, what is the present value of a bond that matures in two years, pays $85 one year from now, and pays $1,085 two years from now?

A.7 The following is from an Associated Press story on the contract of baseball star Carlos Beltran:

Beltran's contract calls for his $11 million signing bonus to be paid in four installments: $5 million upon approval and $2 million each this June 15, 2005, and on Jan. 15, 2006, and Jan. 15, 2007. He gets a $10 million salary this year, $12 million in each of the following two seasons and

$18.5 million in each of the final four seasons, with $8.5 million deferred annually from 2008–11. The players' association calculated the present day value of the contract at $115,726,946, using a 6 percent discount rate (the prime rate [which is the interest rate banks charge on loans to their best customers] plus 1 percent, rounded to the nearest whole number). For purposes of baseball's luxury tax, which currently uses a 3.62 percent discount rate, the contract is valued at $116,695,898.

Briefly explain why the present value of Beltran's contract is lower if a higher interest is used to make the calculation than if a lower interest rate is used.

Source: "Like Pedro, Beltran Gets Suite on Road," Associated Press, January 18, 2005.

A.8 (Related to *Solved Problem A-1*) Before the 2007 season, the Seattle Mariners baseball team signed catcher Kenji Johjima to a contract that would pay him the following amounts: an immediate $1 million signing bonus, $5.1 million for the 2007 season, $5.2 million for the 2008 season, and $5.2 million for the 2009 season. Assume that he receives each of his three seasonal salaries as a lump sum payment at the end of the season and that he receives his 2007 salary one year after he signed the contract.

a. Some newspaper reports described Johjima as having signed a "$16.5 million contract" with the Mariners. Do you agree that $16.5 million was the value of this contract? Briefly explain.

b. What was the present value of Johjima's contract at the time he signed it (assuming an interest rate of 10 percent)?

c. If you use an interest rate of 5 percent, what was the present value of Johjima's contract?

A.9 (Related to *Solved Problem A-1*) A winner of the Pennsylvania Lottery was given the choice of receiving $18 million at once or $1,440,000 per year for 25 years.

a. If the winner had opted for the 25 annual payments, how much in total would she have received?

b. At an interest rate of 10 percent, what would be the present value of the 25 payments?

c. At an interest rate of 5 percent, what would be the present value of the 25 payments?

d. What interest rate would make the present value of the 25 payments equal to the one payment of $18 million? (This question is difficult and requires the use of a financial calculator or a spreadsheet. *Hint:* If you are familiar with the Excel spreadsheet program, use the RATE function. Questions (b) and (c) can be answered by using the Excel NPV—Net Present Value—function.)

A.10 **(Related to *Solved Problem A-1*)** Before the start of the 2000 baseball season, the New York Mets decided they didn't want Bobby Bonilla playing for them any longer. But Bonilla had a contract with the Mets for the 2000 season that would have obliged the Mets to pay him $5.9 million. When the Mets released Bonilla, he agreed to take the following payments in lieu of the $5.9 million the Mets would have paid him in the year 2000: He will receive 25 equal payments of $1,193,248.20 each July 1 from 2011 to 2035. If you were Bobby Bonilla, which would you rather have had, the lump sum $5.9 million or the 25 payments beginning in 2011? Explain the basis for your decision.

A.11 Suppose that eLake, an online auction site, is paying a dividend of $2 per share. You expect this dividend to grow 2 percent per year, and the interest rate is 10 percent. What is the most you would be willing to pay for a share of stock in eLake? If the interest rate is 5 percent, what is the most you would be willing to pay? When interest rates in the economy decline, would you expect stock prices in general to rise or fall? Explain.

A.12 Suppose you buy the bond of a large corporation at a time when the inflation rate is very low. If the inflation rate increases during the time you hold the bond, what is likely to happen to the price of the bond?

A.13 Use the information in the following table for calendar year 2006 to prepare the McDonald's Corporation's income statement. Be sure to include entries for operating income and net income.

Revenue from company restaurants	$16,083 million
Revenue from franchised restaurants	5,503 million
Cost of operating company-owned restaurants	13,542 million
Income taxes	1,293 million
Interest expense	402 million
General and administrative cost	2,338 million
Cost of restaurant leases	1,060 million
Other operating costs	67 million

Source: McDonald's Corporation, *Annual Report, 2006*, February 26, 2007.

A.14 Use the information in the following table on the financial situation of Starbucks Corporation as of December 31, 2006, to prepare the firm's balance sheet. Be sure to include an entry for stockholders' equity.

Current assets	$1,530 million
Current liabilities	1,936 million
Property and equipment	2,288 million
Long-term liabilities	50 million
Goodwill	161 million
Other assets	187 million

Source: Starbucks Corporation, *Annual Report, 2006*.

A.15 The *current ratio* is equal to a firm's current assets divided by its current liabilities. Use the information in Figure A-2 to calculate Google's current ratio on December 31, 2006. Investors generally prefer that a firm's current ratio be greater than 1.5. What problems might a firm encounter if the value of its current assets is low relative to the value of its current liabilities?

>> End Appendix Learning Objective

Technology, Production, and Costs

From Chapter 10 of *Microeconomics*, 2/e. R. Glenn Hubbard. Anthony Patrick O'Brien. Copyright © 2008 by Pearson Prentice Hall. All rights reserved.

Technology, Production, and Costs

Sony Uses a Cost Curve to Determine the Price of Radios

In consumer electronics, rapid technological change leads to new products and lower cost ways of manufacturing existing products. How do firms take costs into account when setting prices? This is an important question that we will explore in the next few chapters and it is a question that Sony Corporation, the Japanese electronics giant, must answer every day. Sony manufactures televisions, computers, satellite systems, semiconductors, telephones, and flat-screen televisions, among other products.

Like most firms, Sony started small. Its early success resulted from the vision and energy of two young entrepreneurs, Akio Morita and Masaru Ibuka.

In 1953, Sony purchased a license that allowed it to use transistor technology developed in the United States at Western Electric's Bell Laboratories.

Sony used the technology to develop a transistor radio that was small enough to fit in a shirt pocket and far smaller than any other radio then available. In 1955, Akio Morita, Sony's chairman, arrived in New York, hoping to convince one of the U.S. department store chains to carry the Sony radios.

Morita offered to sell one department store chain 5,000 radios at a price of $29.95 each. If the chain wanted more than 5,000 radios, the price would change. As Morita described it later:

I sat down and drew a curve that looked something like a lopsided letter U. The price for five thousand would be our regular price. That would be the beginning of the curve. For ten thousand there would be a discount, and that was at the bottom of the curve. For thirty thousand the price would begin to climb. For fifty thousand the price per unit would be higher than for five thousand, and for one hundred thousand units the price per unit would have to be much higher than for the first five thousand.

Why would the prices Morita offered the department store follow a U shape? Because Sony's cost per unit, or *average cost*, of manufacturing the radios would have the same shape. Curves that show the relationship between the level of output and per-unit cost are called *average total cost curves*. Average total cost curves typically have the U shape of Morita's curve. As we explore the relationship between production and costs in this chapter, we will see why average total cost curves have this shape.

Today, Sony is one of the largest electronics firms in the world, but more than 50 years ago, when it was a small, struggling company, Akio Morita used a simple economic tool—the average cost curve—to help make an important business decision. Every day, in companies large and small, managers use economic tools to make decisions. **AN INSIDE LOOK** discusses the effect of lower manufacturing costs on the prices of flat-panel televisions.

Source: Akio Morita, with Edwin M. Reingold and Mitsuko Shimomura. *Made in Japan : Akio Morita and Sony*. New York: 1986, p. 94.

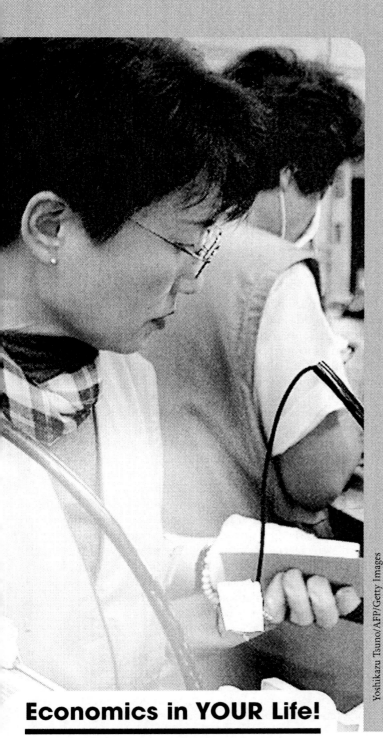

Yoshikazu Tsuno/AFP/Getty Images

LEARNING Objectives

After studying this chapter, you should be able to:

1   Define **technology** and give examples of **technological change**.

2   Distinguish between the economic **short run** and the economic **long run**.

3   Understand the relationship between the **marginal product of labor** and the **average product of labor**

4   Explain and illustrate the relationship between **marginal cost** and **average total cost**

5   **Graph** average total cost, average variable cost, average fixed cost, and marginal cost.

6   Understand how firms use the **long-run average cost curve** in their planning.

APPENDIX Use **isoquants** and **isocost lines** to understand production and cost.

Economics in YOUR Life!

Using Cost Concepts in Your Own Business

Suppose that you have the opportunity to open a store selling recliners. You learn that you can purchase the recliners from the manufacturer for $300 each. Bob's Big Chairs is an existing store that is the same size as your new store will be. Bob's sells the same recliners you plan to sell and also buys them from the manufacturer for $300 each. Your plan is to sell the recliners for a price of $500. After studying how Bob's is operated, you find that they are selling more recliners per month than you expect to be able to sell and that they are selling them for $450. You wonder how Bob's makes a profit at the lower price. Are there any reasons to expect that because Bob's sells more recliners per month, its costs will be lower than your store's costs? You can check your answer against the one we provide at the end of the chapter.

189

In this chapter, we look behind the supply curve to better understand firm decision making. Earlier chapters showed that supply curves are upward sloping because marginal cost increases as firms increase the quantity of a good that they supply. In this chapter, we look more closely at why this is true. In the appendix to this chapter, we extend the analysis by using isoquants and isocost lines to understand the relationship between production and costs. Once we have a good understanding of production and cost, we can proceed in the following chapters to understand how firms decide what level of output to produce and what price to charge.

1 | Define technology and give examples of technological change.

Technology: An Economic Definition

The basic activity of a firm is to use *inputs*, such as workers, machines, and natural resources, to produce *outputs* of goods and services. A pizza parlor, for example, uses inputs such as pizza dough, pizza sauce, cooks, and ovens to produce pizza. A firm's **technology** is the processes it uses to turn inputs into outputs of goods and services. Notice that this economic definition of technology is broader than the everyday definition. When we use the word *technology* in everyday language, we usually refer only to the development of new products. In the economic sense, a firm's technology depends on many factors, such as the skill of its managers, the training of its workers, and the speed and efficiency of its machinery and equipment. The technology of pizza production, for example, includes not only the capacity of the pizza ovens and how quickly they bake the pizza but also how quickly the cooks can prepare the pizza for baking, how well the manager motivates the workers, and how well the manager has arranged the facilities to allow the cooks to quickly prepare the pizzas and get them in the ovens.

Whenever a firm experiences positive **technological change**, it is able to produce more output using the same inputs or the same output using fewer inputs. Positive technological change can come from many sources. The firm's managers may rearrange the factory floor or the layout of a retail store, thereby increasing production and sales. The firm's workers may go through a training program. The firm may install faster or more reliable machinery or equipment. It is also possible for a firm to experience negative technological change. If a firm hires less-skilled workers or if a hurricane damages its facilities, the quantity of output it can produce from a given quantity of inputs may decline.

Technology The processes a firm uses to turn inputs into outputs of goods and services.

Technological change A change in the ability of a firm to produce a given level of output with a given quantity of inputs.

Getty Images, Inc.

Better inventory controls have helped reduce firms' costs.

Making the Connection | Improving Inventory Control at Wal-Mart

Inventories are goods that have been produced but not yet sold. For a retailer such as Wal-Mart, inventories at any point in time include the goods on the store shelves as well as goods in warehouses. Inventories are an input into Wal-Mart's output of goods sold to consumers. Having money tied up in holding inventories is costly, so firms have an incentive to hold as few inventories as possible and to *turn over* their inventories as rapidly as possible by ensuring that goods do not remain on the shelves long. Holding too few inventories, however, results in *stockouts*— that is, sales being lost because the goods consumers want to buy are not on the shelf.

Improvements in inventory control meet the economic definition of positive technological change because they allow firms to produce the same output with fewer inputs. In recent years, many firms have adopted *just-in-time* inventory systems in which firms accept shipments from suppliers as close as possible to the time they will be needed. The just-in-time system was pioneered by Toyota, which used it to reduce the inventories of parts in its automobile assembly plants. Wal-Mart has been a pioneer in using similar inventory control systems in its stores.

Wal-Mart actively manages its *supply chain*, which stretches from the manufacturers of the goods it sells to its retail stores. Entrepreneur Sam Walton, the company founder, built a series of distribution centers spread across the country to supply goods to the retail stores. As goods are sold in the stores, this *point-of-sale* information is sent electronically to the firm's distribution centers to help managers determine what products will be shipped to each store. Depending on a store's location relative to a distribution center, managers can use Wal-Mart's trucks to ship goods overnight. This distribution system allows Wal-Mart to minimize its inventory holdings without running the risk of many stockouts. Because Wal-Mart sells 15 percent to 25 percent of all the toothpaste, disposable diapers, dog food, and many other products sold in the United States, it has been able to involve many manufacturers closely in its supply chain. For example, a company such as Procter & Gamble, which is one of the world's largest manufacturers of toothpaste, laundry detergent, toilet paper, and other products, receives Wal-Mart's point-of-sale and inventory information electronically. Procter & Gamble uses that information to help determine its production schedules and the quantities it should ship to Wal-Mart's distribution centers.

Technological change has been a key to Wal-Mart's becoming one of the largest firms in the world, with 1.9 million employees and revenue of more than $348 billion in 2006.

YOUR TURN: Test your understanding by doing related problem 1.5 at the end of this chapter.

The Short Run and the Long Run in Economics

When firms analyze the relationship between their level of production and their costs, they separate the time period involved into the short run and the long run. In the **short run**, at least one of the firm's inputs is fixed. In particular, in the short run, the firm's technology and the size of its physical plant—its factory, store, or office—are both fixed, while the number of workers the firm hires is variable. In the **long run**, the firm is able to vary all its inputs and can adopt new technology and increase or decrease the size of its physical plant. Of course, the actual length of calendar time in the short run will be different from firm to firm. A pizza parlor may be able to increase its physical plant by adding another pizza oven and some tables and chairs in just a few weeks. BMW, in contrast, may take more than a year to increase the capacity of one of its automobile assembly plants by installing new equipment.

Short run The period of time during which at least one of a firm's inputs is fixed.

Long run The period of time in which a firm can vary all its inputs, adopt new technology, and increase or decrease the size of its physical plant.

The Difference between Fixed Costs and Variable Costs

Total cost is the cost of all the inputs a firm uses in production. We have just seen that in the short run, some inputs are fixed and others are variable. The costs of the fixed inputs are *fixed costs*, and the costs of the variable inputs are *variable costs*. We can also think of **variable costs** as the costs that change as output changes. Similarly, **fixed costs** are costs that remain constant as output changes. A typical firm's variable costs include its labor costs, raw material costs, and costs of electricity and other utilities. Typical fixed costs include lease payments for factory or retail space, payments for fire insurance, and payments for newspaper and television advertising. All of a firm's costs are either fixed or variable, so we can state the following:

Total cost The cost of all the inputs a firm uses in production.

Variable costs Costs that change as output changes.

Fixed costs Costs that remain constant as output changes.

Total Cost = Fixed Cost + Variable Cost

or, using symbols:

$$TC = FC + VC.$$

Publishers consider the salaries of editors to be a fixed cost.

Making the Connection | Fixed Costs in the Publishing Industry

An editor at Cambridge University Press gives the following estimates of the annual fixed cost for a medium-size academic book publisher.

COST	AMOUNT
Salaries and benefits	$437,500
Rent	75,000
Utilities	20,000
Supplies	6,000
Postage	4,000
Travel	8,000
Subscriptions, etc.	4,000
Miscellaneous	5,000
Total	$559,500

Academic book publishers hire editors, designers, and production and marketing managers who help prepare books for publication. Because these employees work on several books simultaneously, the number of people the company hires does not go up and down with the quantity of books the company publishes during any particular year. Publishing companies therefore consider the salaries and benefits of people in these job categories as fixed costs.

In contrast, for a company that *prints* books, the quantity of workers varies with the quantity of books printed. The wages and benefits of the workers operating the printing presses, for example, would be a variable cost.

The other costs listed in the preceding table are typical of fixed costs at many firms.

Source: Beth Luey, *Handbook for Academic Authors*, 4th ed., Cambridge, UK: Cambridge University Press, 2002, p. 244.

YOUR TURN: Test your understanding by doing related problems 2.3, 2.4, and 2.5 at the end of this chapter.

Implicit Costs versus Explicit Costs

It is important to remember that economists always measure costs as *opportunity costs*. The **opportunity cost** of any activity is the highest-valued alternative that must be given up to engage in that activity. Costs are either *explicit* or *implicit*. When a firm spends money, it incurs an **explicit cost**. When a firm experiences a nonmonetary opportunity cost, it incurs an **implicit cost**.

For example, suppose that Jill Johnson owns a pizza restaurant. In operating her store, Jill has explicit costs, such as the wages she pays her workers and the payments she makes for rent and electricity. But some of Jill's most important costs are implicit. Before opening her own restaurant, Jill earned a salary of $30,000 per year managing a restaurant for someone else. To start her restaurant, Jill quit her job, withdrew $50,000 from her bank account—where it earned her interest of $3,000 per year—and used the funds to equip her restaurant with tables, chairs, a cash register, and other equipment. To open her own business, Jill had to give up the $30,000 salary and the $3,000 in interest. This $33,000 is an implicit cost because it does not represent payments that Jill has to make. All the same, giving up this $33,000 per year is a real cost to Jill. In addition, during the course of the year, the $50,000 worth of tables, chairs, and other physical capital in Jill's store will lose some of its value due partly to wear and tear and partly to better furniture, cash registers, and so forth becoming available. *Economic depreciation* is the difference between what Jill paid for her capital at the beginning of the year and what she could sell the capital for at the end of the year. If Jill could sell the capital for $40,000 at the end of the year, then the $10,000 in economic depreciation represents another implicit cost.

Opportunity cost The highest-valued alternative that must be given up to engage in an activity.

Explicit cost A cost that involves spending money.

Implicit cost A nonmonetary opportunity cost.

TABLE 1

Jill Johnson's Costs per Year

Pizza dough, tomato sauce, and other ingredients	$20,000
Wages	48,000
Interest payments on loan to buy pizza ovens	10,000
Electricity	6,000
Lease payment for store	24,000
Foregone salary	30,000
Foregone interest	3,000
Economic depreciation	10,000
Total	$151,000

(Note that the whole $50,000 she spent on the capital is not a cost because she still has the equipment at the end of the year, although it is now worth only $40,000.)

Table 1 lists Jill's costs. The entries in red are explicit costs, and the entries in blue are implicit costs. The rules of accounting generally require that only explicit costs be used for purposes of keeping the company's financial records and for paying taxes. Therefore, explicit costs are sometimes called *accounting costs*. *Economic costs* include both accounting costs and implicit costs.

The Production Function

Let's look at the relationship between the level of production and costs in the short run for Jill Johnson's restaurant. To keep things simpler than in the more realistic situation in Table 1, let's assume that Jill uses only labor—workers—and one type of capital—pizza ovens—to produce a single good: pizzas. Many firms use more than two inputs and produce more than one good, but it is easier to understand the relationship between output and cost by focusing on the case of a firm using only two inputs and producing only one good. In the short run, Jill doesn't have time to build a larger restaurant, install additional pizza ovens, or redesign the layout of her restaurant. So, in the short run, she can increase or decrease the quantity of pizzas she produces only by increasing or decreasing the quantity of workers she employs.

The first three columns of Table 2 show the relationship between the quantity of workers and ovens Jill uses each week and the quantity of pizzas she can produce. The relationship between the inputs employed by a firm and the maximum output it can

TABLE 2 | Short-Run Production and Cost at Jill Johnson's Restaurant

QUANTITY OF WORKERS	QUANTITY OF PIZZA OVENS	QUANTITY OF PIZZAS PER WEEK	COST OF PIZZA OVENS (FIXED COST)	COST OF WORKERS (VARIABLE COST)	TOTAL COST OF PIZZAS	COST PER PIZZA (AVERAGE TOTAL COST)
0	2	0	$800	$0	$800	—
1	2	200	800	650	1,450	$7.25
2	2	450	800	1,300	2,100	4.67
3	2	550	800	1,950	2,750	5.00
4	2	600	800	2,600	3,400	5.67
5	2	625	800	3,250	4,050	6.48
6	2	640	800	3,900	4,700	7.34

Production function The relationship between the inputs employed by a firm and the maximum output it can produce with those inputs.

produce with those inputs is called the firm's **production function**. Because a firm's technology is the processes it uses to turn inputs into output, the production function represents the firm's technology. In this case, Table 2 shows Jill's *short-run* production function because we are assuming that the time period is too short for Jill to increase or decrease the quantity of ovens she is using.

A First Look at the Relationship between Production and Cost

Table 2 gives us information on Jill's costs. We can determine the total cost of producing a given quantity of pizzas if we know how many workers and ovens are required to produce that quantity of pizzas and what Jill has to pay for those workers and pizzas. Suppose Jill has taken out a bank loan to buy two pizza ovens. The cost of the loan is $800 per week. Therefore, her fixed costs are $800 per week. If Jill pays $650 per week to each worker, her variable costs depend on how many workers she hires. In the short run, Jill can increase the quantity of pizzas she produces only by hiring more workers. The table shows that if she hires 1 worker, she produces 200 pizzas during the week; if she hires 2 workers, she produces 450 pizzas; and so on. For a particular week, Jill's total cost of producing pizzas is equal to the $800 she pays on the loan for the ovens plus the amount she pays to hire workers. If Jill decides to hire 4 workers and produce 600 pizzas, her total cost is $3,400: $800 to lease the ovens and $2,600 to hire the workers. Her cost per pizza is equal to her total cost of producing pizzas divided by the quantity of pizzas produced. If she produces 600 pizzas at a total cost of $3,400, her cost per pizza, or *average total cost*, is $3,400/600 = $5.67. A firm's **average total cost** is always equal to its total cost divided by the quantity of output produced.

Average total cost Total cost divided by the quantity of output produced.

Panel (a) of Figure 1 uses the numbers in the next-to-last column of Table 2 to graph Jill's total cost. Panel (b) uses the numbers in the last column to graph her average total

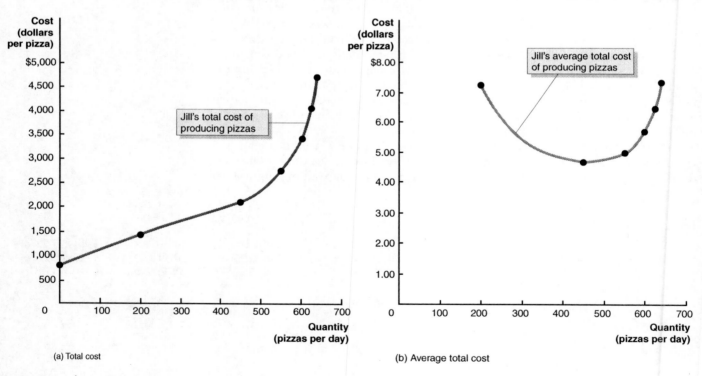

(a) Total cost

(b) Average total cost

Figure 1 | Graphing Total Cost and Average Total Cost at Jill Johnson's Restaurant

We can use the information from Table 2 to graph the relationship between the quantity of pizzas Jill produces and her total cost and average total cost. Panel (a) shows that total cost increases as the level of production increases. In panel (b), we see that the average total cost is roughly U-shaped: As production increases from low levels,

average cost falls before rising at higher levels of production. To understand why average cost has this shape, we must look more closely at the technology of producing pizzas, as shown by the production function.

cost. Notice in panel (b) that Jill's average cost has roughly the same U shape as the average cost curve we saw Akio Morita calculate for Sony transistor radios at the beginning of this chapter. As production increases from low levels, average cost falls. Average cost then becomes fairly flat, before rising at higher levels of production. To understand why average cost has this U shape, we first need to look more closely at the technology of producing pizzas, as shown by the production function for Jill's restaurant. Then we need to look at how this technology determines the relationship between production and cost.

---

3 | Understand the relationship between the marginal product of labor and the average product of labor.

The Marginal Product of Labor and the Average Product of Labor

To better understand the choices Jill faces, given the technology available to her, think first about what happens if she hires only one worker. That one worker will have to perform several different activities, including taking orders from customers, baking the pizzas, bringing the pizzas to the customers' tables, and ringing up sales on the cash register. If Jill hires two workers, some of these activities can be divided up: One worker could take the orders and ring up the sales, and one worker could bake the pizzas. With this division of tasks, Jill will find that hiring two workers actually allows her to produce more than twice as many pizzas as she could produce with just one worker.

The additional output a firm produces as a result of hiring one more worker is called the **marginal product of labor**. We can calculate the marginal product of labor by determining how much total output increases as each additional worker is hired. We do this for Jill's restaurant in Table 3.

Marginal product of labor The additional output a firm produces as a result of hiring one more worker.

When Jill hires only 1 worker, she produces 200 pizzas per week. When she hires 2 workers, she produces 450 pizzas per week. Hiring the second worker increases her production by 250 pizzas per week. So, the marginal product of labor for 1 worker is 200 pizzas. For 2 workers, the marginal product of labor rises to 250 pizzas. This increase in marginal product results from the *division of labor* and from *specialization*. By dividing the tasks to be performed—the division of labor—Jill reduces the time workers lose moving from one activity to the next. She also allows them to become more specialized at their tasks. For example, a worker who concentrates on baking pizzas will become skilled at doing so quickly and efficiently.

The Law of Diminishing Returns

In the short run, the quantity of pizza ovens Jill leases is fixed, so as she hires more workers, the marginal product of labor eventually begins to decline. This happens because at some point, Jill uses up all the gains from the division of labor and from specialization

QUANTITY OF WORKERS	QUANTITY OF PIZZA OVENS	QUANTITY OF PIZZAS	MARGINAL PRODUCT OF LABOR
0	2	0	—
1	2	200	200
2	2	450	250
3	2	550	100
4	2	600	50
5	2	625	25
6	2	640	15

TABLE 3

The Marginal Product of Labor at Jill Johnson's Restaurant

Law of diminishing returns The principle that, at some point, adding more of a variable input, such as labor, to the same amount of a fixed input, such as capital, will cause the marginal product of the variable input to decline.

and starts to experience the effects of the **law of diminishing returns**. This law states that adding more of a variable input, such as labor, to the same amount of a fixed input, such as capital, will eventually cause the marginal product of the variable input to decline. For Jill, the marginal product of labor begins to decline when she hires the third worker. Hiring three workers raises the quantity of pizzas she produces from 450 per week to 550. But the increase in the quantity of pizzas—100—is less than the increase when she hired the second worker—250.

If Jill kept adding more and more workers to the same quantity of pizza ovens, eventually workers would begin to get in each other's way, and the marginal product of labor would actually become negative. When the marginal product is negative, the level of total output declines. No firm would actually hire so many workers as to experience a negative marginal product of labor and falling total output.

Graphing Production

Panel (a) in Figure 2 shows the relationship between the quantity of workers Jill hires and her total output of pizzas, using the numbers from Table 3. Panel (b) shows the marginal product of labor. In panel (a), output increases as more workers are hired, but the increase in output does not occur at a constant rate. Because of specialization and the division of labor, output at first increases at an increasing rate, with each additional worker hired causing production to increase by a *greater* amount than did the hiring of the previous worker. But after the second worker has been hired, hiring more workers while keeping the quantity of ovens constant results in diminishing returns. When the point of diminishing returns is reached, production increases at a decreasing rate. Each additional worker hired after the second worker causes production to increase by a *smaller* amount than did the hiring of the previous worker. In panel (b), the marginal product of labor curve rises initially because of the effects of specialization and division of labor, and then it falls due to the effects of diminishing returns.

© Indranil Mukherjee/AFP/Getty Images

The gains from division of labor and specialization are as important to firms today as they were in the eighteenth century, when Adam Smith first discussed them.

Making the Connection | Adam Smith's Famous Account of the Division of Labor in a Pin Factory

In *The Wealth of Nations*, Adam Smith uses production in a pin factory as an example of the gains in output resulting from the division of labor. The following is an excerpt from his account of how pin making was divided into a series of tasks:

> One man draws out the wire, another straightens it, a third cuts it, a fourth points it, a fifth grinds it at the top for receiving the head; to make the head requires two or three distinct operations; to put it on is a [distinct operation], to whiten the pins is another; it is even a trade by itself to put them into the paper; and the important business of making a pin is, in this manner, divided into eighteen distinct operations.

Because the labor of pin making was divided up in this way, the average worker was able to produce about 4,800 pins per day. Smith speculated that a single worker using the pin-making machinery alone would make only about 20 pins per day. This lesson from more than 225 years ago, showing the tremendous gains from division of labor and specialization, remains relevant to most business situations today.

Source: Adam Smith, *An Inquiry into the Nature and Causes of the Wealth of Nations*, Vol. I, Oxford, UK: Oxford University Press edition, 1976, pp. 14–15.

YOUR TURN: Test your understanding by doing related problem 3.6 at the end of this chapter.

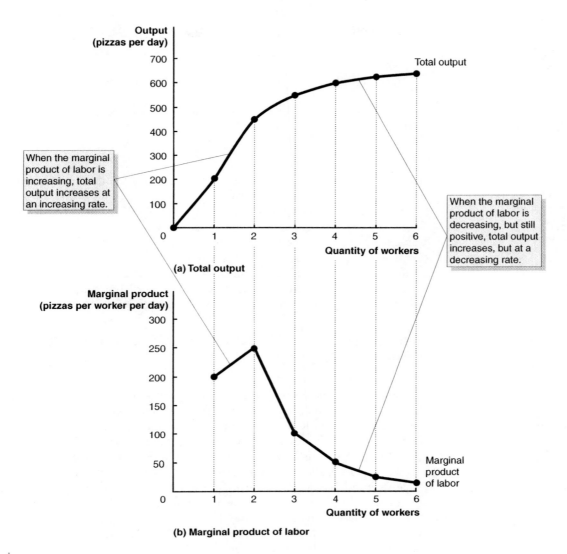

Figure 2 | Total Output and the Marginal Product of Labor

In panel (a), output increases as more workers are hired, but the increase in output does not occur at a constant rate. Because of specialization and the division of labor, output at first increases at an increasing rate, with each additional worker hired causing production to increase by a *greater* amount than did the hiring of the previous worker. After the third worker has been hired, hiring more workers while keeping the number of pizza ovens constant results in diminishing returns. When the point of diminishing returns is reached, production increases at a decreasing rate. Each additional worker hired after the third worker causes production to increase by a *smaller* amount than did the hiring of the previous worker. In panel (b), the *marginal product of labor* is the additional output produced as a result of hiring one more worker. The marginal product of labor rises initially because of the effects of specialization and division of labor, and then it falls due to the effects of diminishing returns.

The Relationship between Marginal and Average Product

The marginal product of labor tells us how much total output changes as the quantity of workers hired changes. We can also calculate how many pizzas workers produce on average. The **average product of labor** is the total output produced by a firm divided by the quantity of workers. For example, using the numbers in Table 3, if Jill hires 4 workers to produce 600 pizzas, the average product of labor is 600/4 = 150.

We can state the relationship between the marginal and average products of labor this way: *The average product of labor is the average of the marginal products of labor.* For example, the numbers from Table 3 show that the marginal product of the first worker Jill hires is 200, the marginal product of the second worker is 250, and the

Average product of labor The total output produced by a firm divided by the quantity of workers.

marginal product of the third worker is 100. Therefore, the average product of labor for three workers is 183.3:

$$183.3 = (200 + 250 + 100) / 3$$

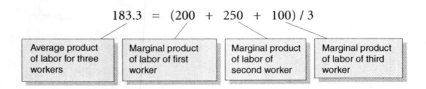

By taking the average of the marginal products of the first three workers, we have the average product of the three workers.

Whenever the marginal product of labor is greater than the average product of labor, the average product of labor must be increasing. This statement is true for the same reason that a person 6 feet, 2 inches tall entering a room where the average height is 5 feet, 9 inches raises the average height of people in the room. Whenever the marginal product of labor is less than the average product of labor, the average product of labor must be decreasing. The marginal product of labor equals the average product of labor for the quantity of workers where the average product of labor is at its maximum.

An Example of Marginal and Average Values: College Grades

The relationship between the marginal product of labor and the average product of labor is the same as the relationship between the marginal and average values of any variable. To see this more clearly, think about the familiar relationship between a student's grade point average (GPA) in one semester and his overall, or cumulative, GPA. The table in Figure 3 shows Paul's college grades for each semester, beginning with fall 2005. The graph in Figure 3 plots the grades from the table. Just as each additional worker hired adds to a firm's total production, each additional semester adds to Paul's total grade points. We can calculate what each individual worker hired adds to total production (marginal product), and we can calculate the average production of the workers hired so far (average product).

Similarly, we can calculate the GPA Paul earns in a particular semester (his "marginal GPA"), and we can calculate his cumulative GPA for all the semesters he has completed so far (his "average GPA"). As the table shows, Paul gets off to a weak start in the fall semester of his freshman year, earning only a 1.50 GPA. In each subsequent semester through the fall of his junior year, his GPA for the semester increases from the previous semester—raising his cumulative GPA. As the graph shows, however, his cumulative GPA does not increase as rapidly as his semester-by-semester GPA because his cumulative GPA is held back by the low GPAs of his first few semesters. Notice that in Paul's junior year, even though his semester GPA declines from fall to spring, his cumulative GPA rises. Only in the fall of his senior year, when his semester GPA drops below his cumulative GPA, does his cumulative GPA decline.

4 LEARNING OBJECTIVE

4 | Explain and illustrate the relationship between marginal cost and average total cost.

The Relationship between Short-Run Production and Short-Run Cost

We have seen that technology determines the values of the marginal product of labor and the average product of labor. In turn, the marginal and average products of labor affect the firm's costs. Keep in mind that the relationships we are discussing are *short-run* relationships: We are assuming that the time period is too short for the firm to change its technology or the size of its physical plant.

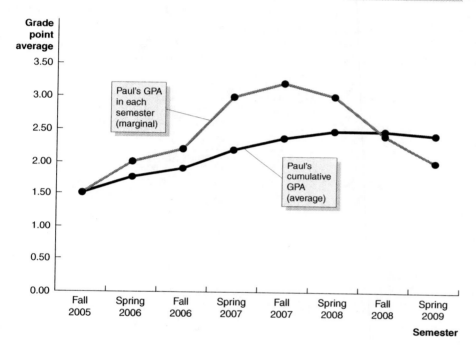

	Semester GPA (Marginal) GPA	Cumulative GPA (Average) GPA
Freshman Year		
Fall	1.50	1.50
Spring	2.00	1.75
Sophomore Year		
Fall	2.20	1.90
Spring	3.00	2.18
Junior Year		
Fall	3.20	2.38
Spring	3.00	2.48
Senior Year		
Fall	2.40	2.47
Spring	2.00	2.41

Average GPA continues to rise, although marginal GPA falls.

With the marginal GPA below the average, the average GPA falls.

Paul's GPA in each semester (marginal)

Paul's cumulative GPA (average)

Figure 3

Marginal and Average GPAs

The relationship between marginal and average values for a variable can be illustrated using GPAs. We can calculate the GPA Paul earns in a particular semester (his "marginal GPA"), and we can calculate his cumulative GPA for all the semesters he has completed so far (his "average GPA"). Paul's GPA is only 1.50 in the fall semester of his freshman year. In each following semester through fall of his junior year, his GPA for the semester increases—raising his cumulative GPA. In Paul's junior year, even though his semester GPA declines from fall to spring, his cumulative GPA rises. Only in the fall of his senior year, when his semester GPA drops below his cumulative GPA, does his cumulative GPA decline.

At the beginning of this chapter, we saw how Akio Morita used an average total cost curve to determine the price of radios. The average total cost curve Morita used and the average total cost curve in Figure 1 for Jill Johnson's restaurant both have a U shape. As we will soon see, the U shape of the average total cost curve is determined by the shape of the curve that shows the relationship between *marginal cost* and the level of production.

Marginal Cost

One of the key ideas in economics is that optimal decisions are made at the margin. Consumers, firms, and government officials usually make decisions about doing a little more or a little less. As Jill Johnson considers whether to hire additional workers to produce additional pizzas, she needs to consider how much she will add to her total cost by producing the additional pizzas. **Marginal cost** is the change in a firm's total cost from producing one more unit of a good or service. We can calculate marginal cost for a particular increase in output by dividing the change in cost by the change in output. We can

Marginal cost The change in a firm's total cost from producing one more unit of a good or service.

express this idea mathematically (remembering that the Greek letter delta, Δ, means "change in"):

$$MC = \frac{\Delta TC}{\Delta Q}.$$

In the table in Figure 4, we use this equation to calculate Jill's marginal cost of producing pizzas.

Why Are the Marginal and Average Cost Curves U-Shaped?

Notice in the graph in Figure 4 that Jill's marginal cost of producing pizzas declines at first and then increases, giving the marginal cost curve a U shape. The table in Figure 4 also shows the marginal product of labor. This table helps us see the important relationship between the marginal product of labor and the marginal cost of production: The marginal product of labor is *rising* for the first two workers, but the marginal cost of the pizzas produced by these workers is *falling*. The marginal product of labor is *falling* for the last four workers, but the marginal cost of pizzas produced by these workers is *rising*. To summarize this point: *When the marginal product of labor is rising, the marginal cost of output is falling. When the marginal product of labor is falling, the marginal cost of production is rising.*

Figure 4

Jill Johnson's Marginal Cost and Average Total Cost of Producing Pizzas

We can use the information in the table to calculate Jill's marginal cost and average total cost of producing pizzas. For the first two workers hired, the marginal product of labor is increasing. This increase causes the marginal cost of production to fall. For the last four workers hired, the marginal product of labor is falling. This causes the marginal cost of production to increase. Therefore, the marginal cost curve falls and then rises—that is, has a U shape—because the marginal product of labor rises and then falls. As long as marginal cost is below average total cost, average total cost will be falling. When marginal cost is above average total cost, average total cost will be rising. The relationship between marginal cost and average total cost explains why the average total cost curve also has a U shape.

Quantity of Workers	Quantity of Ovens	Marginal Product of Labor	Total Cost of Pizzas	Marginal Cost of Pizzas	Average Total Cost of Pizzas
0	0	—	$800	—	—
1	200	200	1,450	$3.25	$7.25
2	450	250	2,100	2.60	4.67
3	550	100	2,750	6.50	5.00
4	600	50	3,400	13.00	5.67
5	625	25	4,050	26.00	6.48
6	640	15	4,700	43.33	7.34

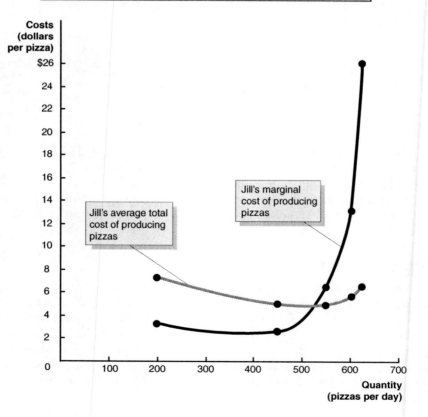

One way to understand why this point is true is first to notice that the only additional cost to Jill from producing more pizzas is the additional wages she pays to hire more workers. She pays each new worker the same $650 per week. So the marginal cost of the additional pizzas each worker makes depends on that worker's additional output, or marginal product. As long as the additional output from each new worker is rising, the marginal cost of that output is falling. When the additional output from each new worker is falling, the marginal cost of that output is rising. *We can conclude that the marginal cost of production falls and then rises—forming a U shape—because the marginal product of labor rises and then falls.*

The relationship between marginal cost and average total cost follows the usual relationship between marginal and average values. As long as marginal cost is below average total cost, average total cost falls. When marginal cost is above average total cost, average total cost rises. Marginal cost equals average total cost when average total cost is at its lowest point. Therefore, the average total cost curve has a U shape because the marginal cost curve has a U shape.

Solved Problem | 4

The Relationship between Marginal Cost and Average Cost

Is Jill Johnson right or wrong when she says the following? "I am currently producing 10,000 pizzas per month at a total cost of $500.00. If I produce 10,001 pizzas, my total cost will rise to $500.11. Therefore, my marginal cost of producing pizzas must be increasing." Draw a graph to illustrate your answer.

SOLVING THE PROBLEM:

Step 1: **Review the chapter material.** This problem requires understanding the relationship between marginal and average cost, so you may want to review the section "Why Are the Marginal and Average Cost Curves U-Shaped?"

Step 2: **Calculate average total cost and marginal cost.** Average total cost is total cost divided by total output. In this case, average total cost is $500.11/10,001 = $0.05. Marginal cost is the change in total cost divided by the change in output. In this case, marginal cost is $0.11/1 = $0.11.

Step 3: **Use the relationship between marginal cost and average total cost to answer the question.** When marginal cost is greater than average total cost, marginal cost must be increasing. You have shown in step 2 that marginal cost is greater than average total cost. Therefore, Jill is right: Her marginal cost of producing pizzas must be increasing.

Step 4: **Draw the graph.**

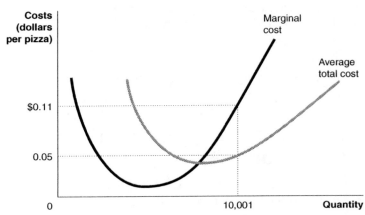

YOUR TURN: For more practice, do related problems 4.5 and 4.6 at the end of this chapter.

>> End Solved Problem 4

5 | Graph average total cost, average variable cost, average fixed cost, and marginal cost.

Graphing Cost Curves

Average fixed cost Fixed cost divided by the quantity of output produced.

Average variable cost Variable cost divided by the quantity of output produced.

We have seen that we calculate average total cost by dividing total cost by the quantity of output produced. Similarly, we can calculate **average fixed cost** by dividing fixed cost by the quantity of output produced. And we can calculate **average variable cost** by dividing variable cost by the quantity of output produced. Or, mathematically, with Q being the level of output, we have:

$$\text{Average total cost} = ATC = \frac{TC}{Q}$$

$$\text{Average fixed cost} = AFC = \frac{FC}{Q}$$

$$\text{Average variable cost} = AVC = \frac{VC}{Q}.$$

Finally, notice that average total cost is the sum of average fixed cost plus average variable cost:

$$ATC = AFC + AVC.$$

The only fixed cost Jill incurs in operating her restaurant is the $800 per week she pays on the bank loan for her pizza ovens. Her variable costs are the wages she pays her workers. The table and graph in Figure 5 show Jill's costs.

We will use graphs like the one in Figure 5 in the next several chapters to analyze how firms decide the level of output to produce and the price to charge. Before going further, be sure you understand the following three key facts about Figure 5:

1 The marginal cost (*MC*), average total cost (*ATC*), and average variable cost (*AVC*) curves are all U-shaped, and the marginal cost curve intersects the average variable cost and average total cost curves at their minimum points. When marginal cost is less than either average variable cost or average total cost, it causes them to decrease. When marginal cost is above average variable cost or average total cost, it causes them to increase. Therefore, when marginal cost equals average variable cost or average total cost, they must be at their minimum points.

2 As output increases, average fixed cost gets smaller and smaller. This happens because in calculating average fixed cost, we are dividing something that gets larger and larger—output—into something that remains constant—fixed cost. Firms often refer to this process of lowering average fixed cost by selling more output as "spreading the overhead." By "overhead" they mean fixed costs.

3 As output increases, the difference between average total cost and average variable cost decreases. This happens because the difference between average total cost and average variable cost is average fixed cost, which gets smaller as output increases.

6 | Understand how firms use the long-run average cost curve in their planning.

Costs in the Long Run

The distinction between fixed cost and variable cost that we just discussed applies to the short run but *not* to the long run. For example, in the short run, Jill Johnson has fixed costs of $800 per week because she signed a loan agreement with a bank when she bought her pizza ovens. In the long run, the cost of purchasing more pizza ovens becomes variable because Jill can choose whether to expand her business by buying

Quantity of Workers	Quantity of Ovens	Quantity of Pizzas	Cost of Ovens (Fixed Cost)	Cost of Workers (Variable Cost)	Total Cost of Pizzas	ATC	AFC	AVC	MC
0	2	0	$800	$0	$800	—	—	—	—
1	2	200	800	650	1,450	$7.25	$4.00	$3.25	$3.25
2	2	450	800	1,300	2,100	4.67	1.78	2.89	2.60
3	2	550	800	1,950	2,750	5.00	1.45	3.55	6.50
4	2	600	800	2,600	3,400	5.67	1.33	4.33	13.00
5	2	625	800	3,250	4,050	6.48	1.28	5.2	26.00
6	2	640	800	3,900	4,700	7.34	1.25	6.09	43.33

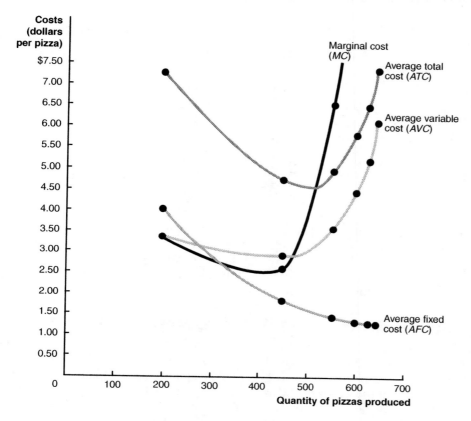

Figure 5

Costs at Jill Johnson's Restaurant

Jill's costs of making pizzas are shown in the table and plotted in the graph. Notice three important facts about the graph: (1) The marginal cost (MC), average total cost (ATC), and average variable cost (AVC) curves are all U-shaped, and the marginal cost curve intersects both the average variable cost curve and average total cost curve at their minimum points. (2) As output increases, average fixed cost (AFC) gets smaller and smaller. (3) As output increases, the difference between average total cost and average variable cost decreases. Make sure you can explain why each of these three facts is true. You should spend time becoming familiar with this graph because it is one of the most important graphs in microeconomics.

more ovens. The same would be true of any other fixed costs a company like Jill's might have. Once a company has purchased a fire insurance policy, the cost of the policy is fixed. But when the policy expires, the company must decide whether to renew it, and the cost becomes variable. The important point here is this: *In the long run, all costs are variable. There are no fixed costs in the long run.* In other words, in the long run, total cost equals variable cost, and average total cost equals average variable cost.

Managers of successful firms simultaneously consider how they can most profitably run their current store, factory, or office and also whether in the long run they would be more profitable if they became larger or, possibly, smaller. Jill must consider how to run her current restaurant, which has only two pizza ovens, and she must also plan what to do when her current bank loan is paid off and the lease on her store ends. Should she buy more pizza ovens? Should she lease a larger restaurant?

Economies of Scale

Short-run average cost curves represent the costs a firm faces when some input, such as the quantity of machines it uses, is fixed. The **long-run average cost curve** shows the lowest cost at which a firm is able to produce a given level of output in the long run, when no inputs are fixed. Many firms experience **economies of scale**, which means the

Long-run average cost curve A curve showing the lowest cost at which a firm is able to produce a given quantity of output in the long run, when no inputs are fixed.

Economies of scale The situation when a firm's long-run average costs fall as it increases output.

Figure 6

The Relationship between Short-Run Average Cost and Long-Run Average Cost

If a small bookstore expects to sell only 1,000 books per month, then it will be able to sell that quantity of books at the lowest average cost of $22 per book if it builds the small store represented by the *ATC* curve on the left of the figure. A larger bookstore will be able to sell 20,000 books per month at a lower cost of $18 per book. A bookstore selling 20,000 books per month and a bookstore selling 40,000 books per month will experience constant returns to scale and have the same average cost. A bookstore selling 20,000 books per month will have reached minimum efficient scale. Very large bookstores will experience diseconomies of scale, and their average costs will rise as sales increase beyond 40,000 books per month.

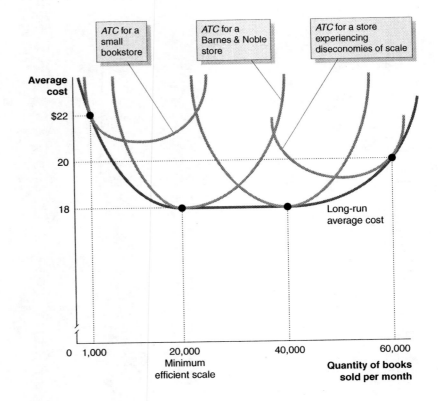

firm's long-run average costs fall as it increases the quantity of output it produces. We can see the effects of economies of scale in Figure 6, which shows the relationship between short-run and long-run average cost curves. Managers can use long-run average cost curves for planning because they show the effect on cost of expanding output by, for example, building a larger factory or store.

Long-Run Average Total Cost Curves for Bookstores

Figure 6 shows long-run average cost in the retail bookstore industry. If a small bookstore expects to sell only 1,000 books per month, then it will be able to sell that quantity of books at the lowest average cost of $22 per book if it builds the small store represented by the *ATC* curve on the left of the figure. A much larger bookstore, such as one run by a national chain like Barnes & Noble, will be able to sell 20,000 books per month at a lower average cost of $18 per book. This decline in average cost from $22 to $18 represents the economies of scale that exist in bookselling. Why would the larger bookstore have lower average costs? One important reason is that the Barnes & Noble store is selling 20 times as many books per month as the small store but might need only six times as many workers. This saving in labor cost would reduce Barnes & Noble's average cost of selling books.

Firms may experience economies of scale for several reasons. First, as in the case of Barnes & Noble, the firm's technology may make it possible to increase production with a smaller proportional increase in at least one input. Second, both workers and managers can become more specialized, enabling them to become more productive, as output expands. Third, large firms, like Barnes & Noble, Wal-Mart, and General Motors, may be able to purchase inputs at lower costs than smaller competitors. In fact, as Wal-Mart expanded, its bargaining power with its suppliers increased, and its average costs fell. Finally, as a firm expands, it may be able to borrow money more inexpensively, thereby lowering its costs.

Economies of scale do not continue forever. The long-run average cost curve in most industries has a flat segment that often stretches over a substantial range of output. As Figure 6 shows, a bookstore selling 20,000 books per month and a bookstore selling 40,000 books per month have the same average cost. Over this range of output, firms in the industry experience **constant returns to scale**. As these firms increase their output, they have to increase their inputs, such as the size of the store and the quantity of

Constant returns to scale The situation when a firm's long-run average costs remain unchanged as it increases output.

workers, proportionally. The level of output at which all economies of scale are exhausted is known as **minimum efficient scale**. A bookstore selling 20,000 books per month has reached minimum efficient scale.

Very large bookstores experience increasing average costs as managers begin to have difficulty coordinating the operation of the store. Figure 6 shows that for sales above 40,000 books per month, firms in the industry experience **diseconomies of scale**. Toyota ran into diseconomies of scale in assembling automobiles. The firm found that as it expanded production at its Georgetown, Kentucky, plant and its plants in China, its managers had difficulty keeping costs from rising. The president of Toyota's Georgetown plant was quoted as saying, "Demand for . . . high volumes saps your energy. Over a period of time, it eroded our focus . . . [and] thinned out the expertise and knowledge we painstakingly built up over the years." One analysis of the problems Toyota faced in expanding production concluded: "It is the kind of paradox many highly successful companies face: Getting bigger doesn't always mean getting better."

Minimum efficient scale The level of output at which all economies of scale are exhausted.

Diseconomies of scale The situation when a firm's long-run average costs rise as the firm increases output.

Solved Problem | 6

Using Long-Run Average Cost Curves to Understand Business Strategy

In fall 2002, Motorola and Siemens were each manufacturing both mobile phone handsets and wireless infrastructure—the base stations needed to operate a wireless communications network. The firms discussed the following arrangement: Motorola would give Siemens its wireless infrastructure busi-

ness in exchange for Siemens giving Motorola its mobile phone handsets business. The main factor motivating the trade was the hope of taking advantage of economies of scale in each business. Use long-run average total cost curves to explain why this trade might make sense for Motorola and Siemens.

SOLVING THE PROBLEM:

Step 1: **Review the chapter material.** This problem is about the long-run average cost curve, so you may want to review the material in the section "Costs in the Long Run."

Step 2: **Draw long-run average cost graphs for Motorola and Siemens.** The question does not provide us with the details of the quantity of each product each firm is producing before the trade or the firms' average costs of production. If economies of scale were an important reason for the trade, we can assume that Motorola and Siemens were not yet at minimum efficient scale in the wireless infrastructure and phone handset businesses. Therefore, we can draw the following graphs:

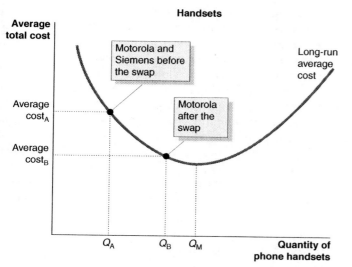

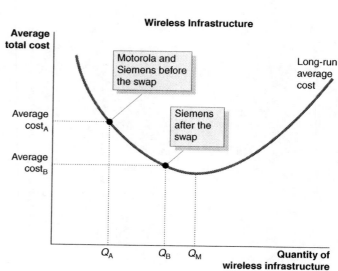

Step 3: **Explain the curves in the graphs.** Before the proposed trade, Motorola and Siemens are producing both products at less than the minimum efficient scale, which is Q_M in both graphs. After the trade, Motorola's production of handsets will increase, moving it from Q_A to Q_B in the first graph. This increase in production will allow it to take advantage of economies of scale and reduce its average cost from Average Cost$_A$ to Average Cost$_B$. Similarly, production of wireless infrastructure by Siemens will increase from Q_A to Q_B, lowering its average cost from Average Cost$_A$ to Average Cost$_B$. As drawn, the graphs show that both firms will still be short of minimum efficient scale after the trade, although their average costs will have fallen.

EXTRA CREDIT: These were new technologies at the time Motorola and Siemens discussed the trade. As a result, companies making these products were only beginning to understand how large minimum efficient scale was. To survive in the industry, the managements of both companies wanted to lower their costs by taking advantage of economies of scale. As one industry analyst put it: "Motorola and Siemens may be driven by the conviction that they have little choice. Most observers believe consolidation in both the [wireless] networking and handset areas is inevitable."

Source for quote: Ray Hegarty, *Rumored Motorola–Siemens Business Unit Swap? A Compelling M&A Story*, www.thefeature.com.

YOUR TURN: For more practice, do related problems 6.4, 6.5, 6.6, and 6.7 at the end of this chapter.

>> **End Solved Problem 6**

Over time, most firms in an industry will build factories or stores that are at least as large as the minimum efficient scale but not so large that diseconomies of scale occur. In the bookstore industry, stores will sell between 20,000 and 40,000 books per month. However, firms often do not know the exact shape of their long-run average cost curves. As a result, they may mistakenly build factories or stores that are either too large or too small.

Making the Connection	The Colossal River Rouge: Diseconomies of Scale at Ford Motor Company

When Henry Ford started the Ford Motor Company in 1903, automobile companies produced cars in small workshops, using highly skilled workers. Ford introduced two new ideas that allowed him to take advantage of economies of scale. First, Ford used identical—or, interchangeable—parts so that unskilled workers could assemble the cars. Second, instead of having groups of workers moving from one stationary automobile to the next, he had the workers remain stationary while the automobiles moved along an assembly line. Ford built a large factory at Highland Park, outside Detroit, where he used these ideas to produce the famous Model T at an average cost well below what his competitors could match using older production methods in smaller factories.

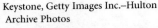
Keystone, Getty Images Inc.–Hulton Archive Photos

Ford believed that he could produce automobiles at an even lower average cost by building a still larger plant along the River Rouge. Unfortunately, Ford's River Rouge plant was too large and suffered from diseconomies of scale. Ford's managers had great difficulty coordinating the production of automobiles in such a large plant. The following description of the River Rouge comes from a biography of Ford by Allan Nevins and Frank Ernest Hill:

A total of 93 separate structures stood on the [River Rouge] site.... Railroad trackage covered 93 miles, conveyors 27 [miles]. About 75,000 men worked in the great plant. A force of 5000 did

Is it possible for a factory to be too big?

nothing but keep it clean, wearing out 5000 mops and 3000 brooms a month, and using 86 tons of soap on the floors, walls, and 330 acres of windows. The Rouge was an industrial city, immense, concentrated, packed with power. . . . By its very massiveness and complexity, it denied men at the top contact with and understanding of those beneath, and gave those beneath a sense of being lost in inexorable immensity and power.

Beginning in 1927, Ford produced the Model A—its only car model at that time—at the River Rouge plant. Ford failed to achieve economies of scale and actually *lost money* on each of the four Model A body styles.

Ford could not raise the price of the Model A to make it profitable because at a higher price, the car could not compete with similar models produced by competitors such as General Motors and Chrysler. He eventually reduced the cost of making the Model A by constructing smaller factories spread out across the country. These smaller factories produced the Model A at a lower average cost than was possible at the River Rouge plant.

Source for quote: Allan Nevins and Frank Ernest Hill, *Ford: Expansion and Challenge, 1915–1933*, New York: Scribner, 1957, pp. 293, 295.

YOUR TURN: Test your understanding by doing related problem 6.8 at the end of this chapter.

Don't Let This Happen to **YOU!**

DON'T CONFUSE DIMINISHING RETURNS WITH DISECONOMIES OF SCALE

The concepts of diminishing returns and diseconomies of scale may seem similar, but, in fact, they are unrelated. Diminishing returns applies only to the short run, when at least one of the firm's inputs, such as the quantity of machinery it uses, is fixed. The law of diminishing returns

tells us that in the short run, hiring more workers will, at some point, result in less additional output. Diminishing returns explains why marginal cost curves eventually slope upward. Diseconomies of scale apply only in the long run, when the firm is free to vary all its inputs, can adopt new technology, and can vary the amount of machinery it uses and the size of its facility. Diseconomies of scale explain why long-run average cost curves eventually slope upward.

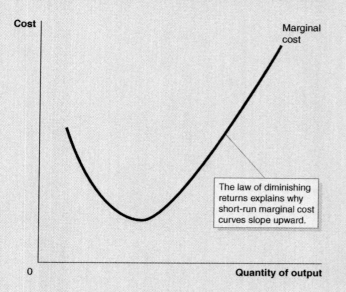

The law of diminishing returns explains why short-run marginal cost curves slope upward.

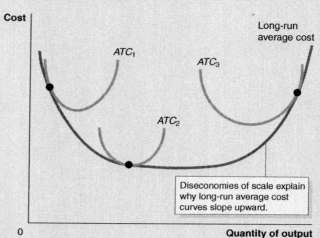

Diseconomies of scale explain why long-run average cost curves slope upward.

YOUR TURN: Test your understanding by doing related problem 6.10 at the end of this chapter.

Economics in YOUR Life!

At the beginning of the chapter, we asked you to consider a situation in which you are about to open a store to sell recliners. Both you and a competing store, Bob's Big Chairs, can buy recliners from the manufacturer for $300 each. But because Bob's sells more recliners per month than you expect to be able to, his costs per recliner are lower than yours. We asked you to think about why this might be true. In this chapter, we have seen that firms often experience declining average costs as the quantity they sell increases. One significant reason Bob's average cost might be lower than yours has to do with fixed costs. Because your stores are the same size, you may be paying about the same amount to lease the store space. You may also be paying about the same amounts for utilities, insurance, and advertising. All these are fixed costs because they do not change as the quantity of recliners you sell changes. Because Bob's fixed costs are the same as yours, but he is selling more recliners, his average fixed costs are lower than yours, and, therefore, so are his average total costs. With lower average total costs, he can sell his recliners for a lower price than you do and still make a profit.

Conclusion

In this chapter, we discussed the relationship between a firm's technology, production, and costs. In the discussion, we encountered a number of definitions of costs. Because we will use these definitions in later chapters, it is useful to bring them together in Table 4 for you to review.

We have seen the important relationship between a firm's level of production and its costs. Just as this information was vital to Akio Morita in deciding which price to charge for his transistor radios, so it remains vital today to all firms as they attempt to decide the optimal level of production and the optimal prices to charge for their products. Read *An Inside Look* to see how we can use long-run average cost curves to understand the effect of lower costs of production on the pricing of flat-panel TVs.

TERM	DEFINITION	SYMBOLS AND EQUATIONS
Total cost	The cost of all the inputs used by a firm, or fixed cost plus variable cost	TC
Fixed cost	Costs that remain constant when a firm's level of output changes	FC
Variable cost	Costs that change when the firm's level of output changes	VC
Marginal cost	Increase in total cost resulting from producing another unit of output	$MC = \dfrac{\Delta TC}{\Delta Q}$
Average total cost	Total cost divided by the quantity of output produced	$ATC = \dfrac{TC}{Q}$
Average fixed cost	Fixed cost divided by the quantity of output produced	$AFC = \dfrac{FC}{Q}$
Average variable cost	Variable cost divided by the quantity of output produced	$AVC = \dfrac{VC}{Q}$
Implicit cost	A nonmonetary opportunity cost	—
Explicit cost	A cost that involves spending money	—

TABLE 4

A Summary of Definitions of Cost

WALL STREET JOURNAL, APRIL 15, 2006

Flat-Panel TVs, Long Touted, Finally Are Becoming the Norm

After years as the Next Big Thing in consumer electronics, flat-panel TVs are finally becoming the mainstream standard. . . .

Last year, flat-screen TVs for the first time accounted for the majority of TVs bought in Japan, Hong Kong and Singapore. That crossover will happen this year or next in the U.S. and most European countries, industry watchers say, and at least one company has already stopped shipping tube TVs in the U.S. "It's happening faster than the most optimistic targets," says Ross Young, president of DisplaySearch, an Austin, Texas, market-research firm.

World-wide, sales this year of liquid-crystal display and plasma flat-panel TVs are on track to total about 44 million units, valued at as much as $54 billion, out of an overall market of 185 million TVs, according to market research firms. In the U.S., sales are expected to reach between 12 million and 14 million flat-panel TVs, or roughly half of all TVs sold. Last year, world-wide sales of flat-panel TVs totaled 25 million units.

Consumers like the thin form and light weight of flat-panel TVs, but until recently, many considered them too expensive. Two years ago, a 30-inch, LCD-TV cost $3,500 to $4,000. Since then, more than a dozen factories producing critical glass and screen components have opened, which has pushed down manufacturing costs, allowing for lower prices.

Competition between LCD and plasma technologies is pushing down prices, too. Plasma models use electricity to light individual points of gas on a screen; in LCDs, a layer of liquid crystal filters a bright light. LCD beat plasma about 15 years ago as the flat-panel of choice in notebook computers. From there, plasma developers jumped to big size screens, where they have since been most cost effective, while technical challenges long limited the size of LCDs. . . .

Increased production is likely to help prices continue to fall throughout the year. Seven new factories are under construction in Asia that will make LCD panels 40 inches or larger, and three new factories for plasma screens are under construction. Several are being optimized for screens that are 50 inches or larger. By late next year, prices of 40-inch models will be closing in on $1,000 as production ramps up. . . .

Japan's Matsushita Electric Industrial Co., maker of Panasonic products, has stopped shipping tube TVs altogether to the U.S., where it expects to sell about 1.5 million plasma-screen TVs this year. Just two years ago, it sold one million tube TVs and 150,000 plasma models in the U.S. Flat-panel TVs of all types have become an easier sell as popular television shows such as "CSI" and "Lost" adopt the widescreen, high-definition look of movies. The U.S. and several other countries are shifting their broadcast systems to digital signals that promise to broaden the availability of HDTV content. Higher-definition DVDs that are emerging this year may also fuel demand. . . .

To meet demand, manufacturers are in a mad dash to build new factories, or change existing ones, to accommodate flat-panel TVs. In one week last month, Sony, LG Electronics Co. and China's Changhong Group announced new factories in Eastern Europe to assemble flat-panel models for the European market. Just this week, Sony and Samsung Electronics Co. said they would expand their LCD-panel joint venture by spending $2 billion on what, for the moment, will be the industry's largest factory. Hitachi Corp. a week earlier said it's considering building factories to quadruple its annual output of LCD-TVs to more than five million annually. . . .

Source: "Flat-Panel TVs, Long Touted, Finally are Becoming the Norm," by Evan Ranstad from *Wall Street Journal Online*, April 15, 2006. Copyright © 2006 Dow Jones. Reprinted by permission of Dow Jones via Copyright Clearance Center.

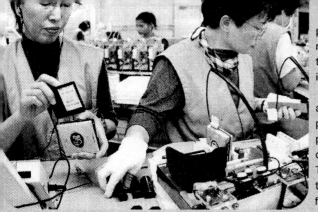

Yoshikazu Tsuno/AFP/Getty Images

Key Points in the Article

This article illustrates how several firms are racing to expand production of flat-panel televisions. The article discusses long-run decisions firms make, such as what plant size to build. It also discusses how the costs of inputs into flat-panel televisions have been declining. Lower costs of production have resulted in sharply lower prices of flat-panel televisions.

Analyzing the News

ⓐ As more factories open to produce components to make flat-panel televisions, the price of the components should fall. As a result, the marginal and average cost of producing flat-panel televisions should decline. In Figure 1, we see that more factories producing components for flat-panel TVs increases the supply of components from S_1 to S_2. The increased sup-

ply causes the price of components to fall from P_1 to P_2, while the quantity of components sold increases from Q_1 to Q_2.

Because these components are inputs in production of flat-panel TVs, as the price of components falls, the costs of producing flat-panel TVs also fall. This is seen in Figure 2, where the marginal cost curve of TVs falls from MC_1 to MC_2 and the average cost curve falls from ATC_1 to ATC_2.

Falling costs, make it possible for firms like Sony to sell TVs at lower prices and still cover their costs. You can see in Figure 2 that prior to the decrease in input prices a firm would need to receive ATC_1 dollars per TV to cover the cost of producing Q_1 TVs. After the reduction in input prices, the average cost of producing Q_1 TVs falls to ATC_2 dollars and the firm is able to cover its costs at lower prices.

ⓑ Increased production moves a firm further to the right on its cost curve. For goods like flat-panel TVs, fixed costs tend to be high relative to marginal costs, because the factories that produce the televisions are expensive to build. So, average cost will decline over large ranges of output, which makes it possible for Sony and other manufacturers to offer the televisions for sale at lower prices.

ⓒ Firms use the long-run average cost curve when choosing what size

manufacturing plant to build. The long-run average cost curve shows the minimum cost of producing at each output level. Choosing the best point to be on the long-run average cost curve requires firms to forecast future sales. In this case, firms are expecting continuing rapid increases in demand for flat-panel televisions and are building increasingly larger plants. They are expecting that economies of scale will make the average costs of production in the larger plants lower than the average costs of production in smaller plants. But as the example of Ford's River Rouge plant shows, when a new industry is rapidly expanding, it is not unusual for at least one firm to build a plant that is too large and to begin experiencing diseconomies of scale. With diseconomies of scale, the average cost of production in a larger plant is actually *higher* than in a smaller plant.

Thinking Critically

1. Suppose you are a manager at Sony and you are asked to determine what size manufacturing plants for flat-panel televisions the firm should be planning to build. What information would you need to gather in order to determine the optimal sized plant?

2. Use the concepts from this chapter to explain why the long-run supply of flat-panel TVs is more elastic than the short-run supply of flat-panel TVs.

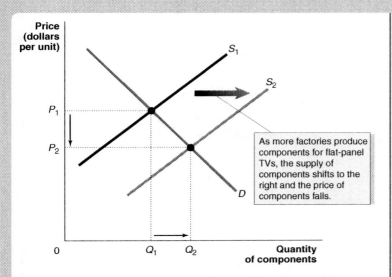

Figure 1. An increased supply of flat-panel televisions components leads to a lower price.

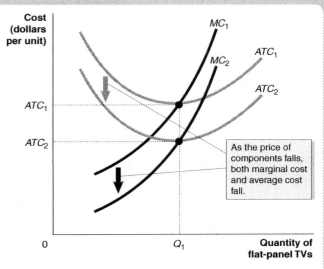

Figure 2. Lower input prices reduce the marginal and average costs of producing flat-panel televisions.

Key Terms

Average fixed cost	Economies of scale	Marginal cost	Technology
Average product of labor	Explicit cost	Marginal product of labor	Total cost
Average total cost	Fixed costs	Minimum efficient scale	Variable costs
Average variable cost	Implicit cost	Opportunity cost	
Constant returns to scale	Law of diminishing returns	Production function	
Diseconomies of scale	Long run	Short run	
	Long-run average cost curve	Technological change	

Technology: An Economic Definition

Summary

The basic activity of a firm is to use inputs, such as workers, machines, and natural resources, to produce goods and services. The firm's **technology** is the processes it uses to turn inputs into goods and services. **Technological change** refers to a change in the ability of a firm to produce a given level of output with a given quantity of inputs.

 Visit www.myeconlab.com to complete these exercises *Get Ahead of the Curve* online and get instant feedback.

Review Questions

1.1 What is the difference between technology and technological change?

1.2 Is it possible for technological change to be negative? If so, give an example.

Problems and Applications

1.3 Briefly explain whether you agree with the following observation: "Technological change refers only to the introduction of new products, so it is not relevant to the operations of most firms."

1.4 Which of the following are examples of a firm experiencing positive technological change?
   a. A firm is able to cut each worker's wage rate by 10 percent and still produce the same level of output.
   b. A training program makes a firm's workers more productive.
   c. An exercise program makes a firm's workers more healthy and productive.
   d. A firm cuts its workforce and is able to maintain its initial level of output.
   e. A firm rearranges the layout of its factory and finds that by using its initial set of inputs, it can produce exactly as much as before.

1.5 (Related to the *Making the Connection*) The Seven-Eleven chain of convenience stores in Japan reorganized its system for supplying its stores with food. This lead to a sharp reduction in the number of trucks the company had to use, while increasing the amount of fresh food on store shelves. Someone discussing Seven-Eleven's new system argues "This is not an example of technological change because it did not require the use of new machinery or equipment." Briefly explain whether you agree with this argument.

>> End Learning Objective 1

The Short Run and the Long Run in Economics

Summary

In the **short run**, a firm's technology and the size of its factory, store, or office are fixed. In the **long run**, a firm is able to adopt new technology and to increase or decrease the size of its physical plant. **Total cost** is the cost of all the inputs a firm uses in production. Variable costs are costs that change as output changes. Fixed costs are costs that remain constant as output changes. Opportunity cost is the highest-valued alternative that must be given up to engage in an activity. An explicit cost is a cost that involves spending money. An implicit cost is a nonmonetary opportunity cost. The relationship between the inputs employed by a firm and the maximum output it can produce with those inputs is called the firm's **production function**.

 Visit www.myeconlab.com to complete these exercises online and get instant feedback.

Review Questions

2.1 What is the difference between the short run and the long run? Is the amount of time that separates the short run from the long run the same for every firm?

2.2 What are implicit costs? How are they different from explicit costs?

Problems and Applications

2.3 (Related to the *Making the Connection*) Many firms consider their wage costs to be variable costs. Why do publishers usually consider their wage and salary costs to be fixed costs? Are the costs of utilities always fixed, always variable, or can they be both? Briefly explain?

2.4 (Related to the *Making the Connection*) For Jill Johnson's pizza restaurant, explain whether each of the following is a fixed cost or a variable cost.
   a. The payment she makes on her fire insurance policy
   b. The payment she makes to buy pizza dough
   c. The wages she pays her workers
   d. The lease payment she makes to her landlord who owns the building where her store is located
   e. The $300-per-month payment she makes to her local newspaper for running her weekly advertisements

2.5 (Related to the *Making the Connection*) The *Statistical Abstract of the United States* is published each year by the U.S. Census Bureau. It provides a summary of business, economic, social, and political statistics. It is available for free on-line and a printed copy can also be purchased from the U.S. Government Printing Office for $35.00. Because government documents are not copyrighted anyone can print copies of the *Statistical Abstract* and sell them. Each year, one or two companies typically will print

and sell copies for a significantly lower price than the Government Printing Office does. The copies of the Statistical Abstract that these companies sell are usually identical to those sold by the government, except for having different covers. How can these companies sell the same book for a lower price than the government and still cover their costs?

2.6 Suppose Jill Johnson operates her pizza restaurant in a building she owns in the center of the city. Similar buildings in the neighborhood rent for $4,000 per month. Jill is considering selling her building and renting space in the suburbs for $3,000 per month. Jill decides not to make the move. She reasons, "I would like to have a restaurant in the suburbs, but I pay no rent for my restaurant now, and I don't want to see my costs rise by $3,000 per month." What do you think of Jill's reasoning?

2.7 When the DuPont chemical company first attempted to enter the paint business, it was not successful. According to a company report, in one year it "lost nearly $500,000 in actual cash in addition to an expected return on investment of nearly $500,000, which made a total loss of income to the company of nearly a million." Why did this report include as part of the company's loss the amount it had expected to earn—but didn't—on its investment in manufacturing paint?

Source: Alfred D. Chandler, Jr., Thomas K. McCraw, and Richard Tedlow, *Management Past and Present*, Cincinnati: South-Western, 2000, pp. 3–92.

2.8 An account of Benjamin Franklin's life notes that he started his career as a printer and publisher of the newspaper the *Pennsylvania Gazette*. He also opened a store where he sold stationery, books, and food. According to this account, "He could without expense apprise the public of items on hand by advertisements in his *Gazette*." Is the author correct that Franklin did not incur a cost when he used space in his newspaper to run advertisements for his store? Briefly explain.

Source: Richard Tedlow, "Benjamin Franklin and the Definition of American Values," in Alfred D. Chandler, Jr., Thomas K. McCaw, and Richard S. Tedlow, *Management Past and Present: A Casebook on the History of American Business*, Cincinnati: South-Western College Publishing, 2000.

>> End Learning Objective 2

3 LEARNING OBJECTIVE   3 | Understand the relationship between the marginal product of labor and the average product of labor

The Marginal Product of Labor and the Average Product of Labor

Summary

The **marginal product of labor** is the additional output produced by a firm as a result of hiring one more worker. Specialization and division of labor cause the marginal product of labor to rise for the first few workers hired. Eventually, the **law of diminishing returns** causes the marginal product of labor to decline. The **average product of labor** is the total amount of output produced by a firm divided by the quantity of workers hired. When the marginal product of labor is greater than the average product of labor, the average product of labor increases. When the marginal product of labor is less than the average product of labor, the average product of labor decreases.

 Visit www.myeconlab.com to complete these exercises online and get instant feedback.

Review Questions

3.1 Draw a graph showing the usual relationship between the marginal product of labor and the average product of labor. Why do the marginal product of labor and the average product of labor have the shapes you drew?

3.2 What is the law of diminishing returns? Does it apply in the long run?

Problems and Applications

3.3 Fill in the missing values in the following table.

QUANTITY OF WORKERS	TOTAL OUTPUT	MARGINAL PRODUCT OF LABOR	AVERAGE PRODUCT OF LABOR
0	0		
1	400		
2	900		
3	1,500		
4	1,900		
5	2,200		
6	2,400		
7	2,300		

3.4 Use the numbers from problem 3.3 to draw one graph showing how total output increases with the quantity of workers hired and a second graph showing the marginal product of labor and the average product of labor.

3.5 A student looks at the data in Table 3 and draws this conclusion: "The marginal product of labor is increasing for the first two workers hired, and then it declines for the next four workers. I guess each of the first two workers must have been hard workers. Then Jill must have had to settle for increasingly poor workers." Do you agree with the student's analysis? Briefly explain.

3.6 (Related to the *Making the Connection*) Briefly explain whether you agree or disagree with the following argument: Adam Smith's idea of the gains to firms from the division of labor makes a lot of sense when the good being manufactured is something complex like automobiles or computers, but it doesn't apply in the manufacturing of less complex goods or in other sectors of the economy, such as retail sales.

3.7 Sally looks at her college transcript and says to Sam, "How is this possible? My grade point average for this semester's courses is higher than my grade point average for last semester's courses, but my cumulative grade point average still went down from last semester to this semester." Explain to Sally how this is possible.

3.8 Is it possible for a firm to experience a technological change that would increase the marginal product of labor while leaving the average product of labor unchanged? Explain.

>> End Learning Objective 3

---

4 LEARNING OBJECTIVE   4 | Explain and illustrate the relationship between marginal cost and average total cost

The Relationship between Short-Run Production and Short-Run Cost

Summary

The **marginal cost** of production is the increase in total cost resulting from producing another unit of output. The marginal cost curve has a U shape because when the marginal product of labor is rising, the marginal cost of output is falling. When the marginal product of labor is falling, the marginal cost of output is rising. When marginal cost is less than average total cost, average total cost falls. When marginal cost is greater than average total cost, average total cost rises.

 Visit www.myeconlab.com to complete these exercises online and get instant feedback.

Review Questions

4.1 If the marginal product of labor is rising, is the marginal cost of production rising or falling? Briefly explain.

4.2 Explain why the marginal cost curve intersects the average total cost curve at the level of output where average total cost is at a minimum.

Problems and Applications

4.3 Is it possible for average total cost to be decreasing over a range of output where marginal cost is increasing? Briefly explain.

4.4 Suppose a firm has no fixed costs, so all of its costs are variable, even in the short run.
a. If the firm's marginal costs are continually increasing (that is, marginal cost is increasing from the first unit of output produced) will the firm's average total cost curve have a U shape?
b. If the firm's marginal costs are $5 at every level of output, what shape will the firm's average total cost have?

4.5 (*Related to Solved Problem 4*) Is Jill Johnson right or wrong when she says the following: "Currently, I am producing 20,000 pizzas per month at a total cost of $750.00. If I produce 20,001 pizzas, my total cost will rise to $750.02. Therefore, my marginal cost of producing pizzas must be increasing." Illustrate your answer with a graph.

4.6 (*Related to Solved Problem 4*) The following problem is somewhat advanced. Using symbols, we can write that the marginal product of labor is equal to $\Delta Q/\Delta L$. Marginal cost is equal to $\Delta TC/\Delta Q$. Because fixed costs by definition don't change, marginal cost is also equal to $\Delta VC/\Delta Q$. If Jill Johnson's only variable cost is labor cost, then her variable cost is just the wage multiplied by the quantity of workers hired, or wL.
a. If the wage Jill pays is constant, then what is ΔVC in terms of w and L?
b. Use your answer to question (a) and the expressions given above for the marginal product of labor and the marginal cost of output to find an expression for marginal cost, $\Delta TC/\Delta Q$, in terms of the wage, w, and the marginal product of labor, $\Delta Q/\Delta L$.
c. Use your answer to question (b) to determine Jill's marginal cost of producing pizzas if the wage is $750 per week and the marginal product of labor is 150. If the wage falls to $600 per week and the marginal product of labor is unchanged, what happens to Jill's marginal cost? If the wage is unchanged at $750 per week and the marginal product rises to 250, what happens to Jill's marginal cost?

>> **End Learning Objective 4**

---

5 LEARNING OBJECTIVE   5 | Graph average total cost, average variable cost, average fixed cost, and marginal cost

Graphing Cost Curves

Summary

Average fixed cost is equal to fixed cost divided by the level of output. **Average variable cost** is equal to variable cost divided by the level of output. Figure 5 shows the relationship among marginal cost, average total cost, average variable cost, and average fixed cost. It is one of the most important graphs in microeconomics.

 Visit www.myeconlab.com to complete these exercises online and get instant feedback.

Review Questions

5.1 As the level of output increases, what happens to the value of average fixed cost?

5.2 As the level of output increases, what happens to the difference between the value of average total cost and average variable cost?

Problems and Applications

5.3 Suppose the total cost of producing 10,000 tennis balls is $30,000, and the fixed cost is $10,000.
a. What is the variable cost?
b. When output is 10,000, what are the average variable cost and the average fixed cost?
c. Assuming that the cost curves have the usual shape, is the dollar difference between the average total cost and the average variable cost greater when the output is 10,000 tennis balls or when the output is 30,000 tennis balls? Explain.

5.4 One description of the costs of operating a railroad makes the following observation: "The fixed ... expenses which attach to the operation of railroads ... are in the nature of a tax upon the business of the road; the smaller the [amount of] business, the larger the tax." Briefly explain why fixed costs are like a tax. In what sense is this tax smaller when the amount of business is larger?

Source for quote: Alfred D. Chandler, Jr., Thomas K. McCraw, and Richard Tedlow, *Management Past and Present*, Cincinnati: South-Western, 2000, pp. 2–27.

5.5 In the ancient world, a book could be produced either on a scroll or as a codex, which was made of folded sheets glued together, something like a modern book. One scholar has estimated the following variable costs (in Greek drachmas) of the two methods:

	SCROLL	CODEX
Cost of writing (wage of a scribe)	11.33 drachmas	11.33 drachmas
Cost of paper	16.50 drachmas	9.25 drachmas

Another scholar points out that a significant fixed cost was involved in producing a codex:

> In order to copy a codex ... the amount of text and the layout of each page had to be carefully calculated in advance to determine the exact number of sheets ... needed. No doubt, this is more time-consuming and calls for more experimentation than the production of a scroll would. But for the next copy, these calculations would be used again.

a. Suppose that the fixed cost of preparing a codex was 58 drachmas and that there was no similar fixed cost for a scroll. Would an ancient book publisher who intended to sell 5 copies of a book be likely to publish it as a scroll or as a codex? What if he intended to sell 10 copies? Briefly explain.

b. Although most books were published as scrolls in the first century A.D., by the third century, most were published as codices. Considering only the factors mentioned in this problem, explain why this change may have taken place.

Sources: T. C. Skeat, "The Length of the Standard Papyrus Roll and the Cost-Advantage of the Codex," *Zeitschrift für Papyrologie und Epigraphik*, 1982, p. 175; and David Trobisch, *The First Edition of the New Testament*, New York: Oxford University Press, 2000, p. 73.

5.6 Use the information in the following graph to find the values for the following at an output level of 1,000.
a. Marginal cost
b. Total cost
c. Variable cost
d. Fixed cost

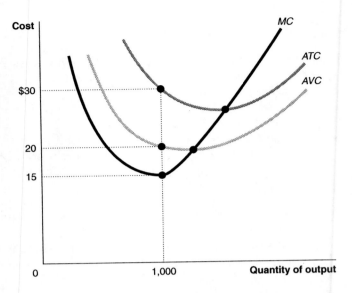

5.7 List the errors in the following graph. Carefully explain why the curves drawn this way are wrong. In other words, why can't these curves be as they are shown in the graph?

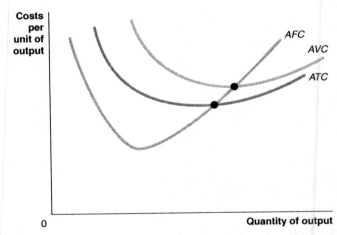

5.8 Explain how the listed events (a–d) would affect the following at Ford Motor Company:
    i. Marginal cost
    ii. Average variable cost
    iii. Average fixed cost
    iv. Average total cost

a. Ford signs a new contract with the United Automobile Workers union that requires the company to pay higher wages.
b. The federal government starts to levy a $1,500-per-vehicle tax on sport-utility vehicles.
c. Ford decides to give its senior executives a one-time $100,000 bonus.
d. Ford decides to increase the amount it spends on designing new car models.

>> **End Learning Objective 5**

Costs in the Long Run

Summary

The **long-run average cost curve** shows the lowest cost at which a firm is able to produce a given level of output in the long run. For many firms, the long-run average cost curve falls as output expands because of **economies of scale**. **Minimum efficient scale** is the level of output at which all economies of scale have been exhausted. After economies of scale have been exhausted, firms experience **constant returns to scale**, where their long-run average cost curve is flat. At high levels of output, the long-run average cost curve turns up as the firm experiences **diseconomies of scale**.

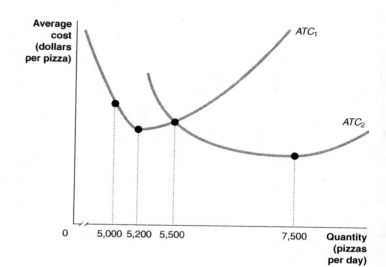

myeconlab Visit www.myeconlab.com to complete these exercises
Get Ahead of the Curve online and get instant feedback.

Review Questions

6.1 What is the difference between total cost and variable cost in the long run?

6.2 What is minimum efficient scale? What is likely to happen in the long run to firms that do not reach minimum efficient scale?

6.3 What are economies of scale? What are diseconomies of scale? What is the main reason that firms eventually encounter diseconomies of scale as they keep increasing the size of their store or factory?

Problems and Applications

6.4 (Related to *Solved Problem 6*) Suppose that Jill Johnson has to choose between building a smaller restaurant and a larger restaurant. In the following graph, the relationship between costs and output for the smaller restaurant is represented by the curve ATC_1, and the relationship between costs and output for the larger restaurant is represented by the curve ATC_2.

a. If Jill expects to produce 5,100 pizzas per week, should she build a smaller restaurant or a larger restaurant? Briefly explain.

b. If Jill expects to produce 6,000 pizzas per week, should she build a smaller restaurant or a larger restaurant? Briefly explain.

c. A student asks, "If the average cost of producing pizzas is lower in the larger restaurant when Jill produces 7,500 pizzas per week, why isn't it also lower when Jill produces 5,200 pizzas per week?" Give a brief answer to the student's question.

6.5 (Related to *Solved Problem 6*) Consider the following description of U.S. manufacturing in the late nineteenth century:

> When . . . Standard Oil . . . reorganized its refinery capacity in 1883 and concentrated almost two-fifths of the nation's refinery production in three huge refineries, the unit cost dropped from 1.5 cents a gallon to 0.5 cents. A comparable concentration of two-fifths of the nation's output of textiles or shoes in three plants would have been impossible, and in any case would have brought huge diseconomies of scale and consequently higher prices.

a. Use this information to draw a long-run average cost curve for an oil-refining firm and a long-run average cost curve for a firm manufacturing shoes.

b. Is it likely that there were more oil refineries or more shoe factories in the United States in the late nineteenth century? Briefly explain.

c. Why would concentrating two-fifths of total shoe output in three factories have led to higher shoe prices?

Source: Alfred D. Chandler, Jr., Thomas K. McCraw, and Richard Tedlow, *Management Past and Present*, Cincinnati: South-Western, 2000, pp. 4–53.

6.6 (Related to *Solved Problem 6*) The company eToys sold toys on the Internet. In 1999, the total value of the company was about $7.7 billion, but by early 2001, the company was in deep financial trouble, and it eventually closed. One of the company's key mistakes was the decision in 2000 to build a large distribution center from which it would ship toys throughout the United States. The following description of this decision appeared in an article in the *Wall Street Journal*:

> [eToys built] a giant automated distribution center in Virginia. . . . Although many analysts agreed that the costly move was a sound decision for the long run . . . [the] decision meant eToys needed to generate much higher sales to justify its costs. . . . Despite a spiffy TV ad campaign and an expanded line of goods, there weren't enough customers.

What does the author mean when she says that eToys "needed to generate much higher sales to justify its costs"? Use a graph like Figure 6 to illustrate your answer.

Source: Lisa Bannon, "The eToys Saga: Costs Kept Rising but Sales Slowed," *Wall Street Journal*, January 22, 2001.

6.7 (Related to *Solved Problem 6*) In 2003, Time Warner and the Walt Disney Company discussed merging their news operations. Time Warner owns the Cable News Network (CNN), and Disney owns ABC News. After analyzing the situation, the companies decided that a combined news operation would have higher average costs than either CNN or ABC News had separately. Use a long-run average cost curve graph to illustrate why the companies did not merge their news operations.

Source: Martin Peers and Joe Flint, "AOL Calls Off CNN–ABC Deal, Seeing Operating Difficulties," *Wall Street Journal*, February 14, 2003.

6.8 (Related to the *Making the Connection*) Suppose that Henry Ford had continued to experience increasing returns to scale, no matter how large an automobile factory he built. Discuss what the implications of this would have been for the automobile industry.

6.9 One scholar has made the following comment on the publishing industry: "If publishers were able to determine exactly what sells a book, they all would feature fewer titles and produce them in larger numbers." What must be true about the costs of publishing books for this statement to be correct? Briefly explain.

Source: David Trobisch, *The First Edition of the New Testament*, New York: Oxford University Press, 2000, p. 75.

6.10 (Related to the *Don't Let This Happen to You!*) Explain whether you agree or disagree with the following statement: "Henry Ford expected to be able to produce cars at a lower average cost at his River Rouge plant. Unfortunately, because of diminishing returns, his costs were actually higher."

6.11 (Related to the *Chapter Opener*) Review the discussion at the beginning of the chapter of Akio Morita selling transistor radios in the United States. Suppose that Morita became convinced that Sony would be able to sell more than 75,000 transistor radios each year in the United States. What steps would he have taken?

6.12 TIAA-CREF is a retirement system for people who work at colleges and universities. For some years, TIAA-CREF also sold long-term care insurance before deciding to sell that business to MetLife, a large insurance company. TIAA-CREF's chairman and chief executive officer explained the decision this way:

> In recent years, the long-term care insurance market has experienced significant consolidation. A few large insurance companies now own most of the business. MetLife has 428,000 policies, for example—nearly 10 times the number we have—and can achieve economies of scale that we can't. Over time, we would have had difficulty holding down premium rates.

Briefly explain what economies of scale have to do with the premiums (that is, the prices buyers have to pay for insurance policies) that insurance companies can charge for their policies.

Source: "Long-Term Care Sale in Best Interest of Policyholders," *Advance*, Spring 2004, p. 6.

6.13 According to one account of the problems DuPont had in entering the paint business, "the du Ponts had assumed that large volume would bring profits through lowering unit costs." In fact, according to one company report, "The more paint and varnish we sold, the more money we lost." Draw an average cost curve graph showing the relationship between paint output and average cost as DuPont expected it to be. Draw another graph that explains the result that the more paint the company sold, the more money it lost.

Source: Alfred D. Chandler, Jr., Thomas K. McCraw, and Richard Tedlow, *Management Past and Present*, Cincinnati: South-Western, 2000, pp. 3–88.

6.14 According to a study of chicken processing plants by the U.S. Department of Agriculture, the largest plants have average costs that are 20 percent lower than the smallest plants. The report concludes, "These cost differentials are consistent with the near-disappearance of small plants." Briefly explain the reasoning behind this conclusion.

Source: Michael Ollinger, James MacDonald, and Milton Madison, *Structural Change in U.S. Chicken and Turkey Slaughter*, Agricultural Economic Report No. 787, Economic Research Service, U.S. Department of Agriculture.

6.15 Michael Korda was for many years editor-in-chief at the Simon & Schuster book publishing company. He has described how during the 1980s many publishing companies merged together to form larger firms. He claims that publishers hoped to take advantage of economies of scale. But, he concludes, "sheer size did not make publishing necessarily more profitable, and most of these big publishing monoliths would continue to disap-point their corporate owners in terms of earnings." On the basis of this information, draw a long-run average cost curve for a publishing firm that reflects the economies of scale expected to result from the mergers. Draw another long-run average cost curve that reflects the actual results experienced by the new larger publishing firms.

Source: Michael Korda, *Making the List: A Cultural History of the American Bestseller, 1900–1999.* New York: Barnes & Noble Books, 2001, p. 166.

>> **End Learning Objective 6**

Appendix

Using Isoquants and Isocosts to Understand Production and Cost

Use isoquants and isocost lines to understand production and cost.

Isoquants

In this chapter, we studied the important relationship between a firm's level of production and its costs. In this appendix, we will look more closely at how firms choose the combination of inputs to produce a given level of output. Firms usually have a choice of how they will produce their output. For example, Jill Johnson is able to produce 5,000 pizzas per week using 10 workers and 2 ovens or using 6 workers and 3 ovens. We will see that firms search for the *cost-minimizing* combination of inputs that will allow them to produce a given level of output. The cost-minimizing combination of inputs depends on two factors: technology—which determines how much output a firm receives from employing a given quantity of inputs—and input prices—which determine the total cost of each combination of inputs.

An Isoquant Graph

We begin by graphing the levels of output that Jill can produce using different combinations of two inputs: labor—the quantity of workers she hires per week—and capital—the quantity of ovens she uses per week. In reality, of course, Jill uses more than just these two inputs to produce pizzas, but nothing important would change if we expanded the discussion to include many inputs instead of just two. Figure A-1 measures capital along the vertical axis and labor along the horizontal axis. The curves in the graph are **isoquants**, which show all the combinations of two inputs, in this case capital and labor, that will produce the same level of output.

The isoquant labeled $Q = 5,000$ shows all the combinations of workers and ovens that enable Jill to produce that quantity of pizzas per week. For example, at point A, she produces 5,000 pizzas using 6 workers and 3 ovens, and at point B, she produces the same output using 10 workers and 2 ovens. With more workers and ovens, she can move to a higher isoquant. For example, with 12 workers and 4 ovens, she can produce at point C on the isoquant $Q = 10,000$. With even more workers and ovens, she could move to the isoquant $Q = 13,000$. The higher the isoquant—that is, the further to the upper right on the graph—the more output the firm produces. Although we have shown only three isoquants in this graph, there are, in fact, an infinite number of isoquants—one for every level of output.

The Slope of an Isoquant

Remember that the slope of a curve is the ratio of the change in the variable on the vertical axis to the change in the variable on the horizontal axis. Along an isoquant, the slope tells us the rate at which a firm is able to substitute one input for another while

Isoquant A curve that shows all the combinations of two inputs, such as capital and labor, that will produce the same level of output.

220

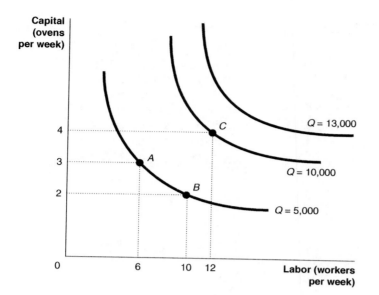

Figure A-1

Isoquants

Isoquants show all the combinations of two inputs, in this case capital and labor, that will produce the same level of output. For example, the isoquant labeled $Q = 5,000$ shows all the combinations of ovens and workers that enable Jill to produce that quantity of pizzas per week. At point A, she produces 5,000 pizzas using 3 ovens and 6 workers, and at point B, she produces the same output using 2 ovens and 10 workers. With more ovens and workers, she can move to a higher isoquant. For example, with 4 ovens and 12 workers, she can produce at point C on the isoquant $Q = 10,000$. With even more ovens and workers, she could move to the isoquant $Q = 13,000$.

keeping the level of output constant. The slope of an isoquant is called the **marginal rate of technical substitution** (*MRTS*).

We expect that the *MRTS* will change as we move down an isoquant. In Figure A-1, at a point like A on isoquant $Q = 5,000$, the isoquant is relatively steep. As we move down the curve, it becomes less steep at a point like B. This shape is the usual one for isoquants: They are bowed in, or convex. The reason isoquants have this shape is that as we move down the curve, we continue to substitute labor for capital. As the firm produces the same quantity of output using less capital, the additional labor it needs increases because of diminishing returns. Remember from the chapter that, as a consequence of diminishing returns, for a given decline in capital, increasing amounts of labor are necessary to produce the same level of output. Because the *MRTS* is equal to the change in capital divided by the change in labor, it will become smaller (in absolute value) as we move down an isoquant.

Marginal rate of technical substitution (*MRTS*) The slope of an isoquant, or the rate at which a firm is able to substitute one input for another while keeping the level of output constant.

Isocost Lines

Any firm wants to produce a given quantity of output at the lowest possible cost. We can show the relationship between the quantity of inputs used and the firm's total cost by using an *isocost* line. An **isocost line** shows all the combinations of two inputs, such as capital and labor, that have the same total cost.

Isocost line All the combinations of two inputs, such as capital and labor, that have the same total cost.

Graphing the Isocost Line

Suppose Jill has $6,000 per week to spend on capital and labor. Suppose, to simplify the analysis, that Jill can rent pizza ovens by the week. The table in Figure A-2 shows the combinations of capital and labor available to her if the rental price of ovens is $1,000 per week and the wage rate is $500 per week. The graph uses the data in the table to construct an isocost line. The isocost line intersects the vertical axis at the maximum number of ovens Jill can rent per week, which is shown by point A. The line intersects the horizontal axis at the maximum number of workers Jill can hire per week, which is point G. As Jill moves down the isocost line from point A, she gives up renting 1 oven for every 2 workers she hires. Any combination of inputs along the line or inside the line can be purchased with $6,000. Any combination that lies outside the line cannot be purchased because it would have a total cost to Jill of more than $6,000.

The Slope and Position of the Isocost Line

The slope of the isocost line is constant and equals the change in the quantity of ovens divided by the change in the quantity of workers. In this case, in moving from any point on the isocost line to any other point, the change in the quantity of ovens equals −1, and

Figure A-2

The isocost line shows the combinations of inputs with a total cost of $6,000. The rental price of ovens is $1,000 per week, so if Jill spends the whole $6,000 on ovens, she can rent 6 ovens (point *A*). The wage rate is $500 per week, so if Jill spends the whole $6,000 on workers, she can hire 12 workers. As she moves down the isocost line, she gives up renting 1 oven for every 2 workers she hires. Any combinations of inputs along the line or inside the line can be purchased with $6,000. Any combinations that lie outside the line cannot be purchased with $6,000.

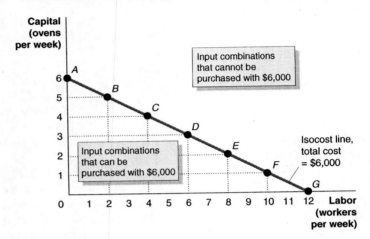

Point	Ovens	Workers	Total Cost
A	6	0	(6 x $1,000) + (0 x $500) = $6,000
B	5	2	(5 x $1,000) + (2 x $500) = 6,000
C	4	4	(4 x $1,000) + (4 x $500) = 6,000
D	3	6	(3 x $1,000) + (6 x $500) = 6,000
E	2	8	(2 x $1,000) + (8 x $500) = 6,000
F	1	10	(1 x $1,000) + (10 x $500) = 6,000
G	0	12	(0 x $1,000) + (12 x $500) = 6,000

the change in the quantity of workers equals 2, so the slope equals −1/2. Notice that with a rental price of ovens of $1,000 per week and a wage rate for labor of $500 per week, the slope of the isocost line is equal to the ratio of the wage rate divided by the rental price of capital, multiplied by −1: −$500/$1,000 = −1/2. In fact, this result will always hold, whatever inputs are involved and whatever their prices may be: *The slope of the isocost line is equal to the ratio of the price of the input on the horizontal axis divided by the price of the input on the vertical axis, multiplied by −1.*

The position of the isocost line depends on the level of total cost. Higher levels of total cost shift the isocost line outward, and lower levels of total cost shift the isocost line inward. This can be seen in Figure A-3, which shows isocost lines for total

Figure A-3

The position of the isocost line depends on the level of total cost. As total cost increases from $3,000 to $6,000 to $9,000 per week, the isocost line shifts outward. For each isocost line shown, the rental price of ovens is $1,000 per week, and the wage rate is $500 per week.

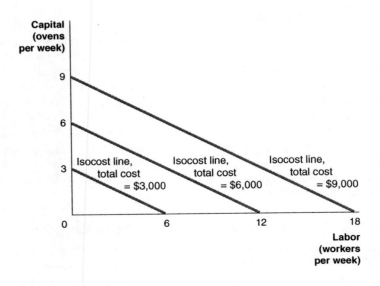

costs of $3,000, $6,000, and $9,000. We have shown only three isocost lines in the graph, but there are, in fact, an infinite number of isocost lines—one for every level of total cost.

Choosing the Cost-Minimizing Combination of Capital and Labor

Suppose Jill wants to produce 5,000 pizzas per week. Figure A-1 shows that there are many combinations of ovens and workers that will allow Jill to produce this level of output. There is only one combination of ovens and workers, however, that will allow her to produce 5,000 pizzas *at the lowest total cost*. Figure A-4 shows the isoquant $Q = 5,000$ along with three isocost lines. Point B is the lowest-cost combination of inputs shown in the graph, but this combination of 1 oven and 4 workers will produce fewer than the 5,000 pizzas needed. Points C and D are combinations of ovens and workers that will produce 5,000 pizzas, but their total cost is $9,000. The combination of 3 ovens and 6 workers at point A produces 5,000 pizzas at the lowest total cost of $6,000.

The graph shows that moving to an isocost line with a total cost of less than $6,000 would mean producing fewer than 5,000 pizzas. Being at any point along the isoquant $Q = 5,000$ other than point A would increase total cost above $6,000. In fact, the combination of inputs at point A is the only one on isoquant $Q = 5,000$ that has a total cost of $6,000. All other input combinations on this isoquant have higher total costs. Notice also that at point A, the isoquant and the isocost lines are tangent, so the slope of the isoquant is equal to the slope of the isocost line at that point.

Different Input Price Ratios Lead to Different Input Choices

Jill's cost-minimizing choice of 3 ovens and 6 workers is determined jointly by the technology available to her—as represented by her firm's isoquants—and by input prices—as represented by her firm's isocost lines. If the technology of making pizzas changes, perhaps because new ovens are developed, her isoquants will be affected, and her choice of inputs may change. If her isoquants remain unchanged but input

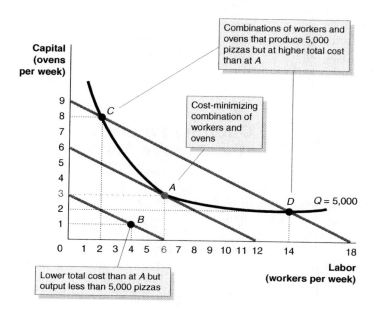

Combinations of workers and ovens that produce 5,000 pizzas but at higher total cost than at A

Cost-minimizing combination of workers and ovens

Lower total cost than at A but output less than 5,000 pizzas

Figure A-4

Choosing Capital and Labor to Minimize Total Cost

Jill wants to produce 5,000 pizzas per week at the lowest total cost. Point B is the lowest-cost combination of inputs shown in the graph, but this combination of 1 oven and 4 workers will produce fewer than the 5,000 pizzas needed. Points C and D are combinations of ovens and workers that will produce 5,000 pizzas, but their total cost is $9,000. The combination of 3 ovens and 6 workers at point A produces 5,000 pizzas at the lowest total cost of $6,000.

Figure A-5

As the graph shows, the input combination at point *A*, which was optimal for Jill, is not optimal for a businessperson in China. Using the input combination at point *A* would cost businesspeople in China more than $6,000. Instead, the Chinese isocost line is tangent to the isoquant at point *B*, where the input combination is 2 ovens and 10 workers. Because ovens cost more in China but workers cost less, a Chinese firm will use fewer ovens and more workers than a U.S. firm, even if it has the same technology as the U.S. firm.

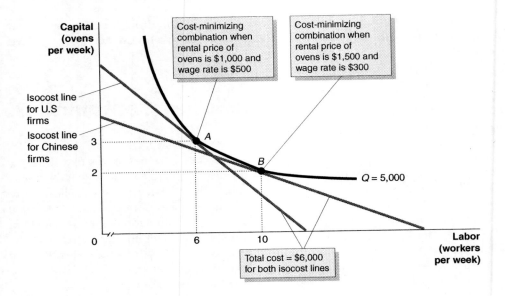

prices change, then her choice of inputs may also change. This fact can explain why firms in different countries that face different input prices may produce the same good using different combinations of capital and labor, even though they have the same technology available.

For example, suppose that in China, pizza ovens are higher priced and labor is lower priced than in the United States. In our example, Jill Johnson pays $1,000 per week to rent pizza ovens and $500 per week to hire workers. Suppose a businessperson in China must pay a price of $1,500 per week to rent the identical pizza ovens but can hire Chinese workers who are as productive as U.S. workers at a wage of $300 per week. Figure A-5 shows how the cost-minimizing input combination for the businessperson in China differs from Jill's.

Remember that the slope of the isocost line equals the wage rate divided by the rental price of capital, multiplied by −1. The slope of the isocost line that Jill and other U.S. firms face is −$500/$1,000, or −1/2. Firms in China, however, face an isocost line with a slope of −$300/$1,500, or −1/5. As the graph shows, the input combination at point *A*, which was optimal for Jill, is not optimal for a firm in China. Using the input combination at point *A* would cost a firm in China more than $6,000. Instead, the Chinese isocost line is tangent to the isoquant at point *B*, where the input combination is 2 ovens and 10 workers. This result makes sense: Because ovens cost more in China, but workers cost less, a Chinese firm will use fewer ovens and more workers than a U.S. firm, even if it has the same technology as the U.S. firm.

Making the Connection | The Changing Input Mix in Walt Disney Film Animation

The inputs used to make feature-length animated films have changed dramatically in the past 15 years. Prior to the early 1990s, the Walt Disney Company dominated the market for animated films. Disney's films were produced using hundreds of animators drawing most of the film by hand. Each film would contain as many as 170,000 individual drawings. Then, two developments dramatically affected how animated films are produced. First, in 1994, Disney had a huge hit with *The Lion King*, which cost only $50 million but earned the company more than $1 billion in profit. As a result of this success, Disney and other film studios began to produce more animated films, increasing the demand for animators and more than doubling their salaries. The second development came in 1995, when Pixar Animation Studios released the film *Toy Story*. This was the first successful feature-length film produced using computers, with no hand-drawn animation. In the following years, technological advance continued to reduce the cost of the computers and software necessary to produce an animated film.

As a result of these two developments, the price of capital—computers and software—fell relative to the price of labor—animators. As the figure shows, the change in the price of computers relative to animators changed the slope of the isocost line and resulted in film studios now producing animated films using many more computers and many fewer animators than in the early 1990s.

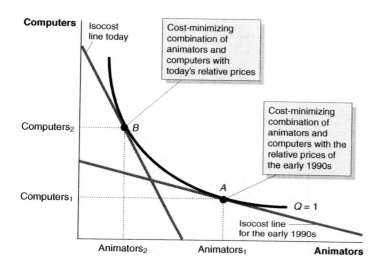

Source: Bruce Orwall, "Disney Delivers 'Lilo and Stitch' on Competition-Driven Budget," *Wall Street Journal*, June 18, 2002, p. A1.

YOUR TURN: Test your understanding by doing related problem A.8 at the end of this chapter.

Another Look at Cost Minimization

We saw that consumers maximize utility when they consume each good up to the point where the marginal utility per dollar spent is the same for every good. We can derive a very similar cost-minimization rule for firms. Remember that at the point of cost minimization, the isoquant and the isocost line are tangent, so they have the same slope. Therefore, *at the point of cost minimization, the marginal rate of technical substitution* (MRTS) *is equal to the wage rate divided by the rental price of capital.*

The slope of the isoquant tells us the rate at which a firm is able to substitute labor for capital, *given existing technology.* The slope of the isocost line tells us the rate at which a firm is able to substitute labor for capital, *given current input prices.* Only at the point of cost minimization are these two rates the same.

When we move from one point on an isoquant to another, we end up using more of one input and less of the other input, but the level of output remains the same. For example, as Jill moves down an isoquant, she uses fewer ovens and more workers but produces the same quantity of pizzas. In this chapter, we defined the *marginal product of labor* (MP_L) as the additional output produced by a firm as a result of hiring one more worker. Similarly, we can define the *marginal product of capital* (MP_K) as the additional output produced by a firm as a result of using one more machine. So, when Jill uses fewer ovens by moving down an isoquant, she loses output equal to:

$$- \text{ Change in the quantity of ovens} \times MP_K.$$

But she uses more workers, so she gains output equal to:

$$\text{Change in the quantity of workers} \times MP_L.$$

We know that the gain in output from the additional workers is equal to the loss from the smaller quantity of ovens because total output remains the same along an isoquant. Therefore, we can write:

$$- \text{ Change in the quantity of ovens} \times MP_K = \text{Change in the quantity of workers} \times MP_L.$$

Loss in output from using fewer ovens

Gain in output from using more workers

If we rearrange terms, we have the following:

$$\frac{-\text{Change in the quantity of ovens}}{\text{Change in the quantity of workers}} = \frac{MP_L}{MP_K}.$$

Because the

$$\frac{-\text{Change in the quantity of ovens}}{\text{Change in the quantity of workers}}$$

is the slope of the isoquant, or the marginal rate of technical substitution (*MRTS*), we can write:

$$\frac{-\text{Change in the quantity of ovens}}{\text{Change in the quantity of workers}} = MRTS = \frac{MP_L}{MP_K}.$$

The slope of the isocost line equals the wage rate (w) divided by the rental price of capital (r). At the point of cost minimization, the slope of the isoquant is equal to the slope of the isocost line. Therefore:

$$\frac{MP_L}{MP_K} = \frac{w}{r}.$$

We can rewrite this to show that at the point of cost minimization:

$$\frac{MP_L}{w} = \frac{MP_K}{r}.$$

This last expression tells us that to minimize cost, a firm should hire inputs up to the point where the last dollar spent on each input results in the same increase in output. If this equality did not hold, a firm could lower its costs by using more of one input and less of the other. For example, if the left-hand side of the equation were greater than the right-hand side, a firm could rent fewer ovens, hire more workers, and produce the same output at lower cost.

Solved Problem | A-1

Determining the Optimal Combination of Inputs

Consider the information in the following table for Jill Johnson's restaurant:

Marginal product of capital	3,000 pizzas
Marginal product of labor	1,200 pizzas
Wage rate	$300 per week
Rental price of ovens	$600 per week

Briefly explain whether Jill is minimizing costs. If she is not minimizing costs, explain whether she should rent more ovens and hire fewer workers or rent fewer ovens and hire more workers.

SOLVING THE PROBLEM:

Step 1: **Review the chapter material.** This problem is about determining the optimal choice of inputs by comparing the ratios of the marginal products of inputs to their prices, so you may want to review the section "Another Look at Cost Minimization."

Step 2: **Compute the ratios of marginal product to input price to determine whether Jill is minimizing costs.** If Jill is minimizing costs, the following relationship should hold:

$$\frac{MP_L}{w} = \frac{MP_K}{r}.$$

In this case, we have:

$$MP_L = 1,200$$

$$MP_K = 3,000$$

$$w = \$300$$

$$r = \$600.$$

So:

$$\frac{MP_L}{w} = \frac{1,200}{\$300} = 4 \text{ pizzas per dollar, and } \frac{MP_K}{r} = \frac{3,000}{\$600} = 5 \text{ pizzas per dollar.}$$

Because the two ratios are not equal, Jill is not minimizing cost.

Step 3: **Determine how Jill should change the mix of inputs she uses.** Jill produces more pizzas per dollar from the last oven than from the last worker. This indicates that she has too many workers and too few ovens. Therefore, to minimize cost, Jill should use more ovens and hire fewer workers.

YOUR TURN: For more practice, do related problem A.7 at the end of this appendix.

>> End Solved Problem A-1

Making the Connection

Do National Football League Teams Behave Efficiently?

In the National Football League (NFL), the "salary cap" is the maximum amount each team can spend each year on salaries for football players. Each year's salary cap results from negotiations between the league and the union representing the players. To achieve efficiency, an NFL team should distribute salaries among players so as to maximize the level of output—in this case, winning football games—given the constant level of cost represented by the salary cap. (Notice that maximizing the level of output for a given level of cost is equivalent to minimizing cost for a given level of output. To see why, think about the situation where an isocost line is tangent to an isoquant. At the point of tangency, the firm has simultaneously minimized the cost of producing the level of output represented by the isoquant and maximized the output produced at the level of cost represented by the isocost line.) In distributing salaries, teams should equalize the marginal productivity of players as represented by their contribution to winning games to the salaries paid. Just as a firm may not use a machine that has a very high marginal product if its rental price is very high, a football team may not want to hire a superstar player if the salary the team would need to pay is too high.

Chris McGrath/Getty Images

Are the Detroit Lions paying too much to Calvin Johnson?

Economists Cade Massey, of Duke University, and Richard Thaler, of the University of Chicago, have analyzed whether NFL teams distribute their salaries efficiently. NFL teams obtain their players either by signing free agents—who are players whose contracts with other teams have expired—or by signing players chosen in the annual draft of eligible college players. The college draft consists of seven rounds, with the teams with the worst records the previous year choosing first. Massey and Thaler find that, in fact, NFL teams do not allocate salaries efficiently. In particular, the players chosen with the first few picks of the first round of the draft tend to be paid salaries that are much higher relative to their marginal products than is true for players taken later in the first round. A typical team with a high draft pick would increase its ability to win football games at the constant cost represented by the salary cap if it traded for lower draft picks. Why do NFL teams apparently make the error of not efficiently distributing salaries? Massey and Thaler argue that managers of NFL teams tend to be overconfident in their ability to forecast how well a college player is likely to perform in the NFL.

Managers of NFL teams are not alone in suffering from overconfidence. Studies have shown that, in general, people tend to overestimate their ability to forecast an uncertain outcome. Because NFL teams tend to overestimate the future marginal productivity of high draft picks, they pay them salaries that are inefficiently high when compared to salaries other draft picks receive.

This example shows that the concepts developed in this chapter provide powerful tools for analyzing whether firms are operating efficiently.

Source: Cade Massey and Richard Thaler, "Overconfidence versus Market Efficiency in the National Football League," Working Paper 11270, Cambridge, MA: National Bureau of Economic Research, April 2005.

YOUR TURN: Test your understanding by doing related problem A.14 at the end of this chapter.

The Expansion Path

We can use isoquants and isocost lines to examine what happens as a firm expands its level of output. Figure A-6 shows three isoquants for a firm that produces bookcases. The isocost lines are drawn, assuming that the machines used in producing bookcases can be rented for $100 per day and the wage rate is $25 per day. The point where each isoquant is tangent to an isocost line determines the cost-minimizing combination of capital and labor for producing that level of output. For example, 10 machines and 40 workers is the cost-minimizing

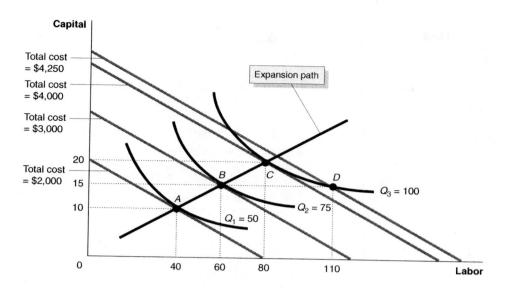

Figure A-6

The Expansion Path

The tangency points *A*, *B*, and *C* lie along the firm's expansion path, which is a curve that shows the cost-minimizing combination of inputs for every level of output. In the short run, when the quantity of machines is fixed, the firm can expand output from 75 bookcases per day to 100 bookcases per day at the lowest cost only by moving from point *B* to point *D* and increasing the number of workers from 80 to 110 In the long run, when it can increase the quantity of machines it uses, the firm can move from point *D* to point *C*, thereby reducing its total costs of producing 100 bookcases per day from $4,250 to $4,000.

combination of inputs for producing 50 bookcases per day. The cost-minimizing points *A*, *B*, and *C* lie along the firm's **expansion path**, which is a curve that shows the cost-minimizing combination of inputs for every level of output.

An important point to note is that the expansion path represents the least-cost combination of inputs to produce a given level of output *in the long run*, when the firm is able to vary the levels of all of its inputs. We know, though, that in the short run, at least one input is fixed. We can use Figure A-6 to show that as the firm expands in the short run, its costs will be higher than in the long run. For example, suppose that the firm is currently at point *B*, using 15 machines and 60 workers to produce 75 bookcases per day. The firm wants to expand its output to 100 bookcases per day, but in the short run, it is unable to increase the quantity of machines it uses. Therefore, to expand output, it must hire more workers. The figure shows that in the short run, to produce 100 bookcases per day using 15 machines, the lowest costs it can attain are at point *D*, where it employs 110 workers. With a rental price of machines of $100 per day and a wage rate of $25 per day, in the short run, the firm will have total costs of $4,250 to produce 100 bookcases per day. In the long run, though, the firm can increase the number of machines it uses from 15 to 20 and reduce the number of workers from 110 to 80. This change allows it to move from point *D* to point *C* on its expansion path and to lower its total costs of producing 100 bookcases per day from $4,250 to $4,000. The firm's minimum total costs of production are lower in the long run than in the short run.

Expansion path A curve that shows a firm's cost-minimizing combination of inputs for every level of output.

Key Terms

Expansion path

Isocost line

Isoquant

Marginal rate of technical
substitution (*MRTS*)

Review Questions

A.1 What is an isoquant? What is the slope of an isoquant?

A.2 What is an isocost line? What is the slope of an isocost line?

A.3 How do firms choose the optimal combination of inputs?

Problems and Applications

A.4 Draw an isoquant–isocost line graph to illustrate the following situation: Jill Johnson can rent pizza ovens for $400 per week and hire workers for $200 per week. She is currently using 5 ovens and 10 workers to produce 20,000 pizzas per week and has total costs of $4,000. Make sure to label your graph showing the cost-minimizing input combination and the maximum quantity of labor and capital she can use with total costs of $4,000.

A.5 Use the following graph to answer the questions.

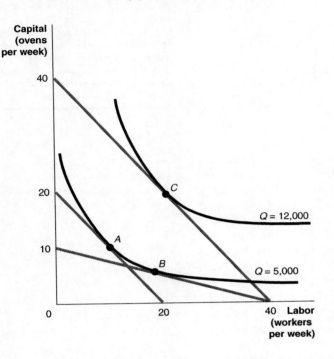

a. If the wage rate and the rental price of machines are both $100 and total cost is $2,000, is the cost-minimizing point A, B, or C? Briefly explain.

b. If the wage rate is $25, the rental price of machines is $100, and total cost is $1,000, is the cost-minimizing point A, B, or C? Briefly explain.

c. If the wage rate and the rental price of machines are both $100 and total cost is $4,000, is the cost-minimizing point A, B, or C? Briefly explain.

A.6 **(Related to *Solved Problem A-1*)** Consider the information in the following table for Jill Johnson's restaurant.

Marginal product of capital	4,000
Marginal product of labor	100
Wage rate	$10
Rental price of pizza ovens	$500

Briefly explain whether Jill is minimizing costs. If she is not minimizing costs, explain whether she should rent more ovens and hire fewer workers or rent fewer ovens and hire more workers.

A.7 **(Related to *Solved Problem A-1*)** Draw an isoquant–isocost line graph to illustrate the following situation: Jill Johnson can rent pizza ovens for

$200 per week and hire workers for $100 per week. Currently, she is using 5 ovens and 10 workers to produce 20,000 pizzas per week and has total costs of $2,000. Jill's marginal rate of technical substitution (*MRTS*) equals −1. Explain why this means that she's not minimizing costs and what she could do to minimize costs.

A.8 **(Related to the *Making the Connection*)** During the eighteenth century, the American colonies had much more land per farmer than did Europe, with the result that the price of labor in the colonies was much higher relative to the price of land than was true in Europe. Assume that Europe and the colonies had access to the same technology for producing food. Use an isoquant-isocost line graph to illustrate why the combination of land and labor used in producing food in the colonies would have been different than the combination used to produce food in Europe.

A.9 Draw an isoquant–isocost line graph to illustrate the following situation and the change that occurs: Jill Johnson can rent pizza ovens for $2,000 per week and hire workers for $1,000 per week. Currently, she is using 5 ovens and 10 workers to produce 20,000 pizzas per week and has total costs of $20,000. Then Jill reorganizes the way things are done in her business and achieves positive technological change.

A.10 Use the following graph to answer the following questions about Jill Johnson's isoquant curve.

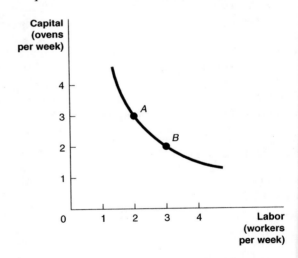

a. Which combination of inputs yields more output: combination A (3 ovens and 2 workers) or combination B (2 ovens and 3 workers)?

b. What will determine whether Jill selects A, B, or some other point along this isoquant curve?

c. Is the marginal rate of technical substitution (*MRTS*) greater at point A or point B?

A.11 Draw an isoquant–isocost line graph to illustrate the following situation: Jill Johnson can rent pizza ovens for $2,000 per week and hire workers for $1,000 per week. She can minimize the cost of producing 20,000 pizzas per week by using 5 ovens and 10 workers, at a total cost of $20,000. She can minimize the cost of producing 45,000 pizzas per week by using 10 ovens and 20 workers, at a total cost of $40,000. And she can minimize the cost of producing 60,000 pizzas per week by using 15 ovens and 30 workers, at a total cost of $60,000. Now draw Jill's long-run average cost curve and discuss its economies and diseconomies of scale.

A.12 In Brazil, a grove of oranges is picked using 20 workers, ladders, and baskets. In Florida, a grove of oranges is picked using 1 worker and a machine that shakes the oranges off the trees and scoops up the fallen oranges. Using an isoquant–isocost line graph, illustrate why these two different methods are used to pick the same number of oranges per day in these two locations.

A.13 Jill Johnson is minimizing the costs of producing pizzas. The rental price of one of her ovens is $2,000 per week, and the wage rate is $600 per week. The marginal product of capital in her business is 12,000 pizzas. What must be the marginal product of her workers?

A.14 **(Related to the *Making the Connection*)** If Massey and Thaler are correct, then should the team that has the first pick in the draft keep the pick or trade it to another team for a lower pick? Explain.

>> **End Appendix Learning Objective**

Monopoly and Antitrust Policy

From Chapter 14 of *Microeconomics*, 2/e. R. Glenn Hubbard. Anthony Patrick O'Brien. Copyright © 2008 by Pearson Prentice Hall.

Monopoly and Antitrust Policy

Time Warner Rul[...] Manhattan

Today most people can hardly imagine life without cable television. In fact, almost 80 percent of U.S. homes have cable television: a larger fraction than have clothes dryers, dishwashers, air conditioning, or personal computers. The first cable systems were established in the 1940s in cities that were too small to support broadcast stations. Those systems consisted of large antennas set up on hills to receive broadcasts from television stations within range. The signals were then transmitted by cable to individual houses.

The cable industry grew slowly because the technology did not exist to rebroadcast the signals of distant stations, so cable systems offered just a few channels. By 1970, only about 7 percent of households had cable television. In addition, the Federal Communications Commission (FCC)—the U.S. government agency that regulates the television industry—placed restrictions on both rebroadcasting the signals of distant stations and the fees that could be charged for "premium channels" that would show movies or sporting events. In the

[...]wo key developments occurred: First, satellite relay technology made it feasible for local cable systems to receive signals relayed by satellite from distant broadcast stations. Second, Congress loosened regulations on rebroadcasting distant stations and premium channels. The result of these developments was the growth of both "superstations," which are local broadcast stations in large cities—such as New York, Chicago, and Atlanta—whose programming is sent by satellite to cable systems around the country, and premium channels, such as Home Box Office (HBO).

One of the most successful of the superstations was WTBS, started by Atlanta entrepreneur Robert Edward "Ted" Turner III. Turner went on to found the Turner Broadcasting System (TBS), which included the Cable News Network (CNN), the first 24-hour news network. In 2001, Turner was involved in the largest merger of entertainment companies in history, when AOL Time Warner was formed. The company—now known as Time Warner—was made up of leading firms from four segments of the entertainment industry: Warner Brothers (movie making), *Time* (magazine publishing), TBS (cable television),

and AOL (Internet). Today, Time Warner operates cable systems in 22 states through Time Warner Cable.

A firm needs a license from the city government to enter a local cable television market. If you live in Manhattan and you want cable television, you have to purchase it from Time Warner Cable. Other cable companies could ask the New York City government for licenses to compete against Time Warner Cable in Manhattan, but none have. This is not an unusual situation for a cable television system: Of the nearly 9,000 markets for cable television in the United States, fewer than 400 have competing cable systems.

As the only provider of cable TV in Manhattan, Time Warner has a *monopoly*. Few firms in the United States are monopolies because in a market system, whenever a firm earns economic profits, other firms will enter its market. Therefore, it is very difficult for a firm to remain the only provider of a good or service. In this chapter, we will develop an economic model of monopoly that can help us analyze how such firms affect the economy. **AN INSIDE LOOK AT POLICY** explores how legislation in California is lowering barriers to entry in the cable TV market.

LEARNING Objectives

After studying this chapter, you should be able to:

1. Define **monopoly**.

2. Explain the four main **reasons monopolies arise**.

3. Explain how a monopoly chooses **price** and **output**.

4. Use a graph to illustrate how a monopoly affects **economic efficiency**.

5. Discuss **government policies** toward monopoly.

Economics in YOUR Life!

Why Can't I Watch the NFL Network?

Are you a fan of the National Football League? Would you like to see more NFL-related programming on television? If so, you're not alone. The NFL felt there was so much demand for more football programming that it began its own football network, the NFL Network.

Unfortunately for many football fans, the NFL Network is not available to most households with cable television. Why are some of the largest cable TV systems unwilling to include the NFL Network in their channel lineups? Why are some systems requiring customers who want the NFL Network to upgrade to more expensive channel packages or digital service? As you read this chapter, see if you can answer these questions. You can check your answers against those we provide at the end of the chapter.

Although few firms are monopolies, the economic model of monopoly can still be quite useful. Even though perfectly competitive markets are rare, this market model provides a benchmark for how a firm acts in the most competitive situation possible: when it is in an industry with many firms that all supply the same product. Monopoly provides a benchmark for the other extreme, where a firm is the only one in its market and, therefore, faces no competition from other firms supplying its product. The monopoly model is also useful in analyzing situations in which firms agree to *collude*, or not compete, and act together as if they were a monopoly. As we will discuss in this chapter, collusion is illegal in the United States, but it occasionally happens.

Monopolies also pose a dilemma for the government. Should the government allow monopolies to exist? Are there circumstances in which the government should actually promote the existence of monopolies? Should the government regulate the prices monopolies charge? If so, will such price regulation increase economic efficiency? In this chapter, we will explore these public policy issues.

1 LEARNING OBJECTIVE

1 | Define monopoly.

Is Any Firm Ever Really a Monopoly?

Monopoly A firm that is the only seller of a good or service that does not have a close substitute.

A **monopoly** is a firm that is the only seller of a good or service that does not have a close substitute. Because substitutes of some kind exist for just about every product, can any firm really be a monopoly? The answer is "yes," provided that the substitutes are not "close" substitutes. But how do we decide whether a substitute is a close substitute? A narrow definition of monopoly that some economists use is that a firm has a monopoly if it can ignore the actions of all other firms. In other words, other firms must not be producing close substitutes if the monopolist can ignore the other firms' prices. For example, candles are a substitute for electric lights, but your local electric company can ignore candle prices because however low the price of candles falls, almost no customers will give up using electric lights and switch to candles. Therefore, your local electric company is clearly a monopoly.

Many economists, however, use a broader definition of monopoly. For example, suppose Joe Santos owns the only pizza parlor in a small town. (We will consider later the question of *why* a market may have only a single firm.) Does Joe have a monopoly? Substitutes for pizzas certainly exist. If the price of pizza is too high, people will switch to hamburgers or fried chicken or some other food instead. People do not have to eat at Joe's or starve. Joe is in competition with the local McDonald's and Kentucky Fried Chicken, among other firms. So, Joe does not meet the narrow definition of a monopoly. But many economists would still argue that it is useful to think of Joe as having a monopoly.

Although hamburgers and fried chicken are substitutes for pizza, competition from firms selling them is not enough to keep Joe from earning economic profits. When firms earn economic profits, we can expect new firms to enter the industry, and in the long run, the economic profits are competed away. Joe's profits will not be competed away as long as he is the *only* seller of pizza. Using the broader definition, Joe has a monopoly because there are no other firms selling a substitute close enough that his economic profits are competed away in the long run.

Making the Connection | Is Xbox 360 a Close Substitute for PlayStation 3?

In the early 2000s, Microsoft's Xbox and Sony's PlayStation 2 (PS2) were the best-selling video game consoles. When the two companies began work on the next generation of consoles, they had important decisions to make. In developing the Xbox, Microsoft had decided to include a hard disk and a version of the Windows computer operating system. As a result, the cost of producing the Xbox was much higher than the cost to Sony of producing the PlayStation 2. Microsoft was not concerned by the higher production cost because it believed it would be able to charge a higher price for Xbox than Sony charged for PlayStation 2. Unfortunately for Microsoft, consumers considered the Sony PS2 a close substitute for the Xbox. Microsoft was forced to charge the same price for the Xbox that Sony charged for the PS2. So, while Sony was able to make a substantial profit at that price, Microsoft initially lost money on the Xbox because of its higher costs.

In developing the next generation of video game consoles, both companies hoped to produce devices that could serve as multipurpose home-entertainment systems. To achieve this goal, the new systems needed to play DVDs as well as games. Sony developed a new type of DVD called Blu-ray. Blu-ray DVDs can store five times as much data as conventional DVDs and can play back high-definition (HD) video. Sony's decision to give the new PlayStation 3 (PS3) the capability to play Blu-ray DVDs was risky in two ways: First, it raised the cost of producing the consoles. Second, because there is a competing second-generation standard for DVDs, called HD-DVD, the PlayStation 3 would not be capable of playing all available second-generation DVDs, thereby reducing its appeal to some consumers. Microsoft decided to sell its Xbox 360 with only the capability of playing older-format DVDs, while making available an add-on component that would play HD-DVDs.

Early indications were that Microsoft may have made the better decision. Consumers seemed to consider the PS3 and the Xbox to be close substitutes. In that case, the fact that the PS3's price was $200 higher than the Xbox 360's price was a significant problem for Sony. Ironically, Sony made the same mistake Microsoft made several years before when it launched the Xbox to compete with PS2.

To many gamers, PlayStation 3 is a close substitute for Xbox.

REUTERS/Toshiyuki Aizawa/Landov

Sources: Stephen H. Wildstrom, "PlayStation 3: It's Got Game," *BusinessWeek*, December 4, 2006; and "Sony: Playing a Long Game," *Economist*, November 16, 2006.

YOUR TURN: Test your understanding by doing related problem 1.7 at the end of this chapter.

2 | Explain the four main reasons monopolies arise.

Where Do Monopolies Come From?

Because monopolies do not face competition, every firm would like to have a monopoly. But to have a monopoly, barriers to entering the market must be so high that no other firms can enter. *Barriers to entry* may be high enough to keep out competing firms for four main reasons:

1. Government blocks the entry of more than one firm into a market.
2. One firm has control of a key resource necessary to produce a good.
3. There are important *network externalities* in supplying the good or service.
4. Economies of scale are so large that one firm has a *natural monopoly*.

Entry Blocked by Government Action

As we will discuss later in this chapter, governments ordinarily try to promote competition in markets, but sometimes governments take action to block entry into a market. In the United States, government blocks entry in two main ways:

1. By granting a *patent* or *copyright* to an individual or firm, giving it the exclusive right to produce a product.
2. By granting a firm a *public franchise*, making it the exclusive legal provider of a good or service.

Patent The exclusive right to a product for a period of 20 years from the date the product is invented.

Patents and Copyrights The U.S. government grants patents to firms that develop new products or new ways of making existing products. A **patent** gives a firm the exclusive right to a new product for a period of 20 years from the date the product is invented. Because Microsoft has a patent on the Windows operating system, other firms cannot sell their own versions of Windows. The government grants patents to encourage firms to spend money on the research and development necessary to create new products. If other firms could have freely copied Windows, Microsoft is unlikely to have spent the money necessary to develop it. Sometimes firms are able to maintain a monopoly in the production of a good without patent protection, provided that they can keep secret how the product is made.

Patent protection is of vital importance to pharmaceutical firms as they develop new prescription drugs. Pharmaceutical firms start research and development work on a new prescription drug an average of 12 years before the drug is available for sale. A firm applies for a patent about 10 years before it begins to sell the product. The average 10-year delay between the government granting a patent and the firm actually selling the drug is due to the federal Food and Drug Administration's requirements that the firm demonstrate that the drug is both safe and effective. Therefore, during the period before the drug can be sold, the firm will have substantial costs to develop and test the drug. If the drug does not make it successfully to market, the firm will have a substantial loss.

Once a drug is available for sale, the profits the firm earns from the drug will increase throughout the period of patent protection—which is usually about 10 years—as the drug becomes more widely known to doctors and patients. After the patent has expired, other firms are free to legally produce chemically identical drugs called *generic drugs.* Gradually, competition from generic drugs will eliminate the profits the original firm had been earning. For example, when patent protection expired for Glucophage, a diabetes drug manufactured by Bristol-Myers Squibb, sales of the drug declined by more than $1.5 billion in the first year due to competition from 12 generic versions of the drug produced by other firms. When the patent expired on Prozac, an antidepressant drug manufactured by Eli Lilly, sales dropped by more than 80 percent. Most economic profits from selling a prescription drug are eliminated 20 years after the drug is first offered for sale.

Making the Connection | The End of the Christmas Plant Monopoly

In December, the poinsettia plant seems to be almost everywhere, decorating stores, restaurants, and houses. Although it may seem strange that anyone can have a monopoly on the production of a plant, for many years the Paul Ecke Ranch in Encinitas, California, had a monopoly on poinsettias.

The poinsettia is a wildflower native to Mexico. It was almost unknown in the United States before Albert Ecke, a German immigrant, began selling it in the early twentieth century at his flower stand in Hollywood, California. Unlike almost every other flowering plant, the poinsettia blossoms in the winter. This timing, along with the plant's striking red and green colors, makes the Poinsettia ideal for Christmas decorating.

Albert Ecke's son, Paul, discovered that by grafting together two varieties of poinsettias, it was possible to have multiple branches grow from one stem. The result was a plant that had more leaves and was much more colorful than conventional poinsettias. Paul Ecke did not attempt to patent his new technique for growing poinsettias. But because the Ecke family kept the technique secret for decades, it was able to maintain a monopoly on the commercial production of the plants. Unfortunately for the Ecke family—but fortunately for consumers—a university researcher discovered the technique and published it in an academic journal.

New firms quickly entered the industry, and the price of poinsettias plummeted. Soon consumers could purchase them for as little as three for $10. At those prices, the Ecke's firm was unable to earn economic profits. Eventually, Paul Ecke III, the owner of the firm, decided to sell off more than half the firm's land to fund new state-of-the-art

At one time, the Ecke family had a monopoly on growing poinsettias, but many new firms entered the industry.

greenhouses and research into new varieties of plants that he hoped would earn the firm economic profits once again. One of the firm's new products was a variety of white poinsettias that could be spray-painted in different colors and sold for $10 or more—double the price of plain poinsettias.

Sources: Bart Ziegler, "What Color Is Your Poinsettia?" *Wall Street Journal*, December 14, 2006; Cynthia Crossen, "Holiday's Ubiquitous Houseplant," *Wall Street Journal*, December 19, 2000; and Mike Freeman and David E. Graham, "Ecke Ranch Plans to Sell Most of Its Remaining Land," *San Diego Union-Tribune*, December 11, 2003.

YOUR TURN: Test your understanding by doing related problem 2.9 at the end of this chapter.

Just as the government grants a new product patent protection, books, films, and software receive **copyright** protection. U.S. law grants the creator of a book, film, or piece of music the exclusive right to use the creation during the creator's lifetime. The creator's heirs retain this exclusive right for 70 years after the creator's death. In effect, copyrights create monopolies for the copyrighted items. Without copyrights, individuals and firms would be less likely to invest in creating new books, films, and software.

Public Franchises In some cases, the government grants a firm a **public franchise** that allows it to be the only legal provider of a good or service. For example, state and local governments often designate one company as the sole provider of electricity, natural gas, or water.

Occasionally, the government may decide to provide certain services directly to consumers through a *public enterprise*. This is much more common in Europe than in the United States. For example, the governments in most European countries own the railroad systems. In the United States, many city governments provide water and sewage service themselves rather than rely on private firms.

Copyright A government-granted exclusive right to produce and sell a creation.

Public franchise A designation by the government that a firm is the only legal provider of a good or service.

Control of a Key Resource

Another way for a firm to become a monopoly is by controlling a key resource. This happens infrequently because most resources, including raw materials such as oil or iron ore, are widely available from a variety of suppliers. There are, however, a few prominent examples of monopolies based on control of a key resource, such as the Aluminum Company of America (Alcoa) and the International Nickel Company of Canada.

For many years until the 1940s, Alcoa either owned or had long-term contracts to buy nearly all of the available bauxite, the mineral needed to produce aluminum. Without access to bauxite, competing firms had to use recycled aluminum, which limited the amount of aluminum they could produce. Similarly, the International Nickel Company of Canada controlled more than 90 percent of available nickel supplies. Competition in the nickel market increased when the Petsamo nickel fields in northern Russia were developed after World War II.

In the United States, a key resource for a professional sports team is a large stadium. The teams that make up the major professional sports leagues—Major League Baseball, the National Football League, and the National Basketball Association—usually have long-term leases with the stadiums in major cities. Control of these stadiums is a major barrier to new professional baseball, football, or basketball leagues forming.

Making the Connection	**Are Diamond Profits Forever? The De Beers Diamond Monopoly**

The most famous monopoly based on control of a raw material is the De Beers diamond mining and marketing company of South Africa. Before the 1860s, diamonds were extremely rare. Only a few pounds of diamonds were produced each year, primarily from Brazil and India. Then in 1870, enormous deposits of diamonds were discovered along the Orange River in South Africa. It became possible to produce thousands of pounds of diamonds per year, and the owners of the new mines feared that the price of diamonds would plummet. To avoid financial disaster, the mine owners decided in 1888 to merge and form De Beers Consolidated Mines, Ltd.

De Beers became one of the most profitable and longest-lived monopolies in history. The company has carefully controlled the supply of diamonds to keep prices high. As new diamond deposits were discovered in Russia and Zaire, De Beers was able to maintain prices by buying most of the new supplies.

Because diamonds are rarely destroyed, De Beers has always worried about competition from the resale of stones. Heavily promoting diamond engagement and wedding rings with the slogan "A Diamond Is Forever" was a way around this problem. Because engagement and wedding rings have great sentimental value, they are seldom resold, even by the heirs of the original recipients. De Beers advertising has been successful even in some countries, such as Japan, that have had no custom of giving diamond engagement rings. As the populations in De Beers's key markets age, its advertising in recent years has focused on middle-aged men presenting diamond rings to their wives as symbols of financial success and continuing love and on professional women buying "right-hand rings" for themselves.

In the past few years, competition has finally come to the diamond business. By 2000, De Beers directly controlled only about 40 percent of world diamond production. The company became concerned about the amount it was spending to buy diamonds from other sources to keep them off the market. It decided to adopt a strategy of differentiating its diamonds by relying on its name recognition. Each De Beers diamond is now marked with a microscopic brand—a "Forevermark"—to reassure consumers of its high quality. Other firms, such as BHP Billiton, which owns mines in northern Canada, have followed suit by branding their diamonds. Sellers of Canadian diamonds stress that they are "mined under ethical, environmentally friendly conditions," as opposed to "blood diamonds," which are supposedly "mined under armed force in war-torn African countries and exported to finance military campaigns." Whether consumers will pay attention to brands on diamonds remains to be seen, although through 2006, the branding strategy had helped De Beers maintain its 40 percent share of the diamond market.

Sources: Edward Jay Epstein, "Have You Ever Tried to Sell a Diamond?" *Atlantic Monthly*, February 1982; Donna J. Bergenstock, Mary E. Deily, and Larry W. Taylor, "A Cartel's Response to Cheating: An Empirical Investigation of the De Beers Diamond Empire," *Southern Economic Journal*, Vol. 73, No. 1, July 2006, pp. 173–189; Bernard Simon, "Adding Brand Names to Nameless Stones," *New York Times*, June 27, 2002; Blythe Yee, "Ads Remind Women They Have Two Hands," *Wall Street Journal*, August 14, 2003; quote in last paragraph from Joel Baglole, "Political Correctness by the Carat," *Wall Street Journal*, April 17, 2003.

YOUR TURN: Test your understanding by doing related problem 2.10 at the end of this chapter.

De Beers promoted the sentimental value of diamonds as a way to maintain its position in the diamond market.

Network Externalities

Network externalities The situation where the usefulness of a product increases with the number of consumers who use it.

There are **network externalities** in the consumption of a product if the usefulness of the product increases with the number of people who use it. If you owned the only cell phone in the world, for example, it would not be very valuable. The more cell phones there are in use, the more valuable they become to consumers.

Some economists argue that network externalities can serve as barriers to entry. For example, in the early 1980s, Microsoft gained an advantage over other software companies by developing MS-DOS, the operating system for the first IBM personal computers. Because IBM sold more computers than any other company, software developers wrote many application programs for MS-DOS. The more people who used MS-DOS–based programs, the greater the usefulness to a consumer of using an MS-DOS–based program. Today, Windows, the program Microsoft developed to succeed MS-DOS, has a 95 percent share in the market for personal computer operating systems (although

Windows has a much lower share in the market for operating systems for servers). If another firm introduced a competing operating system, some economists argue that relatively few people would use it initially, and few applications would run on it, which would limit the operating system's value to other consumers.

eBay was the first Internet site to attract a significant number of people to its online auctions. Once a large number of people began to use eBay to buy and sell collectibles, antiques, and many other products, it became a more valuable place to buy and sell. Yahoo.com, Amazon.com, and other Internet sites eventually started online auctions, but they found it difficult to attract buyers and sellers. On eBay, a buyer expects to find more sellers, and a seller expects to find more potential buyers than on Amazon or other auction sites.

As these examples show, network externalities can set off a *virtuous cycle*: If a firm can attract enough customers initially, it can attract additional customers because its product's value has been increased by more people using it, which attracts even more customers, and so on. With products such as computer operating systems and online auctions, it might be difficult for new firms to enter the market and compete away the profits being earned by the first firm in the market.

Economists engage in considerable debate, however, about the extent to which network externalities are important barriers to entry in the business world. Some economists argue that the dominant positions of Microsoft and eBay reflect the efficiency of those firms in offering products that satisfy consumer preferences more than the effects of network externalities. In this view, the advantages existing firms gain from network externalities would not be enough to protect them from competing firms offering better products. In other words, a firm entering the operating system market with a program better than Windows or a firm offering an Internet auction site better than eBay would be successful despite the effects of network externalities.

Natural Monopoly

Economies of scale exist when a firm's long-run average costs fall as it increases the quantity of output it produces. A **natural monopoly** occurs when economies of scale are so large that one firm can supply the entire market at a lower average total cost than two or more firms. In that case, there is really "room" in the market for only one firm.

Figure 1 shows the average total cost curve for a firm producing electricity and the total demand for electricity in the firm's market. Notice that the average total cost

Natural monopoly A situation in which economies of scale are so large that one firm can supply the entire market at a lower average total cost than can two or more firms.

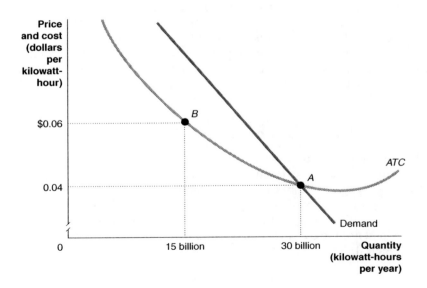

Figure 1

Average Total Cost Curve for a Natural Monopoly

With a natural monopoly, the average total cost curve is still falling when it crosses the demand curve (point *A*). If only one firm is producing electric power in the market and it produces where average cost intersects the demand curve, average total cost will equal $0.04 per kilowatt-hour of electricity produced. If the market is divided between two firms, each producing 15 billion kilowatt-hours, the average cost of producing electricity rises to $0.06 per kilowatt-hour (point *B*). In this case, if one firm expands production, it can move down the average total cost curve, lower its price, and drive the other firm out of business.

curve is still falling when it crosses the demand curve at point *A*. If the firm is a monopoly and produces 30 billion kilowatt-hours of electricity per year, its average total cost of production will be $0.04 per kilowatt-hour. Suppose instead that two firms are in the market, each producing half of the market output, or 15 billion kilowatt-hours per year. Assume that each firm has the same average total cost curve. The figure shows that producing 15 billion kilowatt-hours would move each firm back up its average cost curve so that the average cost of producing electricity would rise to $0.06 per kilowatt-hour (point *B*). In this case, if one of the firms expands production, it will move down the average total cost curve. With lower average costs, it will be able to offer electricity at a lower price than the other firm can. Eventually, the other firm will be driven out of business, and the remaining firm will have a monopoly. Because a monopoly would develop automatically—or *naturally*—in this market, it is a natural monopoly.

Natural monopolies are most likely to occur in markets where fixed costs are very large relative to variable costs. For example, a firm that produces electricity must make a substantial investment in machinery and equipment necessary to generate the electricity and in wires and cables necessary to distribute it. Once the initial investment has been made, however, the marginal cost of producing another kilowatt-hour of electricity is relatively small.

Solved Problem | **2**

Is the "Proxy Business" a Natural Monopoly?

A corporation is owned by its shareholders, who elect members of the corporation's board of directors and who also vote on particularly important issues of corporate policy. The shareholders of large corporations are spread around the country, and relatively few of them are present at the annual meetings at which elections take place. Before each meeting, corporations must provide shareholders with annual reports and forms that allow them to vote by mail. Voting by mail is referred to as "proxy voting." People who work on Wall Street refer to providing annual reports and ballots to shareholders as the "proxy business." Currently, one company, Broadridge, controls almost all of the proxy business.

According to the *Wall Street Journal*, Don Kittell of the Securities Industry Association has explained Broadridge's virtual monopoly by arguing that, "The economies of scale and the efficiencies achieved by Broadridge handling all the brokerage business—rather than multiple companies—resulted in savings to [corporations]."

a. Assuming that Kittell is correct, draw a graph showing the market for handling proxy materials. Be sure that the graph contains the demand for proxy materials and Broadridge's average total cost curve. Explain why cost savings result from having the proxy business handled by a single firm.

b. According to a spokesperson for Broadridge, the proxy business produces a profit rate of about 7 percent, which is lower than the profit rate the company receives from any of its other businesses. Does this information support or undermine Kittell's analysis? Explain.

SOLVING THE PROBLEM:

Step 1: **Review the chapter material.** This problem is about natural monopoly, so you may want to review the section "Natural Monopoly."

Step 2: **Answer question (a) by drawing a natural monopoly graph and discussing the potential cost savings in this industry.** Kittell describes a situation of natural monopoly. Otherwise, the entry of another firm into the market would not raise average cost. Draw a natural monopoly graph, like the one in Figure 1:

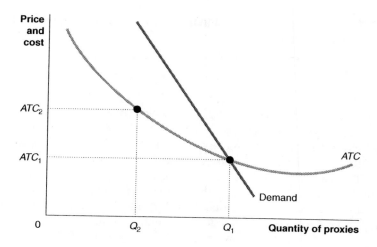

Make sure your average total cost curve is still declining when it crosses the demand curve. If one firm can supply Q_1 proxies at an average total cost of ATC_1, then dividing the business equally between two firms each supplying Q_2 proxies would raise average total cost to ATC_2.

Step 3: Answer question (b) by discussing the implications of Broadridge's low profit rate in the proxy business. If Broadridge earns a low profit rate on its investment in this business even though it has a monopoly, Kittell probably is correct that the proxy business is a natural monopoly.

EXTRA CREDIT: Keep in mind that competition is not good for its own sake. It is good because it can lead to lower costs, lower prices, and better products. In certain markets, however, cost conditions are such that competition is likely to lead to higher costs and higher prices. These markets are natural monopolies that are best served by one firm.

Source. Phyllis Plitch, "Competition Remains Issue in Proxy-Mailing Costs," *Wall Street Journal*, January 16, 2002.

YOUR TURN: For more practice, do related problem 2.11 at the end of this chapter.

>> End Solved Problem 2

3 | Explain how a monopoly chooses price and output.

3 LEARNING OBJECTIVE

How Does a Monopoly Choose Price and Output?

Like every other firm, a monopoly maximizes profit by producing where marginal revenue equals marginal cost. A monopoly differs from other firms in that *a monopoly's demand curve is the same as the demand curve for the product.* The market demand curve for wheat was very different from the demand curve for the wheat produced by any one farmer. If, however, one farmer had a monopoly on wheat production, the two demand curves would be exactly the same.

Marginal Revenue Once Again

Firms in perfectly competitive markets—such as a farmer in the wheat market—face horizontal demand curves. They are *price takers*. All other firms, including monopolies, are *price makers*. If price makers raise their prices, they will lose some, but not all, of their customers. Therefore, they face a downward-sloping demand curve and a downward-sloping marginal revenue curve as well. Let's review why a firm's marginal revenue curve slopes downward if its demand curve slopes downward.

Remember that when a firm cuts the price of a product, one good thing happens, and one bad thing happens:

- **_The good thing._** It sells more units of the product.

- **_The bad thing._** It receives less revenue from each unit than it would have received at the higher price.

For example, consider the table in Figure 2, which shows the demand curve for Time Warner Cable's basic cable package. For simplicity, we assume that the market has only 10 potential subscribers instead of the millions it actually has. If Time Warner charges a price of $60 per month, it won't have any subscribers. If it charges a price of $57, it sells 1 subscription. At $54, it sells 2, and so on. Time Warner's total revenue is equal to the number of subscriptions sold per month multiplied by the price. The firm's average revenue—or revenue per subscription sold—is equal to its total revenue divided by the quantity of subscriptions sold. Time Warner is particularly interested in marginal revenue because marginal revenue tells the firm how much revenue will increase if it cuts the price to sell one more subscription.

Notice that Time Warner's marginal revenue is less than the price for every subscription sold after the first subscription. To see why, think about what happens if Time Warner cuts the price of its basic cable package from $42 to $39, which increases its subscriptions sold from 6 to 7. Time Warner increases its revenue by the $39 it receives for the seventh subscription. But it also loses revenue of $3 per subscription on the first 6 subscriptions because it could have sold them at the old price of $42. So, its marginal

Figure 2

Time Warner Cable faces a downward-sloping demand curve for subscriptions to basic cable. To sell more subscriptions, it must cut the price. When this happens, it gains the revenue from selling more subscriptions but loses revenue from selling at a lower price the subscriptions that it could have sold at a higher price. The firm's marginal revenue is the change in revenue from selling another subscription. We can calculate marginal revenue by subtracting the revenue lost as a result of a price cut from the revenue gained. The table shows that Time Warner's marginal revenue is less than the price for every subscription sold after the first subscription. Therefore, Time Warner's marginal revenue curve will be below its demand curve.

Subscribers per Month (Q)	Price (P)	Total Revenue (TR = P x Q)	Average Revenue (AR = TR/Q)	Marginal Revenue (MR = ΔTR/ΔQ)
0	$60	$0	–	–
1	57	57	$57	$57
2	54	108	54	51
3	51	153	51	45
4	48	192	48	39
5	45	225	45	33
6	42	252	42	27
7	39	273	39	21
8	36	288	36	15
9	33	297	33	9
10	30	300	30	3

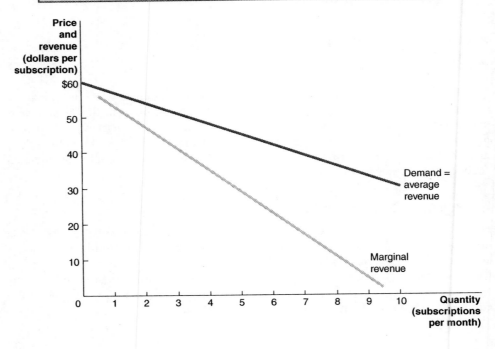

revenue on the seventh subscription is $39 − $18 = $21, which is the value shown in the table. The graph in Figure 2 plots Time Warner's demand and marginal revenue curves, based on the information given in the table.

Profit Maximization for a Monopolist

Figure 3 shows how Time Warner combines the information on demand and marginal revenue with information on average and marginal costs to decide how many subscriptions to sell and what price to charge. We assume that the firm's marginal cost and average total cost curves have the usual U shapes. In panel (a), we see how Time Warner can calculate its profit-maximizing quantity and price. As long as the marginal cost of selling one more subscription is less than the marginal revenue, the firm should sell additional subscriptions because it is adding to its profits. As Time Warner sells more cable subscriptions, rising marginal cost will eventually equal marginal revenue, and the firm will be selling the profit-maximizing quantity of subscriptions. This happens with the sixth subscription, which adds $27 to the firm's costs and $27 to its revenues (point A in panel (a) of Figure 3). The demand curve tells us that Time Warner can sell 6 subscriptions for a price of $42 per month. We can conclude that Time Warner's profit-maximizing quantity of subscriptions is 6 and its profit-maximizing price is $42.

Panel (b) shows that the average total cost of 6 subscriptions is $30 and that Time Warner can sell 6 subscriptions at a price of $42 per month (point B on the demand curve). Time Warner is making a profit of $12 per subscription—the price of $42 minus the average cost of $30. Its total profit is $72 (6 subscriptions × $12 profit per subscription), which is shown by the area of the green-shaded rectangle in the figure. We could also have calculated Time Warner's total profit as the difference between its total revenue and its total cost. Its total revenue from selling 6 subscriptions is $252. Its total cost equals its average cost multiplied by the number of subscriptions sold, or $30 × 6 = $180. So, its profit is $252 − $180 = $72.

It's important to note that even though Time Warner is earning economic profits, new firms will *not* enter the market. Because Time Warner has a monopoly, it will not face competition from other cable operators. Therefore, if other factors remain unchanged, Time Warner will be able to continue to earn economic profits, even in the long run.

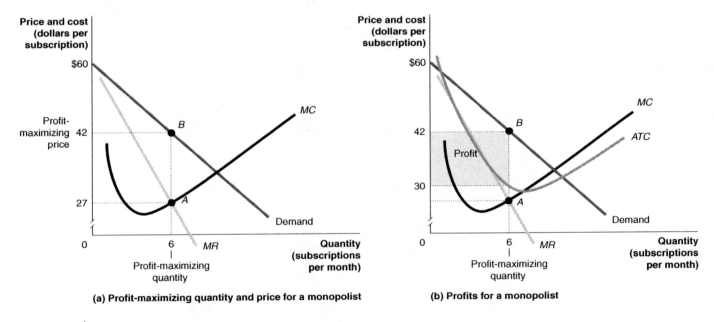

(a) Profit-maximizing quantity and price for a monopolist

(b) Profits for a monopolist

Figure 3 | Profit-Maximizing Price and Output for a Monopoly

Panel (a) shows that to maximize profit, Time Warner should sell subscriptions up to the point that the marginal revenue from selling the last subscription equals its marginal cost (point A). In this case, the marginal revenue from selling the sixth subscription and the marginal cost are both $27. Time Warner maximizes profit by selling 6

subscriptions per month and charging a price of $42 (point B). In panel (b), the green box represents Time Warner's profits. The box has a height equal to $12, which is the price of $42 minus the average total cost of $30, and a base equal to the quantity of 6 cable subscriptions. Time Warner's profit equals $12 × 6 = $72.

Solved Problem | **3**

Finding the Profit-Maximizing Price and Output for a Monopolist

Suppose that Comcast has a cable monopoly in Philadelphia. The following table gives Comcast's demand and costs per month for subscriptions to basic cable (for simplicity, we once again keep the number of subscribers artificially small).

PRICE	QUANTITY	TOTAL REVENUE	MARGINAL REVENUE $(MR = \Delta TR/\Delta Q)$	TOTAL COST	MARGINAL COST $(MC = \Delta TC/\Delta Q)$
$17	3			$56	
16	4			63	
15	5			71	
14	6			80	
13	7			90	
12	8			101	

a. Fill in the missing values in the table.

b. If Comcast wants to maximize profits, what price should it charge and how many cable subscriptions per month should it sell? How much profit will Comcast make? Briefly explain.

c. Suppose the local government imposes a $2.50 per month tax on cable companies. Now what price should Comcast charge, how many subscriptions should it sell, and what will its profits be?

SOLVING THE PROBLEM:

Step 1: **Review the chapter material.** This problem is about finding the profit-maximizing quantity and price for a monopolist, so you may want to review the section "Profit Maximization for a Monopolist."

Step 2: **Answer question (a) by filling in the missing values in the table.** Remember that to calculate marginal revenue and marginal cost, you must divide the change in total revenue or total cost by the change in quantity.

PRICE	QUANTITY	TOTAL REVENUE	MARGINAL REVENUE $(MR = \Delta TR/\Delta Q)$	TOTAL COST	MARGINAL COST $(MC = \Delta TC/\Delta Q)$
$17	3	$51	—	$56	—
16	4	64	$13	63	$7
15	5	75	11	71	8
14	6	84	9	80	9
13	7	91	7	90	10
12	8	96	5	101	11

We don't have enough information from the table to fill in the values for marginal revenue or marginal cost in the first row.

Step 3: **Answer question (b) by determining the profit-maximizing quantity and price.** We know that Comcast will maximize profits by selling subscriptions up to the point where marginal cost equals marginal revenue. In this case, that means selling 6 subscriptions per month. From the information in the first two columns, we know Comcast can sell 6 subscriptions at a price of $14 each. Comcast's profits are equal to the difference between its total revenue and its total cost: Profit = $84 − $80 = $4 per month.

Step 4: **Answer question (c) by analyzing the impact of the tax.** This tax is a fixed cost to Comcast because it is a flat $2.50, no matter how many subscriptions it sells. Because the tax has no impact on Comcast's marginal revenue or marginal cost, the profit-maximizing level of output has not changed. So, Comcast will still sell 6 subscriptions per month at a price of $14, but its profits will fall by the amount of the tax from $4.00 per month to $1.50.

YOUR TURN: For more practice, do related problems 3.3 and 3.4 at the end of this chapter.

>> **End Solved Problem 3**

4 LEARNING OBJECTIVE

4 | Use a graph to illustrate how a monopoly affects economic efficiency.

Does Monopoly Reduce Economic Efficiency?

A perfectly competitive market is economically efficient. How would economic efficiency be affected if instead of being perfectly competitive, a market were a monopoly? Economic surplus provides a way of characterizing the economic efficiency of a perfectly competitive market: *Equilibrium in a perfectly competitive market results in the greatest amount of economic surplus, or total benefit to society, from the production of a good or service.* What happens to economic surplus under monopoly? We can begin the analysis by considering the hypothetical case of what would happen if the market for television sets begins as perfectly competitive and then becomes a monopoly. (In reality, the market for television sets is not perfectly competitive, but assuming that it is simplifies our analysis.)

Comparing Monopoly and Perfect Competition

Panel (a) in Figure 4 illustrates the situation if the market for televisions is perfectly competitive. Price and quantity are determined by the intersection of the demand and supply curves. Remember that none of the individual firms in a perfectly competitive industry has any control over price. Each firm must accept the price determined by the market. Panel (b) shows what happens if the television industry becomes a monopoly. We know that the monopoly will maximize profits by producing where marginal revenue equals marginal cost. To do this, the monopoly reduces the quantity of televisions

Don't Let This Happen to **YOU!**

Don't Assume That Charging a Higher Price Is Always More Profitable for a Monopolist

In answering question (c) of Solved Problem 3, it's tempting to argue that Comcast should increase its price to make up for the tax. After all, Comcast is a monopolist, so why can't it just pass along the tax to its customers? The reason it can't is that Comcast, like any other monopolist, must pay attention to demand. Comcast is not interested in charging high prices for the sake of charging high prices; it is interested in maximizing profits. Charging a price of $1,000 for a basic cable subscription sounds nice, but if no one will buy at that price, Comcast would hardly be maximizing profits.

To look at it another way, before the tax is imposed, Comcast has already determined $14 is the price that will maximize its profits. After the tax is imposed, it must determine whether $14 is still the profit-maximizing price. Because the tax has not affected Comcast's marginal revenue or marginal cost (or had any effect on consumer demand), $14 is still the profit-maximizing price, and Comcast should continue to charge it. The tax cuts into Comcast's profits but doesn't cause it to increase the price of cable subscriptions.

YOUR TURN: Test your understanding by doing related problems 3.7 and 3.8 at the end of this chapter.

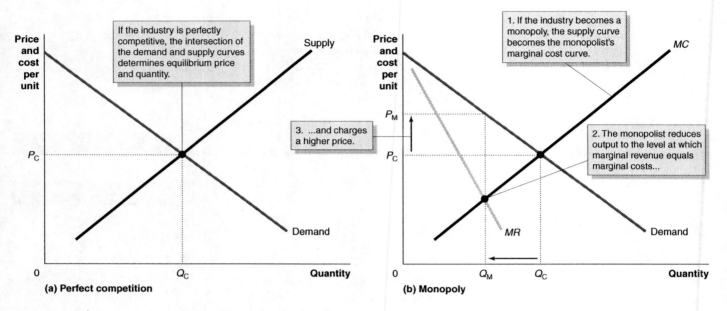

Figure 4 | What Happens If a Perfectly Competitive Industry Becomes a Monopoly?

In panel (a), the market for television sets is perfectly competitive, and price and quantity are determined by the intersection of the demand and supply curves. In panel (b), the perfectly competitive television industry became a monopoly. As a result, the equilibrium quantity falls, and the equilibrium price rises.

1. The industry supply curve becomes the monopolist's marginal cost curve.
2. The monopolist reduces output to where marginal revenue equals marginal cost, Q_M.
3. The monopolist raises the price from P_C to P_M.

that would have been produced if the industry were perfectly competitive and increases the price. Panel (b) illustrates an important conclusion: *A monopoly will produce less and charge a higher price than would a perfectly competitive industry producing the same good.*

Measuring the Efficiency Losses from Monopoly

Figure 5 uses panel (b) from Figure 4 to illustrate how monopoly affects consumers, producers, and the efficiency of the economy. *Consumer surplus* measures the net benefit received by consumers from purchasing a good or service. We measure consumer surplus as the area below the demand curve and above the market price. The higher the price, the smaller the consumer surplus. Because a monopoly raises the market price, it reduces consumer surplus. In Figure 5, the loss of consumer surplus is equal to rectangle A plus triangle B. Remember that *producer surplus* measures the net benefit to producers from selling a good or service. We measure producer surplus as the area above the supply curve and below the market price. The increase in price due to monopoly increases producer surplus by an amount equal to rectangle A and reduces it by an amount equal to triangle C. Because rectangle A is larger than triangle C, we know that a monopoly increases producer surplus compared with perfect competition.

Economic surplus is equal to the sum of consumer surplus plus producer surplus. By increasing price and reducing the quantity produced, the monopolist has reduced economic surplus by an amount equal to the areas of triangles B and C. This reduction in economic surplus is called *deadweight loss* and represents the loss of economic efficiency due to monopoly.

The best way to understand how a monopoly causes a loss of economic efficiency is to recall that price is equal to marginal cost in a perfectly competitive market. As a result, a consumer in a perfectly competitive market is always able to buy a good if she is willing to pay a price equal to the marginal cost of producing it. As Figure 5 shows, the monopolist stops producing at a point where the price is well above marginal cost. Consumers are unable to buy some units of the good for which they would be willing to pay a price greater

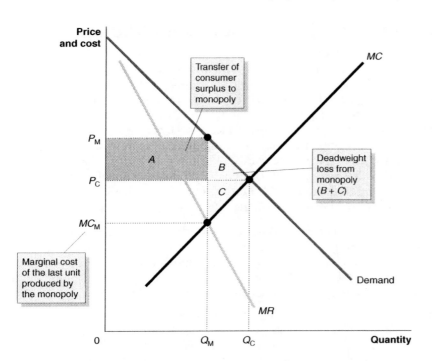

Figure 5

The Inefficiency of Monopoly

A monopoly charges a higher price, P_M, and produces a smaller quantity, Q_M, than a perfectly competitive industry, which charges a price of P_C and produces at Q_C. The higher price reduces consumer surplus by the area equal to the rectangle A and the triangle B. Some of the reduction in consumer surplus is captured by the monopoly as producer surplus, and some becomes deadweight loss, which is the area equal to triangles B and C.

than the marginal cost of producing them. Why doesn't the monopolist produce this additional output? Because the monopolist's profits are greater if it restricts output and forces up the price. A monopoly produces the profit-maximizing level of output but fails to produce the efficient level of output from the point of view of society.

We can summarize the effects of monopoly as follows:

1 Monopoly causes a reduction in consumer surplus.

2 Monopoly causes an increase in producer surplus.

3 Monopoly causes a deadweight loss, which represents a reduction in economic efficiency.

How Large Are the Efficiency Losses Due to Monopoly?

We know that there are relatively few monopolies, so the loss of economic efficiency due to monopoly must be small. Many firms, though, have **market power**, which is the ability of a firm to charge a price greater than marginal cost. The analysis we just completed shows that some loss of economic efficiency will occur whenever a firm has market power and can charge a price greater than marginal cost, even if the firm is not a monopoly. The only firms that do *not* have market power are firms in perfectly competitive markets, who must charge a price equal to marginal cost. Because few markets are perfectly competitive, *some loss of economic efficiency occurs in the market for nearly every good or service.*

Is the total loss of economic efficiency due to market power large or small? It is possible to put a dollar value on the loss of economic efficiency by estimating for every industry the size of the deadweight loss triangle, as in Figure 5. The first economist to do this was Arnold Harberger of the University of Chicago. His estimates—largely confirmed by later researchers—indicated that the total loss of economic efficiency in the U.S. economy due to market power is small. According to his estimates, if every industry in the economy were perfectly competitive, so that price were equal to marginal cost in every market, the gain in economic efficiency would equal less than 1 percent of the value of total production in the United States, or about $450 per person.

The loss of economic efficiency is this small primarily because true monopolies are very rare. In most industries, competition keeps price much closer to marginal cost than would be the case in a monopoly. The closer price is to marginal cost, the smaller the size of the deadweight loss.

Market power The ability of a firm to charge a price greater than marginal cost.

Market Power and Technological Change

Some economists have raised the possibility that the economy may actually benefit from firms having market power. This argument is most closely identified with Joseph Schumpeter, an Austrian economist who spent many years as a professor of economics at Harvard. Schumpeter argued that economic progress depended on technological change in the form of new products. For example, the replacement of horse-drawn carriages by automobiles, the replacement of ice boxes by refrigerators, and the replacement of mechanical calculators by electronic computers all represent technological changes that significantly raised living standards. In Schumpeter's view, new products unleash a "gale of creative destruction" that drives older products—and, often, the firms that produced them—out of the market. Schumpeter was unconcerned that firms with market power would charge higher prices than perfectly competitive firms:

> It is not that kind of [price] competition which counts but the competition from the new commodity, the new technology, the new source of supply, the new type of organization . . . competition which commands a decisive cost or quality advantage and which strikes not at the margins of the profits and outputs of the existing firms but at their foundations and their very lives.

Economists who support Schumpeter's view argue that the introduction of new products requires firms to spend funds on research and development. It is possible for firms to raise this money by borrowing from investors or from banks. But investors and banks are usually skeptical of ideas for new products that have not yet passed the test of consumer acceptance in the market. As a result, firms are often forced to rely on their profits to finance the research and development needed for new products. Because firms with market power are more likely to earn economic profits than are perfectly competitive firms, they are also more likely to carry out research and development and introduce new products. In this view, the higher prices firms with market power charge are unimportant compared with the benefits from the new products these firms introduce to the market.

Some economists disagree with Schumpeter's views. These economists point to the number of new products developed by smaller firms, including, for example, Steve Jobs and Steve Wozniak inventing the first Apple computer in Wozniak's garage, and Larry Page and Sergey Brin inventing the Google search engine as graduate students at Stanford. As we will see in the next section, government policymakers continue to struggle with the issue of whether, on balance, large firms with market power are good or bad for the economy.

5 LEARNING OBJECTIVE

5 | Discuss government policies toward monopoly.

Government Policy toward Monopoly

Collusion An agreement among firms to charge the same price or otherwise not to compete.

Because monopolies reduce consumer surplus and economic efficiency, most governments have policies that regulate their behavior. **Collusion** refers to an agreement among firms to charge the same price or otherwise not to compete. In the United States, government policies with respect to monopolies and collusion are embodied in the *antitrust laws*. These laws make illegal any attempts to form a monopoly or to collude. Governments also regulate firms that are natural monopolies, often by controlling the prices they charge.

Antitrust Laws and Antitrust Enforcement

The first important law regulating monopolies in the United States was the Sherman Act, which Congress passed in 1890 to promote competition and prevent the formation of monopolies. Section 1 of the Sherman Act outlaws "every contract, combination in the form of trust or otherwise, or conspiracy in restraint of trade." Section 2 states that "every person who shall monopolize, or attempt to monopolize, or combine or conspire with any other person or persons, to monopolize any part of the trade or commerce . . . shall be deemed guilty of a felony."

The Sherman Act targeted firms in several industries that had combined together during the 1870s and 1880s to form "trusts." In a trust, the firms were operated independently but gave voting control to a board of trustees. The board enforced collusive agreements for the firms to charge the same price and not to compete for each other's customers. The most notorious of the trusts was the Standard Oil Trust, organized by John D. Rockefeller. After the Sherman Act was passed, trusts disappeared, but the term **antitrust laws** has lived on to refer to the laws aimed at eliminating collusion and promoting competition among firms.

The Sherman Act prohibited trusts and collusive agreements, but it left several loopholes. For example, it was not clear whether it would be legal for two or more firms to merge to form a new, larger firm that would have substantial market power. A series of Supreme Court decisions interpreted the Sherman Act narrowly, and the result was a wave of mergers at the turn of the twentieth century. Included in these mergers was the U.S. Steel Corporation, which was formed from dozens of smaller companies. U.S. Steel, organized by J. P. Morgan, was the first billion-dollar corporation, and it controlled two-thirds of steel production in the United States. The Sherman Act also left unclear whether any business practices short of outright collusion were illegal.

To address the loopholes in the Sherman Act, in 1914, Congress passed the Clayton Act and the Federal Trade Commission Act. Under the Clayton Act, a merger was illegal if its effect was "substantially to lessen competition, or to tend to create a monopoly." The Federal Trade Commission Act set up the Federal Trade Commission (FTC), which was given the power to police unfair business practices. The FTC has brought lawsuits against firms employing a variety of business practices, including deceptive advertising. In setting up the FTC, however, Congress divided the authority to police mergers. Currently, both the Antitrust Division of the U.S. Department of Justice and the FTC are responsible for merger policy. Table 1 lists the most important U.S. antitrust laws and the purpose of each.

Antitrust laws Laws aimed at eliminating collusion and promoting competition among firms.

Mergers: The Trade-off between Market Power and Efficiency

The federal government regulates business mergers because it knows that if firms gain market power by merging, they may use that market power to raise prices and reduce output. As a result, the government is most concerned with **horizontal mergers**, or mergers between firms in the same industry. Horizontal mergers are more likely to increase market power than **vertical mergers**, which are mergers between firms at different stages of the production of a good. An example of a vertical merger would be a merger between a company making personal computers and a company making computer hard drives.

Horizontal merger A merger between firms in the same industry.

Vertical merger A merger between firms at different stages of production of a good.

LAW	DATE	PURPOSE
Sherman Act	1890	Prohibited "restraint of trade," including price fixing and collusion. Also outlawed monopolization.
Clayton Act	1914	Prohibited firms from buying stock in competitors and from having directors serve on the boards of competing firms.
Federal Trade Commission Act	1914	Established the Federal Trade Commission (FTC) to help administer antitrust laws.
Robinson–Patman Act	1936	Prohibited charging buyers different prices if the result would reduce competition.
Cellar–Kefauver Act	1950	Toughened restrictions on mergers by prohibiting any mergers that would reduce competition.

TABLE 1

Important U.S. Antitrust Laws

Regulating horizontal mergers can be complicated by two factors. First, the "market" that firms are in is not always clear. For example, if Hershey Foods wants to merge with Mars, Inc., maker of M&Ms, Snickers, and other candies, what is the relevant market? If the government looks just at the candy market, the newly merged company would have more than 70 percent of the market, a level at which the government would likely oppose the merger. What if the government looks at the broader market for "snacks"? In this market, Hershey and Mars compete with makers of potato chips, pretzels, peanuts, and, perhaps, even producers of fresh fruit. Of course, if the government looked at the very broad market for "food," then both Hershey and Mars have very small market shares, and there would be no reason to oppose their merger. In practice, the government defines the relevant market on the basis of whether there are close substitutes for the products being made by the merging firms. In this case, potato chips and the other snack foods mentioned are not close substitutes for candy. So, the government would consider the candy market to be the relevant market and would oppose the merger on the grounds that the new firm would have too much market power.

The second factor that complicates merger policy is the possibility that the newly merged firm might be more efficient than the merging firms were individually. For example, one firm might have an excellent product but a poor distribution system for getting the product into the hands of consumers. A competing firm might have built a great distribution system but have an inferior product. Allowing these firms to merge might be good for both the firms and consumers. Or, two competing firms might each have an extensive system of warehouses that are only half full, but if the firms merged, they could consolidate their warehouses and significantly reduce their costs.

An example of the government dealing with the issue of greater efficiency versus reduced competition occurred in early 2000, when Time Warner—which owns cable systems with more than 20 million subscribers—and America Online (AOL)—which was the country's largest Internet service provider (ISP), with more than 26 million subscribers—announced plans to merge. The firms argued that the merger would speed the development of high-speed (or "broadband") Internet access and would lead to more rapid growth of services such as interactive television. Some competing firms complained that the new firm created by the merger would have excessive market power. In particular, other ISPs were worried that they would be denied access to the cable systems owned by Time Warner. After more than a year of study, the FTC finally approved the merger, subject to certain conditions. One key condition was that Time Warner was required to allow AOL's competitors to offer their services over Time Warner's high-speed cable lines before AOL would be permitted to offer its services over those lines.

Most of the mergers that come under scrutiny by the Department of Justice and the FTC are between large firms. For simplicity, let's consider a case where all the firms in a perfectly competitive industry want to merge to form a monopoly. As we saw in Figure 5, as a result of this merger, prices will rise and output will fall, leading to a decline in consumer surplus and economic efficiency. But what if the larger, newly merged firm actually is more efficient than the smaller firms had been? Figure 6 shows a possible result.

If costs are unaffected by the merger, we get the same result as in Figure 5: Price rises from P_C to P_M, quantity falls from Q_C to Q_M, consumer surplus is lower, and a loss of economic efficiency results. If the monopoly has lower costs than the competitive firms, it is possible for price to decline and quantity to increase. In Figure 6, to find the new profit-maximizing quantity, note where MR crosses MC after the merger. This new profit-maximizing quantity is Q_{Merge}. The demand curve shows that the monopolist can sell this quantity at a price of P_{Merge}. Therefore, the price declines after the merger from P_C to P_{Merge} and quantity increases from Q_C to Q_{Merge}. We have the following seemingly paradoxical result: *Although the newly merged firm has a great deal of market power, because it is more efficient, consumers are better off and economic efficiency is improved.* Of course, sometimes a merged firm will be more efficient and have lower costs, and other times it won't. Even if a merged firm is more efficient and has lower costs, that may not offset the increased market power of the firm enough to increase consumer surplus and economic efficiency.

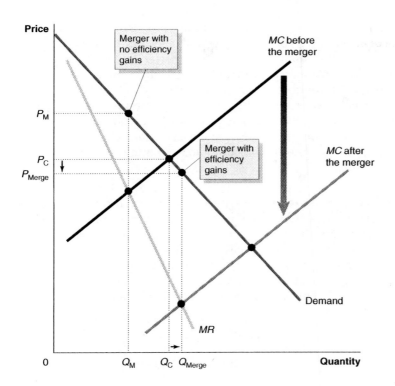

Price

Merger with no efficiency gains

MC before the merger

P_M

Merger with efficiency gains

MC after the merger

P_C
P_{Merge}

Demand

MR

0   Q_M Q_C Q_{Merge} **Quantity**

Figure 6

A Merger That Makes Consumers Better Off

This figure shows the result of all the firms in a perfectly competitive industry merging to form a monopoly. If costs are unaffected by the merger, the result is the same as in Figure 5: Price rises from P_C to P_M, quantity falls from Q_C to Q_M, consumer surplus declines, and a loss of economic efficiency results. If, however, the monopoly has lower costs than the perfectly competitive firms, as shown by the marginal cost curve shifting to MC after the merger, it is possible that the price will actually decline from P_C to P_{Merge} and output will increase from Q_C to Q_{Merge} following the merger.

As you might expect, whenever large firms propose a merger, they claim that the newly merged firm will be more efficient and have lower costs. They realize that without these claims, it is unlikely their merger will be approved. It is up to the Department of Justice and the FTC, along with the court system, to evaluate the merits of these claims.

The Department of Justice and Federal Trade Commission Merger Guidelines

For many years after the passage of the Sherman Antitrust Act in 1890, lawyers from the Department of Justice enforced the antitrust laws. They rarely considered economic arguments, such as the possibility that consumers might be made better off by a merger if economic efficiency were significantly improved. This began to change in 1965, when Donald Turner became the first Ph.D. economist to head the Antitrust Division of the Department of Justice. Under Turner and his successors, economic analysis shaped antitrust policy. In 1973, the Economics Section of the Antitrust Division was established and staffed with economists who evaluate the economic consequences of proposed mergers.

Economists played a major role in the development of merger guidelines by the Department of Justice and the FTC in 1982. The guidelines made it easier for firms considering a merger to understand whether the government was likely to allow the merger or to oppose it. The guidelines have three main parts:

1. Market definition

2. Measure of concentration

3. Merger standards

Market Definition A market consists of all firms making products that consumers view as close substitutes. We can identify close substitutes by looking at the effect of a price increase. If our definition of a market is too narrow, a price increase will cause firms to experience a significant decline in sales—and profits—as consumers switch to buying close substitutes.

Identifying the relevant market involved in a proposed merger begins with a narrow definition of the industry. For the hypothetical merger of Hershey Foods and Mars, Inc., discussed previously in this chapter, we might start with the candy industry. If all firms in the candy industry increased price by 5 percent, would their profits increase or decrease? If profits would increase, the market is defined as being just these firms. If profits would decrease, we would try a broader definition—say, by adding in potato chips and other snacks. Would a price increase of 5 percent by all firms in the broader market raise profits? If profits increase, the relevant market has been identified. If profits decrease, we consider a broader definition. We continue this procedure until a market has been identified.

Measure of Concentration A market is *concentrated* if a relatively small number of firms have a large share of total sales in the market. A merger between firms in a market that is already highly concentrated is very likely to increase market power. A merger between firms in an industry that has a very low concentration is unlikely to increase market power and can be ignored. The guidelines use the *Herfindahl-Hirschman Index (HHI)* of concentration, which squares the market shares of each firm in the industry and adds up the values of the squares. The following are some examples of calculating a Herfindahl-Hirschman Index:

- 1 firm, with 100% market share (a monopoly):

$$HHI = 100^2 = 10,000$$

- 2 firms, each with a 50% market share:

$$HHI = 50^2 + 50^2 = 5,000$$

- 4 firms, with market shares of 30%, 30%, 20%, and 20%:

$$HHI = 30^2 + 30^2 + 20^2 + 20^2 = 2,600$$

- 10 firms, each with market shares of 10%:

$$HHI = 10 \, (10^2) = 1,000$$

Merger Standards The Department of Justice and the FTC use the HHI calculation for a market to evaluate proposed horizontal mergers according to these standards:

- *Post-merger HHI below 1,000.* These markets are not concentrated, so mergers in them are not challenged.

- *Post-merger HHI between 1,000 and 1,800.* These markets are moderately concentrated. Mergers that raise the HHI by less than 100 probably will not be challenged. Mergers that raise the HHI by more than 100 may be challenged.

- *Post-merger HHI above 1,800.* These markets are highly concentrated. Mergers that increase the HHI by less than 50 points will not be challenged. Mergers that increase the HHI by 50 to 100 points may be challenged. Mergers that increase the HHI by more than 100 points will be challenged.

Increases in economic efficiency will be taken into account and can lead to approval of a merger that otherwise would be opposed, but the burden of showing that the efficiencies exist lies with the merging firms:

> The merging firms must substantiate efficiency claims so that the [Department of Justice and the FTC] can verify by reasonable means the likelihood and magnitude of each asserted efficiency. . . . Efficiency claims will not be considered if they are vague or speculative or otherwise cannot be verified by reasonable means.

Making the Connection

Should the Government Prevent Banks from Becoming Too Big?

For many years, state and federal regulations kept banks small. Until the 1990s, federal regulations required a bank to operate in only a single state. This restriction on interstate banking meant that there were no nationwide banks. As recently as the 1980s, some states—including Illinois and Texas—did not allow banks to have branches. So, if a bank opened in Chicago, it could not have branches in other cities in Illinois. Today, these regulations have been repealed, and banks are free to have as many branches as they choose and can operate nationwide. Many economists believe that the old regulations on banks reduced economic efficiency. If there are significant economies of scale in banking, then keeping banks artificially small by not allowing them to operate in more than one state will drive up their average cost of providing banking services. As a result, consumers will have to pay higher interest rates on loans and will receive lower interest rates on deposits.

The elimination of government regulations on nationwide banking and on branch banking led to a sharp decline in the number of banks. In the early 1980s, there were 14,500 banks in the United States; today there are fewer than 7,500. Smaller, less efficient banks were acquired by larger banks or went out of business, and some large banks merged with other large banks. There is, however, still one limit on the size of banks. In 1994, when Congress removed restrictions on interstate banking, it wrote into the law a restriction that no bank mergers would be allowed if they resulted in one bank having more than 10 percent of all bank deposits. This provision was included because some smaller, community-based banks were afraid that they would be unable to compete against large, nationwide banks.

The Top-Five U.S. Banks by Domestic Deposits, Through Sept. 30 of Each Year

2006	Dometic deposits, in billions	Percentage of all U.S. deposits	1994	Dometic deposits, in billions	Percentage of all U.S. deposits
Bank of America	$584.33	9.0%	Bank of America	$125.59	4.0%
J.P. Morgan Chase	447.30	6.9	NationsBank	87.44	2.8
Wachovia/Golden West Financial*	375.61	5.8	Chemical Banking	66.86	2.1
Wells Fargo	295.14	4.6	Banc One	64.74	2.1
Citigroup	226.26	3.5	First Union	52.54	1.7

Note: Deposit share information is based on FDIC quarterly reports. The Federal Reserve, which approves acquisitions, uses a slightly different definition of deposits.
* Figures are combined to reflect merger which took place Oct. 1, 2006
Source: FDIC call reports

As the chart shows, at the time the government removed restrictions on interstate banking, no bank was near the 10 percent limit. But by the end of 2006, Bank of America had 9 percent of all U.S. deposits and was considering mergers that would have brought its share above 10 percent. Bank of America Chairman and Chief Executive Kenneth D. Lewis began to push for Congress to remove the 10 percent limit. He argued that because other countries did not have limits on the size of banks, foreign banks were able to take advantage of economies of scale beyond what was possible for U.S. banks. In a position paper, Bank of America argued, "In time, the mega-foreign banks will be positioned to acquire the largest U.S. banks." Many community banks, though, remained opposed to lifting the 10 percent limit. Some consumer groups also argued that very large banks would have enough market power to raise interest rates on loans and lower interest rates on deposits because they would have less competition. Members of Congress considering the possibility of changing the law had to face the usual question raised by antitrust policy: Will a potential increase in monopoly power made possible by lifting the 10-percent limit be offset by gains in economic efficiency?

Source: Valerie Bauerlein and Damian Paletta, "Bank of America Quietly Targets Barrier to Growth," *Wall Street Journal*, January 16, 2007, p. A1.

YOUR TURN: Test your understanding by doing related problem 5.16 at the end of this chapter.

Regulating Natural Monopolies

If a firm is a natural monopoly, competition from other firms will not play its usual role of forcing price down to the level where the company earns zero economic profit. As a result, local or state *regulatory commissions* usually set the prices for natural monopolies, such as firms selling natural gas or electricity. What price should these commissions set? Economic efficiency requires the last unit of a good or service produced to provide an additional benefit to consumers equal to the additional cost of producing it. We can measure the additional benefit consumers receive from the last unit by the price and the additional cost to the monopoly of producing the last unit by marginal cost. Therefore, to achieve economic efficiency, regulators should require that the monopoly charge a price equal to its marginal cost. There is, however, an important drawback to doing so, which is illustrated in Figure 7. This figure shows the situation of a typical regulated natural monopoly.

Remember that with a natural monopoly, the average total cost curve is still falling when it crosses the demand curve. If unregulated, the monopoly will charge a price equal to P_M and produce Q_M. To achieve economic efficiency, regulators should require the monopoly to charge a price equal to P_E. The monopoly will then produce Q_E. But here is the drawback: P_E is less than average total cost, so the monopoly will be suffering a loss, shown by the area of the red-shaded rectangle. In the long run, the owners of the monopoly will not continue in business if they are experiencing losses. Realizing this, most regulators will set the regulated price, P_R, equal to the level of average total cost at which the demand curve intersects the ATC curve. At that price, the owners of the monopoly are able to break even on their investment by producing the quantity Q_R.

Figure 7

Regulating a Natural Monopoly

A natural monopoly that is not subject to government regulation will charge a price equal to P_M and produce Q_M. If government regulators want to achieve economic efficiency, they will set the regulated price equal to P_E, and the monopoly will produce Q_E. Unfortunately, P_E is below average cost, and the monopoly will suffer a loss, shown by the shaded rectangle. Because the monopoly will not continue to produce in the long run if it suffers a loss, government regulators set a price equal to average cost, which is P_R in the figure.

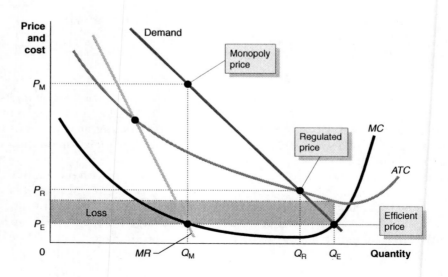

Economics in YOUR Life

At the beginning of the chapter, we asked why many cable systems won't carry the NFL Network. You might think that the cable systems would want to televise one of the most popular sports in the nation. In most cities, a customer of a cable system can't switch to a competing cable system, so many areas cable systems can be the sole source of many programs. (Although some consumers have the option of switching to satellite television.) As a result, a cable system can increase its profits by, for example, not offering popular programming such as the NFL Network as part of its normal programming package, requiring instead that consumers upgrade to digital programming at a higher price.

Conclusion

The more intense the level of competition among firms, the better a market works. In this chapter, we have seen that with monopoly—where competition is entirely absent—price is higher, output is lower, and consumer surplus and economic efficiency decline compared with perfect competition. Fortunately, true monopolies are rare. Even though most firms resemble monopolies in being able to charge a price above marginal cost, most markets have enough competition to keep the efficiency losses from market power quite low.

We've seen that barriers to entry are an important source of market power. Read *An Inside Look at Policy* on the next page for a discussion of how legislation in California is lowering barriers to entry into the cable TV market.

As Barriers Fall, Will Cable TV Competition Rise?

WALL STREET JOURNAL, SEPTEMBER 28, 2006

Cable Guys

In an era of partisan nastiness and gridlock, the California legislature did something on Aug. 31 that was shockingly harmonious, reasonable and beneficial to consumers. Both parties voted overwhelmingly to allow competition into a sector—cable television—where prices have been elevated and service depressed by the most pernicious monopoly in America.

When Gov. Arnold Schwarzenegger signs the bill, as expected, companies that want a statewide video franchise can go straight to the Public Utility Commission and get approval to operate within 44 days. In the past, in California, as in other states, cable companies had to make separate deals with America's 33,760 municipal units—a process that can take years....

The effect was to create cable monopolies that often infuriated captive customers. According to a 2004 study by the Government Accountability Office, "cable subscribers in about 2% of all markets have the opportunity to choose between two or more wire-based operators." As cable rates rose in the 1980s, the federal government tried to fix the market with more regulation. That attempt, of course, failed. For the five years ending January 2004, the Federal Communications Commission reports that average cable rates increased 7.8% annually, compared with a 2.1% increase in the Consumer Price Index.

Very quietly, things are changing. Seven states, comprising about one-third of the U.S. population, have now passed video franchise laws, which will not only lower monthly subscriber costs but also create new technology jobs—10,000 in California alone, according to one estimate—as Verizon and AT&T, along with cable over-builders like RCN, jump in with both feet. To bring high-quality video to the home over a technology called Internet protocol, the telcos will make major investments to drive the fiber—which carries the data—much more deeply into their networks. Broadband service will improve; state and local governments will still get their franchise fees. All that will end is a monopoly that drives consumers nuts....

With a national election coming up, you would expect Congress to get on the bandwagon and embrace a version of the state bills, killing the monopoly and taking the credit. Instead, federal legislation is slowed down by measures promoting "net neutrality"—the concept that telecom companies should be barred from asking content providers, like Amazon, to pay extra for higher-speed service the telcos develop—the way that an airline asks more for a first-class seat....

How much will consumers save? A 2004 study by the GAO looked at six markets with cable competition and found that rates were 15% to 41% below similar markets with no competition. Annual savings for U.S. households through competition will total $8 billion, says the Phoenix Center for Advanced Legal and Economic Public Policy.

In Texas, where a statewide franchising law went into effect last year, a study by the American Consumer Institute surveyed consumers and found that 22% switched cable providers and saved an average of $22.30 per month. Subscribers who stayed with incumbent providers saved $26.83 per month because of the downward pressure on prices. Verizon rolled out a service in Keller, Plano and Lewisville, charging $43.95 a month for 180 video and music channels. "Shortly thereafter," writes the Heartland Institute's Steven Titch, Charter, the erstwhile monopoly cable provider, "began offering a bundle of 240 channels and fast Internet service for $50 a month, compared to $68.99 Charter had been charging for the TV package alone." Savings in Texas this year alone will total $599 million, according to the Phoenix Center. Yale Braunstein, an economist at the University of California at Berkeley, estimates that Californians will save between $692 million and $1 billion a year.

Yes, Americans can choose satellite TV, but, for reasons of convenience and service, many find it an inadequate substitute. There's a reason that cable families far outnumber satellite families. "Overall customer satisfaction among satellite subscribers has declined," says Steve Kirkeby, senior director of telecommunication research for J.D. Power and Associates....

Getty Images, Inc.

Key Points in the Article

This article discusses a change in regulatory policy toward cable television in California. The change should make it easier for new cable firms to enter the market. As a result, prices for cable TV should fall, and we should see more firms offering cable TV in California cities. This article indicates that an increase in quantity and a decrease in price occurs as policy makes entry into the cable TV market easier.

Analyzing the News

a In California, the state government's requirement that a cable provider buy a franchise in each jurisdiction was a barrier to entry because of the high cost of franchises. By allowing firms a statewide license, California has made it easier for them to enter the cable TV market in a given jurisdiction, making competition more likely. In fact, the relative lack of competition in many local cable television markets was partly the result of technology—laying more than one set of cables to an individual home would be very expensive—and partly the result of government regulations, which often allowed only one firm to be in the market.

b Entry, of course, will reduce the economic profit existing firms earn. The figure illustrates what happens as entry occurs and the market becomes competitive. For simplicity, we assume that the marginal cost of providing cable services is constant, so the marginal cost curve is a horizontal line. Notice that output increases from Q_M to Q_C, and price falls from P_M to P_C. You can also see that consumer surplus increases from areas $A + E$ to areas $A + E + B + C + D$, and the deadweight loss in the market (area D) disappears and becomes consumer surplus. In this figure, what were profits to the monopoly (areas $B + C$) are redistributed to consumers as consumer surplus. Economic profits fall to zero.

c One of the benefits of competition is that firms compete not just by cutting prices, but also by improving the services they offer. Here, we see cable systems competing by providing more services and channels to their customers.

Thinking Critically About Policy

1. What is the most a firm would be willing to spend to remain the sole provider of cable television in a market?
2. Even with a statewide franchise, what might prevent new cable TV firms from entering local markets?

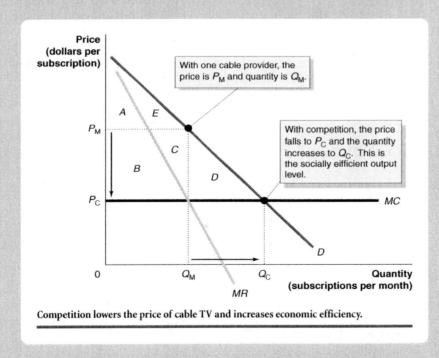

Competition lowers the price of cable TV and increases economic efficiency.

Key Terms

Antitrust laws	Horizontal merger	Natural monopoly	Public franchise
Collusion	Market power	Network externalities	Vertical merger
Copyright	Monopoly	Patent	

---

1 LEARNING OBJECTIVE   1 | Define monopoly

Is Any Firm Ever Really a Monopoly?

Summary

A **monopoly** exists only in the rare situation in which a firm is producing a good or service for which there are no close substitutes. A narrow definition of monopoly that some economists use is that a firm has a monopoly if it can ignore the actions of all other firms. Many economists favor a broader definition of monopoly. Under the broader definition, a firm has a monopoly if no other firms are selling a substitute close enough that the firm's economic profits are competed away in the long run.

 Visit www.myeconlab.com to complete these exercises online and get instant feedback.

Review Questions

1.1 What is a monopoly? Can a firm be a monopoly if close substitutes for its product exist?

1.2 If you own the only hardware store in a small town, do you have a monopoly?

Problems and Applications

1.3 Is "monopoly" a good name for the game *Monopoly*? What aspects of the game involve monopoly? Explain briefly, using the definition of monopoly.

1.4 (Related to the *Chapter Opener*) Some observers say that changes in the past few years have eroded the monopoly power of local cable TV companies, even though no other cable firms have entered their markets. What are these changes? Do these "monopoly" firms still have monopoly power?

1.5 Are there any products for which there are no substitutes? Are these the only products for which it would be possible to have a monopoly? Briefly explain.

1.6 An economist argues, "No firm can remain a monopoly for long in the face of technological change." Do you agree?

1.7 (Related to the *Making the Connection*) Microsoft thought that the initial Xbox was sufficiently different from PS2 that it could charge a significantly higher price for the Xbox than Sony could charge for PS2. As it turns out, Microsoft was wrong. Draw the average total cost and marginal cost curves for Microsoft's Xbox. Now draw the demand curve Microsoft thought would exist for Xbox and the demand curve that actually existed. Why were the two demand curves different? Show on your graph the profits Microsoft would earn with each demand curve.

>> End Learning Objective 1

---

2 LEARNING OBJECTIVE   2 | Explain the four main reasons monopolies arise

Where Do Monopolies Come From?

Summary

To have a monopoly, barriers to entering the market must be so high that no other firms can enter. Barriers to entry may be high enough to keep out competing firms for four main reasons: (1) government blocks the entry of more than one firm into a market by issuing a **patent**, which is the exclusive right to a product for 20 years, or a **copyright**, which is the exclusive right to produce and sell a creation, or giving a firm a **public franchise**, which is the right to be the only legal provider of a good or service (2) one firm has control of a key raw material necessary to produce a good, (3) there are important *network externalities* in supplying the good or service, or (4) economies of scale are so large that one firm has a *natural monopoly*. **Network externalities** refer to the situation where the usefulness of a product increases with the number of consumers who use it. A **natural monopoly** is a situation in which economies of scale are so large that one firm can supply the entire market at a lower average cost than two or more firms.

 Visit www.myeconlab.com to complete these exercises online and get instant feedback.

Review Questions

2.1 What are the four most important ways a firm becomes a monopoly?

2.2 If patents reduce competition, why does the federal government grant them?

2.3 What is a public franchise? Are all public franchises natural monopolies?

2.4 What is "natural" about a natural monopoly?

Problems and Applications

2.5 The U.S. Postal Service (USPS) is a monopoly because the federal government has blocked entry into the market for delivering first-class mail. Is it also a natural monopoly? How can we tell? What would happen if the law preventing competition in this market were removed?

2.6 Patents are granted for 20 years, but pharmaceutical companies can't use their patent-guaranteed monopoly powers for anywhere near this long because it takes several years to acquire FDA approval of drugs. Should the life of drug patents be extended to 20 years *after* FDA approval? What would be the costs and benefits of this extension?

2.7 Just as a new product or a new method of making a product receives patent protection from the government, books, articles, and essays receive copyright protection. Under U.S. law, authors have the exclusive right to their writings during their lifetimes—unless they sell this right, as most authors do to their

publishers—and their heirs retain this exclusive right for 50 years after their death. The historian Thomas Macaulay once described the copyright law as "a tax on readers to give a bounty to authors." In what sense does the existence of the copyright law impose a tax on readers? What "bounty" do copyright laws give authors? Discuss whether the government would be doing readers a favor by abolishing the copyright law.

Source of quote: Thomas Mallon, *Stolen Words: The Classic Book on Plagiarism*, San Diego: Harcourt, 2001 (original ed. 1989), p. 59.

2.8 The German company Koenig & Bauer has 90 percent of the world market for presses that print currency. Discuss the factors that would make it difficult for new companies to enter this market.

2.9 (Related to the *Making the Connection*) Would the Ecke's have been better off if they had patented their process for growing poinsettias? Briefly explain.

2.10 (Related to the *Making the Connection*) Why was De Beers worried that people might resell their old diamonds? How did De Beers attempt to convince consumers that used diamonds were not good substitutes for new diamonds? How did De Beers' strategy affect the demand curve for new diamonds? How were De Beers' profits affected?

2.11 (Related to *Solved Problem 2*) Suppose that the quantity demanded per day for a product is 90 when the price is $35. The following table shows costs for a firm with a monopoly in this market:

QUANTITY (PER DAY)	TOTAL COST
30	$1,200
40	1,400
50	2,250
60	3,000

Briefly explain whether this firm has a natural monopoly in this market.

>> **End Learning Objective 2**

3 LEARNING OBJECTIVE 3 | Explain how a monopoly chooses price and output

How Does a Monopoly Choose Price and Output?

Summary

Monopolists face downward-sloping demand and marginal revenue curves and, like all other firms, maximize profit by producing where marginal revenue equals marginal cost.

Unlike a perfect competitor, a monopolist that earns economic profits does not face the entry of new firms into the market. Therefore, a monopolist can earn economic profits, even in the long run.

Review Questions

3.1 What is the relationship between a monopolist's demand curve and the market demand curve? What is the relationship between a monopolist's demand curve and its marginal revenue curve?

3.2 Draw a graph that shows a monopolist that is earning a profit. Be sure your graph includes the monopolist's demand, marginal revenue, average total cost, and marginal cost curves. Be sure to indicate the profit-maximizing level of output and price.

Problems and Applications

3.3 (Related to *Solved Problem 3*) Ed Scahill has acquired a monopoly on the production of baseballs (don't ask how), and faces the demand and cost situation given in the following table:

PRICE	QUANTITY (PER WEEK)	TOTAL REVENUE	MARGINAL REVENUE	TOTAL COST	MARGINAL COST
$20	15,000			$330,000	
19	20,000			365,000	
18	25,000			405,000	
17	30,000			450,000	
16	35,000			500,000	
15	40,000			555,000	

a. Fill in the remaining values in the table.

b. If Ed wants to maximize profits, what price should he charge and how many baseballs should he sell? How much profit will he make?

c. Suppose the government imposes a tax of $50,000 per week on baseball production. Now what price should Ed charge, how many baseballs should he sell, and what will his profits be?

3.4 (Related to *Solved Problem 3*) Use the information in Solved Problem 3 to answer the following questions.

a. What will Comcast do if the tax is $6.00 per month instead of $2.50? (*Hint:* Will its decision be different in the long run than in the short run?)

b. Suppose that the flat per-month tax is replaced with a tax on the firm of $0.50 per cable subscriber. Now how many subscriptions should Comcast sell if it wants to maximize profit? What

price does it charge? What are its profits? (Assume that Comcast will sell only the quantities listed in the table.)

3.5 Before inexpensive pocket calculators were developed, many science and engineering students used slide rules to make numeric calculations. Slide rules are no longer produced, which means nothing prevents you from establishing a monopoly in the slide rule market. Draw a graph showing the situation your slide rule firm would be in. Be sure to include on your graph your demand, marginal revenue, average total cost, and marginal cost curves. Indicate the price you would charge and the quantity you would produce. Are you likely to make a profit or a loss? Show this area on your graph.

3.6 Does a monopolist have a supply curve? Briefly explain.

3.7 (Related to the *Don't Let This Happen to You!*) A student argues, "If a monopolist finds a way of producing a good at lower cost, he will not lower his price. Because he is a monopolist, he will keep the price and the quantity the same and just increase his profit." Do you agree? Use a graph to illustrate your answer.

3.8 (Related to the *Don't Let This Happen to You!*) Discuss whether you agree or disagree with the following statement: "A monopolist maximizes profit by charging the highest price at which it can sell any of the good at all."

3.9 When home builders construct a new housing development, they usually sell the rights to lay cable to a single cable television company. As a result, anyone buying a home in that development is not able to choose between competing cable companies. Some cities have begun to ban such exclusive agreements. Williams Township, Pennsylvania, decided to allow any cable company to lay cable in the utility trenches of new housing developments. The head of the township board of supervisors argued, "What I would like to see and do is give the consumers a choice. If there's no choice, then the price [of cable] is at the whim of the provider." In a situation in which the consumers in a housing development have only one cable company available, is the price really at the whim of the company? Would a company in this situation be likely to charge, say, $500 per month for basic cable services? Briefly explain why or why not.

Source: Sam Kennedy, "Williams Township May Ban Exclusive Cable Provider Pacts," (Allentown, Pennsylvania) *Morning Call*, November 5, 2004, p. D1.

3.10 Will a monopoly that maximizes profit also be maximizing revenue? Will it be maximizing production? Briefly explain.

Does Monopoly Reduce Economic Efficiency?

Summary

Compared with a perfectly competitive industry, a monopoly charges a higher price and produces less, which reduces consumer surplus and economic efficiency. Some loss of economic efficiency will occur whenever firms have **market power** and can charge a price greater than marginal cost. The total loss of economic efficiency in the U.S. economy due to market power is small, however, because true monopolies are very rare. In most industries, competition will keep price much closer to marginal cost than would be the case in a monopoly.

Visit www.myeconlab.com to complete these exercises online and get instant feedback.

Review Questions

4.1 Suppose that a perfectly competitive industry becomes a monopoly. Describe the effects of this change on consumer surplus, producer surplus, and deadweight loss.

4.2 Explain why market power leads to a deadweight loss. Is the total deadweight loss from market power for the economy large or small?

Problems and Applications

4.3 Review Figure 5 on the inefficiency of monopoly. Will the deadweight loss due to monopoly be larger if the demand is elastic or if it is inelastic? Briefly explain.

4.4 Economist Harvey Leibenstein argued that the loss of economic efficiency in industries that are not perfectly competitive has been understated. He argues that when competition is weak, firms are under less pressure to adopt the best techniques or to hold down their costs. He refers to this effect as "x-inefficiency." If x-inefficiency causes a firm's marginal costs to rise, show that the deadweight loss in Figure 5 understates the true deadweight loss caused by a monopoly.

4.5 In most cities, the city owns the water system that provides water to homes and businesses. Some cities charge a flat monthly fee, while other cities charge by the gallon. Which method of pricing is more likely to result in economic efficiency in the water market? Be sure to refer to the definition of economic efficiency in your answer. Why do you think the same method of pricing isn't used by all cities?

>> End Learning Objective 4

Government Policy toward Monopoly

Summary

Because monopolies reduce consumer surplus and economic efficiency, most governments regulate monopolies. Firms that are not monopolies have an incentive to avoid competition by **colluding**, or agreeing to charge the same price, or otherwise not to compete. In the United States, **antitrust laws** are aimed at deterring monopoly, eliminating collusion, and promoting competition among firms. The Antitrust Division of the U.S. Department of Justice and the Federal Trade Commission share responsibility for enforcing the antitrust laws including regulating mergers between firms. A **horizontal merger** is a merger between firms in the same industry. A **vertical merger** is a merger between firms at different stages of production of a good. Local governments regulate the prices charged by natural monopolies.

Visit www.myeconlab.com to complete these exercises online and get instant feedback.

Review Questions

5.1 What is the purpose of the antitrust laws? Who is in charge of enforcing them?

5.2 What is the difference between a horizontal merger and a vertical merger? Which type of merger is more likely to increase the market power of a newly merged firm?

5.3 Why would it be economically efficient to require a natural monopoly to charge a price equal to marginal cost? Why do most regulatory agencies require natural monopolies to charge a price equal to average cost instead?

Problems and Applications

5.4 Use the following graph for a monopoly to answer the questions.

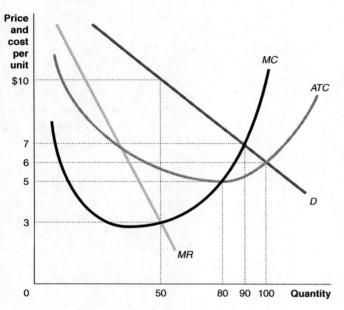

a. What quantity will the monopoly produce, and what price will the monopoly charge?

b. Suppose the monopoly is regulated. If the regulatory agency wants to achieve economic efficiency, what price should it require the monopoly to charge? How much output will the monopoly produce at this price? Will the monopoly make a profit if it charges this price? Briefly explain.

5.5 Use the following graph for a monopoly to answer the questions.

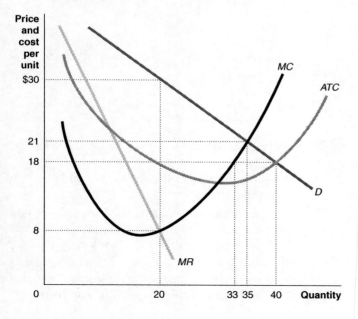

a. What quantity will the monopoly produce, and what price will the monopoly charge?

b. Suppose the government decides to regulate this monopoly and imposes a price ceiling of $18 (in other words, the monopoly can charge less than $18 but can't charge more). Now what quantity will the monopoly produce, and what price will the monopoly charge? Will every consumer who is willing to pay this price be able to buy the product? Briefly explain.

5.6 The following is from an article in the *New York Times*: "United Airlines and US Airways announced today that they had called off their proposed merger after the Justice Department threatened to file a lawsuit to block the $4.2 billion deal, calling it anticompetitive." Why would the Justice Department care if two airlines merge? What is "anticompetitive" about two airlines merging?

Source: Kenneth N. Gilpin and Jack Lynch, "United and US Airways Call Off Merger after U.S. Opposes It," *New York Times*, July 27, 2001.

5.7 A marketing textbook observes, "Pricing actions that violate laws can land executives in jail." Why would executives be thrown in jail because of the prices they charge? Which laws are they likely to have violated?

Source: David W. Cravens, *Strategic Marketing*, 5th ed., Boston: Irwin McGraw-Hill, 1997, p. 343.

5.8 Draw a graph like Figure 6. On your graph, show producer surplus and consumer surplus before a merger and consumer surplus and producer surplus after a merger.

5.9 The following phone call took place in February 1982 between Robert Crandall, the chief executive officer of American Airlines, and Howard Putnam, the chief executive officer of Braniff Airways. Although Crandall didn't know it, Putnam was recording the call:

> *Crandall:* I think it's dumb . . . to sit here and pound the (obscenity) out of each other and neither one of us making a (obscenity) dime . . .
>
> *Putnam:* Do you have a suggestion for me?
>
> *Crandall:* Yes, I have a suggestion for you. Raise your . . . fares 20 percent. I'll raise mine the next morning.
>
> *Putnam:* Robert, we . . .
>
> *Crandall:* You'll make more money and I will, too.
>
> *Putnam:* We can't talk about pricing.
>
> *Crandall:* Oh (obscenity), Howard. We can talk about any . . . thing we want to talk about.

Who had a better understanding of antitrust law, Crandall or Putnam? Briefly explain.

Source: Mark Potts, "American Airlines Charged with Seeking a Monopoly," *Washington Post*, February 24, 1983; "Blunt Talk on the Phone," *New York Times*, February 24, 1983; and Thomas Petzinger Jr., *Hard Landing: The Epic Contest for Power and Profits that Plunged the Airline Industry into Chaos*, New York: Random House, 1995, pp. 149–150.

5.10 Look again at the section "The Department of Justice and Federal Trade Commission Merger Guidelines." Evaluate the following situations.

a. A market initially has 20 firms, each with a 5 percent market share. Of the firms, 4 propose to merge, leaving a total of 17 firms in the industry. Are the Department of Justice and the Federal Trade Commission likely to oppose the merger? Briefly explain.

b. A market initially has 5 firms, each with a 20 percent market share. Of the firms, 2 propose to merge, leaving a total of 4 firms in the industry. Are the Department of Justice and the Federal Trade Commission likely to oppose the merger? Briefly explain.

5.11 In 2007, Sirius Satellite Radio and XM Satellite Radio, the only two satellite radio firms, announced that they would attempt to merge. Maurice McKenzie, an analyst for Signal Hill investment bank, was quoted in the *Wall Street Journal* as arguing, "We believe that governmental approval could hinge on the market definition surrounding radio competition, which we expect to be narrowly defined to include terrestrial and satellite radio operators. . . ." What is a "terrestrial" radio operator? Why would government approval depend on how it defines the relevant market? What other firms—apart from terrestrial radio operators—might the government consider competitors to a newly merged Sirius-XM firm?

Source: "Analysts Like Sirius-XM Merger, but Note Regulatory Difficulties," *Wall Street Journal*, February 20, 2007.

5.12 In a column in the *Wall Street Journal*, David Henderson, an economist at the Hoover Institution, argued that it was possible to judge whether the proposed merger between Sirius and XM would make consumers better or worse off by looking at how owners of "free," or broadcast, radio stations reacted:

> Look at what the "free" broadcasters are saying about the XM-Sirius merger. As this newspaper recently reported, "The radio industry has loudly opposed the deal since it was announced, and broadcasters cite satellite-radio operators as major competitors in securities filings." Traditional radio broadcasters understand that they are competing with satellite radio. And they oppose the merger.

Why would "free" radio broadcasters oppose the merger? If the newly merged Sirius-XM charged higher prices, wouldn't that be good news to "free" radio broadcasters? Does the reaction of the "free" radio broadcasters indicate that consumers would be made better or worse off by the Sirius-XM merger?

Source: David R. Henderson, "Sirius Business," *Wall Street Journal*, February 28, 2007.

5.13 Industrial gases are used in the electronics industry. For example, nitrogen trifluoride is used for cleaning semiconductor wafers. The following table shows the market shares for the companies in this industry.

COMPANY	MARKET SHARE
Air Products	29%
Air Liquide	22
BOC Gases	21
Nippon Sanso	17
Praxair	8
Other	3

In 2000, Air Products discussed a merger with BOC Gases. Use the information in the section "The Department of Justice and Federal Trade Commission Merger Guidelines" to predict whether the Department of Justice and the Federal Trade Commission opposed this merger. Assume that "Other" in the table consists of three firms, each of which has a 1 percent share of the market.

Source for market share data: Dan Shope, "Air Products Turns a Corner," (Allentown, Pennsylvania) *Morning Call*, July 29, 2001.

5.14 The following table gives the market shares of the companies in the U.S. carbonated soft drink industry.

COMPANY	MARKET SHARE
Coca-Cola	37%
PepsiCo	35
Cadbury Schweppes	17
Other	11

Use the information in the section "The Department of Justice and Federal Trade Commission Merger Guidelines" to predict whether the Department of Justice and the Federal Trade Commission would be likely to approve a merger between any two of the first three companies listed. Does your answer depend on how many companies are included in the "Other" category? Briefly explain.

Source: Pepsico *Annual Report*, 2003.

5.15 According to a column in the *New York Times* by Austan Goolsbee of the University of Chicago, the French National Assembly approved a bill:

> . . . that would require Apple Computer to crack open the software codes of its iTunes music store and let the files work on players other than the iPod. . . . If the French gave away the codes, Apple would lose much of its rationale for improving iTunes.

a. Why would Apple no longer want to improve iTunes if its software codes were no longer secret?

b. Why would the French government believe it was a good idea to require Apple to make the codes public?

Source: Austan Goolsbee, "In iTunes War, France Has Met the Enemy. Perhaps It Is France," *New York Times*, April 27, 2006.

5.16 (Related to the *Making the Connection*) Bank of America has attempted to convince Congress to eliminate the rule that banks may not merge if the newly merged bank would have more than a 10 percent share of U.S. deposits. In 2007, Bank of America was expanding its banking activities by, among other things, offering checking accounts and credit cards to illegal immigrants and other people who lacked Social Security numbers. An article in the *Wall Street Journal* observed:

> Unorthodox initiatives like the new credit-card program may be crucial to Bank of America's long-term success. In the past the bank, which operates in 31 states and the District of Columbia, grew mostly by buying up other banks. Now, however, it is bumping up against a regulatory cap that bars any U.S. bank from an acquisition that would give it more than 10% of the nation's total bank deposits. That means Bank of America's only way to grow domestically is to sell more products to existing customers and to attract new ones.

Should the government take this information into account in evaluating the policy of limiting mergers among large banks? The *Wall Street Journal* article also notes, "Illegal immigrants have typically relied on loan sharks and neighborhood finance shops [which charge very high interest rates] for credit." Should the government consider this additional piece of information when formulating policy on bank mergers?

Source: Miriam Jordan and Valerie Bauerlein, "Bank of America Casts Wider Net for Hispanics," *Wall Street Journal*, February 13, 2007, p. A1.

>> **End Learning Objective 5**

Pricing Strategy

From Chapter 15 of *Microeconomics*, 2/e. R. Glenn Hubbard. Anthony Patrick O'Brien. Copyright © 2008 by Pearson Prentice Hall.

Pricing Strategy

Getting into Walt Disney World: One Price Does Not Fit All

When you visit Walt Disney World in Florida, your age, home address, and occupation can determine how much you pay for admission. In the summer of 2007, the price for a one-day ticket for an adult was $71.36. The same ticket for a child, aged three to nine, was $59.64. Children under three were free. Florida residents paid $64.22. Florida residents who were also members of Auto Club South paid $60.30. Active members of the military paid $69. Why does Disney charge so many different prices for the same product?

In previous chapters, we assumed that firms charge all consumers the same price for a given product. In reality, many firms charge customers different prices, based on differences in their willingness to pay for the product. Firms often face complicated pricing problems. For example, the Walt Disney Company faces the problem of determining the profit-maximizing prices to charge different groups of consumers for admission to its Disneyland and Walt Disney World theme parks.

The Walt Disney Company was founded in 1923 by Walt Disney and his brother Roy O. Disney. Several times, the Disney brothers risked financial ruin by investing most of the company's funds in innovative entertainment ideas. In 1927, they released *Steamboat Willie* starring Mickey Mouse, the first cartoon to feature synchronized sound. The profits from *Steamboat Willie* and other short cartoons helped finance production of *Snow White and the Seven Dwarfs*. Released in 1937, this was the first full-length Technicolor cartoon.

In the early 1950s, Walt Disney began to believe there was a market for theme parks. At that time, amusement parks—like Coney Island in New York—were usually collections of unrelated rides, such as roller coasters and Ferris wheels. The parks often had rowdy reputations and appealed more to teenagers and young adults than to families with children. Disney believed that a theme park, with attractions that emphasized storytelling over thrills, would be more attractive to families than were amusement parks. Disney had trouble raising the funds necessary to build his new park, however, because it was so strikingly different from existing parks. Disney hired an economist to evaluate the feasibility of the park. Managers of existing parks gave this advice to the economist: "Tell your boss to save his money. Tell him to stick to what he knows and leave the amusement business to people who know it."

Eventually, Disney convinced the ABC television network to provide funding in exchange for his providing them with a weekly television program.

When Disneyland opened in Anaheim, California, in July 1955, the Disney company had to set ticket prices. Should the company charge for entry into the park—which most amusements parks did not—and also charge for each ride within the park? Disney decided to charge a low price— $1 for adults and $0.50 for children— for admission into the park and also to charge for tickets to the rides. This system of separate charges for admission and for the rides continued until the early 1980s, when Disney decided to switch to a very different pricing strategy. Today, there is a high price for admission to Disneyland and Walt Disney World, but once a customer is in the park, the rides are free. Why did Disney change its pricing strategy? In this chapter, we will study some common pricing strategies, and we will see how Disney and other firms use these strategies to increase their profits. **AN INSIDE LOOK** discusses how colleges also charge different prices to different students.

Sources: Harrison Price, *Walt's Revolution! By the Numbers*, Ripley Entertainment, Inc., 2004, p. 31; and Bruce Gordon and David Mumford, *Disneyland: The Nickel Tour*, Santa Clarita, CA: Camphor Tree Publishers, 2000, pp. 174–175.

John M. Greim/CreativeEye/MIRA.com. Disney characters © Disney Enterprises, Inc. Used by permission from Disney Enterprises, Inc.

LEARNING Objectives

After studying this chapter, you should be able to:

1   Define the **law of one price** and explain the role of **arbitrage**.

2   Explain how a firm can increase its profits through **price discrimination**.

3   Explain how some firms increase their profits through the use of **odd pricing, cost-plus pricing** and **two-part tariffs**.

Economics in YOUR Life!

Why So Many Prices to See a Movie?

Think about the movie theaters in your area. How much do you, as a student, pay to get into a theater? Would your parents pay the same amount? What about your grandparents? How about your little brother or sister? Is the price the same at night as in the afternoon? Why do you suppose movie theaters charge different prices to different groups of consumers?

If you buy popcorn at the movie theater, you pay the same price as everyone else. Why do you suppose people in certain age groups get a discount on movie admission but not on movie popcorn? As you read the chapter, see if you can answer these questions. You can check your answers against those we provide at the end of the chapter.

E ntrepreneurs continually seek out economic profit. Pricing strategies are one way firms can attempt to increase their economic profit. One of these strategies is called *price discrimination*. It involves firms setting different prices for the same good or service, as Disney does when setting admission prices at Disney World. In this chapter, we will see how a firm can increase its profits by charging a higher price to consumers who value the good more and a lower price to consumers who value the good less.

We will also analyze the widely used strategies of *odd pricing* and *cost-plus pricing*. Finally, we will analyze situations in which firms are able to charge consumers one price for the right to buy a good and a second price for each unit of the good purchased. The ability of Disney to charge for admission to Disney World and also to charge for each ride is an example of this situation, which economists call a *two-part tariff*.

---

1 LEARNING OBJECTIVE

1 | Define the law of one price and explain the role of arbitrage.

Pricing Strategy, the Law of One Price, and Arbitrage

We saw in the opening to this chapter that sometimes firms can increase their profits by charging different prices for the same good. In fact, many firms rely on economic analysis to practice *price discrimination* by charging higher prices to some customers and lower prices to others. Firms use technology to gather information on the preferences of consumers and their responsiveness to changes in prices. Managers use the information to rapidly adjust the prices of their goods and services. This practice of rapidly adjusting prices, called *yield management*, has been particularly important to airlines and hotels. There are limits, though, to the ability of firms to charge different prices for the same product. The key limit is the possibility in some circumstances that consumers who can buy a good at a low price will resell it to consumers who would otherwise have to buy at a high price.

Arbitrage

According to the *law of one price*, identical products should sell for the same price everywhere. Let's explore why the law of one price usually holds true. Suppose that a Sony PlayStation Portable (PSP) handheld video game player sells for $249 in stores in Atlanta and for $199 in stores in San Francisco. Anyone who lives in San Francisco could buy PSPs for $199 and resell them for $249 in Atlanta. They could sell them on eBay or ship them to someone they know in Atlanta who could sell them in local flea markets. Buying a product in one market at a low price and reselling it in another market at a high price is referred to as *arbitrage*. The profits received from engaging in arbitrage are referred to as *arbitrage profits*.

As the supply of PSPs in Atlanta increases, the price of PSPs in Atlanta will decline, and as the supply of PSPs in San Francisco decreases, the price of PSPs in San Francisco will rise. Eventually the arbitrage process will eliminate most, but not all, of the price difference. Some price difference will remain because sellers must pay to list PSPs on eBay and to ship them to Atlanta. The costs of carrying out a transaction—by, for example, listing items on eBay and shipping them across the country—are called **transactions costs**. The law of one price holds exactly *only if transactions costs are zero*. As we will soon see, in cases in which it is impossible to resell a product, the law of one price will not hold, and firms will be able to price discriminate. Apart from this important qualification, we expect that arbitrage will result in a product selling for the same price everywhere.

Transactions costs The costs in time and other resources that parties incur in the process of agreeing to and carrying out an exchange of goods or services.

270

Solved Problem | 1

Is Arbitrage Just a Rip-off?

People are often suspicious of arbitrage. Buying something at a low price and reselling it at a high price exploits the person buying at the high price. Or does it? Is this view correct? If so, do the auctions on eBay serve any useful economic purpose?

SOLVING THE PROBLEM:

Step 1: **Review the chapter material.** This problem is about arbitrage, so you may want to review the section "Arbitrage."

Step 2: **Use the discussion of arbitrage and the discussion in earlier chapters of the benefits from trade to answer the questions.** Many of the goods on eBay have been bought at a low price and are being resold at a higher price. In fact, some people supplement their incomes by buying collectibles and other goods at garage sales and reselling them on eBay. Does eBay serve a useful economic purpose? Economists would say that it does. Consider the case of Lou, who buys collectible movie posters and resells them on eBay. Suppose Lou buys a *Spider-Man 3* poster at a garage sale for $30 and resells it on eBay for $60. Both the person who sold to Lou at the garage sale and the person who bought from him on eBay must have been made better off by the deals *or they would not have made them*. Lou has performed the useful service of locating the poster and making it available for sale on eBay. In carrying out this service, Lou has incurred costs, including the opportunity cost of his time spent searching garage sales, the opportunity cost of the funds he has tied up in posters he has purchased but not yet sold, and the cost of the fees eBay charges him. It is easy to sell goods on eBay, so over time, competition among Lou and other movie poster dealers should cause the difference between the prices of posters sold at garage sales and the prices on eBay to shrink until they are equal to the dealers' costs of reselling the posters.

YOUR TURN: For more practice, do related problems 1.5 and 1.6 at the end of this chapter.

>> End Solved Problem 1

Why Don't All Firms Charge the Same Price?

The law of one price may appear to be violated even where transactions costs are zero and a product can be resold. For example, different Internet Web sites may sell what seem to be identical products for different prices. We can resolve this apparent contradiction if we look more closely at what "product" an Internet Web site—or other business—actually offers for sale.

Suppose you want to buy a copy of the book *Harry Potter and the Deathly Hallows*. You use mySimon.com or some other search engine to compare the book's price at various Web sites. You get the results shown in Table 1.

Would you automatically buy the book from one of the last two sites listed rather than from Amazon.com or BarnesandNoble.com? We can think about why you might not. Consider what product is being offered for sale. Amazon.com is not just offering *Harry Potter and the Deathly Hallows*; it is offering *Harry Potter and the Deathly Hallows* delivered quickly to your home, well packaged so it's not damaged in the mail, and charged to your credit card using a secure method that keeps your credit card number safe from computer hackers. Firms differentiate the products they sell in many ways. One way is by providing faster and more reliable delivery than competitors.

TABLE 1

Which Internet Bookseller Would You Buy From?

PRODUCT: *HARRY POTTER AND THE DEATHLY HALLOWS*	
COMPANY	PRICE
Amazon.com	$18.89
BarnesandNoble.com	18.89
WaitForeverForYourOrder.com	17.50
JustStartedinBusinessLastWednesday.com	16.75

Amazon.com and BarnesandNoble.com have built reputations for fast and reliable service. New Internet booksellers who lack that reputation will have to differentiate their products on the basis of price, as the two fictitious firms listed in the table have done. So, the difference in the prices of products offered on Web sites does *not* violate the law of one price. A book Amazon.com offers for sale is not the same product as a book JustStartedinBusinessLastWednesday.com offers for sale.

---

2 LEARNING OBJECTIVE

2 | Explain how a firm can increase its profits through price discrimination.

Price Discrimination: Charging Different Prices for the Same Product

Price discrimination Charging different prices to different customers for the same product when the price differences are not due to differences in cost.

We saw at the beginning of this chapter that the Walt Disney Company charges different prices for the same product: admission to Disney World. Charging different prices to different customers for the same good or service when the price differences are not due to differences in cost is called **price discrimination**. But doesn't price discrimination

---

Don't Let This Happen to **YOU!**

Don't Confuse Price Discrimination with Other Types of Discrimination

Don't confuse price discrimination with discrimination based on race or gender. Discriminating on the basis of arbitrary characteristics, like race or gender, is illegal under the civil rights laws. Price discrimination is legal because it involves charging people different prices on the basis of their willingness to pay rather than on the basis of arbitrary characteristics. There is a gray area, however, when companies charge different prices on the basis of race or gender. For example, insurance companies usually charge women lower prices than men for automobile insurance. The courts have ruled that this is not illegal discrimination under the civil rights laws because women, on average, have better driving records than men. Because the costs of insuring men are higher than the costs of insuring women, insurance companies are allowed to charge them higher prices. Notice that this is not actually price discrimination as we have defined it here. Price discrimination involves charging different prices for the same product *where the price differences are not due to differences in cost.*

Insurance companies have been less successful in defending the practice of charging black people higher life insurance prices than white people. The insurance companies had claimed that this practice, which continued into the 1960s, was based on the shorter average life span of black people. Even though most insurance companies stopped the practice in the 1960s for new policies, most companies continued to collect the higher prices on policies that were already in effect. When this became widely known, several state insurance commissions launched investigations. Eventually, most companies reimbursed policyholders for the higher prices and paid substantial fines to the government. MetLife, the largest publicly held life insurance company in the United States, paid $250 million to settle a lawsuit by policyholders and to pay fines imposed by the New York State Insurance Department.

YOUR TURN: Test your understanding by doing related problem 2.18 at the end of this chapter.

contradict the law of one price? Why doesn't the possibility of arbitrage profits lead people to buy at the low price and resell at the high price?

The Requirements for Successful Price Discrimination

A successful strategy of price discrimination has three requirements:

1. A firm must possess market power.

2. Some consumers must have a greater willingness to pay for the product than other consumers, and the firm must be able to know what prices customers are willing to pay.

3. The firm must be able to divide up—or *segment*—the market for the product so that consumers who buy the product at a low price are not able to resell it at a high price. In other words, price discrimination will not work if arbitrage is possible.

Note that a firm selling in a perfectly competitive market cannot practice price discrimination because it can only charge the market price. But because most firms do not sell in perfectly competitive markets, they have market power and can set the price of the good they sell. Many firms may also be able to determine that some customers have a greater willingness to pay for the product than others. However, the third requirement—that markets be segmented so that customers buying at a low price will not be able to resell the product—can be difficult to fulfill. For example, some people really love Big Macs and would be willing to pay $10 rather than do without one. Other people would not be willing to pay a penny more than $1 for one. Even if McDonald's could identify differences in the willingness of its customers to pay for Big Macs, it would not be able to charge them different prices. Suppose McDonald's knows that Joe is willing to pay $10, whereas Jill will pay only $1. If McDonald's tries to charge Joe $10, he will just have Jill buy his Big Mac for him.

Only firms that can keep consumers from reselling a product are able to practice price discrimination. Because buyers cannot resell the product, the law of one price does not hold. For example, movie theaters know that many people are willing to pay more to see a movie at night than during the afternoon. As a result, theaters usually charge higher prices for tickets to night showings than for tickets to afternoon showings. They keep these markets separate by making the tickets to afternoon showings a different color or by having the time printed on them, and by having a ticket taker examine the tickets. That makes it difficult for someone to buy a lower-priced ticket in the afternoon and use the ticket to gain admission to an evening showing.

Figure 1 illustrates how the owners of movie theaters use price discrimination to increase their profits. The marginal cost to the movie theater owner from another person attending a showing is very small: a little more wear on a theater seat and a few more kernels of popcorn to be swept from the floor. In Figure 1, we assume for simplicity that marginal cost is a constant $0.50, shown as a horizontal line. Panel (a) shows the demand for afternoon showings. In this segment of its market, the theater should maximize profit by selling the number of tickets for which marginal revenue equals marginal cost, or 450 tickets. We know from the demand curve that the theater can sell 450 tickets at a price of $4.50 per ticket. Panel (b) shows the demand for night showings. Notice that charging $4.50 per ticket would *not* be profit maximizing in this market. At a price of $4.50, the theater sells 850 tickets, which is 225 more tickets than the profit-maximizing number of 625. By charging $4.50 for tickets to afternoon showings and $6.75 for tickets to night showings, the theater has maximized profits.

Figure 1 also illustrates another important point about price discrimination: When firms can price discriminate, they will charge customers who are less sensitive to price—those whose demand for the product is *less elastic*—a higher price and charge customers who are more sensitive to price—those whose demand is *more elastic*—a lower price. In this case, the demand for tickets to night showings is less elastic, so the price charged is higher, and the demand for tickets to afternoon showings is more elastic, so the price charged is lower.

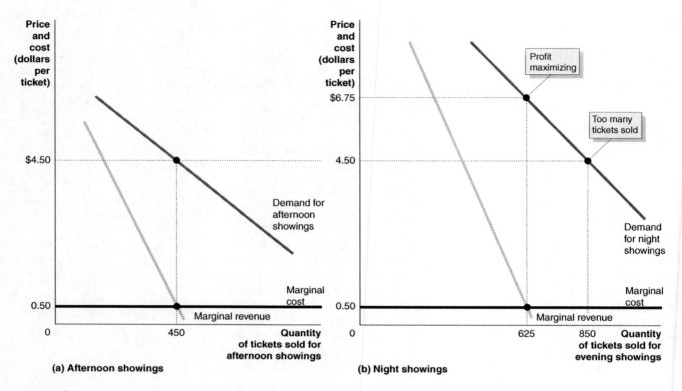

Figure 1 | Price Discrimination by a Movie Theater

Fewer people want to go to the movies in the afternoon than in the evening. In panel (a), the profit-maximizing price for a ticket to an afternoon showing is $4.50. Charging this same price for night showings would not be profit maximizing, as panel (b) shows. At a price of $4.50, 850 tickets would be sold to night showings, which is more than the profit-maximizing number of 625 tickets. To maximize profits, the theater should charge $6.75 for tickets to night showings.

Solved Problem | 2

How Dell Computer Uses Price Discrimination to Increase Profits

According to an article in the *Wall Street Journal*, "On Dell's Web site recently, the same Optiplex business desktop PC priced at $1,498 for education customers was offered at $1,426 on a page devoted to health-care customers." Why would Dell charge different prices for the same computer, depending on whether the buyer is an education customer or a health-care customer? Draw a graph to illustrate your answer.

SOLVING THE PROBLEM:

Step 1: **Review the chapter material.** This problem is about using price discrimination to increase profits, so you may want to review the section "Price Discrimination: Charging Different Prices for the Same Product."

Step 2: **Explain why charging different prices to education customers and health care customers will increase Dell's profits.** It makes sense for Dell to charge different prices if education customers have a different price elasticity of demand than do health-care customers. In that case, Dell will charge the market segment with the less elastic demand a higher price and the market segment with the more elastic demand a lower price. Because education customers are being charged the higher price, they must have a less elastic demand than health-care customers.

Step 3: **Draw a graph to illustrate your answer.** Your graph should look like the one below, where we have chosen hypothetical quantities to illustrate the ideas. As in the case of movie theaters, you can assume for simplicity that the marginal cost is constant; in the graph we assume that marginal cost is $400.

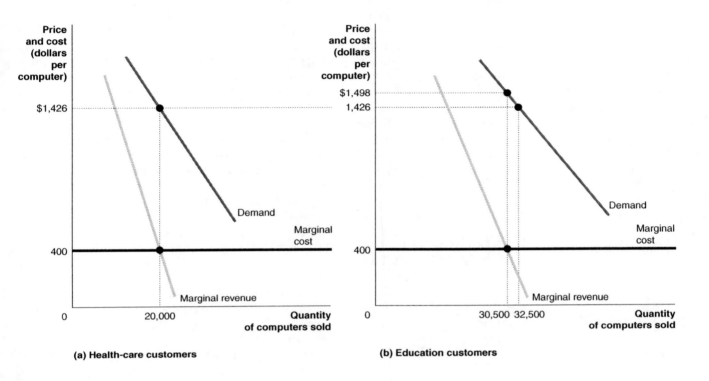

(a) Health-care customers

(b) Education customers

The graph shows that in the health-care customers segment of the market, marginal revenue equals marginal cost at 20,000 computers sold. Therefore, Dell should charge a price of $1,426 to maximize profits. But if Dell also charged $1,426 in the education customers segment of the market, it would sell 32,500 computers, which is more than the profit-maximizing quantity. By charging $1,498 to education customers, Dell will sell 30,500 computers, the profit-maximizing quantity. We have shown that Dell maximizes its profits by charging education customers a higher price than health care customers. Notice that although the demand curve in panel (a) is more elastic, it is also steeper.

Source: David Bank and Gary McWilliams, "Picking a Big Fight with Dell, H-P Cuts PC Profits Razor-Thin," *Wall Street Journal*, May 12, 2004.

YOUR TURN: For more practice, do problem 2.12 at the end of this chapter.   **»» End Solved Problem 2**

Airlines: The Kings of Price Discrimination

Airline seats are a perishable product. Once a plane has taken off from Chicago for Los Angeles, any seat that has not been sold on that particular flight will never be sold. In addition, the marginal cost of flying one additional passenger is low. This situation gives airlines a strong incentive to manage prices so that as many seats as possible are filled on each flight.

Airlines divide their customers into two main categories: business travelers and leisure travelers. Business travelers often have inflexible schedules, can't commit until the last minute to traveling on a particular day, and, most importantly, are not very sensitive to changes in price. The opposite is true for leisure travelers: They are flexible about when they travel, willing to buy their tickets well in advance, and sensitive to changes in price. Based on what we discussed earlier in this chapter, you can see that airlines will maximize profits by charging business travelers higher ticket prices than leisure travelers, but they need to determine who is a business traveler and who is a leisure traveler. Some airlines do this by requiring people who want to buy a ticket at the leisure price to buy 14 days in advance and to stay at their destination over a Saturday night. Anyone unable to meet these requirements must pay a much higher price. Because business travelers often cannot make their plans 14 days in advance of their flight and don't want to stay over a weekend, they end up paying the higher ticket price. The gap between leisure fares and business fares is often very substantial. For example, in April 2007, the price of a leisure-fare ticket between New York and San Francisco on United Airlines was $308. The price of a business-fare ticket was $1,198.

The airlines go well beyond a single leisure fare and a single business fare in their pricing strategies. Although they ordinarily charge high prices for tickets sold only a few days in advance, they are willing to reduce prices for seats that they expect will not be sold at existing prices. Since the late 1980s, airlines have employed economists and mathematicians to construct computer models of the market for airline tickets. To calculate a suggested price each day for each seat, these models take into account factors that affect the demand for tickets, such as the season of the year, the length of the route, the day of the week, and whether the flight typically attracts primarily business or leisure travelers. This practice of continually adjusting prices to take into account fluctuations in demand is called *yield management*.

Since the late 1990s, Internet sites such as Priceline.com have helped the airlines to implement yield management. On Priceline.com, buyers commit to paying a price of their choosing for a ticket on a particular day and agree that they will fly at any time on that day. This gives airlines the opportunity to fill seats that otherwise would have gone empty, particularly on late night or early morning flights, even though the price may be well below the normal leisure fare. In 2001, several airlines combined to form the Internet site Orbitz, which became another means of filling seats at discount prices. In fact, in the past few years, the chance that you paid the same price for your airline ticket as the person sitting next to you has become quite small. Figure 2 shows an actual

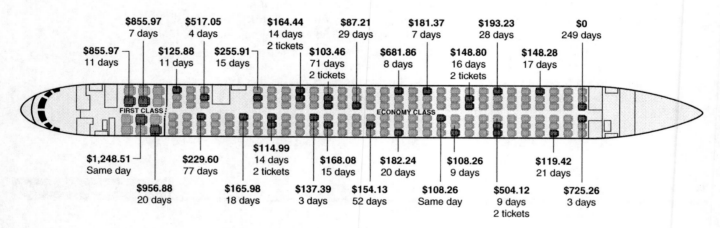

Figure 2 | 33 Customers and 27 Different Prices

To fill as many seats on a flight as possible, airlines charge many different ticket prices. The 33 passengers on this United Airlines flight from Chicago to Los Angeles paid 27 different prices for their tickets, including one passenger who used frequent flyer miles to obtain a free ticket. The first number in the figure is the price paid for the ticket; the second number is the number of days in advance that the ticket was purchased.

Source: Matthew L. Wald, "So, How Much Did You Pay for Your Ticket?" *New York Times*, April 12, 1998. Used with permission of New York Times Agency.

United Airlines flight from Chicago to Los Angeles. The 33 passengers on the flight paid 27 different prices for their tickets, including one passenger who used frequent flyer miles to obtain a free ticket.

Making the Connection | How Colleges Use Yield Management

Some colleges use yield management techniques to determine financial aid.

Traditionally, colleges have based financial aid decisions only on the incomes of prospective students. In recent years, however, many colleges have started using yield management techniques, first developed for the airlines, to determine the amount of financial aid they offer different students. Colleges typically use a name like "financial aid engineering" or "student enrollment management" rather than "yield management" to describe what they are doing. There is an important difference between the airlines and colleges: Colleges are interested not just in maximizing the revenue they receive from student tuition but also in increasing the academic quality of the students who enroll.

The "price" of a college education equals the tuition charged minus any financial aid received. When colleges use yield management techniques, they increase financial aid offers to students likely to be more price sensitive, and they reduce financial aid offers to students likely to be less price sensitive. As Stanford economist Caroline Hoxby puts it, "Universities are trying to find the people whose decisions will be changed by these [financial aid] grants." Some of the factors colleges use to judge how sensitive to price students are likely to be include whether they applied for early admission, whether they came for an on-campus interview, their intended major, their home state, and the level of their family's income. Focusing on one of these factors, William F. Elliot, vice president for enrollment management at Carnegie Mellon University, advises, "If finances are a concern, you shouldn't be applying any place [for] early decision" because you are less likely to receive a large financial aid offer.

Many students (and their parents) are critical of colleges that use yield management techniques in allocating financial aid. Some colleges, such as those in the Ivy League, have large enough endowments to meet all of their students' financial aid needs, so they don't practice yield management. Less well-endowed colleges defend the practice on the grounds that it allows them to recruit the best students at a lower cost in financial aid.

Sources: Jane J. Kim and Anjali Athavaley, "Colleges Seek to Address Affordability," *Wall Street Journal*, May 3, 2007; and Albert B. Crenshaw, "Price Wars on Campus: Colleges Use Discounts to Draw Best Mix of Top Students, Paying Customers," *Washington Post*, October 15, 2002; and Steve Stecklow, "Expensive Lesson: Colleges Manipulate Financial-Aid Offers, *Wall Street Journal*, April 1, 1996.

YOUR TURN: Test your understanding by doing related problem 2.14 at the end of this chapter.

Perfect Price Discrimination

If a firm knew every consumer's willingness to pay—and could keep consumers who bought a product at a low price from reselling it—the firm could charge every consumer a different price. In this case of *perfect price discrimination*—also known as *first-degree price discrimination*—each consumer would have to pay a price equal to the consumer's willingness to pay and, therefore, would receive no consumer surplus. To see why, remember that consumer surplus is the difference between the highest price a consumer is willing to pay for a product and the price the consumer actually pays. But if the price the consumer pays is the maximum the consumer would be willing to pay, there is no consumer surplus.

Figure 3 shows the effects of perfect price discrimination. To simplify the discussion, we assume that the firm is a monopoly and that it has constant marginal and average costs. Panel (a) should be familiar. It shows the case of a monopolist who cannot price discriminate and, therefore, can charge only a single price for its product. The monopolist maximizes profits by producing the level of output where marginal revenue equals marginal cost. Recall that the economically efficient level of output occurs where price is equal to marginal cost, which is the level of output in a perfectly competitive market. Because the monopolist produces where price is greater than marginal cost, it causes a loss of economic efficiency equal to the area of the deadweight loss triangle in the figure.

Panel (b) shows the situation of a monopolist practicing perfect price discrimination. Because the firm can now charge each consumer the maximum the consumer is willing to pay, its marginal revenue from selling one more unit is equal to the price of that unit. Therefore, the monopolist's marginal revenue curve becomes equal to its demand curve, and the firm will continue to produce up to the point where price is equal to marginal cost. It may seem like a paradox, but the ability to perfectly price discriminate causes the monopolist to produce the efficient level of output. By doing so, it converts into profits what in panel (a) had been consumer surplus *and* what had been deadweight loss. In both panel (a) and panel (b), the profit shown is also producer surplus.

Even though the result in panel (b) is more economically efficient than the result in panel (a), consumers clearly are worse off because the amount of consumer surplus has been reduced to zero. We probably will never see a case of perfect price discrimination in the real world because firms typically do not know how much each consumer is willing to pay and therefore cannot charge each consumer a different price. Still, this extreme case helps us to see the two key results of price discrimination:

1 Profits increase.

2 Consumer surplus decreases.

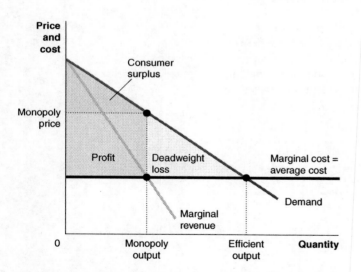

(a) A monopolist who cannot practice price discrimination

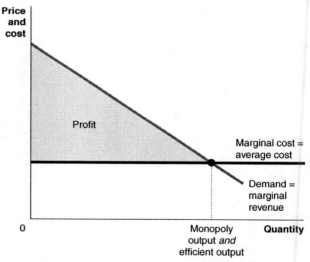

(b) A monopolist practicing perfect price discrimination

Figure 3 | Perfect Price Discrimination

Panel (a) shows the case of a monopolist who cannot price discriminate and, therefore, can charge only a single price for its product. The graph shows that to maximize profits, the monopolist will produce the level of output where marginal revenue equals marginal cost. The resulting profit is shown by the area of the green rectangle. Given the monopoly price, the amount of consumer surplus in this market is shown by the area of the blue triangle. The economically efficient level of

output occurs where price equals marginal cost. Because the monopolist stops production at a level of output where price is above marginal cost, there is a deadweight loss equal to the area of the yellow triangle. In panel (b), the monopolist is able to perfectly price discriminate by charging a different price to each consumer. The result is to convert both the consumer surplus *and* the deadweight loss from panel (a) into profit.

With perfect price discrimination, economic efficiency is improved. Can we also say that this will be the case if price discrimination is less than perfect? Often, less-than-perfect price discrimination will improve economic efficiency. But under certain circumstances, it may actually reduce economic efficiency, so we can't draw a general conclusion.

Price Discrimination across Time

Firms are sometimes able to engage in price discrimination over time. With this strategy, firms charge a higher price for a product when it is first introduced and a lower price later. Some consumers are *early adopters* who will pay a high price to be among the first to own certain new products. This pattern helps explain why DVD players, digital cameras, and flat-screen plasma televisions all sold for very high prices when they were first introduced. After the demand of the early adopters was satisfied, the companies reduced prices to attract more price-sensitive customers. For example, the price of DVD players dropped by 95 percent within five years of their introduction. Some of the price reductions over time for these products was also due to falling costs as companies took advantage of economies of scale, but some represented price discrimination across time.

Book publishers routinely use price discrimination across time to increase profits. Hardcover editions of novels have much higher prices and are published months before paperback editions. For example, the hardcover edition of Stephen King's novel *Lisey's Story* was published in October 2006 at a price of $28. The paperback edition was published in June 2007 for $9.99. Although this difference in price might seem to reflect the higher costs of hardcover books, in fact, it does not. The marginal cost of printing another copy of the hardcover is about $1.50. The marginal cost of printing another copy of the paperback edition is only slightly less, about $1.25. So, the difference in price between the hardcover and paperback is driven primarily by differences in demand. Stephen King's most devoted fans want to read his next book at the earliest possible moment and are not too sensitive to price. Many casual readers are also interested in King's books but will read something else if the price is too high.

As Figure 4 shows, a publisher will maximize profits by segmenting the market—in this case across time—and by charging a higher price to the less elastic market segment and a lower price to the more elastic segment. (This example is similar to our earlier analysis of movie tickets in Figure 1.) If the publisher had skipped the hardcover and issued only the paperback version at a price of $9.99 when the book was first published in October, its revenue would have dropped by the number of readers who bought the hardcover multiplied by the difference between the price of the hardcover and the price of the paperback, or $500,000 \times (\$28 - 9.99) = \$9,005,000$.

Can Price Discrimination Be Illegal?

Congress has passed *antitrust laws* to promote competition. Price discrimination may be illegal if its effect is to reduce competition in an industry. In 1936, Congress passed the Robinson–Patman Act, which outlawed price discrimination that reduced competition, but which also contained language that could be interpreted as making illegal *all* price discrimination not based on differences in cost. In the 1960s, the Federal Trade Commission sued the Borden company under this act because Borden was selling the same evaporated milk for two different prices. Cans with the Borden label were sold for a high price, and cans sold to supermarkets to be repackaged as the supermarkets' private brands were sold for a much lower price. The courts ultimately ruled that Borden had not violated the law because the price differences increased, rather than reduced, competition in the market

279

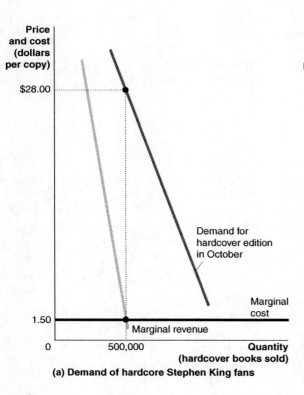

(a) Demand of hardcore Stephen King fans

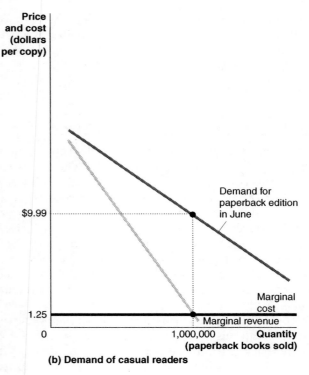

(b) Demand of casual readers

Figure 4 | Price Discrimination across Time

Publishers issue most novels in hardcover at high prices to satisfy the demand of the novelists' most devoted fans. Later, they publish paperback editions at much lower prices to capture sales from casual readers. In panel (a), with a marginal cost of $1.50 per copy for a hardcover, the profit-maximizing level of output is 500,000 copies, which can be sold at a price of $28. In panel (b), the more elastic demand of casual readers and the slightly lower marginal cost result in a profit-maximizing output of 1,000,000 for the paperback edition, which can be sold at a price of $9.99.

for evaporated milk. In recent years, the courts have interpreted Robinson–Patman narrowly, allowing firms to use the types of price discrimination described in this chapter.

Why does renting only a few movies get you better service on Netflix?

Making
the
Connection

Price Discrimination with a Twist at Netflix

Price discrimination usually refers to charging different prices to different consumers for the same good or service. But price discrimination can also involve charging the same price for goods or services of different quality. Netflix, an online DVD rental service, has apparently engaged in this second form of price discrimination. According to a newspaper story, "Netflix customers who pay the same price for the same service are often treated differently, depending on their rental patterns." Netflix subscribers pay a fixed monthly fee to rent a given number of DVDs. For instance, in 2007, Netflix was charging $17.99 per month to rent three DVDs at a time. After a subscriber returns a DVD, Netflix mails that subscriber a new DVD. Subscribers can rent an unlimited number of DVDs per month, although they can have no more than three at any one time. Netflix has become very popular, with more than seven million subscribers by 2007.

But does every Netflix subscriber receive service of the same quality? In particular, does every subscriber have an equal chance of receiving the latest movie released on DVD? Apparently not. Although Netflix does not emphasize it in its advertising, subscribers who rent the fewest movies per month have the best chance of receiving the latest releases and will typically receive their DVDs faster. According to Netflix's Terms of Use (the "fine print" that most subscribers don't read):

> In determining priority for shipping and inventory allocation, we may utilize many different factors. . . . For example, if all other factors are the same, we give priority to those members who receive the fewest DVDs through our service. . . . Also . . . [the service you experience] may be different from the service we provide to other members on the same membership plan.

One Netflix subscriber was quoted in a newspaper article as saying, "Sometimes it would be two or three months before I got [a movie] once it came out on DVD. The longer I was a customer, the worse it got."

Why would Netflix provide better service to subscribers who rent only a few DVDs per month and poorer service to subscribers who rent many DVDs per month? Subscribers who rent many DVDs per month are likely to have less elastic demand—they really like watching movies—than subscribers who rent only a few DVDs per month. As we have seen in this chapter, firms can increase their profits by charging higher prices to consumers with less elastic demand and lower prices to consumers with more elastic demand. But this strategy works only if firms have a way of reliably separating consumers into groups on the basis of how elastic their demand is. When they first subscribe, Netflix has no way of separating their consumers on the basis of how elastic their demand is, so it has to charge the same price to everyone. But after a few months of observing a subscriber's pattern of rentals, Netflix has enough information to determine whether the subscriber's demand is more or less elastic. By reducing the level of service to subscribers with less elastic demand, Netflix is, in effect, raising the price these consumers pay relative to consumers who receive better service. In effect, Netflix is engaging in price discrimination and increasing its profits over what they would be if every subscriber received the same service at the same price.

Sources: Alina Tugend, "Getting Movies from a Store or a Mailbox (or Just a Box)," *New York Times*, August 5, 2006; and "Netflix Critics Slam 'Throttling,'" Associated Press, February 10, 2006.

YOUR TURN: Test your understanding by doing related problem 2.17 at the end of this chapter.

---

3 | Explain how some firms increase their profits through the use of odd pricing, cost-plus pricing, and two-part tariffs.

3 LEARNING OBJECTIVE

Other Pricing Strategies

In addition to price discrimination, firms use many different pricing strategies, depending on the nature of their products, the level of competition in their markets, and the characteristics of their customers. In this section, we consider three important strategies: odd pricing, cost-plus pricing, and two-part tariffs.

Odd Pricing: Why Is the Price $2.99 Instead of $3.00?

Many firms use what is called *odd pricing*—for example, charging $4.95 instead of $5.00, or $199 instead of $200. Surveys show that 80 percent to 90 percent of the products sold in supermarkets have prices ending in "9" or "5" rather than "0." Odd pricing has a long history. In the early nineteenth century, most goods in the United States were sold in general stores and did not have fixed prices. Instead, prices were often determined by haggling, much as prices of new cars are often determined today by haggling on dealers' lots. Later in the nineteenth century, when most products began to sell for a fixed price, odd pricing became popular.

Different explanations have been given for the origin of odd pricing. One explanation is that it began because goods imported from Great Britain had a reputation for high quality. When the prices of British goods in British currency—the pound—were translated into U.S. dollars, the result was an odd price. Because customers connected odd prices with high-quality goods, even sellers of domestic goods charged odd prices. Another explanation is that odd pricing began as an attempt to guard against employee theft. An odd price forced an employee to give the customer change, which reduced the likelihood that the employee would simply pocket the customer's money without recording the sale.

Whatever the origins of odd pricing, why do firms still use it today? The most obvious answer is that an odd price, say $9.99, seems somehow significantly—more than a penny—cheaper than $10.00. But do consumers really have this illusion? To find out, three market researchers conducted a study. Demand curves can be estimated statistically. If consumers have the illusion that $9.99 is significantly cheaper than $10.00, they will demand a greater quantity of goods at $9.99—and other odd prices—than the estimated demand curve predicts. The researchers surveyed consumers about their willingness to purchase six different products—ranging from a block of cheese to an electric blender—at a series of prices. Ten of the prices were either odd cent prices—99 cents or 95 cents—or odd dollar prices—$95 or $99. Nine of these 10 odd prices resulted in an odd-price effect, with the quantity demanded being greater than predicted using the estimated demand curve. The study was not conclusive because it relied on surveys rather than on observing actual purchasing behavior and because it used only a small group of products, but it does provide some evidence that using odd prices makes economic sense.

Why Do Firms Use Cost-Plus Pricing?

Many firms use *cost-plus pricing*, which involves adding a percentage *markup* to average cost. With this pricing strategy, the firm first calculates average cost at a particular level of production, usually equal to the firm's expected sales. It then increases average cost by a percentage amount, say 30 percent, to arrive at the price. For example, if average cost is $100 and the percentage markup is 30 percent, the price will be $130. In a firm selling multiple products, the markup is intended to cover all costs, including those that the firm cannot assign to any particular product. Most firms have costs that are difficult to assign to one particular product. For example, the work performed by the employees in McDonald's accounting and finance departments applies to all of McDonald's products and can't be assigned directly to Big Macs or Happy Meals.

Making
the
Connection | ### Cost-Plus Pricing in the Publishing Industry

Book publishing companies incur substantial costs for editing, designing, marketing, and warehousing books. These costs are difficult to assign directly to any particular book. Most publishers arrive at a price for a book by applying a markup to their production costs, which are usually divided into plant costs and manufacturing costs. Plant costs include typesetting the manuscript and preparing graphics or artwork for printing. Manufacturing costs include the costs of printing, paper, and binding the book.

Consider the following example for the hypothetical new book by Adam Smith, *How to Succeed at Economics without Really Trying*. We will assume that the book is 250 pages long, the publisher expects to sell 5,000 copies, and plant and manufacturing costs are as given in the following table:

PLANT COST

Typesetting	$3,500	
Other plant costs	2,000	

MANUFACTURING COST

Printing	$5,750	
Paper	6,250	
Binding	5,000	

TOTAL PRODUCTION COST

	$22,500

With total production cost of $22,500 and production of 5,000 books, the per-unit production cost is $22,500/5,000 = $4.50. Many publishers multiply the unit production cost number by 7 or 8 to arrive at the retail price they will charge customers in bookstores. In this case, multiplying by 7 results in a price of $31.50 for the book. The markup seems quite high, but publishers typically sell books to bookstores at a 40 percent discount. Although a customer in a bookstore will pay $31.50 for the book—or less, of course, if it is purchased from a bookseller that discounts the retail price—the publisher receives only $18.90. The difference between the $18.90 received from the bookstore and the $4.50 production cost equals the cost of editing, marketing, warehousing, and all other costs, including the opportunity cost of the investment in the firm by its owners, plus any economic profit received by the owners.

Source: Beth Luey, *Handbook for Academic Authors*, 4th ed., New York: Cambridge University Press, 2002.

YOUR TURN: Test your understanding by doing related problem 3.8 at the end of this chapter.

A difficulty that firms face when using cost-plus pricing should be obvious to you. In this chapter, we have emphasized that firms maximize profit by producing the quantity where marginal revenue equals marginal cost and charging a price that will cause consumers to buy this quantity. The cost-plus approach doesn't appear to maximize profits unless the cost-plus price turns out to be the same as the price that will cause the quantity sold to be where marginal revenue is equal to marginal cost. Economists have two views of cost-plus pricing. One is that cost-plus pricing is simply a mistake that firms should avoid. The other view is that cost-plus pricing is a good way to come close to the profit-maximizing price when either marginal revenue or marginal cost is difficult to calculate.

Small firms often like cost-plus pricing because it is easy to use. Unfortunately, these firms can fall into the trap of mechanically applying a cost-plus pricing rule, which can result in charging prices that do not maximize profits. The most obvious problems with cost-plus pricing are that it ignores demand and focuses on average cost rather than marginal cost. If the firm's marginal cost is significantly different from its average cost at its current level of production, cost-plus pricing is unlikely to maximize profits.

Despite these problems, cost-plus pricing is used by some large firms, such as General Motors, that clearly have the knowledge and resources to devise a better method of pricing if cost-plus pricing fails to maximize profits. Economists conclude that cost-plus pricing may be the best way to determine the optimal price in two situations:

1. When marginal cost and average cost are roughly equal
2. When the firm has difficulty estimating its demand curve

In fact, most large firms that use cost-plus pricing do not just mechanically apply a markup to their estimate of average cost. Instead, they adjust the markup to reflect their best estimate of current demand. At General Motors, for example, a pricing policy committee adjusts prices to reflect its views of the current state of competition in the industry and the current state of the economy. If competition is strong in a weak economy, the pricing committee may decide to set price significantly below the cost-plus price—perhaps by offering buyers a rebate.

In general, firms that take demand into account will charge lower markups on products that are more price elastic and higher markups on products that are less elastic. Supermarkets, where cost-plus pricing is widely used, have markups in the 5 percent to 10 percent range for products with more elastic demand, such as soft drinks and breakfast cereals, and markups in the 50 percent range for products with less elastic demand, such as fresh fruits and vegetables.

Pricing with Two-Part Tariffs

Some firms can require consumers to pay an initial fee for the right to buy their product and an additional fee for each unit of the product purchased. For example, many golf and tennis clubs require members to buy an annual membership in addition to paying a fee each time they use the tennis court or golf course. Sam's Club requires consumers to pay a membership fee before shopping at its stores. Cellular phone companies charge a monthly fee and then have a per-minute charge after a certain number of minutes have been used. Economists refer to this situation as a **two-part tariff**.

Two-part tariff A situation in which consumers pay one price (or tariff) for the right to buy as much of a related good as they want at a second price.

The Walt Disney Company is in a position to use a two-part tariff by charging consumers for admission to Walt Disney World or Disneyland and also charging them to use the rides in the parks. As mentioned at the beginning of this chapter, at one time, the admission price to Disneyland was low, but people had to purchase tickets to go on the rides. Today, you must pay a high price for admission to Disneyland or Disney World, but the rides are free once you're in the park. Figure 5 helps us understand which of these pricing strategies is more profitable for Disney. The numbers in the figure are simplified to make the calculations easier.

Once visitors are inside the park, Disney is in the position of a monopolist—no other firm is operating rides in Disney World. So, we can draw panel (a) in Figure 5 to represent the market for rides at Disney World. This graph looks like the standard monopoly graph. (Note that the marginal cost of another rider is quite low. We can assume that it is a constant $2 and equal to the average cost.) It seems obvious—but it will turn out to be wrong!—that Disney should determine the profit-maximizing quantity of ride tickets by setting marginal revenue equal to marginal cost. In this case, that would lead to 20,000 ride tickets sold per day at a price of $26 per ride. Disney's profit from selling *ride tickets* is shown by the area of the light-green rectangle, *B*. It equals the difference between the $26 price and the average cost of $2, multiplied by the 20,000 tickets sold, or ($26 − $2) × 20,000 = $480,000. Disney also has a second source of profit from selling *admission tickets* to the park. Given the $26 price for ride tickets, what price would Disney be able to charge for admission tickets?

Let's assume the following for simplicity: The only reason people want admission to Disney World is to go on the rides, all consumers have the same individual demand curve for rides, and Disney knows what this demand curve is. This last assumption allows Disney to be able to practice perfect price discrimination. More realistic assumptions would make the outcome of the analysis somewhat different but would not affect

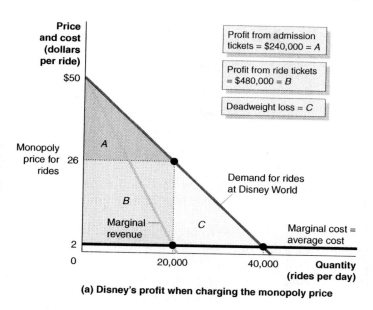

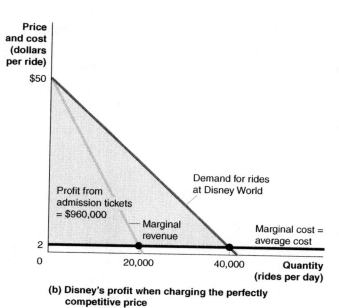

(a) Disney's profit when charging the monopoly price

(b) Disney's profit when charging the perfectly competitive price

Figure 5 | A Two-Part Tariff at Disney World

In panel (a), Disney charges the monopoly price of $26 per ride ticket and sells 20,000 ride tickets. Its profit from *ride tickets* is shown by the area of the light-green rectangle, B, $480,000. If Disney is in the position of knowing every consumer's willingness to pay, it can also charge a price for *admission tickets* that would result in the total amount paid for admission tickets being equal to total consumer surplus from the rides. Total consumer surplus from the rides equals the area of the dark-green triangle, A, or $240,000. So, when charging the monopoly price, Disney's total profit equals $480,000 + $240,000, or $720,000. In panel (b), Disney charges the perfectly competitive price of $2, where marginal revenue equals marginal cost, and sells 40,000 ride tickets. At the lower ride ticket price, Disney can charge a higher price for admission tickets, which will increase its total profits from operating the park to the area of the light-green triangle, or $960,000.

---

the main point of how Disney uses a two-part tariff to increase its profits. With these assumptions, we can use the concept of consumer surplus to calculate the maximum total amount consumers would be willing to pay for admission. Remember that consumer surplus is equal to the area below the demand curve and above the price line, shown by the dark-green triangle, A, in panel (a). The area represents the benefit to buyers from consuming the product. In this case, consumers would not be willing to pay more for admission to the park than the consumer surplus they receive from the rides. In panel (a) of Figure 5, the total consumer surplus when Disney charges a price of $26 per ride is $240,000. (This number is easy to calculate if you remember that the formula for the area of a triangle is ½ × base × height, or ½ × 20,000 × $24.) Disney can set the price of admission tickets so that the *total* amount spent by buyers would be $240,000. In other words, Disney can set the price of admission to capture the entire consumer surplus from the rides. So, Disney's total profit from Disney World would be the $240,000 it receives from admission tickets plus the $480,000 in profit from the rides, or $720,000 per day.

Is this the most profit Disney can earn from selling admission tickets and ride tickets? The answer is "no." The key to seeing why is to notice that *the lower the price Disney charges for ride tickets, the higher the price it can charge for admission tickets.* Lower-priced ride tickets increase consumer surplus from the rides and, therefore, increase the willingness of buyers to pay a higher price for admission tickets. In panel (b) of Figure 5, we assume that Disney acts as it would in a perfectly competitive market and charges a price for ride tickets that is equal to marginal cost, or $2. Charging this price increases consumer surplus— *and* the maximum total amount that Disney can charge for admission tickets—from $240,000 to $960,000. (Once again, we use the formula for the area of a triangle to calculate the light-green area in panel (b): ½ × 40,000 × 48 × $960,000) Disney's profits from the rides will decline to

TABLE 2

Disney's Profits per Day from Different Pricing Strategies

	MONOPOLY PRICE FOR RIDES	COMPETITIVE PRICE FOR RIDES
PROFITS FROM ADMISSION TICKETS	$240,000	$960,000
PROFITS FROM RIDE TICKETS	480,000	0
TOTAL PROFIT	720,000	960,000

zero because it is now charging a price equal to average cost, *but its total profit from Disney World will rise from $720,000 per day to $960,000.* Table 2 summarizes this result.

What is the source of Disney's increased profit from charging a price equal to marginal cost? The answer is that Disney has converted what was deadweight loss when the monopoly price was charged—the area of triangle *C* in panel (a)—into consumer surplus. It then turns this consumer surplus into profit by increasing the price of admission tickets.

It is important to note the following about the outcome of a firm using an optimal two-part tariff:

1. Because price equals marginal cost at the level of output supplied, the outcome is economically efficient.

2. All of consumer surplus is transformed into profit.

Notice that, in effect, Disney is practicing perfect price discrimination. As we noted in our discussion of perfect price discrimination, Disney's use of a two-part tariff has increased the amount of the product—in this case, rides at Disney World—consumers are able to purchase, but has eliminated consumer surplus. Although it may seem paradoxical, consumer surplus was actually higher when consumers were being charged the monopoly price for the rides. The solution to the paradox is that although consumers pay a lower price for the rides when Disney employs a two-part tariff, the overall amount they pay to be at Disney World increases.

Disney actually does follow the profit-maximizing strategy of charging a high price for admission to the park and a very low price—zero—for the rides. It seems that Disney could increase its profits by raising the price for the rides from zero to the marginal cost of the rides. But the marginal cost is so low that it would not be worth the expense of printing ride tickets and hiring additional workers to sell the tickets and collect them at each ride. Finally, note that because the demand curves of Disney's customers are not all the same, and because Disney does not actually know precisely what these demand curves are, Disney is not able to convert all of consumer surplus into profit.

The rides at Disney World are free—once you have paid to get into the park.

Gerd Ludwig, The Image Works

Economics in YOUR Life!

At the beginning of the chapter, we asked you to think about what you pay for a movie ticket and what people in other age groups pay. A movie theater will try to charge different prices to different consumers based on their willingness to pay. If you have two otherwise identical people, one a student and one not, you might assume that the student has less income, and thus a lower willingness to pay, than the non-student, and the movie theater would like to charge the student a lower price. The movie theater employee can ask to see a student ID to ensure that the theater is giving the discount to a student.

But why don't theaters practice price discrimination at the concession stand? It is likely that a student will also have a lower willingness to pay for popcorn, and the theater can check for a student ID at the time of purchase, but unlike the case of the entry ticket, the theater would have a hard time preventing the student from giving the popcorn to a non-student once inside the theater. Since it is easier to limit resale in movie admissions, we often see different prices for different groups. Since it is difficult to limit resale of popcorn and other movie concessions, all groups will typically pay the same price.

Conclusion

Firms in perfectly competitive industries must sell their products at the market price. For firms in other industries—which means, of course, the vast majority of firms—pricing is an important part of the strategy used to maximize profits. We have seen in this chapter, for example, that if firms can successfully segment their customers into different groups on the basis of willingness to pay, they can increase their profits by charging different segments different prices.

Read *An Inside Look* on the next page for a discussion of why colleges do not charge all students the same tuition.

College Tuition: One Price Does Not Fit All

WALL STREET JOURNAL, OCTOBER 11, 2006

Amid Rising Costs and Criticism, Some Colleges Cut Back Merit Aid

As colleges and universities consider whether to join Harvard and Princeton in abandoning early-admissions programs, some are also trying to roll back another popular recruiting tool: merit aid.

Colleges offer merit aid, which is typically awarded on the basis of grades, class rank and test scores, to students who ordinarily wouldn't qualify for financial help. Because merit aid can be a deciding factor in these students' choice of schools, it has become a major weapon in the bidding wars among colleges for high achievers who can help boost their national rankings. . . .

But the cost of such programs has mounted as their use has expanded and tuition has risen. Meanwhile, criticism has grown that they disproportionately benefit students from wealthier communities with better school systems, siphoning resources away from lower-income students with greater financial need. In some cases, students who qualify for neither need- nor merit-based aid end up paying even more to cover a college's costs. As a result, a small but growing number of schools and university systems are trying to reduce their merit offerings. The University of Florida recently slashed the value of its four-year scholarships for in-state scholars who qualified under the National Merit program by 79% to a total of $5,000. . . .

Allegheny College, in Meadville, Pa., where annual tuition and fees total about $28,300, gave its $15,000-a-year merit scholarships to 15% of this year's freshmen, down from about 33% three years ago. To free up funding for more need-based aid, Rhode Island's Providence College scuttled its smaller merit scholarships and raised the eligibility requirements for its larger ones: A grade-point average of about 3.7 on a 4.0 scale used to be good enough; now it takes around a 3.83. Providence's merit scholarships can run as high as full tuition, which is $26,780 this year. . . .

Efforts to cut back on merit aid also risk setting off a backlash from middle- and upper-income families who don't qualify for need-based aid but are finding the rising cost of a college to be a daunting stretch. "Family income isn't keeping pace with the things driving higher-education costs," says Jim Scannell, a partner at Scannell & Kurz Inc., a Pittsford, N.Y., consulting firm that works with colleges on enrollment issues.

Some high-achieving applicants target schools that have merit-aid programs, hoping to win a tuition break. With tuition and fees at many private schools surpassing $40,000 a year, small private liberal-arts colleges that lack the cachet of the Ivy League but whose tuitions far exceed those of state colleges could have the most to lose from any cutbacks in merit aid. . . .

Many institutions have no intention of cutting back on merit aid. Baylor University, a Baptist college in Waco, Texas, recently increased the value of the merit awards it gives to all incoming freshmen who score at least 1,300 points out of a possible 1,600 on SAT reading and math exams. The awards, which rise in value in tandem with a student's SAT scores, range from $2,000 to $4,000 a year. . . .

For some smaller schools, merit aid is less about boosting rankings than adding revenue by swelling enrollment. In most cases, students are still paying substantial sums for tuition even after receiving a scholarship. "I think in many cases it's misleading to call it merit aid," says Michael McPherson, president of the Spencer Foundation, a Chicago-based educational research group. "It's 'get 'em in the door' aid."

At private Wilkes University, Wilkes Barre, Pa., where tuition and fees are about $23,000 a year, only 81 of this year's 580 incoming freshmen didn't get merit aid. To land a scholarship, which starts at $6,000 a year, students have to have graduated in the top half of their high-school class and to have scored a combined total of at least a 900 on the SAT reading and math exams, not much above average. . . .

Although families with earnings of $100,000 or more might qualify for need-based aid, depending on factors such as how many college-aged children they have, college administrators say many such families usually don't bother to apply for need-based aid because they presume they won't get it. . . .

Source: Robert Tomsho, "Amid Rising Costs and Criticism, Some Colleges Cut Back Merit Aid," Wall Street Journal, October 11, 2006.

Key Points in the Article

This article highlights a change in the scholarships offered by universities and colleges. In particular, colleges are reducing merit aid and increasing the amount of need-based financial aid. Because many students receive scholarships and other types of aid, they pay a variety of actual tuition prices, which may be very different from the posted tuition price.

Analyzing the News

(a) High-achieving students are typically offered admission by a number of different universities, many of which are good substitutes for each other. As a result, talented high school seniors would have a relatively elastic demand for attending any particular college. Consumers with more elastic demands tend to pay lower prices for goods.

(b) Need-based aid can be thought of as a form of price discrimination, separating the market into high-income students (with high demand) and low-income students (with low demand). Panel (a) in the figure below shows two demand curves for

college education: one for high-income students and the other for low-income students. Notice that for any quantity, high-income students have a higher willingness to pay for education. So for Q_1 of each type of student to be enrolled, the school could charge P_1 dollars to high-income students but only P_2 dollars to low-income students. Need-based aid makes it possible to charge a lower price to low-income students without changing the tuition price charged to high-income students. You can see in panel (a) that if the school had to charge P_1 to both types of students, it would still enroll Q_1 high-income students but only Q_2 low-income students, so it would not maximize revenue.

(c) An additional student adds very little to the cost of running a college or university. As a result, offering merit aid is usually not the difference between a student paying full tuition or reduced tuition; it is the difference between a student enrolling and paying some tuition or not enrolling and paying $0 to the school. Panel (b) in the figure below shows the demand curve for enrollment at a school. Notice that in this example as the price drops from P_1 to P_2,

there is a large increase in quantity, from Q_1 to Q_2 students. If the demand for education at a particular college is elastic, as it likely is, tuition revenues will increase as the school lowers its price. At the higher price, P_1, with Q_1 students, revenue is shown as areas $A + B$. If tuition drops, revenue at price P_2 with Q_2 students will be areas $B + C$. The school will be better off if the increased revenue from additional students is (area C) greater than the lost revenue from the lower price now charged to the original Q_1 students (area A). In this example, area C is greater than area A, so the college's revenues increase when it cuts its tuition.

Thinking Critically

1. If lowering the tuition to some students increases a university's revenue, why don't universities just lower the tuition for everyone?

2. If customers with less elastic demands will pay more for a product when firms can price discriminate, would you expect to see freshmen or seniors pay higher tuition at your college? How might a college charge different classes different levels of tuition?

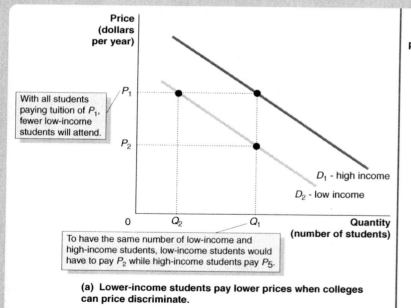

(a) Lower-income students pay lower prices when colleges can price discriminate.

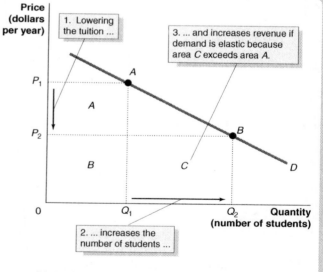

(b) Demand and revenue at different tuition prices.

College tuition strategies.

Key Terms

Price discrimination

Transactions costs

Two-part tariff

1 LEARNING OBJECTIVE   1 | Define the law of one price and explain the role of arbitrage

Pricing Strategy, the Law of One Price, and Arbitrage

Summary

According to the *law of one price*, identical products should sell for the same price everywhere. If a product sells for different prices, it will be possible to make a profit through *arbitrage*: buying a product at a low price and reselling it at a high price. The law of one price will hold as long as arbitrage is possible. Arbitrage is sometimes blocked by high **transactions costs**, which are the costs in time and other resources incurred to carry out an exchange, or because the product cannot be resold. Another apparent exception to the law of one price occurs when companies offset the higher price they charge for a product by providing superior or more reliable service to customers.

myeconlab Visit www.myeconlab.com to complete these exercises
Get Ahead of the Curve online and get instant feedback.

Review Questions

1.1 What is the law of one price? What is arbitrage?

1.2 Does a product always have to sell for the same price everywhere? Briefly explain.

Problems and Applications

1.3 A newspaper article contains the following description:

> For years, shoppers from New York City have played a game of retail arbitrage, traveling to the many malls in northern New Jersey, a state where there is no tax on clothing and shoes. Even accounting for tolls, gas and time, shoppers could save money by visiting the Westfield Garden State Plaza and other malls here, escaping the 8.375 percent sales tax they must pay in New York City on clothing and shoes that cost more than $110 per item.

Does this article use the word *arbitrage* correctly? Briefly explain.

Source: Ken Belson and Nate Schweber, "Sales Tax Cut in City May Dim Allure of Stores Across Hudson," *New York Times*, January 18, 2007.

1.4 The following table contains the actual prices charged by four Web sites for a DVD of the movie *Borat* in March 2007.

Amazon.com	$15.99
Wal-Mart	$15.87
DeepDiscount	$17.21
CDUniverse	$22.19

Briefly explain whether the information in this table contradicts the law of one price.

1.5 **(Related to *Solved Problem 1*)** Suppose California has many apple trees, and the price of apples there is low. Nevada has few apple trees, and the price of apples there is high. Abner buys low-priced California apples and ships them to Nevada, where he resells them at a high price. Is Abner exploiting Nevada consumers by doing this? Is he likely to earn economic profits in the long run? Briefly explain.

1.6 **(Related to *Solved Problem 1*)** Suspicions of arbitrage have a long history. For example, Valerian of Cimiez, a Catholic bishop who lived during the fifth century, wrote, "When something is bought cheaply only so it can be retailed dearly, doing business always means cheating." What might Valerian think of eBay? Do you agree with his conclusion? Explain.

Source for quote: Michael McCormick, *The Origins of the European Economy: Communications and Commerce, A.D. 300–900*, New York: Cambridge University Press, 2001, p. 85.

>> End Learning Objective 1

Price Discrimination: Charging Different Prices for the Same Product

Summary

Price discrimination occurs if a firm charges different prices for the same product when the price differences are not due to differences in cost. Three requirements must be met for a firm to successfully price discriminate: (1) A firm must possess market power. (2) Some consumers must have a greater willingness to pay for the product than other consumers, and firms must be able to know what customers are willing to pay. (3) Firms must be able to divide up—or segment—the market for the product so that consumers who buy the product at a low price cannot resell it a high price. In the case of *perfect price discrimination*, each consumer pays a price equal to the consumer's willingness to pay.

myeconlab Visit www.myeconlab.com to complete these exercises
Get Ahead of the Curve online and get instant feedback.

Review Questions

2.1 What is price discrimination? Under what circumstances can a firm successfully practice price discrimination?

2.2 During a particular week, America West charged $218 for a round-trip ticket on a flight from New York to San Francisco, provided that the ticket was purchased at least 10 days in advance and the ticket buyer was willing to stay over a Saturday night. If the buyer did not meet these conditions, the price for the ticket was $1,361. Why does America West use this pricing strategy?

2.3 What is yield management? Give an example of a firm using yield management to increase profits.

2.4 What is perfect price discrimination? Is it likely to ever occur? Explain. Is perfect price discrimination economically efficient? Explain.

2.5 Is it possible to price discriminate across time? Briefly explain.

Problems and Applications

2.6 An article on the AMC movie theater chain contained the following:

In July, [AMC] announced plans to offer steeply discounted movie tickets to shows on Friday, Saturday and Sunday mornings. "Seventy-five percent of the revenue comes from the weekend," Mr. Brown [AMC's CEO] said. His recent initiatives

are attempts to address the question: "Is there a way with price that you can create opportunity, a new market?"

Why would it be profitable for AMC to sell "steeply discounted" movie tickets for movies being shown on weekend mornings? Wouldn't the firm's revenues be higher if it charged the regular—higher—price for these showings? Briefly explain.

Source: Kate Kelly, "Box-Office Bounty Stirs Theater Deals," *Wall Street Journal*, August 10, 2006, p. C1.

2.7 According to an article in the *Wall Street Journal*, the average price of Ford Explorers sold in Dallas, Texas, was $30,142. During the same period, the average price of identically equipped Explorers in Oklahoma was only $27,939. Briefly explain whether this is an example of price discrimination.

Source: Karen Lundegaard, "How to Buy Your Next Car: First, Get a Plane Ticket," *Wall Street Journal*, April 30, 2002.

2.8 An article on how prices in South Bend, Indiana rise during Notre Dame home football games contained the following:

[Notre Dame football fan Anthony] Gallis ended up reserving a suite at a Hampton Inn and Suites in South Bend, which normally goes for $129 a night, for $400 a night, with a three-night minimum. "It's just insane," says the 42-year-old owner of a State Farm Insurance agency back in Pennsylvania. . . . Indeed, rates for many of the 4,015 hotel rooms in the South Bend area are skyrocketing. Two weeks before the start of the season, the Comfort Suites here was asking $245 a night, with a two-night minimum, for the Penn State weekend. That's up from $109 a night on non-football weekends. For the Sept. 16 game against the University of Michigan, the South Bend Marriott is charging $649 a night for a double room. That's more than the price of a room at the Waldorf-Astoria Hotel in New York. The Marriott's regular weekend price is $149 a night.

Is this an example of price discrimination? Briefly explain.

Source: Ilan Brat, "Notre Dame Football Introduces Its Fans To Inflationary Spiral," *Wall Street Journal*, September 7, 2006, p. A1.

2.9 Political columnist Michael Kinsley writes, "The infuriating [airline] rules about Saturday night stayovers and so on are a crude alternative to administering truth serum and asking, 'So how much are you really willing to pay?'" Would a truth serum—or some other way of knowing how much people would be willing to pay for an airline ticket—really be all the airlines need to price discriminate? Briefly explain.

Source: Michael Kinsley, "Consuming Gets More Complicated," *Slate*, November 21, 2001.

2.10 In a column in the *Wall Street Journal*, Walter Mossberg offered the following opinion:

> There's a sucker in the software business today, and if you're in an average family with a couple of PCs, that sucker is you. . . . Families constitute the only significant customer group not getting a discount on [Microsoft] Office when upgrading multiple PCs. Big corporations, organizations and government agencies get a discount, called a "site license." College students get a discount. Small and medium-size businesses get a discount. But not families.

Why might Microsoft charge families a higher price for Office than it charges the other groups Mossberg mentions?

Source: Walter Mossberg, "Microsoft Should Offer Families a Deal with Its Office Program," *Wall Street Journal*, July 18, 2002.

2.11 According to an article in the *Economist*, "The PS3 [PlayStation 3] is available in two configurations, costing $500 and $600 in America, and ¥50,000 ($425) and ¥60,000 ($510) in Japan." Based on this information, does Sony consider the demand of U.S. consumers for the PS3 to be more elastic or less elastic than the demand of Japanese consumers? Briefly explain.

Source: "Playing a Long Game," *Economist*, November 16, 2006.

2.12 (Related to *Solved Problem 2*) Use the graphs at the bottom of the page to answer the following questions.
   a. If the firm wants to maximize profits, what price will it charge in Market 1, and what quantity will it sell?
   b. If the firm wants to maximize profits, what price will it charge in Market 2, and what quantity will it sell?

2.13 When a firm offers a rebate on a product, the buyer normally has to fill out a form and mail it in to receive a rebate check in the mail. A financial columnist argues:

> When a manufacturer offers a rebate, you needn't be too suspicious. The manufacturer wants to lower the price temporarily (to move an old product or combat a competitor's new low price), but doesn't have faith that the retailer will pass on the savings.

But suppose that a manufacturer wants to engage in price discrimination. Would offering rebates be a way of doing this? Briefly explain.

Source: Carol Vinzant, "The Great Rebate Scam," *Slate*, June 10, 2003.

2.14 (Related to the *Making the Connection*) Assume that the marginal cost of admitting one more student is constant for every university. Also assume that the demand for places in the freshmen class is downward sloping at every university. Now suppose that the public becomes upset that universities charge different prices to different students. Responding to these concerns, the federal government requires universities to charge the same price to each student. Who would gain and who would lose?

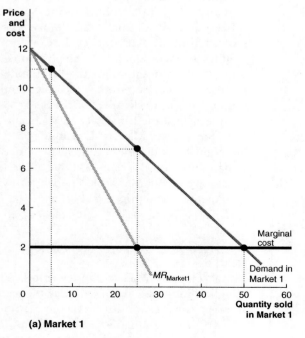

(a) Market 1

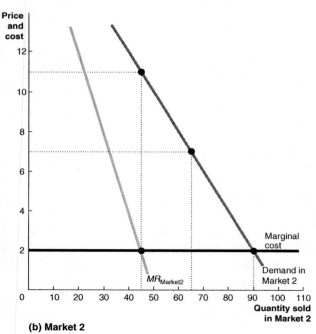

(b) Market 2

2.15 (Related to the *Chapter Opener*) Why does Walt Disney World charge a lower admission price for children aged 3 to 9 than for adults? Why does it categorize a 10-year-old as an adult for this purpose? Why does it admit children under 3 for free? Why does it charge residents of Florida a lower price than residents of other states?

2.16 Are supermarket coupons a form of price discrimination? Briefly explain why or why not.

2.17 (Related to the *Making the Connection*) Netflix offers subscriptions. Some have a higher price and allow more—or unlimited—movies to be rented per month. Others have a lower price and allow fewer movies to be rented per month. Is Netflix practicing price discrimination by offering these different subscriptions? Briefly explain.

2.18 (Related to the *Don't Let This Happen to You!*) Beginning in 2002, a state law in California made it illegal for businesses to charge men and women different prices for dry cleaning, laundry, tailoring, or hair grooming. The state legislator who proposed the law did so after a dry cleaner charged her more to have her shirts dry-cleaned than to have her husband's shirts dry-cleaned: "They charged me $1.50 for each of his, and he wears an extra large. They charged $3.50 for each of mine, and I wear a small." According to a newspaper article, "the dry cleaning proprietor told her that the price difference stemmed from the need for hand ironing her shirts because automatic presses are not made to handle small-sized women's garments."

a. Was the dry cleaner practicing price discrimination, as defined in this chapter? Briefly explain.

b. Do you support laws like this one? Briefly explain.

Source: Harry Brooks, "Law Mandates Equality in Dry Cleaning, Hair Styling," *North County (California) Times*, October 7, 2001.

2.19 Eric Orkin, the president of Opus 2 Revenue Technologies, Inc., which sells yield management systems to hotels, argues, "The price-sensitive person gets what he wants as long as he's willing to have some flexibility." Why would a yield management system for hotels result in lower prices for "price-sensitive" customers than the alternative of charging one price for all customers? Why would a price-sensitive person need to be "flexible" to receive a lower price?

Source: Neal Templin, "Property Report: Your Room Costs $250 . . . No! $200 . . . No . . . ," *Wall Street Journal*, May 5, 1999.

2.20 Draw a graph that shows producer surplus, consumer surplus, and deadweight loss (if any) in a market where the seller practices perfect price discrimination. Profit-maximizing firms select an output at which marginal cost equals marginal revenue. Where is the marginal revenue curve in this graph?

>> End Learning Objective 2

---

3 LEARNING OBJECTIVE | 3 | Explain how some firms increase their profits through the use of odd pricing, cost-plus pricing, and two-part tariffs

Other Pricing Strategies

Summary

In addition to price discrimination, firms also use odd pricing, cost-plus pricing, and two-part tariffs as pricing strategies. Firms use *odd pricing*—for example, charging $1.99 rather than $2.00—because consumers tend to buy more at odd prices than would be predicted from estimated demand curves. With *cost-plus pricing*, firms set the price for a product by adding a percentage markup to average cost. Cost-plus pricing may be a good way to come close to the profit-maximizing price when marginal revenue or marginal cost is difficult to measure. Some firms can require consumers to pay an initial fee for the right to buy their product and an additional fee for each unit of the product purchased. Economists refer to this situation as a **two-part tariff**. Sam's Club, cell phone companies, and many golf and tennis clubs use two-part tariffs in pricing their products.

 **myeconlab** Visit www.myeconlab.com to complete these exercises online and get instant feedback.

Review Questions

3.1 What is odd pricing?

3.2 What is cost-plus pricing? Is using cost-plus pricing consistent with a firm maximizing profits?

3.3 Give an example of a firm using a two-part tariff as part of its pricing strategy.

3.4 Why did the Walt Disney Company switch from charging for admission to Disneyland and charging for the rides to charging for admission and *not* charging for the rides?

Problems and Applications

3.5 One leading explanation for odd pricing is that it allows firms to trick buyers into the illusion that they're paying less than they really are. If this is true, in what types of markets and among what groups of consumers would you be mostly likely to find odd pricing? Should the government ban this practice and force companies to round up their prices to the nearest dollar?

3.6 Emerson Electric Company of St. Louis makes industrial equipment. Jerry Bernstein, the director of its price improvement team, describes how the company previously determined the prices of its products: "You developed a product, worked at the costs, and said, 'I need to make X [profit],' and you marked it up accordingly." Using this approach, Emerson arrived at a cost of $2,650 for a compact sensor used in pharmaceutical factories. In recent years, Emerson has moved away from a policy of cost-plus pricing, so it ended up charging $3,150, rather than $2,650, for the sensor. Discuss the factors that would lead Emerson to charge a price higher than the cost-plus price.

Source: Timothy Aeppel, "Amid Weak Inflation, Firms Turn Creative to Boost Prices," *Wall Street Journal*, September 18, 2002.

3.7 An article in the *Wall Street Journal* gives the following explanation of how products were traditionally priced at Parker-Hannifin Corporation:

> For as long as anyone at the 89-year-old company could recall, Parker used the same simple formula to determine prices of its 800,000 parts—from heat-resistant seals for jet engines to steel valves that hoist buckets on cherry pickers. Company managers would calculate how much it cost to make and deliver each product and add a flat percentage on top, usually aiming for about 35%. Many managers liked the method because it was straightforward. . . .

Is it likely that this system of pricing maximized the firm's profits? Briefly explain.

Source: Timothy Aeppel, "Changing the Formula: Seeking Perfect Prices, CEO Tears Up the Rules," *Wall Street Journal*, March 27, 2007, p. A1.

3.8 **(Related to the *Making the Connection*)** Would you expect a publishing company to use a strict cost-plus pricing system for all of its books? How might you find some indication whether a publishing company actually was using cost-pull pricing for all of its books?

3.9 Some professional sports teams charge fans a one-time lump sum for a "personal seat license." The personal seat license allows a fan the right to buy season tickets each year. No one without a personal seat license can buy season tickets. After the original purchase from the team, the personal seat licenses usually can be bought and sold by fans—whoever owns the seat license in a given year can buy season tickets—but the team does not earn any additional revenue from this buying and selling. Suppose a new sports stadium has been built, and the team is trying to decide on the price to charge for season tickets.

   a. Will the team make more profit from the combination of selling personal seat licenses and season tickets if it keeps the prices of the season tickets low or if it charges the monopoly price? Briefly explain.
   b. After the first year, is the team's strategy for pricing season tickets likely to change?
   c. Will it make a difference in the team's pricing strategy for season tickets if all the personal seat licenses are sold in the first year?

3.10 During the nineteenth century, the U.S. Congress encouraged railroad companies to build transcontinental railways across the Great Plains by giving them land grants. At that time, the federal government owned most of the land on the Great Plains. The land grants consisted of the land on which the railway was built and alternating sections of 1 square mile each on either side of the railway to a distance of 6 to 40 miles, depending on the location. The railroad companies were free to sell this land to farmers or anyone else who wanted to buy it. The process of selling the land took decades. Some economic historians have argued that the railroad companies charged lower prices to ship freight because they owned so much land along the tracks. Briefly explain the reasoning of these economic historians.

3.11 Thomas Kinnaman, an economist at Bucknell University, has analyzed the pricing of garbage collection:

> Setting the appropriate fee for garbage collection can be tricky when there are both fixed and marginal costs of garbage collection. . . . A curbside price set equal to the average total cost of collection would have high garbage generators partially subsidizing the fixed costs of low garbage generators. For example, if the time that a truck idles outside a one-can household and a two-can household is the same, and the fees are set to cover the total cost of garbage collection, then the two-can household paying twice that of the one-can household has subsidized a portion of the collection costs of the one-can household.

Briefly explain how a city might solve this pricing problem by using a two-part tariff in setting the garbage collection fees households are charged.

Source: Thomas C. Kinnaman, "Examining the Justification for Residential Recycling," *Journal of Economic Perspectives*, Vol. 20, No. 4, Fall 2006, p. 224.

>> End Learning Objective 3

Monopolistic Competition: The Competitive Model in a More Realistic Setting

From Chapter 12 of *Microeconomics*, 2/e. R. Glenn Hubbard. Anthony Patrick O'Brien. Copyright © 2008 by Pearson Prentice Hall.

Monopolistic Competition: The Competitive Model in a More Realistic Setting

Starbucks: Growth through Product Differentiation

Starbucks coffee shops seem to be everywhere—in malls, downtown shopping districts, airports, Barnes & Noble bookstores, and practically everywhere else you can imagine. By 2007, Starbucks operated 13,000 stores worldwide, with the company planning to eventually open 40,000. More than 44 million people visit a Starbucks each week.

Like many other firms that are currently large, Starbucks started small. In 1971, entrepreneurs Gordon Bowker, Gerald Baldwin, and Zev Siegl opened the first Starbucks in Seattle. About 10 years later, they hired Howard Schultz to manage the firm's retail sales and marketing. Even though at that point the chain had only five stores, Schultz was determined to make the company first a national chain and then a worldwide chain. By 1993, Starbucks was opening stores on the East Coast, and in 1996, it opened its first store outside North America, in Tokyo, Japan. Today, Starbucks has stores in 38 countries. Schultz had achieved his dream and had become

chairman of the board and chief executive officer of the company.

Of course, fresh-brewed coffee has always been widely available in restaurants, diners, and donut shops. What Howard Schultz and the other Starbucks executives realized, however, was that a significant consumer demand existed for coffeehouses where customers could sit, relax, read newspapers, and drink higher-quality coffee than was typically served in diners or donut shops. The espresso-based coffees served at Starbucks were relatively difficult to find elsewhere during the 1990s, as Starbucks expanded nationally.

Still, Starbucks is *not* unique: You probably know of three or more coffeehouses in your neighborhood. The coffeehouse market is competitive because it is inexpensive to open a new store by leasing store space and buying espresso machines. Hundreds of firms in the United States operate coffeehouses. Some firms are large nationwide chains, such as Caribou Coffee and Diedrich Coffee, which have hundreds of stores. Others are regional chains, such as Dunn Brothers Coffee, which operates 65 stores in four states. Still others are small firms that operate only one store.

We discussed the situation of firms in perfectly competitive markets. These markets share three key characteristics:

1. There are many firms.
2. All firms sell identical products.
3. There are no barriers to new firms entering the industry.

The market Starbucks competes in shares two of these characteristics: There are many other coffeehouses—with the number increasing all the time—and the barriers to entering the market are very low. But consumers do not view the products sold by coffeehouses as being identical. The coffee at Starbucks, as well as the muffins and other snacks, are not identical to what competing coffeehouses offer. Selling coffee in coffeehouses is not like selling wheat: The products that Starbucks and its competitors sell are *differentiated* rather than identical. So, the coffeehouse market is *monopolistically competitive* rather than perfectly competitive. **AN INSIDE LOOK** explores one of the ways that businesses like Starbucks and Dunkin' Donuts attempt to differentiate themselves from the competition.

Bernard Boutrit, Woodfin Camp & Associates

Economics in YOUR Life!

Opening Your Own Restaurant

After you graduate, you plan to realize your dream of opening your own Italian restaurant. You are confident that many people will enjoy the pasta prepared with your grandmother's secret sauce. Although your hometown already has three Italian restaurants, you are convinced that you can enter this market and make a profit.

You have many choices to make in operating your restaurant. Will it be "family style," with sturdy but inexpensive furniture, where families with small—and noisy!—children will feel welcome, or will it be more elegant, with nice furniture, tablecloths, and candles? Will you offer a full menu or concentrate on just pasta dishes that use your grandmother's secret sauce? These and other choices you make will distinguish your restaurant from other competing restaurants. What's likely to happen in the restaurant market in your hometown after you open? How successful are you likely to be? See if you can answer these questions as you read this chapter. You can check your answers against those we provide at the end of the chapter.

Many markets in the U.S. economy are similar to the coffeehouse market: They have many buyers and sellers, and the barriers to entry are low, but the goods and services offered for sale are differentiated rather than identical. Examples of these markets include consumer electronics stores, restaurants, movie theaters, supermarkets, and manufacturers of men's and women's clothing. In fact, the majority of the firms you patronize are competing in **monopolistically competitive** markets.

Perfect competition benefits consumers and results in economic efficiency. Will these same desirable outcomes also hold for monopolistically competitive markets? This question, which we explore in this chapter, is important because monopolistically competitive markets are so common.

Monopolistic competition A market structure in which barriers to entry are low and many firms compete by selling similar, but not identical, products.

1 LEARNING OBJECTIVE

1 | Explain why a monopolistically competitive firm has downward-sloping demand and marginal revenue curves.

Demand and Marginal Revenue for a Firm in a Monopolistically Competitive Market

If the Starbucks coffeehouse located one mile from your house raises the price for a caffè latte from $3.00 to $3.25, it will lose some, but not all, of its customers. Some customers will switch to buying their coffee at another store, but other customers will be willing to pay the higher price for a variety of reasons: This store may be closer to them, or they may prefer Starbucks caffè lattes to similar coffees at competing stores. Because changing the price affects the quantity of caffè lattes sold, a Starbucks store will face a downward-sloping demand curve rather than the horizontal demand curve that a wheat farmer faces.

The Demand Curve for a Monopolistically Competitive Firm

Figure 1 shows how a change in price affects the quantity of caffè lattes Starbucks sells. The increase in the price from $3.00 to $3.25 decreases the quantity of caffè lattes sold from 3,000 per week to 2,400 per week.

Figure 1

The Downward-Sloping Demand for Caffè Lattes at a Starbucks

If a Starbucks increases the price of caffè lattes, it will lose some, but not all, of its customers. In this case, raising the price from $3.00 to $3.25 reduces the quantity of caffè lattes sold from 3,000 to 2,400. Therefore, unlike a perfect competitor, a Starbucks store faces a downward-sloping demand curve.

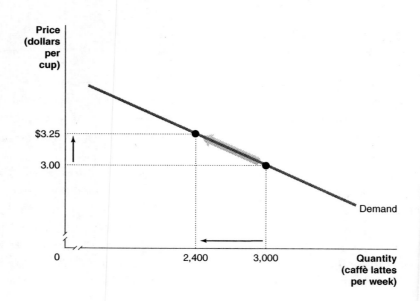

Marginal Revenue for a Firm with a Downward-Sloping Demand Curve

For a firm in a perfectly competitive market, the demand curve and the marginal revenue curve are the same. A perfectly competitive firm faces a horizontal demand curve and does not have to cut the price to sell a larger quantity. A monopolistically competitive firm, however, must cut the price to sell more, so its marginal revenue curve will slope downward and will be below its demand curve.

The data in Table 1 illustrate this point. To keep the numbers simple, let's assume that your local Starbucks coffeehouse is very small and sells at most 10 caffè lattes per week. If Starbucks charges a price of $6.00 or more, all of its potential customers will buy their coffee somewhere else. If it charges $5.50, it will sell 1 caffè latte per week. For each additional $0.50 Starbucks reduces the price, it increases the number of caffè lattes it sells by 1. The third column in the table shows how the firm's *total revenue* changes as it sells more caffè lattes. The fourth column shows the firm's revenue per unit, or its *average revenue*. Average revenue is equal to total revenue divided by quantity. Because total revenue equals price multiplied by quantity, dividing by quantity leaves just price. Therefore, *average revenue is always equal to price*. This result will be true for firms selling in any of the four market structures.

The last column shows the firm's marginal revenue, or the amount that total revenue changes as the firm sells 1 more caffè latte. For a perfectly competitive firm, the additional revenue received from selling 1 more unit is just equal to the price. That will not be true for Starbucks because to sell another caffè latte, it has to reduce the price. When the firm cuts the price by $0.50, one good thing and one bad thing happen:

- **The good thing.** It sells one more caffè latte; we can call this the *output effect*.

- **The bad thing.** It receives $0.50 less for each caffè latte that it could have sold at the higher price; we can call this the *price effect*.

Figure 2 illustrates what happens when the firm cuts the price from $3.50 to $3.00. Selling the sixth caffè latte adds the $3.00 price to the firm's revenue; this is the output effect. But Starbucks now receives a price of $3.00, rather than $3.50, on the first 5 caffè lattes sold; this is the price effect. As a result of the price effect, the firm's revenue

CAFFÈ LATTES SOLD PER WEEK (Q)	PRICE (P)	TOTAL REVENUE (TR = P × Q)	AVERAGE REVENUE $\left(AR = \dfrac{TR}{Q} \right)$	MARGINAL REVENUE $\left(MR = \dfrac{\Delta TR}{\Delta Q} \right)$
0	$6.00	$0.00	—	—
1	5.50	5.50	$5.50	$5.50
2	5.00	10.00	5.00	4.50
3	4.50	13.50	4.50	3.50
4	4.00	16.00	4.00	2.50
5	3.50	17.50	3.50	1.50
6	3.00	18.00	3.00	0.50
7	2.50	17.50	2.50	−0.50
8	2.00	16.00	2.00	−1.50
9	1.50	13.50	1.50	−2.50
10	1.00	10.00	1.00	−3.50

TABLE 1

Demand and Marginal Revenue at a Starbucks

Figure 2

How a Price Cut Affects
a Firm's Revenue

If the local Starbucks reduces the price of a caffè latte from $3.50 to $3.00, the number of caffè lattes it sells per week will increase from 5 to 6. Its marginal revenue from selling the sixth caffè latte will be $0.50, which is equal to the $3.00 additional revenue from selling 1 more caffè latte (the area of the green box) minus the $2.50 loss in revenue from selling the first 5 caffè lattes for $0.50 less each (the area of the red box).

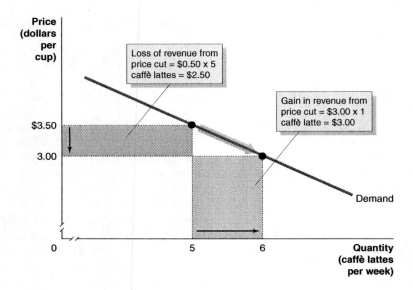

on these 5 caffè lattes is $2.50 less than it would have been if the price had remained at $3.50. So, the firm has gained $3.00 in revenue on the sixth caffè latte and lost $2.50 in revenue on the first 5 caffè lattes, for a net change in revenue of $0.50. Marginal revenue is the change in total revenue from selling one more unit. Therefore, the marginal revenue of the sixth caffè latte is $0.50. Notice that the marginal revenue of the sixth unit is far below its price of $3.00. In fact, for each additional caffè latte Starbucks sells, marginal revenue will be less than price. There is an important general point: *Every firm that has the ability to affect the price of the good or service it sells will have a marginal revenue curve that is below its demand curve.* Only firms in perfectly competitive markets, which can sell as many units as they want at the market price, have marginal revenue curves that are the same as their demand curves.

Figure 3 shows the relationship between the demand curve and the marginal revenue curve for the local Starbucks. Notice that after the sixth caffè latte, marginal

Figure 3

The Demand and Marginal
Revenue Curves for a
Monopolistically Competitive
Firm

Any firm that has the ability to affect the price of the product it sells will have a marginal revenue curve that is below its demand curve. We plot the data from Table 1 to create the demand and marginal revenue curves. After the sixth caffè latte, marginal revenue becomes negative because the additional revenue received from selling 1 more caffè latte is smaller than the revenue lost from receiving a lower price on the caffè lattes that could have been sold at the original price.

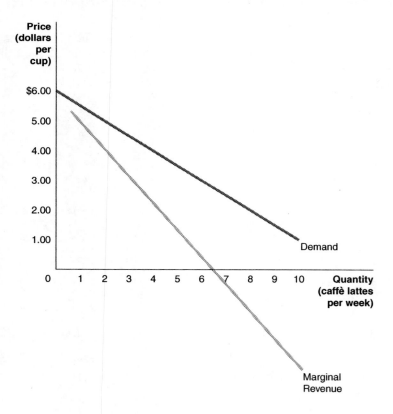

300

revenue becomes negative. Marginal revenue is negative because the additional revenue received from selling 1 more caffè latte is smaller than the revenue lost from receiving a lower price on the caffè lattes that could have been sold at the original price.

How a Monopolistically Competitive Firm Maximizes Profits in the Short Run

All firms use the same approach to maximize profits: They produce where marginal revenue is equal to marginal cost. For the local Starbucks, this means selling the quantity of caffè lattes for which the last caffè latte sold adds the same amount to the firm's revenue as to its costs. To begin our discussion of how monopolistically competitive firms maximize profits, let's consider the situation the local Starbucks faces in the short run. Recall that in the short run, at least one factor of production is fixed and there is not enough time for new firms to enter the market. A Starbucks has many costs, including the cost of purchasing the ingredients for its caffè lattes and other coffees, the electricity it uses, and the wages of its employees. Recall that a firm's *marginal cost* is the increase in total cost resulting from producing another unit of output. We have seen that for many firms, marginal cost has a U shape. We will assume that the Starbucks marginal cost has this usual shape.

In the table in Figure 4, we bring together the revenue data from Table 1 with the cost data for Starbucks. The graphs in Figure 4 plot the data from the table. In panel (a), we see how Starbucks can determine its profit-maximizing quantity and price. As long as the marginal cost of selling one more caffè latte is less than the marginal revenue, the firm should sell additional caffè lattes. For example, increasing the quantity of caffè lattes sold from 3 per week to 4 per week increases marginal cost by $1.00 but increases marginal revenue by $2.50. So, the firm's profits are increased by $1.50 as a result of selling the fourth caffè latte.

As Starbucks sells more caffè lattes, rising marginal cost eventually equals marginal revenue, and the firm sells the profit-maximizing quantity of caffè lattes. Marginal cost equals marginal revenue with the fifth caffè latte, which adds $1.50 to the firm's costs and $1.50 to its revenues—point *A* in panel (a) of Figure 4. The demand curve tells us the price at which the firm is able to sell 5 caffè lattes per week. In Figure 4, if we draw a vertical line from 5 caffè lattes up to the demand curve, we can see that the price at which the firm can sell 5 caffè lattes per week is $3.50 (point *B*). We can conclude that for Starbucks the profit-maximizing quantity is 5 caffè lattes, and its profit-maximizing price is $3.50. If the firm sells more than 5 caffè lattes per week, its profits fall. For example, selling a sixth caffè latte adds $2.00 to its costs and only $0.50 to its revenues. So, its profit would fall from $5.00 to $3.50.

Panel (b) adds the average total cost curve for Starbucks. The panel shows that the average total cost of selling 5 caffè lattes is $2.50. Recall that:

$$\text{Profit} = (P - ATC) \times Q.$$

In this case, profit = ($3.50 − $2.50) × 5 = $5.00. The green box in panel (b) shows the amount of profit. The box has a base equal to Q and a height equal to $(P - ATC)$, so its area equals profit.

Notice that, unlike a perfectly competitive firm, which produces where $P = MC$, a monopolistically competitive firm produces where $P > MC$. In this case, Starbucks is charging a price of $3.50, although marginal cost is $1.50. For the perfectly competitive firm, price equals marginal revenue, $P = MR$. Therefore, to fulfill the $MR = MC$ condition for profit maximization, a perfectly competitive firm will produce where $P = MC$. Because $P > MR$ for a monopolistically competitive firm—which results from the marginal revenue curve being below the demand curve—a monopolistically competitive firm will maximize profits where $P > MC$.

301

Caffè Lattes Sold per Week (Q)	Price (P)	Total Revenue (TR)	Marginal Revenue (MR)	Total Cost (TC)	Marginal Cost (MC)	Average Total Cost (ATC)	Profit
0	$6.00	$0.00	–	$5.00	–	–	–$5.00
1	5.50	5.50	$5.50	8.00	$3.00	$8.00	–2.50
2	5.00	10.00	4.50	9.50	1.50	4.75	0.50
3	4.50	13.50	3.50	10.00	0.50	3.33	3.50
4	4.00	16.00	2.50	11.00	1.00	2.75	5.00
5	3.50	17.50	1.50	12.50	1.50	2.50	5.00
6	3.00	18.00	0.50	14.50	2.00	2.42	3.50
7	2.50	17.50	–0.50	17.00	2.50	2.43	0.50
8	2.00	16.00	–1.50	20.00	3.00	2.50	–4.00
9	1.50	13.50	–2.50	23.50	3.50	2.61	–10.00
10	1.00	10.00	–3.50	27.50	4.00	2.75	–17.50

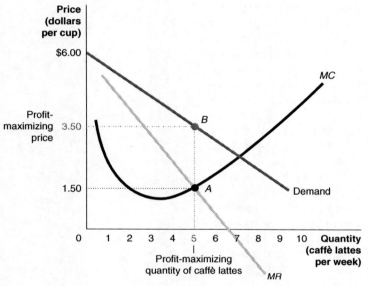

(a) Profit-maximizing quantity and price for a monopolistic competitor

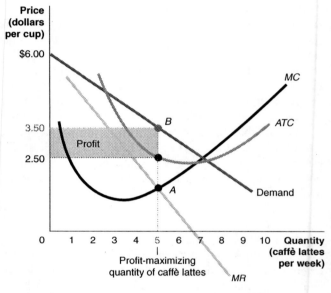

(b) Short-run profits for a monopolistic competitor

Figure 4 | Maximizing Profit in a Monopolistically Competitive Market

To maximize profit, a Starbucks coffeehouse wants to sell caffè lattes up to the point where the marginal revenue from selling the last caffè latte is just equal to the marginal cost. As the table shows, this happens with the fifth caffè latte—point A in panel (a)—which adds $1.50 to the firm's costs and $1.50 to its revenues. The firm then uses the demand curve to find the price that will lead consumers to buy this quantity of caffè lattes (point B). In panel (b), the green box represents the firm's profits. The box has a height equal to $1.00, which is the price of $3.50 minus the average total cost of $2.50, and a base equal to the quantity of 5 caffè lattes. So, this Starbucks profit equals $1 × 5 = $5.00.

Solved Problem | **2**

How Not to Maximize Profits at a Publishing Company

In an article in the *New York Times*, Virginia Postrel states that when deciding the "question of whether printing another copy of a given, already published book, is a profitable thing to do," managers at publishing firms begin by calculating the cost of printing one additional copy. But these managers "often fall prey to the mistake of adding up every expense associated with a book, including the overhead like rent and editors' salaries, and then dividing by the number of copies." Will the process described in the previous sentence give an accurate estimate of marginal cost? If you were a manager at a publishing firm, how would you determine whether producing one more copy of a book will increase your profits?

SOLVING THE PROBLEM:

Step 1: **Review the chapter material.** This problem is about how monopolistically competitive firms maximize profits, so you may want to review the section "How a Monopolistically Competitive Firm Maximizes Profits in the Short Run."

Step 2: **Analyze the costs described in the problem.** We have seen that to maximize profits, firms should produce up to the point where marginal revenue equals marginal cost. Marginal cost is the increase in total cost that results from producing another unit of output. Rent and editors' salaries are part of a publishing company's fixed costs because they do not change as the company increases its output of books. Therefore, managers at publishing companies should not include them in calculating marginal cost.

Step 3: **Explain how a manager at a publishing firm should decide whether to publish one more copy of a book.** To determine whether producing one more copy of a book will increase your profits, you need to compare the marginal revenue received from selling the book with the marginal cost of producing it. If the marginal revenue is greater than the marginal cost, producing the book will increase your profits.

Source: Virginia Postrel, "Often, Basic Concepts in Economics Are Taken for Granted," *New York Times*, January 3, 2002.

YOUR TURN: For more practice, do related problem 2.9 at the end of this chapter.

>> **End Solved Problem 2**

3 | Analyze the situation of a monopolistically competitive firm in the long run.

What Happens to Profits in the Long Run?

Remember that a firm makes an economic profit when its total revenue is greater than all of its costs, including the opportunity cost of the funds invested in the firm by its owners. Because cost curves include the owners' opportunity costs, the Starbucks coffeehouse represented in Figure 4 is making an economic profit. This economic profit gives entrepreneurs an incentive to enter this market and establish new firms. If a Starbucks is earning economic profit selling caffè lattes, new coffeehouses are likely to open in the same area.

How Does the Entry of New Firms Affect the Profits of Existing Firms?

As new coffeehouses open near the local Starbucks, the firm's demand curve will shift to the left. The demand curve will shift because Starbucks will sell fewer caffè lattes at each price when there are additional coffeehouses in the area selling similar drinks. The demand curve will also become more elastic because consumers have additional coffeehouses from which to buy coffee, so Starbucks will lose more sales if it raises its prices. Figure 5 shows how the demand curve for the local Starbucks shifts as new firms enter its market.

In panel (a) of Figure 5, the short-run demand curve shows the relationship between the price of caffè lattes and the quantity of caffè lattes Starbucks sells per week before the entry of new firms. With this demand curve, Starbucks can charge a price above average total cost—shown as point *A* in panel (a)—and make a profit. But this profit attracts additional coffeehouses to the area and shifts the demand curve for the Starbucks caffè lattes to the left. As long as Starbucks is making an economic profit, there is an incentive for additional coffeehouses to open in the area, and the demand curve will continue

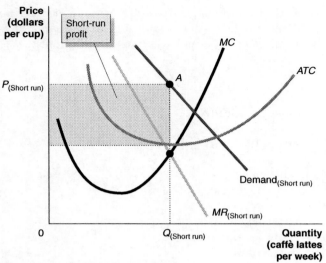

(a) A monopolistic competitor may earn a short-run profit

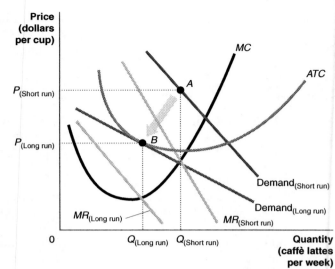

(b) A monopolistic competitor's profits are eliminated in the long run

Figure 5 | How Entry of New Firms Eliminates Profits

In the short run—panel (a)—the local Starbucks faces the demand and marginal revenue curves labeled "Short run." With this demand curve, Starbucks can charge a price above average total cost (point A) and make a profit, shown by the green rectangle. But this profit attracts new firms to enter the market, which shifts the demand and marginal revenue curves to the ones labeled "Long run" in panel (b). Because price is now equal to average total cost (point B), Starbucks breaks even and no longer earns an economic profit.

shifting to the left. As panel (b) shows, eventually the demand curve will have shifted to the point where it is just touching—or tangent to—the average cost curve.

In the long run, at the point at which the demand curve is tangent to the average cost curve, price is equal to average total cost (point B), the firm is breaking even, and it no longer earns an economic profit. In the long run, the demand curve is also more elastic because the more coffeehouses there are in the area, the more sales Starbucks will lose to other coffeehouses if it raises its price.

Of course, it is possible that a monopolistically competitive firm will suffer economic losses in the short run. As a consequence, the owners of the firm will not be covering the opportunity cost of their investment. We expect that, in the long run, firms will exit an industry if they are suffering economic losses. If firms exit, the demand curve for the output of a remaining firm will shift to the right. This process will continue until the representative firm in the industry is able to charge a price equal to its average cost and break even. Therefore, in the long run, monopolistically competitive firms will experience neither economic profits nor economic losses. Table 2 summarizes the short run and the long run for a monopolistically competitive firm.

Don't Let This Happen to **YOU!**

Don't Confuse Zero Economic Profit with Zero Accounting Profit

Remember that economists count the opportunity cost of the owner's investment in a firm as a cost. For example, suppose you invest $200,000 opening a pizza parlor, and the return you could earn on those funds each year in a similar investment—such as opening a sandwich shop—is 10 percent. Therefore, the annual opportunity cost of investing the funds in your own business is 10 percent of $200,000, or $20,000.

This $20,000 is part of your profit in the accounting sense, and you would have to pay taxes on it. But in an economic sense, the $20,000 is a cost. In long-run equilibrium, we would expect that entry of new firms would keep you from earning more than 10 percent on your investment. So, you would end up breaking even and earning zero economic profit, even though you were earning an accounting profit of $20,000.

YOUR TURN: Test your understanding by doing related problem 3.4 at the end of this chapter.

304

TABLE 2 | The Short Run and the Long Run for a Monopolistically Competitive Firm

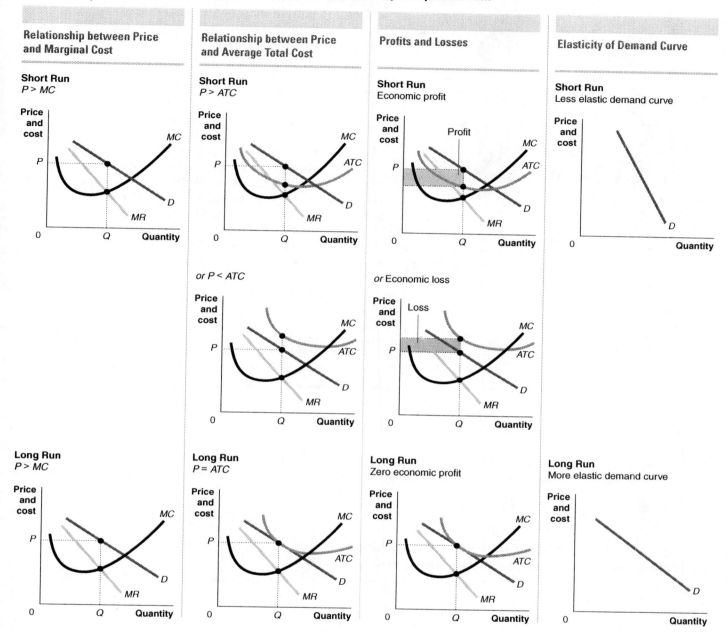

Relationship between Price and Marginal Cost	Relationship between Price and Average Total Cost	Profits and Losses	Elasticity of Demand Curve
Short Run P > MC	**Short Run** P > ATC	**Short Run** Economic profit	**Short Run** Less elastic demand curve
	or P < ATC	or Economic loss	
Long Run P > MC	**Long Run** P = ATC	**Long Run** Zero economic profit	**Long Run** More elastic demand curve

Making the Connection

The Rise and Fall of Apple's Macintosh Computer

In 1983, there were more than 15 firms selling personal computers nationally, as well as many smaller firms in local markets selling computers assembled from purchased components. None of these personal computers operated using the current system of clicking on icons with a mouse. Instead, users had to type in commands to call up word processing, spreadsheet, and other software programs. This awkward system required users to memorize many commands or constantly consult computer manuals. In January 1984, Apple Computer introduced the Macintosh, which used a mouse and could be operated by clicking on icons. The average cost of producing Macintoshes was about $500. Apple sold them for prices between $2,500 and $3,000. This price was more than twice that

Macintosh lost its differentiation, but still has a loyal—if relatively small—following.

of comparable personal computers sold by IBM and other companies, but the Macintosh was so easy to use that it was able to achieve a 15 percent share of the market. Apple had successfully introduced a personal computer that was strongly differentiated from its competitors. One journalist covering the computer industry has gone so far as to call the Macintosh "the most important consumer product of the last half of the twentieth century."

Microsoft produced the operating system known as MS-DOS (for Microsoft disk operating system), which most non-Apple computers used. The financial success of the Macintosh led Microsoft to develop an operating system that would also use a mouse and icons. In 1992, Microsoft introduced the operating system Windows 3.1, which succeeded in reproducing many of the key features of the Macintosh. By August 1995, when Microsoft introduced Windows 95, non-Apple computers had become as easy to use as Macintosh computers. By that time, most personal computers operated in a way very similar to the Macintosh, and Apple was no longer able to charge prices that were significantly above those that its competitors charged. The Macintosh had lost its differentiation. Although the Macintosh (now known as the iMac) continues to have a loyal following, particularly among graphic designers, today it has only a 6 percent share of the personal computer market.

Source for quote: Steven Levy, *Insanely Great: The Life and Times of Macintosh, the Computer that Changed Everything*, New York: Viking, 1994, p. 7.

YOUR TURN: Test your understanding by doing related problem 3.5 at the end of this chapter.

Solved Problem | 3

The Short Run and the Long Run for the Macintosh

Use the information in *Making the Connection* to draw a graph that shows changes in the market for Macintosh computers between 1984 and 1995.

SOLVING THE PROBLEM:

Step 1: **Review the chapter material.** This problem is about how the entry of new firms affected the market for the Macintosh, so you may want to review the section "How Does the Entry of New Firms Affect the Profits of Existing Firms?"

Step 2: **Draw the graph.** The *Making the Connection* about Apple indicates that in 1984, when the Macintosh was first introduced, its differentiation from other computers allowed Apple to make a substantial economic profit. In 1995, the release of Windows 95 meant that non-Macintosh computers were as easy to use as Macintosh computers. Apple's product differentiation was eliminated, as was its ability to earn economic profits. The change over time in Apple's situation is shown in the following graph, which combines panels (a) and (b) from Figure 5 in one graph.

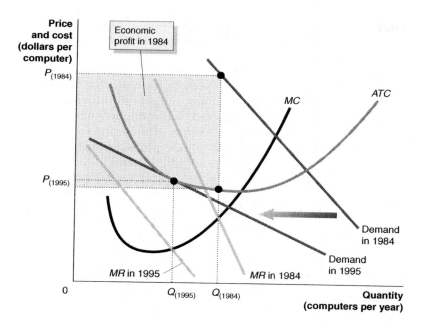

Between 1984 and 1995, Microsoft's development of the Windows operating system eliminated Macintosh's product differentiation. The demand curve for Macintosh shifted to the left and became more elastic throughout the relevant range of prices.

EXTRA CREDIT: Note that this analysis is simplified. The Macintosh of 1995 was a different—and better—computer than the Macintosh of 1984. Apple has made changes to the Macintosh, such as the introduction of the colorful iMac computer in 1999, that have sometimes led to increases in sales. The great success of the Apple iPod has also lead some consumers to switch to Apple computers. But the Macintosh has never been able to regain the high demand and premium prices it enjoyed from the mid-1980s to the early 1990s.

YOUR TURN: For more practice, do related problem 3.6 at the end of this chapter.

>> End Solved Problem 3

Is Zero Economic Profit Inevitable in the Long Run?

The economic analysis of the long run shows the effects of market forces over time. In the case of Starbucks, the effect of market forces is to eliminate the economic profit earned by a monopolistically competitive firm. Owners of monopolistically competitive firms, of course, do not have to passively accept this long-run result. The key to earning economic profits is either to sell a differentiated product or to find a way of producing an existing product at a lower cost. If a monopolistically competitive firm selling a differentiated product is earning profits, these profits will attract the entry of additional firms, and the entry of those firms will eventually eliminate the firm's profits. If a firm introduces new technology that allows it to sell a good or service at a lower cost, competing firms will eventually be able to duplicate that technology and eliminate the firm's profits. *But this result holds only if the firm stands still and fails to find new ways of differentiating its product or fails to find new ways of lowering the cost of producing its product.* Firms continually struggle to find new ways of differentiating their products as they try to stay one step ahead of other firms that are attempting to copy their success. As new coffeehouses enter the area served by the Starbucks coffeehouse, the owners can expect to see their economic profits competed away, unless they can find ways to differentiate their product.

In 2007, Howard Schultz, the chairman of Starbucks, was well aware of this fact. In opening thousands of coffeehouses worldwide, he worried that Starbucks had made the customer experience less distinctive and easier for competitors to copy. Starbucks has used various strategies to differentiate itself from competing coffeehouses. Competitors have found it difficult to duplicate the European espresso bar atmosphere of Starbucks, with its large, comfortable chairs; music playing; and groups of friends dropping in and out during the day. Most importantly, Starbucks has continued to be very responsive to its customers' preferences. As one observer put it, "How many retailers could put up with 'I'll have a grande low-fat triple-shot half-caf white-chocolate mocha, extra hot, easy on the whipped cream. And I'm in a rush'?" But Howard Schultz was worried. In a memo sent to employees, he wrote, "Over the past ten years, in order to achieve the growth, development, and scale necessary to go from less than 1,000 stores to 13,000 stores . . . we have had to make a series of decisions that . . . have led to the watering down of the Starbucks experience." Starbucks has begun serving breakfast sandwiches and installing drive-through windows that make its stores appear similar to other fast-food restaurants. Although at one time Starbucks had been able to maintain greater control over the operations of its coffeehouses, because unlike many of its competitors, all of its coffeehouses were company owned, it now has thousands of *franchises*. A franchise is a business with the legal right to sell a good or service in a particular area. When a firm uses franchises, local businesspeople are able to buy and run the stores in their area. This makes it easier for a firm to finance its expansion but forces the firm to give up some control over its stores.

Starbucks experienced great success during the 1990s and the early 2000s, but history shows that in the long run, competitors will be able to duplicate most of what it does. In the face of that competition, it will be very difficult for Starbucks to continue earning economic profits. As Howard Schultz put it, "Competitors of all kinds, small and large coffee companies, fast food operators, and mom and pops, [have positioned] themselves in a way that creates awareness . . . and loyalty of people who previously have been Starbucks customers." He concluded, "I have said for 20 years that our success is not an entitlement and now it's proving to be a reality."

The owner of a competitive firm is in a position similar to that of Ebenezer Scrooge in Charles Dickens's *A Christmas Carol*. When the Ghost of Christmas Yet to Come shows Scrooge visions of his own death, he asks the ghost, "Are these the shadows of the things that Will be, or are they shadows of things that May be, only?" The shadow of the end of their profits haunts owners of every firm. Firms try to avoid losing profits by reducing costs, by improving their products, or by convincing consumers their products are indeed different from what competitors offer. To stay one step ahead of its competitors, a firm has to offer consumers goods or services that they perceive to have greater *value* than those offered by competing firms. Value can take the form of product differentiation that makes the good or service more suited to consumers' preferences, or it can take the form of a lower price.

Making the Connection	**Staying One Step Ahead of the Competition: Eugène Schueller and L'Oréal**

Today, L'Oréal, with headquarters in the Paris suburb of Clichy, is the largest seller of perfumes, cosmetics, and hair care products in the world. In addition to L'Oréal, its brands include Lancôme, Maybelline, Soft Sheen/Carson, Garnier, Redken, Ralph Lauren, and Matrix. Like most other large firms, L'Oréal was started by an entrepreneur with an idea. Eugène Schueller was a French chemist who experimented in the evenings trying to find a safe and reliable hair coloring for women. In 1907, he founded the firm that became L'Oréal and began selling his hair coloring preparations to Paris hair salons. Schueller was able to take advantage of changes in fashion. In the early twentieth century, women began to cut their hair much shorter than had been typical in the nineteenth century, and it had become socially acceptable to spend time and money styling it. The number of hair salons in Europe and the United States increased rapidly. By the 1920s and 1930s, the international popularity of Hollywood films, many starring "platinum blonde bombshells" such as Jean Harlow, made it fashionable for women to color their hair. By the late 1920s, L'Oréal was selling its products throughout Europe, the United States, and Japan.

Unlike many monopolistically competitive firms, L'Oréal has earned economic profits for a very long time.

Perfumes, cosmetics, and hair coloring are all products that should be easy for rival firms to duplicate. We would expect, then, that the economic profits L'Oréal earned in its early years would have been competed away in the long run through the entry of new firms. In fact, though, the firm has remained profitable through the decades, following a strategy of developing new products, improving existing products, and expanding into new markets. For example, when French workers first received paid holidays during the 1930s, L'Oréal moved quickly to dominate the new market for suntan lotion. Today, the firm's SoftSheen brand is experiencing rapid sales increases in Africa. When L'Oréal launched a new line of men's skin-care products, including shaving cream, one analyst observed that at L'Oréal, "brands don't stay at home serving the same old clientele. They get spruced up, put in a new set of traveling clothes, and sent abroad to meet new customers." L'Oréal has maintained its ability to innovate by spending more on research and development than do competing firms. The firm has a research staff of more than 1,000.

One reason L'Oréal has been able to follow a focused strategy is that the firm has had only three chairmen in its nearly century of existence: founder Eugène Schueller, François Dalle, and Lindsay Owen-Jones, who became chairman in 1988. Owen-Jones has described the firm's strategy: "Each brand is positioned on a very precise [market] segment, which overlaps as little as possible with the others." The story of L'Oréal shows that it is possible for a firm to stay one step ahead of the competition, but it takes top management committed to an entrepreneurial spirit of continually developing new products.

Source for quotes: Richard Tomlinson, "L'Oréal's Global Makeover," *Fortune*, September 30, 2002.

YOUR TURN: Test your understanding by doing related problem 3.9 at the end of this chapter.

---

4 | Compare the efficiency of monopolistic competition and perfect competition.

4 LEARNING OBJECTIVE

Comparing Perfect Competition and Monopolistic Competition

We have seen that monopolistic competition and perfect competition share the characteristic that in long-run equilibrium, firms earn zero economic profits. As Figure 6 shows, however, there are two important differences between long-run equilibrium in the two markets:

- Monopolistically competitive firms charge a price greater than marginal cost.

- Monopolistically competitive firms do not produce at minimum average total cost.

Excess Capacity under Monopolistic Competition

Recall that a firm in a perfectly competitive market faces a perfectly elastic demand curve that is also its marginal revenue curve. Therefore, the firm maximizes profit by producing where price equals marginal cost. As panel (a) of Figure 6 shows, in

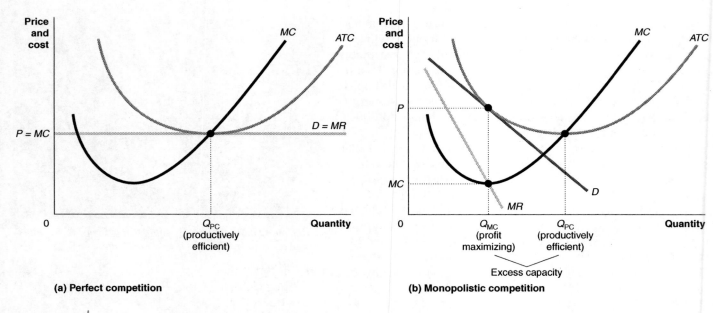

Figure 6 | Comparing Long-Run Equilibrium under Perfect Competition and Monopolistic Competition

In panel (a), the perfectly competitive firm in long-run equilibrium produces at Q_{PC}, where price equals marginal cost, and average total cost is at a minimum. The perfectly competitive firm is both allocatively efficient and productively efficient. In panel (b), the monopolistically competitive firm produces at Q_{MC}, where price is greater than marginal cost, and average total cost is not at a minimum. As a result, the monopolistically competitive firm is neither allocatively efficient nor productively efficient. The monopolistically competitive firm has excess capacity equal to the difference between its profit-maximizing level of output and the productively efficient level of output.

long-run equilibrium, a perfectly competitive firm produces at the minimum point of its average total cost curve.

Panel (b) of Figure 6 shows that the profit-maximizing level of output for a monopolistically competitive firm comes at a level of output where price is greater than marginal cost and the firm is not at the minimum point of its average total cost curve. A monopolistically competitive firm has *excess capacity*: If it increased its output, it could produce at a lower average cost.

Is Monopolistic Competition Inefficient?

Productive efficiency refers to the situation where a good is produced at the lowest possible cost. Allocative efficiency refers to the situation where every good or service is produced up to the point where the last unit provides a marginal benefit to consumers equal to the marginal cost of producing it. For productive efficiency to hold, firms must produce at the minimum point of average total cost. For allocative efficiency to hold, firms must charge a price equal to marginal cost. In a perfectly competitive market, both productive efficiency and allocative efficiency are achieved, but in a monopolistically competitive market, neither is achieved. Does it matter? Economists have debated whether monopolistically competitive markets being neither productively nor allocatively efficient results in a significant loss of well-being to society in these markets compared with perfectly competitive markets.

How Consumers Benefit from Monopolistic Competition

Looking again at Figure 6, you can see that the only difference between the monopolistically competitive firm and the perfectly competitive firm is that the demand curve for the monopolistically competitive firm slopes downward, whereas the demand curve for the perfectly competitive firm is a horizontal line. The demand curve for the monopolistically competitive firm slopes downward because the good or service the firm is selling is differentiated from the goods or services being sold by competing firms. The perfectly competitive firm is selling a good or service identical to those being sold by its competitors. A key point to remember is that *firms differentiate their products to appeal to consumers.* When Starbucks coffeehouses begin offering new flavors of coffee, when Blockbuster stores begin carrying more HD-DVDs and fewer regular DVDs, when General Mills introduces Apple-Cinnamon Cheerios, or when PepsiCo introduces caffeine-free Diet Pepsi, they are all attempting to attract and retain consumers through product differentiation. The success of these product differentiation strategies indicates that some consumers find these products preferable to the alternatives. Consumers, therefore, are better off than they would have been had these companies not differentiated their products.

We can conclude that consumers face a trade-off when buying the product of a monopolistically competitive firm: They are paying a price that is greater than marginal cost, and the product is not being produced at minimum average cost, but they benefit from being able to purchase a product that is differentiated and more closely suited to their tastes.

Making the Connection

Abercrombie & Fitch: Can the Product Be Too Differentiated?

Business managers often refer to differentiating their products as finding a "market niche." The larger the niche you have, the greater the potential profit but the more likely that other firms will be able to compete against you. Too small a niche, however, may reduce competition— but also reduce profits. Some analysts believe that the market niche chosen by the managers of the Abercrombie & Fitch clothing stores is too small. The chief executive, Mike Jeffries, argues that his store's target customer is an "18-to-22 [year old] college guy who has a good body and is aspirational." He admits that this is a narrow niche: "If I exclude people—absolutely. Delighted to do so."

But is A&F excluding too many people? One analyst argues "they've . . . pushed a lot of people out of the brand." A&F's sales results seemed to indicate that this analyst may be correct. Managers of retail stores closely monitor "same-store sales," which measures how much sales have increased in the same stores from one year to the next. To offset the effects of inflation—or general increases in prices in the economy—same-store sales need to increase at least 2 percent to 3 percent each year. A firm whose strategy of product differentiation succeeds will experience increases in same-store sales of at least 5 percent to 6 percent each year. For several years in the early 2000s, A&F's 350 stores experienced *negative* same-store results. Although sales increased from 2004 through early 2006, negative changes in same-store sales returned in late 2006 and continued through mid 2007. A&F may have gone too far in narrowing its market niche.

James A. Finley, AP Wide World Photos

Did Abercrombie and Fitch narrow its target market too much?

Sources: James Covert, "Retail Sales Slide Fuels Concern," *Wall Street Journal*, May 11, 2007; and Shelly Branch, "Maybe Sex Doesn't Sell, A&F Is Discovering," *Wall Street Journal*, December 12, 2003.

YOUR TURN: Test your understanding by doing related problem 4.6 at the end of this chapter.

---

5 | Define marketing and explain how firms use it to differentiate their products.

How Marketing Differentiates Products

Firms can differentiate their products through marketing. **Marketing** refers to all the activities necessary for a firm to sell a product to a consumer. Marketing includes activities such as determining which product to produce, designing the product, advertising the product, deciding how to distribute the product—for example, in retail stores or

Marketing All the activities necessary for a firm to sell a product to a consumer.

through a Web site—and monitoring how changes in consumer tastes are affecting the market for the product. Peter F. Drucker, a leading business strategist, describes marketing as follows: "It is the whole business seen from the point of view of its final result, that is, from the consumer's point of view. . . . True marketing . . . does not ask, 'What do we want to sell?' It asks, 'What does the consumer want to buy?'"

As we have seen, for monopolistically competitive firms to earn economic profits and to defend those profits from competitors, they must differentiate their products. Firms use two marketing tools to differentiate their products: brand management and advertising.

Brand Management

Brand management The actions of a firm intended to maintain the differentiation of a product over time.

Once a firm has succeeded in differentiating its product, it must try to maintain that differentiation over time through **brand management**. As we have seen, whenever a firm successfully introduces a new product or a significantly different version of an old product, it earns economic profits in the short run. But the success of the firm inspires competitors to copy the new or improved product and, in the long run, the firm's economic profits will be competed away. Firms use brand management to postpone the time when they will no longer be able to earn economic profits.

Advertising

An innovative advertising campaign can make even long-established and familiar products, such as Coke or McDonald's Big Mac hamburgers, seem more desirable than competing products. When a firm advertises a product, it is trying to shift the demand curve for the product to the right and to make it more inelastic. If the firm is successful, it will sell more of the product at every price, and it will be able to increase the price it charges without losing as many customers. Of course, advertising also increases a firm's costs. If the increase in revenue that results from the advertising is greater than the increase in costs, the firm's profits will rise.

Needless to say, advertising campaigns are not always successful. In 1957, the Ford Motor Company introduced a new car, the Edsel, designed to compete with the Buick from General Motors. Ford set up a new division of the company to produce the Edsel in five different models and hired the advertising firm of Foote, Cone & Belding to direct a massive advertising campaign. Among other things, Ford purchased an hour of prime television time on the CBS network to broadcast *The Edsel Show*, hosted by Frank Sinatra, Bing Crosby, and Louis Armstrong, three of the biggest stars of the 1950s. Ford set a sales goal of 200,000 cars during the first year of production. Unfortunately, most of the car-buying public found the styling of the Edsel, with its oversized headlights and elaborate front grill, unappealing. First-year sales were only about 63,000 cars. During the same period, General Motors sold more than 230,000 Buicks. Ford decided to shift its advertising account for the Edsel from Foote, Cone & Belding to Kenyon & Eckhardt. Despite a revised advertising campaign, sales of the Edsel remained very low. Ford sold fewer than 45,000 Edsels during the car's second year of production. In November 1959, after only two years in production, Ford stopped making the Edsel. Even one of the largest advertising campaigns in history had failed to make the Edsel successful.

Defending a Brand Name

Once a firm has established a successful brand name, it has a strong incentive to defend it. A firm can apply for a *trademark*, which grants legal protection against other firms using its product's name.

One threat to a trademarked name is the possibility that it will become so widely used for a type of product that it will no longer be associated with the product of a specific company. Courts in the United States have ruled that when this happens, a firm is no longer entitled to legal protection of the brand name. For example, "aspirin," "escalator," and "thermos" were originally all brand names of the products of particular firms, but each became so widely used to refer to a type of product that none remains a legally protected brand name. Firms spend substantial amounts of money trying to make sure that this does not happen to them. Coca-Cola, for example, employs workers to travel around the country stopping at restaurants and asking to be served a "Coke" with their meal. If the restaurant serves Pepsi or some other cola, rather than Coke, Coca-Cola's legal department sends the restaurant a letter reminding that "Coke" is a trademarked name and not a generic name for any cola. Similarly, Xerox Corporation spends money on advertising to remind the public that "Xerox" is not a generic term for making photocopies.

Legally enforcing trademarks can be difficult. Estimates are that each year, U.S. firms lose hundreds of billions of dollars in sales worldwide as a result of unauthorized use of their trademarked brand names. U.S. firms often find it difficult to enforce their trademarks in the courts of some foreign countries, although recent international agreements have increased the legal protections for trademarks.

Firms that sell their products through franchises rather than through company-owned stores encounter the problem that if a franchisee does not run his or her business well, the firm's brand may be damaged. Automobile firms send "roadmen" to visit their dealers to make sure the dealerships are clean and well maintained and that the service departments employ competent mechanics and are well equipped with spare parts. Similarly, McDonald's sends employees from corporate headquarters to visit McDonald's franchises to make sure the bathrooms are clean and the French fries are hot.

6 | Identify the key factors that determine a firm's success.

6 LEARNING OBJECTIVE

What Makes a Firm Successful?

A firm's owners and managers control some of the factors that make a firm successful and allow it to earn economic profits. The most important of these are the firm's ability to differentiate its product and to produce its product at a lower average cost than competing firms. A firm that successfully does these things creates *value* for its customers. Consumers will buy a product if they believe it meets a need not met by competing products or if its price is below that of competitors.

Some factors that affect a firm's profitability are not directly under the firm's control. Certain factors will affect all the firms in a market. For example, rising prices for jet fuel will reduce the profitability of all airlines. If consumers decide that they would rather watch pay-for-view movies delivered to their homes by cable or satellite than buy DVDs, the profitability of all stores selling DVDs will be reduced.

Sheer chance also plays a role in business, as it does in all other aspects of life. A struggling McDonald's franchise may see profits increase dramatically after the county unexpectedly decides to build a new road nearby. Many businesses in New York City, including restaurants, hotels, and theaters, experienced a marked drop in customers and profits following the September 11, 2001, terrorist attacks. Figure 7 illustrates the important point that factors within the firm's control and factors outside the firm's control interact to determine the firm's profitability.

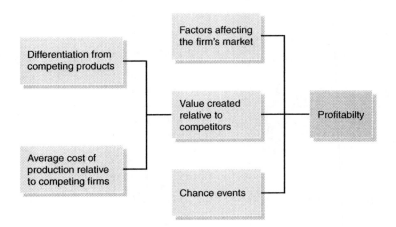

Figure 7

What Makes a Firm Successful?

The factors under a firm's control—the ability to differentiate its product and the ability to produce it at lower cost—combine with the factors beyond its control to determine the firm's profitability.

Source: Adapted from Figure 11.3 in David Besanko, David Dranove, Mark Shanley, and Scott Schaefer, *The Economics of Strategy*, 4th ed., New York: Wiley, 2007.

Making the Connection

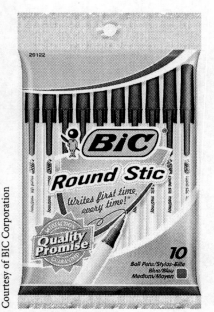

Although not first to market, Bic ultimately was more successful than the firm that pioneered ballpoint pens.

Is Being the First Firm in the Market a Key to Success?

Some business analysts argue that the first firm to enter a market can have important *first-mover advantages*. By being the first to sell a particular good, a firm may find its name closely associated with the good in the public's mind, as, for instance, Amazon is closely associated with ordering books online or eBay is associated with online auctions. This close association may make it more difficult for new firms to enter the market and compete against the first mover.

Surprisingly, though, recent research has shown that the first firm to enter a market often does *not* have a long-lived advantage over later entrants. Consider, for instance, the market for pens. Until the 1940s, the only pens available were fountain pens that had to be refilled frequently from an ink bottle and used ink that dried slowly and smeared easily. In October 1945, entrepreneur Milton Reynolds introduced the first ballpoint pen, which never needed to be refilled. When it went on sale at Gimbel's department store in New York City, it was an instant success. Although the pen had a price of $12.00—the equivalent of about $135.00 at today's prices—hundreds of thousands were sold, and Milton Reynolds became a millionaire. Unfortunately, it didn't last. Although Reynolds had guaranteed that his pen would write for two years—later raised to five years—in fact, the pen often leaked and frequently stopped writing after only limited use. Sales began to collapse, the flood of pens returned under the company's guarantee wiped out its profits, and within a few years, Reynolds International Pen Company stopped selling pens in the United States. By the late 1960s, firms such as Bic selling inexpensive—but reliable—ballpoint pens dominated the market.

What happened to the Reynolds International Pen Company turns out to be more the rule than the exception. For example, Apple's iPod was not the first digital music player to appear on the U.S. market. Both Seahan's MPMan and Diamond's PMP300 were released in the United States in 1998, three years before the iPod. Similarly, although Hewlett-Packard currently dominates the market for laser printers, with a market share of more than 50 percent, it did not invent the laser printer. Xerox invented the laser printer, and IBM sold the first commercial laser printers. Nor was Procter & Gamble the first firm to sell disposable diapers when it introduced Pampers in 1961. Microsoft's Internet Explorer was not the first Web browser: Before Internet Explorer, there was Netscape; before Netscape, there was Mosaic; and before Mosaic, there were several other Web browsers that for a time looked as if they might dominate the market. In all these cases, the firms that were first to introduce a product ultimately lost out to latecomers who did a better job of providing consumers with products that were more reliable, less expensive, more convenient, or otherwise provided greater value.

Sources: Steven P. Schnaars, *Managing Imitation Strategies: How Later Entrants Seize Markets from Pioneers*, New York: The Free Press, 1994; and Gerard J. Tellis and Peter N. Golder, *Will and Vision: How Latecomers Grow to Dominate Markets*, Los Angeles: Figueroa Press, 2002.

YOUR TURN: Test your understanding by doing related problem 6.6 at the end of this chapter.

Economics in YOUR Life!

At the beginning of the chapter, we asked you to think about how successful you are likely to be in opening an Italian restaurant in your hometown. As you learned in this chapter, if your restaurant is successful, other people are likely to open competing restaurants, and all your economic profits will eventually disappear. This occurs because economic profits attract entry of new firms into a market. The new restaurants will sell Italian food, but it won't be exactly like your Italian food—after all, they don't have your grandmother's secret recipe! Each restaurant will have its own ideas on how best to appeal to people who like Italian food. Unless your food is so different from the food competing restaurants offer that your consumers will continue to pay higher prices for your food, you probably won't earn an economic profit in the long run.

In a monopolistically competitive market, free entry will lead to zero economic profits in the long run. But competition will also lead firms to offer somewhat different versions of the same product; for example, two Italian restaurants will rarely be exactly alike.

Conclusion

In this chapter, we have applied many ideas about competition to the common market structure of monopolistic competition. We have seen that these ideas apply to monopolistically competitive markets, just as they do to perfectly competitive markets. The competitive forces of the market impose relentless pressure on firms to produce new and better goods and services at the lowest possible cost. Firms that fail to adequately anticipate changes in consumer tastes or that fail to adopt the latest and most efficient production technology do not survive in the long run. These conclusions are as true for coffeehouses and firms in other monopolistically competitive markets as they are for wheat farmers or apple growers.

Read *An Inside Look* on the next page for a discussion of how Starbucks and Dunkin' Donuts each try to differentiate their product and services.

Can Dunkin' Donuts Really Compete with Starbucks?

WALL STREET JOURNAL, APRIL 8, 2006

Brewing Battle: Dunkin' Donuts Tries to Go Upscale, but Not too Far

Dunkin' Donuts last year paid dozens of faithful customers in Phoenix, Chicago and Charlotte, N.C., $100 a week to buy coffee at Starbucks instead. At the same time, the no-frills coffee chain paid Starbucks customers to make the opposite switch.

When it later debriefed the two groups, Dunkin' says it found them so polarized that company researchers dubbed them "tribes"—each of whom loathed the very things that made the other tribe loyal to their coffee shop. Dunkin' fans viewed Starbucks as pretentious and trendy, while Starbucks loyalists saw Dunkin' as austere and unoriginal.

"I don't' get it," one Dunkin' regular told researchers after visiting Starbucks. "If I want to sit on a couch, I stay at home."

(a) Bridging some of that divide—but not too much—is key to Dunkin' Donuts' ambitious plan to expand its largely Eastern coffee chain into a national powerhouse that's as synonymous with coffee as Starbucks Corp., the nation's largest coffee chain. Armed with fresh capital from December's $2.43 billion private-equity buyout of Dunkin' Brands Inc., Dunkin' plans to remake its nearly 5,000 U.S. stores over the next three years and have triple that number in less than 15 years. . . .

(b) While executives of Canton, Mass.-based Dunkin' insist they aren't trying to emulate their Seattle rival, Dunkin's store makeovers include some similarities to Starbucks. A prototype Dunkin' store in Euclid, Ohio, outside Cleveland, features rounded granite-style coffee bars where workers make espresso drinks face-to-face with customers. Open-air pastry cases brim with yogurt parfaits and fresh fruit while a carefully orchestrated pop-music soundtrack is piped throughout. . . .

Yet Dunkin' built itself on serving simple fare to working-class customers. Inching upscale without alienating that base is proving tricky. There will be no couches in the new stores. And Dunkin' renamed a new hot sandwich a "stuffed melt" after customers complained that calling it a "panini" was too fancy.

Some customers "have remarked along the lines of 'You're trying to be somebody else,'" says Ryan Humphrey, who oversees Dunkin' franchisees in the Cleveland area. Regina Lewis, the chain's vice president, consumer and brand insights, says, "We're walking that line. The thing about the Dunkin' tribe is, they see through the hype."

Anne Saunders, Starbucks senior vice president, global brand, says Starbucks doesn't focus on Dunkin' Donuts as a competitor. While competitors may use elements of its strategy, they can't recreate Starbucks' "unique and differentiated concept," she says. . . .

Company researchers set out to determine whether Dunkin' could draw consumers in new cities, and how to lure customers from fast-food chains, coffee houses and convenience stores. "Consumers love environments," Mr. Luther (Dunkin's Chief Executive) says. "We have to move our environment where the customer is."

(c) Early research showed customers wanted nicer stores, but revealed a potential problem: the loyal Dunkin' tribe was bewildered and turned off by the atmosphere at Starbucks. They groused that crowds of laptop users made it difficulty to find a seat, Dunkin' says. They didn't like Starbucks' "tall," "grande" and "venti" lingo for small, medium and large coffees. And, Dunkin' says, they couldn't understand why anyone would pay as much as $4 for a cup of coffee. . . .

Dunkin' researchers concluded that it wasn't income that set the two tribes apart, as much as an ideal: Dunkin' tribe members wanted to be part of a crowd, while members of the Starbucks tribe had a desire to stand out as individuals. "The Starbucks tribe, they seek out things to make them feel more important," Ms. Lewis says. Members of the Dunkin' Donuts tribe "don't need to be any more important than they are." . . .

Bernard Boutrit, Woodfin Camp & Associates

Key Points in the Article

This article discusses an attempt by Dunkin' Donuts to appeal to some of Starbucks' customers. As we have seen in this chapter, when a firm successfully differentiates its product, its competitors do their best to copy it. Starbucks has experienced great success by reinventing the coffeehouse. But the article notes that many Starbucks customers see Dunkin' Donuts stores as "austere and unoriginal." As Dunkin' Donuts begins to expand nationwide, it is redesigning its stores to make them more like Starbucks. As this chapter has shown, once consumers show they want a particular good or service, firms will compete to offer it to them.

Analyzing the News

a Currently, upscale coffeehouses like Starbucks are earning an economic profit. This would suggest that an existing firm could be represented by point A in the figure selling Q_1 cups of coffee and charging a price of P_1 dollars. The profit-maximizing quantity is found at the point where the marginal revenue curve MR_1 intersects the marginal cost curve MC. The price is determined by the demand curve. The firm is earning economic profits equal to the shaded area. The economic profits earned by coffeehouses like Starbucks explains why as Dunkin' Donuts expands nationwide, it has been building stores that are more upscale than its older stores.

b Dunkin' Donuts is trying to capture the feel of a Starbucks' store in order to attract customers who may like some of the elements of Starbucks, but who may also like some of the elements of Dunkin' Donuts. Dunkin' Donuts will never attract loyal Starbucks' customers, but they do hope to attract customers who like some features about Starbucks but who may prefer a different environment and food selection. As the figure shows, new entrants in a market will take some demand away from current firms in the market. This causes the demand curve to shift to the left from demand curve D_1 to demand curve D_2. The marginal revenue curve also shifts to the left (from MR_1 to MR_2).

The profit-maximizing level of output is now Q_2, where the new marginal revenue curve intersects the marginal cost curve, MC. The new profit maximizing price is P_2. Notice that at this point the demand curve D_2 is tangent to the average total cost curve ATC and the firm is earning zero profits. At equilibrium, all firms in the market will earn zero profits. This is shown as point E in the figure.

c This section illustrates why product differentiation is important in a market. While customers at Dunkin' Donuts and Starbucks are looking for similar products—coffee and food—there are important differences between the customers that cause them to shop at one coffee shop over another. Those who are in the Starbucks tribe or the Dunkin' Donuts tribe are unlikely to go to another coffee shop. There may, however, be a third tribe looking for a home.

Thinking Critically

1. Suppose the government required a license to open a coffeehouse and that the number of licenses was limited. How would this new requirement affect the equilibrium market price and quantity in the coffeehouse market? Who would gain from this requirement, and who would lose?

2. Suppose that the number of people in the Dunkin' Donuts tribe increases as people begin to prefer donuts with their coffee rather than couches. How would Starbucks likely respond to this change in tastes?

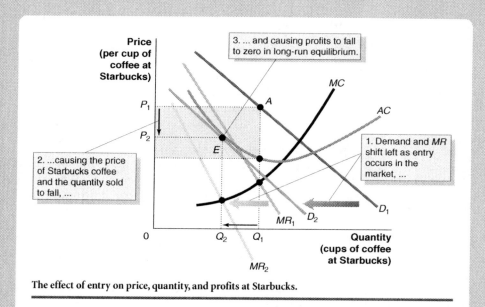

The effect of entry on price, quantity, and profits at Starbucks.

Key Terms

Brand management   Monopolistic competition

Marketing

Demand and Marginal Revenue for a Firm in a Monopolistically Competitive Market

Summary

A firm competing in a **monopolistically competitive** market sells a differentiated product. Therefore, unlike a firm in a perfectly competitive market, it faces a downward-sloping demand curve. When a monopolistically competitive firm cuts the price of its product, it sells more units but must accept a lower price on the units it could have sold at the higher price. As a result, its marginal revenue curve is downward sloping. Every firm that has the ability to affect the price of the good or service it sells will have a marginal revenue curve that is below its demand curve.

 Visit www.myeconlab.com to complete these exercises online and get instant feedback.

Review Questions

1.1 What are the most important differences between perfectly competitive markets and monopolistically competitive markets? Give two examples of products sold in perfectly competitive markets and two examples of products sold in monopolistically competitive markets.

1.2 Why does the local McDonald's face a downward-sloping demand curve for Big Macs? If it raises the price it charges for Big Macs above the prices charged by other McDonald's stores, won't it lose all its customers?

1.3 Explain the differences between total revenue, average revenue, and marginal revenue.

Problems and Applications

1.4 Complete the following table:

DVDS RENTED PER WEEK (Q)	PRICE (P)	TOTAL REVENUE (TR = P × Q)	AVERAGE REVENUE (AR = TR/Q)	MARGINAL REVENUE (MR = ΔTR/ΔQ)
0	$8.00			
1	7.50			
2	7.00			
3	6.50			
4	6.00			
5	5.50			
6	5.00			
7	4.50			
8	4.00			

1.5 A student makes the following argument:

> When a firm sells another unit of a good, the additional revenue the firm receives is equal to the price: If the price is $10, then the additional revenue is also $10. Therefore, this chapter is incorrect when it says that marginal revenue is less than price for a monopolistically competitive firm.

Briefly explain whether you agree with this argument.

1.6 There are many wheat farms in the world, but there are also many Starbucks coffeehouses. Why, then, does a Starbucks coffeehouse face a downward-sloping demand curve when a wheat farmer faces a horizontal demand curve?

1.7 Is it possible for marginal revenue to be negative for a firm selling in a perfectly competitive market? Would a firm selling in a monopolistically competitive market ever produce where marginal revenue is negative?

How a Monopolistically Competitive Firm Maximizes Profits in the Short Run

Summary

A monopolistically competitive firm maximizes profits at the level of output where marginal revenue equals marginal cost. Price equals marginal revenue for a perfectly competitive firm, but price is greater than marginal revenue for a monopolistically competitive firm. Therefore, unlike a perfectly competitive firm, which produces where $P = MC$, a monopolistically competitive firm produces where $P > MC$.

myeconlab Visit www.myeconlab.com to complete these exercises online and get instant feedback.

Review Questions

2.1 Sally runs a McDonald's franchise. She is selling 350 Big Macs per week at a price of $3.25. If she lowers the price to $3.20, she will sell 351 Big Macs. What is the marginal revenue of the 351st Big Mac?

2.2 Sam runs a Hollywood Video store. Sam is currently renting 3,525 DVDs per week. If instead of renting 3,525 DVDs, he rents 3,526 DVDs, he will add $2.95 to his costs and $2.75 to his revenues. What will be the effect on his profits of renting 3,526 DVDs instead of 3,525 DVDs?

2.3 Should a monopolistically competitive firm take into account its fixed costs when deciding how much to produce? Briefly explain.

Problems and Applications

2.4 If Daniel sells 350 Big Macs at a price of $3.25, and his average cost of producing 350 Big Macs is $3.00, what is his profit?

2.5 Alicia manages a Hollywood Video store and has the following information on demand and costs:

DVDS RENTED PER WEEK (Q)	PRICE (P)	TOTAL COST (TC)
0	$6.00	$3.00
1	5.50	7.00
2	5.00	10.00
3	4.50	12.50
4	4.00	14.50
5	3.50	16.00
6	3.00	17.00
7	2.50	18.50
8	2.00	21.00

a. To maximize profit, how many DVDs should Alicia rent, what price should she charge, and how much profit will she make?

b. What is the marginal revenue received by renting the profit-maximizing DVD? What is the marginal cost of renting the profit-maximizing DVD?

2.6 A trucking company investigates the relationship between the gas mileage of its trucks and the average speed at which the trucks are driven on the highway. The company finds the relationship shown in the following graph:

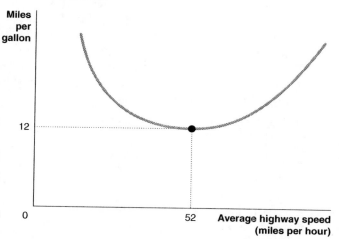

Will the firm maximize profits if it instructs its drivers to maintain an average speed of 52 miles per hour? Briefly explain.

2.7 The following is from an article in the *Wall Street Journal*: "Krispy Kreme Doughnuts Inc. reported its profit fell 56% in its second quarter despite an 11% increase in revenue." Briefly explain how it is possible for a firm's revenue to increase at the same time its profits decrease.

Source: "Krispy Kreme's Net Falls 56%; Company Cuts Sales Forecast," *Wall Street Journal*, August 26, 2004.

2.8 During 2003, General Motors cut the prices of most of its car models. As a result, GM earned a profit of only $184 per car, compared to the profit of $555 per car it had earned in 2002. Does the decline in GM's profits per car indicate that cutting prices was not a profit-maximizing strategy? Briefly explain.

Source: Karen Lundegaard and Sholnn Freeman, "Detroit's Challenge: Weaning Buyers from Years of Deals," *Wall Street Journal*, January 6, 2004.

2.9 **(Related to Solved Problem 2)** William Germano is vice president and publishing director at the Routledge publishing company. He has given the following description of how a publisher might deal with an unexpected increase in the cost of publishing a book:

> It's often asked why the publisher can't simply raise the price [if costs increase]. . . . It's likely that the editor [is already] . . . charging as much as the market will bear. . . . In other words, you might be willing to pay $50.00 for a . . . book on the Brooklyn Bridge, but if . . . production costs [increase] by 25 percent, you might think $62.50 is too much to pay, though that would be what the publisher needs to charge. And indeed the publisher may determine that $50.00 is this book's ceiling—the most you would pay before deciding to rent a movie instead.

According to what you have learned in this chapter, how do firms adjust the price of a good when there is an increase in cost? Use a graph to illustrate your answer. Does the model of monopolistic competition seem to fit Germano's description? If a publisher does not raise the price of a book following an increase in its production cost, what will be the result?

Source: William Germano, *Getting It Published: A Guide to Scholars and Anyone Else Serious about Serious Books*, Chicago: University of Chicago Press, 2001, pp. 110–111.

2.10 The following excerpt is from an article in the *Wall Street Journal*:

> [Amazon.com], whose sales stagnated last year, increased revenue [this quarter] by 21 percent, to $806 million. . . . It attributed the increase to its price-cutting strategy: discounting books that cost more than $15 each and offering free shipping on orders of at least $49.

a. If Amazon.com's revenue increased after it cut the price of books, what must be true about the price elasticity of demand for ordering books online?

b. Suppose that before the price cut, Amazon.com was not selling the profit-maximizing quantity of books, but after the price cut, it was. Draw a graph that shows Amazon.com's situation before and after the price cut. (For simplicity, assume that Amazon charges the same price for all books.) Be sure your graph includes the price Amazon was charging and the quantity of books it was selling before the price cut; the price and quantity after the price cut; Amazon's demand, marginal revenue, average total cost, and marginal cost curves; and the areas representing Amazon's profits before and after the price cut.

Source: Saul Hansell, "Citing Its Price Strategy, Amazon Pares Loss," *Wall Street Journal*, July 24, 2002.

2.11 In 1916, the Ford Motor Company produced 500,000 Model T Fords at a price of $440 each. The company made a profit of $60 million that year. Henry Ford told a newspaper reporter that he intended to reduce the price of the Model T to $360, and he expected to sell 800,000 cars at that price. Ford said, "Less profit on each car, but more cars, more employment of labor, and in the end we get all the total profit we ought to make."

a. Did Ford expect the total revenue he received from selling Model Ts to rise or fall following the price cut?

b. Use the information given above to calculate the price elasticity of demand for Model Ts. Use the midpoint formula to make your calculation. If you need a refresher on the midpoint formula.

c. What would the average total cost of producing 800,000 Model Ts have to be for Ford to make as much profit selling 800,000 Model Ts as it made selling 500,000 Model Ts? Is this smaller or larger than the average total cost of producing 500,000 Model Ts?

d. Assume that Ford would make the same total profit when selling 800,000 cars as when selling 500,000 cars. Was Henry Ford correct in saying he would make less profit per car when selling 800,000 cars than when selling 500,000 cars?

>> End Learning Objective 2

3 LEARNING OBJECTIVE 3 | Analyze the situation of a monopolistically competitive firm in the long run

What Happens to Profits in the Long Run?

Summary

If a monopolistically competitive firm is earning economic profits in the short run, entry of new firms will eliminate those profits in the long run. If a monopolistically competitive firm is suffering economic losses in the short run, exit of existing firms will eliminate those losses in the long run. Monopolistically competitive firms continually struggle to find new ways of differentiating their products as they try to stay one step ahead of other firms that are attempting to copy their success.

Visit www.myeconlab.com to complete these exercises online and get instant feedback.

Review Questions

3.1 What effect does the entry of new firms have on the economic profits of existing firms?

3.2 What is the difference between zero accounting profit and zero economic profit.

Problems and Applications

3.3 Use this graph to answer the questions that follow.

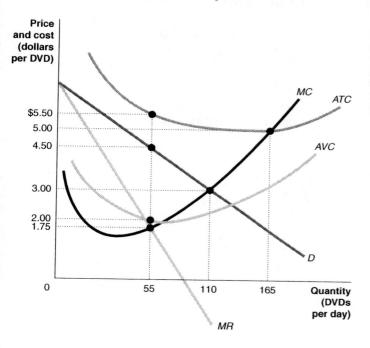

a. If the owner of this video store wants to maximize profits, how many DVDs should she rent per day, and what rental price should she charge? Briefly explain your answer.

b. How much economic profit (or loss) is she making? Briefly explain.

c. Is the owner likely to continue renting this number of DVDs in the long run? Briefly explain.

3.4 (Related to the *Don't Let This Happen to You!*) A student remarks:

> If firms in a monopolistically competitive industry are earning economic profits, new firms will enter the industry. Eventually, the representative firm will find its demand curve has shifted to the left until it is just tangent to its average cost curve and it is earning zero profit. Because firms are earning zero profit at that point, some firms will leave the industry and the representative firm will

find its demand curve will shift to the right. In long-run equilibrium, price will be above average total cost by just enough so that each firm is just breaking even.

Briefly explain whether you agree with this analysis.

3.5 (Related to the *Making the Connection*) Writing in the *Wall Street Journal,* Walter Mossberg argues:

> But the new popularity of the [Macintosh computer] is also partly due to the fact that it can now run Windows along with Apple's superior Mac OS X operating system. That means that if there's a program you need that comes only in a Windows version, you can run it on any current Mac model, speedily and with all its features.

If it is an advantage to Apple that the Macintosh can now run Windows as well as the Mac operating system, would Apple be even better off if it abandoned its own operating system and installed only Windows on the computers it sells?

Source: Walter S. Mossberg, "Fusion is the Latest Way for Macs to Run Windows, PC Software," *Wall Street Journal,* August 2, 2007.

3.6 (Related to *Solved Problem 3*) Michael Porter, an economist at Harvard Business School, argues that firms in the U.S. commercial-printing industry have been "investing heavily in the same new equipment, running their presses faster, and reducing crew sizes. But the resulting major productivity gains are being captured by customers and equipment suppliers, not retained in superior profitability." How would consumers gain from these productivity increases? Why haven't the productivity increases made the printing firms more profitable?

Source: Michael E. Porter, "What Is Strategy?" *Harvard Business Review,* November–December 1996, p. 63.

3.7 Michael Korda was, for many years, editor-in-chief at the Simon & Schuster book publishing company. He has written about the many books that have become bestsellers by promising to give readers financial advice that will make them wealthy, by, for example, buying and selling real estate. Korda is very skeptical about the usefulness of the advice in these books because "I have yet to meet anybody who got rich by buying a book, though quite a few people got rich by writing one." On the basis of the analysis in this chapter, discuss why it may be very difficult to become rich by following the advice found in a book.

Source: Michael Korda, *Making the List: A Cultural History of the American Bestseller, 1900–1999,* New York: Barnes & Noble Books, 2001, p. 168.

3.8 (Related to the *Chapter Opener*) According to an article in *Fortune* magazine, "The big question for [Starbucks' chairman] Howard Schultz is whether Starbucks can keep it up. There are those on Wall

Street who say that Starbucks' game is almost over." What do you think the article means by "Starbucks' game is almost over"? Why would some people on Wall Street be making this prediction about a firm that was making substantial economic profits at the time the article was written?

Source: Andy Serwer, "Hot Starbucks to Go," *Fortune*, January 12, 2004.

3.9 (Related to the *Making the Connection*) L'Oreal devotes significant resources to developing new products and differentiating its products from those of its competitors. Suppose it did not do that. What would be the effect on its profits in the short run? What would be the effect on its profits in the long run?

>> **End Learning Objective 3**

4 LEARNING OBJECTIVE   4 | Compare the efficiency of monopolistic competition and perfect competition

Comparing Perfect Competition and Monopolistic Competition

Summary

Perfectly competitive firms produce where price equals marginal cost and at minimum average total cost. Perfectly competitive firms achieve both allocative and productive efficiency. Monopolistically competitive firms produce where price is greater than marginal cost and above minimum average total cost. Monopolistically competitive firms do not achieve either allocative or productive efficiency. Consumers face a trade-off when buying the product of a monopolistically competitive firm: They are paying a price that is greater than marginal cost, and the product is not being produced at minimum average cost, but they benefit from being able to purchase a product that is differentiated and more closely suited to their tastes.

myeconlab Visit www.myeconlab.com to complete these exercises *Get Ahead of the Curve* online and get instant feedback.

Review Questions

4.1 What are the differences between the long-run equilibrium of a perfectly competitive firm and the long-run equilibrium of a monopolistically competitive firm?

4.2 Does the fact that monopolistically competitive markets are not allocatively or productively efficient mean that there is a significant loss in economic well-being to society in these markets? In your answer, be sure to define what you mean by "economic well-being."

Problems and Applications

4.3 A student asks the following question:

> I can understand why a perfectly competitive firm will not earn profits in the long run because a perfectly competitive firm charges a price equal to marginal cost. But

a monopolistically competitive firm can charge a price greater than marginal cost, so why can't it continue to earn profits in the long run?

How would you answer this question?

4.4 Consider the following graph.

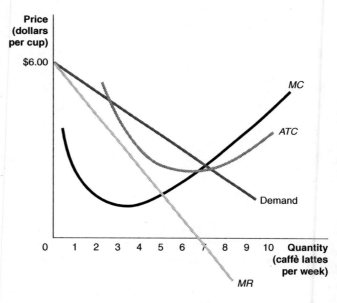

a. Is it possible to say whether this firm is a perfectly competitive firm or a monopolistically competitive firm? If so, explain how you are able to say this.

b. Does the graph show a short-run equilibrium or a long-run equilibrium? Briefly explain.

c. What quantity on the graph represents long-run equilibrium if the firm were perfectly competitive?

4.5 Before the fall of Communism, most basic consumer products in Eastern Europe and the Soviet Union were standardized. For example, government-run stores would offer for sale only one type of bar soap or one type of toothpaste. Soviet economists often argued that this system of standardizing basic consumer products avoided the waste associated with the differentiated goods and services produced in Western Europe and the United States. Do you agree with this argument?

4.6 **(Related to the *Making the Connection*)** Juicy Couture has been successful in selling women's clothing using an unusual strategy. According to an article in the *Wall Street Journal* the key to the firm's strategy is to "Limit distribution to maintain the brand's exclusive cachet, even if that means sacrificing sales, a brand-management technique once used only for high-end luxury brands." In 2006, Juicy clothes were sold in only four department stores: Neiman Marcus, Saks, Bloomingdale's, and Nordstrom. Although Juicy was originally known mainly for the fashion tracksuits it sold, "Juicy Couture doesn't just make tracksuits favored by

celebrities any more. With its edgy contemporary sportswear and accessories, it has become a lifestyle brand for women, men and kids with estimated annual sales of more than $300 million, up from $47 million in 2002. . . . "

a. Why would limiting the number of stores your product was sold in be a successful strategy for a clothing firm? What would be likely to happen to Juicy's sales if it began to sell its clothes at Wal-Mart and similar stores?

b. Compared with the situation Apple Computer faced during the mid 1980s, is Juicy more or less likely to be able to maintain its product differentiation over a long period of time?

Source: Rachel Dodes, "From Track Suits to Fast Track," *Wall Street Journal*, September 13, 2006.

>> **End Learning Objective 4**

---

5 LEARNING OBJECTIVE 5 | Define marketing and explain how firms use it to differentiate their products

How Marketing Differentiates Products

Summary

Marketing refers to all the activities necessary for a firm to sell a product to a consumer. Firms use two marketing tools to differentiate their products: brand management and advertising. **Brand management** refers to the actions of a firm intended to maintain the differentiation of a product over time. When a firm has established a successful brand name, it has a strong incentive to defend it. A firm can apply for a *trademark*, which grants legal protection against other firms using its product's name.

myeconlab Visit www.myeconlab.com to complete these exercises online and get instant feedback.

Review Questions

5.1 Define marketing. Is marketing just another name for advertising?

5.2 Why are many companies so concerned about brand management?

Problems and Applications

5.3 Draw a graph that shows the impact on a firm's profits when it increases spending on advertising and the increased advertising has *no* effect on the demand for the firm's product.

5.4 A skeptic says, "Marketing research and brand management are redundant. If a company wants to find out what customers want, it should simply look at what they're already buying." Do you agree with this comment? Explain.

5.5 The National Football League (NFL) has a trademark on the name "Super Bowl" for its championship game. Advertisers can only use the words Super Bowl in their advertising if they pay the NFL a fee. Many companies attempt to get around this trademark by using the phrase "the big game" in their advertising. For example, just before the Super Bowl is to be played a consumer electronics store might have an advertisement with the phrase "Watch the big game on a new HD TV." In 2007, the National Football League indicated that it might attempt legal action to have the phrase "the big game" included in its Super Bowl trademark.

a. Why does the government allow firms to trademark their products?

b. Would consumers gain or lose if the NFL were allowed to trademark the phrase "the big game"? Briefly explain.

5.6 Some companies have done a poor job protecting their products' images. For example, Hormel's Spam brand name is widely ridiculed and has escaped from the company's control in cyberspace. Think of other cases where companies have failed to protect their brand names. What can they do about it now? Should they re-brand their products?

>> **End Learning Objective 5**

What Makes a Firm Successful?

Summary

A firm's owners and managers control some of the factors that determine the profitability of the firm. Other factors affect all the firms in the market or are the result of chance, so they are not under the control of the firm's owners. The interactions between factors the firm controls and factors it does not control determine its profitability.

 Visit www.myeconlab.com to complete these exercises online and get instant feedback.

Review Questions

6.1 What are the key factors that determine the profitability of a firm in a monopolistically competitive market?

6.2 How might a monopolistically competitive firm continually earn economic profit greater than zero?

Problems and Applications

6.3 According to an article in the *Wall Street Journal*:

> In early January last year, after a disappointing Christmas season and amid worries about competition from discount retailers, Zale Corp. decided to shake things up: The self-proclaimed jeweler to Middle America was going to chase upscale customers. . . . The move was a disaster. The Irving, Texas, retailer lost many of its traditional customers without winning the new ones it coveted.

Why would a firm like Zale abandon one market niche for another market niche? We know that in this case the move was not successful. Can you think of other cases where it has been successful?

Source: Ann Zimmerman and Kris Hudson, "Chasing Upscale Customers Tarnishes Mass-Market Jeweler," *Wall Street Journal*, June 26, 2006, p. A1.

6.4 7-Eleven, Inc., operates more than 20,000 convenience stores worldwide. Edward Moneypenny, 7-Eleven's chief financial officer, was asked to name the biggest risk the company faced. He replied, "I would say that the biggest risk that 7-Eleven faces, like all retailers, is competition . . . because that is something that you've got to be aware of in this business." In what sense is competition a "risk" to a business? Why would a company in the retail business need to be particularly aware of competition?

Source: Company Report, CEO Interview: Edward Moneypenny—7-Eleven, Inc., The Wall Street Transcript Corporation.

6.5 In 2006, Wal-Mart closed its stores in South Korea and Germany. According to an article in the *New York Times*:

> Wal-Mart's most successful markets, like Mexico, are those in which it started big. There, the company bought the country's largest and best-run retail chain, Cifra, and has never looked back. This year, Wal-Mart is spending more than $1 billion in Mexico to open 120 new stores.

What advantages does Wal-Mart gain from buying large retail chains, as it did in Mexico, rather than small chains, as it did in its unsuccessful attempts to enter the South Korean and German markets?

Source: Mark Landler and Michael Barbaro, "Wal-Mart Finds That Its Formula Doesn't Fit Every Culture," *New York Times*, August 2, 2006.

6.6 **(Related to the *Making the Connection*)** A firm that is first to the market with a new product frequently discovers that there are design flaws or problems with the product that were not anticipated. For example, the ballpoint pens made by the Reynolds International Pen Company often leaked. What effect do these problems have on the innovating firm and how do these unexpected problems open up possibilities for other firms to enter the market?

>> End Learning Objective 6

Firms in Perfectly Competitive Markets

From Chapter 11 of *Microeconomics*, 2/e. R. Glenn Hubbard. Anthony Patrick O'Brien. Copyright © 2008 by Pearson Prentice Hall.

Firms in Perfectly Competitive Markets

Perfect Competition in the Market for Organic Apples

The market for organically grown food has expanded rapidly in the United States. As recently as 15 years ago, organic food was sold primarily in small health food stores. By the 2000s, sales of organic foods were growing at a rate of more than 20 percent per year, and organic foods were available in nearly every supermarket. In 2002, the U.S. Department of Agriculture (USDA) established standards for organic food labeling. The standards were intended to protect consumers from false and misleading claims and to make it easier for U.S. farmers to export to foreign countries whose governments also require organic food labeling. According to the USDA, a firm can label and advertise food as "organic" only if that food is "produced without using most conventional pesticides; fertilizers made with synthetic ingredients or sewage sludge; bioengineering; or ionizing radiation."

Organically grown apples became popular with consumers during the late 1990s. Farmers growing apples organically use only organic fertilizers and control insects with sprays made from soil compounds. These growing methods add about 15 percent to the cost of growing apples. The Yakima Valley of Washington State is particularly suited to growing apples organically because of the absence of certain insects. In 1997, Yakima Valley apple farmers were able to sell organically grown apples for a price 50 percent higher than the price of regular apples, more than offsetting the higher costs of organic growing methods. This price difference made organically grown apples considerably more profitable than apples grown using traditional methods.

Between 1997 and 2001, many apple farmers switched from traditional to organic growing methods, increasing production of organically grown apples from 1.2 million boxes per year to more than 3 million boxes. The additional supply of organically grown apples forced down prices and made them no more profitable than apples grown using traditional meth-

ods. As one farmer in the Yakima Valley put it, "It's like anything else in agriculture. If people see an economic opportunity, usually it only lasts for a few years." AN INSIDE LOOK discusses how an organic farmer in South Dakota responds to large firms like Wal-Mart entering the market for organic foods.

What the organic apple farmers in the Yakima Valley experienced is not unique to agriculture. Throughout the economy, entrepreneurs are continually introducing new products, which—when successful—enable them to earn economic profits in the short run. But in the long run, competition among firms force prices to the level where they just cover the costs of production. This process of competition is at the heart of the market system and is the focus of this chapter.

Sources: Lydia Oberholtzer, Carolyn Dimitri, and Catherine Greene, "Price Premiums Hold on as U.S. Organic Produce Market Expands," Agricultural Economic Report No. VGS-308-01, Economic Research Service, U.S. Department of Agriculture, May 2005; Emily Green, "Study Gives Nod to Organic Apples, but It's Crunch Time for All State Growers," Seattle Times, April 19, 2001; quote from farmer from All Things Considered, National Public Radio, www.npr.org, April 18, 2001.

© Bob Daemmrich/The Image Works

LEARNING Objectives

After studying this chapter, you should be able to:

1 Define a **perfectly competitive market** and explain why a perfect competitor faces a **horizontal demand curve**.

2 Explain how a **firm maximizes profits** in a perfectly competitive market.

3 Use **graphs** to show a firm's **profit or loss**.

4 Explain why firms may **shut down** temporarily.

5 Explain how **entry** and **exit** ensure that perfectly competitive firms earn **zero economic profit** in the long run.

6 Explain how **perfect competition** leads to **economic efficiency**

Economics in YOUR Life!

Are You an Entrepreneur?

Were you an entrepreneur during your high school years? Perhaps you didn't have your own store, but you may have worked as a babysitter, or perhaps you mowed lawns for families in your neighborhood. While you may not think of these jobs as being small businesses, that is exactly what they are. How did you decide what price to charge for your services? You may have wanted to charge $25 per hour to babysit or mow lawns, but you probably charged much less. As you read the chapter, think about the competitive situation you faced as a teenaged entrepreneur and try to determine why the prices received by most people who babysit and mow lawns are so low. You can check your answers against those we provide at the end of the chapter.

Organic apple growing is an example of a *perfectly competitive* industry. Firms in perfectly competitive industries are unable to control the prices of the products they sell and are unable to earn an economic profit in the long run. There are two main reasons for this result: Firms in these industries sell identical products, and it is easy for new firms to enter these industries. Studying how perfectly competitive industries operate is the best way to understand how markets answer the fundamental economic questions:

- What goods and services will be produced?

- How will the goods and services be produced?

- Who will receive the goods and services produced?

In fact, though, most industries are not perfectly competitive. In most industries, firms do *not* produce identical products, and in some industries, it may be difficult for new firms to enter. There are thousands of industries in the United States. Although in some ways each industry is unique, industries share enough similarities that economists group them into four market structures. In particular, any industry has three key characteristics:

- The number of firms in the industry

- The similarity of the good or service produced by the firms in the industry

- The ease with which new firms can enter the industry

Economists use these characteristics to classify industries into the four market structures listed in Table 1.

Many industries, including restaurants, hardware stores, and other retailers, have a large number of firms selling products that are differentiated, rather than identical, and fall into the category of *monopolistic competition*. Some industries, such as computers and automobiles, have only a few firms and are *oligopolies*. Finally, a few industries, such as the delivery of first-class mail by the U.S. Postal Service, have only one firm and are *monopolies*. After discussing perfect competition in this chapter, we will devote a chapter to each of these other market structures.

TABLE 1 | The Four Market Structures

	MARKET STRUCTURE			
CHARACTERISTIC	PERFECT COMPETITION	MONOPOLISTIC COMPETITION	OLIGOPOLY	MONOPOLY
Number of firms	Many	Many	Few	One
Type of product	Identical	Differentiated	Identical or differentiated	Unique
Ease of entry	High	High	Low	Entry blocked
Examples of industries	• Wheat • Apples	• Selling DVDs • Restaurants	• Manufacturing computers • Manufacturing automobiles	• First-class mail delivery • Tap water

1 | Define a perfectly competitive market and explain why a perfect competitor faces a horizontal demand curve.

Perfectly Competitive Markets

Why are firms in a **perfectly competitive market** unable to control the prices of the goods they sell, and why are the owners of these firms unable to earn economic profits in the long run? We can begin our analysis by listing the three conditions that make a market perfectly competitive:

1 There must be many buyers and many firms, all of whom are small relative to the market.

2 The products sold by all firms in the market must be identical.

3 There must be no barriers to new firms entering the market.

All three of these conditions hold in the market for organic apples. No single consumer or producer of organic apples buys or sells more than a tiny fraction of the total apple crop. The apples sold by each apple grower are identical, and there are no barriers to a new firm entering the organic apple market by purchasing land and planting apple trees. As we will see, it is the existence of many firms, all selling the same good, that keeps any single organic apple farmer from affecting the price of organic apples.

Although the market for organic apples meets the conditions for perfect competition, the markets for most goods and services do not. In particular, the second and third conditions are very restrictive. In most markets that have many buyers and sellers, firms do not sell identical products. For example, not all restaurant meals are the same, nor is all women's clothing the same. In this chapter, we concentrate on perfectly competitive markets so we can use as a benchmark the situation in which firms are facing the maximum possible competition.

> **Perfectly competitive market**
> A market that meets the conditions of (1) many buyers and sellers, (2) all firms selling identical products, and (3) no barriers to new firms entering the market.

A Perfectly Competitive Firm Cannot Affect the Market Price

Prices in perfectly competitive markets are determined by the interaction of demand and supply. The actions of any single consumer or any single firm have no effect on the market price. Consumers and firms have to accept the market price if they want to buy and sell in a perfectly competitive market.

Because a firm in a perfectly competitive market is very small relative to the market and because it is selling exactly the same product as every other firm, it can sell as much as it wants without having to lower its price. But if a perfectly competitive firm tries to raise its price, it won't sell anything at all because consumers will switch to buying from the firm's competitors. Therefore, the firm will be a **price taker** and will have to charge the same price as every other firm in the market. Although we don't usually think of firms as being too small to affect the market price, consumers are often in the position of being price takers. For instance, suppose your local supermarket is selling bread for $1.50 per loaf. You can load up your shopping cart with 10 loaves of bread, and the supermarket will gladly sell them all to you for $1.50 per loaf. But if you go to the cashier and offer to buy the bread for $1.49 per loaf, he or she will not sell it to you. As a buyer, you are too small relative to the bread market to have any effect on the equilibrium price. Whether you leave the supermarket and buy no bread or you buy 10 loaves, you are unable to change the market price of bread by even 1 cent.

The situation you face as a bread buyer is the same one a wheat farmer faces as a wheat seller. More than 225,000 farmers grow wheat in the United States. The market price of wheat is determined not by any individual wheat farmer but by the interaction

> **Price taker** A buyer or seller that is unable to affect the market price.

Figure 1

A firm in a perfectly competitive market is selling exactly the same product as many other firms. Therefore, it can sell as much as it wants at the current market price, but it cannot sell anything at all if it raises the price by even 1 cent. As a result, the demand curve for a perfectly competitive firm's output is a horizontal line. In the figure, whether the wheat farmer sells 3,000 bushels per year or 7,500 bushels has no effect on the market price of $4.

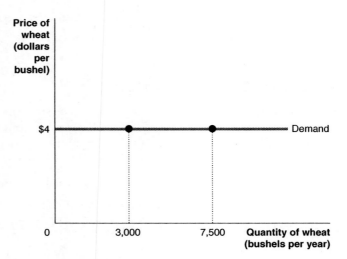

in the wheat market of all the buyers and all the sellers. If any one wheat farmer has the best crop the farmer has ever had, or if any one wheat farmer stops growing wheat altogether, the market price of wheat will not be affected *because the market supply curve for wheat will not shift by enough to change the equilibrium price by even 1 cent.*

The Demand Curve for the Output of a Perfectly Competitive Firm

Suppose Bill Parker grows wheat on a 250-acre farm in Washington State. Farmer Parker is selling wheat in a perfectly competitive market, so he is a price taker. Because he can sell as much wheat as he chooses at the market price—but can't sell any wheat at all at a higher price—the demand curve for his wheat has an unusual shape: It is horizontal, as shown in Figure 1. With a horizontal demand curve, Farmer Parker must accept the market price, which in this case is $4. Whether Farmer Parker sells 3,000 bushels per year or 7,500 has no effect on the market price.

The demand curve for Farmer Parker's wheat is very different from the market demand curve for wheat. Panel (a) of Figure 2 shows the market for wheat. The demand

Don't Let This Happen to **YOU!**

Don't Confuse the Demand Curve for Farmer Parker's Wheat with the Market Demand Curve for Wheat

The demand curve for wheat has the normal downward-sloping shape. If the price of wheat goes up, the quantity of wheat demanded goes down, and if the price of wheat goes down, the quantity of wheat demanded goes up. But the demand curve for the output of a single wheat farmer is *not* downward sloping: It is a horizontal line. If an individual wheat farmer tries to increase the price he charges for his wheat, the quantity demanded falls to zero because buyers will purchase from one of the other 225,000 wheat farmers. But any one farmer can sell as much wheat as the farmer can produce without needing to cut the price. Both of these

things are true because each wheat farmer is very small relative to the overall market for wheat.

When we draw graphs of the wheat market, we usually show the market equilibrium quantity in millions or billions of bushels. When we draw graphs of the demand for wheat produced by one farmer, we usually show the quantity produced in smaller units, such as thousands of bushels. It is important to remember this difference in scale when interpreting these graphs.

Finally, it is not just wheat farmers who have horizontal demand curves for their products; any firm in a perfectly competitive market faces a horizontal demand curve.

YOUR TURN: Test your understanding by doing related problem 1.6 at the end of this chapter.

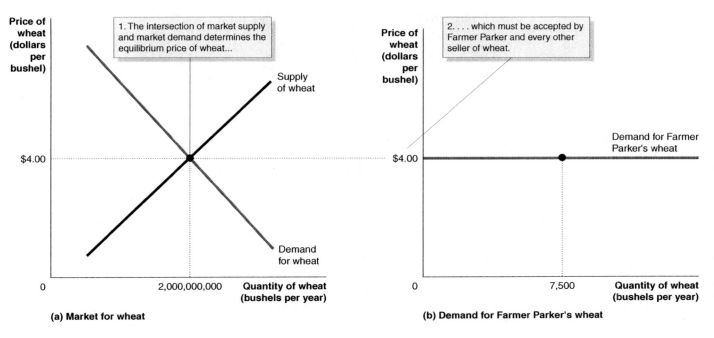

Figure 2 | The Market Demand for Wheat versus the Demand for One Farmer's Wheat

In a perfectly competitive market, price is determined by the intersection of market demand and market supply. In panel (a), the demand and supply curves for wheat intersect at a price of $4 per bushel. An individual wheat farmer like Farmer Parker has no ability to affect the market price for wheat. Therefore, as panel (b) shows, the demand curve for Farmer Parker's wheat is a horizontal line. To understand this figure, it is important to notice that the scales on the horizontal axes in the two panels are very different. In panel (a), the equilibrium quantity of wheat is 2 *billion* bushels, and in panel (b), Farmer Parker is producing only 7,500 bushels of wheat.

curve in panel (a) is the *market demand curve for wheat* and has the normal downward slope we are familiar with from market demand curves. Panel (b) of Figure 2 shows the demand curve for Farmer Parker's wheat, which is a horizontal line. By viewing these graphs side by side, you can see that the price Farmer Parker receives for his wheat in panel (b) is determined by the interaction of all sellers and all buyers of wheat in the wheat market in panel (a). Keep in mind, however, that the scales on the horizontal axes in the two panels are very different. In panel (a), the equilibrium quantity of wheat is 2 *billion* bushels. In panel (b), Farmer Parker is producing only 7,500 bushels, or less than 0.0004 percent of market output. We need to use different scales in the two panels so we can display both of them on one page. Keep in mind the key point: Farmer Parker's output of wheat is very small relative to the total market output.

---

2 | Explain how a firm maximizes profits in a perfectly competitive market.

2 LEARNING OBJECTIVE

How a Firm Maximizes Profit in a Perfectly Competitive Market

We have seen that Farmer Parker cannot control the price of his wheat. In this situation, how does he decide how much wheat to produce? We assume that Farmer Parker's objective is to maximize profits. This is a reasonable assumption for most firms, most of the time. Remember that **profit** is the difference between total revenue (TR) and total cost (TC):

$$\text{Profit} = TR - TC.$$

To maximize his profit, Farmer Parker should produce the quantity of wheat where the difference between the total revenue he receives and his total cost is as large as possible.

Profit Total revenue minus total cost.

TABLE 2	NUMBER OF BUSHELS (Q)	MARKET PRICE (PER BUSHEL) (P)	TOTAL REVENUE (TR)	AVERAGE REVENUE (AR)	MARGINAL REVENUE (MR)
Farmer Parker's Revenue from Wheat Farming	0	$4	$0	—	—
	1	4	4	$4	$4
	2	4	8	4	4
	3	4	12	4	4
	4	4	16	4	4
	5	4	20	4	4
	6	4	24	4	4
	7	4	28	4	4
	8	4	32	4	4
	9	4	36	4	4
	10	4	40	4	4

Revenue for a Firm in a Perfectly Competitive Market

To understand how Farmer Parker maximizes profits, let's first consider his revenue. To keep the numbers simple, we will assume that he owns a very small farm and produces at most 10 bushels of wheat per year. Table 2 shows the revenue Farmer Parker will earn from selling various quantities of wheat if the market price for wheat is $4.

The third column in Table 2 shows that Farmer Parker's *total revenue* rises by $4 for every additional bushel he sells because he can sell as many bushels as he wants at the market price of $4 per bushel. The fourth and fifth columns in the table show Farmer Parker's *average revenue* and *marginal revenue* from selling wheat. His **average revenue (AR)** is his total revenue divided by the quantity of bushels he sells. For example, if he sells 5 bushels for a total of $20, his average revenue is $20/5 = $4. Notice that his average revenue is also equal to the market price of $4. In fact, for any level of output, a firm's average revenue is always equal to the market price. One way to see this is to note that total revenue equals price times quantity ($TR = P \times Q$), and average revenue equals total revenue divided by quantity ($AR = TR/Q$). So, $AR = TR/Q = (P \times Q)/Q = P$.

Farmer Parker's **marginal revenue (MR)** is the change in his total revenue from selling one more bushel:

$$\text{Marginal Revenue} = \frac{\text{Change in total revenue}}{\text{Change in quantity}}, \text{ or } MR = \frac{\Delta TR}{\Delta Q}.$$

Because for each additional bushel sold he always adds $4 to his total revenue, his marginal revenue is $4. Farmer Parker's marginal revenue is $4 per bushel because he is selling wheat in a perfectly competitive market and can sell as much as he wants at the market price. In fact, Farmer Parker's marginal revenue and average revenue are both equal to the market price. This is an important point: *For a firm in a perfectly competitive market, price is equal to both average revenue and marginal revenue.*

Determining the Profit-Maximizing Level of Output

To determine how Farmer Parker can maximize profit, we have to consider his costs as well as his revenue. A wheat farmer has many costs, including seed, fertilizer, and the wages of farm workers. In Table 3, we bring together the revenue data from Table 1 with cost data for Farmer Parker's farm. A firm's *marginal cost* is the increase in total cost resulting from producing another unit of output.

Average revenue (AR) Total revenue divided by the quantity of the product sold.

Marginal revenue (MR) Change in total revenue from selling one more unit of a product.

QUANTITY (BUSHELS) (Q)	TOTAL REVENUE (TR)	TOTAL COST (TC)	PROFIT (TR–TC)	MARGINAL REVENUE (MR)	MARGINAL COST (MC)
0	$0.00	$1.00	–$1.00	—	—
1	4.00	4.00	0.00	$4.00	$3.00
2	8.00	6.00	2.00	4.00	2.00
3	12.00	7.50	4.50	4.00	1.50
4	16.00	9.50	6.50	4.00	2.00
5	20.00	12.00	8.00	4.00	2.50
6	24.00	15.00	9.00	4.00	3.00
7	28.00	19.50	8.50	4.00	4.50
8	32.00	25.50	6.50	4.00	6.00
9	36.00	32.50	3.50	4.00	7.00
10	40.00	40.50	–0.50	4.00	8.00

TABLE 3

Farmer Parker's Profits from Wheat Farming

We calculate profit in the fourth column by subtracting total cost in the third column from total revenue in the second column. The fourth column shows that as long as Farmer Parker produces between 2 and 9 bushels of wheat, he will earn a profit. His maximum profit is $9.00, which he will earn by producing 6 bushels of wheat. Because Farmer Parker wants to maximize his profits, we would expect him to produce 6 bushels of wheat. Producing more than 6 bushels reduces his profit. For example, if he produces 7 bushels of wheat, his profit will decline from $9.00 to $8.50. The values for marginal cost given in the last column of the table help us understand why Farmer Parker's profits will decline if he produces more than 6 bushels of wheat. After the sixth bushel of wheat, rising marginal cost causes Farmer Parker's profits to fall.

In fact, comparing the marginal cost and marginal revenue at each level of output is an alternative method of calculating Farmer Parker's profits. We illustrate the two methods of calculating profits in Figure 3 on the next page. We show the total revenue and total cost approach in panel (a) and the marginal revenue and marginal cost approach in panel (b). Total revenue is a straight line on the graph in panel (a) because total revenue increases at a constant rate of $4 for each additional bushel sold. Farmer Parker's profits are maximized when the vertical distance between the line representing total revenue and the total cost curve is as large as possible. Just as we saw in Table 3, this occurs at an output of 6 bushels.

The last two columns of Table 3 provide information on the marginal revenue (*MR*) Farmer Parker receives from selling another bushel of wheat and his marginal cost (*MC*) of producing another bushel of wheat. Panel (b) is a graph of Farmer Parker's marginal revenue and marginal cost. Because marginal revenue is always equal to $4, it is a horizontal line at the market price. We have already seen that the demand curve for a perfectly competitive firm is also a horizontal line at the market price. *Therefore, the marginal revenue curve for a perfectly competitive firm is the same as its demand curve.* Farmer Parker's marginal cost of producing wheat first falls and then rises, following the usual pattern.

We know from panel (a) that profit is at a maximum at 6 bushels of wheat. In panel (b), profit is also at a maximum at 6 bushels of wheat. To understand why profit is maximized at the level of output where marginal revenue equals marginal cost, remember a key economic principle: *Optimal decisions are made at the margin.* Firms use this principle to decide the quantity of a good to produce. For example, in deciding how much wheat to produce, Farmer Parker needs to compare the marginal revenue he earns from selling another

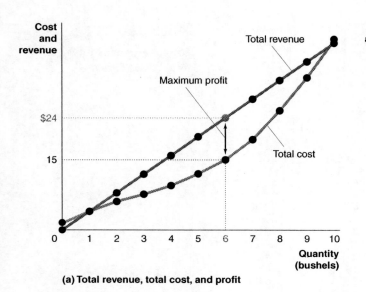

(a) Total revenue, total cost, and profit

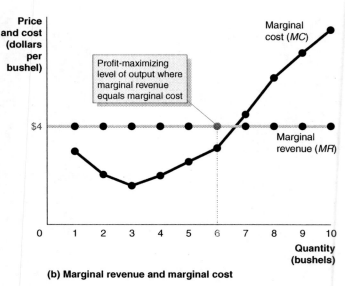

(b) Marginal revenue and marginal cost

Figure 3 | The Profit-Maximizing Level of Output

In panel (a), Farmer Parker maximizes his profit where the vertical distance between total revenue and total cost is the largest. This happens at an output of 6 bushels. Panel (b) shows that Farmer Parker's marginal revenue (*MR*) is equal to a constant $4 per bushel. Farmer Parker maximizes profits by producing wheat up to the point where the marginal revenue of the last bushel produced is equal to its marginal cost, or *MR* = *MC*.

In this case, at no level of output does marginal revenue exactly equal marginal cost. The closest Farmer Parker can come is to produce 6 bushels of wheat. He will not want to continue to produce once marginal cost is greater than marginal revenue because that would reduce his profits. Panels (a) and (b) show alternative ways of thinking about how Farmer Parker can determine the profit-maximizing quantity of wheat to produce.

bushel of wheat to the marginal cost of producing that bushel. The difference between the marginal revenue and the marginal cost is the additional profit (or loss) from producing one more bushel. As long as marginal revenue is greater than marginal cost, Farmer Parker's profits are increasing, and he will want to expand production. For example, he will not stop producing at 5 bushels of wheat because producing and selling the sixth bushel adds $4 to his revenue but only $3 to his cost, so his profit increases by $1. He wants to continue producing until the marginal revenue he receives from selling another bushel is equal to the marginal cost of producing it. At that level of output, he will make no *additional* profit by selling another bushel, so he will have maximized his profits.

By inspecting the table, we can see that at no level of output does marginal revenue exactly equal marginal cost. The closest Farmer Parker can come is to produce 6 bushels of wheat. He will not want to continue to produce once marginal cost is greater than marginal revenue because that would reduce his profits. For example, the seventh bushel of wheat adds $4.50 to his cost but only $4.00 to his revenue, so producing the seventh bushel *reduces* his profit by $0.50.

From the information in Table 3 and Figure 3, we can draw the following conclusions:

1 The profit-maximizing level of output is where the difference between total revenue and total cost is the greatest.

2 The profit-maximizing level of output is also where marginal revenue equals marginal cost, or *MR* = *MC*.

Both these conclusions are true for any firm, whether or not it is in a perfectly competitive industry. We can draw one other conclusion about profit maximization that is true only of firms in perfectly competitive industries: For a firm in a perfectly competitive industry, price is equal to marginal revenue, or *P* = *MR*. So, we can restate the *MR* = *MC* condition as *P* = *MC*.

Illustrating Profit or Loss on the Cost Curve Graph

We have seen that profit is the difference between total revenue and total cost. We can also express profit in terms of *average total cost* (*ATC*). This allows us to show profit on the cost curve graph.

To begin, we need to work through the several steps necessary to determine the relationship between profit and average total cost. Because profit is equal to total revenue minus total cost (*TC*) and total revenue is price times quantity, we can write the following:

$$\text{Profit} = (P \times Q) - TC.$$

If we divide both sides of this equation by Q, we have:

$$\frac{\text{Profit}}{Q} = \frac{(P \times Q)}{Q} - \frac{TC}{Q},$$

or:

$$\frac{\text{Profit}}{Q} = P - ATC,$$

because TC/Q equals ATC. This equation tells us that profit per unit (or average profit) equals price minus average total cost. Finally, we obtain the expression for the relationship between total profit and average total cost by multiplying again by Q:

$$\text{Profit} = (P - ATC) \times Q.$$

This expression tells us that a firm's total profit is equal to the quantity produced multiplied by the difference between price and average total cost.

Showing a Profit on the Graph

Figure 4 shows the relationship between a firm's average total cost and its marginal cost. In this figure, we also show the firm's marginal revenue curve (which is the same as its demand curve) and the area representing total profit. Using the relationship between profit and average total cost that we just determined, we can say that the area representing total profit has a height equal to $(P - ATC)$ and a base equal to Q. This area is shown by the green-shaded rectangle.

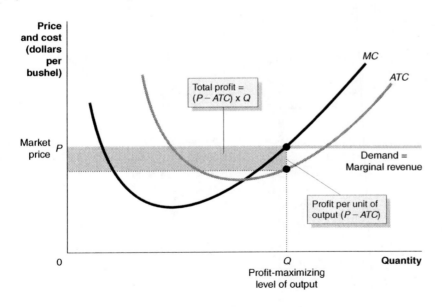

Figure 4

The Area of Maximum Profit

A firm maximizes profit at the level of output at which marginal revenue equals marginal cost. The difference between price and average total cost equals profit per unit of output. Total profit equals profit per unit multiplied by the number of units produced. Total profit is represented by the area of the green-shaded rectangle, which has a height equal to $(P - ATC)$ and a width equal to Q.

Solved Problem | 3

Determining Profit-Maximizing Price and Quantity

Suppose that Andy sells basketballs in the perfectly competitive basketball market. His output per day and his costs are as follows:

OUTPUT PER DAY	TOTAL COST
0	$10.00
1	15.00
2	17.50
3	22.50
4	30.00
5	40.00
6	52.50
7	67.50
8	85.00
9	105.00

a. If the current equilibrium price in the basketball market is $12.50, to maximize profits, how many basketballs will Andy produce, what price will he charge, and how much profit (or loss) will he make? Draw a graph to illustrate your answer. Your graph should be labeled clearly and should include Andy's demand, ATC, AVC, MC, and MR curves; the price he is charging; the quantity he is producing; and the area representing his profit (or loss).

b. Suppose the equilibrium price of basketballs falls to $5.00. Now how many basketballs will Andy produce, what price will he charge, and how much profit (or loss) will he make? Draw a graph to illustrate this situation, using the instructions in question (a).

SOLVING THE PROBLEM:

Step 1: **Review the chapter material.** This problem is about using cost curve graphs to analyze perfectly competitive firms, so you may want to review the section "Illustrating Profit or Loss on the Cost Curve Graph."

Step 2: **Calculate Andy's marginal cost, average total cost, and average variable cost.** To maximize profits, Andy will produce the level of output where marginal revenue is equal to marginal cost. We can calculate marginal cost from the information given in the table. We can also calculate average total cost and average variable cost in order to draw the required graph. Average total cost (ATC) equals total cost (TC) divided by the level of output (Q). Average variable cost (AVC) equals variable cost (VC) divided by output (Q). To calculate variable cost, recall that total cost equals variable cost plus fixed cost. When output equals zero, total cost equals fixed cost. In this case, fixed cost equals $10.00.

OUTPUT PER DAY (Q)	TOTAL COST (TC)	FIXED COST (FC)	VARIABLE COST (VC)	AVERAGE TOTAL COST (ATC)	AVERAGE VARIABLE COST (AVC)	MARGINAL COST (MC)
0	$10.00	$10.00	$0.00	—	—	—
1	15.00	10.00	5.00	$15.00	$5.00	$5.00
2	17.50	10.00	7.50	8.75	3.75	2.50
3	22.50	10.00	12.50	7.50	4.17	5.00
4	30.00	10.00	20.00	7.50	5.00	7.50
5	40.00	10.00	30.00	8.00	6.00	10.00
6	52.50	10.00	42.50	8.75	7.08	12.50
7	67.50	10.00	57.50	9.64	8.21	15.00
8	85.00	10.00	75.00	10.63	9.38	17.50
9	105.00	10.00	95.00	11.67	10.56	20.00

Step 3: **Use the information from the table in step 2 to calculate how many basketballs Andy will produce, what price he will charge, and how much profit he will earn if the market price of basketballs is $12.50.** Andy's marginal revenue is equal to the market price of $12.50. Marginal revenue equals marginal cost when Andy produces 6 basketballs per day. So, Andy will produce 6 basketballs per day and charge a price of $12.50 per basketball. Andy's profits are equal to his total revenue minus his total costs. His total revenue equals the 6 basketballs he sells multiplied by the $12.50 price, or $75.00. So, his profits equal $75.00 − $52.50 = $22.50.

Step 4: **Use the information from the table in step 2 to illustrate your answer to question (a) with a graph.**

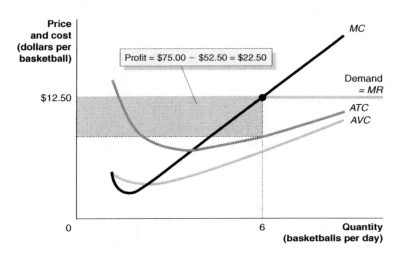

Step 5: **Calculate how many basketballs Andy will produce, what price he will charge, and how much profit he will earn when the market price of basketballs is $5.00.** Referring to the table in step 2, we can see that marginal revenue equals marginal cost when Andy produces 3 basketballs per day. He charges the market price of $5.00 per basketball. His total revenue is only $15.00, while his total costs are $22.50, so he will have a loss of $7.50. (Can we be sure that Andy will continue to produce even though he is operating at a loss? We answer this question in the next section.)

Step 6: **Illustrate your answer to question (b) with a graph.**

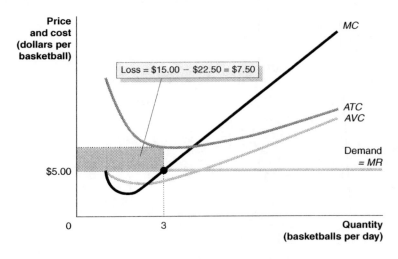

YOUR TURN: For more practice, do related problems 3.3 and 3.4 at the end of this chapter.

>> End Solved Problem 3

Don't Let This Happen to **YOU!**

Remember That Firms Maximize Total Profit, Not Profit per Unit

A student examines the following graph and argues, "I believe that a firm will want to produce at Q_1, not Q_2. At Q_1, the distance between price and average total cost is the greatest. Therefore, at Q_1, the firm will be maximizing its profits per unit." Briefly explain whether you agree with the student's argument.

The student's argument is incorrect because firms are interested in maximizing their *total* profits and not their profits per unit. We know that profits are not maximized at Q_1 because at that level of output, marginal revenue is greater than marginal cost. A firm can always increase its profits by producing any unit that adds more to its revenue than it does to its costs. Only when the firm has expanded production to Q_2 will it have produced every unit for which marginal revenue is greater than marginal cost. At that point, it will have maximized profit.

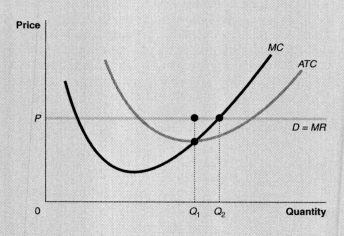

YOUR TURN: Test your understanding by doing related problem 3.5 at the end of this chapter.

Illustrating When a Firm Is Breaking Even or Operating at a Loss

We have already seen that to maximize profits, a firm produces the level of output where marginal revenue equals marginal cost. But will the firm actually make a profit at that level of output? It depends on the relationship of price to average total cost. There are three possibilities:

1. $P > ATC$, which means the firm makes a profit.
2. $P = ATC$, which means the firm *breaks even* (its total cost equals its total revenue).
3. $P < ATC$, which means the firm experiences losses.

Figure 4 shows the first possibility, where the firm makes a profit. Panels (a) and (b) of Figure 5 show the situations where a firm experiences losses or breaks even.

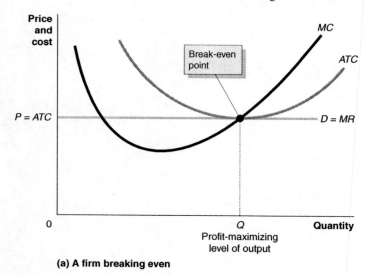

(a) A firm breaking even

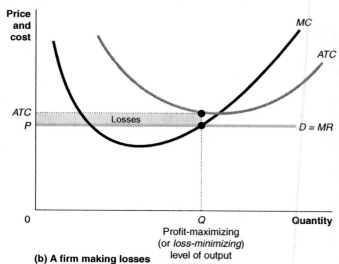

(b) A firm making losses

Figure 5 | A Firm Breaking Even and a Firm Experiencing Losses

In panel (a), price equals average total cost, and the firm breaks even because its total revenue will be equal to its total cost. In this situation, the firm makes zero economic profit. In panel (b), price is below average total cost, and the firm experiences a loss.

The loss is represented by the area of the red-shaded rectangle, which has a height equal to $(ATC - P)$ and a width equal to Q.

In panel (a) of Figure 5, at the level of output at which $MR = MC$, price is equal to average total cost. Therefore, total revenue is equal to total cost, and the firm will break even, making zero economic profit. In panel (b), at the level of output at which $MR = MC$, price is less than average total cost. Therefore, total revenue is less than total cost, and the firm has losses. In this case, maximizing profits amounts to *minimizing* losses.

Making the Connection

Losing Money in the Medical Screening Industry

In a market system, a good or service becomes available to consumers only if an entrepreneur brings the product to market. Thousands of new businesses open every week in the United States. Each new business represents an entrepreneur risking his or her funds trying to earn a profit by offering a good or service to consumers. Of course, there are no guarantees of success, and many new businesses experience losses rather than earn the profits their owners hoped for.

In the early 2000s, technological advance reduced the price of computed tomography (CT) scanning equipment. For years, doctors and hospitals have prescribed CT scans to diagnose patients showing symptoms of heart disease, cancer, and other disorders. The declining price of CT scanning equipment convinced many entrepreneurs that it would be profitable to offer preventive body scans to apparently healthy people. The idea was that the scans would provide early detection of diseases before the customers had begun experiencing symptoms. Unfortunately, the new firms offering this service ran into several difficulties: First, because the CT scan was a voluntary procedure, it was not covered under most medical insurance plans. Second, very few consumers used the service more than once, so there was almost no repeat business. Finally, as with any other medical test, some false positives occurred, where the scan appeared to detect a problem that did not actually exist. Negative publicity from people who had expensive additional—and unnecessary—medical procedures as a result of false-positive CT scans also hurt these new businesses.

As a result of these difficulties, the demand for CT scans was less than most of these entrepreneurs had expected, and the new businesses operated at a loss. For example, the owner of California HeartScan would have broken even if the market price had been $495 per heart scan, but it suffered losses because the actual market price was only $250. The following graphs show the owner's situation.

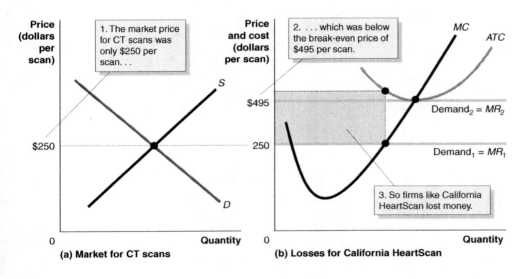

(a) Market for CT scans

(b) Losses for California HeartScan

Why didn't California HeartScan and other medical clinics just raise the price to the level they needed to break even? We have already seen that any firm that tries to raise the price it charges above the market price loses customers to competing firms. By fall 2003, many scanning businesses began to close. Most of the entrepreneurs who had started these businesses lost their investments.

Source: Patricia Callahan, "Scanning for Trouble," *Wall Street Journal*, September 11, 2003, p. B1.

YOUR TURN: Test your understanding by doing related problem 3.8 at the end of this chapter.

---

4 | Explain why firms may shut down temporarily.

Deciding Whether to Produce or to Shut Down in the Short Run

In panel (b) of Figure 5, we assumed that the firm would continue to produce, even though it was operating at a loss. In fact, in the short run, a firm suffering losses has two choices:

1. Continue to produce

2. Stop production by shutting down temporarily

In many cases, a firm experiencing losses will consider stopping production temporarily. Even during a temporary shutdown, however, a firm must still pay its fixed costs. For example, if the firm has signed a lease for its building, the landlord will expect to receive a monthly rent payment, even if the firm is not producing anything that month. Therefore, if a firm does not produce, it will suffer a loss equal to its fixed costs. This loss is the maximum the firm will accept. If, by producing, the firm would lose an amount greater than its fixed costs, it will shut down.

A firm will be able to reduce its loss below the amount of its total fixed cost by continuing to produce, provided the total revenue it receives is greater than its variable cost. A firm can use the revenue over and above variable cost to cover part of its fixed cost. In this case, the firm will have a smaller loss by continuing to produce than if it shut down.

Sunk cost A cost that has already been paid and that cannot be recovered.

In analyzing the firm's decision to shut down, we are assuming that its fixed costs are *sunk costs*. A **sunk cost** is a cost that has already been paid and cannot be recovered. We assume, as is usually the case, that the firm cannot recover its fixed costs by shutting down. For example, if a farmer has taken out a loan to buy land, the farmer is legally required to make the monthly loan payment whether he grows any wheat that season or not. The farmer has to spend those funds and cannot get them back, so the farmer should treat his sunk costs as irrelevant to his decision making. For any firm, whether total revenue is greater or less than *variable costs* is the key to deciding whether to shut down. As long as a firm's total revenue is greater than its variable costs, it should continue to produce no matter how large or small its fixed costs are.

Making the **Connection** | **When to Close a Laundry**

An article in the *Wall Street Journal* describes what happened to Robert Kjelgaard when he quit his job writing software code at Microsoft and bought a laundry by paying the previous owner $80,000. For this payment, he received 76 washers and dryers and the existing lease on the building. The lease had six years remaining and required a monthly payment of $3,300. Unfortunately, Mr. Kjelgaard had difficulty operating the laundry at a profit. His explicit costs were $4,000 per month more than his revenue.

He tried but failed to sell the laundry. As he told a reporter, "It's hard to sell a business that's losing money." He considered closing the laundry, but as a sole proprietor, he would be responsible for the remainder of the lease. At $3,300 per month for six years, he would be responsible for paying almost $200,000 out of his personal savings. Closing the laundry would still seem to be the better choice because his $3,300 per month in sunk costs were less than the $4,000 per month plus the opportunity cost of his time, which he was losing from operating the laundry.

He finally decided to reorganize his business and hire a professional manager. This change allowed him to return to Microsoft and still reduce his losses to $2,000 per month. Because this amount was less than the $3,300 per month he would lose by shutting down, it made sense for him to continue to operate the laundry. But he was still suffering losses and, according to the article, his wife was "counting the days until the lease runs out."

Source: G. Pascal Zachary, "How a Success at Microsoft Washed Out at a Laundry," *Wall Street Journal*, May 30, 1995.

YOUR TURN: Test your understanding by doing related problems 4.5 and 4.6 at the end of this chapter.

Keeping a business open even when suffering losses can sometimes be the best decision for an entrepreneur in the short run.

One option not available to a firm with losses in a perfectly competitive market is to raise its price. If the firm did raise its price, it would lose all its customers, and its sales would drop to zero. For example, in a recent year, the price of wheat in the United States was $3.16 per bushel. At that price, the typical U.S. wheat farmer lost $9,500. At a price of about $4.25 per bushel, the typical wheat farmer would have broken even. But any wheat farmer who tried to raise his price to $4.25 per bushel would have seen his sales quickly disappear because buyers could purchase all the wheat they wanted at $3.16 per bushel from the thousands of other wheat farmers.

The Supply Curve of a Firm in the Short Run

Remember that the supply curve for a firm tells us how many units of a product the firm is willing to sell at any given price. Notice that the marginal cost curve for a firm in a perfectly competitive market tells us the same thing. The firm will produce at the level of output where $MR = MC$. Because price equals marginal revenue for a firm in a perfectly competitive market, the firm will produce where $P = MC$. For any given price, we can determine from the marginal cost curve the quantity of output the firm will supply. *Therefore, a perfectly competitive firm's marginal cost curve also is its supply curve.* There is, however, an important qualification to this. We have seen that if a firm is experiencing losses, it will shut down if its total revenue is less than its variable cost:

$$\text{Total revenue} < \text{Variable cost},$$

or, in symbols:

$$P \times Q < VC.$$

If we divide both sides by Q, we have the result that the firm will shut down if:

$$P < AVC.$$

If the price drops below average variable cost, the firm will have a smaller loss if it shuts down and produces no output. *So, the firm's marginal cost curve is its supply curve only for prices at or above average variable cost.* The red line in Figure 6 shows the supply curve for the firm in the short run.

Recall that the marginal cost curve intersects the average variable cost where the average variable cost curve is at its minimum point. Therefore, the firm's supply curve is its marginal cost curve above the minimum point of the average variable cost curve. For prices below minimum average variable cost (P_{MIN}), the firm will shut down, and its output will fall to zero. The minimum point on the average variable cost curve is called the **shutdown point** and occurs in Figure 6 at output level Q_{SD}.

Shutdown point The minimum point on a firm's average variable cost curve; if the price falls below this point, the firm shuts down production in the short run.

Figure 6

The Firm's Short-Run Supply Curve

The firm will produce at the level of output at which $MR = MC$. Because price equals marginal revenue for a firm in a perfectly competitive market, the firm will produce where $P = MC$. For any given price, we can determine the quantity of output the firm will supply from the marginal cost curve. In other words, the marginal cost curve is the firm's supply curve. But remember that the firm will shut down if the price falls below average variable cost. The marginal cost curve crosses the average variable cost at the firm's shutdown point. This point occurs at output level Q_{SD}. For prices below P_{MIN}, the supply curve is a vertical line along the price axis, which shows that the firm will supply zero output at those prices. The red line in the figure is the firm's short-run supply curve.

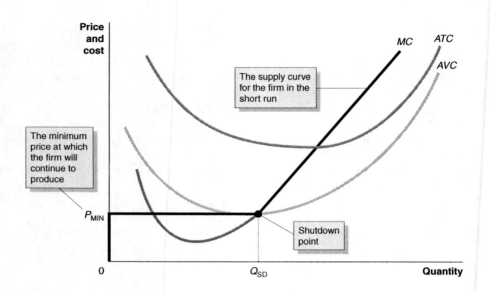

The Market Supply Curve in a Perfectly Competitive Industry

The market demand curve is determined by adding up the quantity demanded by each consumer in the market at each price. Similarly, the market supply curve is determined by adding up the quantity supplied by each firm in the market at each price. Each firm's marginal cost curve tells us how much that firm will supply at each price. So, the market supply curve can be derived directly from the marginal cost curves of the firms in the market. Panel (a) of Figure 7 shows the marginal cost curve for one wheat farmer. At a price of $4, this wheat farmer supplies 8,000 bushels of wheat. If every wheat farmer

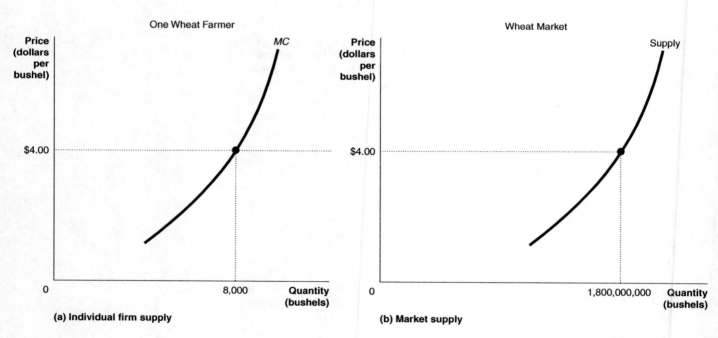

Figure 7 | Firm Supply and Market Supply

We can derive the market supply curve by adding up the quantity that each firm in the market is willing to supply at each price. In panel (a), one wheat farmer is willing to supply 8,000 bushels of wheat at a price of $4 per bushel. If every wheat farmer supplies the same amount of wheat at this price and if there are 225,000 wheat farmers, the total amount of wheat supplied at a price of $4 will equal 8,000 bushels per farmer × 225,000 farmers = 1.8 billion bushels of wheat. This is one point on the market supply curve for wheat shown in panel (b). We can find the other points on the market supply curve by seeing how much wheat each farmer is willing to supply at each price.

supplies the same amount of wheat at this price and if there are 225,000 wheat farmers, the total amount of wheat supplied at a price of $4 will be:

8,000 bushels per farmer × 225,000 farmers = 1.8 billion bushels of wheat.

Panel (b) shows a price of $4 and a quantity of 1.8 billion bushels as a point on the market supply curve for wheat. In reality, of course, not all wheat farms are alike. Some wheat farms supply more at the market price than the typical farm; other wheat farms supply less. The key point is that we can derive the market supply curve by adding up the quantity that each firm in the market is willing to supply at each price.

5 LEARNING OBJECTIVE

5 | Explain how entry and exit ensure that perfectly competitive firms earn zero economic profit in the long run.

"If Everyone Can Do It, You Can't Make Money at It": The Entry and Exit of Firms in the Long Run

In the long run, unless a firm can cover all its costs, it will shut down and exit the industry. In a market system, firms continually enter and exit industries. In this section, we will see how profits and losses provide signals to firms that lead to entry and exit.

Economic Profit and the Entry or Exit Decision

To begin, let's look more closely at how economists characterize the profits earned by the owners of a firm. Suppose Anne Moreno decides to start her own business. After considering her interests and preparing a business plan, she decides to start an organic apple farm rather than open a restaurant or gift shop. After 10 years of effort, Anne has saved $100,000 and borrowed another $900,000 from a bank. With these funds, she has bought the land, apple trees, and farm equipment necessary to start her organic apple business. When someone invests her own funds in her firm, the opportunity cost to the firm is the return the funds would have earned in their best alternative use. If Farmer Moreno could have earned a 10 percent return on her $100,000 in savings in their best alternative use—which might have been, for example, to buy a small restaurant—then her apple business incurs a $10,000 opportunity cost. We can also think of this $10,000 as being the minimum amount that Farmer Moreno needs to earn on her $100,000 investment in her farm to remain in the industry in the long run.

Table 4 lists Farmer Moreno's costs. In addition to her explicit costs, we assume that she has two implicit costs: the $10,000, which represents the opportunity cost of the

EXPLICIT COSTS	
Water	$10,000
Wages	$15,000
Organic fertilizer	$10,000
Electricity	$5,000
Payment on bank loan	$45,000
IMPLICIT COSTS	
Foregone salary	$30,000
Opportunity cost of the $100,000 she has invested in her farm	$10,000
Total cost	$125,000

TABLE 4

Farmer Moreno's Costs per Year

Economic profit A firm's revenues minus all its costs, implicit and explicit.

funds she invested in her farm, and the $30,000 salary she could have earned managing someone else's farm instead of her own. Her total costs are $125,000. If the market price of organic apples is $15 per box and Farmer Moreno sells 10,000 boxes, her total revenue will be $150,000 and her economic profit will be $25,000 (total revenue of $150,000 minus total costs of $125,000). **Economic profit** equals a firm's revenues minus all of its costs, implicit and explicit. So, Farmer Moreno is covering the $10,000 opportunity cost of the funds invested in her firm, and she is also earning an additional $25,000 in economic profit.

Economic Profit Leads to Entry of New Firms

Unfortunately, Farmer Moreno is unlikely to earn an economic profit for very long. Suppose other apple farmers are just breaking even by growing apples using conventional methods. In that case, they will have an incentive to convert to organic growing methods so they can begin earning an economic profit. Remember that the more firms there are in an industry, the further to the right the market supply curve is. Panel (a) of Figure 8 shows that more farmers entering the market for organically grown apples will cause the market supply curve to shift to the right. Farmers will continue entering the market until the market supply curve has shifted from S_1 to S_2.

With the supply curve at S_2, the market price will have fallen to $10 per box. Panel (b) shows the effect on Farmer Moreno, whom we assume has the same costs as other organic apple farmers. As the market price falls from $15 to $10 per box, Farmer Moreno's demand curve shifts down, from D_1 to D_2. In the new equilibrium, Farmer Moreno is selling 8,000 boxes at a price of $10 per box. She and the other organic apple growers are no longer earning any economic profit. They are just breaking even, and the return on their investment is just covering the opportunity cost of these funds. New farmers will stop entering the market for organic apples because the rate of return is no better than they can earn elsewhere.

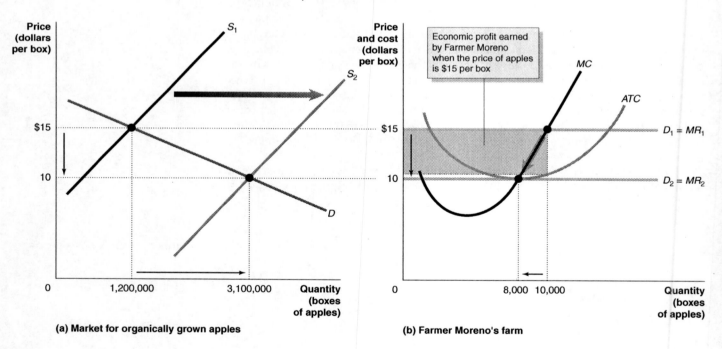

(a) Market for organically grown apples

(b) Farmer Moreno's farm

Figure 8 | The Effect of Entry on Economic Profits

We assume that Farmer Moreno's costs are the same as the costs of other organic apple growers. Initially, she and other producers of organically grown apples are able to charge $15 per box and earn an economic profit. Farmer Moreno's economic profit is represented by the area of the green box. Panel (a) shows that as other farmers begin to grow apples using organic methods, the market supply curve shifts to the right, from S_1 to S_2, and the market price drops to $10 per box. Panel (b) shows that the falling price causes Farmer Moreno's demand curve to shift down from D_1 to D_2, and she reduces her output from 10,000 boxes to 8,000. At the new market price of $10 per box, organic apple growers are just breaking even: Their total revenue is equal to their total cost, and their economic profit is zero. Notice the difference in scale between the graph in panel (a) and the graph in panel (b).

Will Farmer Moreno continue to grow organic apples even though she is just breaking even? She will because growing organic apples earns her as high a return on her investment as she could earn elsewhere. It may seem strange that new firms will continue to enter a market until all economic profits are eliminated and that established firms remain in a market despite not earning any economic profit. It only seems strange because we are used to thinking in terms of accounting profits, rather than *economic* profits. Remember that accounting rules generally require that only explicit costs be included on a firm's financial statements. The opportunity cost of the funds Farmer Moreno invested in her firm—$10,000—and her foregone salary—$30,000—are economic costs, but neither is an accounting cost. So, although an accountant would see Farmer Moreno as earning a profit of $40,000, an economist would see her as just breaking even. Farmer Moreno must pay attention to her accounting profit when preparing her financial statements and when paying her income tax. But because economic profit takes into account all her costs, it gives a truer indication of the financial health of her farm.

Economic Losses Lead to Exit of Firms Suppose some consumers decide there are no important benefits from eating organically grown apples and they switch back to buying conventionally grown apples. Panel (a) of Figure 9 shows that the demand curve for organically grown apples will shift to the left, from D_1 to D_2, and the market price will fall from $10 per box to $7. Panel (b) shows that as the price falls, a typical organic apple farmer, like Anne Moreno, will move down her marginal cost curve to a lower level of output. At the lower level of output and lower price, she will be suffering an **economic loss** because she will not cover all her costs. As long as price is above average variable cost, she will continue to produce in the short run, even when suffering losses. But in the long run, firms will exit an industry if they are unable to cover all their costs. In this case, some organic apple growers will switch back to growing apples using conventional methods.

Panel (c) of Figure 9 shows that firms exiting the organic apple industry will cause the market supply curve to shift to the left. Firms will continue to exit, and the supply curve will continue to shift to the left until the price has risen back to $10 and the market supply curve is at S_2. Panel (d) shows that when the price is back to $10, the remaining firms in the industry will be breaking even.

Economic loss The situation in which a firm's total revenue is less than its total cost, including all implicit costs.

Long-Run Equilibrium in a Perfectly Competitive Market

We have seen that economic profits attract firms to enter an industry. The entry of firms forces down the market price until the typical firm is breaking even. Economic losses cause firms to exit an industry. The exit of firms forces up the equilibrium market price until the typical firm is breaking even. This process of entry and exit results in *long-run competitive equilibrium*. In **long-run competitive equilibrium**, entry and exit have resulted in the typical firm breaking even. The *long-run equilibrium market price* is at a level equal to the minimum point on the typical firm's average total cost curve.

The long run in the organic apple market is three to four years, which is the amount of time it takes farmers to convert from conventional growing methods to organic growing methods. As discussed at the beginning of this chapter, only during the years from 1997 to 2001 was it possible for organic apple farmers to earn economic profits. By 2002, the entry of new firms had eliminated economic profits in the industry.

Firms in perfectly competitive markets are in a constant struggle to stay one step ahead of their competitors. They are always looking for new ways to provide a product, such as growing apples organically. It is possible for firms to find ways to earn an economic profit for a while, but to repeat the quote from a Yakima Valley organic apple farmer at the beginning of this chapter, "It's like anything else in agriculture. If people see an economic opportunity, usually it only lasts for a few years." This observation is not restricted to agriculture. In any perfectly competitive market, an opportunity to make economic profits never lasts long. As Sharon Oster, an economist at Yale University, has put it, "If everyone can do it, you can't make money at it."

Long-run competitive equilibrium The situation in which the entry and exit of firms has resulted in the typical firm breaking even.

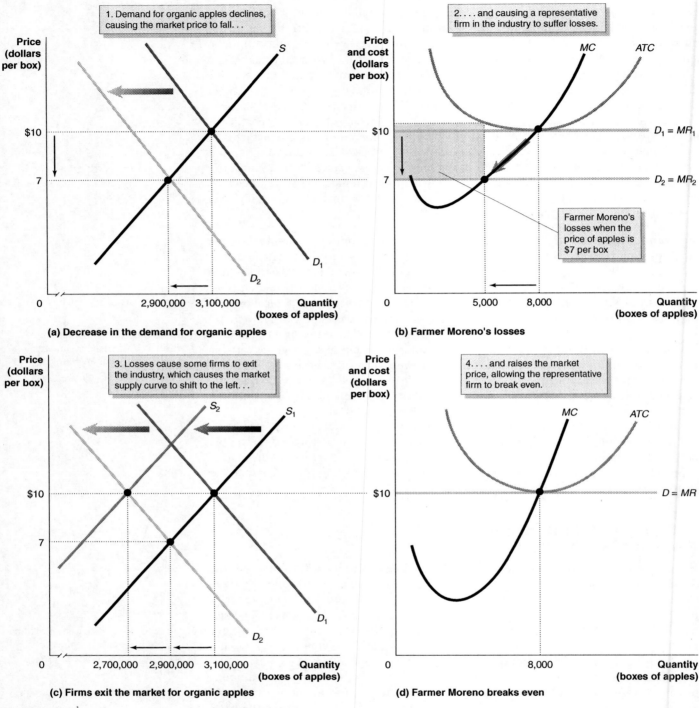

Figure 9 | The Effect of Exit on Economic Losses

When the price of apples is $10 per box, Farmer Moreno and other producers of organi- cally grown apples are breaking even. A total quantity of 3,100,000 boxes is sold in the market. Farmer Moreno sells 8,000 boxes. Panel (a) shows a decline in the demand for organically grown apples from D_1 to D_2 that reduces the market price to $7 per box. Panel (b) shows that the falling price causes Farmer Moreno's demand curve to shift down from D_1 to D_2 and her output to fall from 8,000 to 5,000 boxes. At a market price of

$7 per box, farmers have economic losses, represented by the area of the red box. As a result, some farmers will exit the market, which shifts the market supply curve to the left. Panel (c) shows that exit continues until the supply curve has shifted from S_1 to S_2 and the market price has risen from $7 back to $10. Panel (d) shows that with the price back at $10, Farmer Moreno will break even. In the new market equilibrium, total production of organic apples has fallen from 3,100,000 to 2,700,000 boxes.

The Long-Run Supply Curve in a Perfectly Competitive Market

If the typical organic apple grower breaks even at a price of $10 per box, in the long run, the market price will always return to this level. If an increase in demand causes the market price to rise above $10, farmers will be earning economic profits. This profit will attract additional farmers into the market, and the market supply curve will shift to the right until the price is back to $10. Panel (a) in Figure 10 illustrates the long-run effect of an increase in demand. An increase in demand from D_1 to D_2 causes the market price to temporarily rise from $10 per box to $15. At this price, farmers are making economic profits growing organic apples, but these profits attract entry of new farmers' organic apples. The result is an increase in supply from S_1 to S_2, which forces the price back down to $10 per box and eliminates the economic profits.

Similarly, if a decrease in demand causes the market price to fall below $10, farmers will experience economic losses. These losses will cause some farmers to exit the market, the supply curve will shift to the left, and the price will return to $10. Panel (b) in Figure 10 illustrates the long-run effect of a decrease in demand. A decrease in demand from D_1 to D_2 causes the market price to fall temporarily from $10 per box to $7. At this price, farmers are suffering economic losses growing organic apples, but these losses cause some farmers to exit the market for organic apples. The result is a decrease in supply from S_1 to S_2, which forces the price back up to $10 per box and eliminates the losses.

The **long-run supply curve** shows the relationship in the long run between market price and the quantity supplied. In the long run, the price in the organic apple market will be $10 per box, no matter how many boxes of apples are produced. So, as Figure 10 shows, the long-run supply curve (S_{LR}) for organic apples is a horizontal line at a price of $10. Remember that the reason the price returns to $10 in the long run is that this is the price at which the typical firm in the industry just breaks even. The typical firm breaks even at this

Long-run supply curve A curve that shows the relationship in the long run between market price and the quantity supplied.

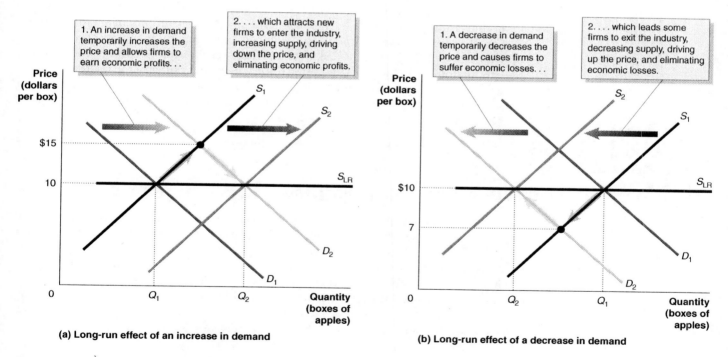

(a) Long-run effect of an increase in demand

(b) Long-run effect of a decrease in demand

Figure 10 | The Long-Run Supply Curve in a Perfectly Competitive Industry

Panel (a) shows that an increase in demand for organic apples will lead to a temporary increase in price from $10 to $15 per box, as the market demand curve shifts to the right, from D_1 to D_2. The entry of new firms shifts the market supply curve to the right, from S_1 to S_2, which will cause the price to fall back to its long-run level of $10. Panel (b) shows that a decrease in demand will lead to a temporary decrease in price

from $10 to $7 per box, as the market demand curve shifts to the left, from D_1 to D_2. The exit of firms shifts the market supply curve to the left, from S_1 to S_2, which causes the price to rise back to its long-run level of $10. The long-run supply curve (S_{LR}) shows the relationship between market price and the quantity supplied in the long run. In this case, the long-run supply curve is a horizontal line.

price because it is at the minimum point on the firm's average total cost curve. We can draw the important conclusion that *in the long run, a perfectly competitive market will supply whatever amount of a good consumers demand at a price determined by the minimum point on the typical firm's average total cost curve.*

Because the position of the long-run supply curve is determined by the minimum point on the typical firm's average total cost curve, anything that raises or lowers the costs of the typical firm in the long run will cause the long-run supply curve to shift. For example, if a disease infects apple trees and the costs of treating the disease adds $2 per box to the cost of producing apples, the long-run supply curve will shift up by $2.

Increasing-Cost and Decreasing-Cost Industries

Any industry in which the typical firm's average costs do not change as the industry expands production will have a horizontal long-run supply curve, like the one in Figure 10. Industries, like the apple industry, where this holds true are called *constant-cost industries*. It's possible, however, for the typical firm's average costs to change as an industry expands.

For example, if an input used in producing a good is available in only limited quantities, the cost of the input will rise as the industry expands. If only a limited amount of land is available on which to grow the grapes to make a certain variety of wine, an increase in demand for wine made from these grapes will result in competition for the land and will drive up its price. As a result, more of the wine will be produced in the long run only if the price rises to cover the higher average costs of the typical firm. In this case, the long-run supply curve will slope upward. Industries with upward-sloping long-run supply curves are called *increasing-cost industries*.

Finally, in some cases, the typical firm's costs may fall as the industry expands. Suppose that someone invents a new microwave that uses as an input a specialized memory chip that is currently produced only in small quantities. If demand for the microwave increases, firms that produce microwaves will increase their orders for the memory chip. If there are economies of scale in producing a good, its average cost will decline as output increases. If there are economies of scale in producing this memory chip, the average cost of producing it will fall, and competition will result in its price falling as well. This price decline, in turn, will lower the average cost of producing the new microwave. In the long run, competition will force the price of the microwave to fall to the level of the new lower average cost of the typical firm. In this case, the long-run supply curve will slope downward. Industries with downward-sloping long-run supply curves are called *decreasing-cost industries*.

6 LEARNING OBJECTIVE

6 | Explain how perfect competition leads to economic efficiency.

Perfect Competition and Efficiency

Notice how powerful consumers are in a market system. If consumers want more organic apples, the market will supply them. This happens not because a government bureaucrat in Washington, DC, or an official in an apple growers' association gives orders. The additional apples are produced because an increase in demand results in higher prices and a higher rate of return on investments in organic growing techniques. Apple growers, trying to get the highest possible return on their investment, begin to switch from using conventional growing methods to using organic growing methods. If consumers lose their taste for organic apples and demand falls, the process works in reverse.

Making | **The Decline of Apple Production**
the | **in New York State**
Connection | Although New York State is second only to Washington State in production of apples, its production has been declining during the past 20 years. The decline has been particularly steep in counties close to New York City. In 1985, there were more than 11,000 acres of apple orchards in Ulster County, which

is 75 miles north of New York City. Today, fewer than 5,000 acres remain. As it became difficult for apple growers in the county to compete with lower-cost producers elsewhere, the resources these entrepreneurs were using to produce apples—particularly land—became more valuable in other uses. Many farmers sold their land to housing developers. As one apple farmer put it, "Over the last ten years or so, [apple] prices have been stagnant or going down. I didn't see a return on the money, and I didn't want to continue."

In a market system, entrepreneurs will not continue to employ economic resources to produce a good or service unless consumers are willing to pay a price at least high enough for them to break even. Consumers were not willing to pay a high enough price for apples for many New York State apple growers to break even on their investments. As a result, resources left apple production in that state.

Sources: Lisa W. Foderaro, "Where Apples Don't Pay, Developers Will," *New York Times*, June 23, 2001; and USDA, *2002 Census of Agriculture, Volume 1, Chapter 2*, New York County Level Data, Table 31.

When apple growers in New York State stopped breaking even, many sold their land to housing developers.

Richard Heinzen, SuperStock, Inc.

YOUR TURN: Test your understanding by doing related problem 6.7 at the end of this chapter.

Productive Efficiency

In the market system, consumers get as many apples as they want, produced at the lowest average cost possible. The forces of competition will drive the market price to the minimum average cost of the typical firm. **Productive efficiency** refers to the situation in which a good or service is produced at the lowest possible cost. As we have seen, perfect competition results in productive efficiency.

The managers of every firm strive to earn an economic profit by reducing costs. But in a perfectly competitive market, other firms quickly copy ways of reducing costs, so that in the long run, only the consumer benefits from cost reductions.

Productive efficiency The situation in which a good or service is produced at the lowest possible cost.

Solved Problem | 6

How Productive Efficiency Benefits Consumers

Writing in the *New York Times* on the technology boom of the late 1990s, Michael Lewis argues "The sad truth, for investors, seems to be that most of the benefits of new technologies are passed right through to consumers free of charge."

a. What do you think Lewis means by the benefits of new technology being "passed right through to consumers free of charge"? Use a graph like Figure 8 to illustrate your answer.
b. Explain why this result is a "sad truth" for investors.

SOLVING THE PROBLEM:

Step 1: **Review the chapter material.** This problem is about perfect competition and efficiency, so you may want to review the section "Perfect Competition and Efficiency."

Step 2: **Use the concepts from this chapter to explain what Lewis means.** By "new technologies," Lewis means new products—like cell phones or plasma television sets—or lower-cost ways of producing existing products. In either case, new technologies will allow firms to earn economic profits for a while, but these profits will lead new firms to enter the market in the long run.

Step 3: **Use a graph like Figure 8 to illustrate why the benefits of new technologies are "passed right through to consumers free of charge."** Figure 8 shows the situation in which a firm is making economic profits in the short run but has these profits eliminated by entry in the long run. We can draw a similar graph to analyze what happens in the long run in the market for plasma televisions:

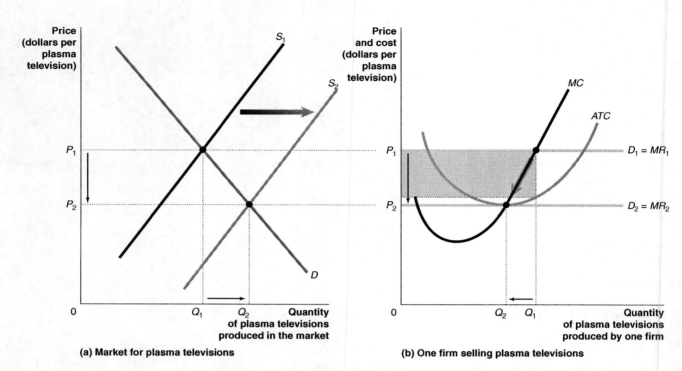

(a) Market for plasma televisions

(b) One firm selling plasma televisions

When plasma televisions were first introduced, prices were high, and only a few firms were in the market. Panel (a) shows that the initial equilibrium price in the market for plasma televisions is P_1. Panel (b) shows that at this price, the typical firm in the industry is earning an economic profit, which is shown by the green-shaded box. The economic profit attracts new firms into the industry. This entry shifts the market supply curve from S_1 to S_2 in panel (a) and lowers the equilibrium price from P_1 to P_2. Panel (b) shows that at the new market price, P_2, the typical firm is breaking even. Therefore, plasma televisions are being produced at the lowest possible cost, and productive efficiency is achieved. Consumers receive the new technology "free of charge" in the sense that they only have to pay a price equal to the lowest possible cost of production.

Step 4: **Answer question (b) by explaining why the result in question (a) is a "sad truth" for investors.** We have seen in answering question (a) that in the long run, firms only break even on their investment in producing high-technology goods. That result implies that investors in these firms are also unlikely to earn an economic profit in the long run.

EXTRA CREDIT: Lewis is using a key result from this chapter: In the long run, entry of new firms competes away economic profits. We should notice that, strictly speaking, the high-technology industries Lewis is discussing are not perfectly competitive. Cell phones or plasma televisions, for instance, are not identical, and each cell phone company produces a quantity large enough to affect the market price. However, these deviations from perfect competition do not change the important conclusion that the entry of new firms benefits consumers by forcing prices down to the level of average cost. In fact, the price of plasma televisions dropped by more than 75 percent within five years of their first becoming widely available.

Source: Michael Lewis, "In Defense of the Boom," *New York Times*, October 27, 2002.

YOUR TURN: For more practice, do related problems 6.4, 6.5, and 6.6 at the end of this chapter.

>> End Solved Problem 6

Allocative Efficiency

Not only do perfectly competitive firms produce goods and services at the lowest possible cost, they also produce the goods and services that consumers value most. Firms will produce a good up to the point where the marginal cost of producing another unit is equal to the marginal benefit consumers receive from consuming that unit. In other words, firms will supply all those goods that provide consumers with a marginal benefit at least as great as the marginal cost of producing them. We know this is true because:

1. The price of a good represents the marginal benefit consumers receive from consuming the last unit of the good sold.

2. Perfectly competitive firms produce up to the point where the price of the good equals the marginal cost of producing the last unit.

3. Therefore, firms produce up to the point where the last unit provides a marginal benefit to consumers equal to the marginal cost of producing it.

These statements are another way of saying that entrepreneurs in a market system efficiently *allocate* labor, machinery, and other inputs to produce the goods and services that best satisfy consumer wants. In this sense, perfect competition achieves **allocative efficiency**. As we will explore in the next few chapters, many goods and services sold in the U.S. economy are not produced in perfectly competitive markets. Nevertheless, productive efficiency and allocative efficiency are useful benchmarks against which to compare the actual performance of the economy.

Allocative efficiency A state of the economy in which production represents consumer preferences; in particular, every good or service is produced up to the point where the last unit provides a marginal benefit to consumers equal to the marginal cost of producing it.

Economics in YOUR Life!

At the beginning of the chapter, we asked you to think about why you can charge only a relatively low price for performing services such as babysitting or lawn mowing. In the chapter, we saw that firms selling products in competitive markets are unable to charge prices higher than those being charged by competing firms. The market for babysitting and lawn mowing is very competitive. In most neighborhoods, there are a lot of teenagers willing to supply these services. The price you can charge for babysitting may not be worth your while at age 20 but is enough to cover the opportunity cost of a 14-year-old eager to enter the market. (Or, as we put it in Table 1, the ease of entry into babysitting and lawn mowing is high.) So, in your career as a teenage entrepreneur, you may have become familiar with one of the lessons of this chapter: A firm in a competitive market has no control over price.

Conclusion

The competitive forces of the market impose relentless pressure on firms to produce new and better goods and services at the lowest possible cost. Firms that fail to adequately anticipate changes in consumer tastes or that fail to adopt the latest and most efficient technology do not survive in the long run. In the nineteenth century, the biologist Charles Darwin developed a theory of evolution based on the idea of the "survival of the fittest." Only those plants and animals that are best able to adapt to the demands of their environment are able to survive. Darwin first realized the important role that the struggle for existence plays in the natural world after reading early nineteenth-century economists' descriptions of the role it plays in the economic world. Just as "survival of the fittest" is the rule in nature, so it is in the economic world.

At the start of this chapter, we saw that there are four market structures: perfect competition, monopolistic competition, oligopoly, and monopoly. Now that we have studied perfect competition, in the following chapters we move on to the other three market structures. Before turning to those chapters, read *An Inside Look* on the next page to learn how firms are rushing to enter the market for organic snacks.

Why Are Organic Farmers Worried about Wal-Mart?

BUSINESSWEEK, MARCH 29, 2006

Wal-Mart's Organic Offensive

Richard DeWilde has a long history with organic farming. His grandfather, Nick Hoogshagen, adopted the organic approach five decades ago on his farm in South Dakota, well before it became popular with consumers and fueled the popularity of retailers like Whole Foods Market.

Now, DeWilde, 57 is a working farmer himself, carrying on the family tradition of avoiding pesticides and other chemicals that can contaminate food in favor of a more natural approach. He's co-owner of Harmony Valley Farm, which grows Swiss chard, parsnips, turnips, and kale on 100 acres in the southwestern corner of Wisconsin. So you might think that DeWilde would be overjoyed at the news that Wal-Mart has finally come around to his grandfather's philosophy. The juggernaut retailer said recently that it plans to double its offering of organic product, including produce, dairy, and dry goods.

But DeWilde isn't thrilled. Instead, he's dismayed at the prospect of Wal-Mart becoming a player in the organic market. He fears that the company will use its market strength to drive down prices and hurt U.S. farmers. "Wal-Mart has the reputation of beating up on its suppliers," says DeWilde. "I certainly don't see 'selling at a lower price' as an opportunity."

He's hardly the only one. Many farmers who have benefited from the strong demand and healthy margins for organic goods are fretting that the market's newfound success also brings with it newfound risks. As large companies enter the market, from Kraft and Dean Foods to Wal-Mart, farmers worry that the corporatization of organic foods could have negative consequences.

Large corporations have taken sizable steps into the organic market, even if it isn't always obvious from the brands on store shelves. Silk, the best-selling branded soy milk, is a product from Dean Foods, the $10 billion behemoth that sells the most milk in the country. Cascadian Farms, which makes organic cereal, frozen fruits, and other products, is a brand of cereal giant General Mills. And Kraft owns Boca Burgers. . . .

Organic farmers are straining to meet rising demand, one of the reasons that legislators have been willing to drop certain requirements for organic foods. In the past year, the demand for organic milk outstripped the supply by 10% and created acute shortages. That even prompted organic dairy company Stonyfield Farms to stop producing its fat-free 32-ounce cups of yogurt. Now Stonyfield has resumed its production, but organic milk consumption nationwide is growing 30% annually.

Wal-Mart is making its aggressive move into organics at the same time it's trying to improve its environmental image. Last year, it embarked on a new green policy and has several initiatives to demonstrate how serious it is. The company recently said that it will require that all its wild-caught fresh and frozen fish meet the Marine Stewardship Council's standard for sustainable and well-managed fisheries. Fish accounts for a third of all the chain's seafood sales. . . .

While some farmers are concerned that Wal-Mart may try to squeeze them financially, there could be a more benign impact. Farmers who now use pesticides and other chemicals could turn to organic farming, as they see increased demand. Consider what's happening in California.

Last year, the state showed an increase of 40,000 acres, or 27%, in organic livestock production. The number of acres dedicated to organic vegetable production increased by 5,000 acres, or 12%, according to the California Certified Organic Farmers, an organics trade association. "Strong demand is creating markets here," says Jake Lewin, director of marketing at the organization.

Meanwhile, back in Wisconsin, DeWilde is preparing for warmer weather and the spring planting season. He is worried about how the increasing attention from Wal-Mart and other large companies may change the business of organic foods. Yet he's more convinced than ever of the benefits of the approach his grandfather helped champion. "It's the future of farming," he says.

Source: Pallavi Gogoi, "Wal-Mart's Organic Offensive," *BusinessWeek*, March 29, 2006 (from *BusinessWeek* Online).

© Bob Daemmrich/The Image Works

Key Points in the Article

The increasing popularity of organic food has caught the attention of large food producers, such as Dean Foods, which produces Silk, the best-selling brand of soy milk. Wal-Mart, which is the largest seller of groceries in the United States, has also begun to offer more organic foods for sale. Some farmers who supply organic foods are concerned that Wal-Mart may offer lower prices than they have been receiving from supermarkets. Other farmers believe that if Wal-Mart begins selling more organic foods it may increase the popularity of these products and increase the demand for them.

Analyzing the News

a One of the key points of this chapter is that, ultimately, it is *consumers* who decide which goods will be produced. If consumers increase their demand for organic foods, then firms will redirect workers, machines, and natural resources toward producing those goods. One industry analyst (not quoted in the article) observed, "Organic is a niche, but a very profitable niche. Give consumers what they truly want/need and they will dig deeply into their pockets."

In fact, it is those profits that signal to entrepreneurs that demand for organic foods has increased. We know from the analysis in this chapter, though, that these profits will not persist in the long run. Figure 1 shows that an increase in demand for organic food raises the price from P_1 to P_2, which results in the typical firm earning economic profits.

b Figure 2 shows the long-run result. The economic profit earned by producing organic foods will attract additional firms to enter the industry. As the article mentions, farmers in California are taking resources out of non-organic farming and putting them into organic farming. The entrance of new firms will eventually cause the market price to fall back to P_1. At a price

of P_1, the typical firm is once again breaking even. The increase in consumer demand for organic foods results in the quantity supplied rising in the long run, as new firms enter the industry. In the long run the typical firm in a perfectly competitive industry breaks even, as economic profits are competed away.

Thinking Critically

1. Use a demand and supply graph and a cost curve graph to show what would happen if the government tightened its regulations, making it more difficult for foods to be labeled as "organic."

2. Suppose that farmers who produce organic foods protest to Congress as prices decline. Use a demand and supply graph to show the impact on the market for organic foods if Congress decides to impose a price floor above the equilibrium price. What happens to consumer surplus and producer surplus as a result of the price floor?

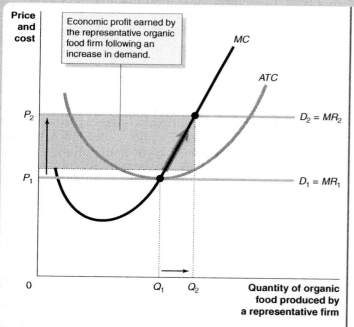

Figure 1. The short-run effects of an increase in demand for organic food.

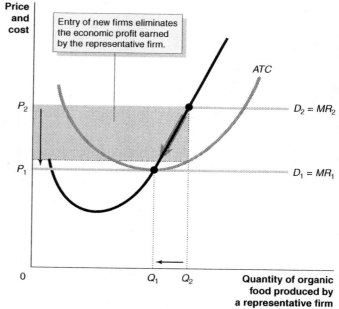

Figure 2. The long-run effects of an increase in demand for organic foods.

Key Terms

Allocative efficiency

Average revenue (*AR*)

Economic loss

Economic profit

Long-run competitive
equilibrium

Long-run supply curve

Marginal revenue (*MR*)

Perfectly competitive market

Price taker

Productive efficiency

Profit

Shutdown point

Sunk cost

---

1 LEARNING OBJECTIVE   1 | Define a perfectly competitive market and explain why a perfect competitor faces a horizontal demand curve

Perfectly Competitive Markets

Summary

A **perfectly competitive market** must have many buyers and sellers, firms must be producing identical products, and there must be no barriers to entry of new firms. The demand curve for a good or service produced in a perfectly competitive market is downward sloping, but the demand curve for the output of one firm in a perfectly competitive market is a horizontal line at the market price. Firms in perfectly competitive markets are **price takers** and see their sales drop to zero if they attempt to charge more than the market price.

 Visit www.myeconlab.com to complete these exercises online and get instant feedback.

Review Questions

1.1 What are the three conditions for a market to be perfectly competitive?

1.2 What is a price taker? When are firms likely to be price takers?

1.3 Draw a graph showing the market demand and supply for corn and the demand for the corn produced by one corn farmer. Be sure to indicate the market price and the price received by the corn farmer.

Problems and Applications

1.4 Explain whether each of the following is a perfectly competitive market. For each market that is not perfectly competitive, explain why it is not.
a. Corn farming
b. Retail bookselling
c. Automobile manufacturing
d. New home construction

1.5 Why are consumers usually price takers when they buy most goods and services, while relatively few firms are price takers?

1.6 **(Related to the *Don't Let This Happen to You!*)** Explain whether you agree or disagree with the following remark:

> According to the model of perfectly competitive markets, the demand for wheat should be a horizontal line. But this can't be true: When the price of wheat rises, the quantity of wheat demanded falls, and when the price of wheat falls, the quantity of wheat demanded rises. Therefore, the demand for wheat is not a horizontal line.

1.7 The financial writer Andrew Tobias has described an incident when he was a student at the Harvard Business School: Each student in the class was given large amounts of information about a particular firm and asked to determine a pricing strategy for the firm. Most of the students spent hours preparing their answers and came to class carrying many sheets of paper with their calculations. Tobias came up with the correct answer after just a few minutes and without having made any calculations. When his professor called on him in class for an answer, Tobias stated, "The case said the XYZ Company was in a very competitive industry . . . and the case said that the company had all the business it could handle." Given this information, what price do you think Tobias argued the company should charge? Briefly explain. (Tobias says the class greeted his answer with "thunderous applause.")

Source: Andrew Tobias, *The Only Investment Guide You'll Ever Need*, San Diego: Harcourt, 2005, pp. 6–8.

>> End Learning Objective 1

How a Firm Maximizes Profit in a Perfectly Competitive Market

Summary

Profit is the difference between total revenue (TR) and total cost (TC). **Average revenue (AR)** is total revenue divided by the quantity of the product sold. A firm maximizes profit by producing the level of output where the difference between revenue and cost is the greatest. This is the same level of output where marginal revenue is equal to marginal cost. **Marginal revenue** is the change in total revenue from selling one more unit.

 Visit www.myeconlab.com to complete these exercises online and get instant feedback.

Review Questions

2.1 Explain why it is true that for a firm in a perfectly competitive market that $P = MR = AR$.

2.2 Explain why it is true that for a firm in a perfectly competitive market, the profit-maximizing condition $MR = MC$ is equivalent to the condition $P = MC$.

Problems and Applications

2.3 A student argues: "To maximize profit, a firm should produce the quantity where the difference between marginal revenue and marginal cost is the greatest. If it produces more than this quantity, then the profit made on each additional unit will be falling." Briefly explain whether you agree with this reasoning.

2.4 Why don't firms maximize revenue rather than profit? If a firm decided to maximize revenue, would it be likely to produce a smaller or a larger quantity than if it were maximizing profit? Briefly explain.

2.5 Refer to Table 2 and Table 3. Suppose the price of wheat rises to $6.00 per bushel. How many bushels of wheat will Farmer Parker produce, and how much profit will he make? Briefly explain.

2.6 Refer to Table 2 and Table 3. Suppose that the marginal cost of wheat is $0.50 higher for every bushel of wheat produced. For example, the marginal cost of producing the eighth bushel of wheat is now $6.50. Assume that the price of wheat remains $4 per bushel. Will this increase in marginal cost change the profit-maximizing level of production for Farmer Parker? Briefly explain. How much profit will Farmer Parker make now?

>> End Learning Objective 2

Illustrating Profit or Loss on the Cost Curve Graph

Summary

From the definitions of profit and average total cost, we can develop the following expression for the relationship between total profit and average total cost: Profit = $(P - ATC) \times Q$. Using this expression, we can determine the area showing profit or loss on a cost-curve graph: The area of profit or loss is a box with a height equal to price minus average total cost (for profit) or average total cost minus price (for loss) and a base equal to the quantity of output.

 Visit www.myeconlab.com to complete these exercises online and get instant feedback.

Review Questions

3.1 Draw a graph showing a firm in a perfectly competitive market that is making a profit. Be sure your graph includes the firm's demand curve, marginal revenue curve, marginal cost curve, average total cost curve, and average variable cost curve and make sure to indicate the area representing the firm's profits.

3.2 Draw a graph showing a firm in a perfectly competitive market that is operating at a loss. Be sure your graph includes the firm's demand curve, marginal revenue curve, marginal cost curve, average total cost curve, and average variable cost curve and make sure to indicate the area representing the firm's losses.

Problems and Applications

3.3 (Related to *Solved Problem 3*) Frances sells earrings in the perfectly competitive earring market. Her output per day and costs are as follows:

OUTPUT PER DAY	TOTAL COST
0	$1.00
1	2.50
2	3.50
3	4.20
4	4.50
5	5.20
6	6.80
7	8.70
8	10.70
9	13.00

a. If the current equilibrium price in the earring market is $1.80, how many earrings will Frances produce, what price will she charge, and how much profit (or loss) will she make? Draw a graph to illustrate your answer. Your graph should be clearly labeled and should include Frances's demand, *ATC*, *AVC*, *MC*, and *MR* curves; the price she is charging; the quantity she is producing; and the area representing her profit (or loss).

b. Suppose the equilibrium price of earrings falls to $1.00. Now how many earrings will Frances produce, what price will she charge, and how much profit (or loss) will she make? Show your work. Draw a graph to illustrate this situation, using the instructions in question (a).

c. Suppose the equilibrium price of earrings falls to $0.25. Now how many earrings will Frances produce, what price will she charge, and how much profit (or loss) will she make?

3.4 (Related to *Solved Problem 3*) Review Solved Problem 3 and then answer the following: Suppose the equilibrium price of basketballs falls to $2.50. Now how many basketballs will Andy produce? What price will he charge? How much profit (or loss) will he make?

3.5 (Related to the *Don't Let This Happen to You!*) A student examines the following graph and argues, "I believe that a firm will want to produce at Q_1, not Q_2.

At Q_1, the distance between price and marginal cost is the greatest. Therefore, at Q_1, the firm will be maximizing its profits." Briefly explain whether you agree with the student's argument.

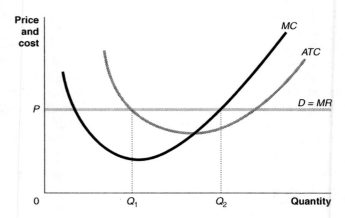

3.6 According to a report in the *Wall Street Journal*, during the fourth quarter of 2003, the profits of British Airways rose to £83 million, from £13 million one year earlier. At the same time, "the average amount the airline makes on each paying passenger fell 0.8%." If profit per passenger fell, how could total profits rise? Illustrate your answer with a graph. Be sure to indicate profit per passenger and total profit on the graph.

Source: Emma Blake, "British Airways Reports Sharp Jump in Net Profits," *Wall Street Journal*, February 9, 2004.

3.7 The following is from an article in the *Los Angeles Times* : "Gerald Lasseigne, a 53-year-old information systems technician in Donaldsonville, La., lost his job last month when steep natural gas prices forced Triad Nitrogen to shut down its fertilizer plant on the banks of the Mississippi River." Draw a graph showing the Triad Nitrogen company earning a profit from its fertilizer plant before the increase in the price of natural gas. Draw a second graph showing why Triad Nitrogen shut down the plant following the increase in the price of natural gas.

Source: Warren Vieth and Aparna Kumar, "Higher Oil Prices Ooze into Economy," *Los Angeles Times*, March 25, 2003, p. C1.

3.8 (Related to the *Making the Connection*) Suppose the medical screening firms had run an effective advertising campaign which convinced a large number of people that yearly CT scans were critical for good health. How would this have changed the fortunes of these firms? Illustrate your answer with a graph showing the situation for a representative firm in the industry. Be sure your graph includes the firm's demand curve, marginal revenue curve, marginal cost curve, and average total cost curve.

>> End Learning Objective 3

Deciding Whether to Produce or to Shut Down in the Short Run

Summary

In deciding whether to shut down or produce during a given period, a firm should ignore its *sunk costs*. A **sunk cost** is a cost that has already been paid and that cannot by recovered. In the short run, a firm continues to produce as long as its price is at least equal to its average variable cost. A perfectly competitive firm's **shutdown point** is the minimum point on the firm's average variable cost curve. If price falls below average variable cost, the firm shuts down in the short run. For prices above the shutdown point, a perfectly competitive firm's marginal cost curve is also its supply curve.

myeconlab Visit www.myeconlab.com to complete these exercises online and get instant feedback.

Review Questions

4.1 What is the difference between a firm's shutdown point in the short run and in the long run? Why are firms willing to accept losses in the short run but not in the long run?

4.2 What is the relationship between a perfectly competitive firm's marginal cost curve and its supply curve?

Problems and Applications

4.3 Edward Scahill produces table lamps in the perfectly competitive desk lamp market.
a. Fill in the missing values in the table.

OUTPUT PER WEEK	TOTAL COSTS	AFC	AVC	ATC	MC
0	$100				
1	150				
2	175				
3	190				
4	210				
5	240				
6	280				
7	330				
8	390				
9	460				
10	540				

b. Suppose the equilibrium price in the desk lamp market is $50. How many table lamps should Edward produce, and how much profit will he make?
c. If next week the equilibrium price of desk lamps drops to $30, should Edward shut down? Explain.

4.4 The graph represents the situation of a perfectly competitive firm.

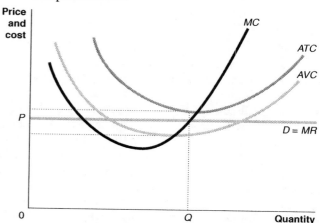

Indicate on the graph the areas that represent the following:
a. Total cost
b. Total revenue
c. Variable cost
d. Profit or loss
   Briefly explain whether the firm will continue to produce in the short run.

4.5 (Related to the *Making the Connection*) Suppose you decide to open a copy store. You rent store space (signing a one-year lease to do so), and you take out a loan at a local bank and use the money to purchase 10 copiers. Six months later, a large chain opens a copy store two blocks away from yours. As a result, the revenue you receive from your copy store, while sufficient to cover the wages of your employees and the costs of paper and utilities, doesn't cover all your rent and the interest and repayment costs on the loan you took out to purchase the copiers. Should you continue operating your business?

4.6 (Related to the *Making the Connection*) Club Mediterranee operates 120 Club Med resorts around the world. Following the September 11, 2001, terrorist attacks on the United States, many American tourists were reluctant to travel to foreign resorts. As a result, the prices Club Med could charge visitors to its resorts declined. In November 2001, Club Med decided to temporarily shut down 15 of its resorts. Analyze possible reasons for Club Med's decision. Be sure to discuss the likely relationship between the revenue Club Med received from operating these resorts and the resorts' fixed and variable costs.

Source: Rafer Guzman, "Club Med Plans to Temporarily Close 15 Resorts," *Wall Street Journal,* November 9, 2001, p. B1.

>> End Learning Objective 4

"If Everyone Can Do It, You Can't Make Money at It": The Entry and Exit of Firms in the Long Run

Summary

Economic profit is a firm's revenues minus all its costs, implicit and explicit. **Economic loss** is the situation in which a firm's total revenue is less than its total cost, including all implicit costs. If firms make economic profits in the short run, new firms enter the industry until the market price has fallen enough to wipe out the profits. If firms make economic losses, firms exit the industry until the market price has risen enough to wipe out the losses. **Long-run competitive equilibrium** is the situation in which the entry and exit of firms has resulted in the typical firm breaking even. The **long-run supply curve** shows the relationship between market price and the quantity supplied.

 Visit www.myeconlab.com to complete these exercises online and get instant feedback.

Review Questions

5.1 When are firms likely to enter an industry? When are they likely to exit an industry?

5.2 Would a firm earning zero economic profit continue to produce, even in the long run?

5.3 Discuss the shape of the long-run supply curve in a perfectly competitive market. Suppose that a perfectly competitive market is initially at long-run equilibrium and then there is a permanent decrease in the demand for the product. Draw a graph showing how the market adjusts in the long run.

Problems and Applications

5.4 Suppose an assistant professor of economics is earning a salary of $65,000 per year. One day she quits her job, sells $100,000 worth of bonds that had been earning 5 percent per year, and uses the funds to open a bookstore. At the end of the year, she shows an accounting profit of $80,000 on her income tax return. What is her economic profit?

5.5 Suppose that you and your sister both decide to open copy stores. Your parents always liked your sister better than you, so they purchase and give to her free of charge the three copiers she needs to operate her store. You, however, have to rent your copiers for $1,500 per month each. Does your sister have lower costs in operating her copy store than you have in operating your copy store because of this? Explain.

5.6 Consider the following statement: "The products for which demand is the greatest will also be the products that are most profitable to produce." Briefly explain whether you agree with this statement.

5.7 In panel (b) of Figure 9, Anne Moreno reduces her output from 8,000 to 5,000 boxes of apples when the price falls to $7. At this price and this output level, she is operating at a loss. Why doesn't she just continue charging the original $10 and continue producing 8,000 boxes of apples?

5.8 The following statement appeared in a Congressional analysis of the airline industry: "In lean times, airlines can operate for extended periods of time [while making losses] . . . because revenues will cover a large part of their costs (Pan Am lost money for about a decade before finally closing down)." Why would Pan Am—or any other airline—continue losing money for 10 years rather than shut down immediately? In the statement "revenues will cover a large part of their costs," does it matter if the costs being referred to are fixed costs or variable costs? Briefly explain.

Source: Joint Economic Committee, Democratic Staff, *Assessing Losses for the Airline Industry and Its Workers in the Aftermath of the Terrorist Attacks,* October 3, 2001.

5.9 A student in a principles of economics course makes the following remark: "The economic model of perfectly competitive markets is fine in theory but not very realistic. It predicts that in the long run, a firm in a perfectly competitive market will earn no profits. No firm in the real world would stay in business if it earned zero profits." Do you agree with this remark?

5.10 Suppose that the laptop computer industry is perfectly competitive and that the firms that assemble laptops do not also make the displays, or screens, for them. Suppose that the laptop display industry is also perfectly competitive. Finally, suppose that because the demand for laptop displays is currently relatively small, firms in the laptop display industry have not been able to take advantage of all the economies of scale in laptop display production. Use a graph of the laptop computer market to illustrate the long-run effects on equilibrium price and quantity in the laptop computer market of a substantial and sustained increase in the demand for laptop computers. Use another graph to show the impact on the cost curves of a typical firm in the laptop computer industry. Briefly explain your graphs. Do your graphs indicate that the laptop computer industry is a constant-cost industry, an increasing-cost industry, or a decreasing-cost industry?

5.11 **(Related to the *Chapter Opener*)** If in the long run apple growers who use organic methods of cultivation make no greater rate of return on their investment than apple growers who use conventional methods, why did a significant number of apple growers switch from conventional to organic methods in the first place?

>> End Learning Objective 5

6 LEARNING OBJECTIVE

6 | Explain how perfect competition leads to economic efficiency

Perfect Competition and Efficiency

Summary

Perfect competition results in **productive efficiency,** which means that goods and services are produced at the lowest possible cost. Perfect competition also results in **allocative efficiency,** which means the goods and services are produced up to the point where the last unit provides a marginal benefit to consumers equal to the marginal cost of producing it.

myeconlab Visit www.myeconlab.com to complete these exercises online and get instant feedback.

Review Questions

6.1 What is meant by allocative efficiency? What is meant by productive efficiency? Briefly discuss the difference between these two concepts.

6.2 How does perfect competition lead to allocative and productive efficiency?

Problems and Applications

6.3 The chapter states, "Firms will supply all those goods that provide consumers with a marginal benefit at least as great as the marginal cost of producing them." A student objects to this statement by making the following argument: "I doubt that firms will really do this. After all, firms are in business to make a profit; they don't care about what is best for consumers." Evaluate the student's argument.

6.4 **(Related to *Solved Problem 6*)** Discuss the following statement: "In a perfectly competitive market, in the long run consumers benefit from reductions in costs, but firms don't." Don't firms also benefit from cost reductions because they are able to earn greater profits?

6.5 **(Related to *Solved Problem 6*)** Suppose you read the following item in a newspaper article under the headline "Price Gouging Alleged in Pencil Market":

Consumer advocacy groups charged at a press conference yesterday that there is widespread price gouging in the sale of pencils. They released a study showing that whereas the average retail price of pencils was $1.00, the average cost of producing pencils was only $0.50. "Pencils can be produced without complicated machinery or highly skilled workers, so there is no justification for companies charging a price that is twice what it costs them to produce the product. Pencils are too important in the life of every American for us to tolerate this sort of price gouging any longer," said George Grommet, chief spokesperson for the consumer groups. The consumer groups advocate passage of a law that would allow companies selling pencils to charge a price no more than 20 percent greater than their average cost of production.

Do you believe such a law would be advisable in a situation like this? Explain.

6.6 **(Related to *Solved Problem 6*)** In early 2007, Pioneer and JVC, two Japanese electronics firms, each announced that their profits were going to be lower than expected because they were both forced to cut prices for LCD and plasma television sets. Given the strong consumer demand for plasma television sets, shouldn't firms have been able to raise prices and increase their profits? Briefly explain.

Source: Hiroyuki Kachi, "Pioneer's Net Rises 74%, JVC Posts Loss," *Wall Street Journal*, February 1, 2007.

6.7 **(Related to the *Making the Connection*)** Suppose a nutritionist develops a revolutionary new diet that involves eating 10 apples per day. The new diet becomes wildly popular. What effect is the new diet likely to have on the number of apple orchards within 100 miles of New York City? What effect is the diet likely to have on housing prices in New York City?

>> End Learning Objective 6

Oligopoly: Firms in Less Competitive Markets

From Chapter 13 of *Microeconomics*, 2/e. R. Glenn Hubbard. Anthony Patrick O'Brien. Copyright © 2008 by Pearson Prentice Hall.

Oligopoly: Firms in Less Competitive Markets

Competing with Wal-Mart

Many of the largest corporations in the United States began as small businesses. In 1975, Bill Gates and Paul Allen founded the Microsoft Corporation in Albuquerque, New Mexico, with themselves as the only employees. Michael Dell started the Dell computer company in 1984 from his dorm room at the University of Texas. Sam Walton, founder of Wal-Mart, bought his first store in 1945 with $20,000 borrowed from his father-in-law. Eventually, Wal-Mart would become the largest company in the world. Today, Wal-Mart employs nearly 1.8 million people, which is four times as many as McDonalds, the second largest employer.

When each of these firms was founded, their industries included many more firms than they do now. Today, in the software and computer industries, fewer than 10 firms account for the great majority of sales. Wal-Mart accounts for a large share of several segments of retail sales. In 2007, Wal-Mart was the leading seller of groceries in the United States. It sells more than 25 percent of all the disposable diapers, toothpaste, dog food, and photographic film sold in

the United States. It is also the leading seller of CDs and DVDs, with market shares of 15 to 20 percent. More than 93 percent of U.S. families shop at Wal-Mart at least once per year.

An industry with only a few firms is an *oligopoly*. In an oligopoly, a firm's profitability depends on its interactions with other firms. In these industries, firms must develop *business strategies*, which involve not just deciding what price to charge and how many units to produce but also how much to advertise, which new technologies to adopt, how to manage relations with suppliers, and which new markets to enter.

A key part of Sam Walton's business strategy for Wal-Mart involved placing stores in small towns, where the main competition was from small, locally owned stores. By buying in bulk directly from manufacturers, Walton was able to lower costs, which enabled him to charge lower prices than his competitors. As early as the 1970s, Wal-Mart also made large investments in information technology (IT). Unlike most of its competitors, which had to count unsold goods by hand to find out how many were left in inventory, Wal-Mart had a computerized system for tracking goods. To aid this system, Wal-Mart insisted in the early 1980s that its suppliers use UPC barcodes on

products. This helped spread the use of barcodes to nearly every product sold in the United States. Today, Wal-Mart is pioneering the use of radio frequency identification (RFID) tracking tags that may ultimately replace barcodes. With this system, employees will no longer have to manually scan barcodes. Instead, a radio signal will automatically record the arrival of a product in the warehouse, its shipment to a Wal-Mart store, and its purchase by the consumer. By 2007, many of Wal-Mart's largest suppliers had implemented RFID systems.

In recent years, Wal-Mart has been criticized for several practices, including selling goods produced in foreign factories by low-paid workers, paying low wages to its own workers, providing limited health care benefits, and driving smaller competitors into bankruptcy. As a result, Wal-Mart has run into some difficulty getting local government approvals to open new stores. Wal-Mart's competitors, however, continue to search for ways to successfully compete. **AN INSIDE LOOK** discusses Target's attempts to compete with Wal-Mart in the market for generic prescription drugs.

Source: "The Bulldozer of Bentonville Slows," *Economist*, February 15, 2007.

Ralf-Finn Hestoft, Corbis/Bettmann

Economics in YOUR Life!

Why Can't You Find a Cheap PlayStation 3?

It's the end of finals, and you and your roommate decide to treat yourselves to a PlayStation 3 game system—provided that you can find one that has a relatively low price. First you check Amazon.com and find a price of $499.99. Then you check Best Buy, but the price is also $499.99. Then you check Target; $499.99 again! Finally, you check Wal-Mart, and you find a lower price: $499. *82*, a whopping discount of $0.17. Why isn't one of these big retailers willing to charge a lower price? What happened to price competition? As you read the chapter, see if you can answer these questions. You can check your answers against those we provide at the end of the chapter.

363

Oligopoly A market structure in which a small number of interdependent firms compete.

Firms maximize profit by producing where marginal revenue equals marginal cost. To determine marginal revenue and marginal cost, we use graphs that include the firm's demand, marginal revenue, and marginal cost curves. In this chapter, we will study **oligopoly**, a market structure in which a small number of interdependent firms compete. In analyzing oligopoly, we cannot rely on the same types of graphs we use in analyzing perfect competition and monopolistic competition—for two reasons.

First, we need to use economic models that allow us to analyze the more complex business strategies of large oligopoly firms. Second, even in determining the profit-maximizing price and output of an oligopoly firm, demand curves and cost curves are not as useful as in the cases of perfect competition and monopolistic competition. We are able to draw the demand curves for competitive firms by assuming that the prices these firms charge have no impact on the prices other firms in their industries charge. This assumption is realistic when each firm is small relative to the market. It is not a realistic assumption, however, for firms that are as large relative to their markets as Microsoft, Dell, or Wal-Mart.

When large firms cut their prices, their rivals in the industry often—but not always—respond by also cutting their prices. Because we don't know for sure how other firms will respond to a price change, we don't know the quantity an oligopolist will sell at a particular price. In other words, it is difficult to know what an oligopolist's demand curve will look like. As we have seen, a firm's marginal revenue curve depends on its demand curve. If we don't know what an oligopolist's demand curve looks like, we also don't know what its marginal revenue curve looks like. Not knowing marginal revenue, we can't calculate the profit-maximizing level of output and the profit-maximizing price the way we did for competitive firms.

The approach we use to analyze competition among oligopolists is called *game theory*. Game theory can be used to analyze any situation in which groups or individuals interact. In the context of economic analysis, game theory is the study of the decisions of firms in industries where the profits of each firm depend on its interactions with other firms. It has been applied to strategies for nuclear war, for international trade negotiations, and for political campaigns, among many other examples. In this chapter, we use game theory to analyze the business strategies of large firms.

1 LEARNING OBJECTIVE

1 | Show how barriers to entry explain the existence of oligopolies.

Oligopoly and Barriers to Entry

Oligopolies are industries with only a few firms. This market structure lies between competitive industries which have many firms, and monopolies, which have only a single firm. One measure of the extent of competition in an industry is the *concentration ratio*. Every five years, the U.S. Bureau of the Census publishes four-firm concentration ratios that state the fraction of each industry's sales accounted for by its four largest firms. Most economists believe that a four-firm concentration ratio of greater than 40 percent indicates that an industry is an oligopoly.

The concentration ratio has some flaws as a measure of the extent of competition in an industry. For example, concentration ratios do not include sales in the United States by foreign firms. In addition, concentration ratios are calculated for the national market, even though the competition in some industries, such as restaurants or college bookstores, is mainly local. Finally, competition sometimes exists between firms in different industries. For example, Wal-Mart is included in the discount department stores industry but also competes with firms in the supermarket industry and the retail toy store industry. Some economists prefer another measure of competition, known as the *Herfindahl-Hirschman Index*. Despite their shortcomings, concentration ratios can be useful in providing a general idea of the extent of competition in an industry.

Table 1 lists examples of oligopolies in manufacturing and retail trade. Notice that the "Discount Department Stores" industry that includes Wal-Mart is highly concentrated. Wal-Mart also operates Sam's Club stores, which are in the highly concentrated "Warehouse Clubs and Supercenters" industry.

Barriers to Entry

Why do oligopolies exist? Why aren't there many more firms in the discount department store industry, the beer industry, or the automobile industry? Recall that new firms will enter industries where existing firms are earning economic profits. But new firms often have difficulty entering an oligopoly. Anything that keeps new firms from entering an industry in which firms are earning economic profits is called a **barrier to entry**. Three barriers to entry are economies of scale, ownership of a key input, and government-imposed barriers.

Economies of Scale The most important barrier to entry is economies of scale. **Economies of scale** exist when a firm's long-run average costs fall as it increases output. The greater the economies of scale, the fewer the number of firms that will be in the industry. Figure 1 illustrates this point.

If economies of scale are relatively unimportant in the industry, the typical firm's long-run average cost curve (*LRAC*) will reach a minimum at a level of output (Q_1 in Figure 1) that is a small fraction of total industry sales. The industry will have room for a large number of firms and will be competitive. If economies of scale are significant, the typical firm will not reach the minimum point on its long-run average cost curve (Q_2 in Figure 1) until it has produced a large fraction of industry sales. Then the industry will have room for only a few firms and will be an oligopoly.

Barrier to entry Anything that keeps new firms from entering an industry in which firms are earning economic profits.

Economies of scale The situation when a firm's long-run average costs fall as it increases output.

RETAIL TRADE		MANUFACTURING	
INDUSTRY	FOUR-FIRM CONCENTRATION RATIO	INDUSTRY	FOUR-FIRM CONCENTRATION RATIO
Discount Department Stores	95%	Cigarettes	95%
Warehouse Clubs and Supercenters	92%	Beer	91%
Hobby, Toy, and Game Stores	72%	Aircraft	81%
Athletic Footwear Stores	71%	Breakfast Cereal	78%
College Bookstores	70%	Automobiles	76%
Radio, Television, and Other Electronic Stores	69%	Computers	76%
Pharmacies and Drugstores	53%	Dog and Cat Food	64%

TABLE 1

Examples of Oligopolies in Retail Trade and Manufacturing

Source: U.S. Census Bureau, *Concentration Ratios, 2002*, May 2006; and U.S. Census Bureau, *Establishment and Firm Size, 2002*, November 2005.

Figure 1

Economies of Scale Help Determine the Extent of Competition in an Industry

An industry will be competitive if the minimum point on the typical firm's long-run average cost curve ($LRAC_1$) occurs at a level of output that is a small fraction of total industry sales, like Q_1. The industry will be an oligopoly if the minimum point comes at a level of output that is a large fraction of industry sales, like Q_2.

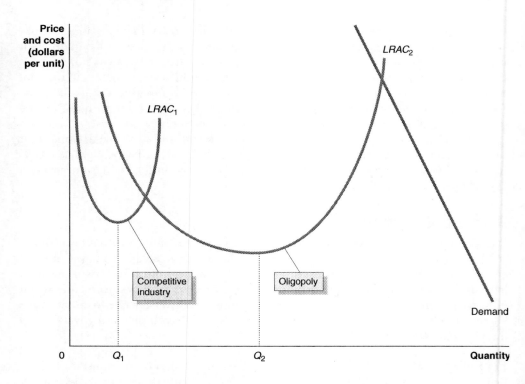

Economies of scale can explain why there is much more competition in the restaurant industry than in the discount department store industry. Because very large restaurants do not have lower average costs than smaller restaurants, the restaurant industry has room for many firms. In contrast, large discount department stores, such as Wal-Mart, have much lower average costs than small discount department stores, for the reasons we discussed in the chapter opener. As a result, just four firms—Wal-Mart, Target, Kmart, and Costco—account for about 95 percent of all sales in this industry.

Ownership of a Key Input If production of a good requires a particular input, then control of that input can be a barrier to entry. For many years, the Aluminum Company of America (Alcoa) controlled most of the world's supply of high-quality bauxite, the mineral needed to produce aluminum. The only way other companies could enter the industry to compete with Alcoa was to recycle aluminum. The De Beers Company of South Africa was able to block competition in the diamond market by controlling the output of most of the world's diamond mines. Until the 1990s, Ocean Spray had very little competition in the market for fresh and frozen cranberries because it controlled almost the entire supply of cranberries. Even today, it controls about 80 percent of the cranberry crop.

Government-Imposed Barriers Firms sometimes try to have the government impose barriers to entry. Many large firms employ *lobbyists* to convince state legislators and members of Congress to pass laws favorable to the economic interests of the firms. There are tens of thousands of lobbyists in Washington, DC, alone. Top lobbyists command annual salaries of $300,000 or more, which indicates the value firms place on their activities. Examples of government-imposed barriers to entry are patents, licensing requirements, and barriers to international trade. A **patent** gives a firm the exclusive right to a new product for a period of 20 years from the date the product is invented. Governments use patents to encourage firms to carry out research and development of new and better products and better ways of producing existing products. Output and living standards increase faster when firms devote resources to research and development, but a firm that spends money to develop a new product may not earn much profit if other firms can copy the product. For example, the pharmaceutical company Merck spends more than $3 billion per year to develop new prescription drugs. If rival companies

Patent The exclusive right to a product for a period of 20 years from the date the product is invented.

366

could freely produce these new drugs as soon as Merck developed them, most of the firm's investment would be wasted. Because Merck can patent a new drug, the firm can charge higher prices during the years the patent is in force and make an economic profit on its successful innovation.

The government also restricts competition through *occupational licensing*. The United States currently has about 500 occupational licensing laws. For example, doctors and dentists in every state need licenses to practice. The justification for the laws is to protect the public from incompetent practitioners, but by restricting the number of people who can enter the licensed professions, the laws also raise prices. Studies have shown that states that make it harder to earn a dentist's license have prices for dental services that are about 15 percent higher than in other states. Similarly, states that require a license for out-of-state firms to sell contact lenses have higher prices for contact lenses. When state licenses are required for occupations like hair braiding, which was done several years ago in California, restricting competition is the main result.

Government also imposes barriers to entering some industries by imposing tariffs and quotas on foreign competition. A *tariff* is a tax on imports, and a *quota* limits the quantity of a good that can be imported into a country. A quota on foreign sugar imports severely limits competition in the U.S. sugar market. As a result, U.S. sugar companies can charge prices that are more than twice as high as those charged by companies outside the United States.

In summary, to earn economic profits, all firms would like to charge a price well above average cost, but earning economic profits attracts new firms to enter the industry. Eventually, the increased competition forces price down to average cost, and firms just break even. In an oligopoly, barriers to entry prevent—or at least slow down—entry, which allows firms to earn economic profits over a longer period.

---

2 | Use game theory to analyze the strategies of oligopolistic firms.

Using Game Theory to Analyze Oligopoly

As we noted at the beginning of the chapter, economists analyze oligopolies using *game theory*, which was developed during the 1940s by the mathematician John von Neumann and the economist Oskar Morgenstern. **Game theory** is the study of how people make decisions in situations in which attaining their goals depends on their interactions with others. In oligopolies, the interactions among firms are crucial in determining profitability because the firms are large relative to the market.

In all games—whether poker, chess, or Monopoly—the interactions among the players are crucial in determining the outcome. In addition, games share three key characteristics:

1 *Rules* that determine what actions are allowable

2 *Strategies* that players employ to attain their objectives in the game

3 *Payoffs* that are the results of the interaction among the players' strategies

In business situations, the rules of the "game" include not just laws that a firm must obey but also other matters beyond a firm's control—at least in the short run—such as its production function. A **business strategy** is a set of actions that a firm takes to achieve a goal, such as maximizing profits. The *payoffs* are the profits earned as a result of a firm's strategies interacting with the strategies of the other firms. The best way to understand the game theory approach is to look at an example.

Game theory The study of how people make decisions in situations in which attaining their goals depends on their interactions with others; in economics, the study of the decisions of firms in industries where the profits of each firm depend on its interactions with other firms.

Business strategy Actions taken by a firm to achieve a goal, such as maximizing profits.

A Duopoly Game: Price Competition between Two Firms

In this simple example, we use game theory to analyze price competition in a *duopoly*— an oligopoly with two firms. Suppose that an isolated town in Alaska has only two stores: Wal-Mart and Target. Both stores sell the new Sony PlayStation 3. For simplicity, let's

Figure 2

A Duopoly Game

Wal-Mart's profits are in blue, and Target's profits are in red. Wal-Mart and Target would each make profits of $10,000 per month on sales of PlayStation 3 if they both charged $600. However, each store manager has an incentive to undercut the other by charging a lower price. If both charge $400, they would each make a profit of only $7,500 per month.

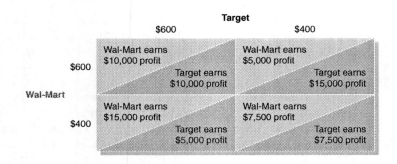

Payoff matrix A table that shows the payoffs that each firm earns from every combination of strategies by the firms.

Collusion An agreement among firms to charge the same price or otherwise not to compete.

Dominant strategy A strategy that is the best for a firm, no matter what strategies other firms use.

Nash equilibrium A situation in which each firm chooses the best strategy, given the strategies chosen by other firms.

assume that no other stores stock PlayStation 3 and that consumers in the town can't buy it on the Internet or through mail-order catalogs. The manager of each store decides whether to charge $400 or $600 for the PlayStation. Which price will be more profitable depends on the price the other store charges. The decision regarding what price to charge is an example of a business strategy. In Figure 2, we organize the possible outcomes that result from the actions of the two firms into a *payoff matrix*. A **payoff matrix** is a table that shows the payoffs that each firm earns from every combination of strategies by the firms.

Wal-Mart's profits are shown in blue, and Target's profits are shown in red. If Wal-Mart and Target both charge $600 for the PlayStation, each store will make a profit of $10,000 per month from sales of the game console. If Wal-Mart charges the lower price of $400, while Target charges $600, Wal-Mart will gain many of Target's customers. Wal-Mart's profits will be $15,000, and Target's will be only $5,000. Similarly, if Wal-Mart charges $600, while Target is charging $400, Wal-Mart's profits will be only $5,000, while Target's profits will be $15,000. If both stores charge $400, each will earn profits of $7,500 per month.

Clearly, the stores will be better off if they both charge $600 for the PlayStation. But will they both charge this price? One possibility is that the manager of the Wal-Mart and the manager of the Target will get together and *collude* by agreeing to charge the higher price. **Collusion** is an agreement among firms to charge the same price or otherwise not to compete. Unfortunately, for Wal-Mart and Target—but fortunately for their customers—collusion is against the law in the United States. The government can fine companies that collude and send the managers involved to jail.

The manager of the Wal-Mart store legally can't discuss his pricing decision with the manager of the Target store, so he has to predict what the other manager will do. Suppose the Wal-Mart manager is convinced that the Target manager will charge $600 for the PlayStation. In this case, the Wal-Mart manager will definitely charge $400 because that will increase his profit from $10,000 to $15,000. But suppose instead the Wal-Mart manager is convinced that the Target manager will charge $400. Then the Wal-Mart manager also definitely will charge $400 because that will increase his profit from $5,000 to $7,500. In fact, whichever price the Target manager decides to charge, the Wal-Mart manager is better off charging $400. So, we know that the Wal-Mart manager will choose a price of $400 for the PlayStation.

Now consider the situation of the Target manager. The Target manager is in the identical position to the Wal-Mart manager, so we can expect her to make the same decision to charge $400 for the PlayStation. In this situation, each manager has a *dominant strategy*. A **dominant strategy** is the best strategy for a firm, no matter what strategies other firms use. The result is an equilibrium where both managers charge $400 for the PlayStation. This situation is an equilibrium because each manager is maximizing profits, *given the price chosen by the other manager*. In other words, neither firm can increase its profits by changing its price, given the price chosen by the other firm. An equilibrium where each firm chooses the best strategy, given the strategies chosen by other firms, is called a **Nash equilibrium**, named after Nobel laureate John Nash of Princeton University, a pioneer in the development of game theory.

Making the Connection

A Beautiful Mind: Game Theory Goes to the Movies

John Nash is the most celebrated game theorist in the world, partly because of his achievements and partly because of his dramatic life. In 1948, at the age of 20, Nash received bachelor's and master's degrees in mathematics from the Carnegie Institute of Technology (now known as Carnegie Mellon University). Two years later, he received a Ph.D. from Princeton for his 27-page dissertation on game theory. It was in this dissertation that he first discussed the concept that became known as the *Nash equilibrium*. Nash appeared to be on his way to a brilliant academic career until he developed schizophrenia in the 1950s. He spent decades in and out of mental hospitals. During these years, he roamed the Princeton campus, covering blackboards in unused classrooms with indecipherable writings. He became known as the "Phantom of Fine Hall." In the 1970s, Nash gradually began to recover. In 1994, he shared the Nobel Prize in Economics with John Harsanyi of the University of California, Berkeley, and Reinhard Selten of Rheinische Friedrich–Wilhelms Universität, Germany, for his work on game theory.

In 1998, Sylvia Nasar of the *New York Times* wrote a biography of Nash, titled *A Beautiful Mind*. Three years later, the book was adapted into an award-winning film starring Russell Crowe. Unfortunately, the (fictitious) scene in the film that shows Nash discovering the idea of Nash equilibrium misstates the concept. In the scene, Nash is in a bar with several friends when four women with brown hair and one with blonde hair walk in. Nash and all of his friends prefer the blonde to the brunettes. One of Nash's friends points out that if they all compete for the blonde, they are unlikely to get her. In competing for the blonde, they will also insult the brunettes, with the result that none of them will end up with a date. Nash then gets a sudden insight. He suggests that they ignore the blonde and each approach one of the brunettes. That is the only way, he argues, that each of them will end up with a date.

Nash immediately claims that this is also an economic insight. He points out that Adam Smith had argued that the best result comes from everyone in the group doing what's best for himself. Nash argues, however, "The best result comes from everyone in the group doing what's best for himself *and* the group." But this is not an accurate description of the Nash equilibrium. As we have seen, in a Nash equilibrium, each player uses a strategy that will make him as well off as possible, *given the strategies of the other players*. The bar situation would not be a Nash equilibrium. Once the other men have chosen a brunette, each man will have an incentive to switch from the brunette he initially chose to the blonde.

In the film A Beautiful Mind, *Russell Crowe played John Nash, winner of the Nobel Prize in Economics.*

YOUR TURN: Test your understanding by doing related problem 2.11 at the end of this chapter.

Don't Let This Happen to **YOU!**

Don't Misunderstand Why Each Manager Ends Up Charging a Price of $400

It is tempting to think that the Wal-Mart manager and the Target manager would each charge $400 rather than $600 for the PlayStation because each is afraid that the other manager will charge $400. In fact, fear of being undercut by the other firm's charging a lower price is not the key to understanding each manager's pricing strategy. Notice that charging $400 is the most profitable strategy for each manager, no matter which price the other manager decides to charge. For example, even if the Wal-Mart manager somehow knew for sure that the Target manager intended to charge $600, he would still charge $400 because his profits would be $15,000 instead of $10,000. The Target manager is in the same situation. That is why charging $400 is a dominant strategy for both managers.

YOUR TURN: Test your understanding by doing related problem 2.15 at the end of the chapter.

Firm Behavior and the Prisoners' Dilemma

Cooperative equilibrium An equilibrium in a game in which players cooperate to increase their mutual payoff.

Noncooperative equilibrium An equilibrium in a game in which players do not cooperate but pursue their own self-interest.

Prisoners' dilemma A game in which pursuing dominant strategies results in noncooperation that leaves everyone worse off.

Notice that the equilibrium in Figure 2 is not very satisfactory for either firm. The firms earn $7,500 profit each month by charging $400, but they could have earned $10,000 profit if they had both charged $600. By "cooperating" and charging the higher price, they would have achieved a *cooperative equilibrium*. In a **cooperative equilibrium**, players cooperate to increase their mutual payoff. We have seen, though, that the outcome of this game is likely to be a **noncooperative equilibrium**, in which each firm pursues its own self-interest.

A situation like this, in which pursuing dominant strategies results in noncooperation that leaves everyone worse off, is called a **prisoners' dilemma**. The game gets its name from the problem faced by two suspects the police arrest for a crime. If the police lack other evidence, they may separate the suspects and offer each a reduced prison sentence in exchange for confessing to the crime and testifying against the other criminal. Because each suspect has a dominant strategy to confess to the crime, they will both confess and serve a jail term, even though they would have gone free if they had both remained silent.

Solved Problem | 2

Is Advertising a Prisoners' Dilemma for Coca-Cola and Pepsi?

Coca-Cola and Pepsi both advertise aggressively, but would they be better off if they didn't? Their commercials are not designed to convey new information about the products. Instead, they are designed to capture each other's customers. Construct a payoff matrix using the following hypothetical information:

- If neither firm advertises, Coca-Cola and Pepsi both earn profits of $750 million per year.

- If both firms advertise, Coca-Cola and Pepsi both earn profits of $500 million per year.

- If Coca-Cola advertises and Pepsi doesn't, Coca-Cola earns profits of $900 million and Pepsi earns profits of $400 million.

- If Pepsi advertises and Coca-Cola doesn't, Pepsi earns profits of $900 million and Coca-Cola earns profits of $400 million.

a. If Coca-Cola wants to maximize profit, will it advertise? Briefly explain.

b. If Pepsi wants to maximize profit, will it advertise? Briefly explain.

c. Is there a Nash equilibrium to this advertising game? If so, what is it?

SOLVING THE PROBLEM:

Step 1: **Review the chapter material.** This problem uses payoff matrixes to analyze a business situation, so you may want to review the section "A Duopoly Game: Price Competition between Two Firms."

Step 2: **Construct the payoff matrix.**

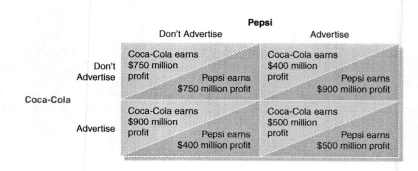

Step 3: **Answer question (a) by showing that Coca-Cola has a dominant strategy of advertising.** If Pepsi doesn't advertise, then Coca-Cola will make $900 million if it advertises but only $750 million if it doesn't. If Pepsi advertises, then Coca-Cola will make $500 million if it advertises but only $400 million if it doesn't. Therefore, advertising is a dominant strategy for Coca-Cola.

Step 4: **Answer question (b) by showing that Pepsi has a dominant strategy of advertising.** Pepsi is in the same position as Coca-Cola, so it also has a dominant strategy of advertising.

Step 5: **Answer question (c) by showing that there is a Nash equilibrium for this game.** Both firms advertising is a Nash equilibrium. Given that Pepsi is advertising, Coca-Cola's best strategy is to advertise. Given that Coca-Cola is advertising, Pepsi's best strategy is to advertise. Therefore, advertising is the optimal decision for both firms, *given the decision by the other firm.*

EXTRA CREDIT: This is another example of the prisoners' dilemma game. Coca-Cola and Pepsi would be more profitable if they both refrained from advertising, thereby saving the enormous expense of television and radio commercials and newspaper and magazine ads. Each firm's dominant strategy is to advertise, however, so they end up in an equilibrium where both advertise, and their profits are reduced.

YOUR TURN: For more practice, do related problems 2.12, 2.13, and 2.14 at the end of this chapter.

>> **End Solved Problem 2**

Making the Connection

Is There a Dominant Strategy for Bidding on eBay?

An auction is a game in which bidders compete to buy a product. The payoff in winning an auction is equal to the difference between the subjective value you place on the product being auctioned and the amount of the winning bid. On the online auction site eBay, more than 200 million items valued at more than $10 billion are auctioned each year.

eBay is run as a *second-price auction*, where the winning bidder pays the price of the second-highest bidder. If the high bidder on a DVD of *Spider-Man 3* bids $15, and the second bidder bids $10, the high bidder wins the auction and pays $10. It may seem that your best strategy when bidding on eBay is to place a bid well below the subjective value you place on the item in the hope of winning it at a low price. In fact, bidders on eBay have a dominant strategy of entering a bid equal to the maximum value they place on the item. For instance, suppose you are looking for a present for your parents' anniversary. They are Rolling Stones fans, and someone is auctioning a pair of Stones concert tickets. If the maximum value you place on the tickets is $200, that should be your bid. To see why, consider the results of strategies of bidding more or less than $200.

There are two possible outcomes of the auction: Either someone else bids more than you do, or you are the high bidder. First, suppose you bid $200 but someone else bids more than you do. If you had bid less than

On eBay, bidding the maximum value you place on an item is a dominant strategy.

$200, you would still have lost. If you had bid more than $200, you might have been the high bidder, but because your bid would be for more than the value you place on the tickets, you would have a negative payoff. Second, suppose you bid $200 and you are the high bidder. If you had bid less than $200, you would have run the risk of losing the tickets to someone whose bid you would have beaten by bidding $200. You would be worse off than if you had bid $200 and won. If you had bid more than $200, you would not have affected the price you ended up paying—which, remember, is equal to the amount bid by the second-highest bidder. Therefore, a strategy of bidding $200—the maximum value you place on the tickets—dominates bidding more or less than $200.

Even though making your first bid your highest bid is a dominant strategy on eBay, many bidders don't use it. After an auction is over, a link leads to a Web page showing all the bids. In many auctions, the same bidder bids several times, showing that the bidder had not understood his or her dominant strategy.

YOUR TURN: Test your understanding by doing related problem 2.16 at the end of this chapter.

Can Firms Escape the Prisoners' Dilemma?

Although the prisoners' dilemma game seems to show that cooperative behavior always breaks down, we know it doesn't. People often cooperate to achieve their goals, and firms find ways to cooperate by not competing on price. The reason the basic prisoners' dilemma story is not always applicable is that it assumes the game will be played only once. Most business situations, however, are repeated over and over. Each month, the Target and Wal-Mart managers will decide again what price they will charge for PlayStation 3. In the language of game theory, the managers are playing a *repeated game*. In a repeated game, the losses from not cooperating are greater than in a game played once, and players can also employ *retaliation strategies* against those who don't cooperate. As a result, we are more likely to see cooperative behavior.

Figure 2 shows that Wal-Mart and Target are earning $2,500 less per month by both charging $400 instead of $600 for the PlayStation 3. Every month that passes with both stores charging $400 increases the total amount lost: Two years of charging $400 will cause each store to lose $60,000 in profit. This lost profit increases the incentive for the store managers to cooperate by *implicitly* colluding. Remember that *explicit* collusion—such as the managers meeting and agreeing to charge $600—is illegal. But if the managers can find a way to signal each other that they will charge $600, they may be within the law.

Suppose, for example, that Wal-Mart and Target both advertise that they will match the lowest price offered by any competitor—in our simple example, they are each other's only competitor. These advertisements are signals to each other that they intend to charge $600 for the PlayStation. The signal is clear because each store knows that if it charges $400, the other store will automatically retaliate by also lowering its price to $400. The offer to match prices is a good *enforcement mechanism* because it guarantees that if either store fails to cooperate and charges the lower price, the competing store will automatically punish that store by also charging the lower price. As Figure 3 shows, the stores have changed the payoff matrix they face.

With the original payoff matrix (a), there is no matching offer, and each store makes more profit if it charges $400 when the other charges $600. The matching offer changes the payoff matrix to (b). Now the stores can charge $600 and receive a profit of $10,000 per month, or they can charge $400 and receive a profit of $7,500 per month. The equilibrium shifts from the prisoners' dilemma result of both stores charging the low price and receiving low profits to a result where both stores charge the high price and receive high profits. An offer to match competitors' prices might seem to benefit consumers, but game theory shows that it actually may hurt consumers by helping to keep prices high.

Target

(a) The payoff matrix with no offer to match prices

	Target $600	Target $400
Wal-Mart $600	Wal-Mart earns $10,000 profit / Target earns $10,000 profit	Wal-Mart earns $5,000 profit / Target earns $15,000 profit
Wal-Mart $400	Wal-Mart earns $15,000 profit / Target earns $5,000 profit	Wal-Mart earns $7,500 profit / Target earns $7,500 profit

If Target and Wal-Mart each advertise that they will match the price of their competitors, it changes the payoff matrix from the matrix in part (a) to the matrix in part (b).

Equilibrium changes from this outcome in part (a) to this outcome in part (b).

Target

(b) The payoff matrix with an offer to match prices

	Target $600	Target $400
Wal-Mart $600	Wal-Mart earns $10,000 profit / Target earns $10,000 profit	Wal-Mart earns $7,500 profit / Target earns $7,500 profit
Wal-Mart $400	Wal-Mart earns $7,500 profit / Target earns $7,500 profit	Wal-Mart earns $7,500 profit / Target earns $7,500 profit

Figure 3

Changing the Payoff Matrix in a Repeated Game

Wal-Mart and Target can change the payoff matrix by advertising that they will match their competitor's price. This retaliation strategy provides a signal that one store charging a lower price will be met automatically by the other store charging a lower price. In payoff matrix (a), there is no matching offer, and each store benefits if it charges $400 when the other charges $600. In payoff matrix (b), with the matching offer, the companies have only two choices: They can charge $600 and receive a profit of $10,000 per month, or they can charge $400 and receive a profit of $7,500 per month. The equilibrium shifts from the prisoners' dilemma result of both stores charging the low price and receiving low profits to both stores charging the high price and receiving high profits.

One form of implicit collusion occurs as a result of *price leadership*. With **price leadership**, one firm takes the lead in announcing a price change, which is then matched by the other firms in the industry. For example, through the 1970s, General Motors would announce a price change at the beginning of a model year and Ford and Chrysler would match GM's price change. In some cases, such as the airline industry, firms have attempted to act as price leaders, but failed when other firms in the industry declined to cooperate.

Price leadership A form of implicit collusion where one firm in an oligopoly announces a price change, which is matched by the other firms in the industry.

Making the Connection | American Airlines and Northwest Airlines Fail to Cooperate on a Price Increase

Coordinating prices is easier in some industries than in others. Fixed costs in the airline industry are very large, and marginal costs are very small. The marginal cost of flying one more passenger from New York to Chicago is no more than a few dollars: the cost of another snack served and a small amount of additional jet fuel. As a result, airlines often engage in last-minute price cutting to fill the remaining empty seats on a flight. Even a low-price ticket will increase marginal revenue more than marginal cost. As with other oligopolies, if all airlines cut prices, industry profits will decline. Airlines therefore continually adjust their prices while at the same time monitoring their rivals' prices and retaliating against them either for cutting prices or failing to go along with price increases.

The airlines have trouble raising the price this business traveler pays for a ticket.

Ken Reid, Getty Images, Inc.–Taxi

Consider the following fairly typical events from the spring of 2002. American Airlines decided to raise some of its ticket prices in a roundabout way. Business travelers are usually willing to pay higher prices for airline tickets than are leisure travelers. Business travelers also often must make their flight plans only a few days before they leave. Airlines take advantage of this fact by requiring 10- to 14-day advance reservations to get a fully discounted ticket. A smaller discount is available with a 3-day advance reservation. This smaller discount is aimed at business travelers. American decided to increase to 7 days the advance purchase requirement for the business travel discount. Because many business travelers cannot make their reservations that far in advance, they would have to buy full-fare tickets.

Continental Airlines matched American's change, but the other airlines refused to go along. They hoped that by not matching American's price increase, they would gain some of its customers. American then retaliated by offering very low $99 one-way tickets in 10 markets where Northwest Airlines, United Airlines, Delta Air Lines, and US Airways offered nonstop service. American did not offer the $99 fares in the markets where Continental offered nonstop service. An airline industry consultant observed that "American is trying to slap the hands of people who wouldn't go along with its increase."

Northwest immediately responded by offering $99 fares in 20 markets where American offers nonstop service. American retaliated by offering the low fare in 10 additional markets served by Northwest. Northwest then further retaliated by offering the low fare in a total of 160 markets served by American. After several days of very low fares and lost profits, American and Northwest restored their normal fares, and American went back to a 3-day advance reservation requirement for discounted business-travel tickets.

Did American's aggressive retaliation make it easier for airlines to agree on ticket price increases in the future? Apparently not. A few weeks later, Continental raised its prices for round-trip discounted tickets by $20. Every airline but Northwest matched the price increase. Rather than lose customers to Northwest, Continental and the other airlines rolled back the price increase.

Sources: Scott McCartney, "Airfare Wars Show Why Deals Arrive and Depart," *Wall Street Journal*, March 19, 2002; and Scott McCartney, "Airlines Drop $20 Fare Increase after Northwest Fails to Join In," *Wall Street Journal*, April 16, 2002.

YOUR TURN: Test your understanding by doing related problems 2.18, 2.19, and 2.20 at the end of this chapter.

Cartels: The Case of OPEC

In the United States, firms cannot legally meet to agree on what prices to charge and how much to produce. But suppose they could. Would this be enough to guarantee that their collusion would be successful? The example of the Organization of Petroleum Exporting Countries (OPEC) indicates that the answer to this question is "no." OPEC has 11 members, including Saudi Arabia, Kuwait, and other Arab countries, as well as Iran, Venezuela, Nigeria, and Indonesia. Together, these countries own 75 percent of the world's proven oil reserves, although they pump a smaller share of the total oil sold each year. OPEC operates as a **cartel**, which is a group of firms that collude to restrict output to increase prices and profits. The members of OPEC meet periodically and agree on quotas, quantities of oil that each country agrees to produce. The quotas are intended to reduce oil production well below the competitive level, to force up the price of oil, and to increase the profits of member countries.

Figure 4 shows world oil prices from 1972 to 2006. The blue line shows the price of a barrel of oil in each year. Prices in general have risen since 1972, which has reduced the amount of goods and services that consumers can purchase with a dollar. The red line corrects for general price increases by measuring oil prices in terms of the dollar's purchasing power in 2006. Although political unrest in the Middle East and other factors also affect the price of oil, the figure shows that OPEC had considerable success in raising the price of oil during the mid-1970s and early 1980s. Oil prices, which had been below $3 per barrel in 1972, rose to more than $35 per barrel in 1981, which was almost

Cartel A group of firms that collude by agreeing to restrict output to increase prices and profits.

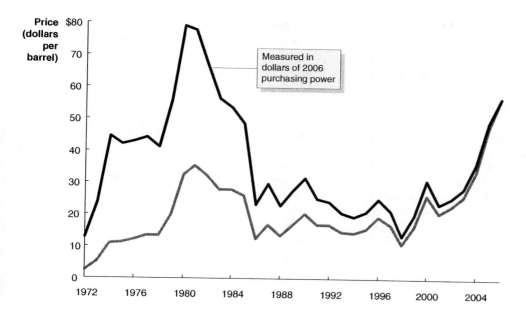

Figure 4

World Oil Prices, 1972–2006

The blue line shows the price of a barrel of oil in each year. The red line measures the price of a barrel of oil in terms of the purchasing power of the dollar in 2006. By reducing oil production, the Organization of Petroleum Exporting Countries (OPEC) was able to raise the world price of oil in the mid-1970s and early 1980s. Sustaining high prices has been difficult over the long run, however, because members often exceed their output quotas.

Source: U.S. Energy Information Agency, *Monthly Energy Review*, March 2007, Table 9.1.

$78 measured in dollars of 2006 purchasing power. The figure also shows that OPEC has had difficulty sustaining the high prices of 1981 in later years, although beginning in 2004, oil prices rose, in part due to increasing demand from China and India.

Game theory helps us understand why oil prices have fluctuated. If every member of OPEC cooperates and produces the low output level dictated by its quota, prices will be high, and the cartel will earn large profits. Once the price has been driven up, however, each member has an incentive to stop cooperating and to earn even higher profits by increasing output beyond its quota. But if no country sticks to its quota, total oil output will increase, and profits will decline. In other words, OPEC is caught in a prisoners' dilemma.

If the members of OPEC always exceeded their production quotas, the cartel would have no effect on world oil prices. In fact, the members of OPEC periodically meet and assign new quotas that, at least for a while, enable them to restrict output enough to raise prices. OPEC's occasional success at behaving as a cartel can be explained by two factors. First, the members of OPEC are participating in a repeated game. As we have seen, this increases the likelihood of a cooperative outcome. Second, Saudi Arabia has far larger oil reserves than any other member of OPEC. Therefore, it has the most to gain from high oil prices and a greater incentive to cooperate. To see this, consider the payoff matrix shown in Figure 5. To keep things simple, let's assume that OPEC has only two members:

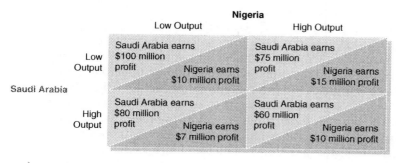

Figure 5 | The OPEC Cartel with Unequal Members

Because Saudi Arabia can produce so much more oil than Nigeria, its output decisions have a much larger effect on the price of oil. In the figure, "low output" corresponds to cooperating with the OPEC-assigned output quota, and "high output" corresponds to producing at maximum capacity. Saudi Arabia has a dominant strategy to cooperate and produce a low output. Nigeria, however, has a dominant strategy not to cooperate and produce a high output. Therefore, the equilibrium of this game will occur with Saudi Arabia producing a low output and Nigeria producing a high output.

Saudi Arabia and Nigeria. In Figure 5, "low output" corresponds to cooperating with the OPEC-assigned output quota, and "high output" corresponds to producing at maximum capacity. The payoff matrix shows the profits received per day by each country.

We can see that Saudi Arabia has a strong incentive to cooperate and maintain its low output quota. By keeping output low, Saudi Arabia can by itself significantly raise the world price of oil, increasing its own profits as well as those of other members of OPEC. Therefore, Saudi Arabia has a dominant strategy of cooperating with the quota and producing a low output. Nigeria, however, cannot by itself have much effect on the price of oil. Therefore, Nigeria has a dominant strategy of not cooperating and producing a high output. The equilibrium of this game will occur with Saudi Arabia producing a low output and Nigeria producing a high output. In fact, OPEC often operates in just this way. Saudi Arabia will cooperate with the quota, while the other 10 members produce at capacity. Because this is a repeated game, however, Saudi Arabia will occasionally produce more oil than its quota to intentionally drive down the price and retaliate against the other members for not cooperating.

---

3 LEARNING OBJECTIVE

3 | Use sequential games to analyze business strategies.

Sequential Games and Business Strategy

We have been analyzing games in which both players move simultaneously. In many business situations, however, one firm will act first, and then other firms will respond. These situations can be analyzed using *sequential games*. We will use sequential games to analyze two business strategies: deterring entry and bargaining between firms. To keep things simple, we consider situations that involve only two firms.

Deterring Entry

We saw earlier that barriers to entry are a key to firms continuing to earn economic profits. Can firms create barriers to deter new firms from entering an industry? Some recent research in game theory has focused on this question. To take a simple example, suppose a town in South Dakota currently has no discount department stores. Executives at Wal-Mart decide to enter the market and are considering what size store to build. To break even by covering the opportunity cost of the funds involved, the store must provide a minimum rate of return of 15 percent on the firm's investment. If Wal-Mart builds a small store in the town, it will earn economic profits by receiving a return of 30 percent. If Wal-Mart builds a large store, its costs will be somewhat higher, and it will receive a return of only 22 percent.

It seems clear that Wal-Mart should build the small store, but the executives are worried that Target may also build a store in this market. If Wal-Mart builds a small store and Target enters the market, both firms will earn an 18 percent return on their investment in this market. If Wal-Mart builds a large store and Target enters, the stores will have to cut prices, and the firms will each earn only 10 percent return on their investments, which is below the 15 percent return necessary for either firm to break even.

We can analyze a sequential game by using a *decision tree*, like the one shown in Figure 6. The boxes in the figure represent *decision nodes*, which are points when the firms must make the decisions contained in the boxes. At the left, Wal-Mart makes the initial decision of what size store to build, and then Target responds by either entering the market or not. The decisions made are shown beside the arrows. The *terminal nodes* at the right side of the figure show the resulting rates of return.

Let's start with Wal-Mart's initial decision. If Wal-Mart builds a large store, then the arrow directs us to the upper red decision node for Target. If Target decides to enter, it will earn only a 10 percent rate of return on its investment, which represents an economic loss because it is below the opportunity cost of the funds involved. If Target doesn't enter, Wal-Mart will earn 22 percent, and Target will not earn anything in this

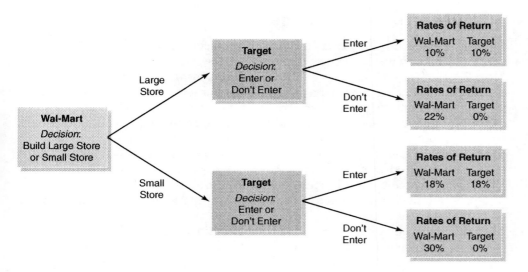

Figure 6

The Decision Tree for an Entry Game

Wal-Mart earns its highest return if it builds a small store and Target doesn't enter the market. If Wal-Mart builds a small store, Target will enter because it will earn economic profit by receiving an 18 percent return on its investment. Therefore, the best decision for Wal-Mart is to build a large store to deter Target's entry. Once Wal-Mart has built a large store, Target knows that if it enters this market, it will earn only 10 percent on its investment, which represents an economic loss, so it won't enter the market.

market. Wal-Mart executives can conclude that if they build a large store, Target will not enter, and Wal-Mart will earn 22 percent on its investment.

If Wal-Mart decides to build a small store, then the arrow directs us to the lower red decision node for Target. If Target decides to enter, it will earn an 18 percent rate of return. If it doesn't enter, Wal-Mart will earn 30 percent, and Target will not earn anything in this market. Wal-Mart executives can conclude that if they build a small store, Target will enter, and Wal-Mart will earn 18 percent on its investment.

This analysis should lead Wal-Mart executives to conclude that they can build a small store and earn 18 percent—because Target will enter—or they can build a large store and earn 22 percent by deterring Target's entry.

Solved Problem | **3**

Is Deterring Entry Always a Good Idea?

Whether deterring entry makes sense depends on how costly it is to the firm doing the deterring. Use the following decision tree to decide whether Wal-Mart should deter Target from entering this market. Assume that each firm must earn a 15 percent return on its investment to break even.

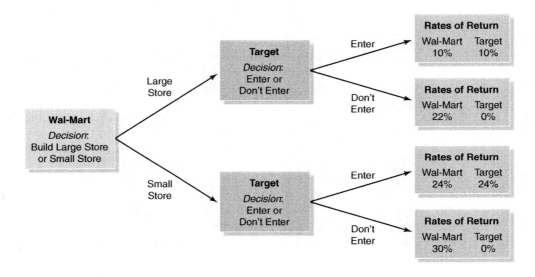

SOLVING THE PROBLEM:

Step 1: **Review the chapter material.** This problem is about sequential games, so you may want to review the section "Deterring Entry."

Step 2: **Determine how Target will respond to Wal-Mart's decision.** If Wal-Mart builds a large store, Target will not enter this market because the return on its investment represents an economic loss. If Wal-Mart builds a small store, Target will enter because it will earn a return that represents an economic profit.

Step 3: **Given how Target will react, determine which strategy maximizes profits for Wal-Mart.** If Wal-Mart builds the large store, it will have deterred Target's entry, and the rate of return on its investment will be 22 percent. If it builds the small store, Target will enter, but Wal-Mart will actually earn a higher return of 24 percent.

Step 4: **State your conclusion.** Like any other business strategy, deterrence is worth pursuing only if its costs are not too high. In this case, the high cost of building a large store lowers Wal-Mart's economic profits below what it earns by building a small store, even given that Target will enter the market.

>> **End Solved Problem 3**

YOUR TURN: For more practice, do related problem 3.3 at the end of this chapter.

Bargaining

The success of many firms depends on how well they bargain with other firms. For example, firms often must bargain with their suppliers over the prices they pay for inputs. Suppose that TruImage is a small firm that has developed software that improves how pictures from a digital camera are displayed on computer screens. TruImage currently sells its software only on its Web site and earns profits of $2 million per year. Dell Computer informs TruImage that it is considering installing the software on every new computer Dell sells. Dell expects to sell more computers at a higher price if it can install TruImage's software on its computers. The two firms begin bargaining over what price Dell will pay TruImage for its software.

The decision tree in Figure 7 illustrates this bargaining game. At the left, Dell makes the initial decision on what price to offer TruImage for its software, and then TruImage responds by either accepting or rejecting the contract offer. First, suppose that Dell offers TruImage a contract price of $30 per copy for its software. If TruImage accepts this contract, its profits will be $5 million per year, and Dell will earn $10 million in additional profits. If TruImage rejects the contract, its profits will be the $2 million per year it earns selling its software on its Web site, and Dell will earn zero additional profits.

Now, suppose Dell offers TruImage a contract price of $20 per copy. If TruImage accepts this contract, its profits will be $3 million per year, and Dell will earn $15 million in additional profits. If TruImage rejects this contract, its profits will be the $2 million it earns selling its software on its Web site, and Dell will earn zero additional profits. Clearly, for Dell, a contract of $20 per copy is more profitable, while for TruImage, a contract of $30 per copy is more profitable.

Suppose TruImage attempts to obtain a favorable outcome from the bargaining by telling Dell that it will reject a $20-per-copy contract. If Dell believes this threat, then it will offer TruImage a $30-per-copy contract because Dell is better off with the $10 million profit that will result from TruImage's accepting the contract than with the zero profits Dell will earn if TruImage rejects the $20-per-copy contract. This result is a Nash equilibrium because neither firm can increase its profits by changing its choice—*provided that Dell believes TruImage's threat*. But is TruImage's threat credible? Once Dell has offered TruImage the $20 contract, TruImage's choices are to accept the contract and earn $3 million or reject the contract and earn only $2 million. Because rejecting the

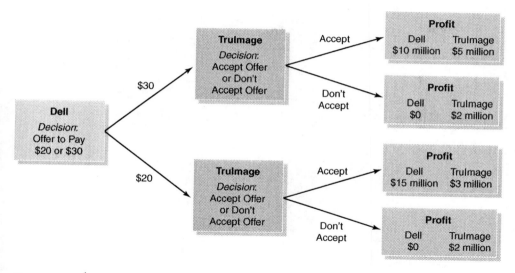

Figure 7 | The Decision Tree for a Bargaining Game

Dell earns the highest profit if it offers a contract price of $20 per copy and TruImage accepts the contract. TruImage earns the highest profit if Dell offers it a contract of $30 per copy and it accepts the contract. TruImage may attempt to bargain by threatening to reject a $20-per-copy contract. But Dell knows this threat is not credible because once Dell has offered a $20-per-copy contract, TruImage's profits are higher if it accepts the contract than if it rejects it.

contract reduces TruImage's profits, TruImage's threat to reject the contract is not credible, and Dell should ignore it.

As a result, we would expect Dell to use the strategy of offering TruImage a $20-per-copy contract and TruImage to use the strategy of accepting the contract. Dell will earn additional profits of $15 million per year, and TruImage will earn profits of $3 million per year. This outcome is called a *subgame-perfect equilibrium*. A subgame-perfect equilibrium is a Nash equilibrium in which no player can make himself better off by changing his decision at any decision node. In our simple bargaining game, each player has only one decision to make. As we have seen, Dell's profits are highest if it offers the $20-per-copy contract, and TruImage's profits are highest if it accepts the contract. Typically, in sequential games of this type, there is only one subgame-perfect equilibrium.

Managers use decision trees like those in Figures 6 and 7 in business planning because they provide a systematic way of thinking through the implications of a strategy and of predicting the reactions of rivals. We can see the benefits of decision trees in the simple examples we considered here. In the first example, Wal-Mart managers can conclude that building a large store is more profitable than building a smaller store. In the second example, Dell managers can conclude that TruImage's threat to reject a $20-per-copy contract is not credible.

4 | Use the five competitive forces model to analyze competition in an industry.

The Five Competitive Forces Model

We have seen that the number of competitors in an industry affects a firm's ability to charge a price above average cost and earn an economic profit. The number of firms is not the only determinant of the level of competition in an industry, however. Michael Porter of Harvard Business School has drawn on the research of a number of economists to develop a model that shows how five competitive forces determine the overall level of competition in an industry. Figure 8 illustrates Porter's model.

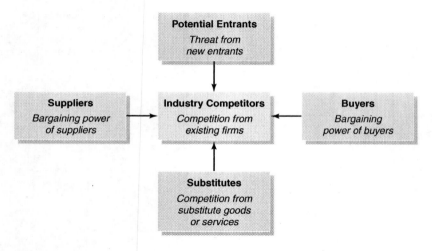

Figure 8 | The Five Competitive Forces Model

Michael Porter's model identifies five forces that determine the level of competition in an industry: (1) competition from existing firms, (2) the threat from new entrants, (3) competition from substitute goods or services, (4) the bargaining power of buyers, and (5) the bargaining power of suppliers.

Source: Reprinted with the permission of The Free Press, a Division of Simon & Schuster Adult Publishing Group, from Michael E. Porter, *Competitive Strategy: Techniques for Analyzing Industries and Competitors.* Copyright © 1980, 1998 by The Free Press. All rights reserved.

We now look at each of the five competitive forces: (1) competition from existing firms, (2) the threat from potential entrants, (3) competition from substitute goods or services, (4) the bargaining power of buyers, and (5) the bargaining power of suppliers.

Competition from Existing Firms

We have already seen that competition among firms in an industry can lower prices and profits. To take another example: The Educational Testing Service (ETS) produces the Scholastic Aptitude Test (SAT) and the Graduate Record Exam (GRE). The GRE is taken by students applying to graduate school. In 2007, the Educational Testing Service charged a price of $43 to take the SAT, but $140 to take the GRE. Part of the explanation for these large price differences is that ETS faces competition in the market for tests given to high school seniors applying to college, where the SAT competes with the ACT Assessment, produced by ACT, Inc. But there is no competition for the GRE test. As we saw earlier in this chapter, when there are only a few firms in a market, it is easier for them to implicitly collude and to charge a price close to the monopoly price. In this case, however, competition from a single firm was enough to cause ETS to keep the price of the SAT near the competition level.

Competition in the form of advertising, better customer service, or longer warranties can also reduce profits by raising costs. For example, online booksellers Amazon.com, BarnesandNoble.com, and Buy.com have competed by offering low-cost—or free—shipping, by increasing their customer service staffs, and by building more warehouses to provide faster deliveries. These activities have raised the booksellers' costs and reduced their profits.

The Threat from Potential Entrants

Firms face competition from companies that currently are not in the market but might enter. We have already seen how actions taken to deter entry can reduce profits. In our hypothetical example in the previous section, Wal-Mart built a larger store and earned less profit to deter Target's entry. Business managers often take actions aimed at deterring entry. Some of these actions include advertising to create product loyalty, introducing new products—such as slightly different cereals or toothpastes—to fill market niches, and setting lower prices to keep profits at a level that would make entry less attractive.

Competition from Substitute Goods or Services

Firms are always vulnerable to competitors introducing a new product that fills a consumer need better than their current product does. Consider the encyclopedia business. For decades, many parents bought expensive and bulky encyclopedias for their children attending high school or college. By the 1990s, computer software companies were offering electronic encyclopedias that sold for a small fraction of the price of the printed encyclopedias. Encyclopedia Britannica and the other encyclopedia publishers responded by cutting prices and launching advertising campaigns aimed at showing the superiority of printed encyclopedias. Still, profits continued to decline, and by the end of the 1990s, most printed encyclopedias had disappeared.

The Bargaining Power of Buyers

If buyers have enough bargaining power, they can insist on lower prices, higher-quality products, or additional services. Automobile companies, for example, have significant bargaining power in the tire market, which tends to lower tire prices and limit the profitability of tire manufacturers. Some retailers have significant buying power over their suppliers. For instance, Wal-Mart has required many of its suppliers to alter their distribution systems to accommodate Wal-Mart's need to control the stocks of goods in its stores.

The Bargaining Power of Suppliers

If many firms can supply an input and the input is not specialized, the suppliers are unlikely to have the bargaining power to limit a firm's profits. For instance, suppliers of paper napkins to McDonald's restaurants have very little bargaining power. With only a single or a few suppliers of an input, the purchasing firm may face a high price. During the 1930s and 1940s, for example, the Technicolor Company was the only producer of the cameras and film that studios needed to produce color movies. Technicolor charged the studios high prices to use its cameras, and it had the power to insist that only its technicians could operate the cameras. The only alternative for the movie studios was to make black-and-white movies.

As with other competitive forces, the bargaining power of suppliers can change over time. For instance, when IBM chose Microsoft to supply the operating system for its personal computers, Microsoft was a small company with very limited bargaining power. As Microsoft's Windows operating system became standard in more than 90 percent of personal computers, this large market share increased Microsoft's bargaining power.

Making the Connection | Is Southwest's Business Strategy More Important Than the Structure of the Airline Industry?

For years, economists and business strategists believed that market structure was the most important factor in explaining the ability of some firms to continue earning economic profits. For example, most economists argued

Southwest's business strategy allowed it to remain profitable when many other airlines faced heavy losses.

that during the first few decades after World War II, steel companies in the United States earned economic profits because barriers to entry were high, there were few firms in the industry, and competition among firms was low. In contrast, restaurants were seen as less profitable because barriers to entry were low and the industry was intensely competitive. One problem with this approach to analyzing the profitability of firms is that it does not explain how firms in the same industry can have very different levels of profit.

Today, economists and business strategists put greater emphasis on the characteristics of individual firms and the strategies their managements use to continue to earn economic profits. This approach helps explain why Nucor continues to be a profitable steel company while Bethlehem Steel, at one time the second-largest steel producer in the United States, was forced into bankruptcy. It also explains why Dell, which began as a small company run by Michael Dell from his dorm room at the University of Texas, went on to become extremely profitable and an industry leader, while other computer companies have disappeared.

Many economists argue that the best strategy for a company is to identify a segment of the market and then shape the company to fit that segment. This strategy makes it more difficult for rivals to compete in that part of the market. For example, Southwest Airlines concentrates on customers who fly relatively short distances and who want a low-price, no-frills airline flight. Every aspect of the company is focused on this goal. Southwest's planes have no first-class or business sections—only coach seats are available. By flying primarily between midsize cities, Southwest can avoid the delays at the crowded airports near big cities and can keep its planes at the airport gate for only 15 minutes—much less time than other airlines. This lowers its costs by allowing it to keep its planes in the air longer and to offer more flights with fewer planes. Southwest also lowers costs by not serving meals, flying only Boeing 737s to standardize maintenance, not assigning passengers to particular seats, and not checking luggage through to connecting flights.

It is very difficult for the other full-service airlines, such as Delta, American, and United, to compete with Southwest. Because they fly out of larger, more congested airports, those airlines have no hope of turning around their planes at the gate as quickly as Southwest does. Because many of their passengers are flying longer distances—often using connecting flights—they have to serve meals and check luggage through. Many of the other airlines' customers want upgraded seats and service, so those airlines must offer first-class and business-class seats. Even when Delta, American, and United have tried to offer stripped-down service on certain routes in direct competition with Southwest, they have not been successful. Southwest's complete focus on providing low-cost, low-price service has proven very difficult for the other airlines to copy. While other airlines suffered heavy losses in 2003–2004 as fuel prices rose and demand declined as a result of the war in Iraq and the spread of the disease SARS (severe acute respiratory syndrome), Southwest continued to earn profits. In 2006, it remained the leading airline in on-time arrivals and fewest customer complaints.

Southwest's corporate strategy, rather than the structure of the airline industry, explains why Southwest earns economic profits.

Source: Scott McCartney, "A Report Card on the Nation's Airlines," *Wall Street Journal,* February 6, 2007, p. D1.

YOUR TURN: Test your understanding by doing related problem 4.5 at the end of this chapter.

Economics in YOUR Life!

At the beginning of this chapter, we asked you to consider why the price of the PlayStation 3 game system is almost the same at every large retailer, from Amazon.com to Wal-Mart. Why don't these retailers seem to compete on price for this type of product? In this chapter, we have seen that if big retailers were engaged in a one-time game of pricing PlayStations, they would be in a prisoner's dilemma and probably all charge a low price. However, we have also seen that pricing PlayStations is actually a repeated game because the retailers will be selling the game system in competition over a long period of time. In this situation, it is more likely that a cooperative equilibrium will be arrived at in which the retailers will all charge a high price. This is good news for the profits of the retailers but bad news for consumers! This is one of many insights that game theory provides into the business strategies of oligopolists.

Conclusion

Firms are locked in a never-ending struggle to earn economic profits. As noted in the two preceding chapters, competition erodes economic profits. Even in the oligopolies discussed in this chapter, firms have difficulty earning economic profits in the long run. We have seen that firms attempt to avoid the effects of competition in various ways. For example, they can stake out a secure niche in the market, they can engage in implicit collusion with competing firms, or they can attempt to have the government impose barriers to entry. Read *An Inside Look* on the next page for a discussion of the business strategy Target uses to compete with Wal-Mart in the market for generic prescription drugs.

Can Target Compete with Wal-Mart in the Market for Generic Drugs?

USA TODAY, SEPTEMBER 23, 2006

Target Says It Will Match Wal-Mart's $4 Generic Drug Price

Chain store Target said late Thursday that it will match rival Wal-Mart's $4 price on 150 generic drug prescriptions in the Tampa Bay area. Target's brief press release didn't say whether it would keep pace with Wal-Mart's plan to take the lower prices nationwide, but it did say it has a "long-standing practice to be price competitive with Wal-Mart."

Wal-Mart, the nation's third-largest seller of prescription drugs, said earlier Thursday that it will offer the $4 price on about 150 generic drugs to the insured and uninsured alike, starting immediately in the Tampa area, and will take the program statewide by January.

"We intend to take it nationwide next year," says Bill Simon, Wal-Mart's executive vice president of the Professional Services Division. For uninsured consumers, the $4 price for some generics is below what they would pay at most pharmacy counters and is less than typical $10 to $15 co-payments on generics offered by many insurance plans.

Wal-Mart's move could save modest amounts for some consumers. It may also draw more customers to its stores or prompt a price war with other pharmacies. Savings could be less than $1 per prescription to more than $20, depending on the drug and pharmacy where customers shop, according to information from Wal-Mart and prices of other retailers posted at MyFloridarx.com, a state-run website.

That could draw more customers to Wal-Mart, already the largest seller of groceries and toys, possibly forcing other chain drugstores to cut their prices, says Ed Kaplan of the Segal Co., a benefits consulting firm. "Customers who take five or seven medications a month and can save $10 on each might switch," says Kaplan.

The move caused share prices for generic drug and pharmacy companies to drop Thursday.

Wal-Mart says the $4 for 30-day supply price would save customers $7.98 a month for blood-pressure drug Lisinopril, $3.85 for diabetes drug metformin and 80 cents for blood-pressure drug atenolol.

Simon says the $4 generics are not expected to be a "loss leader," meaning Wal-Mart doesn't expect to lose money on the drugs in hopes of attracting more customers to buy other products. That's because the drugs offered are longtime generics that have multiple manufacturers and they are already inexpensive on the wholesale market. Large companies such as Wal-Mart can often buy in bulk for less than the $4 cost.

Wal-Mart's press release said 291 drugs will be covered, a total that includes different dosage strengths of the same drugs. When the differing dosage strengths are taken out, the list includes fewer than 150 products, including treatments for high blood pressure, infection and diabetes, along with some vitamins and painkiller ibuprofen. That's a fraction of the estimated 2,100 generic products available.

"This is a much narrower list than they're giving the impression it is," says drug-industry expert Stephen Schondelmeyer at the University of Minnesota. Simon says the drugs chosen for the list represent 20% of the prescriptions Wal-Mart currently fills and cover a wide range of medical needs. More products may be added, he says.

The move comes as Wal-Mart works to counter critics who say the firm doesn't make health insurance affordable for many of its workers. "Providing low-cost drugs is a good thing. But not providing affordable health care to workers is not a good thing. Why can't Wal-Mart address the serious health care crisis in its own stores?" says Chris Kofinis, with WakeUpWalmart.com.

Some praised Wal-Mart's move. "That's a great price for a 30-day supply of drugs and will be a tremendous boon for seniors," says Devon Herrick, economist at the National Center for Policy Analysis.

Source: "Savings, Shakeup Seen in $4 Drug Plan; Wal-Mart May 'Take It Nationwide Next Year' " by Julie Appleby from *USA TODAY*, September 22, 2006, p. 1A. Reprinted by permission of *USA TODAY*.

Ralf-Finn Hestoft, Corbis/Bettmann

Key Points in the Article

This article illustrates Target's plan to match Wal-Mart's low price on generic prescription drugs. As we have seen in this chapter, when a market is an oligopoly, there are only a few firms. So, each firm must take into account the actions of its competitors. When a competitor changes the price it charges, the other firms in the industry must decide how to react. In this case, Target determined that its profits would be higher by matching Wal-Mart's price.

Analyzing the News

In an oligopoly market, a firm's profits depend not only on the price it chooses, but on the price its rivals choose. In this case, Target had to choose how to respond to Wal-Mart's pricing decision. From Target's action, we can assume that it believes its profits will be higher with a low price, given that Wal-Mart is charging a low price. The figure is helpful in analyzing whether Wal-Mart can profitably sell generic

drugs at a price of $4. In both panel (a) and panel (b), the rate of return by Wal-Mart is higher when it offers generics at $4 regardless of what Target does. So, Wal-Mart has a dominant strategy of charging $4.

Target faces the choice of whether to match this price. In panel (a), if Target matches the price it earns an 8 percent return, while if it does not match the price it will earn a return of 0 percent. Target prefers the 8 percent return and will choose to match Wal-Mart's $4 generic drug price.

But suppose that Target determines that given its competitive position relative to Wal-Mart the situation is actually that shown in panel (b). Wal-Mart still has a dominant strategy of charging $4 for generic prescription, but now Target faces the choice of a 3 percent return if it matches Wal-Mart's price, or a 5 percent return if it does not match Wal-Mart's price. In this case, Target would be better off not matching the $4 generic price.

Larger stores sometimes cut the price of a product even if this means they will take a loss on sales of the product, if the store manager believes the low price will attract new customers. If low prescription prices attract more customers to Wal-Mart stores, we would expect that Wal-Mart would earn additional profits from the other goods those customers purchased while in Wal-Mart.

As mentioned in the chapter opener, Wal-Mart is facing increased criticism over its corporate policies. Just as Wal-Mart has to decide how to respond to the market behavior of its rivals, such as pricing, it must also decide how to respond to the behavior of its critics.

Thinking Critically

1. Suppose that you manage a small pharmacy in a local town. How will you decide whether to match the lower generic drug prices of Wal-Mart and Target?
2. Suppose that Congress passes legislation that places a price floor on generic drugs. Who would likely gain from such a law? Who would likely lose? Use a graph to show changes in producer surplus and consumer surplus.

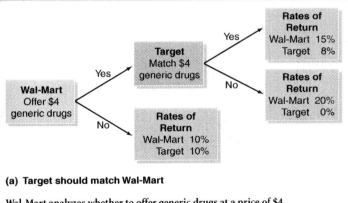

(a) Target should match Wal-Mart

Wal-Mart analyzes whether to offer generic drugs at a price of $4.

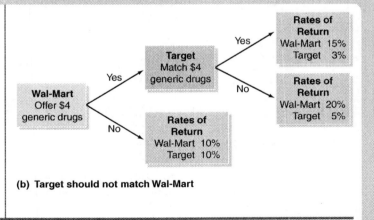

(b) Target should not match Wal-Mart

Key Terms

Barrier to entry	Cooperative equilibrium	Nash equilibrium	Payoff matrix
Business strategy	Dominant strategy	Noncooperative equilibrium	Price leadership
Cartel	Economies of scale	Oligopoly	Prisoners' dilemma
Collusion	Game theory	Patent	

1 LEARNING OBJECTIVE 1 | Show how barriers to entry explain the existence of oligopolies

Oligopoly and Barriers to Entry

Summary

An **oligopoly** is a market structure in which a small number of interdependent firms compete. **Barriers to entry** keep new firms from entering an industry. The three most important barriers to entry are economies of scale, ownership of a key input or raw material, and government barriers. Economies of scale are the most important barrier to entry. **Economies of scale** exist when a firm's long-run average costs fall as it increases output. Government barriers include patents, licensing, and barriers to international trade. A **patent** is the exclusive right to a product for a period of 20 years from the date the product is invented.

Visit www.myeconlab.com to complete these exercises online and get instant feedback.

Review Questions

1.1 What is an oligopoly? Give three examples of oligopolistic industries in the United States.

1.2 What do barriers to entry have to do with the extent of competition, or lack thereof, in an industry? What are the most important barriers to entry?

1.3 Give an example of a government-imposed barrier to entry. Why would the government be willing to erect barriers to entering an industry?

Problems and Applications

1.4 Michael Porter has argued, "The intensity of competition in an industry is neither a matter of coincidence nor bad luck. Rather, competition in an industry is rooted in its underlying economic structure." What does Porter mean by "economic structure"? What factors, other than economic structure, might be expected to determine the intensity of competition in an industry?

Source: Michael Porter, *Competitive Strategy: Techniques for Analyzing Industries and Competitors*, New York: The Free Press, 1980, p. 3.

1.5 "Less-than-truckload" trucking companies include goods from several shippers in their highway trailers. According to an article in the *Wall Street Journal*: "Unlike [the truckload industry, which is] a fiercely competitive business it is relatively easy to enter, less-than-truckload companies face a higher entry barrier due to the cost of an extensive network of terminals to consolidate shipments." Would you expect truckload companies or less-than-truckload companies to charge higher prices to ship freight? Which companies are likely to earn economic profits? Briefly explain.

Source: Daniel Machalaba, "Yellow Freight to Raise Rates 4.9% on Bet about Lower Inventory Costs," *Wall Street Journal*, July 5, 2001.

1.6 Thomas McCraw, a professor at Harvard Business School, has written the following: "Throughout American history, entrepreneurs have tried, sometimes desperately, to create big businesses out of naturally small-scale operations. It has not worked." What advantage would entrepreneurs expect to gain from creating "big businesses"? Why would entrepreneurs fail to create big businesses with "naturally small-scale operations"? Illustrate your answer with a graph showing long-run average costs.

Source: Thomas K. McCraw, ed., *Creating Modern Capitalism*, Cambridge, MA: Harvard University Press, 1997, p. 323.

1.7 The graph below illustrates the average total cost curves for two automobile manufacturing firms: Little Auto and Big Auto. Under which of the following

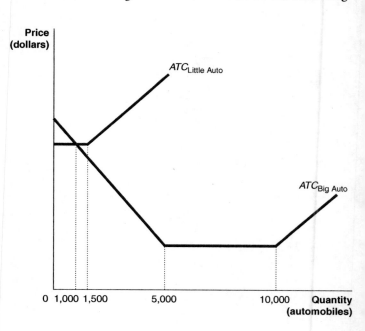

conditions would you expect to see the market composed of firms like Little Auto, and under which conditions would you expect to see the market dominated by firms like Big Auto?

a. When the market demand curve intersects the quantity axis at less than 1,000 units

b. When the market demand curve intersects the quantity axis at more than 1,000 units but less than 10,000 units

c. When the market demand curve intersects the quantity axis at more than 10,000 units

1.8 The following graph contains two long-run average cost curves. Briefly explain which cost curve would most likely be associated with an oligopoly and which would most likely be associated with a perfectly competitive industry.

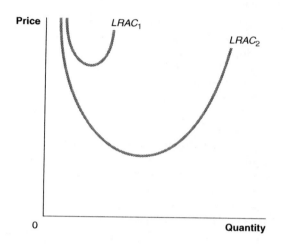

1.9 Alfred Chandler, who was a professor at Harvard Business School, observed, "Imagine the diseconomies of scale—the great increase in unit costs—that would result from placing close to one-fourth of the world's production of shoes, or textiles, or lumber into three factories or mills!" The shoe, textiles, and lumber industries are very competitive, with many firms producing each of these products. Briefly explain whether Chandler's observation helps us explain why.

Source: Alfred D. Chandler, Jr., "The Emergence of Managerial Capitalism," in Alfred D. Chandler, Jr., and Richard S. Tedlow, *The Coming of Managerial Capitalism*, New York: Irwin, 1985, p. 406.

1.10 A historical account of the development of the cotton textile industry in England argues the following:

The cotton textile industry was shaped by ruthless competition. Rapid growth in demand, low barriers to entry, frequent technological innovations, and a high rate of firm bankruptcy all combined to form an environment in which . . . oligopolistic competition became almost impossible.

Explain how each of the factors described here would contribute to making the cotton textile industry competitive rather than oligopolistic.

Source: Thomas K. McCraw, ed., *Creating Modern Capitalism*, Cambridge, MA: Harvard University Press, pp. 61–62.

>> End Learning Objective 1

---

2 LEARNING OBJECTIVE 2 | Use game theory to analyze the strategies of oligopolistic firms

Using Game Theory to Analyze Oligopoly

Summary

Because an oligopoly has only a few firms, interactions among those firms are particularly important. **Game theory** is the study of how people make decisions in situations in which attaining their goals depends on their interactions with others; in economics, it is the study of the decisions of firms in industries where the profits of each firm depend on its interactions with other firms. A **business strategy** refers to actions taken by a firm to achieve a goal, such as maximizing profits. Oligopoly games can be illustrated with a **payoff matrix**, which is a table that shows the payoffs that each firm earns from every combination of strategies by the firms. One possible outcome in oligopoly is **collusion**, which is an agreement among firms to charge the same price or otherwise not to compete. A **cartel** is a group of firms that collude by agreeing to restrict output to increase prices and profits. In a **cooperative equilibrium**, firms cooperate to increase their mutual payoff. In a **noncooperative equilibrium**, firms do not cooperate but pursue their own self-interest. A **dominant strategy** is a strategy that is the best for a firm, no matter what strategies other firms use. A **Nash equilibrium** is a situation in which each firm chooses the best strategy, given the strategies chosen by other firms. A situation in which pursuing dominant strategies results in noncooperation that leaves everyone worse off is called a **prisoners' dilemma**. Because many business situations are repeated games, firms may end up implicitly colluding to keep prices high. With **price leadership**, one firm takes the lead in announcing a price change, which is then matched by the other firms in the industry.

Visit www.myeconlab.com to complete these exercises online and get instant feedback.

Review Questions

2.1 Give brief definitions of the following concepts.
   a. Game theory
   b. Cooperative equilibrium
   c. Noncooperative equilibrium
   d. Dominant strategy
   e. Nash equilibrium

2.2 Why do economists refer to the methodology for analyzing oligopolies as game theory?

2.3 Why do economists refer to the pricing strategies of oligopoly firms as a prisoners' dilemma game?

2.4 What is the difference between explicit collusion and implicit collusion? Give an example of each.

2.5 How is the prisoners' dilemma result changed in a repeated game?

Problems and Applications

2.6 Bob and Tom are two criminals who have been arrested for burglary. The police put Tom and Bob in separate cells. They offer to let Bob go free if he confesses to the crime and testifies against Tom. Bob also is told that he will serve a 15-year sentence if he remains silent while Tom confesses. If he confesses and Tom also confesses, they will each serve a 10-year sentence. Separately, the police make the same offer to Tom. Assume that if Bob and Tom both remain silent, the police have only enough evidence to convict them of a lesser crime, and they will both serve 3-year sentences.
   a. Use the information provided to write a payoff matrix for Bob and Tom.
   b. Does Bob have a dominant strategy? If so, what is it?
   c. Does Tom have a dominant strategy? If so, what is it?
   d. What sentences do Bob and Tom serve? How might they have avoided this outcome?

2.7 Explain how collusion makes firms better off. Given the incentives to collude, briefly explain why every industry doesn't become a cartel.

2.8 Under "early decision" college admission plans, students apply to a college in the fall and, if they are accepted, they must enroll in that college. According to an article in *BusinessWeek*, Yale president Richard Levin argues that early decision plans put too much pressure on students to decide early in their senior years which college they wish to attend. Levin has proposed abolishing early decision plans. But the author of the article is doubtful that this will succeed because "as long as some big-name schools offer early admissions, the others feel they must, too, or lose out

on the best talent." Do you agree with this conclusion? How can game theory help us analyze this situation?

2.9 Baseball players who hit the most home runs *relative to other players* usually receive the highest pay. Beginning in the mid-1990s, the typical baseball player became significantly stronger and more muscular. As one baseball announcer put it, "The players of 20 years ago look like stick figures compared with the players of today." As a result, the average number of home runs hit each year increased dramatically. Some of the increased strength that baseball players gained came from more weight training and better conditioning and diet. As some players admitted, though, some of the increased strength came from taking steroids and other illegal drugs. Taking steroids can significantly increase the risk of developing cancer and other medical problems.
   a. In these circumstances, are baseball players in a prisoners' dilemma? Carefully explain.
   b. Suppose that Major League Baseball begins testing players for steroids and firing players who are caught using them (or other illegal muscle-building drugs). Will this testing make baseball players as a group better off or worse off? Briefly explain.

2.10 Soldiers in battle may face a prisoners' dilemma. If all soldiers stand and fight, the chance that the soldiers, as a unit, will survive is maximized. If there is a significant chance that the soldiers will lose the battle, an individual soldier may maximize his chance of survival by running away while the other soldiers hold off the enemy by fighting. If all soldiers run away, however, many of them are likely to be killed or captured by the enemy because no one is left to hold off the enemy. In ancient times, the Roman army practiced "decimation." If a unit of soldiers was guilty of running away during a battle or committing other cowardly acts, all would be lined up, and every tenth soldier would be killed by being run through with a sword. No attempt was made to distinguish between soldiers in the unit who had fought well and those who had been cowardly. Briefly explain under what condition the Roman system of decimation was likely to have solved the prisoners' dilemma of soldiers running away in battle.

2.11 **(Related to the *Making the Connection*)** Convert the scene from the bar into a game. There are two players John and Steve. They each have the same possible strategies: "approach the blonde" or "approach the brunette." Think of the payoffs in the matrices as measures of utility. Choose payoffs so that there is no Nash equilibrium.

2.12 **(Related to *Solved Problem 2*)** Would a ban on advertising beer on television be likely to increase or decrease the profits of beer companies? Briefly explain.

2.13 (Related to *Solved Problem 2*) Beginning in 2003, the U.S. government spent billions of dollars rebuilding the infrastructure damaged by the war in Iraq. Much of the work was carried out by construction and engineering firms that had to bid for the business. Suppose, hypothetically, that only two companies—Bechtel and Halliburton—enter the bidding and that each firm is deciding whether to bid either $4 billion or $5 billion. (Remember that in this type of bidding, the winning bid is the *low* bid because the bid represents the amount the government will have to pay to have the work done.) Each firm will have costs of $2.5 billion to do the work. If they both make the same bid, they will both be hired and will split the work and the profits. If one makes a low bid and one makes a high bid, only the low bidder will be hired, and it will receive all the profits. The result is the following payoff matrix.

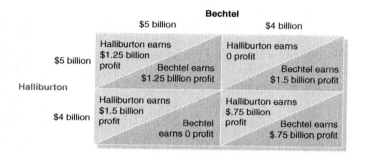

a. Is there a Nash equilibrium in this game? Briefly explain.

b. How might the situation be changed if the two companies expect to be bidding on many similar projects in future years?

2.14 (Related to *Solved Problem 2* and the *Chapter Opener*) Suppose that Wal-Mart and Target are independently deciding whether to stick with bar codes or switch to RFID tags to monitor the flow of products. Because many suppliers sell to both Wal-Mart and Target, it is much less costly for suppliers to use one system or the other rather than to use both. The following payoff matrix shows the profits per year for each company resulting from the interaction of their strategies.

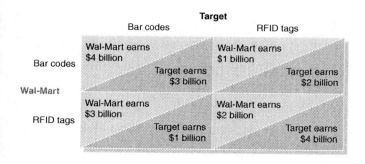

a. Briefly explain whether Wal-Mart has a dominant strategy.

b. Briefly explain whether Target has a dominant strategy.

c. Briefly explain whether there is a Nash equilibrium in this game.

2.15 (Related to the *Don't Let This Happen to You!*) A student argues, "The prisoners' dilemma game is unrealistic. Each player's strategy is based on the assumption that the other player won't cooperate. But if each player assumes that the other player *will* cooperate, the 'dilemma' disappears." Briefly explain whether you agree with this argument.

2.16 (Related to the *Making the Connection*) We made that argument that a bidder on an eBay auction has a dominant strategy of bidding only once, with that bid being the maximum the bidder would be willing to pay.

a. Is it possible that a bidder might receive useful information during the auction, particularly from the dollar amounts other bidders are bidding? If so, how does that change a bidder's optimal strategy?

b. Many people recommend the practice of "sniping," or placing your bid at the last second before the auction ends. Is there connection between sniping and your answer to part a.?

2.17 Consider two oligopolistic industries. In the first industry, firms always match price changes by any other firm in the industry. In the second industry, firms always ignore price changes by any other firm. In which industry are firms likely to charge higher prices? Briefly explain.

2.18 (Related to the *Making the Connection*) Airlines often find themselves in price wars. Consider the following game: Northwest and Continental are the only two airlines flying the route from Houston to Omaha. Each firm has two strategies: charge a high price or charge a low price.

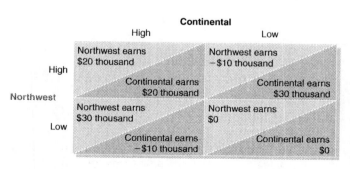

a. What (if any) is the dominant strategy for each firm?

b. Is this game a prisoner's dilemma?

c. How could repeated playing of the game change the strategy each firm uses?

2.19 (Related to the *Making the Connection*)
Consider the following two excerpts from articles in the *Wall Street Journal*:

[From February 2003] An attempt by major airlines to raise fares $20 per round-trip ticket fell apart over the weekend as Northwest Airlines, the fourth-largest carrier, refused to go along. . . . By yesterday morning, all airlines had rolled back prices.

[From August 2003] Northwest Airlines triggered a major round of discounting last week when it launched a fare sale for late summer and early fall travel—setting off a chain reaction in the industry. During the course of one day, airlines cut fares on nearly 35,881 routes.

Briefly explain why airlines might be more likely to match price cuts than price increases.

Sources: Scott McCartney and Susan Carey, "Airlines' Move to Raise Fares Falls Apart as Northwest Balks," *Wall Street Journal*, February 18, 2003; and Eleena De Lisser, "Fall Travel Deals Arrive Early," *Wall Street Journal*, August 14, 2003.

2.20 (Related to the *Making the Connection*)
Until the late 1990s, airlines would post proposed changes in ticket prices on computer reservations systems several days before the new ticket prices went into effect. Then the federal government took action to end the practice. Now airlines can only post prices on their reservations systems for tickets that are immediately available for sale. Why would the federal government object to the old system of posting prices before they went into effect?

Source: Scott McCartney, "Airfare Wars Show Why Deals Arrive and Depart," *Wall Street Journal*, March 19, 2002.

2.21 Finding dominant strategies is often a very effective way of analyzing a game. Consider the following

game: Microsoft and Apple are the two firms in the market for operating systems. Each firm has two strategies: charge a high price or charge a low price.

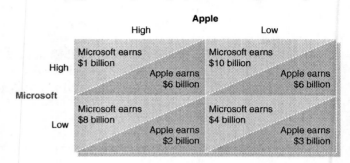

a. What (if any) is the dominant strategy for each firm?
b. Is there a Nash equilibrium? Briefly explain.

2.22 One day in October 2006, oil prices dropped 93 cents per barrel, to their lowest level in almost one year. As an article in the *Wall Street Journal* noted: "The drop Wednesday came even as the Organization of Petroleum Exporting Countries said it will cut global production by one million barrels a day to boost prices, Nigerian oil minister and OPEC president Edmund Daukoru said." Why would oil prices drop at the same time that OPEC was announcing a cut in production. Shouldn't lower production lead to higher prices?

Source: Worth Civils, "Stocks Decline Amid Fed Minutes, Alcoa Earnings, Lower Oil Prices," *Wall Street Jurnal*, October 11, 2006.

2.23 In 2007, some countries that export natural gas discussed forming a cartel, modeled on the OPEC oil cartel. The head of Libya's energy sector was quoted as saying: "We are trying to strengthen the cooperation among gas producers to avoid harmful competition."
a. What is a cartel?
b. What is "harmful competition"? Is competition typically harmful to consumers?
c. What factors would help the cartel succeed? What factors would reduce the cartels chances for success?

Source: Ayesha Daya and James Herron, "Gas Exporters to Study Cartel," *Wall Street Journal*, April 10, 2007, p. A6.

>> End Learning Objective 2

3 LEARNING OBJECTIVE   3 | Use sequential games to analyze business strategies

Sequential Games and Business Strategy

Summary

Recent work in game theory has focused on actions firms can take to deter the entry of new firms into an industry. Deterring entry can be analyzed using a sequential game, where first one firm makes a decision and then another firm reacts to that decision. Sequential games can be illustrated using decision trees.

Visit www.myeconlab.com to complete these exercises online and get instant feedback.

Review Questions

3.1 What is a sequential game?

3.2 How are decision trees used to analyze sequential games?

Problems and Applications

3.3 (Related to *Solved Problem 3*) Bradford is a small town that currently has no fast-food restaurants. McDonald's and Burger King are both considering entering this market. Burger King will wait until McDonald's has made its decision before deciding whether to enter. Use the following decision tree to decide the optimal strategy for each company. Does your answer depend on the rate of return that owners of fast-food restaurants must earn on their investments in order to break even? Briefly explain.

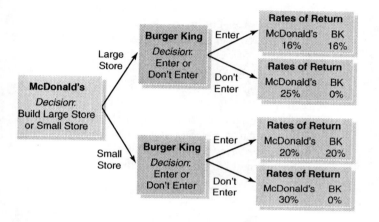

3.4 Suppose that in the situation shown in Figure 7 TruImage's profits are $1.5 million if the firm accepts Dell's contract offer of $20 per copy. Now will Dell offer TruImage a contract of $20 per copy or a contract of $30 per copy? Briefly explain.

3.5 Refer to Figure 5. Consider the entries in the row of the payoff matrix that correspond to Saudi Arabia choosing "low output." Suppose the numbers change so that Nigeria's profit is $15 million when Nigeria chooses "low output" and $10 million when it chooses "high output."
a. Create the payoff matrix for this new situation, assuming that Saudi Arabia and Nigeria choose their output levels simultaneously. Is there a Nash equilibrium to this game? If so, what is it?
b. Now draw the decision tree for this situation, (using the values from the payoff matrix you created in part a), assuming that Saudi Arabia and Nigeria make their decisions sequentially: First Saudi Arabia chooses its output level, and then Nigeria responds by choosing its output level. Is there a Nash equilibrium to this game? If so, what is it?
c. Compare your answers to parts a and b. Briefly explain the reason for any differences in the outcomes of these two games.

>> End Learning Objective 3

4 LEARNING OBJECTIVE | 4 | Use the five competitive forces model to analyze competition in an industry

The Five Competitive Forces Model

Summary

Michael Porter of Harvard Business School argues that the state of competition in an industry is determined by five competitive forces: the degree of competition among existing firms, the threat from new entrants, competition from substitute goods or services, the bargaining power of buyers, and the bargaining power of suppliers.

Visit www.myeconlab.com to complete these exercises online and get instant feedback.

Review Questions

4.1 List the competitive forces in the five competitive forces model.

4.2 Does the strength of each of the five competitive forces remain constant over time? Briefly explain.

Problems and Applications

4.3 Michael Porter has argued that in many industries, "strategies converge and competition becomes a series of races down identical paths that no one can win." Briefly explain whether firms in these industries likely will earn economic profits.

Source: Michael E. Porter, "What Is Strategy?" *Harvard Business Review*, November–December 1996, p. 64.

4.4 According to an article in the *Wall Street Journal*:

The big car makers are pushing a wide array of new technology into production, responding to relentless competitive pressure, rising energy prices and consumer demand for better safety. Once, side-curtain airbags were rare. Now they're becoming standard equipment on a growing number of vehicles. Car makers are racing to deploy fuel-saving technologies such as cylinder shutdown (variously known as "active fuel management" or "multi-displacement system"), six-speed transmissions and, of course, various kinds of gas-electric hybrid drives.

a. What does the article mean by "relentless competitive pressure"? Which of the five competitive forces is being referred to?

b. In the long run, will the car maker who first successfully incorporates these new technologies in its cars earn economic profits? Which group is likely to benefit the most from these innovations: the car companies or consumers?

Source: Joseph B. White, "Ford, GM Eye Shift in Buying Habits," *Wall Street Journal*, May 22, 2006.

4.5 **(Related to *Making the Connection*)** An article in the *Wall Street Journal* argues, "Finally, American [Airlines] has figured out what Southwest Airlines and others have known for some time: There is a cost to complexity." What does the author mean by a "cost to complexity"? How does Southwest Airlines avoid this cost?

Source: Scott McCartney, "Large Carriers Are Beginning to Discover the Benefits of Simplicity," *Wall Street Journal*, August 15, 2002, p. D4.

4.6 In early 2004, Yahoo was set to challenge Google as the leading online search engine. According to an article in the *Wall Street Journal*, Yahoo's strategy was "not simply to match what Google does now but to add features its rival can't easily match." The article quoted a senior vice president at Yahoo as stating, "We're not going to beat the competition by being the competition." Briefly explain what the Yahoo executive means by "being the competition." Briefly discuss whether the strategy of "being the competition" ever makes sense.

Source: Mylene Mangalindan, "Yahoo Gets Set to Give Google a Run for Its Money," *Wall Street Journal*, January 6, 2004.

4.7 The following is from an article in the *Wall Street Journal*:

As U.S. car makers continue to offer generous cash discounts and cut-rate financing to woo buyers, top Japanese manufacturers are taking a different pricing approach that seems to be working: Hold sticker prices steady but pack cars with alluring new features.

What happens to the profit a car company makes on each car sold if it cuts the price while holding the car's features constant? What happens to the company's profit per car if the company adds new features while holding the price constant? Briefly discuss how a car company might decide which of these strategies to use.

Source: Todd Zaun, "Japanese Battle U.S. Discounts with Extras," *Wall Street Journal*, January 6, 2004.

>> End Learning Objective 4

The **Markets** for **Labor** and **Other Factors** of **Production**

From Chapter 16 of *Microeconomics*, 2/e. R. Glenn Hubbard. Anthony Patrick O'Brien. Copyright © 2008 by Pearson Prentice Hall.

The **Markets** for **Labor** and **Other Factors** of **Production**

Why Are the Chicago Cubs Paying Alfonso Soriano $18 Million per Year?

Few businesses arouse in their customers the level of passion that sports teams do. Unlike most other industries, the sports industry has an entire section devoted to it in most newspapers. Jerry Jones made a fortune in the oil and gas exploration business in Oklahoma, but few people knew who he was until he bought the Dallas Cowboys football team. Of course, the best-known people in sports are not the owners of teams but some of their employees—the players.

Sports fans admire the skills of star athletes, but many are also fascinated by their high salaries. How is it, fans often wonder, that some athletes are paid salaries in the millions of dollars "just for playing a game"? Many baseball fans also wonder why a few teams, such as the New York Yankees, Boston Red Sox, and Chicago Cubs, are able to pay higher salaries than other teams. For example, before the 2007 baseball season, the Chicago Cubs signed Alfonso Soriano to a contract worth an average of $18 million per season. This represented a significant raise from the $10 million the Washington Nationals, his previous team, had paid him the year before.

The University of Illinois, Chicago pays professors on its faculty an average salary of $80,000. Why are the Cubs willing to pay a baseball player so much more than the University of Illinois, Chicago is willing to pay a professor?

The key to answering these questions is to understand that wages are determined in the labor market by the demand and supply of labor, just as the price of apples is determined by the demand and supply of apples and the price of DVDs is determined by the demand and supply of DVDs. We developed a model for analyzing the demand and supply of goods and services. We will use some of the same concepts in this chapter to analyze the demand and supply of labor and other factors of production. But there are important ways in which the markets for factors of production are not like markets for goods. The most obvious difference is that in factor markets, firms are demanders, and households are suppliers.

Another difference between the labor market and the markets for goods and services is that concepts of fairness arise more frequently in labor markets. When an athlete like Alfonso Soriano signs a contract for millions of dollars, people often wonder "Why should someone playing a game get paid so much more than teachers, nurses, and other people

Getty Images, Inc.

394

doing more important jobs?" Because people typically earn most of their income from wages and salaries, they often view the labor market as being the most important market they participate in. **AN INSIDE LOOK** discusses the salaries of ex-college athletes who work for NASCAR pit crews.

LEARNING Objectives

After studying this chapter, you should be able to:

1   Explain how firms choose the **profit-maximizing quantity of labor** to employ.

2   Explain how people choose the quantity of **labor** to **supply**.

3   Explain how **equilibrium wages** are determined in labor markets.

4   Use demand and supply analysis to explain how **compensating differentials, discrimination,** and **labor unions** cause wages to differ.

5   Discuss the role **personnel economics** can play in helping firms deal with human resources issues.

6   Show how equilibrium prices are determined in the markets for **capital** and **natural resources**

Economics in YOUR Life!

Why Is It So Hard to Get a Raise?

Imagine that you have worked for a local sandwich shop for over a year and are preparing to ask for a raise. You might tell the manager that you are a good employee, with a good attitude and work ethic. You might also explain that you have learned more about your job and are now able to make sandwiches quicker, track inventory more accurately, and work the cash register more effectively than when you were first hired. Will this be enough to convince your manager to give you a raise? How can you convince your manager that you are worth more money than you are currently being paid? As you read this chapter, see if you can answer these questions. You can check your answers against those we provide at the end of the chapter.

Factors of production Labor, capital, natural resources, and other inputs used to produce goods and services.

F irms use **factors of production**—such as labor, capital, and natural resources—to produce goods and services. For example, the Chicago Cubs use labor (baseball players), capital (Wrigley Field), and natural resources (the land on which Wrigley Field sits) to produce baseball games. In this chapter, we will explore how firms choose the profit-maximizing quantity of labor and other factors of production. The interaction between firm demand for labor and household supply of labor determines the equilibrium wage rate.

Because there are many different types of labor, there are many different labor markets. The equilibrium wage in the market for baseball players is much higher than the equilibrium wage in the market for college professors. We will explore why this is true. We will also explore how factors such as discrimination, unions, and compensation for dangerous or unpleasant jobs help explain differences among wages. We will then look at *personnel economics*, which is concerned with how firms can use economic analysis to design their employee compensation plans. Finally, we will analyze the markets for other factors of production.

1 LEARNING OBJECTIVE

1 | Explain how firms choose the profit-maximizing quantity of labor to employ.

The Demand for Labor

Up until now we have concentrated on consumer demand for final goods and services. The demand for labor is different from the demand for final goods and services because it is a *derived demand*. A **derived demand** is the demand for a factor of production that is based on the demand for the good the factor produces. You demand an Apple iPod because of the utility you receive from listening to music. Apple's demand for the labor to make iPods is derived from the underlying consumer demand for iPods. As a result, we can say that Apple's demand for labor depends primarily on two factors:

Derived demand The demand for a factor of production that is derived from the demand for the good the factor produces.

1 The additional iPods Apple will be able to produce if it hires one more worker

2 The additional revenue Apple receives from selling the additional iPods

The Marginal Revenue Product of Labor

Consider the following example. To keep the main point clear, let's assume that in the short run, Apple can increase production of iPods only by increasing the quantity of labor it employs. The table in Figure 1 shows the relationship between the quantity of workers Apple hires, the quantity of iPods it produces, the additional revenue from selling the additional iPods, and the additional profit from hiring each additional worker.

For simplicity, we are keeping the scale of Apple's factory very small. We will also assume that Apple is a perfect competitor both in the market for selling digital music players and in the market for hiring labor. This means that Apple is a *price taker* in both markets. Although this is not realistic, the basic analysis would not change if we assumed that Apple can affect the price of digital music players and the wage paid to workers. Given these assumptions, suppose that Apple can sell as many iPods as it wants at a price of $200 and can hire as many workers as it wants at a wage of $600 per week. The additional output a firm produces as a result of hiring one more worker is called the **marginal product of labor**. In the table, we calculate the marginal product of labor as the change in total output as each additional worker is hired. We saw *the law of diminishing returns*, the marginal product of labor declines as a firm hires more workers.

Marginal product of labor The additional output a firm produces as a result of hiring one more worker.

When deciding how many workers to hire, a firm is not interested in how much *output* will increase as it hires another worker but in how much *revenue* will increase as it hires another worker. In other words, what matters is how much the firm's revenue will rise when it sells the additional output it can produce by hiring one more worker.

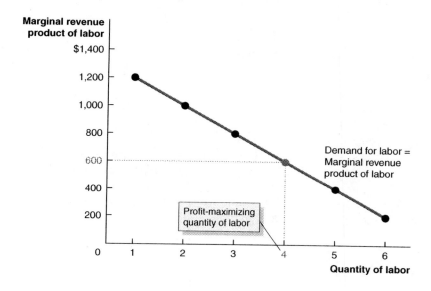

Number of Workers	Output of iPods per Week	Marginal Product of Labor (iPods per week)	Product Price	Marginal Revenue Product of Labor (dollars per week)	Wage (dollars per week)	Additional Profit from Hiring One More Worker (dollars per week)
L	Q	MP	P	MRP = P x MP	W	MRP − W
0	0	—	$200	—	$600	—
1	6	6	200	$1,200	600	$600
2	11	5	200	1,000	600	400
3	15	4	200	800	600	200
4	18	3	200	600	600	0
5	20	2	200	400	600	−200
6	21	1	200	200	600	−400

Figure 1

The Marginal Revenue Product of Labor and the Demand for Labor

The marginal revenue product of labor equals the marginal product of labor multiplied by the price of the good. The marginal revenue product curve slopes downward because diminishing returns cause the marginal product of labor to decline as more workers are hired. A firm maximizes profits by hiring workers up to the point where the wage equals the marginal revenue product of labor. The marginal revenue product of labor curve is the firm's demand curve for labor because it tells the firm the profit-maximizing quantity of workers to hire at each wage. For example, using the demand curve shown in this figure, if the wage is $600, the firm will hire 4 workers.

We can calculate this amount by multiplying the additional output produced by the product price. This amount is called the **marginal revenue product of labor** (*MRP*). For example, consider what happens if Apple increases the number of workers hired from 2 to 3. The table in Figure 1 shows that hiring the third worker allows Apple to increase its weekly output of iPods from 11 to 15, so the marginal product of labor is 4 iPods. The price of the iPods is $200, so the marginal revenue product of the third worker is 4 × $200, or $800. In other words, Apple adds $800 to its revenue as a result of hiring the third worker. In the graph, we plot the values of the marginal revenue product of labor at each quantity of labor.

To decide how many workers to hire, Apple must compare the additional revenue it earns from hiring another worker to the increase in its costs from paying that worker. The difference between the additional revenue and the additional cost is the additional profit (or loss) from hiring one more worker. This additional profit is shown in the last column of the table in Figure 1 and is calculated by subtracting the wage from the marginal revenue product of labor. As long as the marginal revenue product of labor is greater than the wage, Apple's profits are increasing, and it should continue to hire more workers. When the marginal revenue product of labor is less than the wage, Apple's profits are falling, and it should hire fewer workers. When the marginal revenue product of labor is equal to the wage, Apple has maximized its profits by hiring the optimal number of workers. The values in the table show that Apple should hire 4 workers. If the company hires a fifth worker, the marginal revenue product of $400 will be less than the wage of $600, and its profits will fall by $200. Table 1 summarizes the relationship between the marginal revenue product of labor and the wage.

Marginal revenue product of labor (*MRP*) The change in a firm's revenue as a result of hiring one more worker.

TABLE 1

The Relationship between the Marginal Revenue Product of Labor and the Wage

WHEN . . .	THEN THE FIRM . . .
$MRP > W$,	should hire more workers to increase profits.
$MRP < W$,	should hire fewer workers to increase profits.
$MRP = W$,	is hiring the optimal number of workers and is maximizing profits.

We can see from Figure 1 that if Apple has to pay a wage of $600 per week, it should hire 4 workers. If the wage were to rise to $1,000, then applying the rule that profits are maximized where the marginal revenue product of labor equals the wage, Apple should hire only 2 workers. Similarly, if the wage is only $400 per week, Apple should hire 5 workers. In fact, the marginal revenue product curve tells a firm how many workers it should hire at any wage rate. In other words, *the marginal revenue product of labor curve is the demand curve for labor.*

Solved Problem | 1

Hiring Decisions by a Firm That Is a Price Maker

We have assumed that Apple can sell as many iPods as it wants without having to cut the price. This is the case for firms in perfectly competitive markets. These firms are *price takers.* Suppose instead that a firm has market power and is a *price maker*, so that to increase sales, it must reduce the price.

Suppose Apple faces the situation shown in the following table. Fill in the blanks and then determine the profit-maximizing number of workers for Apple to hire. Briefly explain why hiring this number of workers is profit maximizing.

(1) QUANTITY OF LABOR	(2) OUTPUT OF iPODS PER WEEK	(3) MARGINAL PRODUCT OF LABOR	(4) PRODUCT PRICE	(5) TOTAL REVENUE	(6) MARGINAL REVENUE PRODUCT OF LABOR	(7) WAGE	(8) ADDITIONAL PROFIT FROM HIRING ONE ADDITIONAL WORKER
0	0	—	$200		—	$500	—
1	6	6	180			500	
2	11	5	160			500	
3	15	4	140			500	
4	18	3	120			500	
5	20	2	100			500	
6	21	1	80			500	

SOLVING THE PROBLEM:

Step 1: **Review the chapter material.** This problem is about determining the profit-maximizing quantity of labor for a firm to hire, so you may want to review the section "The Demand for Labor."

Step 2: **Fill in the blanks in the table.** As Apple hires more workers, it sells more iPods and earns more revenue. You can calculate how revenue increases by multiplying the number of iPods produced—shown in column 2—by the price—shown in column 4. Then you can calculate the marginal revenue product of labor as the change in revenue as each additional worker is hired. (Notice that in this case marginal revenue product is *not* calculated by multiplying the

398

marginal product by the product price. Because Apple is a price maker, its marginal revenue from selling additional iPods is less than the price of iPods.) Finally, you can calculate the additional profit from hiring one more worker by subtracting the wage—shown in column 7—from each worker's marginal revenue product.

(1) QUANTITY OF LABOR	(2) OUTPUT OF iPODS PER WEEK	(3) MARGINAL PRODUCT OF LABOR	(4) PRODUCT PRICE	(5) TOTAL REVENUE	(6) MARGINAL REVENUE PRODUCT OF LABOR	(7) WAGE	(8) ADDITIONAL PROFIT FROM HIRING ONE ADDITIONAL WORKER
0	0	—	$200	$0	—	$500	—
1	6	6	180	1,080	$1,080	500	$580
2	11	5	160	1,760	680	500	180
3	15	4	140	2,100	340	500	−160
4	18	3	120	2,160	60	500	−440
5	20	2	100	2,000	−160	500	−660
6	21	1	80	1,680	−320	500	−820

Step 3: **Use the information in the table to determine the profit-maximizing quantity of workers to hire.** To determine the profit-maximizing quantity of workers to hire, you need to compare the marginal revenue product of labor with the wage. Column 8 does this by subtracting the wage from the marginal revenue product. As long as the values in column 8 are positive, the firm should continue to hire workers. The marginal revenue product of the second worker is $680, and the wage is $500, so column 8 shows that hiring the second worker will add $180 to Apple's profits. The marginal revenue product of the third worker is $340, and the wage is $500, so hiring the third worker would reduce Apple's profits by $160. Therefore, Apple will maximize profits by hiring 2 workers.

YOUR TURN: For more practice, do problem 1.5 at the end of this chapter.

>> End Solved Problem 1

The Market Demand Curve for Labor

We can determine the market demand curve for labor in the same way we determine a market demand curve for a good. The market demand curve for a good is determined by adding up the quantity of the good demanded by each consumer at each price. Similarly, the market demand curve for labor is determined by adding up the quantity of labor demanded by each firm at each wage, holding constant all other variables that might affect the willingness of firms to hire workers.

Factors That Shift the Market Demand Curve for Labor

In constructing the demand curve for labor, we held constant all variables that would affect the willingness of firms to demand labor—except for the wage. An increase or a decrease in the wage causes *an increase or a decrease in the quantity of labor demanded*, which we show by a movement along the demand curve. If any variable other than the wage changes, the result is *an increase or a decrease in the demand for labor*, which we show by a shift of the demand curve. The five most important variables that cause the labor demand curve to shift are the following:

- *Increases in human capital.* **Human capital** represents the accumulated training and skills that workers possess. For example, a worker with a college education generally has more skills and is more productive than a worker who has only a high school diploma. If workers become more educated and are therefore able to produce

Human capital The accumulated training and skills that workers possess.

more output per day, the demand for their services will increase, shifting the labor demand curve to the right.

- *Changes in technology.* As new and better machinery and equipment are developed, workers become more productive. This effect causes the labor demand curve to shift to the right over time.

- *Changes in the price of the product.* The marginal revenue product of labor depends on the price a firm receives for its output. A higher price increases the marginal revenue product and shifts the labor demand curve to the right. A lower price shifts the labor demand curve to the left.

- *Changes in the quantity of other inputs.* Workers are able to produce more if they have more machinery and other inputs available to them. The marginal product of labor in the United States is higher than the marginal product of labor in other countries in large part because U.S. firms provide workers with more machinery and equipment. Over time, workers in the United States have had increasing amounts of other inputs available to them, and that has increased their productivity and caused the demand for labor to shift to the right.

- *Changes in the number of firms in the market.* If new firms enter the market, the demand for labor will shift to the right. If firms exit the market, the demand for labor will shift to the left. This effect is similar to that which increasing or decreasing the number of consumers in a market has on the demand for a good.

2 LEARNING OBJECTIVE   2 | Explain how people choose the quantity of labor to supply.

The Supply of Labor

Having discussed the demand for labor, we can now consider the supply of labor. Of the many trade-offs each of us faces in life, one of the most important is how to divide up the 24 hours in the day between labor and leisure. Every hour spent watching television, walking on the beach, or in other forms of leisure is one less hour spent working. Because in devoting an hour to leisure, we give up an hour's earnings from working, the *opportunity cost* of leisure is the wage. The higher the wage we could earn working, the higher the opportunity cost of leisure. Therefore, as the wage increases, we tend to take less leisure and work more. This relationship explains why the labor supply curve for most people is upward sloping, as Figure 2 shows.

Figure 2

The Labor Supply Curve

As the wage increases, the opportunity cost of leisure increases, causing individuals to supply a greater quantity of labor. Therefore, the labor supply curve is upward sloping.

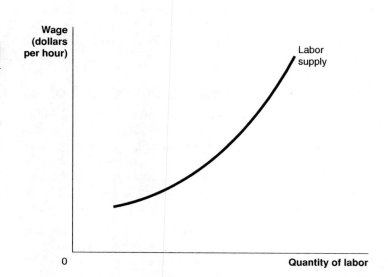

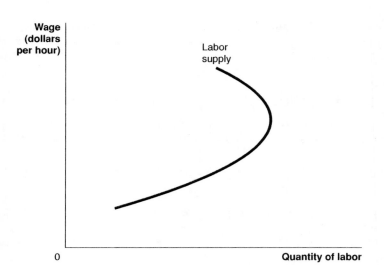

Wage
(dollars
per hour)

Labor
supply

0

Quantity of labor

Figure 3

A Backward-Bending Labor Supply Curve

As the wage rises, a greater quantity of labor is usually supplied. As the wage climbs above a certain level, the individual is able to afford more leisure even though the opportunity cost of leisure is high. The result may be a smaller quantity of labor supplied.

Although we normally expect the labor supply curve for an individual to be upward sloping, it is possible that at very high wage levels, the supply curve of an individual might be *backward bending*, so that higher wages actually result in a *smaller* quantity of labor supplied, as shown in Figure 3. To understand why, recall the definitions of the *substitution effect* and the *income effect*. The substitution effect of a price change refers to the fact that an increase in price makes a good more expensive *relative* to other goods. In the case of a wage change, the substitution effect refers to the fact that an increase in the wage raises the opportunity cost of leisure and causes a worker to devote *more* time to working and less time to leisure.

The income effect of a price change refers to the change in the quantity demanded of a good that results from changes in consumer purchasing power as a result of a price change. An increase in the wage will clearly increase a consumer's purchasing power for any given number of hours worked. For a normal good, the income effect leads to a larger quantity demanded. Because leisure is a normal good, the income effect of a wage increase will cause a worker to devote *less* time to working and more time to leisure. So, the substitution effect of a wage increase causes a worker to supply a larger quantity of labor, but the income effect causes a worker to supply a smaller quantity of labor. Whether a worker supplies more or less labor following a wage increase depends on whether the substitution effect is larger than the income effect. Figure 3 shows the typical case of the substitution effect being larger than the income effect at low levels of wages—so the worker supplies a larger quantity of labor as the wage rises—and the income effect being larger than the substitution effect at high levels of wages—so the worker supplies a smaller quantity of labor as the wage rises. For example, suppose an attorney has become quite successful and can charge clients very high fees. Or suppose a rock band has become very popular and receives a large payment for every concert it performs. In these cases, there is a high opportunity cost for the lawyer to turn down another client to take a longer vacation or for the band to turn down another concert. But because their incomes are already very high, they may decide to give up additional income for more leisure. For the lawyer or the rock band, the income effect is larger than the substitution effect, and a higher wage causes them to supply *less* labor.

The Market Supply Curve of Labor

We can determine the market supply curve of labor in the same way we determine a market supply curve of a good. The market supply curve of a good is determined by adding up the quantity of the good supplied by each firm at each price. Similarly, the market supply curve of labor is determined by adding up the quantity of labor supplied by each worker at each wage, holding constant all other variables that might affect the willingness of workers to supply labor.

Factors That Shift the Market Supply Curve of Labor

In constructing the market supply curve of labor, we hold constant all other variables that would affect the willingness of workers to supply labor, except the wage. If any of these other variables change, the market supply curve will shift. The following are the three most important variables that cause the market supply curve of labor to shift:

- *Increases in population.* As the population grows because of natural increase and immigration, the supply curve of labor shifts to the right. The effects of immigration on labor supply are largest in the markets for unskilled workers. In some large cities in the United States, for example, the majority of taxi drivers and workers in hotels and restaurants are immigrants. Some supporters of reducing immigration argue that wages in these jobs have been depressed by the increased supply of labor from immigrants.

- *Changing demographics.* *Demographics* refers to the composition of the population. The more people who are between the ages of 16 and 65, the greater the quantity of labor supplied. During the 1970s and 1980s, the U.S. labor force grew particularly rapidly as members of the baby boom generation—born between 1946 and 1964—first began working. In contrast, a low birth rate in Japan has resulted in an aging population. The number of working-age people in Japan actually began to decline during the 1990s, causing the labor supply curve to shift to the left.

  A related demographic issue is the changing role of women in the labor force. In 1900, only 21 percent of women in the United States were in the labor force. By 1950, this had risen to 30 percent, and today, it is 60 percent. This increase in the *labor force participation* of women has significantly increased the supply of labor in the United States.

- *Changing alternatives.* The labor supply in any particular labor market depends, in part, on the opportunities available in other labor markets. For example, the telecommunications industry bust in 2001 reduced the opportunities for optical engineers. Many workers left this market—causing the labor supply curve to shift to the left—and entered other markets, causing the labor supply curves to shift to the right in those markets. People who have lost jobs or who have low incomes are eligible for unemployment insurance and other payments from the government. The more generous these payments are, the less pressure unemployed workers have to quickly find another job. In many European countries, it is much easier than in the United States for unemployed workers to receive a greater replacement of their wage income from government payments. In one case that received widespread publicity, an unemployed German banker received payments of $2,400 per month from the German government to help pay for his apartment in Miami Beach in a gated community with a swimming pool and sauna. The banker's psychiatrist reportedly argued that the banker needed to remain in sunny Florida because the overcast weather in his hometown in Germany might worsen his depression. Although cases like this are extreme, many economists believe generous unemployment benefits help explain the higher unemployment rates experienced in Europe. For example, in the 10 years from 1997 to 2006, the average of the unemployment rates in the United Kingdom, France, Germany, Italy, and Spain was 9 percent, while in the United States, the unemployment rate averaged just under 5 percent. There have been proposals in some European countries to reduce the size of these government payments in the hope of increasing the labor supply.

402

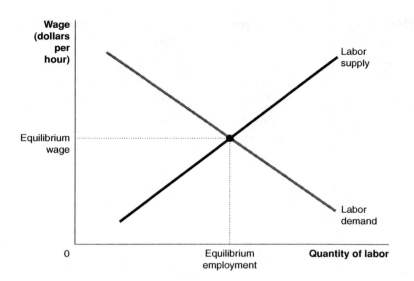

Figure 4

Equilibrium in the Labor Market

As in other markets, equilibrium in the labor market occurs where the demand curve for labor and the supply curve of labor intersect.

Equilibrium in the Labor Market

In Figure 4, we bring labor demand and labor supply together to determine equilibrium in the labor market. We can use demand and supply to analyze changes in the equilibrium wage and the level of employment for the entire labor market, or we can use it to analyze markets for different types of labor, such as baseball players or college professors.

The Effect on Equilibrium Wages of a Shift in Labor Demand

In many labor markets, increases over time in labor productivity will cause the demand for labor to increase. As Figure 5 shows, if labor supply is unchanged, an increase in labor demand will increase both the equilibrium wage and the number of workers employed.

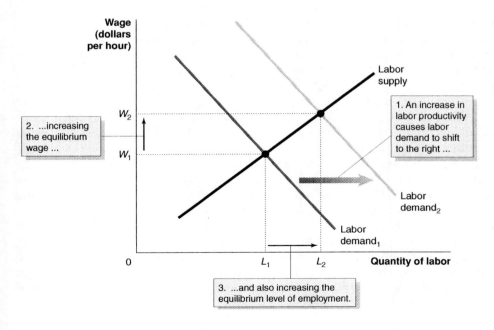

Figure 5

The Effect of an Increase in Labor Demand

Increases in labor demand will cause the equilibrium wage and the equilibrium level of employment to rise.

1. If the productivity of workers rises, the marginal revenue product increases, causing the labor demand curve to shift to the right.
2. The equilibrium wage rises from W_1 to W_2.
3. The equilibrium level of employment rises from L_1 to L_2.

Making the Connection

Will Your Future Income Depend on Which Courses You Take in College?

Most people realize the value of a college education. As the following chart shows, in 2007, full-time workers ages 25 and over with a college degree earned more per week than other workers; for example, they earned 2.5 times as much as high school dropouts.

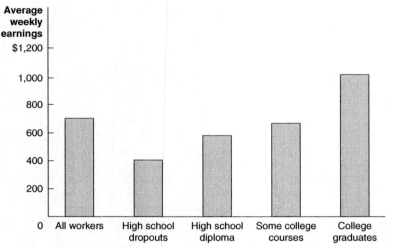

Source: U.S. Bureau of Labor Statistics, "Usual Weekly Earnings of Wage and Salary Workers," April 18, 2007.

Why do college graduates earn more than others? The obvious answer would seem to be that a college education provides skills that increase productivity. Some economists, though, advocate an alternative explanation, known as the *signaling hypothesis*, first proposed by Nobel laureate A. Michael Spence of Stanford University. This hypothesis is based on the idea that job applicants will always have more information than will potential employers about how productive the applicants are likely to be. Although employers attempt through job interviews and background checks to distinguish "good workers" from "bad workers," they are always looking for more information.

According to the signaling hypothesis, employers see a college education as a signal that workers possess certain desirable characteristics: self-discipline, the ability to meet deadlines, and the ability to make a sustained effort. Even if these characteristics are not related to the specifics of a particular job, employers value them because they usually lead to success in any activity. People generally believe that college graduates possess these characteristics, so employers often require a college degree for their best-paying jobs. In this view, the signal that a college education sends about a person's inherent characteristics—which the person presumably already possessed *before* entering college—is much more important than any skills the person may have learned in college. Or, as a college math professor of one of the authors put it (only half-jokingly), "The purpose of college is to show employers that you can succeed at something that's boring and hard."

Recently, though, several economic studies have provided evidence that the higher incomes of college graduates are due to their greater productivity rather than the signal that a college degree sends to employers. Orley Ashenfelter and Cecilia Rouse of Princeton University studied the relationship between schooling and income among 700 pairs of identical twins. Identical twins have identical genes, so differences in their inherent abilities should be relatively small. Therefore, if they have different numbers of years in school, differences in their earnings should be mainly due to the effect of schooling on their productivity. Ashenfelter and Rouse found that identical twins had returns of about 9 percent per additional year of schooling, enough to account for most of the gap in income between high school graduates and college graduates.

Daniel Hamermesh and Stephen G. Donald of the University of Texas have studied the determinants of the earnings of college graduates 5 to 25 years after graduation. They collected extensive information on each person in their study, including the person's SAT scores, rank in high school class, grades in every college course taken, and college major. Hamermesh and Donald discovered that, holding constant all other factors, business and engineering majors earned more than graduates with other majors. They also discovered a large impact on future earnings of taking science and math courses: "A student who takes 15 credits of upper-division science and math courses and obtains a B average in them will earn about 10 percent more than an otherwise identical student in the same major . . . who takes no upper-division classes in these areas." This result held even after adjusting for a student's SAT score. The study by Hamermesh and Donald contradicts the signaling hypothesis because if the signaling hypothesis is correct, the choice of courses taken in college should be of minor importance compared with the signal workers send to employers just by having completed college.

Sources: Orley Ashenfelter and Cecilia Rouse, "Income, Schooling, and Ability: Evidence from a New Sample of Identical Twins," *Quarterly Journal of Economics*, Vol. 113, No. 1 (February 1998), pp. 253–284; Daniel S. Hamermesh and Stephen G. Donald, "The Effect of College Curriculum on Earnings: Accounting for Non-Ignorable Non-Response Bias," National Bureau of Economic Research working paper 10809, September 2004.

YOUR TURN: Test your understanding by doing related problem 3.3 at the end of this chapter.

The Effect on Equilibrium Wages of a Shift in Labor Supply

What is the effect on the equilibrium wage of an increase in labor supply due to population growth? As Figure 6 shows, if labor demand is unchanged, an increase in labor supply will decrease the equilibrium wage but increase the number of workers employed.

Whether the wage rises in a market depends on whether demand increases faster than supply. For example, after the success of Walt Disney's animated film *The Lion King* in 1994, most movie studios increased production of animated films, increasing the

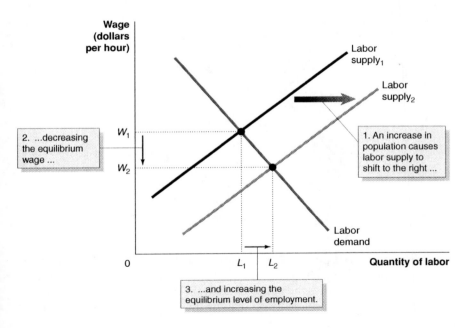

Figure 6

The Effect of an Increase in Labor Supply

Increases in labor supply will cause the equilibrium wage to fall but the equilibrium level of employment to rise.

1. As population increases, the labor supply curve shifts to the right.
2. The equilibrium wage falls from W_1 to W_2.
3. The equilibrium level of employment increases from L_1 to L_2.

demand for animators much faster than the supply of animators was increasing. The annual salary for a top animator rose from about $125,000 in 1994 to $550,000 in 1999. These high salaries led more people with artistic ability to choose to get training as film animators, causing the supply of animators to increase after 1999. Several of the animated films released between 1999 and 2001 failed to earn profits, which caused some companies to stop making these films, thereby decreasing the demand for animators. The decrease in demand for animators and the increase in supply caused the salaries of top animators to fall from $550,000 in 1999 to $225,000 in 2002.

Getty Images, Inc.

The flower industry is one of many industries in the United States that rely on immigrant workers.

Making the Connection | Immigration and Wages, Then and Now

Between 1900 and the outbreak of World War I in 1914, about 13.4 million immigrants arrived in the United States. Relative to the U.S. population—which was about 76 million in 1900—this was the largest wave of immigration in the history of the world. Many commentators at the time predicted that this great increase in the U.S. labor supply would cause a sharp fall in wages. Figure 6 shows that this is a reasonable prediction of the effect of an increase in labor supply on the equilibrium wage, *but only if the demand for labor remains unchanged.* In fact, the demand for labor increased rapidly during these years as technological progress, such as electrification and the development of mass-production techniques, increased the productivity of labor.

As a result, the demand for labor shifted to the right faster than the supply of labor, and wages rose. The following figure shows the situation in manufacturing. Both demand and supply increased, but because the shift in demand was greater than the shift in supply, average hourly earnings rose from less than $0.18 in 1900 to $0.22 in 1914, or by almost 25 percent. (The data for both years use 1914 prices to correct for the effects of inflation.) During the same years, employment in manufacturing rose from about 5.5 million workers to almost 9 million.

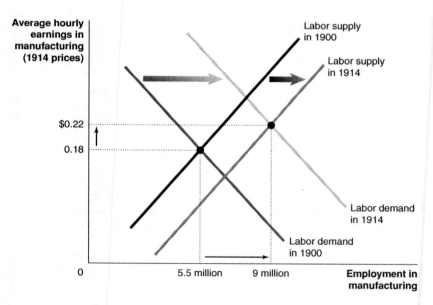

In 2007, the economics of immigration was once again in the forefront during the debate over a proposal by President George W. Bush to revise the immigration laws. President Bush proposed allowing the approximately 12 million illegal immigrants in the United States to enter a process that would allow them to become legal permanent residents. He also proposed strengthening security at the country's borders to reduce future illegal immigration. The figure below shows estimates by the Pew Hispanic Center indicating that illegal immigrants had become a substantial part of the labor supply in a number of industries.

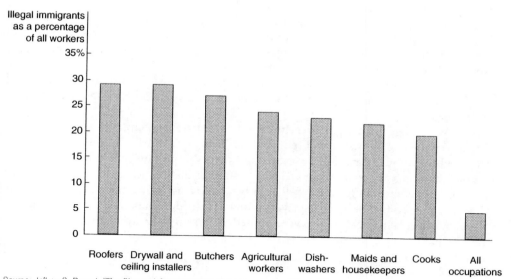

Source: Jeffrey S. Passel, "The Size and Characteristics of the Unauthorized Migrant Population in the U.S.," Pew Hispanic Center Research Report, March 7, 2006, Table 1, p. 12.

Economists have debated the impact of illegal immigrants on the wages of unskilled workers. As the figure indicates, illegal immigrants have substantially increased the supply of labor in some occupations. Some economists argue that illegal immigration may have significantly contributed to the distribution of income becoming more unequal in recent years. Illegal immigration increases income inequality if the supply of illegal workers reduces the wages of low-income workers relative to high-income workers. Claudia Goldin and Lawrence Katz, economists at Harvard University, have recently estimated that immigration—both legal and illegal—can explain only about 10 percent of the increase in the gap between the wages of college-educated workers and the wages of high school-educated workers during the years between 1980 and 2005. George Borjas, of Harvard, Jeffrey Grogger, of the University of Chicago, and Gordon Hanson, of the University of California, San Diego, find a significant impact of immigration on the employment opportunities of African Americans. They find that if as a result of immigration there is a 10 percent increase in the supply of labor with a particular skill, the wages of African Americans with that skill fall by 4 percent, the employment rate of African Americans falls by 3.5 percentage points, and the fraction of African Americans in jail increases by 1 percentage point.

The economic impact of immigration is certain to remain a hotly debated issue for the foreseeable future.

Source: U.S. Department of Commerce, *Historical Statistics of the United States*, Washington, DC: USGPO, 1976; Jeffrey S. Passel, "The Size and Characteristics of the Unauthorized Migrant Population in the U.S.," Pew Hispanic Center Research Report, March 7, 2006; Claudia Goldin and Lawrence F. Katz, "The Race Between Education and Technology," NBER Working Paper, No. 12984, March 2007; and George J. Borjas, Jeffrey Grogger, and Gordon H. Hanson, "Immigration and African-American Employment Opportunities," NBER Working Paper No. 12518, May 2007.

YOUR TURN: Test your understanding by doing related problems 3.5, 3.6, 3.7, and 3.8 at the end of this chapter.

4 LEARNING OBJECTIVE

4 | Use demand and supply analysis to explain how compensating differentials, discrimination, and labor unions cause wages to differ.

Explaining Differences in Wages

A key conclusion of our discussion of the labor market is that the equilibrium wage equals the marginal revenue product of labor. The more productive workers are and the higher the price workers' output can be sold for, the higher the wages workers will receive. At the beginning of the chapter, we raised the question of why major league baseball players are paid so much more than college professors. We are now ready to use demand and supply analysis to answer this question. Figure 7 shows the demand and supply curves for major league baseball players and the demand and supply curves for college professors.

Consider first the marginal revenue product of baseball players, which is the additional revenue a team owner will receive from hiring one more player. Baseball players are hired to produce baseball games that are then sold to fans who pay admission to baseball stadiums and to radio and television stations that broadcast the games. Because a major league baseball team can sell each baseball game for a large amount, the marginal revenue product of baseball players is high. The supply of people with the ability to play major league baseball is also very limited. As a result, the average annual salary of the 750 major league baseball players is about $2,700,000.

The marginal revenue product of college professors is much lower than for baseball players. College professors are hired to produce college educations that are then sold to students and their parents. Although one year's college tuition is quite high at many colleges, hiring one more professor allows a college to admit at most a few more students. So, the marginal revenue product of a college professor is much lower than the marginal revenue product of a baseball player. There are also many more people who possess the skills to be a college professor than possess the skills to be a major league baseball player. As a result, the country's 663,000 college professors are paid an average salary of about $73,000.

This still leaves unanswered the question raised at the beginning of this chapter: Why are the Chicago Cubs willing to pay Alfonso Soriano more than the Washington Nationals were? Soriano's marginal product—which we can think of as the extra games a

Figure 7

Baseball Players Are Paid More Than College Professors

The marginal revenue product of baseball players is very high, and the supply of people with the ability to play major league baseball is low. The result is that the 750 major league baseball players receive an average wage of $2,700,000. The marginal revenue product of college professors is much lower, and the supply of people with the ability to be college professors is much higher. The result is that the 663,000 college professors in the United States receive an average wage of $73,000, far below that of baseball players.

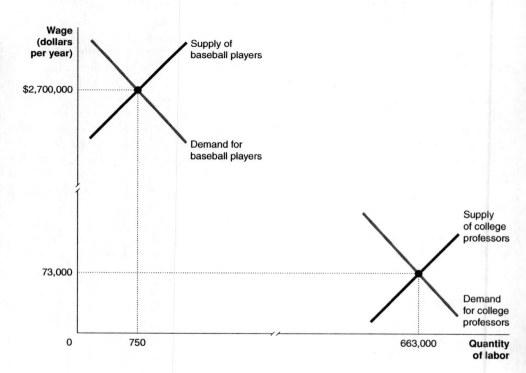

Don't Let This Happen to **YOU!**

Remember That Prices and Wages Are Determined at the Margin

You have probably heard some variation of the following remark: "We could live without baseball, but we can't live without the garbage being hauled away. In a more rational world, garbage collectors would be paid more than baseball players." This remark seems logical: The total value to society of having the garbage hauled away certainly is greater than the total value of baseball games. But wages—like prices—do not depend on total value but on *marginal* value. The *additional* baseball games the Chicago Cubs expect to win by signing Alfonso Soriano will result in millions of dollars in increased revenue. The supply of people with the ability to play major league baseball is very limited. The supply of people with the ability to be trash haulers is much greater. If a trash-hauling firm hires another worker, the *additional* trash-hauling services it can

now offer will bring in a relatively small amount of revenue. The *total* value of baseball games and the *total* value of trash hauling are not relevant in determining the relative salaries of baseball players and garbage collectors.

This point is related to the diamond and water paradox first noted by Adam Smith. On the one hand, water is very valuable—we literally couldn't live without it—but its price is very low. On the other hand, apart from a few industrial uses, diamonds are used only for jewelry, yet their prices are quite high. We resolve the paradox by noting that the price of water is low because the supply is very large and the additional benefit consumers receive from the last gallon purchased is low. The price of diamonds is high because the supply is very small, and the additional benefit consumers receive from the last diamond purchased is high.

YOUR TURN: Test your understanding by doing related problem 4.6 at the end of this chapter.

team will win by employing him—should be about the same in Chicago as it was in Washington, DC. But his *marginal revenue product* will be higher in Chicago. Because the population of the Chicago metropolitan area is about twice as large as the population of the Washington metropolitan area, winning more games will result in a greater increase in attendance at Chicago Cubs games than it would at Washington Nationals games. It will also result in a greater increase in viewers for Cubs games on television. Therefore, the Cubs are able to sell the extra wins that Soriano produces for much more than the Washington Nationals can. This difference explains why the Cubs were willing to pay Soriano $18 million per year when he had made "only" $10 million with the Nationals.

Making the Connection | Technology and the Earnings of "Superstars"

The gap between Alfonso Soriano's salary and the salary of the lowest-paid baseball players is much greater than the gap between the salaries paid during the 1950s and 1960s to top players such as Mickey Mantle and Willie Mays and the salaries of the lowest-paid players. Similarly, the gap between the $20 million Julia Roberts is paid to star in a movie and the salary paid to an actor in a minor role is much greater than the gap between the salaries paid during the 1930s and 1940s to stars such as Clark Gable and Cary Grant and the salaries paid to bit players. In fact, in most areas of sports and entertainment, the highest-paid performers—the "superstars"—now have much higher incomes relative to other members of their professions than was true a few decades ago.

The increase in the relative incomes of superstars is mainly due to technological advances. The spread of cable television has increased the number of potential viewers of Cubs games, but many of those viewers will watch only if the Cubs are winning. This increases the value to the Cubs of winning games and, therefore, increases Soriano's marginal revenue product and the salary he can earn.

With DVDs, Internet streaming video, and pay-per-view cable, the value to movie studios of producing a hit movie has risen greatly. Not surprisingly, movie studios have also increased their willingness to pay large salaries to stars like Julia Roberts or Brad Pitt because they think these superstars will significantly raise the chances of a film being successful.

Why does Julia Roberts earn more today relative to the typical actor than stars did in the 1940s?

The Kobal Collection/Columbia Pictures

This process has been going on for a long time. For instance, before the invention of the motion picture, anyone who wanted to see a play had to attend the theater and see a live performance. Limits on the number of people who could see the best actors and actresses perform created an opportunity for many more people to succeed in the acting profession, and the gap between the salaries earned by the best actors and the salaries earned by average actors was relatively small. Today, when a hit movie starring Julia Roberts appears on DVD, millions of people will buy or rent it, and they will not be forced to spend money to see a lesser actress, as their great-great-grandparents might have been.

YOUR TURN: Test your understanding by doing related problems 4.9 and 4.10 at the end of this chapter.

___

Differences in marginal revenue products are the most important factor in explaining differences in wages, but they are not the whole story. To provide a more complete explanation for differences in wages, we must take into account three important aspects of labor markets: compensating differentials, discrimination, and labor unions. We begin with compensating differentials.

Compensating Differentials

Compensating differentials Higher wages that compensate workers for unpleasant aspects of a job.

Suppose Paul runs a video rental store and acquires a reputation for being a bad boss who yells at his workers and is generally unpleasant. Two blocks away, Brendan also runs a video rental store, but Brendan is always very polite to his workers. We would expect in these circumstances that Paul will have to pay a higher wage than Brendan to attract and retain workers. Higher wages that compensate workers for unpleasant aspects of a job are called **compensating differentials**.

If working in a dynamite factory requires the same degree of training and education as working in a semiconductor factory but is much more dangerous, a larger number of workers will want to work making semiconductors than will want to work making dynamite. As a consequence, the wages of dynamite workers will be higher than the wages of semiconductor workers. We can think of the difference in wages as being the price of risk. As each worker decides on his or her willingness to assume risk and decides how much higher the wage must be to compensate for assuming more risk, wages will adjust so that dynamite factories will end up paying wages that are just high enough to compensate workers who choose to work there for the extra risk they assume. Only when workers in dynamite factories have been fully compensated with higher wages for the additional risk they assume will dynamite companies be able to attract enough workers.

One surprising implication of compensating differentials is that *laws protecting the health and safety of workers may not make workers better off*. To see this, suppose that dynamite factories pay wages of $25 per hour, and semiconductor factories pay wages of $20 per hour, with the $5 difference in wages being a compensating differential for the greater risk of working in a dynamite factory. Suppose that the government passes a law regulating the manufacture of dynamite in order to improve safety in dynamite factories. As a result of this law, dynamite factories are no longer any more dangerous than semiconductor factories. Once this happens, the wages in dynamite factories will decline to $20 per hour, the same as in semiconductor factories. Are workers in dynamite factories any better or worse off? Before the law was passed, their wages were $25 per hour, but $5 per hour was a compensating differential for the extra risk they were exposed to. Now their wages are only $20 per hour, but the extra risk has been eliminated. The conclusion seems to be that dynamite workers are no better off as a result of the safety legislation.

This conclusion is only true, though, if the compensating differential actually does compensate workers fully for the additional risk. George Akerlof of the University of California, Berkeley, and William Dickens of the Brookings Institution have argued that the psychological principle known as *cognitive dissonance* might cause workers to underestimate the true risk of their jobs. According to this principle, people prefer to think of themselves as intelligent and rational and tend to reject evidence that seems to contradict this image. Because working in a very hazardous job may seem irrational, workers in such jobs may refuse to believe that the jobs really are hazardous. Akerlof and Dickens present evidence that workers in chemical plants producing benzene and workers in nuclear power plants underestimate the hazards of their jobs. If this is true, the wages of these workers will not be high enough to compensate them fully for the risk they have assumed. So, in this situation, safety legislation may make workers better off.

Discrimination

Table 2 shows that in the United States, white males on average earn more than other groups. One possible explanation for this is **economic discrimination**, which involves paying a person a lower wage or excluding a person from an occupation on the basis of an irrelevant characteristic such as race or gender.

Economic discrimination Paying a person a lower wage or excluding a person from an occupation on the basis of an irrelevant characteristic such as race or gender.

If employers discriminate by hiring only white males for high-paying jobs or by paying white males higher wages than other groups working the same jobs, white males would have higher earnings, as Table 2 shows. However, excluding groups from certain jobs or paying one group more than another has been illegal in the United States since the passage of the Equal Pay Act of 1963 and the Civil Rights Act of 1964. Nevertheless, it is possible that employers are ignoring the law and practicing economic discrimination.

Most economists believe that only a small amount of the gap between the wages of white males and the wages of other groups is due to discrimination. Instead, most of the gap is explained by three main factors:

1. Differences in education
2. Differences in experience
3. Differing preferences for jobs

Differences in Education Some of the difference between the incomes of whites and the incomes of blacks can be explained by differences in education. Historically, African Americans have had less schooling than whites. Although the gap has closed significantly over the years, 90 percent of adult non-Hispanic white males in 2005 had graduated from high school, but only 80 percent of adult African American males had. Whereas 33 percent of white males had graduated from college, only 17 percent of African American males had. These statistics understate the true gap in education between blacks and whites because many blacks receive a substandard education in inner-city schools. Not surprisingly, studies have shown that differing levels of education can account for a significant part of the gap between the earnings of white and black males.

GROUP	ANNUAL EARNINGS
White males	$46,746
White females	34,464
Black males	33,248
Black females	29,749
Hispanic males	26,769
Hispanic females	24,402

TABLE 2

Why Do White Males Earn More Than Other Groups?

Note: The values are median annual earnings for persons who worked full time, year round in 2005. Persons of Hispanic origin can be of any race.

Source: U.S. Bureau of the Census, Table PINC-10, Current Population Survey, Annual Social and Economic Supplement, March 2006.

Differences in Experience Women are much more likely than men to leave their jobs for a period of time after having a child. Women with several children will sometimes have several interruptions in their careers. Some women leave the workforce for several years until their children are of school age. As a result, on average, women with children have less workforce experience than do men of the same age. Because workers with greater experience are, on average, more productive, the difference in levels of experience helps to explain some of the difference in earnings between men and women. One indication of this is that, on average, married women earn about 39 percent less than married men, but women who have never been married—and whose careers are less likely to have been interrupted—earn only about 10 percent less than men who have never been married.

Differing Preferences for Jobs Significant differences exist between the types of jobs held by women and men. As Table 3 shows, women are overrepresented in some jobs where average weekly earnings are less than $500 per week, and men are overrepresented in some jobs where weekly earnings are greater than $700 per week.

Although the patterns shown in Table 3 could be explained by women being excluded from some occupations, it is likely that they reflect differences in job preferences between men and women. For example, because many women interrupt their careers—at least briefly—when their children are born, they are more likely to take jobs where work experience is less important. Women may also be more likely to take jobs, such as teaching, that allow them to be home in the afternoons when their children return from school.

TABLE 3

"Men's Jobs" Often Pay More Than "Women's Jobs"

"WOMEN'S JOBS"			"MEN'S JOBS"		
OCCUPATION	WEEKLY EARNINGS	PERCENTAGE OF WORKERS WHO ARE WOMEN	OCCUPATION	WEEKLY EARNINGS	PERCENTAGE OF WORKERS WHO ARE WOMEN
Preschool and kindergarten teachers	$521	96%	Electricians	$713	2%
Dental assistants	474	95	Fire fighters	944	4
Childcare workers	332	93	Aircraft mechanics	919	6
Receptionists	466	92	Aircraft pilots	1,366	6
Hairdressers	416	91	Engineering managers	1,788	10
Teacher assistants	398	91	Aerospace engineers	1,366	11
Nursing aides	388	89	Civil engineers	1,138	13
Maids and housekeeping cleaners	335	87	Computer software engineers	1,401	21
Cashiers	336	75	Chief executives	1,834	24

Note: Earnings are for men and women in the occupation and are "median usual weekly earnings of full-time wage and salary workers."

Source: U.S. Department of Labor, Bureau of Labor Statistics, *Highlights of Women's Earnings in 2005*, Report 995, Table 2, September 2006.

Solved Problem | 4

Is "Comparable Worth" Legislation the Answer to Closing the Gap between Men's and Women's Pay?

As we have seen, either because of discrimination or differing preferences, certain jobs are filled primarily by men, and other jobs are filled primarily by women. On average, the "men's jobs" have higher wages than the "women's jobs." Some observers have argued that many "men's jobs" are more highly paid than "women's jobs," despite the jobs being comparable in terms of the education and skills required and the working conditions involved. These observers have argued that the earnings gap between men and women could be closed at least partially if the government required employers to pay the same wages for jobs that have *comparable worth*. Many economists are skeptical of these proposals because they believe allowing markets to determine wages results in a more efficient outcome.

Suppose that electricians are currently being paid a market equilibrium wage of $700 per week, and dental technicians are being paid a market equilibrium wage of $400 per week. Comparable-worth legislation is passed, and a study finds that an electrician and a dental technician have comparable jobs, so employers will now be required to pay workers in both jobs $550 per week. Analyze the effects of this requirement on the market for electricians and on the market for dental technicians. Be sure to use demand and supply graphs.

SOLVING THE PROBLEM:

Step 1: **Review the chapter material.** This problem is about economic discrimination, so you may want to review the section "Discrimination."

Step 2: **Draw the graphs.** When the government sets the price in a market, the result is a surplus or a shortage, depending on whether the government-mandated price is above or below the competitive market equilibrium. A wage of $550 per week is below the market wage for electricians and above the market wage for dental technicians. Therefore, we expect the requirement to result in a shortage of electricians and a surplus of dental technicians.

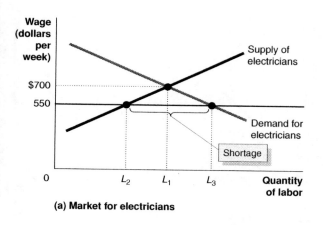

(a) Market for electricians

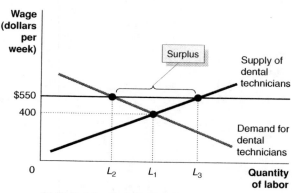

(b) Market for dental technicians

In panel (a), without comparable-worth legislation, the equilibrium wage for electricians is $700, and the equilibrium quantity of electricians hired is L_1. Setting the wage for electricians below equilibrium at $550 reduces the quantity of labor supplied in this occupation from L_1 to L_2 but increases the quantity of labor demanded by employers from L_1 to L_3. The result is a shortage of electricians equal to $L_3 - L_2$, as shown by the bracket in the graph.

In panel (b), without comparable-worth legislation, the equilibrium wage for dental technicians is $400, and the equilibrium quantity of dental technicians

413

hired is L_1. Setting the wage for dental technicians above equilibrium at $550 increases the quantity of labor supplied in this occupation from L_1 to L_3 but reduces the quantity of labor demanded by employers from L_1 to L_2. The result is a surplus of dental technicians equal to $L_3 - L_2$, as shown by the bracket in the graph.

EXTRA CREDIT: Most economists are skeptical of government attempts to set wages and prices, as comparable-worth legislation would require. Supporters of comparable-worth legislation, by contrast, see differences between men's and women's wages as being mainly due to discrimination and are looking to government legislation as a solution.

YOUR TURN: For more practice, do related problems 4.15 and 4.16 at the end of this chapter.

>> End Solved Problem 4

The Difficulty of Measuring Discrimination When two people are paid different wages, discrimination may be the explanation. But differences in productivity or preferences may also be an explanation. Labor economists have attempted to measure what part of differences in wages between blacks and whites and between men and women is due to discrimination and what part is due to other factors. Unfortunately, it is difficult to measure precisely differences in productivity or in worker preferences. As a result, we can't know exactly the extent of economic discrimination in the United States today. Most economists do believe, however, that most of the differences in wages between different groups are due to factors other than discrimination.

Does It Pay to Discriminate? Many economists argue that economic discrimination is no longer a major factor in labor markets in the United States. One reason is that *employers who discriminate pay an economic penalty*. To see why this is true, let's consider a simplified example. Suppose that men and women are equally qualified to be airline pilots and that, initially, airlines do not discriminate. In Figure 8, we divide the airlines

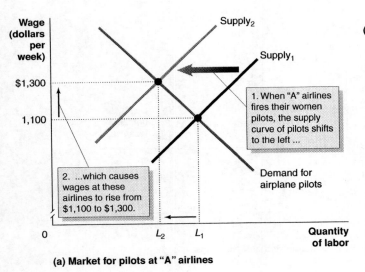

(a) Market for pilots at "A" airlines

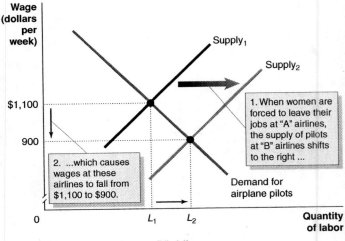

(b) Market for pilots at "B" airlines

Figure 8 | Discrimination and Wages

In this hypothetical example, we assume that initially neither "A" airlines nor "B" airlines discriminate. As a result, men and women pilots receive the same wage of $1,100 per week at both groups of airlines. We then assume that "A" airlines discriminates by firing all their women pilots. Panel (a) shows that this reduces the supply of pilots to "A" airlines and raises the wage paid by these airlines from $1,100 to $1,300. Panel (b)

shows that this increases the supply of pilots to "B" airlines and lowers the wage paid by these airlines from $1,100 to $900. All the women pilots will end up being employed at the nondiscriminating airlines and will be paid a lower wage than the men who are employed by the discriminating airlines.

into two groups: "A" airlines and "B" airlines. If neither group of airlines discriminates, we would expect them to pay an equal wage of $1,100 per week to both men and women pilots. Now suppose that "A" airlines decide to discriminate and to fire all their women pilots. This action will reduce the supply of pilots to these airlines and, as shown in panel (a), that will force up the wage from $1,100 to $1,300. At the same time, as women fired from the jobs with "A" airlines apply for jobs with "B" airlines, the supply of pilots to "B" airlines will increase, and the equilibrium wage will fall from $1,100 to $900. All the women pilots will end up being employed at the nondiscriminating airlines and be paid a lower wage than the men who are employed by the discriminating airlines.

But this situation cannot persist for two reasons. First, male pilots employed by "B" airlines will also receive the lower wage. This lower wage gives them an incentive to quit their jobs at "B" airlines and apply at "A" airlines, which will shift the labor supply curve for "B" airlines to the left and the labor supply curve for "A" airlines to the right. Second, "A" airlines are paying $1,300 per week to hire pilots who are no more productive than the pilots being paid $900 per week by "B" airlines. As a result, "B" airlines will have lower costs and will be able to charge lower prices. Eventually, "A" airlines will lose their customers to "B" airlines and be driven out of business. The market will have imposed an economic penalty on the discriminating airlines. So, discrimination will not persist, and the wages of men and women pilots will become equal.

Can we conclude from this analysis that competition in markets will eliminate all economic discrimination? Unfortunately, this optimistic conclusion is not completely accurate. We know that until the Civil Rights Act of 1964 was passed, many firms in the United States refused to hire blacks. Even though this practice had persisted for decades, nondiscriminating competitors did not drive these firms out of business. Why not? There were three important factors:

1 *Worker discrimination.* In many cases, white workers refused to work alongside black workers. As a result, some industries—such as the important cotton textile industry in the South—were all white. Because of discrimination by white workers, a businessperson who wanted to use low-cost black labor might need to hire an all-black workforce. Some businesspeople tried this, but because blacks had been excluded from these industries, they often lacked the skills and experience to form an effective workforce.

2 *Customer discrimination.* Some white consumers were unwilling to buy from companies in certain industries if they employed black workers. This was not a significant barrier in manufacturing industries, where customers would not know the race of the workers producing the good. It was, however, a problem for firms in industries in which workers came into direct contact with the public.

3 *Negative feedback loops.* Our analysis in Figure 8 assumed that men and women pilots were equally qualified. However, if discrimination makes it difficult for a member of a group to find employment in a particular occupation, his or her incentive to be trained to enter that occupation is reduced. Consider the legal profession as an example. In 1952, future Supreme Court Justice Sandra Day O'Connor graduated third in her class at Stanford University Law School and was an editor of the *Stanford Law Review*, but for some time she was unable to find a job as a lawyer because in those years, many law firms would not hire women. Facing such bleak job prospects, it's not surprising that relatively few women entered law school. As a result, a law firm that did not discriminate would have been unable to act like the nondiscriminating airlines in our example by hiring women lawyers at a lower salary and using this cost advantage to drive discriminating law firms out of business. In this situation, an unfortunate feedback loop was in place: Few women prepared to become lawyers because many law firms discriminated against women, and nondiscriminating law firms were unable to drive discriminating law firms out of business because there were too few women lawyers available.

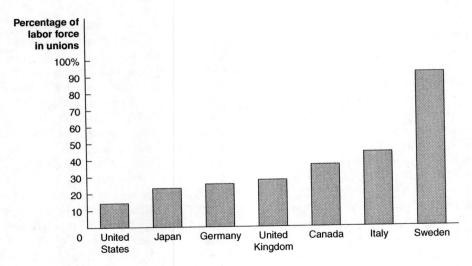

Figure 9 | The United States Is Less Unionized Than Most Industrial Countries

In 2006, the percentage of the labor force belonging to unions was lower in the United States than in most other industrial countries.
Source: International Labour Organization.

Most economists agree that the market imposes an economic penalty on firms that discriminate, but because of the factors just discussed, it may take the market a very long time to eliminate discrimination entirely. The passage of the Civil Rights Act of 1964, which outlawed hiring discrimination on the basis of race and sex, greatly sped up the process of reducing economic discrimination in the United States.

Labor Unions

Labor union An organization of employees that has the legal right to bargain with employers about wages and working conditions.

Workers' wages can differ depending on whether the workers are members of labor unions. **Labor unions** are organizations of employees that have the legal right to bargain with employers about wages and working conditions. If a union is unable to reach an agreement with a company, it has the legal right to call a *strike*, which means its members refuse to work until a satisfactory agreement has been reached. As Figure 9 shows, a smaller fraction of the U.S. labor force is unionized than in most other industrial countries.

As Table 4 shows, in the United States, workers in unions receive higher wages than workers who are not in unions. Do union members earn more than nonunion members because they are in unions? The answer might seem to be "yes," but many union workers are in industries, such as automobile manufacturing, in which their marginal revenue products are high, so their wages would be high even if they were not unionized. Economists who have attempted to estimate statistically the impact of unionization on wages have concluded that being in a union increases a worker's wages about 10 percent, holding constant other factors, such as the industry the worker is in. A related

TABLE 4

Union Workers Earn More Than Nonunion Workers

	AVERAGE WEEKLY EARNINGS
UNION WORKERS	$833
NONUNION WORKERS	642

Note: "Union workers" includes union members as well as workers who are represented by unions but who are not members of them.

Source: U.S. Bureau of Labor Statistics, *Union Members Summary*, January 25, 2007.

416

question is whether unions raise the total amount of wages received by all workers, whether unionized or not. Because the share of national income received by workers has remained roughly constant over many years, most economists do not believe that unions have raised the total amount of wages received by workers.

5 | Discuss the role personnel economics can play in helping firms deal with human resources issues.

Personnel Economics

Traditionally, labor economists have focused on issues such as the effects of labor unions on wages or the determinants of changes in average wages over time. They have spent less time analyzing *human resources issues*, which address how firms hire, train, and promote workers and set their wages and benefits. In recent years, some labor economists, including Edward Lazear of Stanford University and William Neilson of Texas A&M University, have begun exploring the application of economic analysis to human resources issues. This new focus has become known as **personnel economics**.

Personnel economics analyzes the link between differences among jobs and differences in the way workers are paid. Jobs have different skill requirements, require more or less interaction with other workers, have to be performed in more or less unpleasant environments, and so on. Firms need to design compensation policies that take into account these differences. Personnel economics also analyzes policies related to other human resources issues, such as promotions, training, and pensions. In this brief overview, we look only at compensation policies.

Personnel economics The application of economic analysis to human resources issues.

Should Workers' Pay Depend on How Much They Work or on How Much They Produce?

One issue personnel economics addresses is when workers should receive *straight-time pay*—a certain wage per hour or salary per week or month—and when they should receive *commission* or *piece-rate pay*—a wage based on how much output they produce.

Suppose, for example, that Anne owns a car dealership and is trying to decide whether to pay her salespeople a salary of $800 per week or a commission of $200 on each car they sell. Figure 10 compares the compensation a salesperson would receive under the two systems, according to the number of cars the salesperson sells.

With a straight salary, the salesperson receives $800 per week, no matter how many cars she sells. This outcome is shown by the horizontal line in Figure 10. If she receives a commission of $200 per car, her compensation will increase with every car she sells. This outcome is shown by the upward-sloping line. A salesperson who sells fewer than 4 cars per week would earn more by receiving a straight salary of $800 per week. A salesperson who sells more than 4 cars per week would be better off receiving the $200-per-car commission. We can identify two advantages Anne would receive from paying her salespeople commissions rather than salaries: She would attract and retain the most productive employees, and she would provide an incentive to her employees to sell more cars.

Suppose that other car dealerships were all paying salaries of $800 per week. If Anne pays her employees on commission, any of her employees who are unable to sell at least 4 cars per week can improve their pay by going to work for one of her competitors. By the same token, any salespeople at Anne's competitors who can sell more than 4 cars per week can raise their pay by quitting and coming to work for Anne. Over time, Anne will find her least productive employees leaving, while she is able to hire new employees who are more productive.

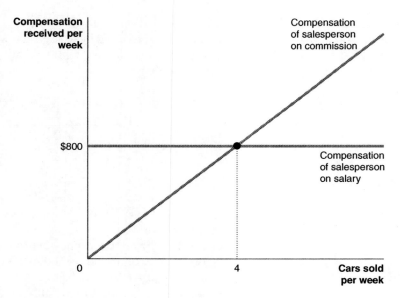

Figure 10 | Paying Car Salespeople by Salary or by Commission

This figure compares the compensation a car salesperson receives if she is on a straight salary of $800 per week or if she receives a commission of $200 for each car she sells. With a straight salary, she receives $800 per week, no matter how many cars she sells. This outcome is shown by the horizontal line in the figure. If she receives a commission of $200 per car, her compensation will increase with every car she sells. This outcome is shown by the upward-sloping line. If she sells fewer than 4 cars per week, she would be better off with the $800 salary. If she sells more than 4 cars per week, she would be better off with the $200-per-car commission.

Paying a commission also increases the incentive Anne's salespeople have to sell more cars. If Anne paid a salary, her employees would receive the same amount no matter how few cars they sold. An employee on salary might decide on a particularly hot or cold day that it was less trouble to stay inside the building than to go out on the car lot to greet potential customers. An employee on commission would know that the additional effort expended on selling more cars would be rewarded with additional compensation.

Making the Connection | **Raising Pay, Productivity, and Profits at Safelite AutoGlass**

Safelite Group, headquartered in Columbus, Ohio, is the parent company of Safelite AutoGlass, the nation's largest installer of auto glass, with 600 repair shops. In the mid-1990s, Safelite shifted from paying its glass installers hourly wages to paying them on the basis of how many windows they installed. Safelite already had in place a computer system that allowed it to track easily how many windows each worker installed per day. To make sure quality did not suffer, Safelite added a rule that if a workmanship-related defect occurred with the installed windshield, the worker would have to install a new windshield and would not be paid for the additional work.

Edward Lazear analyzed data provided by the firm and discovered that under the new piece-rate system, the number of windows installed per worker jumped 44 percent. Lazear estimates that half of this increase was due to increased productivity from workers who continued with the company and half was due to new hires being more productive than the workers they replaced who had left the company. Worker pay rose on average by about 9.9 percent. Ninety-two percent of workers experienced a pay increase, and one-quarter received an increase of at least 28 percent. Safelite's profits also increased as the

A piece-rate system at Safelite AutoGlass led to increased worker wages and firm profits.

Safelite Group

418

cost to the company per window installed fell from $44.43 under the hourly wage system to $35.24 under the piece-rate system.

Sociologists sometimes question whether worker productivity can be increased through the use of monetary incentives. The experience of Safelite AutoGlass provides a clear example of workers reacting favorably to the opportunity to increase output in exchange for higher compensation.

Source: Edward P. Lazear, "Performance Pay and Productivity," *American Economic Review*, Vol. 90, No. 5, December 2000, pp. 1346–1361.

YOUR TURN: Test your understanding by doing related problem 5.7 at the end of this chapter.

Other Considerations in Setting Compensation Systems

The discussion so far indicates that companies will find it more profitable to use a commission or piece-rate system of compensation rather than a salary system. In fact, many firms continue to pay their workers salaries, which means they are paying their workers on the basis of how long they work rather than on the basis of how much they produce. Firms may choose a salary system for several good reasons:

- *Difficulty in measuring output.* Often it is difficult to attribute output to any particular worker. For example, projects carried out by an engineering firm may involve teams of workers whose individual contributions are difficult to distinguish. On assembly lines, such as those used in the automobile industry, the amount produced by each worker is determined by the speed of the line, which is set by managers rather than by workers. Managers at many firms perform such a wide variety of tasks that measuring their output would be costly, if it could be done at all.

- *Concerns about quality.* If workers are paid on the basis of the number of units produced, they may become less concerned about quality. An office assistant who is paid on the basis of the quantity of letters typed may become careless about how many typos the letters contain. In some cases, there are ways around this problem; for example, the assistant may be required to correct the mistakes on his or her own time without pay.

- *Worker dislike of risk.* Piece-rate or commission systems of compensation increase the risk to workers because sometimes output declines for reasons not connected to the worker's effort. For example, if there is a very snowy winter, few customers may show up at Anne's auto dealership. Through no fault of their own, her salespeople may have great difficulty selling any cars. If they are paid a salary, their income will not be affected, but if they are on commission, their incomes may drop to low levels. The flip side of this is that by paying salaries, Anne assumes a greater risk. During a snowy winter, her payroll expenses will remain high even though her sales are low. With a commission system of compensation, her payroll expenses will decline along with her sales. But owners of firms are typically better able to bear risk than are workers. As a result, some firms may find that workers who would earn more under a commission system will prefer to receive a salary to reduce their risk. In these situations, paying a lower salary may reduce the firm's payroll expenses compared with what they would have been under a commission or piece-rate system.

Personnel economics is a relatively new field, but it holds great potential for helping firms deal more efficiently with human relations issues.

6 LEARNING OBJECTIVE

6 | Show how equilibrium prices are determined in the markets for capital and natural resources.

The Markets for Capital and Natural Resources

The approach we have used to analyze the market for labor can also be used to analyze the markets for other factors of production. We have seen that the demand for labor is determined by the marginal revenue product of labor because the value to a firm from hiring another worker equals the increase in the firm's revenue from selling the additional output it can produce by hiring the worker. The demand for capital and natural resources is determined in a similar way.

The Market for Capital

Physical capital includes machines, equipment, and buildings. Firms sometimes buy capital, but we will focus on situations in which firms rent capital. A chocolate manufacturer renting a warehouse and an airline leasing a plane are examples of firms renting capital. Like the demand for labor, the demand for capital is a derived demand. When a firm is considering increasing its capital by, for example, employing another machine, the value it receives equals the increase in the firm's revenue from selling the additional output it can produce by employing the machine. The *marginal revenue product of capital* is the change in the firm's revenue as a result of employing one more unit of capital, such as a machine. We have seen that the marginal revenue product of labor curve is the demand curve for labor. Similarly, the marginal revenue product of capital curve is also the demand curve for capital.

Firms producing capital goods face increasing marginal costs, so the supply curve of capital goods is upward sloping, as are the supply curves for other goods and services. Figure 11 shows equilibrium in the market for capital. In equilibrium,

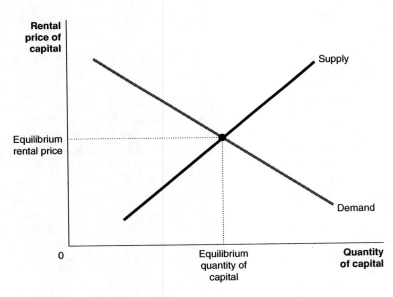

Figure 11 | Equilibrium in the Market for Capital

The rental price of capital is determined by equilibrium in the market for capital. In equilibrium, the rental price of capital is equal to the marginal revenue product of capital.

suppliers of capital receive a rental price equal to the marginal revenue product of capital, just as suppliers of labor receive a wage equal to the marginal revenue product of labor.

The Market for Natural Resources

The market for natural resources can be analyzed in the same way as the markets for labor and capital. When a firm is considering employing more natural resources, the value it receives equals the increase in the firm's revenue from selling the additional output it can produce by buying the natural resources. So, the demand for natural resources is also a derived demand. The *marginal revenue product of natural resources* is the change in the firm's revenue as a result of employing one more unit of natural resources, such as a barrel of oil. The marginal revenue product of natural resources curve is also the demand curve for natural resources.

Although the total quantity of most natural resources is ultimately fixed—as the humorist Will Rogers once remarked, "Buy land; They ain't making any more of it"— in many cases, the quantity supplied still responds to the price. For example, although the total quantity of oil deposits in the world is fixed, an increase in the price of oil will result in an increase in the quantity of oil supplied during a particular period. The result, as shown in panel (a) of Figure 12, is an upward-sloping supply curve. In some cases, however, the quantity of a natural resource that will be supplied is fixed and will not change as the price changes. The land available at a busy intersection is fixed, for example. In panel (b) of Figure 12, we illustrate this situation with a supply curve that is a vertical line, or perfectly inelastic. The price received by a factor of production that is in fixed supply is called an **economic rent** (or **pure rent**) because, in this case, the price of the factor is determined only by demand. For example, if a new highway diverts much of the traffic from a previously busy intersection, the demand for the

Economic rent (or **pure rent**) The price of a factor of production that is in fixed supply.

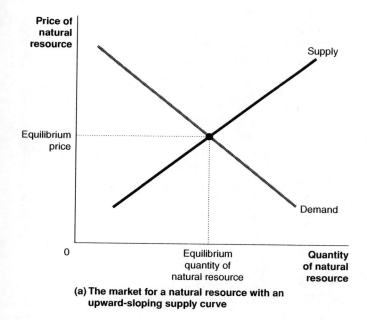

(a) The market for a natural resource with an upward-sloping supply curve

(b) The market for a natural resource with a vertical supply curve

Figure 12 | Equilibrium in the Market for Natural Resources

In panel (a), the supply curve of a natural resource is upward sloping. The price of the natural resource is determined by the interaction of demand and supply. In panel (b), the supply curve of the natural resource is a vertical line, indicating that the quantity supplied does not respond to changes in price. In this case, the price of the natural resource is determined only by demand. The price of a factor of production with a vertical supply curve is called an *economic rent* or a *pure rent*.

land will decline and the price of the land will fall, but the quantity of the land will not change.

Monopsony

What happens if a firm is the sole *buyer* of a factor of production? This case, which is known as **monopsony**, is comparatively rare. An example is a firm in an isolated town—perhaps a lumber mill in a small town in Washington or Oregon—that is the sole employer of labor in that location. In the nineteenth and early twentieth centuries, some coal mining firms were the sole employers in certain small towns in West Virginia and some pineapple plantations were the sole employers on certain small

Monopsony The sole buyer of a factor of production.

With only one lumber mill in town, the wages of these loggers won't be as high.

islands in Hawaii. In these cases, not only would the firm own the mill, mine, or plantation, but it would also own the stores and other businesses in the town. Workers would have the choice of working for the sole employer in the town or moving to another town.

We know that a firm with a monopoly in an output market takes advantage of its market power to reduce the quantity supplied to force up the market price and increase its profits. A firm that has a monopsony in a factor market would employ a similar strategy: It would restrict the quantity of the factor demanded to force down the price of the factor and increase profits. A firm with a monopsony in a labor market will hire fewer workers and pay lower wages than would be the case in a competitive market. Because fewer workers are hired than would be true in a competitive market, monopsony results in a deadweight loss. Monopoly and monopsony have similar effects on the economy: In both cases a firm's market power results in a lower equilibrium quantity, a deadweight loss, and a reduction in economic efficiency compared with a competitive market.

In some cases, monopsony in labor markets is offset by worker membership in a labor union. A notable example of this is professional sports. For instance, Major League Baseball (MLB) effectively has a monopsony on employing professional baseball players. (Although independent baseball leagues exist, none of the best players play for these teams, and the teams pay salaries that are a small fraction of those paid by MLB teams.) The monopsony power of the owners of MLB teams is offset by the power of the Major League Baseball Players Association, the union that represents baseball players. Bargaining between the representatives of MLB and the players union has resulted in baseball players being paid something close to what they would be receiving in a competitive market.

The Marginal Productivity Theory of Income Distribution

We have seen that in equilibrium, each factor of production receives a price equal to its marginal revenue product. We can use this fact to explain the distribution of income. Marginal revenue product represents the value of a factor's marginal contribution to producing goods and services. Therefore, individuals will receive income equal to the marginal contributions to production from the factors of production they own, including their labor. The more factors of production an individual owns and the more productive those factors are, the higher the individual's income will be. This approach to explaining the distribution of income is called the **marginal productivity theory of income distribution**. The marginal productivity theory of income distribution was developed by John Bates Clark, who taught at Columbia University in the late nineteenth and early twentieth centuries.

Marginal productivity theory of income distribution The theory that the distribution of income is determined by the marginal productivity of the factors of production that individuals own.

Economics in YOUR Life!

At the beginning of the chapter, we asked you to imagine that you work at a local sandwich shop and that you plan to ask your manager for a raise. One way to show the manager your worth is to demonstrate how many dollars your work earns for the sandwich shop: your marginal revenue product. You could certainly suggest that as you have become better at your job and have gained new skills that you are a more productive employee, but more importantly, that your productivity results in increased revenue to the sandwich shop. By showing how your employment contributes to higher revenue and profit for the shop, you may be able to convince your manager to raise your pay.

Conclusion

In this chapter, we used the demand and supply model to explain why wages differ among workers. The demand for workers depends on their productivity and on the price that firms receive for the output the workers produce. The supply of workers to an occupation depends on the wages and working conditions offered by employers and on the skills required. The demand and supply for labor can also help us analyze such issues as economic discrimination and the impact of labor unions.

Read *An Inside Look* on the next page to see how demand and supply determine the salaries of ex-college athletes who work for NASCAR pit crews.

An Inside **LOOK**

Are Race Car Drivers Athletes? We Don't Know, but the Pit-Crew Members Are

WALL STREET JOURNAL, JUNE 16, 2005

Racing Teams Recruit Athletes and Train Them Hard; The $60,000 Tire Carrier

After Bob Dowens finished playing college football, he turned pro. But not in the NFL—in the National Association for Stock Car Auto Racing.

Once a defensive back at Fairleigh Dickinson University, the 28-year-old Mr. Dowens is now a professional tire carrier in a Nascar pit crew. At Evernham Motorsports, the stock-car racing team for which Mr. Dowens works, pit-crew members practice five days a week. A pit coach studies videos to hone their footwork and hand speed. A trainer has them lift weights and run sprints.

Years ago, mechanics who worked on race cars during the week simply did double duty on Sundays in the pits. Nobody thought about athletic fitness, and beer bellies were OK. The crew was too busy during the week welding and machining to practice pit stops.

Today, teams like Evernham look increasingly for college jocks whose strength and speed can save precious tenths of a second in a race. One of Mr. Dowens's teammates, jack-man Ed Watkins, was a 300-pound offensive lineman at East Carolina University. The Chip Ganassi Racing team's pit crew includes baseball players from Wake Forest University; football players from Wake, the University of Kentucky and the University of North Carolina; and a hockey player from Dartmouth.

Top tire-changers—the guys who air-wrench lug nuts off and on—can make $100,000 a year. The average at Evernham is about $60,000. Mr. Dowens figures he'll be a bit over that, with bonuses, this year.

Big money is what drives the demand for world-class tire-changers. In the 1990s, Nascar's popularity exploded, bringing hundreds of millions of dollars in television and sponsorship revenue into the sport. With more money at stake, competition intensified, and pit stops often affected the outcome of a race. Twenty years ago, pit crews were doing pretty well to change four tires in less than 30 seconds. Today, taking more than 16 seconds can be disastrous.

"These guys are serious athletes," says Evernham's pit coach, Greg Miller, 33. A car going 200 miles per hour covers nearly 300 feet in a second, so a half-second advantage in the pit can put a driver ahead two or three spots. "In our world, two seconds is a lifetime." . . .

That brought Mr. Dowens under the tutelage of Evernham's coach, Mr. Miller. A former fitness trainer with a master's degree in physiology, he thought he could combine his profession with his love of Nascar and joined a team in 1998. At Evernham, Mr. Miller keeps a thick binder with details of every practice and race-day pit stop of the three crews he coaches, with times of each man's tasks, the car's position entering and leaving the pit.

Last year, Mr. Miller got approval to add a full-time strength coach. It started badly: The first running drill left the former East Carolina lineman, Mr. Watkins, with torn tendons in both knees. Now it's paying off. At 5 feet 10 inches, Mr. Dowens weighs 190 pounds, 20 pounds less than in his football days. The 6-foot-3-inch Mr. Watkins is a buff 230. In May, an Evernham crew came in second in a Nascar pit competition. Two weeks later, a different Evernham pit crew took the title and shared $75,000 in bonus money. . . .

On Sunday at the race, the Coca-Cola 600 in Charlotte, fans strolled the pit area seeking autographs and souvenir lug nuts. . . .

On this day Mr. Dowens was carrying for the No. 19 car driven by Jeremy Mayfield. Early in the 600-mile race, Mr. Mayfield's Charger screamed into the pit; 14.32 seconds later, it was gone. On the next stop, a tire changer slipped on an air hose. The time: 15.39. Mr. Miller grimaced.

As the 600-mile race wore on, the pit times edged below 14 seconds. Mr. Dowens was doing well, indexing tires at under seven-tenths of a second. With their car hanging on in a crash-filled race, Mr. Miller shouted, "Need a good one, boys." With 59 laps to go, the car pulled in for four tires and two cans of gas. It was out in 13.95 seconds, a time that helped Mr. Mayfield leap from 14th to ninth. With that momentum, he finished the race in fourth place, tying his best finish this year.

The pit crew did well, too. "We can do better, but no major problems," Mr. Miller said. "All it takes is one to screw up the race."

Source: "Racing Teams Recruit Athletes and Train Them Hard; The $60,000 Tire Carrier" by Neal E. Boudette, Staff Reporter of Wall Street Journal, June 16, 2005, p. A1. Copyright © 2005 Dow Jones. Reprinted by permission of Dow Jones via Copyright Clearance Center.

Key Points in the Article

This article highlights college athletes who have found a career working on pit crews for NASCAR races. Productivity and the value of the output produced are the two key factors that determine the wages of these pit-crew workers.

Analyzing the News

ⓐ Changes in marginal product will shift the demand for labor. You can see this in the figure as the demand curve shifts to the right from D_1 to D_2. Because labor demand is based on the marginal revenue product of labor, as the marginal product increases, so too will the demand for labor. For race teams, faster pit times would represent an increase in productivity. By hiring athletes, a race team hopes that the speed of its pit stops will fall, which will improve its finishing spot in the race. Holding the value

of winning a NASCAR race constant, this would increase the demand for labor.

ⓑ As NASCAR has become more popular, sponsors are willing to pay more money to place logos on the cars, and prize money for races has increased. Sponsors will pay more money for cars with better finishing positions. If a pit crew can improve the finishing position of a team, the value of the output increases. As the value of the output increases, the value of the marginal product of labor increases, holding productivity constant. This will also increase the demand for labor, as shown in the figure as the demand curve shifts from D_1 to D_2. So, the article indicates that the demand for pit crews has increased for two reasons: pit crews have become more productive and the value of winning a NASCAR race has increased. As labor demand increases, the wages paid to pit-crew workers increases from W_1 to W_2.

ⓒ How can we measure the value of a pit crew? A quick pit stop allowed Jeremy Mayfield to advance five spots in the field. The additional prize money—not only per race but over the 36-race season—adds a large amount of revenue to the race team. The value of a better pit crew could be measured by the additional prize money and sponsorship money the team receives from higher race finishes.

Thinking Critically

1. Suppose NASCAR loses popularity over the next few years. What do you suppose will happen to the wages offered to pit-crew members?
2. The United Auto Workers labor union and an automotive company, such as Ford or General Motors, will sometimes jointly sponsor a NASCAR race. Why would a labor union want to help a company sell more cars?

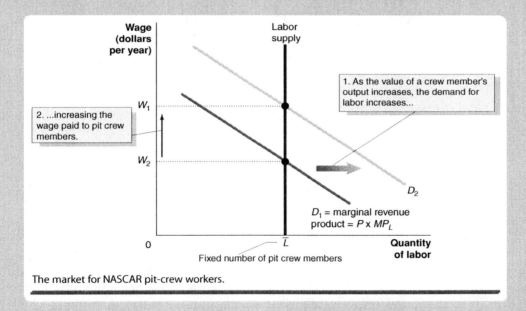

The market for NASCAR pit-crew workers.

Key Terms

Compensating differentials	Economic rent (or pure rent)	Marginal product of labor	Marginal revenue product of labor (*MRP*)
Derived demand	Factors of production	Marginal productivity theory of income distribution	Monopsony
Economic discrimination	Human capital		Personnel economics
	Labor union		

1 LEARNING OBJECTIVE 1 | Explain how firms choose the profit-maximizing quantity of labor to employ

The Demand for Labor

Summary

The demand for labor is a **derived demand** because it depends on the demand consumers have for goods and services. The additional output produced by a firm as a result of hiring another worker is called the **marginal product of labor**. The amount by which the firm's revenue will increase as a result of hiring one more worker is called the **marginal revenue product of labor** (*MRP*). A firm's marginal revenue product of labor curve is its demand curve for labor. Firms maximize profit by hiring workers up to the point where the wage is equal to the marginal revenue product of labor. The market demand curve for labor is determined by adding up the quantity of labor demanded by each firm at each wage, holding constant all other variables that might affect the willingness of firms to hire workers. The most important variables that shift the labor demand curve are changes in human capital, technology, the price of the product, the quantity of other inputs, and the number of firms in the market. **Human capital** is the accumulated training and skills that workers possess.

myeconlab Visit www.myeconlab.com to complete these exercises
Get Ahead of the Curve online and get instant feedback.

Review Questions

1.1 What is the difference between the marginal product of labor and the marginal revenue product of labor?

1.2 Why is the demand curve for labor downward sloping?

1.3 What are the five most important variables that cause the market demand curve for labor to shift?

Problems and Applications

1.4 Frank Gunter owns an apple orchard. He employs 87 apple pickers and pays them each $8 per hour to pick apples, which he sells for $1.60 per box. If Frank is maximizing profits, what is the marginal revenue product of the last worker he hired? What is that worker's marginal product?

1.5 (Related to *Solved Problem 1*) Fill in the blanks in the following table for Tommy's Televisions:

NUMBER OF WORKERS (*L*)	OUTPUT OF TELEVISIONS PER WEEK (*Q*)	MARGINAL PRODUCT OF LABOR (TELEVISION SETS PER WEEK) (*MP*)	PRODUCT PRICE (*P*)	MARGINAL REVENUE PRODUCT OF LABOR (DOLLARS PER WEEK)	WAGE (DOLLARS PER WEEK) (*W*)	ADDITIONAL PROFIT FROM HIRING ONE MORE WORKER (DOLLARS PER WEEK)
0	0	—	$300	—	$1,800	—
1	8	—	300	—	1,800	—
2	15	—	300	—	1,800	—
3	21	—	300	—	1,800	—
4	26	—	300	—	1,800	—
5	30	—	300	—	1,800	—
6	33	—	300	—	1,800	—

a. From the information in the table, can you determine whether this firm is a price taker or a price maker? Briefly explain.

b. Use the information in the table to draw a graph like Figure 1 that shows the demand for labor by this firm. Be sure to indicate the profit-maximizing quantity of labor on your graph.

1.6 State whether each of the following events will result in a movement along the market demand curve for labor in electronics factories in Japan or whether it will cause the market demand curve for labor to shift. If the demand curve shifts, indicate whether it will shift to the left or to the right and draw a graph to illustrate the shift.

a. The wage rate declines.

b. The price of televisions declines.

c. Several firms exit the television market in Japan.

d. Japanese high schools introduce new vocational courses in assembling electronic products.

1.7 Under what circumstances would a firm's demand curve for labor be a horizontal line?

>> End Learning Objective 1

2 LEARNING OBJECTIVE   2 | Explain how people choose the quantity of labor to supply

The Supply of Labor

Summary

As the wage increases, the opportunity cost of leisure increases, causing individuals to supply a greater quantity of labor. Normally, the labor supply curve is upward sloping, but it is possible that at very high wage levels, the supply curve might be backward bending. This outcome occurs when someone with a high income is willing to accept a somewhat lower income in exchange for more leisure. The market labor supply curve is determined by adding up the quantity of labor supplied by each worker at each wage, holding constant all other variables that might affect the willingness of workers to supply labor. The most important variables that shift the labor supply curve are increases in population, changing demographics, and changing alternatives.

myeconlab Visit www.myeconlab.com to complete these exercises online and get instant feedback.

Review Questions

2.1 How can we measure the opportunity cost of leisure? Why is the supply curve of labor usually upward sloping?

2.2 What are the three most important variables that cause the market supply curve of labor to shift?

Problems and Applications

2.3 Daniel had been earning $65 per hour and working 45 hours per week. Then Daniel's wage rose to $75 per hour, and as a result, he now works 40 hours per week.

What can we conclude from this information about the income effect and the substitution effect of a wage change for Daniel?

2.4 Most labor economists believe that many adult males are on the vertical section of their labor supply curves. Explain when and why someone's supply of labor curve would be vertical, using the concepts of income and substitution effects.

Source: Robert Whaples, "Is There Consensus among American Labor Economists: Survey Results on Forty Propositions," *Journal of Labor Research*, Vol. 17, No. 4, Fall 1996.

2.5 Suppose that a large oil field is discovered in Michigan. By imposing a tax on the oil, the state government is able to eliminate the state income tax on wages. What is likely to be the effect on the labor supply curve in Michigan?

2.6 State whether each of the following events will result in a movement along the market supply curve of agricultural labor in the United States or whether it will cause the market supply curve of labor to shift. If the supply curve shifts, indicate whether it will shift to the left or to the right and draw a graph to illustrate the shift.

a. The agricultural wage rate declines.

b. Wages outside of agriculture increase.

c. The law is changed to allow for unlimited immigration into the United States.

>> End Learning Objective 2

3 LEARNING OBJECTIVE   3 | Explain how equilibrium wages are determined in labor markets

Equilibrium in the Labor Market

Summary

The intersection between labor supply and labor demand determines the equilibrium wage and the equilibrium level of employment. If labor supply is unchanged, an increase in labor demand will increase both the equilibrium wage and the number of workers employed. If labor demand is unchanged, an increase in labor supply will lower the equilibrium wage and increase the number of workers employed.

myeconlab Visit www.myeconlab.com to complete these exercises online and get instant feedback.

Review Questions

3.1 If the labor demand curve shifts to the left and the labor supply curve remains unchanged, what will happen to the equilibrium wage and the equilibrium level of employment? Illustrate your answer with a graph.

3.2 If the labor supply curve shifts to the left and the labor demand curve remains unchanged, what will happen to the equilibrium wage and the equilibrium level of employment? Illustrate your answer with a graph.

Problems and Applications

3.3 (Related to the *Making the Connection*) Over time, the gap between the wages of workers with a college degree and the wages of workers without a college degree has been increasing. Shouldn't this gap have increased the incentive for workers to earn a college degree, thereby increasing the supply of college-educated workers, and reducing the size of the gap?

3.4 Reread the discussion of changes in the salaries of film animators. Use a graph to illustrate this situation. Make sure your graph has labor demand and supply curves for 1994, 1999, and 2002 and that the equilibrium point for each year is clearly indicated.

3.5 (Related to the *Making the Connection*) Francis Walker served as commissioner general of the U.S. Immigration Service and as first president of the American Economic Association. In 1896, he wrote the following:

> The question today is protecting the American rate of wages, the American standard of living, and the quality of American citizenship from degradation through the tumultuous access of vast throngs of ignorant and brutalized peasantry from the countries of Eastern and Southern Europe.
>
> Why would Walker have feared that immigration to the United States would drive down wages? Did wages, in fact, fall as he predicted? Briefly explain.

Source: Quoted in Julian L. Simon and Rita James Simon, "Do We Really Need All These Immigrants?" in D. N. McCloskey, *Second Thoughts: Myths and Morals of U.S. Economic History*, New York: Oxford University Press, 1993, p. 20.

3.6 (Related to the *Making the Connection*) Suppose the United States had not allowed any immigration between 1900 and 1914. Which groups would have benefited from prohibiting immigration and which groups would have lost?

3.7 (Related to the *Making the Connection*) Former presidential candidate Patrick J. Buchanan has argued, "The U.S. labor supply has grown by more tens of millions in the past twenty-five years than in any other period in history. How could the price of labor *not* fall?" Answer Buchanan's question: If there is an increase in labor supply, does the equilibrium wage have to fall?

Source: Patrick J. Buchanan, *The Great Betrayal: How American Sovereignty and Social Justice Are Being Sacrificed to the Gods of the Global Economy*, Boston: Little, Brown, 1998, p.

3.8 (Related to the *Making the Connection*) According to an article in the *Wall Street Journal*:

> Through the 1990s, U.S.-bound immigration was split between the poor fleeing hunger or oppression and wealthy elites seeking high-paying jobs. Now, more middle-class, middle-skilled emigrants are heading to the U.S.
>
> Most of the "middle-class, middle-skilled emigrants" referred to in the article were legal immigrants to the United States. Suppose that more effective border control measures reduce the number of low-skilled, illegal immigrants to the United States and the fraction of immigrants who are "middle-skilled" increases significantly. What difference would this change make in the economic impact of immigration? Would it be likely to affect the political debate over immigration?

Source: Joel Millman, "Tidy Business: Immigrant Group Puts a New Spin On Cleaning Niche, *Wall Street Journal*, February 16, 2006, p. A1.

3.9 In 541 A.D., an outbreak of bubonic plague hit the Byzantine Empire. Because the plague was spread by flea-infested rats that often lived on ships, ports were hit particularly hard. In some ports, more than 40 percent of the population died. The emperor, Justinian, was concerned that the wages of sailors were rising very rapidly as a result of the plague. In 544 A.D., he placed a ceiling on the wages of sailors. Use a demand and supply graph of the market for sailors to show the effect of the plague on the wages of sailors. Use the same graph to show the effect of Justinian's wage ceiling. Briefly explain what is happening in your graph.

Source: Michael McCormick, *The Origins of the European Economy: Communications and Commerce, A.D., 300–900*, New York: Cambridge University Press, 2001, p. 109.

>> End Learning Objective 3

---

4 LEARNING OBJECTIVE 4 | Use demand and supply analysis to explain how compensating differentials, discrimination, and labor unions cause wages to differ

Explaining Differences in Wages

Summary

The equilibrium wage is determined by the intersection of the labor demand and labor supply curves. Some differences in wages are explained by **compensating differentials**, which are higher wages that compensate workers for unpleasant aspects of a job. Wages can also differ because of **economic discrimination**, which involves paying a person a lower wage or excluding a person from an occupation on the basis of irrelevant characteristics, such as race or gender. **Labor unions** are organizations of employees that have the legal right to bargain with employers about wages and working conditions. Being in a union increases a worker's wages about 10 percent, holding constant other factors, such as the industry in question.

 Visit www.myeconlab.com to complete these exercises online and get instant feedback.

Review Questions

4.1 What is a compensating differential? Give an example.

4.2 Define economic discrimination. Is the fact that one group in the population has higher earnings than other groups evidence of economic discrimination? Briefly explain.

4.3 Is the fraction of U.S. workers in labor unions larger or smaller than in other countries?

Problems and Applications

4.4 The journalist Michael Kinsley has argued, "Free-market capitalism . . . works well for almost all by rewarding some people more than others." Discuss whether you agree.

Source: Michael Kinsley, "Curse You, Robert Caro!" *Slate*, November 21, 2002.

4.5 **(Related to the *Chapter Opener*)** A student remarks, "I don't think the idea of marginal revenue product really helps explain differences in wages. After all, a ticket to a baseball game costs much less than college tuition, yet baseball players are paid much more than college professors." Do you agree with the student's reasoning?

4.6 **(Related to the *Don't Let This Happen to You!*)** Joe Morgan is a sportscaster and former baseball player. After he stated that he thought the salaries of major league baseball players were justified, a baseball fan wrote the following to ESPN.com columnist, Rob Neyer:

> Mr. Neyer,
>
> What are your feelings about Joe Morgan's comment that players are justified in being paid what they're being paid? How is it ok for A-Rod [New York Yankees infielder Alex Rodriguez] to earn $115,000 per GAME while my boss works 80 hour weeks and earns $30,000 per year?
>
> How would you answer this fan's questions?

Source: ESPN.com, August 30, 2002.

4.7 Buster Olney, a columnist for ESPN.com, wonders why baseball teams pay the teams' managers and general managers less than they pay most baseball players:

> About two-thirds of the players on the [New York] Mets' roster will make more money than [manager Willie] Randolph; Willie will get somewhere in the neighborhood of half of an average major league salary for 2007. But Randolph's deal is right in line with what other managers are making, and right in the range of what the highest-paid general managers are making. . . . I have a hard time believing that Randolph or general manager Omar Minaya will have less impact on the Mets than left-handed reliever Scott Schoeneweis, who will get paid more than either the manager or GM.

Provide an economic explanation of why baseball managers and general managers are generally paid less than baseball players.

Source: Buster Olney, "Managers Low on Pay Scale," ESPN.com, January 25, 2007.

4.8 In early 2007, Nick Saban agreed to leave his job as head coach of the Miami Dolphins National Football League team to take a job as head football coach at the University of Alabama at a salary of $4 million per year for eight years. Ivan Maisel, a columnist for ESPN.com, wondered whether Saban was worth such a large salary: "Is Saban eight times better than the coach who outmaneuvered Bob Stoops of Oklahoma on Monday night? Boise State paid Chris Petersen $500,000 this season—and he still hasn't lost a game." Might Saban still be a worth a salary of $4 million per year to Alabama even if he is not "eight times better" than a coach being paid $500,000 at another school? In your answer, be sure to refer to the difference between the marginal product of labor and the marginal revenue product of labor.

Source: Ivan Maisel, "Saban Will Find Crowded Pond in Tuscaloosa," ESPN.com, January 3, 2007.

4.9 **(Related to the *Making the Connection*)** According to Alan Krueger, an economist at Princeton University, the share of concert ticket revenue received by the top 1 percent of all acts rose from 26 percent in 1982 to 56 percent in 2003. Does this information indicate that the top acts in 2003 must have been much better performers relative to other acts than was the case in 1982? If not, can you think of another explanation?

Source: Eduardo Porter, "More Than Ever, It Pays to Be the Top Executive," *New York Times*, May 25, 2007.

4.10 **(Related to the *Making the Connection*)** Why are there superstar basketball players but no superstar automobile mechanics?

4.11 Tennis stars Venus Williams and Serena Williams do not play for teams. They enter tennis tournaments as individuals. Is the concept of marginal revenue product as important in explaining their earnings as it is in explaining the earnings of major league baseball players? Briefly explain.

4.12 **(Related to the *Chapter Opener*)** The number of players on each major league baseball team is determined by negotiation between the players' union and the owners of major league teams. How does this fact affect the explanation given in the text of why baseball players are paid more than college professors? Briefly explain.

4.13 Prior to the early twentieth century, a worker who was injured on the job could collect damages only by suing his employer. To sue successfully, the worker—or his family, if the worker had been killed—had to show that the injury was due to the employer's negligence, that the worker did not know the job was hazardous, and that the worker's own negligence had not contributed to the accident. These lawsuits were difficult for workers to win, and even workers who had been seriously injured on the job often were unable to collect any damages from their employers. Beginning in 1910, most states passed "workers' compensation" laws that required employers to purchase insurance that would compensate workers for injuries suffered on the job. A study by Price Fishback and Shawn Kantor of the University of Arizona shows that after the passage of workers' compensation laws, wages received by workers in the coal and lumber industries fell. Briefly explain why passage of workers' compensation laws would lead to a fall in wages in some industries.

Source: Price V. Fishback and Shawn Everett Kantor, "Did Workers Pay for the Passage of Workers' Compensation Laws?" *Quarterly Journal of Economics*, Vol. 100, No. 3, August 1995, pp. 713–742.

4.14 The following table is similar to Table 2, except that it includes the earnings of Asian males and females. Does the fact that Asian males are the highest-earning group in the table affect the likelihood that economic discrimination is the best explanation for why earnings differ among the groups listed in the table? Briefly explain your argument.

GROUP	ANNUAL EARNINGS
Asian males	$48,103
White males	46,746
Asian females	36,549
White females	34,464
Black males	33,248
Black females	29,749
Hispanic males	26,769
Hispanic females	24,402

Source: U.S. Bureau of the Census, Current Population Survey, *Annual Social and Economic Supplement*, Table PINC-10, March 2006.

4.15 **(Related to *Solved Problem 4*)** Use the following graphs to answer the questions.

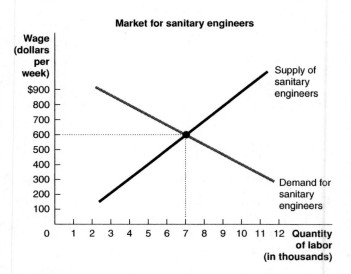

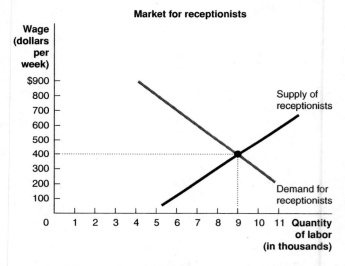

a. What is the equilibrium quantity of sanitary engineers hired, and what is the equilibrium wage?

b. What is the equilibrium quantity of receptionists hired, and what is the equilibrium wage?

c. Briefly discuss why sanitary engineers might earn a higher weekly wage than receptionists.

d. Suppose that comparable-worth legislation is passed and the government requires that sanitary engineers and receptionists must be paid the same wage of $500 per week. Now how many sanitary engineers will be hired and how many receptionists will be hired?

4.16 **(Related to *Solved Problem 4*)** In most universities, economics professors receive larger salaries than English professors. Suppose that the government requires that from now on, all universities must pay economics professors the same salaries as English professors. Use demand and supply graphs to analyze the effect of this requirement.

4.17 During the 1970s, many women changed their minds about whether they would leave the labor force after marrying and having children or whether they would be in the labor force most of their adult lives. In 1968, the National Longitudinal Survey asked a representative sample of women aged 14 to 24 whether they expected to be in the labor force at age 35. Twenty-nine percent of white women and 59 percent of black women responded that they expected to be in the labor force at that age. In fact, when these women were 35, 60 percent of those who were married and 80 percent of those who were unmarried were in the labor force. In other words, many more women ended up being in the labor force than expected to be when they were of high school and college age. What impact did this fact have on the earnings of these women? Briefly explain.

Source: Claudia Goldin, *Explaining the Gender Gap: An Economic History of American Women*, New York: Oxford University Press, 1990, p. 155.

4.18 In the early twentieth century, black people in the U.S. South were excluded from some occupations, but in jobs such as agriculture that employed both white and black workers, black workers received about the same wages as white workers. Briefly discuss why economic discrimination in the South took this form.

>> **End Learning Objective 4**

5 LEARNING OBJECTIVE 5 | Discuss the role personnel economics can play in helping firms deal with human resources issues.

Personnel Economics

Summary

Personnel economics is the application of economic analysis to human resources issues. One insight of personnel economics is that the productivity of workers often can be increased if firms move from straight-time pay to commission or piece-rate pay.

 Visit www.myeconlab.com to complete these exercises online and get instant feedback.

Review Questions

5.1 What is personnel economics?

5.2 If piece-rate or commission systems of compensating workers have important advantages for firms, why don't more firms use them?

Problems and Applications

5.3 According to a recent economic study, the number of jobs in which firms used bonuses, commission, or piece rates to tie workers' pay to their performance increased from an estimated 30 percent of all jobs in the 1970s to 40 percent in the 1990s. Why would systems that tie workers pay to how much they produce have become increasingly popular with firms? The same study found that these pay systems were more common in higher-paid jobs than in lower-paid jobs. What explains this result?

Source: Thomas Lemieux, W. Bentley MacLeod, and Daniel Parent, "Performance Pay and Wage Inequality," NBER Working Paper No. 13128, May 2007.

5.4 Many companies that pay workers an hourly wage require some minimum level of acceptable output. Suppose a company that has been using this system decides to switch to a piece-rate system under which workers are compensated on the basis of how much output they produce but under which they are also free to choose how much to produce. Is it likely that workers under a piece-rate system will end up choosing to produce less than the minimum output required under the hourly wage system? Briefly explain.

5.5 In most jobs, the harder you work, the more you earn. Some workers would rather work harder and earn more; others would rather work less hard, even though as a result they earn less. Suppose, though, that all workers at a company fall into the "work harder and earn more" group. Suppose, also, that the workers all have the same abilities. In these circumstances, would output per worker be the same under an hourly wage compensation system as under a piece-rate system? Briefly explain.

5.6 For years, the Goodyear Tire & Rubber Company compensated its sales force by paying a salesperson a salary plus a bonus based on the number of tires he or she sold. In early 2002, Goodyear made two changes to this policy: (1) The basis for the bonus was changed from the *quantity* of tires sold to the *revenue* from the tires sold, and (2) salespeople were required to get approval from corporate headquarters in Akron, Ohio, before offering to sell tires to customers at reduced prices. Explain why these changes were likely to increase Goodyear's profits.

Source: Timothy Aeppel, "Amid Weak Inflation, Firms Turn Creative to Boost Prices," *Wall Street Journal*, September 18, 2002.

5.7 (Related to the *Making the Connection*) What affect did the incentive pay system have on Safelite's marginal cost of installing replacement car windows? If all firms that replace car windows adopted an incentive pay system, what would happen to the price of replacing automobile glass? Who ultimately would benefit?

>> End Learning Objective 5

6 LEARNING OBJECTIVE 6 | Show how equilibrium prices are determined in the markets for capital and natural resources

The Markets for Capital and Natural Resources

Summary

The approach used to analyze the market for labor can also be used to analyze the markets for other factors of production. In equilibrium, the price of capital is equal to the marginal revenue product of capital, and the price of natural resources is equal to the marginal revenue product of natural resources. The price received by a factor that is in fixed supply is called an *economic rent*, or pure rent. A **monopsony** is the sole buyer of a factor of production. According to the **marginal productivity theory of income distribution**, the distribution of income is determined by the marginal productivity of the factors of production individuals own.

myeconlab Visit www.myeconlab.com to complete these exercises
Get Ahead of the Curve online and get instant feedback.

Review Questions

6.1 In equilibrium, what determines the price of capital? What determines the price of natural resources? What is the marginal productivity theory of income distribution?

6.2 What is an economic rent? What is a monopsony?

Problems and Applications

6.3 Adam operates a pin factory. Suppose Adam faces the situation shown in the following table and the cost of renting a machine is $550 per week.

a. Fill in the blanks in the table and determine the profit-maximizing number of machines for Adam to rent. Briefly explain why renting this number of machines is profit maximizing.

b. Draw Adam's demand curve for capital.

6.4 Many people have predicted, using a model like the one in panel (b) of Figure 12, that the price of natural resources should rise consistently over time in comparison with the prices of other goods because the demand curve for natural resources is continually shifting to the right while the supply curve must be shifting to the left as natural resources are used up. However, the relative prices of most natural resources have not been increasing. Draw a graph that shows the demand and supply for natural resources that can explain why prices haven't risen even though demand has.

6.5 In 1879, economist Henry George published *Progress and Poverty*, which became one of the best-selling books of the nineteenth century. In this book, George argued that all existing taxes should be replaced with a single tax on land. If land is taxed, how will the burden of the tax be divided between the sellers of land and the buyers of land? Illustrate your answer with a graph of the market for land.

6.6 The total amount of oil in the earth is not increasing. Does this mean that in the market for oil, the supply curve is perfectly inelastic? Briefly explain.

6.7 In a competitive labor market, imposing a minimum wage should reduce the equilibrium level of employment. Will this also be true if the labor market is a monopsony? Briefly explain.

NUMBER OF MACHINES	OUTPUT OF PINS (BOXES PER WEEK)	MARGINAL PRODUCT OF CAPITAL	PRODUCT PRICE (DOLLARS PER BOX)	TOTAL REVENUE	MARGINAL REVENUE PRODUCT OF CAPITAL	RENTAL COST PER MACHINE	ADDITIONAL PROFIT FROM RENTING ONE ADDITIONAL MACHINE
0	0	—	$100		—	$550	
1	12		100			550	
2	21		100			550	
3	28		100			550	
4	34		100			550	
5	39		100			550	
6	43		100			550	

>> End Learning Objective 6

The Economics of Information

From Chapter 17 of *Microeconomics*, 2/e. R. Glenn Hubbard. Anthony Patrick O'Brien. Copyright © 2008 by Pearson Prentice Hall.

The **Economics** of **Information**

Why Does State Farm Charge Young Men So Much More Than Young Women for Auto Insurance?

In 2006, if you were a 21-year-old male in Denver, Colorado, driving a car of average value an average number of miles per year, you had to pay State Farm Insurance $1,069 for automobile insurance. If you were a 21-year-old female, you paid only $879. A 35-year-old male paid $625, and a 68-year-old female paid just $444. Was State Farm practicing age and sex discrimination? Was the company practicing price discrimination of the type we discussed? Actually, State Farm was attempting to match up the prices they charged for automobile insurance with the costs they were likely to incur on each policy. Young males are involved in many more auto accidents than young females, or middle-aged males, so they cost State Farm more to insure.

With corporate headquarters in Bloomington, Illinois, State Farm is the largest automobile insurance company in the United States, insuring one out of five automobiles. State Farm was founded in 1922 by George J. Mecherle. Mecherle had started life as a farmer, but later took a job selling insurance. The company he worked for charged the same price for automobile insurance to people living in the city of Bloomington as it did to farmers living outside town. Mecherle realized that farmers had far fewer accidents than did city drivers. So he started the State Farm Mutual Automobile Insurance Company to offer farmers automobile insurance polices at lower prices.

Mecherle's success highlights the importance to insurance companies of correctly pricing policies. A key difficulty facing insurance companies is that drivers know more about how likely they are to have accidents than do the companies. As a result, insurance companies may charge safe drivers prices that are too high—causing these drivers to buy policies from other companies—and charge risky drivers prices that are too low. The difficulties insurance companies face in pricing their policies are caused by *asymmetric information*, which exists when one party to an economic transaction has less information than the other party. In the market for insurance, asymmetric information leads to two problems: *adverse selection* and *moral hazard*. Adverse selection can result in an insurance company attracting more high-risk drivers than it would like, given the prices of its policies. Moral hazard occurs when people change their behavior *after* purchasing insurance. Whether drivers have an accident depends partly on how safely they drive. If drivers did not have insurance to pay for the repairs needed after accidents, they would be likely to drive more cautiously.

In recent years, insurance companies have changed how they price policies. Insurance companies have always aimed at charging high prices to drivers likely to have more accidents and file more claims and lower prices to safer drivers. Usually, though, companies had divided drivers into just a few categories, based on their ages and driving records. Today, many companies use sophisticated computer models that employ thousands of variables to predict the chance that a driver will have an accident. The result has been an increase in the different prices being charged to drivers. For example, until recently, most companies lumped all drivers aged 21 to 70 into one category. But more sophisticated analysis of accident data shows that more categories would be better. As one executive of an insurance company put it, "Now we know a 22-year-old married woman is not as good a driving risk as a 45-year-old married woman." The differing prices State Farm charges drivers in Denver were the result of implementing the new pricing models.

AN INSIDE LOOK examines how insurance companies use credit reports to decide who is likely to be a risky driver.

Sources: Information on State Farm pricing from the Colorado State Department of Regulatory Agencies, Division of Insurance Web site; Denise Trowbridge, "State Farm to Lower Auto Rates," *The Columbus (Ohio) Dispatch*, March 23, 2007, p. 01H; and Christopher Oster, "Auto Insurers Cut Rates—For Some," *Wall Street Journal*, April 22, 2004, p. D1.

© Bubbles Photolibrary/Alamy

LEARNING Objectives

After studying this chapter, you should be able to:

1   Define **asymmetric information** and distinguish between **adverse selection** and **moral hazard**.

2   Apply the concepts of adverse selection and moral hazard to **financial markets**

3   Apply the concepts of adverse selection and moral hazard to **labor markets**

4   Explain the **winner's curse** and why it occurs.

Economics in YOUR Life!

Have You Ever Tried to Sell a Car?

The classified sections of newspapers are filled with ads from people trying to sell cars. Many colleges also have online bulletin boards where students can list cars for sale. Some people also list cars for sale on eBay. Car buyers choose between buying from individual sellers or buying from used car dealers. If you have tried to sell a car through a newspaper or an online ad, you have probably had trouble selling at a price as high as car dealers receive.

Why are used car buyers only willing to pay relatively low prices for cars they buy from individual sellers? If you found two seemingly identical cars, one at a local car dealer and the other for sale by an individual on eBay, would you be willing to pay the same amount for the two cars? As you read this chapter, see if you can answer these questions. You can check your answers against those we provide at the end of the chapter.

We often assume that buyers and sellers in a market possess the same amount of information. In the market for insurance, buyers often have more information than sellers. Later in this chapter, we will see that the reverse is often true in financial markets: Firms selling stocks and bonds usually have more information than buyers. In other markets, buyers and sellers may both lack complete information. For example, when an oil company bids for the right to drill on tracts of government land, neither the company nor the government has complete information on how much oil the tracts contain. When telecommunications companies bid in U.S. Federal Communications Commission auctions for licenses to provide mobile phone services, they don't have complete information on how valuable the licenses may be.

In this chapter, we discuss the economics of information and how imperfect information can affect the decisions of both households and firms. After reading this chapter, you will better understand situations such as auctions and the markets for insurance and stocks and bonds, in which the role of imperfect information is particularly important.

---

1 LEARNING OBJECTIVE

1 | Define asymmetric information and distinguish between adverse selection and moral hazard.

Asymmetric Information

Asymmetric information A situation in which one party to an economic transaction has less information than the other party.

The difficulty in correctly pricing insurance policies arises from the problem of **asymmetric information**, which occurs when one party to an economic transaction has less information than the other party. As we will see, in some markets, it is difficult to understand the actions of buyers and sellers without understanding the effects of asymmetric information. In fact, guarding against the effects of asymmetric information is a major objective of sellers in the insurance market and of buyers in financial markets. The market for used automobiles was the first in which economists began to carefully study the problem of asymmetric information.

Adverse Selection and the Market for "Lemons"

The study of asymmetric information began with an analysis of the used car market by Nobel laureate George Akerlof, of the University of California, Berkeley. Akerlof pointed out that the seller of a used car will always have more information on the true condition of the car than will potential buyers. A car that has been poorly maintained—by, for instance, not having its oil changed regularly—may have damage that could be difficult to detect even by a trained mechanic.

If potential buyers of used cars know that they will have difficulty separating the good used cars from the bad used cars, or "lemons," they will take this into account in the prices they are willing to pay. Consider the following simple example: Suppose that half of the 2006 Volkswagen Jettas offered for sale have been well maintained and are good, reliable used cars. The other half have been poorly maintained and are lemons that will be unreliable. Suppose that potential buyers of 2006 Jettas would be willing to pay $10,000 for a reliable one but only $5,000 for an unreliable one. The sellers know how well they have maintained their cars and whether they are reliable, but the buyers do not have this information and so have no way of telling the reliable cars from the unreliable ones.

In this situation, buyers will generally offer a price somewhere between the price they would be willing to pay for a good car and the price they would be willing to pay for a lemon. In this case, with a 50–50 chance of buying a good car or a lemon, buyers might offer $7,500, which is halfway between the price they would pay if they knew for certain the car was a good one and the price they would pay if they knew it was a lemon.

Unfortunately for used car buyers, a major glitch arises at this point. From the buyers' perspective, given that they don't know whether any particular car offered for sale is a good car or a lemon, an offer of $7,500 seems reasonable. But the sellers *do* know whether the cars they are offering are good cars or lemons. To a seller of a good car, an offer of $7,500 is $2,500 below the true value of the car, and the seller will be reluctant to sell. But to a seller of a lemon, an offer of $7,500 is $2,500 *above* the true value of the car, and the seller will be quite happy to sell. As sellers of lemons take advantage of knowing more about the cars they are selling than buyers do, the used car market will fall victim to **adverse selection**: Most used cars offered for sale will be lemons. In other words, because of asymmetric information, the market has selected adversely the cars that will be offered for sale. Notice as well that the problem of adverse selection reduces the total quantity of used cars bought and sold in the market because few good cars are offered for sale. From this example we can conclude that information problems reduce economic efficiency in a market.

Adverse selection The situation in which one party to a transaction takes advantage of knowing more than the other party to the transaction.

Reducing Adverse Selection in the Car Market: Warranties and Reputations

There are ways of reducing the adverse selection problem in the used car market. Car manufacturers provide warranties when cars are sold new. These warranties cover the costs of major repairs and can be transferred to a new owner when a car is resold. Warranties give prospective buyers some assurance that they will not be stuck with all the cost of repairs. In addition, used car dealers take steps to assure buyers that the cars they are selling are not lemons. They do this by building a reputation for selling reliable used cars and by offering their own warranties if the manufacturer's warranty has expired or can't be transferred. If a used car dealer can convince buyers that the dealer is selling reliable cars, then, using the numbers from our earlier example, buyers would be willing to pay $10,000 rather than $7,500 for a used Jetta.

Some states have passed "lemon laws" to help reduce information problems in the car market. Most lemon laws have two main provisions:

1 New cars that need several major repairs during the first year or two after the date of the original purchase may be returned to the manufacturer for a full refund.

2 Car manufacturers must indicate whether a used car they are offering for sale was repurchased from the original owner as a lemon.

Although lemon laws are popular with consumers, opposition from manufacturers has resulted in these laws being enacted in fewer than 20 states.

Asymmetric Information in the Market for Insurance

Asymmetric information problems are particularly severe in the market for insurance. Buyers of insurance policies will always know more about the likelihood of the event being insured against happening than will insurance companies. For example, buyers of health insurance policies know more about the state of their health—and, therefore, how likely they are to submit medical bills to the insurance company—than will the insurance company that sells them the policies. Similarly, drivers know more about whether they are reckless drivers, homeowners know more about potential fire hazards in their homes, and so on than do the insurance companies selling them policies. Insurance companies will cover their costs, including the opportunity cost of funds invested in them by their owners, only if they set the prices—or *premiums*—of policies at levels that cover the claims for payment insured people are likely to submit.

Reducing Adverse Selection in the Insurance Market

Adverse selection problems arise because sick people are more likely to want health insurance than are healthy people, reckless drivers are more likely to want automobile insurance than are careful drivers, and people living in homes that are fire hazards are more likely to want fire insurance than are people living in safe homes. If insurance companies have trouble determining who is healthy and who is sick or who is a reckless driver and who is a safe driver, they will end up setting their premiums too low and will fail to cover their costs. To reduce the problem of adverse selection, insurance companies gather as much information as they can on people applying for policies. For example, people applying for individual health insurance policies or life insurance policies usually need to submit their medical records to the insurance company. Insurance companies usually also carry out their own medical examinations. People applying for automobile insurance have their driving record reviewed. Insurance companies charge higher premiums to people who have caused accidents or who have speeding tickets. As we saw in the chapter opener, insurance companies like State Farm will remain profitable only if they succeed in identifying the riskiest drivers so as to charge them higher premiums.

Sometimes the adverse selection problem leads insurance companies simply to refuse to offer insurance policies to certain people at any price. Someone with a terminal or chronic illness, for example, may find it difficult to buy an individual health insurance or life insurance policy. The owner of a home or warehouse in an area that is prone to arson fires may have difficulty getting fire insurance. An alternative to refusing to sell policies to these people would be for insurance companies to charge very high premiums for coverage. This may make the adverse selection problem worse, however. When premiums are very high, only people who are almost certain to make a claim will purchase a policy.

The adverse selection problem can also be reduced if people are automatically covered by insurance. For example, state governments require that every driver buy automobile insurance. This policy reduces the problem of insurance being purchased primarily by bad drivers. As we saw at the beginning of the chapter, however, State Farm and other insurance companies still face the problem of determining the profit-maximizing prices to charge for their policies.

Insurance companies can reduce adverse selection problems in selling health insurance and life insurance by offering *group coverage* to large firms—including colleges and universities—or to alliances of smaller firms. With group coverage, everyone employed by a firm is automatically covered. As long as the group is large enough, the coverage is likely to represent the proportions of healthy and unhealthy people found in the general population. As a result of this *risk pooling*, it is much easier for insurance companies to estimate the average number of claims likely to be filed under a group health insurance or life insurance policy than it would be to predict the number of claims likely to be filed under an individual policy. Because everyone in the group must pay the premium—or have it paid for them by their employer—insurance companies avoid the problem of only sick people buying the insurance. Group coverage that allows healthy people not to participate is still subject to adverse selection problems, however. If healthy people don't participate, the number of claims filed per participating employee is likely to be high. This level of claims may cause the insurance company to raise the price it charges to the firm for the group policy. If the firm then raises the monthly payment required of employees, the higher price will discourage additional numbers of healthy employees from participating.

Making the Connection | Does Adverse Selection Explain Why Some People Do Not Have Health Insurance?

More that 45 million people in the United States do not have health insurance. As the chart shows, more than two-thirds of Americans are covered by private health insurance plans—primarily plans provided by firms to their employees—and more than one-quarter of people are covered by government health insurance plans—such as the Medicare program for people over age 65 or the Medicaid program for poor people. But about 16 percent of people are not covered by health insurance. (Note that the percentages in the chart sum to more than 100 because some people are covered by both private health insurance and government health insurance.)

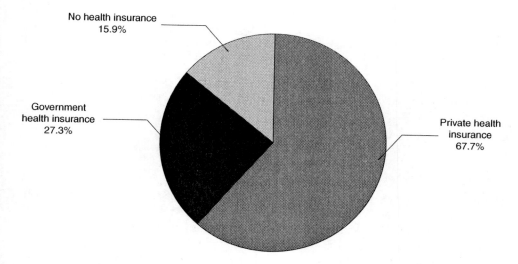

Source: U.S. Bureau of the Census, *Income, Poverty and Health Insurance in the United States, 2005*, P60-231, Figure 6, August 2006. www.census.gov/prod/2006pubs/p60-231.pdf.

There are number of reasons people may not have health insurance. Some healthy young adults don't expect to need medical care and so do not want to pay the monthly premiums to buy insurance they don't expect to need. As a result, although 15.9 percent of the total population lacks health insurance, the proportion of people between the ages of 18 and 24 who do not have insurance is almost twice as large, at 30.6 percent. And more than one-quarter of those between the ages of 25 and 34 do not have insurance. Many low-income people qualify for government health insurance through the Medicaid program. But some low-income people either do not take advantage of Medicaid or are not eligible for it. For these people, their low incomes may be the main reason that they do not have insurance. However, only about 20 percent of the uninsured have incomes below the official U.S. poverty line; more than 30 percent of the uninsured have incomes more than three times greater than the poverty line. Kate Bundorf of Stanford University and Mark Pauly of the University of Pennsylvania have estimated that as many as three-quarters of the uninsured can afford to buy health insurance.

Some economists have argued that adverse selection may be an important explanation for the significant percentage of people lacking health insurance in the United States. We have seen that one effect of adverse selection in a market is that the equilibrium quantity of the good or service may be smaller than it would have been if there were no information problems. Because insurance companies are aware of the adverse selection problem, they may sometimes offer health insurance policies at prices higher than young, healthy consumers are willing to pay. Similarly, as we have already seen, insurance companies will sometimes refuse to offer insurance to people with chronic illnesses.

In recent years, state governments may have unintentionally made the adverse selection problem worse by regulating the terms of the policies insurance companies are allowed to offer small firms. These state regulations generally restrict the ability of insurance companies to offer policies that charge higher premiums to employees with existing health conditions. Research by Kosali Ilayperuma Simon of Cornell University indicates that insurance companies responded to the regulations by raising the prices of the policies they offer to small companies. When the companies, in turn, raised the prices their employees have to pay to participate in the health plans, some younger, healthier employees dropped out of the plans and became uninsured.

So, although no one factor provides a complete explanation of why some people in the United States lack health insurance, adverse selection appears to play a significant role.

Sources: M. Kate Bundorf and Mark V. Pauly, "Is Health Insurance Affordable for the Uninsured," *Journal of Health Economics*, Vol. 25, No. 4, July 2006, pp. 650–673; and Kosali Ilayperuma Simon, "Adverse Selection in Health Insurance Markets? Evidence from State Small-Group Health Insurance Reforms," *Journal of Public Economics*, Vol. 89, Nos. 9–10, September 2005, pp. 1865–1877.

YOUR TURN: Test your understanding by doing related problem 1.11 and 1.12 at the end of this chapter.

Moral Hazard

Moral hazard The actions people take after they have entered into a transaction that make the other party to the transaction worse off.

The insurance market is subject to a second consequence of asymmetric information, called *moral hazard*. **Moral hazard** refers to actions people take after they have entered into a transaction that make the other party to the transaction worse off. Moral hazard in the insurance market occurs when people change their behavior after becoming insured. For example, once a firm has taken out a fire insurance policy on a warehouse, it may be a little less careful about avoiding fire hazards. Similarly, someone with health insurance may visit the doctor for treatment of a cold or other minor illness, when he or she would not do so without the insurance.

Insurance companies can take steps to reduce moral hazard problems. For example, a fire insurance company may insist that a firm install a sprinkler system in a warehouse to offset any increased carelessness once the policy is in place, or it may reserve the right to inspect the warehouse periodically to check for fire hazards. Insurance companies also use *deductibles* and *coinsurance* to reduce moral hazard. A deductible requires the holder of the insurance policy to pay a certain dollar amount of a claim. With coinsurance, the insurance company pays only a percentage of any claim. Suppose you have a health insurance policy with a $200 deductible and 20 percent coinsurance, and you have a medical bill of $1,000. You must pay the first $200 of the bill and 20 percent of the remaining $800. Deductibles and coinsurance give the holders of insurance policies incentives to avoid filing claims.

Don't Let This Happen to **YOU!**

Don't Confuse Adverse Selection with Moral Hazard

The two key consequences of asymmetric information are adverse selection and moral hazard. It is easy to get these concepts mixed up. One way to keep the concepts straight is to remember that adverse selection refers to what happens *at the time* of entering into the transaction. An example would be an insurance company that sells a life insurance policy to a terminally ill person because the company lacks full information on the state of the person's health. Moral hazard refers to what happens *after* entering into the transaction. For example, a nonsmoker buys a life insurance policy and then starts smoking four packs of cigarettes a day. (It may help to remember that *a* comes before *m* in the alphabet just as *a*dverse selection comes before *m*oral hazard.)

YOUR TURN: Test your understanding by doing related problems 1.14 and 3.3 at the end of this chapter.

Adverse Selection and Moral Hazard in Financial Markets

Adverse selection and moral hazard pose problems for firms and investors in the markets for stocks and bonds. Most firms have to raise funds by borrowing from banks. Asymmetric information is a key reason only large corporations are able to raise funds by selling stocks and bonds. Every firm knows more about its financial situation than does any potential investor. Because investors have trouble distinguishing between well-run and poorly run firms, they are reluctant to buy the stocks and bonds of firms unless a great deal of public information about those firms is available. As a result, this means only firms that are studied closely by investment analysts working for brokerage firms and investment companies can succeed in selling stocks and bonds to investors. The investment analysts state their opinions of the true financial health of firms in reports that are available to the investing public. A great deal of public information about Microsoft is available, and investment analysts follow the firm closely. Not much public information is available about small firms like Anisul's Software Solutions, and no investment analysts follow the firm. As a result, Microsoft can raise funds by selling stocks and bonds, but Anisul's Software Solutions can't.

Investors also worry about moral hazard. Once a firm has sold stocks and bonds, what will it do with the funds it has raised? Of course, investors expect that the firm will use the funds in ways that will make the firm more profitable. But the possibility exists that the firm will use the funds in ways that actually reduce profits, which is obviously not in the best interests of investors. For instance, a firm might use the funds to pay high salaries to the firm's managers or to open an unneeded branch office in Paris, to which the managers can make frequent visits. In the worst case, the firm's managers might actually steal the funds. Once again, the larger the firm is and the more carefully investment analysts follow its activities, the less likely moral hazard is to be a problem. This explains, in part, why investors are willing to buy the stocks and bonds of large firms but not of small firms. Note that we are using a broader definition of moral hazard here than we did when discussing insurance. In this case, moral hazard refers to actions taken by one party to a transaction that are different from what the other party expected at the time of the transaction.

Reducing Adverse Selection and Moral Hazard in Financial Markets

The decline in stock prices that followed the great stock market crash of 1929 wiped out the savings of many investors. Some investors complained that firms had failed to provide them with accurate financial information. Congress responded in 1934 by establishing the *Securities and Exchange Commission (SEC)* to regulate the stock and bond markets. The SEC requires that firms register stocks or bonds they wish to sell with the SEC. The firms must also provide potential investors with a *prospectus* that contains all relevant financial information on the firms. Although investors sometimes complain that a firm's prospectus is difficult to understand, the SEC did succeed in increasing the amount of information available to potential investors. This additional information helped reduce the adverse selection and moral hazard problems in financial markets and increased the number of firms that have been able to raise funds by selling stocks and bonds.

The steep decline in stock prices that occurred from 2000 to 2002 made it clear that information problems still exist in financial markets. During the stock market boom of the late 1990s, many investors became less cautious and more willing to invest in firms about which they had relatively little information. As investors became more focused on stock prices during those years, pressure increased for firms to report that they had earned profits at least as high as investment analysts were forecasting. Firms reporting profits that were lower than analysts had forecast could experience a sharp decline in the price of their stock. The managers of some firms gave in to the temptation to "cook the books" by falsely reporting that their profits were much higher than they really were. This cheating could not be concealed forever. During 2002, a number of scandals involving the reporting of inflated profits came to light. These scandals served as a reminder to investors of the difficulty of overcoming adverse selection and moral hazard problems in financial markets.

Making *the* Connection | Using Government Policy to Reduce Moral Hazard in Investments

The basic information on the financial condition of a company is contained in its *financial statements*, particularly its income statement and balance sheet. A firm's income statement reports its profits over a period of time, and its balance sheet shows the net value of the firm, based on the value of everything it owns minus the value of everything it owes. Investment analysts at brokerage firms and individual investors rely on this information when evaluating firms. All firms that issue stock to the public have their statements *audited* by certified public accountants (CPAs). A CPA is an employee of an accounting firm, *not* of the company being audited. The audit is intended to provide investors with an independent opinion as to whether the company's financial statements reflect the true financial condition of the firm.

Unfortunately, a series of spectacular scandals during 2002 revealed that the financial statements of even some very large firms were not reliable. In July 2002, WorldCom, the second-largest provider of long-distance telephone service in the United States, filed for bankruptcy. In June, WorldCom executives had admitted to misstating more than $3.8 billion in expenses on WorldCom's financial statements. As a result, instead of the profit it initially reported earning during 2001 and the first quarter of 2002, it had actually lost $1.2 billion. Investors saw the value of the 3 billion shares of stock issued by WorldCom drop to zero. Enron, an energy trading company, had managed to keep much of its debt from being included on its balance sheet. Eventually, it too had to declare bankruptcy. Members of the Rigas family, which controlled Adelphia Communications, one of the largest cable television companies in the United States, were accused of using more than $250 million of the firm's money for personal expenses—a striking example of moral hazard. The firm also filed for bankruptcy, and two Rigas family members were convicted of looting the company and are serving prison terms of 15 to 20 years.

The news that these and other firms had "cooked the books" illustrates the difficulty that moral hazard poses for investors. The management of a firm knows far more about the firm's finances than any outside investor can. If investors believe they cannot rely on the firm's financial statements to represent the true financial condition of the firm, they will be extremely reluctant to invest in the firm. Many observers have argued that a general loss of confidence in the reliability of financial statements was behind the wave of selling that hit U.S. stock markets in the summer of 2002.

Getty Images, Inc.

The government has intervened to increase the confidence of investors in the securities traded on the New York Stock Exchange and in other financial markets.

To help restore confidence in financial statements, Congress passed and President George W. Bush signed into law the Sarbanes-Oxley Act of 2002, which is aimed at strengthening the country's security laws. The bill authorizes the SEC to set up a government board to oversee the auditing of financial statements. The role of the board was to address the problem of outside auditors who failed to ensure the accuracy of corporate financial statements. Under the provisions of the bill, auditors who willfully violate accounting rules face five-year prison sentences. The bill also requires chief executive officers and chief financial officers to personally certify the accuracy of financial statements. The maximum prison term for violating the securities laws was raised to 25 years.

YOUR TURN: Test your understanding by doing related problem 2.7 at the end of this chapter.

---

3 LEARNING OBJECTIVE

Adverse Selection and Moral Hazard in Labor Markets

Economists refer to the conflict between the interests of shareholders and the interests of top management as a **principal–agent problem**. This problem occurs when agents—in this case, a firm's top management—pursue their own interests rather than the interests of the principal—in this case, the shareholders of the corporation—who hired them. There is also the potential for a principal–agent problem between the managers of a firm and its workers. The moral hazard behind the principal–agent problem is that workers, once hired, may shirk their obligations and not work hard.

Employers can ensure that workers are doing their jobs by closely monitoring them. Telemarketing firms, for example, can monitor their employees electronically to ensure that they make the required number of telephone calls per hour. Not all firms, however, can monitor their employees so closely. Often firms must rely on workers being sufficiently motivated so they do not shirk their responsibilities. One way to motivate workers is to increase the value to them of their current jobs, relative to other jobs they might have. If you consider your current job to be more valuable than the alternatives, you will be reluctant to shirk because you won't want to risk being fired. Firms have several ways to make a worker's job seem more valuable:

Principal–agent problem A problem caused by agents pursuing their own interests rather than the interests of the principals who hired them.

- *Efficiency wages.* There is a market for every kind of labor, just as there is a market for every good and service. A firm's demand for labor is determined by how much output workers can produce for the firm—the workers' *productivity*—and by the price the firm receives when it sells the output the workers produce. The supply of labor is determined by the willingness of workers to supply a given amount of work at a particular wage. The equilibrium wage equates the quantity of labor demanded to the quantity of labor supplied. If a firm offers to pay a wage above the equilibrium wage, a worker will consider the job to be valuable and will be less likely to shirk and risk losing the job. An *efficiency wage* is a higher-than-equilibrium wage firms pay to give workers an incentive to work harder.

- *Seniority system.* Many firms use a seniority system under which workers who have been with the firm longer receive higher pay and other benefits, such as the choice of better or more interesting jobs. A worker who early in his career at a firm is fired for shirking will give up the possibility of participating in the benefits of seniority. A seniority system can have an effect similar to that of an efficiency wage in giving workers an incentive to work harder.

- *Profit sharing.* The harder employees work, the more profits a firm makes, but employees don't share in these increased profits if they are paid a fixed wage or salary. Under a profit-sharing plan, employees receive a share of the profits earned by the firm. The harder the employee works, the more profit the firm earns, and the higher the employee's income. Profit sharing increases the incentive of an employee to work hard. One problem with some profit-sharing plans is that they don't increase the incentive very much. For example, suppose you work at a firm with 100 employees, and by working harder, you can increase the firm's profits by $10,000 per year. If each employee shares equally in the increased profits, your income will rise, but only by $100 per year. This increase is probably not enough to compensate you for the additional effort required. In addition, a firm's profits can be affected by many factors, such as a slowdown in the economy, that are unrelated to how hard a particular employee works. So, you might work very hard during a given period and actually see the profits of the firm fall for reasons you can't control. In that case, your hard work would not have increased your income at all.

Solved Problem | 3

Changing Workers' Compensation to Reduce Adverse Selection and Moral Hazard

Jill runs a clothing store. She is concerned that her salespeople are not making much effort to be friendly to customers or to persuade them to buy more clothes. Because Jill has to be out of the store most of the day, it isn't easy for her to monitor the activities of her salespeople. Jill is paying her workers an hourly wage, but she is considering switching to paying them on commission: They would be compensated on the basis of how much clothing they sold.

a. What effect would this change have on the types of workers Jill attracts?

b. Briefly explain whether this change is likely to increase Jill's profits.

SOLVING THE PROBLEM:

Step 1: **Review the chapter material.** This problem is about adverse selection and moral hazard in labor markets, so you may want to review the section "Adverse Selection and Moral Hazard in Labor Markets."

Step 2: **Use the ideas of adverse selection and moral hazard in labor markets to answer question (a).** When workers are not monitored, they have an incentive to expend as little effort as possible, which is the moral hazard problem in labor markets. When salespeople are paid an hourly wage, their compensation is determined by how many hours they are at work rather than how much they sell. If Jill switches to a system in which compensation depends on how much workers sell, she is likely to attract more workers who have the ability and interest to sell clothes. Workers who don't have much interest in selling clothes are unlikely to stay because their compensation will be reduced. Jill's new compensation scheme will reduce the adverse selection problem she faces when hiring workers.

Step 3: **Answer question (b) by analyzing the effect of the new compensation system on Jill's profits.** Whether Jill's profits rise under the new compensation system depends on whether she is correct that her workers are not making much effort to sell clothes. If she is correct, switching from paying hourly wages to paying commissions is likely to reduce both the adverse selection and moral hazard problems she faces. She will attract people willing to work harder, and she will provide them with an incentive to sell more clothes, so her sales and profits should increase.

YOUR TURN: For more practice, do related problem 3.4 at the end of this chapter.

>> End Solved Problem 3

The Winner's Curse: When Is It Bad to Win an Auction?

Information problems can occur in auctions. In some auctions, neither the bidder nor the seller has complete information about what is being auctioned. For example, when the government auctions off land for oil drilling, neither the government nor the oil companies bidding in the auctions know with certainty how much oil is in the land. In the 1950s and 1960s, the oil companies that won bids to drill on the North Slope of Alaska and in the Gulf of Mexico did not earn the profits they expected. Three engineers with the Atlantic Richfield oil company argued that this was not due to bad luck but was the result of a general tendency for the winners of auctions, like the ones held for the oil fields, to bid too high. This outcome, called the **winner's curse**, applies to other auctions as well. Knowledge of the winner's curse can make it possible for a savvy firm to win an auction with a high bid that is low enough to be very profitable.

Why were the winning bidders in government auctions of oil fields disappointed with their profits? Three Atlantic Richfield engineers, E. C. Capen, R. V. Clapp, and W. M. Campbell, proposed an explanation. They noted that each firm participating in the auctions used geological data, data on how productive nearby wells had been, and other information to estimate how much oil was likely to be available in each tract of land up for bid. Because of the uncertainty in interpreting the information available, companies made very different bids. Figure 1 shows the actual bids made by seven oil companies in 1967 on a tract of land off the Louisiana coast.

Clearly, Company A, with a bid of $32.5 million, was the most optimistic about how much oil the tract contained. Company G, which bid only $3.3 million, was the least optimistic. Who was right? Capen, Clapp, and Campbell argued that as the companies bid on many tracts using the best available information, each company would overestimate the amount of oil in some tracts and underestimate the amount of oil in other tracts. Their mistakes of sometimes being too high would tend to offset their mistakes of sometimes being too low, so *on average their estimates would be correct*. For example, in the case of the tract in Figure 1, it was likely that the true amount of oil in the tract was worth about $11.6 million, or the average of the seven bids. The problem for Company A is that it won the auction with a bid of $32.5 million, which was much too high given the

Winner's curse The idea that the winner in certain auctions may have overestimated the value of the good, thus ending up worse off than the losers.

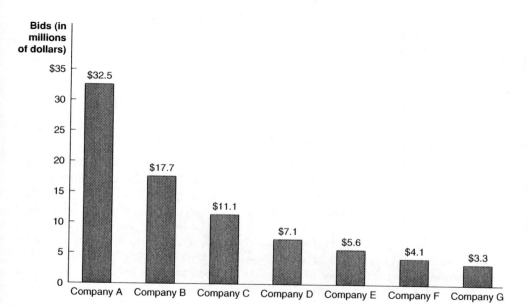

Figure 1

Oil Company Bids to Drill Off the Louisiana Coast

In 1967, seven oil companies bid to drill on land off the Louisiana coast. Because the amount of oil contained in any particular tract of land up for bid is very uncertain, the bids by oil companies differ widely. The company that has the most optimistic estimate is likely to win the auction. It is also likely to be disappointed in the profits it earns from the tract.

Source: E. C. Capen, R. V. Clapp, and W. M. Campbell, "Competitive Bidding in High-Risk Situations," *Journal of Petroleum Engineering*, June 1971, p. 642.

amount of oil that was likely to actually be in the tract. Capen, Clapp, and Campbell came to two conclusions:

1. "In competitive bidding, the winner tends to be the player who most overestimates true tract value."

2. "He who bids on a parcel what he thinks it is worth will, in the long run, be taken to the cleaners."

These conclusions became known as the *winner's curse* because they indicate that the winner of an auction may end up worse off than the losers. In fact, Capen, Clapp, and Campbell concluded that the oil companies would have made a greater return on their investments if they had taken the funds and put them in a savings account in a bank rather than using them to bid on oil tracts.

Making the Connection | Is There a Winner's Curse in the Marriage Market?

In the United States, about 43 percent of all marriages end in divorce. Why the divorce rate is so high is a complicated question. But economics can provide some insight, even if it can't provide a full explanation. Economists have proposed thinking of the interactions of men and women looking for marriage partners as a *marriage market*. Of course, the marriage market is not a typical market in which a good or service is bought and sold for money. But like participants in other markets, the men and women in the marriage market are trying to make themselves as well off as possible, and they are competing against each other to find the best partners.

A life of bliss or the winner's curse?

It's hard to tell how good a marriage partner someone will make until you are actually married to him or her. Like oil companies trying to estimate the amount of oil in a tract of land, men and women use all the information they can to estimate how good a spouse someone will be. But which potential mate are you likely to pursue most strongly? And which potential mate is most likely to find your romantic ardor greater than that of other potential marriage partners? The answer to both questions is the person whose value as a marriage partner you have most greatly overestimated. In other words, if your estimate of how desirable someone is as a marriage partner is much higher than other people's estimates, you have a good chance of marrying that person—but also a good chance of discovering later that your estimate was wrong. The idea of the winner's curse can help explain not only why oil companies can be dissatisfied with the profits from winning oil field auctions but also why many people are apparently dissatisfied with their marriages.

YOUR TURN: Test your understanding by doing related problem 4.7 at the end of this chapter.

When Does the Winner's Curse Apply?

Does the winner's curse indicate that the winner of every auction would have been better off losing? No, because the winner's curse applies only to auctions of *common-value* assets—such as oil fields—that would be given the same value by all bidders if they had perfect information. The winner's curse does not apply to auctions of *private-value* assets where the value to each bidder depends on the bidder's own preferences. For example, if you win an auction on eBay for a DVD player, you are not subject to the winner's curse if the DVD player is new and the auction described it completely. You had all the information you needed to evaluate the DVD player, and your bid was based on your preference for a DVD player relative to other things you could have purchased.

Solved Problem | 4

Auctions, Available Information, and the Winner's Curse

Suppose that the government has decided to auction off oil fields in Alaska. Suppose, also, that advances in geology have increased the accuracy with which oil companies can predict how much oil will be found in a tract of land. Are these advances likely to increase or decrease the amount of revenue the government receives from the auction?

SOLVING THE PROBLEM:

Step 1: **Review the chapter material.** This problem is about the winner's curse, so you may want to review the section "The Winner's Curse: When Is It Bad to Win an Auction?"

Step 2: **Use the information on the winner's curse to answer the problem.** This is an example of a common-value auction where the bidders lack full information about what is being auctioned. We've already seen that oil companies run the risk of the winner's curse when they do not know exactly how much oil is in each tract being auctioned. As shown in Figure 1, the winning bidder may significantly overestimate the true amount of oil and end up earning little, if any, profit, from its investment.

If the oil companies knew with certainty how much oil was in each tract, the bids would all be close together and close to the true value of the tract. The amount of revenue received by the government would be lower in this case because the highest bid would be lower. In this problem, however, some uncertainty remains about how much oil is in each tract, so the winner's curse may still arise. Because advances in geology have allowed the companies to make more accurate estimates, the highest bid is likely to be lower than it would have been. Therefore, the advances in geology are likely to *decrease* the amount of revenue the government receives from the auction.

YOUR TURN: For more practice, do related problem 4.5 at the end of this chapter.

>> End Solved Problem 4

Pacific Telesis Uses the Winner's Curse to Its Own Advantage

In late 1994, the Federal Communications Commission began auctioning 99 licenses that would allow firms to operate wireless communication networks—for mobile phones and similar devices—in specific geographic areas. Pacific Telesis (now part of AT&T) was the local telephone provider in California at that time. It was determined to win the FCC auctions to provide wireless service in California.

Pacific Telesis hired several economists to help plan its bidding strategy. There was no doubt that the licenses being auctioned were valuable, but given the rapid evolution of the market for mobile phones and other wireless devices, no firm had enough information to determine exactly how valuable. In these circumstances, the Pacific Telesis economists knew that the problem of the winner's curse meant that the firm ran the risk of either overpaying or losing the auction to another firm that would overpay. To avoid this outcome, Pacific Telesis launched a campaign to warn other firms that it was far more knowledgeable about this market than they were and that to win the auction, another firm would have to pay more than the licenses were worth. Pacific Telesis took out full-page ads in newspapers in the cities where the corporate headquarters of

Fear of the winner's curse affected the bidding in auctions for wireless service in California.

Bruce Laurance/Image Bank/Getty Images

their competitors were located. The ads emphasized that Pacific Telesis had significant cost advantages over its rivals in California and that it was determined to win the licenses there. Lyndon Daniels, president of wireless operations at Pacific Telesis, stated in an interview with the *Wall Street Journal*, "If somebody takes California away from us, they'll never make any money." Finally, in an effort to ensure that other firms understood the potential dangers of overbidding, Pacific Telesis hired a prominent economist to give seminars on the winner's curse to the other telecommunications firms.

The strategy Pacific Telesis used proved successful. Most other firms bid very cautiously on the California licenses—at least partly to avoid the winner's curse—and Pacific Telesis won the auctions with relatively low bids. For example, it paid only $437 million—or about $23 per person—for the Los Angeles license. This amount was less than other companies paid for licenses in other U.S. cities where the licenses were thought to be less valuable because of lower incomes, less concentrated populations, and slower population growth than in Los Angeles. Not only had Pacific Telesis avoided the winner's curse, it had used it to help hold down bids from rival companies.

Making the Connection

Want to Make Some Money? Try Auctioning a Jar of Coins

A simple experiment illustrates the winner's curse. Fill a jar with coins. Let a group of people—everyone in your economics class?—inspect the jar. Then auction off the jar: Whoever makes the highest bid gets the jar. The winner will, of course, be the person with the highest estimate of how many coins are in the jar. Just as with oil companies bidding on oil fields, the winner is also likely to have *overestimated* the value of the coins in the jar. Because the high bid is likely to be greater than the value of the coins in the jar, you should end up with a profit—equal to the difference between what the high bidder pays and the value of the coins in the jar.

Will the winner's curse really apply in this situation? Max Bazerman of Harvard University and William Samuelson of Boston University tested this possibility using MBA students enrolled in economics classes at Boston University. In each of 12 classes, they auctioned off four jars containing either coins or paper clips. The students were told that large paper clips were worth 4 cents and small paper clips were worth 2 cents. They were also told that the winning bidder would receive the value of the jar minus the value of his bid. For example, if the value of the coins or paper clips in a jar was $20, and the high bid for a jar was $15, the winner would receive $5. In addition, they asked students to submit written estimates of the value of the coins in the jars. They offered a $2 prize for the best estimate of each jar.

The highest bidder on this jar of coins could lose money.

© 2005 Kristen Brochmann/Fundamental Photographs

Although the students didn't know it, each jar contained exactly $8 worth of coins or paper clips. The students' average estimate of the value of the coins or paper clips in the jar was too low—just $5.13. Despite this, the average of the winning bids in the 48 auctions for the jars was $10.01, so on average the high bidders lost $2.01. These MBA students had fallen victim to the winner's curse.

Sources: Richard H. Thaler, *The Winner's Curse: Paradoxes and Anomalies of Economic Life*, New York: The Free Press, 1992, Chapter 5; and Max Bazerman and William Samuelson, "I Won the Auction but Don't Want the Prize," *Journal of Conflict Resolution*, Vol. 27, December 1983, pp. 618–634.

YOUR TURN: Test your understanding by doing related problem 4.10 at the end of this chapter.

Economics in YOUR Life!

At the beginning of the chapter, we asked you to consider why an individual will only be able to sell a used car for a much lower price than a dealer can. The key to the answer is that asymmetric information is a major problem in the used car market. Most buyers are aware that the seller of a used car knows much more about the condition of the car than the buyer does. In fact, most people get their primary information about a car from the seller of the car. The seller has some incentive to overstate the condition of the car: The better the seller makes the car sound, the higher the price the seller can hope to get. When you sell a car as an individual, the buyer is unlikely to ever buy a car from you again or to know anyone who has bought a car from you in the past. So, the buyer knows you don't have much incentive to be honest in the hopes of attracting future buyers. Car dealers, however, are hoping to continue to sell cars to many people, and their need for a good reputation keeps them from too greatly overstating the true condition of the car. So, if you have a good, well-maintained used car for sale, you may have to accept a price considerably below what a used car dealer with a good reputation could sell the car for.

Conclusion

In this chapter, we looked at situations of asymmetric information, where either the buyer or the seller has information not available to the other. We also looked at situations where both the buyer and the seller lack full information, which can lead to outcomes such as the winner's curse. Markets, including financial markets and labor markets, are more efficient when buyers and sellers have full information. Because information problems are significant in many markets, the economics of information is an important area of study.

Read *An Inside Look* on the next page to learn how insurance companies use information on a person's credit to determine premiums.

Should Bad Credit Increase Your Car Insurance Rate?

USA TODAY, JUNE 11, 2007

Your Money: Bad Credit Can Inflate Car Insurance Premiums

(a) You always use your turn signal and observe the speed limit. The only ticket you've ever gotten was for an expired parking meter. You should be eligible for lower car-insurance premiums than that bozo who cut you off this morning is, right? Not necessarily.

If your credit report is blemished, you might not get the lowest insurance rates, despite your spotless driving record. And as a result of a Supreme Court decision last week, your insurer doesn't have to tell you that you're not getting the best rates.

The high court overturned a 9th Circuit Court of Appeals ruling that said the federal Fair Credit Reporting Act requires insurers to notify customers whenever their credit history prevents them from getting the best available rate.

(b) Insurers argued that credit histories are just one of many factors they use to set rates. They also contended that the ruling would have required insurers to send out millions of notices to customers to avoid costly class-action lawsuits.

For about a decade, most insurers have considered a customer's credit history when setting rates, says Joseph Annotti, a spokesman for the Property Casualty Insurers Association of America. Annotti says research has shown that drivers with poor credit are more likely to file insurance claims.

(c) A credit report "is a solid predictor of risk," Annotti says. "People can get tickets taken off their record, DUIs get changed into running a stop sign—there are lots of ways to play with your motor vehicle record. It's less likely for a person who is inherently financial irresponsible to, all of a sudden overnight, change their behavior."

Consumer groups disagree. The insurance industry's contention that people with damaged credit are high-risk drivers is a "pretty disturbing moral hypothesis," says Chi Chi Wu, of the National Consumer Law Center. Many people have poor credit because of divorce, job loss or serious illness, she says. "They're not bad people. They're people who have fallen on hard times."

In addition, credit reports are "notorious for errors," Wu says. Identity theft could also damage an individual's record, she notes.

In November, Oregon voters defeated a measure that would have barred insurers from using credit histories to set auto and home insurance rates. Still, 26 states have adopted a model law that requires insurers to notify consumers that their credit history might affect their rates. The law also bars insurers from refusing to insure someone based solely on the individual's credit history.

The model law also encourages insurers to take into account "extraordinary life events," such as a catastrophic illness or the loss of a spouse, when evaluating a consumer's credit history.

Know Your Score

Consumer groups contend that a notification requirement would encourage people to check their credit reports more frequently. Most consumers aren't aware that their credit histories can affect their insurance rates, says Scott Shorr, a lawyer in Portland, Ore., who represented the plaintiffs in the insurance case.

Now, though, "If you want to know whether there's some inaccuracy in your credit report that's resulting in your paying more for insurance or credit generally, then you're going to have to check your credit report yourself," says Scott Nelson, an attorney for Public Citizen, a consumer-advocacy group.

How to protect yourself:

- When applying for insurance, ask the insurer what factors will be considered in determining your rates. Insurers won't tell you how they weigh them, but the company might tell you the factors it considers when reviewing a potential customer's credit report, Annotti says.

  For example, he says, some insurers are interested only in major credit events, such as foreclosures and bankruptcies....

- Monitor your credit reports regularly for errors. You're entitled to a free copy of a credit report from the three credit-reporting agencies—TransUnion, Equifax and Experian—once a year....

  If you find errors in your credit report, contact the credit agency that issued the report. The agencies are required by law to investigate disputed items.

- Beware of companies that claim they can "repair" your credit report.

Source: "Your Money: Bad Credit Can Inflate Car Insurance Premiums," by Sandra Block from USA TODAY, June 11, 2007. Reprinted by permission USA TODAY.

Key Points in the Article

This article discusses the controversy over insurance companies using credit records to set the policy premiums they charge their customers. Because the buyers of insurance know more about their driving habits and risk-taking than do the sellers of insurance, sellers are looking for some signal that will indicate which buyers are likely to be good risks and which are likely to be bad risks.

Analyzing the News

a In markets where one side of the market has more information than the other, the less informed party will seek ways to gain information. Because credit records can provide information about how responsible a person acts, insurance companies may find it valuable to use credit records to separate consumers who are likely to be safe drivers from those who are more likely to have accidents. Insurance companies are using credit histories both to decide whether or not to offer insurance to a particular applicant,

but also to decide what premiums to charge.

b When a firm uses a credit report to determine whether a person is a good or bad insurance risk, the firm is relying on the statistical correlation between a person's credit history and the likelihood that the person will have an accident. Having bad credit does not cause a person to be a bad driver, but bad credit may be a signal that a person has some unobservable characteristic that results in the person making bad decisions. A person's credit history may be a good signal that reveals to the insurance companies information that is relevant to setting insurance premiums. When insurance companies have better information about the risks they face from different consumers, the companies will be better able to judge the profitability of the policies, and the supply of insurance in the market should increase. You can see the increase in the figure as the supply curve shifts from S_1 to S_2. When this occurs, the market price of insurance falls from P_1 to P_2, and the quantity of insurance sold in the market increases from Q_1 to Q_2.

c How does the information insurance companies obtain from credit histories affect the market for insurance? Suppose that there are only two types of consumers: good risks and bad risks. A good risk will have insurance claims of $100 per year, and a bad risk will have insurance claims of

$5,000 per year. If the insurance company believes that half of its customers are of each type, the expected payout for the insurance company is $2,550 per year, calculated as 0.5($100) + 0.5($5,000). If the company charged that premium, bad risks would happily seek coverage, and good risks would not. Suppose instead that the insurance company could use credit records to identify which customers are likely to be good risks and charge them close to $100 per year, and which are likely to be bad risks and charge them close to $5,000 per year. This would make it less likely that only bad risks would seek insurance. The insurance companies would be more likely to cover their costs (which they must do to stay in business) and encourage drivers who are good risks to purchase insurance.

Thinking Critically About Policy

1. Suppose states banned the use of credit checks by insurance companies in setting premiums. What would happen to the price and quantity of insurance offered in those states? Who would benefit from this change?
2. What would be the benefits and the costs of states requiring that insurance companies charge all drivers the same premium?

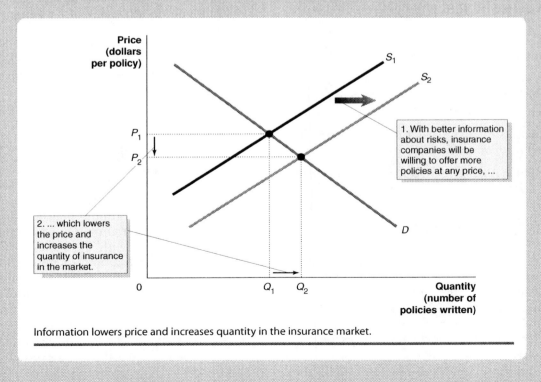

Information lowers price and increases quantity in the insurance market.

Key Terms

Adverse selection

Asymmetric information

Moral hazard

Principal–agent problem

Winner's curse

Asymmetric Information

Summary

Asymmetric information is a situation in which one party to an economic transaction has less information than the other party. Asymmetric information can lead to **adverse selection**, which occurs when one party to a transaction takes advantage of knowing more than the other party to the transaction. An example is the "lemons" problem, where adverse selection may lead to only unreliable used cars being offered for sale. Asymmetric information can also lead to **moral hazard**, which refers to actions people take after they have entered into a transaction that make the other party to the transaction worse off. For example, a firm that has taken out a fire insurance policy on a warehouse may be less careful in the future about avoiding fire hazards. Information problems result in the equilibrium quantity in markets being smaller than it would be if these problems did not exist. Therefore, there is a reduction in economic efficiency.

myeconlab Visit www.myeconlab.com to complete these exercises *Get Ahead of the Curve* online and get instant feedback.

Review Questions

1.1 What is asymmetric information? How does asymmetric information show up in the market for used cars?

1.2 What is the difference between adverse selection and moral hazard? Which is a bigger problem for consumers in the market for used cars?

1.3 Briefly discuss how adverse selection and moral hazard affect the market for insurance.

1.4 What methods do insurance companies use to reduce adverse selection and moral hazard?

Problems and Applications

1.5 Suppose you see a 2006 Volkswagen Jetta GLS Turbo Sedan advertised in the campus newspaper for $10,000. If you knew the car was reliable, you would be willing to pay $12,000 for it. If you knew the car was unreliable, you would only be willing to pay $8,000 for it. Under what circumstances should you buy the car?

1.6 Why are there lemon laws for the car market but not for the television market or the toothbrush market?

1.7 Michael Kinsley, a political columnist, observes that, "The idea of insurance is to share the risks of bad outcomes." In what sense does insurance involve sharing risks? How does the problem of adverse selection affect the ability of insurance to provide the benefit of sharing risk?

Source: Michael Kinsley, "Congress on Drugs," *Slate*, August 1, 2002.

1.8 Under the Social Security retirement system, the federal government collects a tax on most people's wage income and makes payments to retired workers above a certain age who are covered by the system. (The age to receive full Social Security retirement benefits varies based on the year the worker was born.) The Social Security retirement system is sometimes referred to as a program of social insurance. Is Social Security an insurance program in the same sense as a group life insurance or health insurance policy that a company provides to its workers? Briefly explain.

1.9 There are 10,000 houses in Lawrence. Suppose that houses cost $100,000, and 5 percent of the houses burn down each year. Which 5 percent of houses will burn down in any particular year is impossible for anyone, including the owners, to predict. There is no fire insurance available to Lawrence residents, so you decide to start an insurance company and begin offering policies. Your policy will pay the purchaser $100,000 if his or her house burns down. You charge a premium of $22,000 per year.

a. Are the residents of Lawrence likely to buy your policies? Briefly explain.

b. Now suppose that 5 percent of the owners know with certainty that their houses will burn down and that the other 95 percent of the owners know with certainty that their houses will not burn down. You offer everyone the same insurance policy with the same $22,000 premium. What is your accounting profit likely to be for the year? Assume that you have no explicit costs except for the payments you make to people who bought your policies and had their houses burn down.

c. Now suppose that people do not know with certainty whether their houses will burn down and that some houses are significantly more likely to burn down than others. Unfortunately, the owners of the houses that are significantly more likely to burn down know it, but you do not. Is it possible for you to restructure the insurance policies you offer—that is, change the terms of how much you pay out and the premium you charge—in order to deal with this problem?

1.10 Every state requires that drivers have an automobile insurance policy that covers any car they own and operate. Some people have such bad driving records that they are unable to find any insurance company willing to sell them a policy. These drivers are placed in an "assigned risk pool." Every insurance company that sells automobile insurance in the state is required to insure some drivers from the assigned risk pool. The state government usually sets the rates these drivers pay for insurance. Why is this system necessary? Why don't insurance companies voluntarily insure these bad drivers and charge them very high rates? Why does the state government have to force insurance companies to insure bad drivers?

1.11 **(Related to the *Making the Connection*)** Suppose a large firm allows its employees to choose whether to participate in its health insurance plan. The firm is trying to decide whether to offer a plan with a high deductible, but a low monthly premium, or one with a low deductible, but a high monthly premium. Under which plan is adverse selection likely to be a bigger problem? Briefly explain.

1.12 **(Related to the *Making the Connection*)** An editorial in the *Wall Street Journal* argues that regulations imposed by state governments are responsible

for making health insurance "so expensive to buy." The editorial singles out "'community rating' (insurers can't price based on differing risk factors such as age) and 'guaranteed issue' (you can wait until you're sick to buy insurance)." What problems do these regulations cause for insurance companies? How might insurance companies respond to these regulations? Do these regulations make consumers better off? The editorial concludes:

> The real scandal in American health insurance isn't that some people lack coverage for this or that treatment, but that tens of millions of Americans risk financial ruin because of [government] policies that make basic insurance difficult or impossible to buy.

Briefly explain whether you agree or disagree with this conclusion.

Source: "Why Can't You Buy Insurance?" *Wall Street Journal*, October 1, 2002.

1.13 **(Related to the *Chapter Opener*)** Why have auto insurers like State Farm started collecting more information on drivers and using computer models that employ thousands of variables to predict the chance that a driver will have an accident? Why didn't these firms do this sooner if these differences among drivers always existed?

1.14 **(Related to the *Don't Let This Happen to You!*)** Briefly explain whether you agree with the following statement: "The reluctance of healthy young adults to buy medical insurance creates a moral hazard problem for insurance companies."

>> **End Learning Objective 1**

2 LEARNING OBJECTIVE   2 | Apply the concepts of adverse selection and moral hazard to financial markets

Adverse Selection and Moral Hazard in Financial Markets

Summary

Adverse selection and moral hazard are serious problems in financial markets. When firms sell stocks and bonds, they know much more about their true financial condition than do potential investors. Investors are reluctant to buy stocks and bonds issued by small and medium-sized firms because they lack sufficient information about these firms. Investors also worry about the moral hazard problem of firms misusing the funds they raise through the sale of stocks and bonds. The Securities and Exchange Commission (SEC) has the authority to regulate the stock and bond markets and attempts to reduce adverse selection and moral hazard problems. The scandals of 2002 that involved the top managers in a number of corporations misusing funds and

reporting inflated profits indicate the extent of information problems in financial markets.

Review Questions

2.1 Explain why asymmetric information makes it difficult for small firms to sell stocks and bonds.

2.2 What is the Securities and Exchange Commission? Why was it founded?

2.3 What additional responsibility did the SEC receive in 2002? Why did Congress and the president decide that the SEC needed to take on this additional responsibility?

Problems and Applications

2.4 In an article in the *New York Times*, Warren Buffett, one of the most successful investors of the past 30 years, wrote, "For many years, I've had little confidence in the earnings reported by corporations." Why might he be suspicious that firms were not reporting their profits accurately?

Source: Warren Buffett, "Who Really Cooks the Books?" *New York Times*, July 24, 2002.

2.5 Many firms provide information about their plans and financial health to investment analysts who have no stake in the firm. Why would firms divulge such secrets?

2.6 After the countries of Eastern Europe converted from Communism to the market system, they tried to set up stock and bond markets. Most of these markets have remained very small, with few firms being able to find buyers for their stocks or bonds. One economist remarked that the reason these financial markets have been unsuccessful is that "the lemons problem has been too great." Explain what the economist meant.

2.7 (Related to the *Making the Connection*) In 2002, Congress prohibited firms from making loans to members of their boards of directors or to their top managers. Do you think this prohibition is meant to reduce asymmetric information problems? Briefly explain.

>> **End Learning Objective 2**

---

3 LEARNING OBJECTIVE 3 | Apply the concepts of adverse selection and moral hazard to labor markets

Adverse Selection and Moral Hazard in Labor Markets

Summary

The potential for a **principal–agent problem** exists between employers and workers. This problem is caused by agents—workers—pursuing their own interests rather than the interests of the principals who hired them. When workers are not monitored, they may have no incentive to work hard. Employers try to avoid this moral hazard problem by increasing the value to a worker of the worker's current job. Three ways to increase the value of a worker's job are offering efficiency wages, using a seniority system, and offering profit sharing.

myeconlab Visit www.myeconlab.com to complete these exercises online and get instant feedback.

Review Questions

3.1 What problems can adverse selection and moral hazard cause in labor markets? What steps do firms take to deal with these problems?

3.2 What are efficiency wages? What role can they play in reducing the principal-agent problem?

Problems and Applications

3.3 (Related to the *Don't Let This Happen to You!*) Briefly explain whether you agree with the following:

From an employer's point of view, the moral hazard problem in labor markets is that the potential employees who don't intend to work hard are the ones who are most eager for you to hire them. The adverse selection problem is that once you have hired a worker, he or she has an incentive to work hard only if monitored.

3.4 (Related to *Solved Problem 3*) What role do tips play in dealing with the principal–agent problem in the market for restaurant servers? Suppose that a law is passed that outlaws tips, so that now restaurant servers just receive a wage, instead of a wage plus tips. Is the total income of servers likely to rise or fall? Briefly explain.

3.5 Colleges and universities grant tenure to many professors, making it virtually impossible to fire them after they've worked there for six or seven years. Analyze this labor market strategy in light of asymmetric information, adverse selection, and moral hazard.

3.6 The going wage for janitors is $6 per hour. The Executive Building decides to pay its janitors $10 per hour. Will this higher wage increase or decrease the firm's profits? Or could it go either way? In your answer, discuss asymmetric information and efficiency wages.

>> **End Learning Objective 3**

The Winner's Curse: When Is It Bad to Win an Auction?

Summary

In auctions where bidders do not know the true value of what is being auctioned, the winner, by overestimating the value of what is being bid for, can end up worse off than the losers. This is known as the **winner's curse**, and it occurs in auctions of common-value assets that would be given the same value by all bidders if they had perfect information.

Review Questions

4.1 What is the winner's curse? Is it a problem for the winner of every auction? Briefly explain why or why not.

4.2 Briefly explain whether you agree or disagree with the following statement: "The more information bidders have on the true value of what is being auctioned, the less likely they are to fall victim to the winner's curse."

Problems and Applications

4.3 Suppose you are advising one of the oil companies involved in the oil field bidding shown in Figure 1. What bidding strategy would you recommend to the company so it could avoid the winner's curse?

4.4 After playing for six years in the major leagues, baseball players are free to sign a contract to play for any team. (Before that time, they are obligated to play for the team that first signed them.) In this situation, players often sign a contract to play for several years with the team that offers them the highest salary. Consider two players: Joe is a minor star who performs at about the same level each year. Sam's performance has been more uneven: Some years, he seems like one of the best players in baseball, but in other years, his performance has not been very good. Suppose Joe signs with the Cleveland Indians and Sam signs with the Cincinnati Reds. Three years later, is Cleveland or Cincinnati likely to be most satisfied that the player they signed played well enough to justify his salary? Briefly explain.

4.5 **(Related to Solved Problem 4)** Suppose that everyone in an auction has perfect information about the value of whatever is being auctioned. Will the winner's curse still apply? Briefly explain.

4.6 A corporate takeover occurs when one firm—or a group of outside investors—buys up a majority of the stock in another firm. The usual aim of a takeover is to take advantage of the efficiencies possible with the newly merged firm or to bring in new management and run the acquired firm more profitably. In either case, the investors taking over the acquired firm are expecting to profit from the takeover. However, studies of corporate takeovers by Richard Roll of UCLA show that although the stockholders of the firm being taken over receive substantial gains—because the acquiring firm or investors bid up the price of the stock of the acquired firm as they try to take it over—the firm or investors carrying out the takeover earn small gains, if any. Relate Roll's finding to the problem of the winner's curse.

Source: Richard Roll, "The Hubris Hypothesis of Corporate Takeovers," *Journal of Business*, Vol. 59, No. 2, Pt. 1, April 1986, pp. 197–216.

4.7 **(Related to the Making the Connection)** The winner's curse may apply to the marriage market. The winner's curse usually applies in markets with common-value assets but not in markets with private-value assets. Discuss whether it is more accurate to think of the marriage market as a market with common-value assets, private-value assets, or some combination of the two.

4.8 Well-known novelists often auction off the rights to publish their latest books. John Dessauer has described the process:

> Major books are often "auctioned off" among publishers, *i.e.*, literally sold to the highest bidder. . . . The problem is, simply, that most of the auctioned books are not earning [the amounts paid for them]. In fact, very often such books have turned out to be dismal failures whose value was more perceived than real and which benefited from the ability of a plausible agent to sell the big sizzle on a small, tough steak.

Why do publishers who win auctions for books often end up paying more than the book turns out to be worth?

Source: John P. Dessauer, *Book Publishing: What It Is, What It Does*, 2nd ed., New York: Bowker, 1981, pp. 34–35.

4.9 In ancient Rome, the Praetorian Guards were the personal bodyguards of the emperor. The guard was made up of thousands of troops, and occasionally an emperor would lose control over them. In 193 A.D., the Praetorian Guard revolted and murdered Emperor

Pertinax. The guard then decided to auction off the office of emperor. The ancient historian Dio described the situation:

> Then ensued a most disgraceful business and one unworthy of Rome. For, just as if it had been in some market or auction-room, both the City and its entire empire were auctioned off. The sellers were the ones who had slain their emperor, and the would-be buyers were Sulpicianus and Julianus.

Didius Julianus won the auction with a bid that would be the equivalent of more than $1 billion today. Unfortunately, he greatly overestimated the value of becoming emperor in this way. His reign was very short. The general Septimius Severus brought his army from the Danube to Rome, deposed Didius Julianus, and was proclaimed emperor. In the words of the historian Edward Gibbon, Didius Julianus was "beheaded as a common criminal, after having purchased, with an immense treasure, an anxious and precarious reign of only sixty-six days." Does the analysis in this chapter help you understand what happened to Didius Julianus?

Source: Paul Klemperer and Peter Temin, "An Early Example of the 'Winner's Curse' in an Auction," *Journal of Political Economy*, December 2001.

4.10 **(Related to the *Making the Connection*)** Suppose that a $100 bill is auctioned off instead of a jar containing an unknown number of coins. Will the winner's curse still apply? Briefly explain.

>> **End Learning Objective 4**

Consumer Choice and Behavioral Economics

From Chapter 9 of *Microeconomics*, 2/e. R. Glenn Hubbard. Anthony Patrick O'Brien. Copyright © 2008 by Pearson Prentice Hall. All rights reserved.

Consumer Choice and Behavioral Economics

Can Jay-Z Get You to Drink Cherry Coke?

Coca-Cola hired rapper Shawn "Jay-Z" Carter to appear in television commercials as part of the marketing campaign to relaunch Cherry Coke. Why would the Coca-Cola Company hire Jay-Z? Lucia James, of the consulting firm Agenda, explains: "Jay-Z brings a sense of genuine hip-hop authenticity to the brands. . . . There's reassurance that [the brands] won't appear like an out-of-touch uncle trying to act cool." Over the years, Coca-Cola has used other celebrities, including LeBron James, Lance Armstrong, Paula Abdul, and Ray Charles, to advertise its products. Coca-Cola is not alone in using celebrity endorsements. From Britney Spears and Sean "P. Diddy" Combs endorsing Pepsi to Michael Jordan endorsing Nike basketball shoes to Oprah Winfrey endorsing Pontiac cars, celebrities appear constantly in television, magazine, and online advertising. What do firms hope to gain from celebrity endorsements? The obvious answer is that firms expect that celebrity advertising will increase sales of their products. But why should consumers buy more of a product just because a celebrity endorses it? In this chapter, we will examine how consumers make decisions about which products to buy. Firms must understand consumer behavior to determine whether strategies such as using celebrities in their advertising are likely to be effective.

Coca-Cola has been a leader in innovative advertising, including the use of celebrity endorsements. Coca-Cola was founded in Atlanta, Georgia, in 1886 by John Styth Pemberton. After Asa G. Candler bought the company in 1891, Coke began to be sold nationally, first primarily in drugstore soda fountains. The firm's advertising in magazines, newspapers, billboards, and calendars featured pictures of attractive young women drinking Coke—instead of emphasizing the taste or other qualities of the cola.

By the 1910s, Coca-Cola had moved from using unnamed women in its advertising to using movie stars. The attempt to associate Coke with celebrities in the minds of consumers continued through the following decades. From the 1950s on, Coke's television commercials often featured popular singers or sports figures of the time, including the Supremes, the Moody Blues, and football star "Mean" Joe Greene.

Firms' attempts to distinguish their products in the minds of consumers from the products of rival firms will be an important theme in several of the following chapters. Advertising is one way in which firms try to distinguish their products. **AN INSIDE LOOK** discusses whether Elizabeth Arden made a good decision in hiring Mariah Carey to endorse its products.

Source: Can Jay-Z Get You to Drink Cherry Coke? from Kenneth Hein, "Cherry Coke Gets Fresh Jay-Z Remix," *Brandweek*, January 29, 2007, p. 4.

© Frank Micelotta/Getty Images

LEARNING Objectives

After completing this chapter, you should be able to:

1 Define **utility** and explain how consumers choose goods and services to maximize their utility.

2 Use the concept of **utility** to explain the **law of demand**

3 Explain how **social influences** can affect **consumption choices**

4 Describe the **behavioral economics** approach to understanding decision making.

APPENDIX Use **indifference curves** and **budget lines** to understand consumer behavior.

Economics in YOUR Life!

Do You Make Consistent Decisions?

Economists generally assume that people make decisions in a rational, consistent way. But are people actually as consistent as economists assume? Consider the following situation: You bought a concert ticket for $75, which is the most you were willing to pay. While you are in line to enter the concert hall, someone offers you $90 for the ticket. Would you sell the ticket? Would an economist think it is rational to sell the ticket? As you read the chapter, see if you can answer these questions. You can check your answers against those we provide at the end of the chapter.

W̶e begin this chapter by exploring how consumers make decisions. Economists usually assume that people act in a rational, self-interested way. In explaining consumer behavior, this means economists believe consumers make choices that will leave them as satisfied as possible, given their *tastes*, their *incomes*, and the *prices* of the goods and services available to them. We will see how downward-sloping demand curves result from the economic model of consumer behavior. We will also see that in certain situations, knowing the best decision to make can be difficult. In these cases, economic reasoning provides a powerful tool for consumers to improve their decision making. Finally, we will see that *experimental economics* has shown that factors such as social pressure and notions of fairness can affect consumer behavior. We will look at how businesses take these factors into account when setting prices. In the appendix to this chapter, we extend the analysis by using indifference curves and budget lines to understand consumer behavior.

1 LEARNING OBJECTIVE

1 | Define utility and explain how consumers choose goods and services to maximize their utility.

Utility and Consumer Decision Making

The model of demand and supply is a powerful tool for analyzing how prices and quantities are determined. We also saw that, according to the *law of demand*, whenever the price of a good falls, the quantity demanded increases. In this section, we will show how the economic model of consumer behavior leads to the law of demand.

The Economic Model of Consumer Behavior in a Nutshell

Imagine walking through a shopping mall, trying to decide how to spend your clothing budget. If you had an unlimited budget, your decision would be easy: Just buy as much of everything as you want. Given that you have a limited budget, what do you do? Economists assume that consumers act so as to make themselves as well off as possible. Therefore, you should choose the one combination of clothes that makes you as well off as possible from among those combinations that you can afford. Stated more generally, the economic model of consumer behavior predicts that consumers will choose to buy the combination of goods and services that makes them as well off as possible from among all the combinations that their budgets allow them to buy.

This prediction may seem obvious and not particularly useful. But as we explore the implication of this prediction, we will see that it leads to conclusions that are both useful and not obvious.

Utility

Ultimately, how well off you are from consuming a particular combination of goods and services depends on your tastes, or preferences. There is an old saying—"There's no accounting for tastes"—and economists don't try to. If you buy Cherry Coke instead of Pepsi, even though Pepsi has a lower price, you must receive more enjoyment or satisfaction from drinking Cherry Coke. Economists refer to the enjoyment or satisfaction people receive from consuming goods and services as **utility**. So we can say that the goal of a consumer is to spend available income so as to maximize utility. But utility is a difficult concept to measure because there is no way of knowing exactly how much enjoyment or satisfaction someone receives from consuming a product. Similarly, it is not possible to compare utility across consumers. There is no way of knowing for sure whether Jill receives more or less satisfaction than Jack from drinking a bottle of Cherry Coke.

Utility The enjoyment or satisfaction people receive from consuming goods and services.

Two hundred years ago, economists hoped to measure utility in units called "utils." The util would be an objective measure in the same way that temperature is: If it is 70 degrees in New York and 70 degrees in Los Angeles, it is just as warm in both cities. These economists wanted to say that if Jack's utility from eating a hamburger is 10 utils and Jill's utility is 5 utils, then Jack receives exactly twice the satisfaction from eating a hamburger that Jill does. In fact, it is *not* possible to measure utility across people. It turns out that none of the important conclusions of the economic model of consumer behavior depend on utility being directly measurable (a point we demonstrate in the appendix to this chapter). Nevertheless, the economic model of consumer behavior is easier to understand if we assume that utility is something directly measurable, like temperature.

The Principle of Diminishing Marginal Utility

To make the model of consumer behavior more concrete, let's see how a consumer makes decisions in a case involving just two products: pepperoni pizza and Coke. To begin, consider how the utility you receive from consuming a good changes with the amount of the good you consume. For example, suppose that you have just arrived at a Super Bowl party where the hosts are serving pepperoni pizza, and you are very hungry. In this situation, you are likely to receive quite a lot of enjoyment, or utility, from consuming the first slice of pizza. Suppose this satisfaction is measurable and is equal to 20 units of utility, or *utils*. After eating the first slice, you decide to have a second slice. Because you are no longer as hungry, the satisfaction you receive from eating the second slice of pizza is less than the satisfaction you received from eating the first slice. Consuming the second slice increases your utility by only an *additional* 16 utils, which raises your *total* utility from eating the two slices to 36 utils. If you continue eating slices, each additional slice gives you less and less additional satisfaction.

The table in Figure 1 shows the relationship between the number of slices of pizza you consume while watching the Super Bowl and the amount of utility you receive. The second column in the table shows the total utility you receive from eating a particular number of slices. The third column shows the additional utility, or **marginal utility** (**MU**), you receive from consuming one additional slice. (Remember that in economics, "marginal" means additional.) For example, as you increase your consumption from 2 slices to 3 slices, your total utility increases from 36 to 46, so your marginal utility from consuming the third slice is 10 utils. As the table shows, by the time you eat the fifth slice of pizza that evening, your marginal utility is very low: only 2 utils. If you were to eat a sixth slice, you would become slightly nauseated, and your marginal utility would actually be a *negative* 3 utils.

Figure 1 also plots the numbers from the table as graphs. Panel (a) shows how your total utility rises as you eat the first five slices of pizza and then falls as you eat the sixth slice. Panel (b) shows how your marginal utility declines with each additional slice you eat and finally becomes negative when you eat the sixth slice. The height of the marginal utility line at any quantity of pizza in panel (b) represents the change in utility as a result of consuming that additional slice. For example, the change in utility as a result of consuming 4 slices instead of 3 is 6 utils, so the height of the marginal utility line in panel (b) is 6 utils.

The relationship illustrated in Figure 1 between consuming additional units of a product during a period of time and the marginal utility received from consuming each additional unit is referred to as the **law of diminishing marginal utility**. For nearly every good or service, the more you consume during a period of time, the less you increase your total satisfaction from each additional unit you consume.

Marginal utility (MU) The change in total utility a person receives from consuming one additional unit of a good or service.

Law of diminishing marginal utility The principle that consumers experience diminishing additional satisfaction as they consume more of a good or service during a given period of time.

The Rule of Equal Marginal Utility per Dollar Spent

The key challenge for consumers is to decide how to allocate their limited incomes among all the products they wish to buy. Every consumer has to make trade-offs: If you have $100 to spend on entertainment for the month, then the more DVDs you buy, the

Figure 1

Total and Marginal Utility from Eating Pizza on Super Bowl Sunday

The table shows that for the first 5 slices of pizza, the more you eat, the more your total satisfaction or utility increases. If you eat a sixth slice, you start to feel ill from eating too much pizza, and your total utility falls. Each additional slice increases your utility by less than the previous slice, so your marginal utility from each slice is less than the one before. Panel (a) shows your total utility rising as you eat the first 5 slices and falling with the sixth slice. Panel (b) shows your marginal utility falling with each additional slice you eat and becoming negative with the sixth slice. The height of the marginal utility line at any quantity of pizza in panel (b) represents the change in utility as a result of consuming that additional slice. For example, the change in utility as a result of consuming 4 slices instead of 3 is 6 utils, so the height of the marginal utility line in panel (b) for the fourth slice is 6 utils.

Number of Slices	Total Utility from Eating Pizza	Marginal Utility from the Last Slice Eaten
0	0	--
1	20	20
2	36	16
3	46	10
4	52	6
5	54	2
6	51	−3

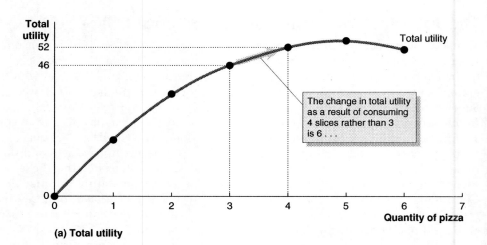

(a) Total utility

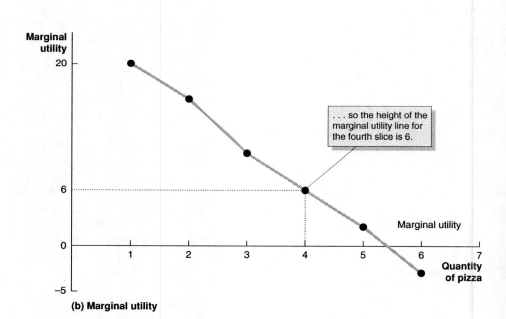

(b) Marginal utility

fewer movies you can see in the theater. Economists refer to the limited amount of income you have available to spend on goods and services as your **budget constraint**. The principle of diminishing marginal utility helps us understand how consumers can best spend their limited incomes on the products available to them.

Budget constraint The limited amount of income available to consumers to spend on goods and services.

Suppose you attend a Super Bowl party at a restaurant, and you have $10 to spend on refreshments. Pizza is selling for $2 per slice, and Coke is selling for $1 per cup. Table 1 shows the relationship between the amount of pizza you eat, the amount of Coke you drink, and the amount of satisfaction, or utility, you receive. The values for pizza are repeated from the table in Figure 1. The values for Coke also follow the principle of diminishing marginal utility.

How many slices of pizza and how many cups of Coke do you buy if you want to maximize your utility? If you did not have a budget constraint, you would buy 5 slices of pizza and 5 cups of Coke because that would give you total utility of 107 (54 + 53), which is the maximum utility you can achieve. Eating another slice of pizza or drinking another cup of Coke during the evening would lower your utility. Unfortunately, you do have a budget constraint: You have only $10 to spend. To buy 5 slices of pizza (at $2 per slice) and 5 cups of Coke (at $1 per cup), you would need $15.

To select the best way to spend your $10, remember this key economic principle: *Optimal decisions are made at the margin.* That is, most of the time, economic decision makers—consumers, firms, and the government—are faced with decisions about whether to do a little more of one thing or a little more of an alternative. In this case, you are choosing to consume a little more pizza or a little more Coke. BMW chooses to manufacture more roadsters or more SUVs in its South Carolina factory. Congress and the president choose to spend more for research on heart disease or more for research on breast cancer. Every economic decision maker faces a budget constraint, and every economic decision maker faces trade-offs.

The key to making the best consumption decision is to maximize utility by following the *rule of equal marginal utility per dollar spent.* As you decide how to spend your income, you should buy pizza and Coke up to the point where the last slice of pizza purchased and the last cup of Coke purchased give you equal increases in utility *per dollar*. By doing this, you will have maximized your total utility.

It is important to remember that to follow this rule, you must equalize your marginal utility per dollar spent, *not* your marginal utility from each good. Buying season tickets for your favorite NFL team or for the opera or buying a BMW may give you a lot more satisfaction than drinking a cup of Coke, but the NFL tickets may well give you less

TABLE 1 | Total Utility and Marginal Utility from Eating Pizza and Drinking Coke

NUMBER OF SLICES OF PIZZA	TOTAL UTILITY FROM EATING PIZZA	MARGINAL UTILITY FROM THE LAST SLICE	NUMBER OF CUPS OF COKE	TOTAL UTILITY FROM DRINKING COKE	MARGINAL UTILITY FROM THE LAST CUP
0	0	—	0	0	—
1	20	20	1	20	20
2	36	16	2	35	15
3	46	10	3	45	10
4	52	6	4	50	5
5	54	2	5	53	3
6	51	−3	6	52	−1

TABLE 2 | Converting Marginal Utility to Marginal Utility per Dollar

(1) SLICES OF PIZZA	(2) MARGINAL UTILITY (MU_{PIZZA})	(3) MARGINAL UTILITY PER DOLLAR $\left(\dfrac{MU_{pizza}}{P_{pizza}}\right)$	(4) CUPS OF COKE	(5) MARGINAL UTILITY (MU_{COKE})	(6) MARGINAL UTILITY PER DOLLAR $\left(\dfrac{MU_{Coke}}{P_{Coke}}\right)$
1	20	10	1	20	20
2	16	8	2	15	15
3	10	5	3	10	10
4	6	3	4	5	5
5	2	1	5	3	3
6	−3	−1.5	6	−1	−1

satisfaction *per dollar* spent. To decide how many slices of pizza and how many cups of Coke to buy, you must convert the values for marginal utility in Table 1 into marginal utility per dollar. You can do this by dividing marginal utility by the price of each good, as shown in Table 2.

In column (3), we calculate marginal utility per dollar spent on pizza. Because the price of pizza is $2 per slice, the marginal utility per dollar from eating one slice of pizza equals 20 divided by $2, or 10 utils per dollar. Similarly, we show in column (6) that because the price of Coke is $1 per cup, the marginal utility per dollar from drinking 1 cup of Coke equals 20 divided by $1, or 20 utils per dollar. To maximize the total utility you receive, you must make sure that the utility per dollar of pizza for the last slice of pizza is equal to the utility per dollar of Coke for the last cup of Coke. Table 2 shows that there are three combinations of slices of pizza and cups of Coke where marginal utility per dollar is equalized. Table 3 lists the combinations, the total amount of money needed to buy each combination, and the total utility received from consuming each combination.

If you buy 4 slices of pizza, the last slice gives you 3 utils per dollar. If you buy 5 cups of Coke, the last cup also gives you 3 utils per dollar, so you have equalized your marginal utility per dollar. Unfortunately, as the third column in the table shows, to buy 4 slices and 5 cups, you would need $13, and you have only $10. You could also equalize your marginal utility per dollar by buying 1 slice and 3 cups, but that would cost just $5, leaving you with $5 to spend. Only when you buy 3 slices and 4 cups have you equalized your marginal utility per dollar and spent neither more nor less than the $10 available.

TABLE 3 | Equalizing Marginal Utility per Dollar Spent

COMBINATIONS OF PIZZA AND COKE WITH EQUAL MARGINAL UTILITIES PER DOLLAR	MARGINAL UTILITY PER DOLLAR (MARGINAL UTILITY/PRICE)	TOTAL SPENDING	TOTAL UTILITY
1 slice of pizza and 3 cups of Coke	10	$2 + $3 = $5	20 + 45 = 65
3 slices of pizza and 4 cups of Coke	5	$6 + $4 = $10	46 + 50 = 96
4 slices of pizza and 5 cups of Coke	3	$8 + $5 = $13	52 + 53 = 105

We can summarize the two conditions for maximizing utility:

1. $\dfrac{MU_{Pizza}}{P_{Pizza}} = \dfrac{MU_{Coke}}{P_{Coke}}$

2. Spending on pizza + Spending on Coke = Amount available to be spent

The first condition shows that the marginal utility per dollar spent must be the same for both goods. The second condition is the budget constraint, which states that total spending on both goods must equal the amount available to be spent. Of course, these conditions for maximizing utility apply not just to pizza and Coke but to any two pairs of goods.

Solved Problem | 1

Finding the Optimal Level of Consumption

The following table shows Lee's utility from consuming ice cream cones and cans of Lime Fizz soda.

NUMBER OF ICE CREAM CONES	TOTAL UTILITY FROM ICE CREAM CONES	MARGINAL UTILITY FROM LAST CONE	NUMBER OF CANS OF LIME FIZZ	TOTAL UTILITY FROM CANS OF LIME FIZZ	MARGINAL UTILITY FROM LAST CAN
0	0	—	0	0	—
1	30	30	1	40	40
2	55	25	2	75	35
3	75	20	3	101	26
4	90	15	4	119	18
5	100	10	5	134	15
6	105	5	6	141	7

a. Ed inspects this table and concludes, "Lee's optimal choice would be to consume 4 ice cream cones and 5 cans of Lime Fizz because with that combination, his marginal utility from ice cream cones is equal to his marginal utility from Lime Fizz." Do you agree with Ed's reasoning? Briefly explain.

b. Suppose that Lee has an unlimited budget to spend on ice cream cones and cans of Lime Fizz. Under these circumstances, how many ice cream cones and how many cans of Lime Fizz will he consume?

c. Suppose that Lee has $7 per week to spend on ice cream cones and Lime Fizz. The price of an ice cream cone is $2, and the price of a can of Lime Fizz is $1. If Lee wants to maximize his utility, how many ice cream cones and how many cans of Lime Fizz should he buy?

SOLVING THE PROBLEM:

Step 1: **Review the chapter material.** This problem involves finding the optimal consumption of two goods, so you may want to review the section "The Rule of Equal Marginal Utility per Dollar Spent."

Step 2: **Answer question (a) by analyzing Ed's reasoning.** Ed's reasoning is incorrect. To maximize utility, Lee needs to equalize marginal utility per dollar for the two goods.

Step 3: **Answer question (b) by determining how Lee would maximize utility with an unlimited budget.** With an unlimited budget, consumers maximize utility by continuing to buy each good as long as their utility is increasing. In this case, Lee will maximize utility by buying 6 ice cream cones and 6 cans of Lime Fizz.

Step 4: **Answer question (c) by determining Lee's optimal combination of ice cream cones and cans of Lime Fizz.** Lee will maximize his utility if he spends his $7 per week so that the marginal utility of ice cream cones divided by the price of ice cream cones is equal to the marginal utility of Lime Fizz divided by the price of Lime Fizz. We can use the following table to solve this part of the problem:

QUANTITY	ICE CREAM CONES		CANS OF LIME FIZZ	
	MU	$\frac{MU}{P}$	MU	$\frac{MU}{P}$
1	30	15	40	40
2	25	12.5	35	35
3	20	10	26	26
4	15	7.5	18	18
5	10	5	15	15
6	5	2.5	7	7

Lee will maximize his utility by buying 1 ice cream cone and 5 cans of Lime Fizz. At this combination, the marginal utility of each good divided by its price equals 15. He has also spent all of his $7.

YOUR TURN: For more practice, do related problems 1.7 and 1.8 at the end of this chapter.

>> End Solved Problem 1

What if the Rule of Equal Marginal Utility per Dollar Does Not Hold?

The idea of getting the maximum utility by equalizing the ratio of marginal utility to price for the goods you are buying can be difficult to grasp, so it is worth thinking about in another way. Suppose that instead of buying 3 slices of pizza and 4 cups of Coke, you buy 4 slices and 2 cups. Four slices and 2 cups cost $10, so you would meet your budget constraint by spending all the money available to you, but would you have gotten the maximum amount of utility? No, you wouldn't have. From the information in Table 1, we can list the additional utility per dollar you are getting from the last slice and the last cup and the total utility from consuming 4 slices and 2 cups:

Marginal utility per dollar for the fourth slice of pizza = 3 utils per dollar

Marginal utility per dollar for the second cup of Coke = 15 utils per dollar

Total utility from 4 slices of pizza and 2 cups of Coke = 87 utils

Obviously, the marginal utilities per dollar are not equal. The last cup of Coke gave you considerably more satisfaction per dollar than did the last slice of pizza. You could raise your total utility by buying less pizza and more Coke. Buying 1 less slice of pizza frees up $2 that will allow you to buy 2 more cups of Coke. Eating 1 less slice of pizza reduces your utility by 6 utils, but drinking 2 additional cups of Coke raises your utility by 15 utils (make sure you see this), for a net increase of 9. You end up equalizing your marginal utility per dollar (5 utils per dollar for both the last slice and the last cup) and raising your total utility from 87 utils to 96 utils.

Don't Let This Happen to **YOU!**

Equalize Marginal Utilities *per Dollar*

Consider the information in the following table, which gives Harry's utility from buying CDs and DVDs.

HARRY'S UTILITY FROM BUYING CDS AND DVDS

QUANTITY OF CDs	TOTAL UTILITY FROM CDs	MARGINAL UTILITY FROM LAST CD	QUANTITY OF DVDs	TOTAL UTILITY FROM DVDs	MARGINAL UTILITY FROM LAST DVD
0	0	—	0	0	—
1	50	50	1	60	60
2	85	35	2	105	45
3	110	25	3	145	40
4	130	20	4	175	30
5	140	10	5	195	20
6	145	5	6	210	15

Can you determine from this information the optimal combination of CDs and DVDs for Harry? It is very tempting to say that Harry should buy 4 CDs and 5 DVDs because his marginal utility from CDs is equal to his marginal utility from DVDs with that combination. In fact, we can't be sure this is the best combination because we are lacking some critical information: Harry's budget constraint—how much he has available to spend on CDs and DVDs—and the prices of CDs and DVDs.

Let's say that Harry has $100 to spend this month, the price of CDs is $10, and the price of DVDs is $20. Using the information from the first table, we can now calculate Harry's marginal utility per dollar for both goods, as shown in the following table.

HARRY'S MARGINAL UTILITY AND MARGINAL UTILITY PER DOLLAR FROM BUYING CDS AND DVDS

QUANTITY OF CDs	MARGINAL UTILITY FROM LAST CD (MU_{CD})	MARGINAL UTILITY PER DOLLAR $\left(\dfrac{MU_{CD}}{P_{CD}}\right)$	QUANTITY OF DVDs	MARGINAL UTILITY FROM LAST DVD (MU_{DVD})	MARGINAL UTILITY PER DOLLAR $\left(\dfrac{MU_{DVD}}{P_{DVD}}\right)$
1	50	5	1	60	3
2	35	3.5	2	45	2.25
3	25	2.5	3	40	2
4	20	2	4	30	1.5
5	10	1	5	20	1
6	5	0.5	6	15	0.75

Harry's marginal utility per dollar is the same for two combinations of CDs and DVDs, as shown in the following table.

COMBINATIONS OF CDs AND DVDs WITH EQUAL MARGINAL UTILITIES PER DOLLAR	MARGINAL UTILITY PER DOLLAR (MARGINAL UTILITY/PRICE)	TOTAL SPENDING	TOTAL UTILITY
5 CDs and 5 DVDs	1	$50 + $100 = $150	140 + 195 = 335
4 CDs and 3 DVDs	2	$40 + $60 = $100	130 + 145 = 275

Unfortunately, 5 CDs and 5 DVDs would cost Harry $150, and he has only $100. The best Harry can do is to buy 4 CDs and 3 DVDs. This combination provides him with the maximum amount of utility attainable, given his budget constraint.

The key point, which we also saw in Solved Problem 1, is that consumers maximize their utility when they equalize marginal utility *per dollar* for every good they buy, not when they equalize marginal utility.

YOUR TURN: Test your understanding by doing related problem 1.10 at the end of this chapter.

The Income Effect and Substitution Effect of a Price Change

We can use the rule of equal marginal utility per dollar to analyze how consumers adjust their buying decisions when a price changes. Suppose you are back at the restaurant for the Super Bowl party, but this time the price of pizza is $1.50 per slice, rather than $2. You still have $10 to spend on pizza and Coke.

When the price of pizza was $2 per slice and the price of Coke was $1 per cup, your optimal choice was to consume 3 slices of pizza and 4 cups of Coke. The fall in the price of pizza to $1.50 per slice has two effects on the quantity of pizza you consume: the *income effect* and the *substitution effect*. First, consider the income effect. When the price of a good falls, you have more purchasing power. In our example, 3 slices of pizza and 4 cups of Coke now cost a total of only $8.50 instead of $10.00. An increase in purchasing power is essentially the same thing as an increase in income. The change in the quantity of pizza you will demand because of this increase in purchasing power—holding all other factors constant—is the **income effect** of the price change. If a product is a *normal good*, a consumer increases the quantity demanded as the consumer's income rises, but if a product is an *inferior good*, a consumer decreases the quantity demanded as the consumer's income rises. So, if we assume that for you pizza is a normal good, the income effect of a fall in price causes you to consume more pizza. If pizza had been an inferior good for you, the income effect of a fall in the price would have caused you to consume less pizza.

The second effect of the price change is the substitution effect. When the price of pizza falls, pizza becomes cheaper *relative* to Coke, and the marginal utility per dollar for each slice of pizza you consume increases. If we hold constant the effect of the price change on your purchasing power and just focus on the effect of the price being lower relative to the price of the other good, we have isolated the **substitution effect** of the price change. The lower price of pizza relative to the price of Coke has lowered the *opportunity cost* to you of consuming pizza because now you have to give up less Coke to consume the same quantity of pizza. Therefore, the substitution effect from the fall in the price of pizza relative to the price of Coke will cause you to eat more pizza and drink less Coke. In this case, both the income effect and the substitution effect of the fall in price cause you to eat more pizza. If the price of pizza had risen, both the income effect and the substitution effect would have caused you to eat less pizza. Table 4 summarizes the effect of a price change on the quantity demanded.

We can use Table 5 to determine the effect of the fall in the price of pizza on your optimal consumption. Table 5 has the same information as Table 2, with one change: The marginal utility per dollar from eating pizza has been changed to reflect the new lower price of $1.50 per slice. Examining the table, we can see that the fall in the price of pizza will result in your eating 1 more slice of pizza, so your optimal consumption now becomes 4 slices of pizza and 4 cups of Coke. You will be spending all of your $10, and the last dollar you spend on pizza will provide you with about the same marginal utility per dollar as the last dollar you spend on Coke. You will not be receiving

Income effect The change in the quantity demanded of a good that results from the effect of a change in price on consumer purchasing power, holding all other factors constant.

Substitution effect The change in the quantity demanded of a good that results from a change in price making the good more or less expensive relative to other goods, holding constant the effect of the price change on consumer purchasing power.

TABLE 4

Income Effect and Substitution Effect of a Price Change

		INCOME EFFECT		SUBSTITUTION EFFECT
PRICE DECREASE	Increases the consumer's purchasing power, which . . .	. . . if a normal good, causes the quantity demanded to increase.	. . . if an inferior good, causes the quantity demanded to decrease.	Lowers the opportunity cost of consuming the good, which causes the quantity of the good demanded to increase.
PRICE INCREASE	Decreases the consumer's purchasing power, which . . .	. . . if a normal good, causes the quantity demanded to decrease.	. . . if an inferior good, causes the quantity demanded to increase.	Raises the opportunity cost of consuming the good, which causes the quantity of the good demanded to decrease.

TABLE 5 | Adjusting Optimal Consumption to a Lower Price of Pizza

NUMBER OF SLICES OF PIZZA	MARGINAL UTILITY FROM LAST SLICE (MU_{Pizza})	MARGINAL UTILITY PER DOLLAR $\left(\dfrac{MU_{Pizza}}{P_{Pizza}}\right)$	NUMBER OF CUPS OF COKE	MARGINAL UTILITY FROM LAST CUP (MU_{COKE})	MARGINAL UTILITY PER DOLLAR $\left(\dfrac{MU_{Coke}}{P_{Coke}}\right)$
1	20	13.33	1	20	20
2	16	10.67	2	15	15
3	10	6.67	3	10	10
4	6	4	4	5	5
5	2	1.33	5	3	3
6	−3	—	6	−1	—

exactly the same marginal utility per dollar spent on the two products. As Table 5 shows, the last slice of pizza gives you 4 utils per dollar, and the last cup of Coke gives you 5 utils per dollar. But this is as close as you can come to equalizing marginal utility per dollar for the two products, unless you can buy a fraction of a slice of pizza or a fraction of a cup of Coke.

2 | Use the concept of utility to explain the law of demand.

2 LEARNING OBJECTIVE

Where Demand Curves Come From

According to the *law of demand*, whenever the price of a product falls, the quantity demanded increases. Now that we have covered the concepts of total utility, marginal utility, and the budget constraint, we can look more closely at why the law of demand holds.

In our example of optimal consumption of pizza and Coke at the Super Bowl party, we found the following:

Price of pizza = $2 per slice ⇒ Quantity of pizza demanded = 3 slices

Price of pizza = $1.50 per slice ⇒ Quantity of pizza demanded = 4 slices

In panel (a) of Figure 2, we plot the two points showing the optimal number of pizza slices you choose to consume at each price. In panel (b) of Figure 2, we draw a line connecting the two points. This downward-sloping line represents your demand curve for pizza. We could find more points on the line by changing the price of pizza and using the information in Table 2 to find the new optimal number of slices of pizza you would demand at each price.

To this point in this chapter, we have been looking at an individual demand curve. However, economists are typically interested in market demand curves. We can construct the market demand curve from the individual demand curves for all the consumers in the market. To keep things simple, let's assume that there are only three consumers in the market for pizza: you, David, and Sharon. The table in Figure 3 shows the individual demand schedules for the three consumers. Because consumers differ in their incomes and their preferences for products, we would not expect every consumer to demand the same quantity of a given product at each price. The final column gives the market demand, which is simply the sum of the quantities demanded by each of the three consumers at each price. For example, at a price of $1.50 per slice, your quantity demanded is 4 slices, David's quantity demanded is 6 slices, and Sharon's quantity demanded is 5 slices. So, at a price of $1.50, a quantity of 15 slices is demanded in the market. The graphs in the figure show that we can obtain the market demand curve by adding horizontally the individual demand curves.

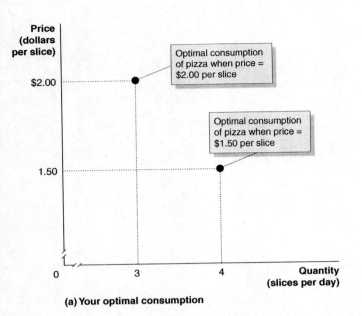

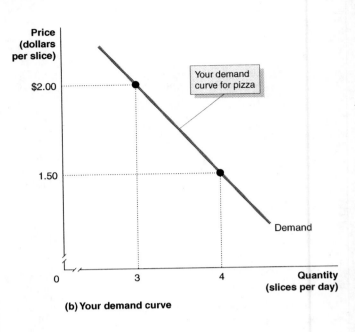

Figure 2 | Deriving the Demand Curve for Pizza

A consumer responds optimally to a fall in the price of a product by consuming more of that product. In panel (a), the price of pizza falls from $2 per slice to $1.50, and the optimal quantity of slices consumed rises from 3 to 4. When we graph this result in panel (b), we have the consumer's demand curve.

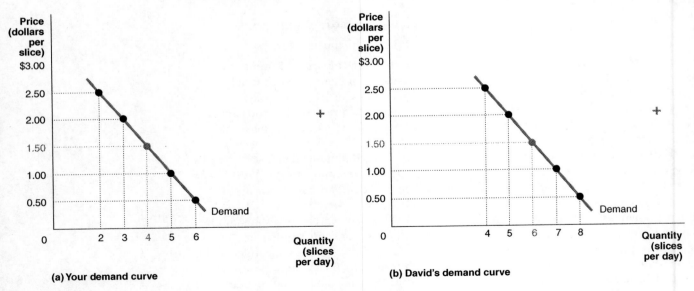

Figure 3 | Deriving the Market Demand Curve from Individual Demand Curves

The table shows that the total quantity demanded in a market is the sum of the quantities demanded by each buyer. We can find the market demand curve by adding horizontally the individual demand curves in parts (a), (b), and (c). For instance, at a price of $1.50, your quantity demanded is 4 slices, David's quantity demanded is 6 slices, and Sharon's quantity demanded is 5 slices. Therefore, part (d) shows a price of $1.50, and a quantity demanded of 15 is a point on the market demand curve.

Remember that according to the law of demand, market demand curves always slope downward. We now know that this is true because the income and substitution effects of a fall in price cause consumers to increase the quantity of the good they demand. There is a complicating factor, however. As we discussed earlier, only for normal goods will the income effect result in consumers increasing the quantity of the good they demand when the price falls. If the good is an inferior good, then the income effect leads consumers to *decrease* the quantity of the good they demand. The substitution effect, on the other hand, results in consumers increasing the quantity they demand of both normal and inferior goods when the price falls. So, when the price of an inferior good falls, the income and substitution effects work in opposite directions: The income effect causes consumers to decrease the quantity of the good they demand, whereas the substitution effect causes consumers to increase the quantity of the good they demand. Is it possible, then, that consumers might actually buy less of a good when the price falls? If this happened, the demand curve would be upward sloping.

For a demand curve to be upward sloping, the good would have to be an inferior good, and the income effect would have to be larger than the substitution effect. Goods that have both of these characteristics are called *Giffen goods*. Although we can conceive of there being Giffen goods, none has ever been discovered because for all actual goods, the substitution effect is larger than the income effect. Therefore, even for an inferior good, a fall in price leads to an increase in quantity demanded, and a rise in price leads to a decrease in the quantity demanded.

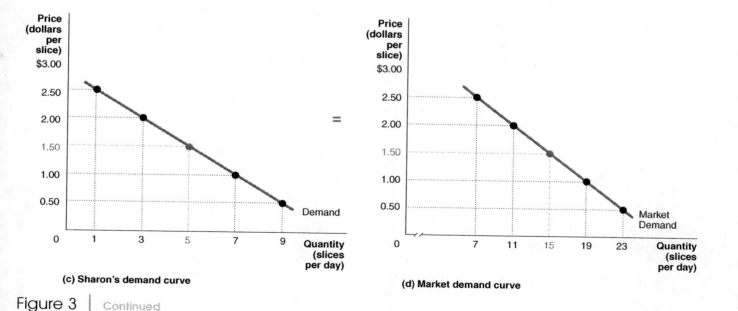

(c) Sharon's demand curve

(d) Market demand curve

Figure 3 Continued

3 | Explain how social influences can affect consumption choices.

Social Influences on Decision Making

Sociologists and anthropologists have argued that social factors such as culture, customs, and religion are very important in explaining the choices consumers make. Economists have traditionally seen such factors as being relatively unimportant, if they take them into consideration at all. Recently, however, some economists have begun to study how social factors influence consumer choice.

For example, people seem to receive more utility from consuming goods they believe are popular. As the economists Gary Becker and Kevin Murphy put it:

> The utility from drugs, crime, going bowling, owning a Rolex watch, voting Democratic, dressing informally at work, or keeping a neat lawn depends on whether friends and neighbors take drugs, commit crimes, go bowling, own Rolex watches, vote Democratic, dress informally, or keep their lawns neat.

This reasoning can help to explain why one restaurant is packed, while another restaurant that serves essentially the same food and has a similar décor has many fewer customers. Consumers decide which restaurant to go to partly on the basis of food and décor but also on the basis of the restaurant's popularity. People receive utility from being seen eating at a popular restaurant because they believe it makes them appear knowledgeable and fashionable. Whenever consumption takes place publicly, many consumers base their purchasing decisions on what other consumers are buying. Examples of public consumption include eating in restaurants, attending sporting events, wearing clothes or jewelry, and driving cars. In all these cases, the decision to buy a product depends partly on the characteristics of the product and partly on how many other people are buying the product.

The Effects of Celebrity Endorsements

In many cases, it is not just the number of people who use a product that makes it desirable but the types of people who use it. If consumers believe that movie stars or professional athletes use a product, demand for the product will often increase. This may be partly because consumers believe public figures are particularly knowledgeable about products: "Tiger Woods knows more about cars than I do, so I'll buy the same car he drives." But many consumers also feel more fashionable and closer to famous people if they use the same products these people do. These considerations help to explain why companies are willing to pay millions of dollars to have celebrities endorse their products. As we saw at the beginning of this chapter, Coke has been using celebrities in its advertising for decades.

Making the Connection | Why Do Firms Pay Tiger Woods to Endorse Their Products?

Tiger Woods may be the best golfer who's ever lived. In his first five years as a professional, he won 27 tournaments on the Professional Golfers' Association (PGA) tour. When he won the Masters in 2001, he became the first golfer ever to win all four major professional golf championships in the same year. In late 2006 and early 2007, Tiger seemed hotter than ever when he won seven straight tournaments on the PGA tour. Even though Tiger Woods is a great golfer, should consumers care what products he uses? A number of major companies apparently believe consumers do care. The General Motors, Nike, Titleist, American Express, and Rolex companies collectively pay him more than $50 million per year to endorse their products.

There seems little doubt that consumers care what products Tiger uses, but *why* do they care? It might be that they believe Tiger has better information than they do about the products he endorses. The average weekend golfer might believe that if Tiger

In 2006, Tiger Woods earned $12 million from playing golf and $100 million from product endorsements.

endorses Titleist golf clubs, maybe Titleist clubs are better than other golf clubs. But it seems more likely that people buy products associated with Tiger Woods or other celebrities because using these products makes them feel closer to the celebrity endorser or because it makes them appear to be fashionable.

YOUR TURN: Test your understanding by doing related problem 3.9 at the end of this chapter.

Network Externalities

Technology can play a role in explaining why consumers buy products that many other consumers are already buying. There is a **network externality** in the consumption of a product if the usefulness of the product increases with the number of consumers who use it. For example, if you owned the only cell phone in the world, it would not be very useful. The usefulness of cell phones increases with the number of people who own them. Similarly, your willingness to buy an iPod depends in part on the number of other people who own iPods. The more people who own iPods, the more music that will be available to download and the more useful an iPod is to you.

Network externality This situation where the usefulness of a product increases with the number of consumers who use it.

Some economists have suggested the possibility that network externalities may have a significant downside because they might result in consumers buying products that contain inferior technologies. This outcome could occur because network externalities can create significant *switching costs* to changing products: When a product becomes established, consumers may find it too costly to switch to a new product that contains a better technology. The selection of products may be *path dependent*. This means that because of switching costs, the technology that was first available may have advantages over better technologies that were developed later. In other words, the path along which the economy has developed in the past is important.

One example of path dependency and the use of an inferior technology is the QWERTY order of the letters along the top row of most computer keyboards. This order became widely used when manual typewriters were developed in the late nineteenth century. The metal keys on manual typewriters would stick together if a user typed too fast, and the QWERTY keyboard was designed to slow down typists and minimize the problem of the keys sticking together. With computers, the problem that QWERTY was developed to solve no longer exists, so keyboards could be changed easily to have letters in a more efficient layout. But because the overwhelming majority of people have learned to use keyboards with the QWERTY layout, there might be significant costs to them if they had to switch, even if a new layout ultimately made them faster typists.

Other products that supposedly embodied inferior technologies are VHS video recorders—supposedly inferior to Sony Betamax recorders—and the Windows computer operating system—supposedly inferior to the Macintosh operating system. Some economists have argued that because of path dependence and switching costs, network externalities can result in *market failures*. A market failure is a situation in which the market fails to produce the efficient level of output. If network externalities result in market failure, government intervention in these markets might improve economic efficiency. Many economists are skeptical, however, that network externalities really do lead to consumers being locked into products with inferior technologies. In particular, economists Stan Leibowitz of the University of Texas, Dallas, and Stephen Margolis of North Carolina State University have argued that in practice, the gains from using a superior technology are larger than the losses due to switching costs. After carefully studying the cases of the QWERTY keyboard, VHS video recorders, and the Windows computer operating system, they have concluded that there is no good evidence that the alternative technologies were actually superior. The implications of network externalities for economic efficiency remain controversial among economists.

Does Fairness Matter?

If people were only interested in making themselves as well off as possible in a material sense, they would not be concerned with fairness. There is a great deal of evidence, however, that people like to be treated fairly and that they usually attempt to treat others fairly, even if doing so makes them worse off financially. Tipping servers in restaurants is an example. Diners in restaurants typically add 15 percent to their food bills as tips to their servers. Tips are not *required*, but most people see it as very unfair not to tip, unless the service has been exceptionally bad. You could argue that people leave tips not to be fair but because they are afraid that if they don't leave a tip, the next time they visit the restaurant, they will receive poor service. Studies have shown, however, that most people leave tips at restaurants even while on vacation or in other circumstances where they are unlikely to visit the restaurant again.

There are many other examples where people willingly part with money when they are not required to do so and when they receive nothing material in return. The most obvious example is making donations to charity. Apparently, donating money to charity or leaving tips in restaurants that they will never visit again gives people more utility than they would receive from keeping the money and spending it on themselves.

A Test of Fairness in the Economic Laboratory: The Ultimatum Game Experiment Economists have used experiments to increase their understanding of the role that fairness plays in consumer decision making. Experimental economics has been widely used during the past two decades, and a number of experimental economics laboratories exist in the United States and Europe. Economists Maurice Allais, Reinhard Selten, and Vernon Smith were awarded the Nobel Prize in Economics in part because of their contributions to experimental economics. Experiments make it possible to focus on a single aspect of consumer behavior. The *ultimatum game*, first popularized by Werner Güth of the Max Planck Institute of Economics, is an experiment that tests whether fairness is important in consumer decision making. Various economists have conducted the ultimatum game experiment under slightly different conditions, but with generally the same result. In this game, a group of volunteers—often college students—are divided into pairs. One member of each pair is the "allocator," and the other member of the pair is the "recipient."

Each pair is given an amount of money, say $20. The allocator decides how much of the $20 each member of the pair will get. There are no restrictions on how the allocator divides up the money. He or she could keep it all, give it all to the recipient, or anything in between. The recipient must then decide whether to accept the allocation or reject it. If the recipient decides to accept the allocation, each member of the pair gets to keep his or her share. If the recipient decides to reject the allocation, both members of the pair receive nothing.

If neither the allocator nor the recipient cared about fairness, optimal play in the ultimatum game is straightforward: The allocator should propose a division of the money in which the allocator receives $19.99 and the recipient receives $0.01. The allocator has maximized his or her gain. The recipient should accept the division because the alternative is to reject the division and receive nothing at all: Even a penny is better than nothing.

In fact, when the ultimatum game experiment is carried out, both allocators and recipients act as if fairness is important. Allocators usually offer recipients at least a 40 percent share of the money, and recipients almost always reject offers of less than a 10 percent share. Why do allocators offer recipients more than a negligible amount? It might be that allocators do not care about fairness but fear that recipients do care and will reject offers they consider unfair. This possibility was tested in an experiment known as the *dictator game* carried out by Daniel Kahneman (a psychologist who shared the Nobel Prize in Economics), Jack Knetsch, and Richard Thaler, using students at Cornell University. In this experiment, the allocators were given only two possible divisions of $20: either $18 for themselves and $2 for the recipient or an even division of $10 for themselves and $10 for the recipient. One important difference from the ultimatum game was that *the recipient was not allowed to reject the division*. Of the 161 allocators, 122 chose the even division of the $20. Because there was no possibility of the $18/$2 split being rejected, the allocators must have chosen the even split because they valued acting fairly.

Why would recipients in the ultimatum game ever reject any division of the money in which they receive even a very small amount, given that even a small amount of money is better than nothing? Apparently, most people value fairness enough that they will refuse to participate in transactions they consider unfair, even if they are worse off financially as a result.

Business Implications of Fairness If consumers value fairness, how does that affect firms? One consequence is that firms will sometimes not raise prices of goods and services, even when there is a large increase in demand, because they are afraid their customers will consider the price increases unfair and may buy elsewhere.

For example, the Broadway play *The Producers* was extremely popular during its first year in production. Even though ticket prices were an average of $75, on most nights, many more people wanted to buy tickets at that price than could be accommodated in the St. James Theater, where the play was running. Figure 4 illustrates this situation.

Notice that the supply curve in Figure 4 is a vertical line, which indicates that the capacity of the St. James Theater is fixed at 1,644 seats. At a price of $75 per ticket, there was a shortage of more than 400 tickets. Why didn't the theater raise ticket prices to $125, where the quantity supplied would equal the quantity demanded?

Let's look at two other examples in which it seems that businesses could increase their profits by raising prices. First, each year, many more people would like to buy tickets to see the Super Bowl than there are tickets for them to buy at the price the National Football League charges. Why doesn't the National Football League raise prices? Second, at popular restaurants, there are often long lines of people waiting to be served. Some of the people will wait hours to be served, and some won't be served at all before the restaurant closes. Why doesn't the restaurant raise prices high enough to eliminate the lines?

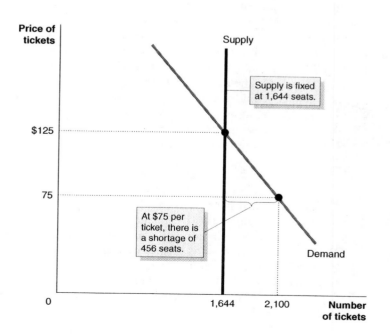

Figure 4

The Market for Tickets to *The Producers*

The St. James Theater could have raised prices for the Broadway musical *The Producers* to $125 per ticket and still sold all of the 1,644 tickets available. Instead, the theater kept the price of tickets at $75, even though the result was a shortage of more than 400 seats. Is it possible that this strategy maximized profits?

475

In each of these cases, it appears that a firm could increase its profits by raising prices. The seller would be selling the same quantity—of seats in a theater or a football stadium or meals in a restaurant—at a higher price, so profits should increase. Economists have provided two explanations why firms sometimes do not raise prices in these situations. Gary Becker, winner of the Nobel Prize in Economics, has suggested that the products involved—theatrical plays, football games, rock concerts, or restaurant meals—are all products that buyers consume together with other buyers. In those situations, the amount consumers wish to buy may be related to how much of the product other people are consuming. People like to consume, and be seen consuming, a popular product. In this case, a popular restaurant that increased its prices enough to eliminate lines might find that it had also eliminated its popularity.

Daniel Kahneman, Jack Knetsch, and Richard Thaler have offered another explanation for why firms don't always raise prices when doing so would seem to increase their profits. In surveys of consumers, these researchers found that most people considered it fair for firms to raise their prices following an increase in costs but unfair to raise prices following an increase in demand. For example, Kahneman, Knetsch, and Thaler conducted a survey in which people were asked their opinion of the following situation: "A hardware store has been selling snow shovels for $15. The morning after a large snowstorm, the store raises the price to $20." Eighty-two percent of those surveyed responded that they considered the hardware store's actions to be unfair. Kahneman, Knetsch, and Thaler have concluded that firms may sometimes not raise their prices even when the quantity demanded of their product is greater than the quantity supplied out of fear that in the long run, they will lose customers who believe the price increases were unfair.

These explanations share the same basic idea: Sometimes firms will give up some profits in the short run to keep their customers happy and increase their profits in the long run.

Making the Connection

Professor Krueger Goes to the Super Bowl

Economist Alan Krueger of Princeton University has studied the question of why the National Football League does not charge a price for Super Bowl tickets that is high enough to make the quantity of tickets demanded equal to the quantity of tickets available. The prices may seem high—$400 for the best seats, $325 for the rest—but the quantity demanded still greatly exceeds the quantity supplied. Most Super Bowl tickets are allocated to the two teams playing in the game or to the league's corporate sponsors. To give ordinary fans a chance to attend the game, in 2001, the NFL set aside 500 pairs of tickets. They held a lottery for the opportunity to buy these tickets, and more than 36,000 people applied. Some fans were willing to pay as much as $5,000 to buy a ticket from ticket scalpers. (Scalpers buy tickets at their face value and then resell them at much higher prices, even though in Florida, where the 2001 Super Bowl was held, ticket scalping is illegal.)

Why didn't the NFL simply raise the price of tickets to clear the market? Krueger decided to survey football fans attending the game to see if their views could help explain this puzzle. Krueger's survey provides support for the Kahneman, Knetsch, and Thaler explanation of why companies do not always raise prices when the quantity demanded is greater than the quantity supplied. When asked whether it would "be fair for the NFL to raise the [price of tickets] to $1,500 if that is still less than the amount most people are willing to pay for tickets," 92 percent of the fans surveyed answered "no." Even 83 percent of the fans who had paid more than $1,500 for their tickets answered "no." Krueger concluded

Should the NFL raise the price of Super Bowl tickets?

Getty Images, Inc.

476

that whatever the NFL might gain in the short run from raising ticket prices, it would more than lose in the long run by alienating football fans.

Source: Alan B. Krueger, "Supply and Demand: An Economist Goes to the Super Bowl," *Milken Institute Review*, Second Quarter 2001.

YOUR TURN: Test your understanding by doing related problems 3.11 and 3.12 at the end of this chapter.

---

4 | Describe the behavioral economics approach to understanding decision making

4 LEARNING OBJECTIVE

Behavioral Economics: Do People Make Their Choices Rationally?

When economists say that consumers and firms are behaving "rationally," they mean that consumers and firms are taking actions that are appropriate to reach their goals, given the information available to them. In recent years, some economists have begun studying situations in which people do not appear to be making choices that are economically rational. This new area of economics is called **behavioral economics**. Why might consumers or businesses not act rationally? The most obvious reason would be that they do not realize that their actions are inconsistent with their goals. One of the objectives of economics is to suggest ways to make better decisions. In this section, we discuss ways in which consumers can improve their decisions by avoiding some common pitfalls.

Behavioral economics The study of situations in which people make choices that do not appear to be economically rational.

Consumers commonly commit the following three mistakes when making decisions:

- They take into account monetary costs but ignore nonmonetary opportunity costs.

- They fail to ignore sunk costs.

- They are overly optimistic about their future behavior.

Ignoring Nonmonetary Opportunity Costs

The **opportunity cost** of any activity is the highest-valued alternative that must be given up to engage in that activity. For example, if you own something you could sell, using it yourself involves an opportunity cost. It is often difficult for people to think of opportunity costs in these terms.

Opportunity cost The highest-valued alternative that must be given up to engage in an activity.

Consider the following example: Some of the fans at the 2001 Super Bowl participated in a lottery run by the National Football League that allowed the winners to purchase tickets at their face value, which was either $325 or $400, depending on where in the stadium the seats were located. Alan Krueger surveyed the lottery winners, asking them two questions:

Question 1: If you had not won the lottery, would you have been willing to pay $3,000 for your ticket?
Question 2: If after winning your ticket (and before arriving in Florida for the Super Bowl) someone had offered you $3,000 for your ticket, would you have sold it?

In answer to the first question, 94 percent said that if they had not won the lottery, they would not have paid $3,000 for a ticket. In answer to the second question, 92 percent said they would not have sold their ticket for $3,000. But these answers are contradictory! If someone offers you $3,000 for your ticket, then by using the ticket rather than selling it, you incur an opportunity cost of $3,000. There really is a $3,000 cost involved in using that ticket, even though you do not pay $3,000 in cash. The alternatives of either paying $3,000 or not receiving $3,000 amount to exactly the same thing.

If the ticket is really not worth $3,000 to you, you should sell it. If it is worth $3,000 to you, you should be willing to pay $3,000 in cash to buy it. Not being willing to sell a ticket you already own for $3,000, while at the same time not being willing to buy a ticket for $3,000 if you didn't already own one is inconsistent behavior. The inconsistency comes from a failure to take into account nonmonetary opportunity costs. Behavioral economists believe this inconsistency is caused by the **endowment effect**, which is the tendency of people to be unwilling to sell a good they already own even if they are offered a price that is greater than the price they would be willing to pay to buy the good if they didn't already own it.

The failure to take into account opportunity costs is a very common error in decision making. Suppose, for example, that a friend is in a hurry to have his room cleaned—it's the Friday before parents' weekend—and he offers you $50 to do it for him. You turn him down and spend the time cleaning your own room, even though you know somebody down the hall who would be willing to clean your room for $20. Leave aside complicating details—the guy who asked you to clean his room is a real slob, or you don't want the person who offered to clean your room for $20 to go through your stuff—and you should see the point we are making. The opportunity cost of cleaning your own room is $50—the amount your friend offered to pay you to clean his room. It is inconsistent to turn down an offer from someone else to clean your room for $20 when you are doing it for yourself at a cost of $50. The key point here is this: *Nonmonetary opportunity costs are just as real as monetary costs and should be taken into account when making decisions.*

Endowment effect The tendency of people to be unwilling to sell a good they already own even if they are offered a price that is greater than the price they would be willing to pay to buy the good if they didn't already own it.

Business Implications of Consumers Ignoring Nonmonetary Opportunity Costs

Behavioral economist Richard Thaler has studied several examples of how businesses make use of consumers' failure to take into account opportunity costs. Whenever you buy something with a credit card, the credit card company charges the merchant a fee to process the bill. Credit card companies generally do not allow stores to charge higher prices to customers who use credit cards. A bill was introduced in Congress that would have made it illegal for credit card companies to enforce this rule. The credit card industry was afraid that if this law passed, credit card usage would drop because stores might begin charging a fee to credit card users. They attempted to have the law amended so that stores would be allowed to give a cash discount to people not using credit cards but would not be allowed to charge a fee to people using credit cards. There really is no difference in terms of opportunity cost between being charged a fee and not receiving a discount. The credit card industry was relying on the fact that *not* receiving a discount is a nonmonetary opportunity cost—and, therefore, likely to be ignored by consumers—but a fee is a monetary cost that people do take into account.

Film processing companies provide another example. Many of these companies have a policy of printing every picture on a roll of film, even if the picture is very fuzzy. Customers are allowed to ask for refunds on pictures they don't like. Once again, the companies are relying on the fact that passing up a refund once you have already paid for a picture is a nonmonetary opportunity cost rather than a direct monetary cost. In fact, customers rarely ask for refunds.

Making the Connection | Why Do Hilton Hotels and other Firms Hide Their Prices?

Economists recently began to use ideas from behavioral economics to understand a puzzling aspect of how some businesses price their products. David Laibson of Harvard University and Xavier Gabaix of New York University note that some products consist of a "base good" and "add-ons." For instance, to use a printer, you buy the printer itself—the base good—and replacement ink cartridges—the add-on. Typically, firms compete on the price of the base good but do their best to hide the prices of the add-ons. Because consumers sometimes spend more on the add-ons than on the base good, it may seem surprising that firms are able to successfully hide the prices of add-ons. For instance, over the life of a printer, consumers spend, on average, 10 times the price of the printer in buying ink cartridges. Yet one survey indicates that only 3 percent of consumers know the true cost of using a printer, including the cost of the ink cartridges. Similarly, many consumers are unaware of the add-on charges from using a checking account, such as ATM fees, returned check charges, and minimum balance fees. Many consumers making a hotel reservation are unaware of the hotel's charges for Internet access, for food from minibars, for breakfast at the hotel restaurant, or for local phone calls.

How are firms able to hide the prices of add-ons? Why doesn't competition lead some firms to offer lower-priced add-ons and advertise that their competitors' add-ons are higher priced? Laibson and Gabaix explain this puzzle by arguing that there are two types of consumers: sophisticated consumers, who pay attention to prices of add-ons, and myopic consumers, who ignore the prices of add-ons. It turns out that using advertising to convert myopic consumers into sophisticated consumers is not a profitable strategy. Consider the following example: Suppose that Hilton Hotels charges $80 per night for a room and the typical myopic consumer also spends $20 per night on local phone calls, food from the minibar, high-priced breakfasts, and other add-ons. Could a competing hotel, such as Marriott, attract Hilton's customers by advertising that Marriott's add-ons were more fairly priced than Hilton's? Laibson and Gabaix argue that this strategy would not work because its main effect would be to turn myopic consumers into sophisticated consumers. Once Hilton's customers become sophisticated, they will avoid the add-on fees, by, for instance, using their cell phones rather than the hotel phones to make calls or by eating breakfast in nearby restaurants rather than in the hotel. According to Laibson and Gabaix, Marriott's advertising campaign, "hurts Hilton—which sells fewer add-ons—but helps Hilton's customers, who are taught to substitute away from add-ons." But these sophisticated consumers are no more likely to switch from Hilton to Marriott than they were before Marriott incurred the cost of its advertising campaign. Exposing a competitor's hidden costs, say Laibson and Gabaix, "is good for the consumer and bad for both firms. Neither firm has an incentive to do it." As a result, many consumers remain unaware of the true prices of some of the products they purchase.

Some hotels hide what they charge for room service and Internet access.

Sources: Christopher Shay, "The Hidden-Fee Economy," *New York Times*, December 10, 2006; and Xavier Gabaix and David Laibson, "Shrouded Attributes, Consumer Myopia, and Information Suppression in Competitive Markets," *Quarterly Journal of Economics*, Vol. 121, No. 2, May 2006, pp. 351–397.

YOUR TURN: Test your understanding by doing related problem 4.10 at the end of this chapter.

Failing to Ignore Sunk Costs

A **sunk cost** is a cost that has already been paid and cannot be recovered. Once you have paid money and can't get it back, you should ignore that money in any later decisions you make. Consider the following two situations:

Situation 1: You bought a ticket to a play for $75. The ticket is nonrefundable and must be used on Tuesday night, which is the only night the play will be performed. On Monday, a friend calls and invites you to a local comedy club to see a comedian you both like who is appearing only on Tuesday night. Your friend offers to pay the cost of going to the club.

Situation 2: It's Monday night, and you are about to buy a ticket for the Tuesday night performance of the same play as in situation 1. As you are leaving to buy the ticket, your friend calls and invites you to the comedy club.

Sunk cost A cost that has already been paid and cannot be recovered.

Would your decision to go to the play or to the comedy club be different in situation 1 than in situation 2? Most people would say that in situation 1, they would go to the play, because otherwise they would lose the $75 they had paid for the ticket. In fact, though, the $75 is "lost" no matter what you do because the ticket is not refundable. The only real issue for you to decide is whether you would prefer to see the play or prefer to go with your friend to the comedy club. If you would prefer to go to the club, the fact that you have already paid $75 for the ticket to the play is irrelevant. Your decision should be the same in situation 1 and situation 2.

Psychologists Daniel Kahneman and Amos Tversky explored the tendency of consumers to not ignore sunk costs by asking two samples of people the following questions:

Question 1: One sample of people was asked the following question: "Imagine that you have decided to see a play and have paid the admission price of $10 per ticket. As you enter the theater, you discover that you have lost the ticket. The seat was not marked, and the ticket cannot be recovered. Would you pay $10 for another ticket?" Of those asked, 46 percent answered "yes," and 54 percent answered "no."

Question 2: A different sample of people was asked the following question: "Imagine that you have decided to see a play where admission is $10 per ticket. As you enter the theater, you discover that you have lost a $10 bill. Would you still pay $10 for a ticket to the play?" Of those asked, 88 percent answered "yes," and 12 percent answered "no."

The situations presented in the two questions are actually the same and should have received the same fraction of yes and no responses. Many people, though, have trouble seeing that in question 1, when deciding whether to see the play, they should ignore the $10 already paid for a ticket because it is a sunk cost.

Being Unrealistic about Future Behavior

Studies have shown that a majority of adults in the United States are overweight. Why do many people choose to eat too much? One possibility is that they receive more utility from eating too much than they would from being thin. A more likely explanation, however, is that many people eat a lot today because they expect to eat less tomorrow. But they never do eat less, and so they end up overweight. (Of course, some people also suffer from medical problems that lead to weight gain.) Similarly, some people continue smoking today because they expect to be able to give it up sometime in the future. Unfortunately, for many people that time never comes, and they suffer the health consequences of prolonged smoking. In both these cases, people are overvaluing the utility from current choices—eating chocolate cake or smoking—and undervaluing the utility to be received in the future from being thin or not getting lung cancer.

Economists who have studied this question argue that many people have preferences that are not consistent over time. In the long run, you would like to be thin or give up smoking or achieve some other goal, but each day, you make decisions (such as to eat too much or to smoke) that are not consistent with this long-run goal. If you are unrealistic about your future behavior, you underestimate the costs of choices—like overeating or smoking—that you make today. A key way of avoiding this problem is to be realistic about your future behavior.

Making the Connection | Why Don't Students Study More?

Government statistics show that students who do well in college earn at least $10,000 more per year than students who fail to graduate or who graduate with low grades. So, over the course of a career of 40 years or more, students who do well in college will have earned upwards of $400,000 more than students who failed to graduate or who received low grades. Most colleges advise that students study at least two hours outside of class for every hour they spend in class. Surveys show that students often ignore this advice.

If the payoff to studying is so high, why don't students study more?

If the opportunity cost of not studying is so high, why do many students choose to study relatively little? Some students have work or family commitments that limit the amount of time they can study. But many other students study less than they would if they were more realistic about their future behavior. On any given night, a student has to choose between studying and other activities—like watching television, going to the movies, or going to a party—that may seem to provide higher utility in the short run. Many students choose one of these activities over studying because they expect to study tomorrow or the next day, but tomorrow they face the same choices and make similar decisions. As a result, they do not study enough to meet their long-run goal of graduating with high grades. If they were more realistic about their future behavior, they would not make the mistake of overvaluing the utility from activities like watching television or partying because they would realize that those activities can endanger their long-run goal of graduating with honors.

YOUR TURN: Test your understanding by doing related problem 4.13 at the end of this chapter.

Solved Problem | **4**

How Do You Get People to Save More of Their Income?

An article in the *New York Times* states the following:

> When it comes to saving for retirement, Americans . . . know they do not put away enough. . . . But ask them to save more in their [retirement] plans and they balk. A buck in the hand is irresistibly spent. Try a different approach. Ask them to commit now to increasing their savings in the future, make the increase coincide with the next raise, and they cheerfully sign up.

Why would people refuse to increase their savings now but agree to increase their savings in the future?

Source: Louis Uchitelle, "Why It Takes Psychology to Make People Save," *New York Times*, January 13, 2002.

SOLVING THE PROBLEM:

Step 1: **Review the chapter material.** This problem is about how people are not always realistic about their future behavior, so you may want to review the section "Being Unrealistic about Future Behavior."

Step 2: **Use your understanding of consumer decision making to show that this plan may work.** We have seen that many people are unrealistic about their future behavior. They spend money today that they should be saving for retirement, partly because they expect to increase their saving in the future. A savings plan that gets people to commit today to saving in the future takes advantage of people's optimism about their future behavior. They agree to save more in the future because they expect to be doing that anyway. In fact, without being part of a plan that automatically saves their next raise, they probably would not have increased their savings.

YOUR TURN: For more practice, do related problems 4.11 and 4.12 at the end of this chapter.

>> **End Solved Problem 2**

Taking into account nonmonetary opportunity costs, ignoring sunk costs, and being more realistic about future behavior are three ways in which consumers are able to improve the decisions they make.

Economics in YOUR Life!

At the beginning of the chapter, we asked you to consider a situation in which you had paid $75 for a concert ticket, which is the most you would be willing to pay. Just before you enter the concert hall, someone offers you $90 for the ticket. We posed two questions: Would you sell the ticket? and Would an economist think it is rational to sell the ticket? If you answered that you would sell, then your answer is rational in the sense in which economists use the term. The cost of going to see the concert is what you have to give up for the ticket. Initially, the cost was just $75—the dollar price of the ticket. This amount was also the most you were willing to pay. However, once someone offers you $90 for the ticket, the cost of seeing the concert rises to $90. The reason the cost of the concert is now $90 is that once you turn down an offer of $90 for the ticket you have incurred a nonmonetary opportunity cost of $90 if you use the ticket yourself. The endowment effect explains why some people would not sell the ticket. People seem to value things that they have more than things that they do not have. Therefore, a concert ticket you already own may be worth more to you than a concert ticket you have yet to purchase. Behavioral economists study situations like this where people make choices that do not appear to be economically rational.

Conclusion

In a market system, consumers are in the driver's seat. Goods are produced only if consumers want them to be. Therefore, how consumers make their decisions is an important area for economists to study, a fact that was highlighted when Daniel Kahneman—whose research was mentioned several times in this chapter—shared the Nobel Prize in Economics. Economists expect that consumers will spend their incomes so that the last dollar spent on each good provides them with equal additional amounts of satisfaction, or utility. In practice, there are significant social influences on consumer decision making, particularly when a good or service is consumed in public. Fairness also seems to be an important consideration for most consumers. Finally, many consumers could improve the decisions they make if they would take into account non-monetary opportunity costs and ignore sunk costs.

In this chapter, we studied consumers' choices. In the next several chapters, we will study firms' choices. Before moving on to the next chapter, read *An Inside Look* on the next page for a discussion of whether Elizabeth Arden made a good decision in hiring Mariah Carey to endorse its products.

Can Mariah Carey Get You to Buy Elizabeth Arden Perfume?

WOMEN'S WEAR DAILY, APRIL 7, 2006

Mariah Signs Scent Deal with Arden

NEW YORK - The celebrity fragrance craze has a new player—Mariah Carey.

The Grammy Award-winning singer has signed with Elizabeth Arden to develop and market her own line of fragrance products, the first of which are to be launched in spring 2007 in what the company described as "prestige department stores."

Financial terms of the deal, announced on Thursday, were not disclosed. However, industry experts have speculated that such agreements often include an up-front payout of $1 million to $2 million, and 1 to 3 percent of fragrance sales after the scent is on the counter.

Carey, whose projects include a self-branded line sold by costume jewelry retailer Claire's, will be involved with all aspects of the fragrance's development, Arden said in a statement. "I've already been involved with the team at Elizabeth Arden in the early stages of the creative process," Carey said.

The deal further amps up the significance of celebrities in the beauty world—particularly in the fragrance arena. Coty is arguably the most entrenched, with Jennifer Lopez, Sarah Jessica Parker, Kimora Lee Simmons, David and Victoria Beckham, Mary-Kate and Ashley Olsen, Shania Twain and the "Desperate Housewives" in its stable.

Arden's deal with Britney Spears, signed in March 2004, has yielded two top-five hits: Curious Britney Spears and Fantasy Britney Spears. Arden has had teen queen Hilary Duff under contract for beauty products since September (the first fruits of that deal have not yet been released), and it signed Catherine Zeta-Jones in February 2002 to be the face of its core Elizabeth Arden brand. In addition, NASCAR star Jeff Gordon has been the face of its Halston Z-14 brand since May 2004, and the original celebrity fragrance maven, Elizabeth Taylor, is also part of the company's constellation.

"Mariah has immense popularity with a very diverse consumer base— from teenagers to grandmothers," Ron Rolleston, executive vice president of global marketing for Elizabeth Arden, said in an interview. "She is global in terms of her appeal, which spans generations and cultures, which we believe will translate well into sales when the fragrance is launched.... She has already met with the four major fragrance houses that we work with, and has very definite ideas." Rolleston noted that Federated Department Stores, Belk and Dillard's are stores that would be likely to carry the scent.

Part of the reason retailers applaud the category is that many of the celebrities are drawing lapsed department store consumers back into the beauty department. "In Mariah, Arden has someone who is a proven hit-maker and an undervalued asset," said Steve Stoute—managing partner of Carol's Daughter and chairman and chief creative officer, Translation— who has brokered celebrity endorsement deals. "Her music has always been bigger than her personality, and she not only appeals to a younger consumer, she has a consumer who has grown up with her. I believe that Arden has her at the right time. I just hope that they have the bandwidth to market all of these celebrity brands.

Key Points in the Article

This article discusses how firms benefit from using celebrity endorsements in their advertising. Elizabeth Arden clearly believes that hiring Mariah Carey to endorse a new line of fragrances will pay off financially. The firm believes that because Carey is a popular celebrity, some of that popularity will rub off on the new fragrance products. Essentially, the firm is betting that a large number of consumers will see Carey's endorsement and purchase the fragrance because of that endorsement. Consumers may purchase the fragrance to be like Mariah Carey or just to signal that they are like Mariah Carey. However, celebrity endorsements come with risks. Mary-Kate and Ashley Olson were dropped from the "Got Milk?" campaign after Mary-Kate was reportedly hospitalized for an eating disorder. In addition, Slim-Fast dropped Whoopi Goldberg from its advertisements after she made critical and vulgar comments about President George W. Bush. Once a firm hires a celebrity, consumers associate the product with the celebrity. This association can be a good or a bad thing depending on the celebrity's actions.

Analyzing the News

a Elizabeth Arden is giving Mariah Carey a large up-front payment and a significant part of the revenues from the fragrance sales. The firm is willing to hire Carey because it believes doing so will increase its profits. Her endorsement could lead to higher prices or a greater quantity sold, but the firm's profits will increase only if its increase in revenue is greater than the required payments to Carey.

When consumers' taste for a product increases, the demand curve will shift to the right, and when consumers' taste for a product decreases, the demand curve for the product will shift to the left. When a firm hires a celebrity to endorse its products, it is hoping to increase consumers' taste for its product. The figure shows that if the endorsement is successful, the demand curve for Elizabeth Arden fragrances shifts from D_1 to D_2. The increase in demand allows the firm to sell more fragrance bottles at every price. For example, at a price of P_1 it could sell Q_1 bottles without the endorsement but Q_2 fragrances with the endorsement.

b Elizabeth Arden's experience with celebrity endorsements has been very positive. The firm has used many celebrity endorsements in the past and the collaboration with Britney Spears produced two very successful fragrances. Therefore, the firm's experience suggests that celebrity endorsements can increase sales.

Thinking Critically

1. Celebrity endorsements may be rewarding to firms, but they can also be risky. Elizabeth Arden has committed a significant amount of money to hiring Mariah Carey and developing the fragrances that she will endorse. What do you think would happen to the demand curve for these fragrances if Mariah Carey gets involved in an embarrassing scandal?

2. Celebrity endorsements are also expensive. Should a firm whose celebrity endorser was just arrested make its decision about whether or not to cancel its ad campaign based on the amount it has already spent on making the ads? Briefly explain.

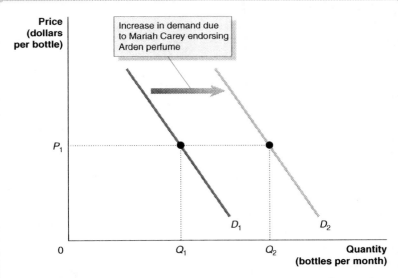

When successful, a celebrity endorsement can shift the demand curve for a product to the right, from D_1 to D_2.

© Frank Micelotta/Getty Images

Key Terms

Behavioral economics

Budget constraint

Endowment effect

Income effect

Law of diminishing marginal utility

Marginal utility (*MU*)

Network externality

Opportunity cost

Substitution effect

Sunk cost

Utility

Utility and Consumer Decision Making

Summary

Utility is the enjoyment or satisfaction that people receive from consuming goods and services. The goal of a consumer is to spend available income so as to maximize utility. **Marginal utility** is the change in total utility a person receives from consuming one additional unit of a good or service. The **law of diminishing marginal utility** states that consumers receive diminishing additional satisfaction as they consume more of a good or service during a given period of time. The **budget constraint** is the amount of income consumers have available to spend on goods and services. To maximize utility, consumers should make sure they spend their income so that the last dollar spent on each product gives them the same marginal utility. The **income effect** is the change in the quantity demanded of a good that results from the effect of a change in the price on consumer purchasing power. The **substitution effect** is the change in the quantity demanded of a good that results from a change in price making the good more or less expensive relative to other goods, holding constant the effect of the price change on consumer purchasing power.

 Visit www.myeconlab.com to complete these exercises online and get instant feedback.

Review Questions

1.1 What is the economic definition of utility? Is utility measurable?

1.2 What is the definition of marginal utility? What is the law of diminishing marginal utility? Why is marginal utility more useful than total utility in consumer decision making?

1.3 What is meant by a consumer's budget constraint? What is the rule of equal marginal utility per dollar spent?

Problems and Applications

1.4 Does the law of diminishing marginal utility hold true in every situation? Is it possible to think of goods for which consuming additional units will result in increasing marginal utility?

1.5 If consumers should allocate their income so that the last dollar spent on every product gives them the same amount of additional utility, how should they decide the amount of their income to save?

1.6 You have six hours to study for two exams tomorrow. The relationship between hours of study and test scores is shown in the following table.

ECONOMICS		PSYCHOLOGY	
HOURS	SCORE	HOURS	SCORE
0	54	0	54
1	62	1	60
2	69	2	65
3	75	3	69
4	80	4	72
5	84	5	74
6	87	6	75

a. Use the rule for determining optimal purchases to decide how many hours you should study each subject. Treat each point on an exam like 1 unit of utility and assume that you are equally interested in doing well in economics and psychology.

b. Now suppose that you are a psychology major, and that you value each point you earn on a psychology exam as being worth three times as much as each point you earn on an economics exam. Now how many hours will you study each subject?

1.7 (Related to *Solved Problem 1*) Joe has $16 to spend on Twinkies and Ho-Hos. Twinkies have a price of $1 per pack, and Ho-Hos have a price of $2 per pack. Use the information in the graphs on the following page to determine the number of Twinkies packs and the number of Ho-Hos packs Joe should buy to maximize his utility. Briefly explain your reasoning.

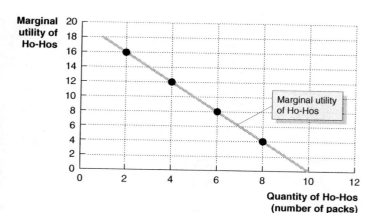

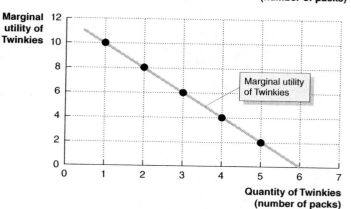

1.8 **(Related to Solved Problem 1)** Joe has $55 to spend on apples and oranges. Given the information in the following table, is Joe maximizing utility? Briefly explain.

PRODUCT	PRICE	QUANTITY	TOTAL UTILITY	MARGINAL UTILITY OF LAST UNIT
Apples	$0.50	50	1,000	20
Oranges	$0.75	40	500	30

1.9 Suppose the price of a bag of Frito's corn chips declines from $0.69 to $0.59. Which is likely to be larger: the income effect or the substitution effect? Briefly explain.

1.10 **(Related to the Don't Let This Happen to You!)** Mary is buying corn chips and soda. She has four bags of corn chips and five bottles of soda in her shopping cart. The marginal utility of the fourth bag of corn chips is 10, and the marginal utility of the fifth bottle of soda is also 10. Is Mary maximizing utility? Briefly explain.

1.11 When the price of pizza falls in the Super Bowl example, both the income and the substitution effect cause you to want to consume more pizza. If pizza were an inferior good, how would the analysis be changed? In this case, is it possible that a lower price of pizza might lead you to buy less pizza? Briefly explain.

>> End Learning Objective 1

---

2 LEARNING OBJECTIVE 2 | Use the concept of utility to explain the law of demand

Where Demand Curves Come From

Summary

When the price of a good declines, the ratio of the marginal utility to price rises. This leads consumers to buy more of that good. As a result, whenever the price of a product falls, the quantity demanded increases. This is known as the *law of demand*. The market demand curve can be constructed from the individual demand curves for all the consumers in the market.

 Visit www.myeconlab.com to complete these exercises online and get instant feedback.

Review Questions

2.1 Explain how a downward-sloping demand curve results from consumers adjusting their consumption choices to changes in price.

2.2 What would need to be true for a demand curve to be upward sloping?

Problems and Applications

2.3 Considering only the income effect, if the price of an inferior good declines, would a consumer want to buy a larger quantity or a smaller quantity of the good? Does this mean that the demand curves for inferior goods should slope upward? Briefly explain.

2.4 The chapter states that "when the price of an inferior good falls, the income and substitution effects work in opposite directions." Explain what this statement means.

2.5 Suppose the market for ice cream cones is made up of three consumers: Josh, Curt, and Tim. Use the information in the following table to construct the market demand curve for ice cream cones. Show the information in a table and in a graph.

| | JOSH | CURT | TIM |
| | QUANTITY DEMANDED (CONES PER WEEK) | QUANTITY DEMANDED (CONES PER WEEK) | QUANTITY DEMANDED (CONES PER WEEK) |
PRICE			
$1.75	2	1	0
1.50	4	3	2
1.25	6	4	3
1.00	7	6	4
0.75	9	7	5

2.6 Suppose the wage you are being paid increases. Is there an income and substitution effect involved? If so, what is being substituted for what?

>> End Learning Objective 2

3 LEARNING OBJECTIVE

3 | Explain how social influences can affect consumption choices

Social Influences on Decision Making

Summary

Social factors can have an influence on consumption. For example, the amount of utility people receive from consuming a good often depends on how many other people they know who also consume the good. There is a **network externality** in the consumption of a product if the usefulness of the product increases with the number of consumers who use it. There is also evidence that people like to be treated fairly and that they usually attempt to treat others fairly, even if doing so makes them worse off financially. This result has been demonstrated in laboratory experiments, such as the ultimatum game. When firms set prices, they take into account consumers' preference for fairness. For example, hardware stores often do not increase the price of snow shovels to take advantage of a temporary increase in demand following a snowstorm.

myeconlab Visit www.myeconlab.com to complete these exercises online and get instant feedback.

Review Questions

3.1 In which of the following situations are social influences on consumer decision making likely to be greater: choosing a restaurant for dinner or choosing a brand of toothpaste to buy? Briefly explain.

3.2 Why do consumers pay attention to celebrity endorsements of products?

3.3 What are network externalities? For what types of products are network externalities likely to be important? What is path dependence?

3.4 What is the ultimatum game? What insight does it provide into consumer decision making?

3.5 How does the fact that consumers apparently value fairness affect the decisions that businesses make?

Problems and Applications

3.6 Which of the following products are most likely to have significant network externalities? Explain.
a. Fax machines
b. Dog food
c. Board games
d. Conventional (CRT) television sets
e. Plasma television sets

3.7 Linux is a computer operating system that is an alternative to Microsoft's Windows system. According to a newspaper article:

> The dominance of the Windows operating system, which runs 95 per cent of the world's PCs, is coming under greater attack in Asia than in any other part of the world, analysts say. Linux for PCs sold three times as many copies in Asia as in the US last year. . . . "In emerging markets such as India and China, where PC growth rates are the highest, Linux's momentum seems to be accelerating," said Robert Stimson, a Bank of America analyst in San Francisco.

If network externalities are important in choosing a computer operating system, why might Linux be more successful in Asia than in the United States?

Source: "Gates Blitzes Asia to Stem Linux Threat," *New Zealand Herald*, June 29, 2004.

3.8 **(Related to the *Chapter Opener*)** Think of some firms that don't use celebrities to endorse their products. Why do some firms, like Coca-Cola, use celebrity endorsers, while other firms don't?

3.9 **(Related to the *Making the Connection*)** Tiger Woods is a professional golfer who knows more about golfing and golf related products than most consumers. However, this is not necessarily the case for Buicks, Rolexes, and American Express products. Consider the model of utility maximizing behavior described in this chapter. For Buick's use of Tiger Woods as a celebrity endorser to make economic sense, then how must Woods's endorsement affect the marginal utility that at least some consumers receive from driving Buicks? What will this do to the demand curve for Buicks?

3.10 An article in the *New York Times* published during the 2002 Winter Olympics held in Utah indicated that many businesses raised prices during the two-week event. The article described one incident as follows:

> Susanne and Heather McDonald, sisters from the northwest Wyoming town of Moose, said a friend was having sushi at a restaurant in Park City, where skiing

events are held, and the waiter was adding $3 for every side dish until the man identified himself as a local resident. "Then he got them for free," Susanne McDonald said.

When setting the price for a meal, why would it matter to the restaurant whether the customer was a local resident?

Source: Michael Janofsky, "Olympic Boom Leaves Visitors Feeling Busted," *New York Times*, February 19, 2002.

3.11 **(Related to the *Making the Connection*)** Suppose the rock band U2 can sell out a concert at Madison Square Garden with tickets priced at $45. U2's manager estimates that they could still sell out the Garden at $85 per ticket. Why might U2 and their manager want to keep ticket prices at $45?

3.12 **(Related to the *Making the Connection*)** Suppose that *Spider-Man 4* comes out, and hundreds of people arrive at a theater and discover that the movie is already sold out. Meanwhile, the theater is also showing a boring movie in its third week of release in a mostly empty theater. Why would this firm charge the same $7.50 for a ticket to either movie, when the quantity of tickets demanded is much greater than the quantity supplied for one movie, and the quantity of tickets demanded is much less than the quantity supplied for the other?

>> **End Learning Objective 3**

---

4 LEARNING OBJECTIVE   4 | Describe the behavioral economics approach to understanding decision making

Behavioral Economics: Do People Make Their Choices Rationally?

Summary

Behavioral economics is the study of situations in which people act in ways that are not economically rational. **Opportunity cost** is the highest-value alternative that must be given up to engage in an activity. People would improve their decision making if they took into account nonmonetary opportunity costs. People sometimes ignore nonmonetary opportunity costs because of the *endowment effect*. The **endowment effect** is the tendency of people to be unwilling to sell something they already own even if they are offered a price that is greater than the price they would be willing to pay to buy the good if they didn't already own it. People would also improve their decision making if they ignored *sunk costs*. A **sunk cost** is a cost that has already been paid and cannot be recovered. Finally, people would improve their decision making if they were more realistic about their future behavior.

Review Questions

4.1 What does it mean to be economically rational?

4.2 Define behavioral economics and give an example of three common mistakes that consumers often make.

Problems and Applications

4.3 Suppose your little brother tells you on Tuesday that one of his friends offered him $20 for his Albert Pujols rookie baseball card, but your brother decided not to sell the card. On Wednesday, your brother loses the card. Your parents feel sorry for him and give him $20 to make up the loss. Instead of buying another

Albert Pujols card with the money (which we will assume he could have done), your brother uses the money to go to the movies. Explain your brother's actions by using the concepts in this chapter.

4.4 Economist Richard Thaler has argued that the behavior of professional football teams during the college draft is an example of the endowment effect. Professional football teams take turns drafting eligible college players. Suppose that the New England Patriots now have a turn to pick, and the best college player not yet drafted is a quarterback. Suppose also that the Patriots already have a great quarterback and don't need another one. What should they do? Their optimal choice would appear to be to draft the quarterback and then trade him to another team that needs a quarterback. The Patriots could then receive in return a player from the other team who plays a position for which the Patriots need help. In fact, teams very rarely draft a college player and immediately trade him. Explain how the endowment effect could be involved here. (*Hint:* Consider the potential reaction of a team's fans to the team drafting a star college player and immediately trading him.)

Source: Richard Thaler, *Quasi Rational Economics*, New York: Russell Sage, 1991, p. 10.

4.5 Oldies 93 has a promotion in which it announces that a local gas station will sell gasoline at 93 cents per gallon beginning in 30 minutes. Jack hops in his car and drives to the station to fill up his half-empty tank. He pays only $9.30 for 10 gallons instead of the going price of $19.30. Did Jack save $10.00? Is the radio station doing its listeners a favor by offering this promotion? Briefly explain.

4.6 You have tickets to see Bruce Springsteen in concert at a stadium 50 miles away. A severe thunderstorm on the night of the concert makes driving hazardous. Will your decision to attend the concert be different if you paid $70 for the tickets than if you received the tickets for free? Explain your answer.

4.7 Rob Neyer is a baseball writer for ESPN.com. He described attending a Red Sox game at Fenway Park in Boston and having a seat in the sun on a hot, humid day: "Granted, I could have moved under the overhang and enjoyed today's contest from a nice, cool, shady seat. But when you paid forty-five dollars for a ticket in the fourth row, it's tough to move back to the twenty-fourth [row]." Evaluate Neyer's reasoning.

Source: Rob Neyer, *Feeding the Green Monster*, New York: iPublish.com, 2001, p. 50.

4.8 After owning a used car for two years, you start having problems with it. You take it into the shop, and a mechanic tells you that repairs will cost $4,000. What factors will you take into account in deciding whether to have the repairs done or to junk the car and buy another one? Will the price you paid for the car be one of those factors? Briefly explain.

4.9 The following excerpt is from a letter sent to a financial advice columnist: "My wife and I are trying to decide how to invest a $250,000 windfall. She wants to pay off our $114,000 mortgage, but I'm not eager to do that because we refinanced only nine months ago, paying $3,000 in fees and costs." Briefly discuss what effect the $3,000 refinancing cost should have on this couple's investment decision.

Source: Liz Pulliam, *Los Angeles Times* advice column, March 24, 2004.

4.10 **(Related to the *Making the Connection*)** Consumers tend to ignore the prices of "add-on" goods like ATM fees for checking accounts. Does this mean that if the government were to ban ATM fees that consumers would benefit?

4.11 **(Related to *Solved Problem 4*)** In an article in the *Quarterly Journal of Economics*, Ted O'Donoghue and Matthew Rabin make the following observation: "People have self-control problems caused by a tendency to pursue immediate gratification in a way that their 'long-run selves' do not appreciate." What do they mean by a person's "long-run self"? Give two examples of people pursuing immediate gratification that their long-run selves would not appreciate.

Source: Ted O'Donoghue and Matthew Rabin, "Choice and Procrastination," *Quarterly Journal of Economics*, February 2001, pp. 125–126.

4.12 **(Related to *Solved Problem 4*)** Data from health clubs show that members who choose a contract with a flat monthly fee over $70 attend, on average, 4.8 times per month. They pay a price per expected visit of more than $14, even though a $10-per-visit fee is also available. Why would these consumers choose a monthly contract when they lose money on it?

4.13 **(Related to the *Making the Connection*)** Briefly explain whether you agree or disagree with the following statement: "If people were more realistic about their future behavior, the demand curve for potato chips would shift to the left."

>> End Learning Objective 4

Appendix

Using Indifference Curves and Budget Lines to Understand Consumer Behavior

Use indifference curves and budget lines to understand consumer behavior.

Consumer Preferences

In this chapter, we analyzed consumer behavior, using the assumption that satisfaction, or *utility*, is measurable in utils. Although this assumption made our analysis easier to understand, it is unrealistic. Instead, we can use the more realistic assumption that consumers are able to *rank* different combinations of goods and services in terms of how much utility they provide. In other words, a consumer is able to determine whether he or she prefers 2 slices of pizza and 1 can of Coke or 1 slice of pizza and 2 cans of Coke, even if the consumer is unsure exactly how much utility he or she would receive from consuming these goods. This approach has the advantage that it allows us to actually draw a map of a consumer's preferences.

To begin with, suppose that a consumer is presented with the following alternatives, or *consumption bundles:*

CONSUMPTION BUNDLE A	CONSUMPTION BUNDLE B
2 slices of pizza and 1 can of Coke	1 slice of pizza and 2 cans of Coke

We assume that the consumer will always be able to decide which of the following is true:

- The consumer prefers bundle A to bundle B.

- The consumer prefers bundle B to bundle A.

- The consumer is indifferent between bundle A and bundle B; that is, the consumer receives equal utility from the two bundles.

For consistency, we also assume that the consumer's preferences are *transitive*. For example, if a consumer prefers pepperoni pizza to mushroom pizza and prefers mushroom pizza to anchovy pizza, the consumer must prefer pepperoni pizza to anchovy pizza.

Indifference Curves

Given the assumptions in the preceding section, we can draw a map of a consumer's preferences by using indifference curves. An **indifference curve** shows combinations of consumption bundles that give the consumer the same utility. In reality, consumers choose among consumption bundles containing many goods and services, but to make

Indifference curve A curve that shows the combinations of consumption bundles that give the consumer the same utility.

491

Figure A-1

Every possible combination of pizza and Coke will have an indifference curve passing through it, although in the graph we show just four of Dave's indifference curves. Dave is indifferent among all the consumption bundles that are on the same indifference curve. So, he is indifferent among bundles E, B, and F because they all lie on indifference curve I_3. Moving to the upper right in the graph increases the quantities of both goods available for Dave to consume. Therefore, the further to the upper right the indifference curve is, the greater the utility Dave receives.

Consumption Bundle	Slices of Pizza	Cans of Coke
A	1	2
B	3	4
C	4	5
D	1	6
E	2	8
F	5	2

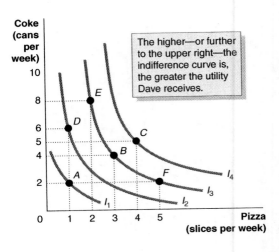

The higher—or further to the upper right—the indifference curve is, the greater the utility Dave receives.

the discussion easier to follow, we will assume that only two goods are involved. Nothing important would change if we expanded the discussion to include many goods instead of just two.

The table in Figure A-1 gives Dave's preferences for pizza and Coke. The graph plots the information from the table. Every possible combination of pizza and Coke will have an indifference curve passing through it, although in the figure we have shown only four of Dave's indifference curves. Dave is indifferent among all the consumption bundles that are on the same indifference curve. So, he is indifferent among bundles E, B, and F because they all lie on indifference curve I_3. Even though Dave has 4 fewer cans of Coke with bundle B than with bundle E, the additional slice of pizza he has in bundle B means he has the same amount of utility at both points.

Even without looking at Dave's indifference curves, we know he will prefer consumption bundle D to consumption bundle A because in D he receives the same quantity of pizza as in A but 4 additional cans of Coke. But we need to know Dave's preferences, as shown by his indifference curves, to know how he will rank bundle B and bundle D. Bundle D contains more Coke but less pizza than bundle B, so Dave's ranking will depend on how much pizza he would be willing to give up to receive more Coke. The higher the indifference curve—that is, the further to the upper right on the graph—the greater the amounts of both goods that are available for Dave to consume and the greater his utility. In other words, Dave receives more utility from the consumption bundles on indifference curve I_2 than from the consumption bundles on indifference curve I_1, more utility from the bundles on I_3 than from the bundles on I_2, and so on.

The Slope of an Indifference Curve

Remember that the slope of a curve is the ratio of the change in the variable on the vertical axis to the change in the variable on the horizontal axis. Along an indifference curve, the slope tells us the rate at which the consumer is willing to trade off one product for another while keeping the consumer's utility constant. The slope of an indifference curve is referred to as the **marginal rate of substitution** (*MRS*).

Marginal rate of substitution (*MRS*) The slope of an indifference curve, which represents the rate at which a consumer would be willing to trade off one good for another.

We expect that the *MRS* will change as we move down an indifference curve. In Figure A-1, at a point like E on indifference curve I_3, Dave's indifference curve is relatively steep. As we move down the curve, it becomes less steep until it becomes relatively flat at a point like F. This is the usual shape of indifference curves: They are bowed in, or convex. A consumption bundle like E contains a lot of Coke and not much pizza. We would expect that Dave could give up a significant quantity of Coke for a smaller quantity of additional pizza and still have the same level of utility. Thus, the *MRS* will be high. As we move down the indifference curve, Dave moves to bundles, like B and F, that have more pizza and less Coke. As a result, Dave is willing to trade less Coke for pizza, and the *MRS* declines.

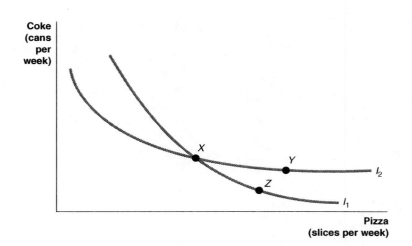

Figure A-2

Indifference Curves Cannot Cross

Because bundle X and bundle Z are both on indifference curve I_1, Dave must be indifferent between them. Similarly, because bundle X and bundle Y are on indifference curve I_2, Dave must be indifferent between them. The assumption of transitivity means that Dave should also be indifferent between bundle Z and bundle Y. We know that this is not true, however, because bundle Y contains more pizza and more Coke than bundle Z. So Dave will definitely prefer bundle Y to bundle Z, which violates the assumption of transitivity. *Therefore, none of Dave's indifference curves can cross.*

Can Indifference Curves Ever Cross?

Remember that we assume that consumers have transitive preferences. That is, if Dave prefers consumption bundle X to consumption bundle Y and he prefers consumption bundle Y to consumption bundle Z, he must prefer bundle X to bundle Z. If indifference curves cross, this assumption is violated. To understand why, look at Figure A-2, which shows two of Dave's indifference curves crossing.

Because bundle X and bundle Z are both on indifference curve I_1, Dave must be indifferent between them. Similarly, because bundle X and bundle Y are on indifference curve I_2, Dave must be indifferent between them. The assumption of transitivity means that Dave should also be indifferent between bundle Z and bundle Y. We know that this is not true, however, because bundle Y contains more pizza and more Coke than bundle Z. So, Dave will definitely prefer bundle Y to bundle Z, which violates the assumption of transitivity. Therefore, none of Dave's indifference curves can cross.

The Budget Constraint

Remember that a consumer's *budget constraint* is the amount of income he or she has available to spend on goods and services. Suppose that Dave has $10 per week to spend on pizza and Coke. The table in Figure A-3 shows the combinations that he can afford to buy if the price of pizza is $2 per slice and the price of Coke is $1 per can. As you can see, all the points lie on a straight line. This line represents Dave's budget constraint. The line intersects the vertical axis at the maximum number of cans of Coke Dave can afford to buy with $10, which is consumption bundle G. The line intersects the horizontal axis at the maximum number of slices of pizza Dave can afford to buy with $10, which is consumption bundle L. As he moves down his budget constraint from bundle G, he gives up 2 cans of Coke for every slice of pizza he buys.

Any consumption bundle along the line or inside the line is *affordable* for Dave because he has the income to buy those combinations of pizza and Coke. Any bundle that lies outside the line is *unaffordable* because those bundles cost more than the income Dave has available to spend.

The slope of the budget constraint is constant because the budget constraint is a straight line. The slope of the line equals the change in the number of cans of Coke divided by the change in the number of slices of pizza. In this case, moving down the budget constraint from one point to another point, the change in the number of cans of Coke equals −2, and the change in the number of slices of pizza equals 1, so the slope equals −2/1, or −2. Notice that with the price of pizza equal to $2 per slice and the price of Coke equal to $1 per can, the slope of the budget constraint is equal to the ratio of the price of pizza to the price of Coke (multiplied by −1). In fact, this

Figure A-3

Dave's budget constraint shows the combinations of slices of pizza and cans of Coke he can buy with $10. The price of Coke is $1 per can, so if he spends all of his $10 on Coke, he can buy 10 cans (bundle G). The price of pizza is $2 per slice, so if he spends all of his $10 on pizza, he can buy 5 slices (bundle L). As he moves down his budget constraint from bundle G, he gives up 2 cans of Coke for every slice of pizza he buys. Any consumption bundles along the line or inside the line are affordable. Any bundles that lie outside the line are unaffordable.

Combinations of Pizza and Coke Dave Can Buy with $10			
Consumption Bundle	Slices of Pizza	Cans of Coke	Total Spending
G	0	10	$10.00
H	1	8	10.00
I	2	6	10.00
J	3	4	10.00
K	4	2	10.00
L	5	0	10.00

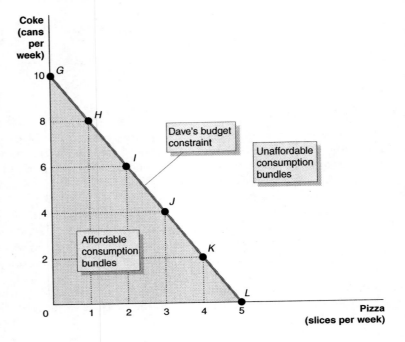

result will always hold: *The slope of the budget constraint is equal to the ratio of the price of the good on the horizontal axis divided by the price of the good on the vertical axis, multiplied by −1.*

Choosing the Optimal Consumption of Pizza and Coke

Dave would like to be on the highest possible indifference curve because higher indifference curves represent more pizza and more Coke. But Dave can only buy the bundles that lie on or inside his budget constraint. In other words, *to maximize utility, a consumer needs to be on the highest indifference curve, given his budget constraint.*

Figure A-4 plots the consumption bundles from Figure A-1 along with the budget constraint from Figure A-3. The figure also shows the indifference curves that pass through each consumption bundle. In Figure A-4, the highest indifference curve shown is I_4. Unfortunately, Dave lacks the income to purchase consumption bundles—like C— that lie on I_4. He has the income to purchase bundles like A and D, but he can do better. If he consumes bundle B, he will be on the highest indifference curve he can reach, given his budget constraint of $10. The resulting combination of 3 slices of pizza and 4 cans of Coke represents optimal consumption of pizza and Coke, given Dave's preferences and given his budget constraint. Notice that at point B, Dave's budget constraint just touches—or is *tangent* to—I_3. In fact, bundle B is the only bundle on I_3 that Dave is able to purchase for $10.

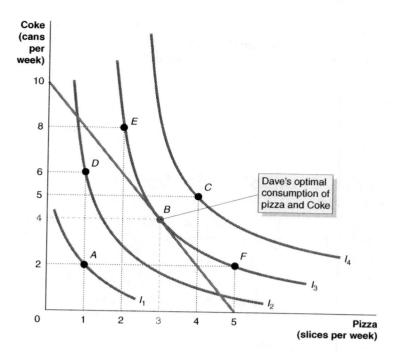

Figure A-4

Finding Optimal Consumption

Dave would like to be on the highest possible indifference curve, but he cannot reach indifference curves like I_4 that are outside his budget constraint. Dave's optimal combination of slices of pizza and cans of Coke comes at point B, where his budget constraint just touches—or is *tangent* to—the highest indifference curve he can reach. At point B, he buys 3 slices of pizza and 4 cans of Coke.

Making the Connection

Dell Determines the Optimal Mix of Products

Consumers have different preferences, which helps explain why many firms offer products with a variety of characteristics. For example, Dell sells laptop computers with different screen sizes, processor speeds, hard drive sizes, graphics cards, and so on. We can use the model of consumer choice to analyze a simplified version of the situation Dell faces in deciding which features to offer consumers.

Assume that consumers have $1,000 each to spend on laptops and that they are concerned with only two laptop characteristics: screen size and processor speed. Because larger screens and faster processors increase Dell's cost of producing laptops, consumers face a trade-off: The larger the screen, the slower the processor speed. Consumers in panel (a) of the figure prefer screen size to processor speed. For this group, the point of tangency between a typical consumer's indifference curve and the budget constraint shows an optimal choice of a 17-inch screen and a 1.5-gigahertz processor. Consumers in panel (b) prefer processor speed to screen size. For this group, the point of tangency between a typical consumer's indifference curve and the budget constraint shows an optimal choice of a 12-inch screen and 3.0-gigahertz processor.

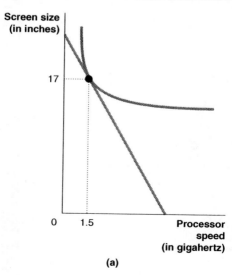

(a)

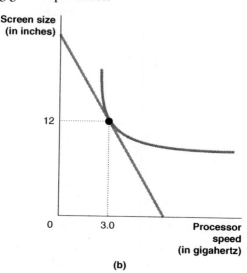

(b)

Companies like Dell use surveys and other means to gather information about consumer preferences. With knowledge of consumers' preferences and data on the costs of producing different laptop components, Dell can determine the mix of components to offer consumers.

YOUR TURN: Test your understanding by doing related problem A.8 at the end of this chapter.

How a Price Change Affects Optimal Consumption

Suppose the price of pizza falls from $2 per slice to $1 per slice. How will this affect Dave's decision about which combination of pizza and Coke is optimal? First, notice what happens to Dave's budget constraint when the price of pizza falls. As Figure A-5 shows, when the price of pizza is $2 per slice, the maximum number of slices Dave can buy is 5. After the price of pizza falls to $1 per slice, Dave can buy a maximum of 10 slices. His budget constraint rotates outward from point A to point B to represent this. (Notice that the fall in the price of pizza does not affect the maximum number of cans of Coke Dave can buy with his $10.)

When his budget constraint rotates outward, Dave is able to purchase consumption bundles that were previously unaffordable. Figure A-6 shows that the combination of 3 slices of pizza and 4 cans of Coke was optimal when the price of pizza was $2 per slice, but the combination of 7 slices of pizza and 3 cans of Coke is optimal when the price of pizza falls to $1. The lower price of pizza causes Dave to consume more pizza and less Coke and to end up on a higher indifference curve.

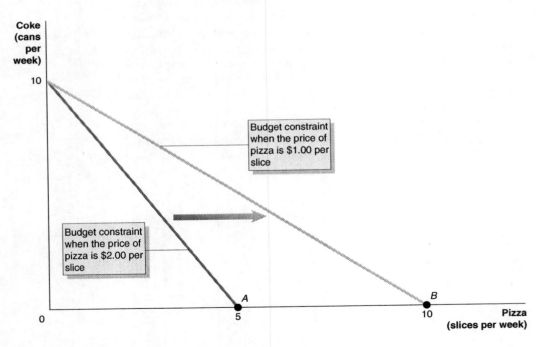

Figure A-5 | How a Price Decrease Affects the Budget Constraint

A fall in the price of pizza from $2 per slice to $1 per slice increases the maximum number of slices Dave can buy with $10 from 5 to 10. The budget constraint rotates outward from point A to point B to show this.

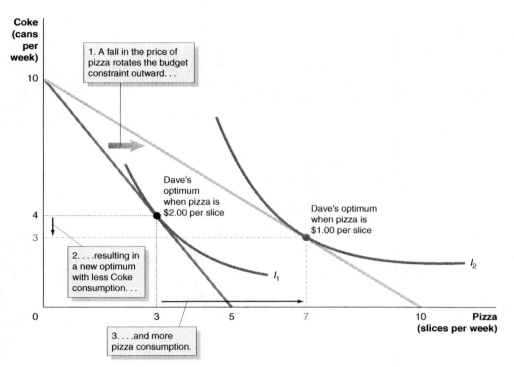

How a Price Change Affects Optimal Consumption

A fall in the price of pizza results in Dave consuming less Coke and more pizza.
1. A fall in the price of pizza rotates the budget constraint outward because Dave can now buy more pizza with his $10.
2. In the new optimum on indifference curve I_2, Dave changes the quantities he consumes of both goods. His consumption of Coke falls from 4 cans to 3 cans.
3. In the new optimum, Dave's consumption of pizza increases from 3 slices to 7 slices.

Solved Problem | **A-1**

When Does a Price Change Make a Consumer Better Off?

Dave has $300 to spend each month on DVDs and CDs. DVDs and CDs both currently have a price of $10, and Dave is maximizing his utility by buying 20 DVDs and 10 CDs. Suppose Dave still has $300 to spend, but the price of CDs rises to $20, while the price of DVDs drops to $5. Is Dave better or worse off than he was before the price change? Use a budget constraint–indifference curve graph to illustrate your answer.

SOLVING THE PROBLEM:

Step 1: **Review the chapter material.** This problem concerns the effect of price changes on optimal consumption, so you may want to review the section "How a Price Change Affects Optimal Consumption."

Step 2: **Answer the problem by drawing the appropriate graph.** We Begin by drawing the budget constraint, indifference curve, and point of optimal consumption for the original prices:

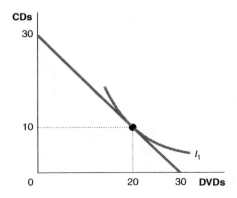

Now draw a graph that shows the results of the price changes. Notice that in this problem, the prices of *both* goods change. However, you can determine the position of the new budget constraint by calculating the maximum quantity of DVDs and CDs Dave can buy after the price changes. You should also note that after the price changes, Dave can still buy his original optimal consumption bundle—20 DVDs and 10 CDs—by spending all of his $300, so his new budget constraint must pass through this point.

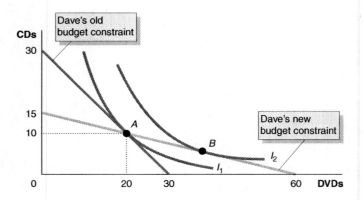

At the new prices, Dave can buy a maximum of 60 DVDs or 15 CDs. Both his old and his new budget constraints pass through the consumption bundle at point *A*. This consumption bundle is no longer optimal, however, because with the new prices, it is possible for him to reach an indifference curve that is higher than I_1. We can draw in the new highest indifference curve he can reach—I_2—and show the new optimal consumption bundle—point *B*.

Because Dave can now reach a higher indifference curve, we can conclude that he is better off as a result of the price change.

YOUR TURN: For more practice, do related problem A.10 at the end of this appendix.

>> End Solved Problem A-1

Deriving the Demand Curve

The change in Dave's optimal consumption of pizza as the price changes explains why demand curves slope downward. Dave adjusted his consumption of pizza as follows:

Price of pizza = $2 per slice ⇒ Quantity of pizza demanded = 3 slices

Price of pizza = $1 per slice ⇒ Quantity of pizza demanded = 7 slices

In panel (a) of Figure A-7, we plot the two points of optimal consumption. In panel (b) of Figure A-7, we draw a line connecting the points. This downward-sloping line is Dave's demand curve for pizza. We could find more points on the demand curve by changing the price of pizza and finding the new optimal number of slices of pizza Dave would demand.

Remember that according to the law of demand, demand curves always slope downward. We have just shown that the law of demand results from the optimal adjustment by consumers to changes in prices. A fall in the price of a good will rotate *outward* the budget constraint and make it possible for a consumer to reach higher indifference curves. As a result, the consumer will increase the quantity of the good demanded. An increase in price will rotate *inward* the budget constraint and force the

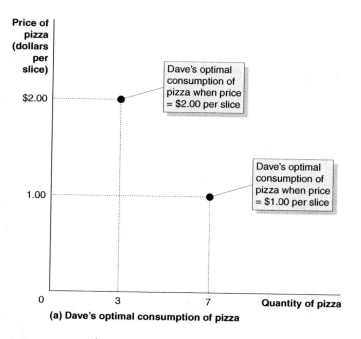

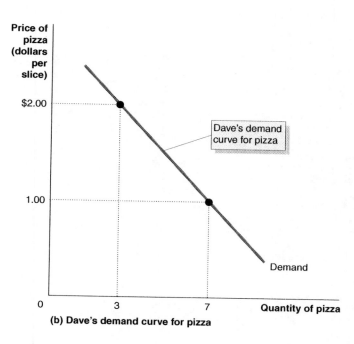

Figure A-7 | Deriving a Demand Curve

Dave responds optimally to the fall in the price of a product by consuming more of that product. In panel (a), the price of pizza falls from $2 per slice to $1, and the opti-

mal quantity of slices consumed rises from 3 to 7. When we graph this result in panel (b), we have Dave's demand curve for pizza.

consumer to a lower indifference curve. As a result, the consumer will decrease the quantity of the good demanded.

The Income Effect and the Substitution Effect of a Price Change

We saw in this chapter that a price change has two effects on the quantity of a good consumed: the *income effect* and the *substitution effect*. The income effect is the change in the quantity demanded of a good that results from the effect of a change in price on consumer purchasing power, holding all other factors constant. The substitution effect is the change in the quantity demanded of a good that results from a change in price making the good more or less expensive relative to other goods, holding constant the effect of the price change on consumer purchasing power. We can use indifference curves and budget constraints to analyze these two effects more exactly.

Figure A-8 illustrates the same situation as Figure A-7: The price of pizza has fallen from $2 per slice to $1 per slice, and Dave's budget constraint has rotated outward. As before, Dave's optimal consumption of pizza increases from 3 slices (point *A* in Figure A-8) per week to 7 slices per week (point *C*). We can think of this movement from point *A* to point *C* as taking place in two steps: The movement from point *A* to point *B* represents the substitution effect, and the movement from point *B* to point *C* represents the income effect. To isolate the substitution effect, we have to hold constant the effect of the price change on Dave's income. We do this by changing the price of pizza relative to the price of Coke *but at the same time holding his utility constant by keeping Dave on the same indifference curve*. In Figure A-8, in moving from point *A* to point *B*, Dave remains on indifference curve I_1. Point *A* is a point of tangency between I_1 and Dave's original budget constraint. Point *B* is a point of tangency

499

Figure A-8

Following a decline in the price of pizza, Dave's optimal consumption of pizza increases from 3 slices (point *A*) per week to 7 slices per week (point *C*). We can think of this movement from point *A* to point *C* as taking place in two steps: The movement from point *A* to point *B* along indifference curve I_1 represents the substitution effect, and the movement from point *B* to point *C* represents the income effect. Dave increases his consumption of pizza from 3 slices per week to 5 slices per week because of the substitution effect of a fall in the price of pizza and from 5 slices per week to 7 slices per week because of the income effect.

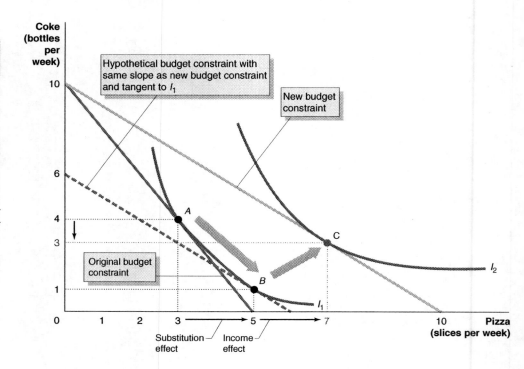

between I_1 and a new, *hypothetical* budget constraint that has a slope equal to the new ratio of the price of pizza to the price of Coke. At point *B*, Dave has increased his consumption of pizza from 3 slices to 5 slices. Because we are still on indifference curve I_1, we know that this increase is Dave's response only to the change in the relative price of pizza and, therefore, that the increase represents the substitution effect of the fall in the price of pizza.

At point *B*, Dave has not spent all his income. Remember that the fall in the price of pizza has increased Dave's purchasing power. In Figure A-8, we illustrate the additional pizza Dave consumes because of the income effect of increased purchasing power by the movement from point *B* to point *C*. Notice that in moving from point *B* to point *C*, the price of pizza relative to the price of Coke is constant because the slope of the new budget constraint is the same as the slope of the hypothetical budget constraint that is tangent to I_1 at point *B*.

We can conclude that Dave increases his consumption of pizza from 3 slices per week to 5 slices per week because of the substitution effect of a fall in the price of pizza and from 5 slices per week to 7 slices per week because of the income effect. Recall from our discussion of income and substitution effects in this chapter that the income effect of a price decline causes consumers to buy more of a normal good and less of an inferior good. Because the income effect causes Dave to increase his consumption of pizza, pizza must be a normal good for him.

How a Change in Income Affects Optimal Consumption

Suppose that the price of pizza remains at $2 per slice, but the income Dave has to spend on pizza and Coke increases from $10 to $20. Figure A-9 shows how this affects his budget constraint. With an income of $10, Dave could buy a maximum of 5 slices of pizza or 10 cans of Coke. With an income of $20, he can buy 10 slices of pizza or 20 cans of Coke. The additional income allows Dave to increase his consumption of both pizza and Coke and to move to a higher indifference curve. Figure A-10 shows Dave's new optimum. Dave is able to increase his consumption of pizza from 3 slices per week to 7 and his consumption of Coke from 4 cans per week to 6.

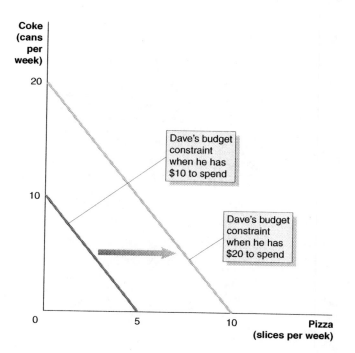

Figure A-9

How a Change in Income Affects the Budget Constraint

When the income Dave has to spend on pizza and Coke increases from $10 to $20, his budget constraint shifts outward. With $10, Dave could buy a maximum of 5 slices of pizza or 10 cans of Coke. With $20, he can buy a maximum of 10 slices of pizza or 20 cans of Coke.

The Slope of the Indifference Curve, the Slope of the Budget Line, and the Rule of Equal Marginal Utility per Dollar Spent

In this chapter, we saw that consumers maximize utility when they consume each good up to the point where the marginal utility per dollar spent is the same for every good. This condition seems different from the one we stated earlier in this appendix that to

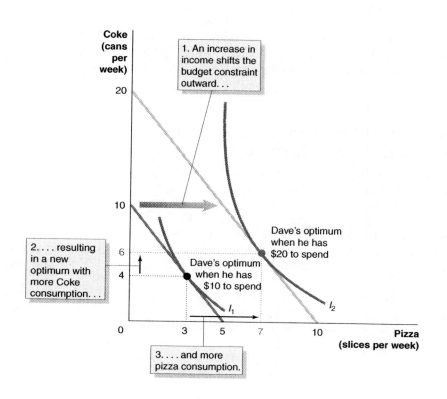

Figure A-10

How a Change in Income Affects Optimal Consumption

An increase in income leads Dave to consume more Coke and more pizza.

1. An increase in income shifts Dave's budget constraint outward because he can now buy more of both goods.
2. In the new optimum on indifference curve I_2, Dave changes the quantities he consumes of both goods. His consumption of Coke increases from 4 cans to 6 cans.
3. In the new optimum, Dave's consumption of pizza increases from 3 slices to 7 slices.

Figure A-11

At the point of optimal consumption, the marginal rate of substitution is equal to the ratio of the price of the product on the horizontal axis to the price of the product on the vertical axis.

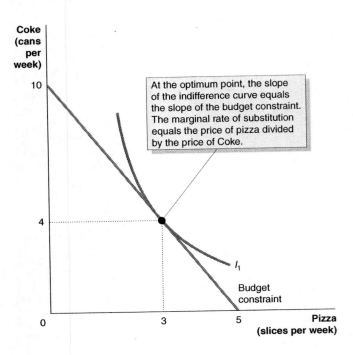

At the optimum point, the slope of the indifference curve equals the slope of the budget constraint. The marginal rate of substitution equals the price of pizza divided by the price of Coke.

maximize utility, a consumer needs to be on the highest indifference curve, given his budget constraint. In fact, though, the two conditions are equivalent. To see this, begin by looking at Figure A-11, which again combines Dave's indifference curve and budget constraint. Remember that at the point of optimal consumption, the indifference curve and the budget constraint are tangent, so they have the same slope. Therefore: *At the point of optimal consumption, the marginal rate of substitution* (MRS) *is equal to the ratio of the price of the product on the horizontal axis to the price of the product on the vertical axis.*

The slope of the indifference curve tells us the rate at which a consumer is *willing* to trade off one good for the other. The slope of the budget constraint tells us the rate at which a consumer is *able* to trade off one good for the other. Only at the point of optimal consumption is the rate at which a consumer is willing to trade off one good for the other equal to the rate at which he can trade off one good for the other.

The Rule of Equal Marginal Utility per Dollar Spent Revisited

Recall from this chapter the *rule of equal marginal utility per dollar*, which states that to maximize utility, consumers should spend their income so that the last dollar spent on each product gives them the same marginal utility. We can use our indifference curve and budget constraint analysis to see why this rule holds. When we move from one point on an indifference curve to another, we end up with more of one product and less of the other product but the same amount of utility. For example, as Dave moves down an indifference curve, he consumes less Coke and more pizza, but he has the same amount of utility.

Remember that marginal utility (MU) tells us how much additional utility a consumer gains (or loses) from consuming more (or less) of a good. So when Dave consumes less Coke by moving down an indifference curve, he loses utility equal to:

$$-\text{Change in the quantity of Coke} \times MU_{Coke}$$

but he consumes more pizza, so he gains utility equal to:

$$\text{Change in the quantity of pizza} \times MU_{Pizza}.$$

We know that the gain in utility from the additional pizza is equal to the loss from the smaller quantity of Coke because Dave's total utility remains the same along an indifference curve. Therefore we can write:

$$-(\text{Change in the quantity of Coke} \times MU_{Coke}) = (\text{Change in the quantity of pizza} \times MU_{Pizza}).$$

| Loss in utility from consuming less Coke | Gain in utility from consuming more pizza |

If we rearrange terms, we have:

$$\frac{-\text{Change in the quantity of Coke}}{\text{Change in the quantity of pizza}} = \frac{MU_{Pizza}}{MU_{Coke}}$$

because the

$$\frac{-\text{Change in the quantity of Coke}}{\text{Change in the quantity of pizza}}$$

is the slope of the indifference curve, or the marginal rate of substitution, we can write:

$$\frac{-\text{Change in the quantity of Coke}}{\text{Change in the quantity of pizza}} = MRS = \frac{MU_{Pizza}}{MU_{Coke}}.$$

The slope of Dave's budget constraint equals the price of pizza divided by the price of Coke. At the point of optimal consumption, the slope of the indifference curve is equal to the slope of the budget line. Therefore:

$$\frac{MU_{Pizza}}{MU_{Coke}} = \frac{P_{Pizza}}{P_{Coke}}.$$

We can rewrite this to show that at the point of optimal consumption:

$$\frac{MU_{Pizza}}{P_{Pizza}} = \frac{MU_{Coke}}{P_{Coke}}.$$

This last expression is the rule of equal marginal utility per dollar that we first developed in this chapter. So we have shown how this rule follows from the indifference curve and budget constraint approach to analyzing consumer choice.

Key Terms

Indifference curve

Marginal rate of substitution (MRS)

Use indifference curves and budget lines to understand consumer behavior

Review Questions

A.1 What are the two assumptions economists make about consumer preferences?

A.2 What is an indifference curve? What is a budget constraint?

A.3 How do consumers choose the optimal consumption bundle?

Problems and Applications

A.4 Jacob receives an allowance of $5 per week. He spends all his allowance on ice cream cones and cans of Lemon Fizz soda.

   a. If the price of ice cream cones is $0.50 per cone and the price of Lemon Fizz is $1 per can, draw a graph showing Jacob's budget constraint. Be sure to indicate on the graph the maximum number of ice cream cones and the maximum number of cans of Lemon Fizz that Jacob can buy.

   b. Jacob buys 8 cones and 1 can of Lemon Fizz. Draw an indifference curve representing Jacob's choice, assuming that he has chosen the optimal combination.

   c. Suppose that the price of ice cream cones rises to $1 per cone. Draw in Jacob's new budget constraint and his new optimal consumption of ice cream cones and Lemon Fizz.

A.5 Suppose that Jacob's allowance in problem A.4 climbs from $5 per week to $10 per week.

   a. Show how the increased allowance alters Jacob's budget constraint.

   b. Draw a set of indifference curves showing how Jacob's choice of cones and Lemon Fizz changes when his allowance increases. Assume that both goods are normal.

   c. Draw a set of indifference curves showing how Jacob's choice of cones and Lemon Fizz changes when his allowance increases. Assume that Lemon Fizz is normal but cones are inferior.

A.6 Suppose that Calvin considers Pepsi and Coke to be perfect substitutes. They taste the same to him, and he gets exactly the same amount of enjoyment from drinking a can of Pepsi or a can of Coke.

   a. Will Calvin's indifference curves showing his trade-off between Pepsi and Coke have the same curvature as the indifference curves drawn in the figures in this appendix? Briefly explain.

   b. How will Calvin decide whether to buy Pepsi or to buy Coke?

A.7 In the following budget constraint–indifference curve graph, Nikki has $200 to spend on blouses and skirts.

   a. What is the price of blouses? What is the price of skirts?

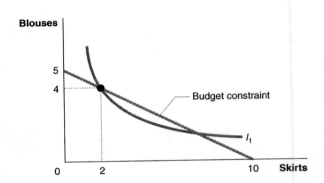

   b. Is Nikki making the optimum choice if she buys 4 blouses and 2 skirts? Explain how you know this.

A.8 (Related to the *Making the Connection*) Marilou and Hunter both purchase milk and doughnuts at the same Quik Mart. They have different tastes for milk and doughnuts and different incomes. They both buy some milk and some doughnuts, but they buy considerably different quantities of the two goods. Can we conclude that their marginal rate of substitution between milk and doughnuts is the same? Draw a graph showing their budget constraints and indifference curves and explain.

A.9 Sunsweet decides that prune juice has a bad image problem, so it launches a slick advertising campaign to convince young people that prune juice is very hip. They hire Eminem, Ludacris, and Trick Daddy to tout their product. The campaign works! Prune juice sales soar, even though Sunsweet hasn't cut the price. Draw a budget constraint and indifference curve diagram with Sunsweet Prune Juice on one axis and other drinks on the other axis and show how the celebrity endorsements have changed things.

A.10 (Related to *Solved Problem A-1*) Dave has $300 to spend each month on DVDs and CDs.

DVDs and CDs both currently have a price of $10, and Dave is maximizing his utility by buying 20 DVDs and 10 CDs. Suppose Dave still has $300 to spend, but the price of DVDs rises to $12, while the price of CDs drops to $6. Is Dave better or worse off than he was before the price change? Use a budget constraint–indifference curve graph to illustrate your answer.

>> End Appendix Learning Objective

Index